BOYD COUNTY
FEB 19 2013
PUBLIC LIBRARY

2013

CHEAT CODE OVERLOAD

Look for faces like this throughout Cheat Code Overload to find the latest and greatest games and the cheats to make playing them even more fun!

MOBILE GAMES

GAMES

ANGRY BIRDS

GOLDEN EGGS

#	LOCATION	DESCRIPTION
1	World Select	At the world select, tap the sun until another Golden Egg pops out.
2	Credits	Select i from the Options and scroll up to find the Golden Egg.
3	Help Screen	This Golden Egg becomes available once you unlock the white bird. Then, during any level, pause the game and select the question mark. At the white bird help screen, touch the golden egg.
4	Poached Eggs	Earn three stars on all of the Poached Eggs levels.
5	Poached Eggs 1-8	Simply tap the treasure chest until you get the egg.
6	Poached Eggs 2-2	Destroy the beach ball that sits among the ice cubes.
7	Mighty Hoax	Earn three stars on all of the Mighty Hoax levels.
8	Mighty Hoax 4-7	Zoom out to spot the egg on the right cliff. Launch the yellow bird into a high arc and tap when it lines up with the egg.
9	Mighty Hoax 5-19	The egg is located above the rocket ship. Zoom out and use a yellow or white bird to get it. Fire the yellow bird almost straight up and then tap when it reaches the clouds. If done correctly, the bird will get the egg as it comes back down.
10	Danger Above Level Select	Select Danger Above and scroll the level select screens as far as you can to the right to find this egg.
11	Danger Above	Earn three stars on all of the Danger Above levels.
12	Danger Above 6-14	Pop the yellow balloon floating below the structure on the right to get this one. Send the boomerang bird over the house and tap to have it come back to the balloon. This requires very good timing with the boomerang.

OVERLOAD

13	Danger Above 8-15	The golden egg is located behind the two boxes below the slingshot. Zoom out to see it. Bounce a yellow bird off the pink cushion located to the right.
14	The Big Setup	Earn three stars on all of The Big Setup levels.
15	The Big Setup 9-14	This egg hides under a hard hat on the far side of the area. Send a bird over or through the structure to get it.
16	The Big Setup 10-3	Destroy the rubber duck located below the bridge to get another Golden Egg.
17	The Big Setup 11-15	Zoom out to spot an egg below and to the left of your location. Fire the boomerang bird to the left and tap the screen to bring it back to the egg.
18	Ham 'Em High	Earn three stars on all of the Ham 'Em High levels.
19	Ham 'Em High 12-12	Destroy the cup that sits on the small platform below the big structure. Destroy the building and then send a bird through the opening to get it.
20	Ham 'Em High 13-10	Zoom out to see the egg hanging on the far side of the map. Send the white bird toward the middle of the structure, just above the two concrete bars on top. At this time, tap the screen to send the bird into the egg.
21	Ham 'Em High 13-12	You cannot see this egg until you get it. Zoom out so that you see the entire hill that you sit upon. Send a white bird to the left and quickly drop an explosive egg to reveal the Golden Egg.
22	Ham 'Em High 14-4	Zoom out so that you can see the Golden Egg that sits high on the mountain in the upper-right corner. Launch the yellow bird at about a 60 degree angle and then tap the screen to send it toward the egg.
23	Mine and Dine 15-12	Zoom out and an egg becomes visible in the top-right corner. Getting this one is very similar to 20. Send the yellow bird up and tap when it lines up with the egg.
24	Mine and Dine 16-9	Zoom out to spot the egg on the rock formation to the right. Aim a yellow bird just to the left of the first platform above the slingshot. Immediately tap the screen and if done correctly, the bird will reach the egg on the descent.
25	Mine and Dine	Earn three stars on all Mine and Dine levels.
26	Mine and Dine 17-12	Zoom out and a treasure chest can be seen on a rock high above. The first two birds cannot reach it, so use them up. Then fire the yellow bird at about a sixty degree angle up and to the right. As it lines up with the chest, tap the screen to get it.

ANGRY BIRDS HD

UNLOCKING WORLDS THE EASY WAY

At the world select, center on a locked world. Back out all the way out of the game. Go back into Angry Birds. At the Play button, tap it very quickly. Pass the first level to unlock the world.

SOUND BOARD

Earn three stars for all levels on worlds 1 through 3.

ANGRY BIRDS SPACE

GOLDEN EGGSTEROID

Golden Eggsteroids are hidden in six levels. These unlock bonus levels that are based on classic video games.

EGGSTEROID #	WORLD	LEVEL	LOCATION
1	Pig Bang	1-9	In brush below two pigs in bubbles.
2	Pig Bang	1-20	In brush on top of the planet.
3	Cold Cuts	2-13	In brush on planet below slingshot.
4	Cold Cuts	2-25	Under slingshot.
5	Cold Cuts	2-28	Hidden in snow, being pointed out by arrow.
6	Fry Me to the Moon	3-10	In bush on west side of planet.

BAG IT!

COMBOS

There are combos that get you extra rewards when bagging the groceries. Place the following items next to each other to create the combo. The characters names are as follows: Lucky is the cereal, Spilt is the milk, Sunshine is juice, Crusteau is the baguette, Chica Sister is either of the bananas, Sir Eggward is the carton of eggs, Nacho is the chips, and Seedy is the watermelon.

COMBO NAME	REQUIRED ITEMS
Balanced Breakfast	Spilt + Sunshine + Lucky + Sir Eggward
Banana Split	Both Chica Sisters
Breakfast Club	Lucky (x3)
Crusty Rivals	Sir Eggward + Crusteau
Double Date	Spilt (x2) + Sunshine (x2)
Eggcelent	Sir Eggward (x4)
Fiesta of Flavor	Nacho (x6)
Milky Way	Spilt (x4)
Mutiny!	Seedy (x5)
Nice Melons	Seedy (x2)
Scallywags	Seedy (x4)
Slumber Party	Sunshine (x3)
Sweethearts	Spilt + Sunshine
Three Amigos	Nacho (x3)
Well Bread	Crusteau (x4)

BATTLESHIP CRAFT

MIKASA

Go to options, select Code, and enter Jmsdf.

CHU CHU ROCKET HD

HARD PUZZLES

Complete all 25 Normal puzzles.

SPECIAL PUZZLES

Complete all 25 Hard puzzles.

MANIA PUZZLES

Complete all 25 Special puzzles.

CRAZY TAXI

EXPERT MODE

In Crazy Box, complete 1-x stages. Select Special from Help & Options to access this option.

TOGGLE ARROW AND DESTINATION MARK ON AND OFF

In Crazy Box, complete 2-x stages. Select Special from Help & Options to access this option.

ANOTHER DAY MODE AND RICKSHAW BIKE

In Crazy Box, complete 3-x stages. Select Special from Help & Options to access this option.

THE CREEPS! HD

DOODLER FROM DOODLE JUMP TOWER

Look at the Credits and click on the word AWESOME 100 times. Doodler shows up on the right side. Tap him to enable the secret. Now you can toggle Doodler on and off in the help menu.

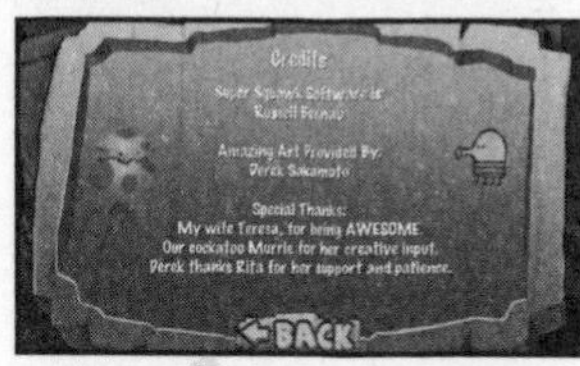

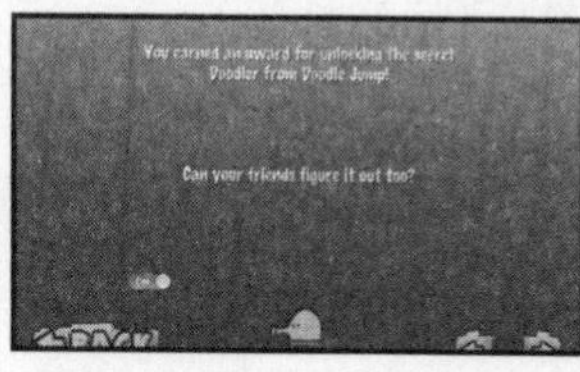

PYGMIES FROM POCKET GOD ENEMIES

Look at the Credits and click on the egg on the left side to enable this secret. Now you can toggle the Pygmies on and off in the help menu.

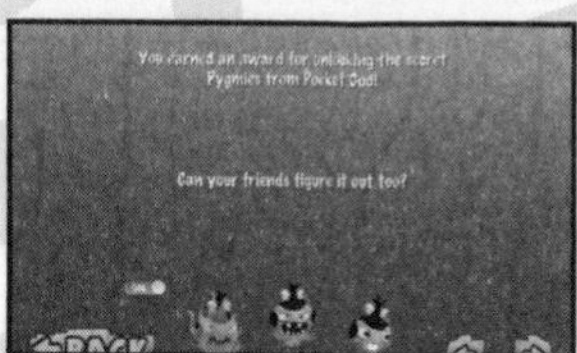

CRIMSON DRAGON: SIDE STORY

WINDOWS PHONE AVATAR AWARDS

AVATAR	EARNED BY
White T-Shirt	Clear the First Level.
Dragon Head	Clear the Second Level.

CUT THE ROPE (IOS)

OM NOM'S DRAWINGS

In 12 levels, if you tap on a certain spot of the background a drawing will be revealed. This spot can be something like a caution exclamation point or peeling wallpaper. Just look for something that looks a little off in the following levels: 1-16, 2-18, 3-3, 3-20, 4-14, 5-1, 5-15, 6-7, 7-3, 7-21, 8-17, and 9-21. Select Om Nom's Drawings to look at your collection.

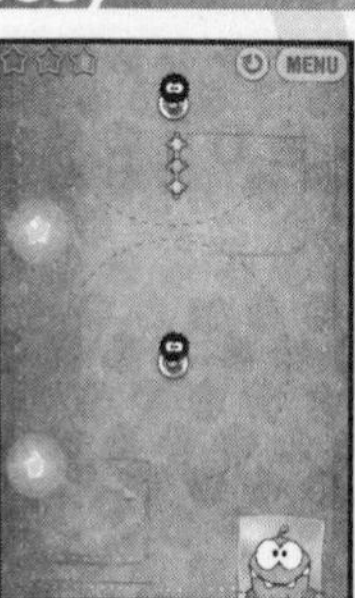

DOODLE JUMP (IOS)

OOG FROM POCKET GOD

After falling, enter Ooga, Klik, or Klak as your name. This only works with version 1.2.1 or later.

MONSTERS FROM THE CREEPS

After falling, enter Creeps as a name.

EASTER LEVEL

After falling, enter E.B., HOP, or Bunny as your name.

SNOW THEME

After falling, enter Snow as a name.

HALLOWEEN THEME

After falling, enter Boo as a name.

FLIGHT CONTROL

ACHIEVEMENTS

ACHIEVEMENT	DESCRIPTION
Safety Card	Read the Game Tutorial.
First Flights	Land an aircraft on each airfield.
Jet Power	Land 20 jets in a game.
Centurion	Reach 100 Total Aircraft Landed.
Helicopter Love	Land 5 helicopters in a row.
Rush Hour	Land 7 aircraft within 12 seconds.
Holding Pattern	Keep the same aircraft in the sky for 5 minutes.
Restrainer	Land no aircraft for 1.5/2 minutes.
Perfect Timing	Land 3 aircraft at the same time.
Crowded Sky	Reach 15/20 Most Aircraft on Screen.
Veteran	Play 250 games in total.
Wings	Land 200 aircraft in a game.

FRUIT NINJA

BLADES

Unlock the following blades by completing the task. These can be found in Sensei's Swag in the Dojo.

BLADE	EARNED BY
Disco Blade	Slice 50 bananas.
Mr. Sparkle	Slice 3 pineapples in a row in Classic Mode.
Old Glory	Finish a game with a score matching the number of stars on the U.S. Flag.
Butterfly Knife	Get a combo with a strawberry 40 times.
Flame Blade	Slice a combo after the timer ends in Zen Mode.
Ice Blade	Slice 20 freeze bananas in Arcade Mode to unlock.
The Shadow	Get a score of exactly 234 in Arcade Mode.
Pixel Love	Get 50 combos in classic mode.
Piano Blade	Slice 100 criticals to unlock.
Party Time	Slice every strawberry (and nothing else) in a game of Arcade Mode!
The Firecracker	Get the same score as the year of the Battle of Red Cliffs (208).
Bamboo Shoot	Play a full game of Zen Mode every day, 5 days in a row.

BACKGROUNDS

Unlock the following backgrounds by completing the task. These can be found in Sensei's Swag in the Dojo.

BACKGROUND	EARNED BY
Fruit Ninja	Get 125 points without dropping a fruit in Classic Mode.
I Heart Sensei	Read 3 of Sensei's Fruit Facts that are about strawberries.
Great Wave	Slice 250 watermelons.
Yin Yang	Slice 75 passion fruit.
Chinese Zodiac	Slice 384 peaches.

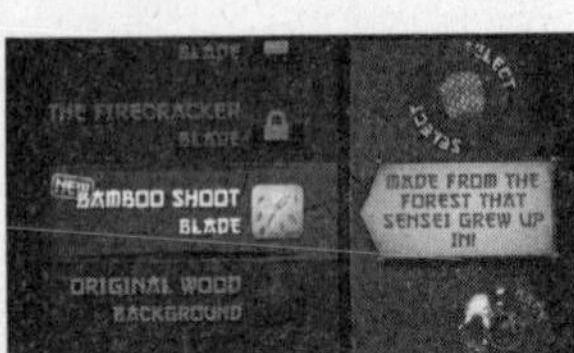

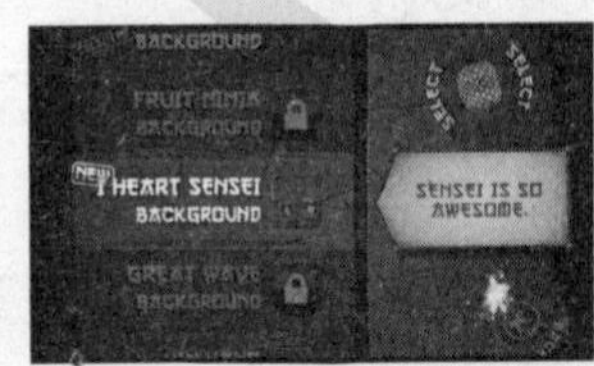

GRAND THEFT AUTO: CHINATOWN WARS

$10,000

In the safe house at the mission replay board, move the letters around to enter CASHIN.

FULL HEALTH

In the safe house at the mission replay board, move the letters around to enter LIFEUP.

FULL ARMOR

In the safe house at the mission replay board, move the letters around to enter SHELLY.

WEAPON CHEAT 1

In the safe house at the mission replay board, move the letters around to enter LOADOA. This gives you the Pistol, Nightsick, Minigun, Assualt Rifle, Micro SMG, Stubby Shotgun, and Grenades.

WEAPON CHEAT 2

In the safe house at the mission replay board, move the letters around to enter LOADOB. This gives you the Twin Pistol, Teaser, Flame Thrower, Carbine Rifle, SMG, Double Barreled Shotgun, and Molotovs.

WEAPON CHEAT 3

In the safe house at the mission replay board, move the letters around to enter LOADOC. This gives you the Revolver, Chainsaw, Flamethrower, Carbine Rifle, SMG, Double Barreled Shotgun, and Proximity Mines.

WEAPON CHEAT 4

In the safe house at the mission replay board, move the letters around to enter LOADOD. This gives you the Pistol, Baseball Bat, Carbine Rifle, RPG, Micro SMG, Shotgun, and Flash Bangs.

EXPLOSIVE EAGLE – PISTOL HAS EXPLOSIVE BULLETS

In the safe house at the mission replay board, move the letters around to enter BOOMCAN.

ALL DRUG DEALER LOCATIONS

In the safe house at the mission replay board, move the letters around to enter TRIPPY.

INCREASE WANTED LEVEL ONE STAR

In the safe house at the mission replay board, move the letters around to enter COPIN.

DECREASE WANTED LEVEL ONE STAR

In the safe house at the mission replay board, move the letters around to enter COPOUT.

ADVANCE TIME AN HOUR

In the safe house at the mission replay board, move the letters around to enter JUMPHR.

ADVANCE TIME SIX HOURS

In the safe house at the mission replay board, move the letters around to enter JUMPHRS.

ADVANCE TIME A DAY

In the safe house at the mission replay board, move the letters around to enter JUMPDAY.

GRAND THEFT AUTO 3 - 10 YEAR ANNIVERSARY EDITION

KEYBOARD CHEATS

If you have an external keyboard for your iOS or Android device or are able to bring up the device's keyboard during the game, the following codes can be entered during gameplay. The cheats may not work on your game. Do not save your game after entering cheats as they may also be saved.

EFFECT	CODE
Full Health	gesundheit
Full Armor	turtoise
All Weapons	gunsgunsguns
More Money	ifiwerearichman
Higher Wanted Level	morepoliceplease
Lose Wanted Level	nopoliceplease
Change to Other Peds	ilikedressingup
Crazy Peds	itsallgoingmaaad
Peds Attack You	nobodylikesme
All Peds are Armed	weaponsforall
Blow Up Cars	bangbangbang
Only Wheels are Visible	wheelsonlyplease
Flying Car	chittychittybb

EFFECT	CODE
Spawn Random Vehicle (Including Tank)	giveusatank
Improved Handling	cornerslikemad
Gore Mode	nastylimbcheat
Fast Game Clock	madweather
Faster Game Play	booooooring
Clear Weather	skincancerforme
Cloudy Weather	ilikescotland
Foggy Weather	peasoup
Rainy Weather	ilovescotland

HEAD SOCCER

CAMEROON TEAM

In Arcade mode, defeat 12 characters. Alternatively, you can purchase it for 100,000 points.

NIGERIA TEAM

Win 30 times in a tournament. Alternatively, you can purchase it for 200,000 points.

INFINITY BLADE

NEGATIVE BLOODLINE

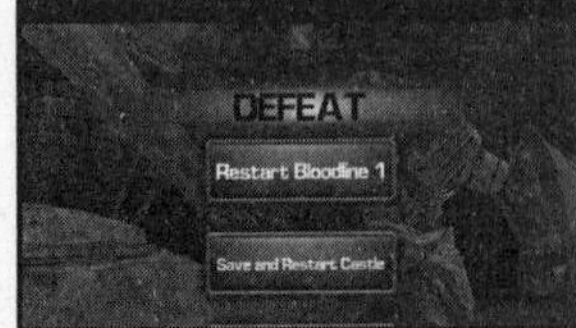

After starting Bloodline 3, lose to anyone except the God King. Restart from Bloodline 1 to be taken to the tutorial. Lose to the Dark Knight by tapping the shield instead of holding. After you die, select Save and Restart Castle. This takes you to Bloodlines -1 with Dark Mech gear equipped. If you have enough money, this is a good time to purchase some great equipment. When you return to Bloodline 1, you keep anything in your inventory but the Dark gear is gone.

NEW GAME +

After unlocking the Infinity Blade, defeat each monster behind the three doors at the bottom of the castle followed by the final two high-level enemies. Select New Game + to restart from Bloodline 1 with all of your stats intact. You do lose your inventory, but much better items wait in the Store.

KINGDOM RUSH

ACHIEVEMENTS

ACHIEVEMENT	DESCRIPTION
First Blood	Kill one Enemy.
Daring	Call 10 early waves.
Constructor	Build 30 Towers.
Bloodlust	Kill 500 Enemies.
Armaggedon [sic]	Use Rain of Fire 5 times in a single stage.
Home Improvement	Upgrade all basic Tower types to level 3.
Starry	Earn 15 Stars.
Whats That?	Open 10 Enemy information cards.
Supermario	Earn 30 Stars.
Nuts and Bolts	Defeat The Juggernaut.
Engineer	Build 100 Towers.
Is He Dead Yeti?	Defeat J.T.
Slayer	Kill 2500 Enemies.
Death From Above	Kill 100 Enemies with Meteor Shower.
Tactician	Change Soldiers rally point 200 times.
Superstar	Earn 45 Stars.
The architect	Build 150 Towers.
This is the End!	Defeat Vez'nan.
Terminator	Kill 10,000 Enemies.
Die Hard	Have your Soldiers regenerate a total of 50,000 life.
G.I. Joe	Train 1,000 Soldiers.
Cannon Fodder	Send 1,000 Soldiers to their deaths.
Fearless	Call all waves early in a single mission.
Real Estate	Sell 30 Towers.
Indecisive	Sell 5 Towers in a single mission.
Impatient	Call an early wave within 3 seconds of the icon showing up.
Forest Diplomacy	Recruit max Elves at The Silveroak Outpost.
Like a Henderson	Free the Sasquatch on the Icewind Pass.
Sunburner!	Fire the Sunray 20 times.
Imperial Saviour	Complete The Citadel with at least 3 surviving Imperial Guards.
Specialist	Build all 8 Tower specializations.
50 Shots 50 Kills	Snipe 50 Enemies.
Toxicity	Kill 50 Enemies by poison damage.
Entangled	Hold 500 or more Enemies with Wrath of the Forest.
Dust to Dust	Desintegrate [sic] 50 or more Enemies.
Beam Me Up Scotty	Teleport 250 or more Enemies.
Shepherd	Polymorph 50 Enemies into sheeps [sic].
Elementalist	Summon 5 rock elementals in any one stage.
Axe Rain	Throw 500 or more axes.
Are You Not Entertained?	Have a single Barbarian kill 10 Enemies.
Medic	Have your Paladins heal a total of 7,000 life.
Holy Chorus	Have your Paladins perform 100 Holy Strike.
Rocketeer	Shoot 100 Missiles.
Clustered	Drop 1,000 or more bomblets with the cluster bomb.
Energy Network	Build 4 Tesla towers in any stage.
AC/DC	Kill 300 Enemies with electricity.
Ovinophobia	Kill 10 or more Sheep with your hands
Twin Rivers Angler	Catch a Fish.
Great Defender	Complete all Campaign stages in Normal difficulty.
Heroic Defender	Complete all Heroic stages in Normal difficulty.
Iron Defender	Complete all Iron stages in Normal difficulty.

LET'S GOLF 2 HD

WIZZY THE WIZARD IN INSTANT PLAY
Select Profile from the Options and then tap Edit. Enter Wizzy10.

MAGIC: THE GATHERING - DUELS OF THE PLANESWALKERS 2013

PROMO UNLOCK 01
At the Player Status screen, select Promotional Unlocks. Click Enter Code and enter WMKFGC.

PROMO UNLOCK 02
At the Player Status screen, select Promotional Unlocks. Click Enter Code and enter KWPMZW.

PROMO UNLOCK 03
At the Player Status screen, select Promotional Unlocks. Click Enter Code and enter FNMDGP.

PROMO UNLOCK 04
At the Player Status screen, select Promotional Unlocks. Click Enter Code and enter MWTMJP.

PROMO UNLOCK 05
At the Player Status screen, select Promotional Unlocks. Click Enter Code and enter FXGJDW.

PROMO UNLOCK 06
At the Player Status screen, select Promotional Unlocks. Click Enter Code and enter GDZDJC.

PROMO UNLOCK 07
At the Player Status screen, select Promotional Unlocks. Click Enter Code and enter HTRNPW.

PROMO UNLOCK 08
At the Player Status screen, select Promotional Unlocks. Click Enter Code and enter NCTFJN.

PROMO UNLOCK 09
At the Player Status screen, select Promotional Unlocks. Click Enter Code and enter PCNKGR.

PROMO UNLOCK 10
At the Player Status screen, select Promotional Unlocks. Click Enter Code and enter GPCRSX.

MIRROR'S EDGE

ALL WALLPAPERS
Earn all 28 Badges.

PEWPEW 2

AMALGAM STAGE
Complete 50% of Campaign.

CHROMATIC CONFLICT
Complete 100% of Campaign.

PLANTS VS. ZOMBIES

ZOMBIE YETI
Complete Adventure Mode. Then, play the mode again to 4-10.

QUICK PLAY
Complete Adventure Mode.

ACHIEVEMENTS
All achievements are not available on all platforms.

ACHIEVEMENT	DESCRIPTION
Home Lawn Security	Complete Adventure Mode.
Spudow!	Blow up a zombie using a Potato Mine.
Explodonator	Take out 10 full-sized zombies with a single Cherry Bomb.
Morticulturalist	Collect all 49 plants (including plants from Crazy Dave's Shop).
Don't Pea in the Pool	Complete a daytime pool level without using Pea Shooters of any kind.
Roll Some Heads	Bowl over 5 Zombies with a single Wall-nut.
Grounded	Defeat a normal Roof level without using any catapult plants.
Zombologist	Discover the Yeti Zombie.
Penny Pincher	Pick up 30 coins in a row on a single level without letting any disappear.
Sunny Days	Accumulate 8,000 sun during a single level
Popcorn Party	Defeat 2 Gargantuars with Corn Cob missiles in a single level
Good Morning	Complete daytime level by planting only Mushrooms and Coffee Beans.
No Fungus Among Us	Complete a nighttime Level without planting any Mushrooms.
Last Mown Standing	Defeat the last zombie in a level with a lawn mower.
20 Below Zero	Immobilize 20 full-sized zombies with a single Ice-shroom.
Flower Power	Keep 10 Twin Sunflowers alive in a single level.
Pyromaniac	Complete a level using only explosive plants to kill zombies.
Lawn Mower Man	Kill 10 zombies with a single lawn mower.
Chill Out	Feel the rhythm, feel the rhyme, you've one level to destroy 3 bobsleds, its jalapeno time!
Defcorn 5	Build 5 Cob Cannons in a single level.
Monster Mash	Crush 5 zombies with a single Squash.
Blind Faith	Complete an extremely foggy level without using Planterns or Blovers.
Pool's Closed	Complete a pool level without using water plants.
Melon-y Lane	Plant a Winter Melon on every lane.
Second Life	Complete Adventure Mode a second time.
Lucky Spin	Get 3 diamonds in Slot Machine.
Chilli Free	Complete Column Like You See 'Em without using Jalapenos.
Enlighted	Collect all Zen Garden, Mushroom Garden, and Aquarium Garden plants.
Diamond Beghouler	Upgrade all your plants in Beghouled.
Sultan of Spin	Upgrade all your plants in Beghouled Twist.
Green Fingers	Grow 10 Zen Garden plants to full size.
Wall-Not-Attack	Complete ZomBotany with no Wall-Nuts, Tall-Nuts, or Pumpkins.
Beyond the Grave	Beat all 18 mini-games.
Down the Hole!	Dig your way to see the Chinese Zombies.
Thrilling the Zombies	Hypnotize the lead Dancer Zombie.
Alive and Planting	Survive 40 waves of pure zombie ferocity.

POCKET GOD

OOGA JUMP JET PACK BONUS

At an island, click the arrow in the upper-left corner and then select the 3-star graphic. Tap the star and then Pocket God Comic Pre-Order Bonus. Enter journey to uranus. You can participate in the promotion and get the jet pack otherwise you need to score 6000 in Ooga Jump.

QUELL

ACHIEVEMENTS

ACHIEVEMENT	DESCRIPTION
Magpie	Collect 25 pearls
Hunter	Collect 50 pearls
Hoarder	Collect 100 pearls
Pearl Jammer	Collect 150 pearls
Pearl Harboring	Collect 200 pearls

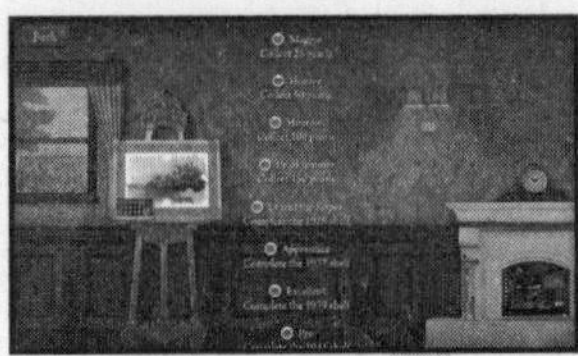

ACHIEVEMENT	DESCRIPTION
Learnt the Ropes	Complete the 1928 shelf
Apprentice	Complete the 1937 shelf
Excellent	Complete the 1939 shelf
Pro	Complete the 1941 shelf
Expert	Complete the 1943 shelf
Champion	Complete the 1945 shelf
Complete	Complete every Quell level
Minimalist	Complete 3 levels perfectly
Accomplished	Complete 10 levels perfectly
Flawless	Complete 20 levels perfectly
Impeccable	Complete 40 levels perfectly
Precise	Complete a stage in perfect moves
Meticulous	Complete a shelf in perfect moves
Perfect	Complete every Quell level in perfect moves
Keep Going!	Play for 10 minutes
Time Flies	Play for 30 minutes
High Stamina	Play for 1 hour
Suicidal	Die on a first move
Ouch!	Spiked 3 times
Fearless	Spiked 10 times
Funeral Bill	Spiked 20 times
Road to Nowhere	Get stuck in a loop 5 times
Groundhog Day	Retry a level 20 times
Matchmaker	Push 2 sets of blocks together
Tired	Push 10 blocks
Ring Leader	Use the ring 5 times
Quick Thinking	Complete a level in under 5 seconds
Defiant	Take over 10 minutes to complete a level
Scenic Route	Take twice as many moves as necessary

RPG ALPHADIA

CHEAT MODE

Defeat the game to unlock cheat mode. This gives you the ability to double experience, gold, and skill points and skip enemy encounters.

THE SIMPSONS: TAPPED OUT

10 Extra Doughnuts and Jebediah Springfield Statue

During a game, select Homer to get his task menu. Tap Homer ten times to get a message for performing the code correctly.

THE SIMS 3

500 SIMOLEONS

Click the ... in the corner and select Help & About. Go to Gardening Tips and shake your device. Repeat as desired.

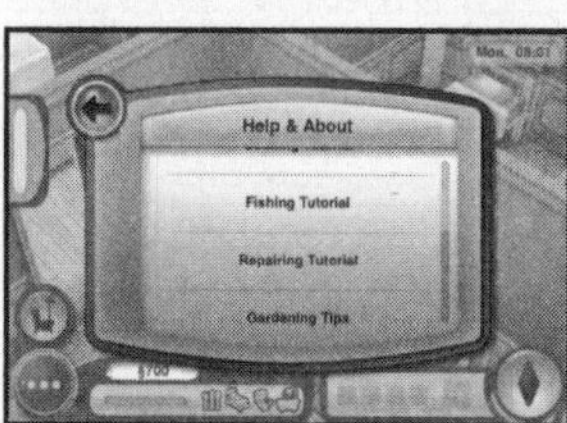

SPIDER-MAN: TOTAL MAYHEM HD

ULTIMATE DIFFICULTY

Defeat the game.

BLACK SUIT

Defeat the game. Access the suit on the level select with an icon in upper-left corner.

SUPER STICKMAN GOLF

ACHIEVEMENTS

ACHIEVEMENTS	DESCRIPTION	POINTS
Sticky Ball	Unlocked the Sticky Ball	10
Ice Ball	Unlocked the Ice Ball	10
Hazard Swap	Unlock the Hazard Swap	20
Air Brakes	Unlock the Air Brakes	20
Super Ball	Unlock the Super Ball	30
Nitro Ball	Unlock the Nitro Ball – Get 30 Achievements	30
Thats A Bingo	Get a hole in one	10
Eagle	Get an eagle	10
Nothing But Net	Get a hole in one without touching the green	20
500 Strokes	Reach a combined 500 shots	10
Lunar Lander	Get a hole in one on the first hole in The Moon Base	10
Funky Dry	Score under par on Funky Town without getting wet	10
The Slew Sniper	Score under par on The Slew without hitting a sand trap	10
Parnage	Beat Dapper Dunes without getting a single bogey	10
1000 Strokes	Take a combined 1000 shots	20
Jacob's Cabin	Can you find Jacob's Cabin? (Dapper Dunes – Hole 1)	10
The Tire Swing	Can you find The Tire Swing? (Lofstrom Links – Hole 8)	10
The Locksmith	Unlock all the courses	20
Cool It Down	Shoot a superball into a water hazard	10
The Trio	Bag three hole in one's in a row	10
2000 Strokes	Take a combined 2000 shots	30
3000 Strokes, Hardcore	Take a combined 3000 shots	50
The Impossible Shot	Get a hole in one on the second hole in The Ice Flows	20
Nil Score	Score a zero on a hole	20

ACHIEVEMENTS	DESCRIPTION	POINTS
Negative Score	Score a negative number on a hole	20
Purple Passion	Score a hole in one on hole 6 in Purple Haze	10
Purple Zero	Score a zero or less on hole 7 in Purple Haze	10
The Woodsman	Score a hole in one on hole 8 in The Woods	10
10 Clean Balls	Score under par on 10 courses without powerups	10
The Long One	Sink a super long putt	10
Look Up	Get a negative score on hole 3 in The Graveyard	10
Iced Temple	Freeze all the hazards on hole 3 in The Temple	10
Parkland Dry	Score under par on Parkland without getting wet	10
Freeze, Bounce, Drop	Beat hole 2 in Parkland In 3 strokes	10
Tropical Slide	Score a hole in one on hole 4 in The Tropics	10
Ride The Boundary	Score a hole in one on hole 3 in Key Lime Links	10
1 Multiplayer Win	Win 1 multiplayer game	10
5 Multiplayer Wins	Win 5 multiplayer games	10
10 Multiplayer Wins	Win 10 multiplayer games	20
10 Multiplayer Points	Reach a combined 10 awarded multiplayer points	10
50 Multiplayer Points	Reach a combined 50 awarded multiplayer points	10
100 Multiplayer Points	Reach a combined 100 awarded multiplayer points	20
200 Multiplayer Points	Reach a combined 200 awarded multiplayer points	50
Haunted Hazards	Score under par on Haunted Hills, without getting wet	10
Haunted Drop-in	Score a hole-in-one on hole 7 in the Haunted Hills	10
All Aces	Score all hole-in-one's in Parkland without powerups	50
Cinnamon Bounce	Score a hole-in-one on hole 7 in the Cinnamon Bluffs	20
Nitro Master	Score a hole-in-one on hole 7 on the Pipes	30
Food For Thought	Score a hole-in-one on hole 6 in the Belts	20
Belts Nil	Beat Belts hole 7 in zero or less strokes	20
Cinnamon Nil	Beat Cinnamon Bluffs hole 2 in zero or less strokes	20

TEMPLE RUN

These codes do not work if you have updated to 1.4. You need the ability to bring up the keyboard to enter them.

EXTRA CHARACTERS

At the title screen, enter rxh7nigh.

INVINCIBILITY

At the title screen, enter samhines86.

PURCHASABLE CHARACTERS

As of version 1.4.1, you can purchase the following characters with the given amount of coins from the store.

CHARACTER	COST
Scarlett Fox	10,000
Barry Bones	10,000
Karma Lee	25,000
Montana Smith	25,000
Francisco Montoya	25,000
Zack Wonder	25,000

PURCHASABLE WALLPAPERS

The following wallpapers can also be purchased at the store.

WALLPAPER	COST
Temple Wall	5000
Guy Dangerous	5000
Evil Demon Monkeys	5000

OBJECTIVES

OBJECTIVE	DESCRIPTION
Novice Runner	Run 500 meters
Pocket Change	Collect 100 coins
Adventurer	Scored 25,000 points
Sprinter	Ran 1000 meters
Miser Run	500 m collecting no coins
Piggy Bank	Collect 250 coins
Treasure Hunter	Scored 50,000 points
Mega Bonus	Fill the bonus meter 4x
Athlete	Ran 2500 meters
Lump Sum	Collected 500 coins
Resurrection	Resurrected after dying
Basic Powers	All level 1 Powerups
High Roller	Scored 100,000 points
Payday	Collected 750 coins
Head Start	Used a Head Start
Steady Feet	Ran 2500 m without tripping
Allergic to Gold	1000 m collecting no coins
5k Runner	Ran 5000 meters
No Trip Runner	Ran 5000 meters without tripping
1/4 Million Club	Scored 250,000 points
Double Resurrection	Resurrected twice in one run
Money Bags	Collected 1000 coins
1/2 Million Club	Scored 500,000 points
Super Powers	All level 5 powerups
Dynamic Duo	Unlocked two characters
Million Club	Scored 1,000,000 points
Money Bin	Collected 2,500 coins
Fantastic Four	Unlocked Four Characters
Sexy Six	Unlocked 6 characters
Interior Decorator	Unlocked 3 wallpapers
10k Runner	Run 10,000 meters
Fort Knox	Collect 5,000 coins
2.5 Million Club	Scored 2,500,000 points
5 Million Club	Scored 5,000,000 points
The Spartan	1 million without power ups
10 Million Club	Score 10,000,000 points

TEXAS HOLD'EM

CHEAT MENU

Select New Player from the Options menu and enter YOUCHEAT as the player name. Hold down the center button until you get confirmation. This gives you a cheat menu with the following five options: Unlock All Tournaments, Start with $100,000, Show Tells and/or Down Cards, and Adjust AI Folding frequency.

APPLE CONFERENCE ROOM TOURNAMENT

Select New Player from the Options menu and enter THREEAMI as the player name. Hold down the center button until you get confirmation.

DOG TOURNAMENT

Select New Player from the Options menu and enter PLAYDOGS as the player name. Hold down the center button until you get confirmation.

FUTURISTIC TOURNAMENT

Select New Player from the Options menu and enter SPACEACE as the player name. Hold down the center button until you get confirmation.

ITUNES BAR TOURNAMENT

Select New Player from the Options menu and enter BARTUNES as the player name. Hold down the center button until you get confirmation.

STONEHENGE TOURNAMENT

Select New Player from the Options menu and enter BIGROCKS as the player name. Hold down the center button until you get confirmation.

SEE SECRET CHARACTERS

Select New Player from the Options menu and enter ALLCHARS as the player name. Hold down the center button until you get confirmation.

WHERE'S MY WATER?

HIDDEN PLANETARIUM LEVEL

Go to the Achievements screen and scroll all the way to the top. Continue to scroll up until you see a drawing of a planet. Tap it to enter the level.

JELLY CAR BONUS LEVEL

If Jelly Car is installed on your device, view the credits. When a Jelly Car goes by, tap it to unlock this level.

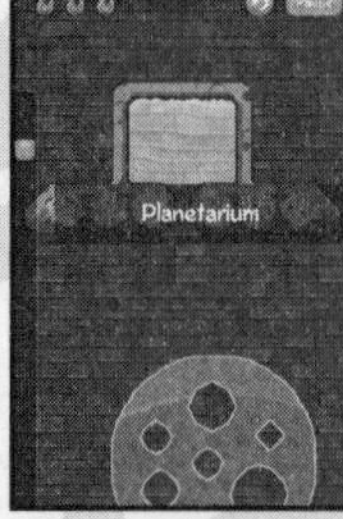

COLLECTION SCREEN EASTER EGG

Go to the Collection screen and scroll all the way to the bottom. Continue to scroll and you will see someone carved a message into the wall.

EMBARASSED ACHIEVEMENT

Clicking on Swampy during a level causes him to perform a random action. If he hides behind the curtain, this achievement is earned.

WORLD OF GOO

WHISTLE ITEM

Complete Leap Hole level.

WORLD OF GOO CORPORATION MINI GAME

Complete Hang Low level.

MICROSOFT XBOX 360®

GAMES

OVERLOAD

XBOX 360

2010 FIFA WORLD CUP SOUTH AFRICA

ADIDAS U11 TEAM

Go to EA Extras in My 2010 FIFA World Cup. Select Unlockable Code Entry and enter WSBJPJYODFYQIIGK.

FINAL MATCH BALL

Go to EA Extras in My 2010 FIFA World Cup. Select Unlockable Code Entry and enter FGWIXGFXTNSICLSS

ADIDAS ADIPURE III TRX (BLACK/SUN)

Go to EA Extras in My 2010 FIFA World Cup. Select Unlockable Code Entry and enter HHDOPWPMIXZQOJOZ

ADIDAS F50 ADIZERO (BLACK/SUN/SUN)

Go to EA Extras in My 2010 FIFA World Cup. Select Unlockable Code Entry and enter SGFSTZPPXCHHMJMH

ADIDAS F50 ADIZERO (CHAMELEON)

Go to EA Extras in My 2010 FIFA World Cup. Select Unlockable Code Entry and enter VOKMNEZTJOQPULUT

ADIDAS F50 ADIZERO (SUN/BLACK/GOLD)

Go to EA Extras in My 2010 FIFA World Cup. Select Unlockable Code Entry and enter YOZCCVIFJGKQJWTW

ADIDAS PREDATOR X (BLACK/SUN)

Go to EA Extras in My 2010 FIFA World Cup. Select Unlockable Code Entry and enter OCEGZCUHXOBSBNFU

COCA-COLA CELEBRATIONS

Go to EA Extras in My 2010 FIFA World Cup. Select Unlockable Code Entry and enter the following:

CELEBRATION	CODE	HOW TO PERFORM
Baby Cradle	UGSIMLBHLFPUBFJY	Left Trigger + A
Dance	KBRRWKUIRSTWUJQW	Left Trigger + B
Dying Fly	DVMNJPBTLHJZGECP	Left Trigger + X
Flying Dive	DBQDUXQTRWTVXYDC	Left Trigger + Y
Prancing Bird	TWVBIXYACAOLGOWO	Right Bumper + B
River Dance	MIKAKPUMEEWNTQVE	Right Bumper + X
Side Slide	VNDWDUDLMGRNHDNV	Right Bumper + Y
Speed Skating	LHEHJZTPYYQDJQXB	Right Bumper + A

AAH IMPOSSIBLE RESCUE

NARRATOR

At the main menu, enter the following codes to change the narrator.

NARRATOR	CODE
Anime-L22	Y, Y, Y, Y, X
Carole Clark	X, Y, Y, Y, X
Geoff-Li	X, Y, X, X, X
Hoegoeshinseki	Y, X, X, X, Y
Lilfirebender	X, X, Y, Y, X
Lucas Wilheim	Y, X, Y, X, Y
Meika	X, X, X, X, X
Michelle Rakar	X, X, X, X, Y
Ofebriso	Y, Y, X, X, X
Pia Lehtinen	X, X, Y, X, X
Sanjikunsgirl	X, Y, X, Y, X
Skimlines	Y, Y, X, X, Y
Teisei	Y, X, X, X, X

ALAN WAKE'S AMERICAN NIGHTMARE

AVATAR AWARDS

AVATAR	EARNED BY
American Nightmare Hoodie	Purchase the Game and Meet Emma in the Game.
Night Springs T-Shirt	Unlock the first Nightmare Difficulty Arcade Level.
Old Gods of Asgard Tour T-Shirt	Complete Story Mode.

ANOMALY: WARZONE EARTH

AVATAR AWARDS

AVATAR	EARNED BY
Anomaly Battle Pants	Complete any tactical trial mission to unlock these pants.
Anomaly Battle Shirt	Complete 1st mission to unlock the battle shirt.
Anomaly Commander's Helmet	Finish the campaign to unlock the commander's helmet.

APPLES TO APPLES

BUMBLEBEE APPLE AVATAR

Select Enter Code from Unlockables and enter buzzworthy.

NINJA APPLE AVATAR

Select Enter Code from Unlockables and enter silentslice.

ASSASSIN'S CREED: BROTHERHOOD

CAPES

Select Outfits from the Inventory screen to access.

CAPE	HOW TO OBTAIN
Auditore Cape	100% Rebuilding Rome
Borgia Cape	Collect 100 Borgia Flags
Medici and Venetian Capes	Complete Auditore Trail Mnemonic in Assassin's Creed: Project Legacy

CHEATS

Select Cheats from the Options menu when replaying a memory.

CHEAT	OBTAIN 100% SYNC IN THIS SEQUENCE
Ride the Unicorn	1
Buns of Steel	2
Killing Spree	3
Sisterhood	4
Ultimate Guild	5
Unlimited Assassins Signals	6
Desmond	8

ASSASSIN'S CREED: REVELATIONS

100% SYNC CHEATS

Completing the sequences with 100% sync unlocks various cheats. They can be used when replaying a memory and are accessed through the Options.

CHEAT	COMPLETE SEQUENCE WITH 100% SYNC
Buns of Steel	2
Killing Spree	3
Ultimate Guild	4
Calling All Assassins	5
Permanent Secrecy	6
Infinite Ammunition	7
The Old Eagle Outfit	8

BAKUGAN BATTLE BRAWLERS

1,000 BP

Enter 33204429 as your name.

5,000 BP

Enter 42348294 as your name.

10,000 BP

Enter 46836478 as your name.

100,000 BP

Enter 18499753 as your name.

500,000 BP

Enter 26037947 as your name.

BAKUGAN: DEFENDERS OF THE CORE

HIDDEN ITEMS

Select Unlock Codes from Collection and enter HXV6Y7BF. Now you can enter up to 8 of your unique Bakugan Dimensions codes.

The codes unlock the following:

- 10,000 Core Energy
- Ten Vexos Passes
- Earthen Armor
- Fire Spirit
- Light Arrow
- Tornado Vortex
- Water Pillar
- Zorch Thunder

Here are 8 codes:

- 2FKRRMNCDQ
- 82D77YK6P8
- HUUH8ST7AR
- JJUZDEACXX
- QY8CLD5NJE
- TD4UMFSRW3
- YJ7RGG7WGZ
- YQLHBBSMDC

BANJO-TOOIE

REGAIN ENERGY

Go to the Code Chamber in the Mayahem Temple and access the scroll on the wall. If you have been awarded this cheat by Cheato, enter HONEYBACK. If not, enter CHEATOKCABYENOH.

FALLS DON'T HURT

Go to the Code Chamber in the Mayahem Temple and access the scroll on the wall. If you have been awarded this cheat by Cheato, enter FALLPROOF. If not, enter CHEATOFOORPLLAF.

HOMING EGGS

Go to the Code Chamber in the Mayahem Temple and access the scroll on the wall. If you have been awarded this cheat, enter HOMING. If not, enter CHEATOGNIMOH.

DOUBLES MAXIMUM EGGS

Go to the Code Chamber in the Mayahem Temple and access the scroll on the wall. If you have been awarded this cheat by Cheato, enter EGGS. If not, enter CHEATOSGGE.

DOUBLES MAXIMUM FEATHERS

Go to the Code Chamber in the Mayahem Temple and access the scroll on the wall. If you have been awarded this cheat by Cheato, enter FEATHERS. If not, enter CHEATOSREHTAEF.

JOLLY ROGER LAGOON'S JUKEBOX

Go to the Code Chamber in the Mayahem Temple and access the scroll on the wall. If you have been awarded this cheat, enter JUKEBOX. If not, enter CHEATOXOBEKUJ.

SIGNS IN JIGGYWIGGY'S TEMPLE GIVE HINTS TO GET EACH JIGGY

Go to the Code Chamber in the Mayahem Temple and access the scroll on the wall. If you have been awarded this cheat, enter GETJIGGY. If not, enter CHEATOYGGIJTEG.

ALL LEVELS

Go to the Code Chamber in the Mayahem Temple and enter JIGGYWIGGYSPECIAL.

SPEED BANJO

Go to the Code Chamber in the Mayahem Temple and enter SUPERBANJO.

SPEED ENEMIES

Go to the Code Chamber in the Mayahem Temple and enter SUPERBADDY.

INFINITE EGGS & FEATHERS

Go to the Code Chamber in the Mayahem Temple and enter NESTKING.

INFINITE HONEY

Go to the Code Chamber in the Mayahem Temple and enter HONEYKING.

BATMAN: ARKHAM CITY

ALL BATMAN SKINS

This code allows you to start the campaign with all of the skins that you have downloaded, purchased, or unlocked. After selecting your save slot, press Left, Left, Down, Down, Left, Left, Right, Up, Up, Down at the main menu. You are then given the opportunity to select a skin.

BIG HEAD MODE

In the game, select the Cryptographic Sequencer. Hold Left Trigger and then hold Right Trigger to get Batman to use the device. Next, rotate the right Thumbstick clockwise while rotating the left Thumbstick counter-clockwise. Eventually, you notice Batman's head enlarge. Enemies and other characters' heads are also big. This works in Normal, Hard, and New Game +.

BATTLEFIELD: BAD COMPANY

M60

Select Unlocks from the Multiplayer menu, press Start, and enter try4ndrunf0rcov3r.

QBU88

Select Unlocks from the Multiplayer menu, press Start, and enter your3mynextt4rget.

UZI

Select Unlocks from the Multiplayer menu, press Start, and enter cov3r1ngthecorn3r.

FIND ALL FIVE WEAPONS

SNIPER RIFLE

You received a weapon unlock code for this gun if you pre-ordered the game.

MACHINE GUN

Receive a weapon unlock code for this gun after signing up for the newsletter at www.findallfive.com.

SUB-MACHINE GUN

Download the demo and reach rank 4 to receive an unlock code for this weapon.

ASSAULT RIFLE

Go to veteran.battlefield.com and register your previous Battlefield games to receive an unlock code for this weapon.

SEMI-AUTOMATIC SHOTGUN

Check your online stats at www.findallfive.com to get an unlock code for this weapon.

BAYONETTA

In Chapter 2, after Verse 3, find the phones in the plaza area. Stand in front of the appropriate phone and enter the following codes. The left phone is used for Weapons, the right phone is for Accessories, and the far phone is for Characters.

These codes require a certain amount of halos to be used. You will lose these halos immediately after entering the code.

WEAPONS

BAZILLIONS

Required Halos: 1 Million

Up, Up, Up, Up, Down, Down, Down, Down, Left, Right, Left, Right, Y

PILLOW TALK

Required Halos: 1 Million

Up, Up, Up, Up, Down, Down, Down, Down, Left, Right, Left, Right, A

RODIN

Required Halos: 5 Million

Up, Up, Up, Up, Down, Down, Down, Down, Left, Right, Left, Right, Left Bumper

ACCESSORIES

BANGLE OF TIME

Required Halos: 3 Million

Up, Up, Up, Up, Down, Down, Down, Down, Left, Right, Left, Right, Left Trigger

CLIMAX BRACELET

Required Halos: 5 Million

Up, Up, Up, Up, Down, Down, Down, Down, Left, Right, Left, Right, Right Trigger

ETERNAL TESTIMONY

Required Halos: 2 Million

Up, Up, Up, Up, Down, Down, Down, Down, Left, Right, Left, Right, Right Bumper

CHARACTERS

JEANNE

Required Halos: 1 Million

Up, Up, Up, Up, Down, Down, Down, Down, Left, Right, Left, Right, B

LITTLE ZERO

Required Halos: 5 Million

Up, Up, Up, Up, Down, Down, Down, Down, Left, Right, Left, Right, X

BEN 10: ALIEN FORCE VILGAX ATTACKS

Level Skip Pause the game and enter Portal in the Cheats menu.

UNLOCK ALL SPECIAL ATTACKS FOR ALL FORMS

Pause the game and enter Everythingproof in the Cheats menu.

UNLOCK ALL ALIEN FORMS

Pause the game and enter Primus in the Cheats menu.

TOGGLE INVULNERABILITY ON AND OFF

Pause the game and enter Xlmrsmoothy in the Cheats menu.

GIVES PLAYER FULL HEALTH

Pause the game and enter Herotime in the Cheats menu.

QUICK ENERGY REGENERATION

Pause the game and enter Generator in the Cheats menu.

BEN 10 GALACTIC RACING

KINECELARATOR

Select Promotional Codes from Extras and enter Ben, Spidermonkey, Kevin Levin, Ultimate Echo Echo.

BIONIC COMMANDO REARMED

The following challenge rooms can be found in the Challenge Room list. Only one code can be active at a time.

AARON SEDILLO'S CHALLENGE ROOM (CONTEST WINNER)

At the Title screen, press Right, Down, Left, Up, Left Bumper, Right Bumper, Y, Y, X, X, Start.

EUROGAMER CHALLENGE ROOM:

At the Title screen, press Down, Up, Down, Up, Left, Left Bumper, X, Left Bumper, X, Y, Start.

GAMESRADAR CHALLENGE ROOM:

At the Title screen, press Right Bumper, Y, X, X, Up, Down, Left Bumper, Left Bumper, Up, Down, Start.

IGN CHALLENGE ROOM:

At the Title screen, press Up, Down, Y, X, X, Y, Down, Up, Left Bumper, Left Bumper, Start.

MAJOR NELSON CHALLENGE ROOM

At the Title screen, press Left Bumper, X, X, X, Right, Down, Left Bumper, Left, Y, Down, Start.

BLACKLIGHT: TANGO DOWN

UNLOCK CODES

Select Unlock Code from Help & Options and enter the following. These tags can be used on your customized weapons.

TAG	UNLOCK CODE
Alienware Black	Alienwarec8pestU
Alienware	Al13nwa4re5acasE
AMD VISION	4MDB4quprex
AMD VISION	AMD3afrUnap
ATi	AT1hAqup7Su
Australia Flag	AUS9eT5edru
Austria Flag	AUTF6crAS5u
Belgium Flag	BELS7utHAsP
Blacklight	R41nB0wu7p3
Blacklight	Ch1pBLuS9PR
Canada Flag	CANfeprUtr5
Denmark Flag	DENdathe8HU
E3 Dog Tags	E3F6crAS5u
Famitsu Magazine	Fam1tsuprusWe2e
Finland Flag	FINw3uthEfe
France Flag	FRApRUyUT4a
Germany Flag	GERtRE4a4eS
Holland Flag	HOLb8e6UWuh
Hong Kong Flag	HOKYeQuKuw3
India Flag	INDs4u8RApr
Ireland Flag	IRE8ruGejec
Italy Flag	ITAQ7Swu9re
Jace Hall Show	J4ceH4llstuFaCh4
Japan Flag	JPNj7fazebR
Korea Flag	KORpaphA9uK
Mexico Flag	MEX5Usw2YAd
New Zealand Flag	NZLxut32eSA
Norway Flag	NOR3Waga8wa

TAG	UNLOCK CODE
Orange Scorpion	Ch1pMMRSc0rp
Order Logo Chip	Ch1p0RD3Ru02
Pink Brass Knuckles	H4rtBr34kerio4u
Portugal Flag	PORQ54aFrEY
Razer	R4z3erzu8habuC
Russia Flag	RUS7rusteXe
Singapore Flag	SINvuS8E2aC
Spain Flag	ESPChE4At5p
Storm Lion Comics	StormLion9rAVaZ2
Storm Lion Comics	St0rmLi0nB4qupre
Sweden Flag	SWEt2aPHutr
Switzerland Flag	SWIsTE8tafU
Taiwan Flag	TAW8udukUP2
United Kingdom Flag	UKv4D3phed
United States Flag	USAM3spudre
Upper Playground	UPGr0undv2FUDame
Upper Playground	UPGr0undWupraf4u
UTV Lightning Logo chip	Ch1p1GN1u0S
Yellow Teddy Bear	Denek1Ju3aceH7
Zombie Studios Logo Chip	Ch1pZ0MB1Et7

BLITZ: THE LEAGUE II

TOUCHDOWN CELEBRATIONS

Press these button combinations when given the chance after scoring a touchdown

CELEBRATION	CODE
Ball Spike	A, A, A, B
Beer Chug	A, A, B, B
Dance Fever	Y, Y, Y, A
Get Down	B, A, B, Y
Golf Putt	A, X, Y, B
Helmet Fling	A, X, A, X

CELEBRATION	CODE
Knockout	X, X, Y, Y
Man Crush	X, X, X, Y
Nut Shot	Y, Y, B, A
Pylon Darts	A, B, A, B
The Pooper	Y, X, A, B

BLUR

BMW CONCEPT 1 SERIES TII CHROME

In the Multiplayer Showroom, highlight the BMW Concept 1 Series tii and press Left Trigger, Right Trigger, Left Trigger, Right Trigger.

FULLY UPGRADE FORD BRONCO

In the Multiplayer Showroom, highlight the Ford Bronco and press Left Trigger, Right Trigger, Left Trigger, Right Trigger.

AVATAR AWARDS

AWARD	EARNED BY
Wreck Tee	Earn the Been there, got the T-shirt Achievement
Friend Rechallenge Tee	Defeat a friends rechallenge.
Legend Tee	Unlock first Legend Rank in multiplayer.
Showdown Tee	Complete Showdown
Sticker Tee	Complete the Sticker Book.

BORDERLANDS 2

BORDERLANDS 1 SKIN

With a Borderlands save game on your system, veteran skins from the first game is unlocked. Find them in the Extras menu.

MINECRAFT SKINS

Go to Caustic Caverns, which is reached by cutting through Sanctuary Hole. Find the train tracks to the northwest and follow them to a big door. Move around it, turn right and hop over the blocks. Move along the left wall until you find Minecraft dirt. Break through them until a Badass Creeper appears. Defeat it to unlock the skins.

EXTRA WUBS

At the title screen, press Up, Up, Down, Down, Left, Right, Left, Right, B, A, Start. This is a pretty useless code as Wubs do not do anything.

BROTHERS IN ARMS: HELL'S HIGHWAY

ALL CHAPTERS

Select Enter Codes from the Options and enter GIMMECHAPTERS.

ALL RECON POINTS

Select Enter Codes from the Options and enter 0ZNDRBICRA.

KILROY DETECTOR

Select Enter Codes from the Options and enter SH2VYIVNZF.

TWO MULTIPLAYER SKINS

Select Enter Codes from the Options and enter HI9WTPXSUK.

CALL OF DUTY: BLACK OPS

ACCESS TERMINAL

At the main menu, alternately press aim and fire until you break free of the restraints. Find the terminal behind the chair. Here you can enter the following.

TERMINAL COMMANDS

EFFECT	COMMAND
List Commands	Help
Root directory (use ls to list codes)	cd .. [enter] cd .. [enter] cd bin [enter]
List directory	ls
List audio files and pictures	DIR
Open file	CAT [filename found from DIR command]
View a file	TYPE (filename.extension)
List CIA e-mail	mail
List login names (does not give passwords)	WHO
FI FIE FOE	FOOBAR
All Intel	3ARC INTEL
Dead Ops Arcade	DOA
Dead Ops Arcade and Presidential Zombie Mode	3ARC UNLOCK
Virtual Therapist Software	Alicia
Zork I: The Great Underground Adventure	ZORK

CIA DATA SYSTEM LOGINS

Use the following IDs and Passwords to access users' files and mail.

USER ACCOUNT	ID	PASSWORD
Alex Mason	amason	PASSWORD
Bruce Harris	bharris	GOSKINS
D. King	dking	MFK
Dr. Adrienne Smith	asmith	ROXY
Dr. Vannevar Bush	vbush	MANHATTAN
Frank Woods	fwoods	PHILLY
Grigori "Greg" Weaver	gweaver	GEDEON
J. Turner	jturner	CONDOR75
Jason Hudson	jhudson	BRYANT1950
John McCone	jmccone	BERKLEY22
Joseph Bowman	jbowman	UWD
President John Fitzgerald Kennedy	jfkennedy	LANCER
President Lyndon Baines Johnson	lbjohnson	LADYBIRD

USER ACCOUNT	ID	PASSWORD
President Richard Nixon	rnixon	CHECKERS
Richard Helms	rhelms	LEROSEY
Richard Kain	rkain	SUNWU
Ryan Jackson	rjackson	SAINTBRIDGET
T. Walker	twalker	RADIO
Terrance Brooks	tbrooks	LAUREN
William Raborn	wraborn	BROMLOW

FRANK WOODS GAMER PICTURE

Escape from interrogation chair by pressing the aim and fire buttons at the main menu.

JASON HUDSON GAMER PICTURE

Use the terminal to login as Jason Hudson.

CALL OF DUTY: BLACK OPS - ANNIHILATION

GAMER PICTURES

DEMPSEY & RICHTOFEN GAMER PICTURES

Earn the Time Travel Will Tell Achievement.

CALL OF DUTY: MODERN WARFARE 3

ARCADE MODE

After a complete playthrough of the game, Arcade Mode becomes available from the Main menu.

UNLOCKABLE CHEATS

After completing the game, cheats are unlocked based on how many intelligence pieces were gathered. These cheats cannot be used during Arcade Mode. They may also disable the ability to earn Achievements.

CHEAT	INTEL ITEMS	DESCRIPTION
CoD Noir	2	Black and white
Photo-Negative	4	Inverses colors
Super Contrast	6	Increases contrast
Ragtime Warfare	8	Black and white, scratches fill screen, double speed, piano music
Cluster Bombs	10	Four extra grenade explosions after frag grenade explodes
A Bad Year	15	Enemies explode into a bunch of old tires when killed
Slow-Mo Ability	20	Melee button enables/disables slow-motion mode
Infinite Ammo	30	Unlimited ammo and no need to reload. Doesn't work for single-shot weapons such as RPG.

CALL OF DUTY: WORLD AT WAR

ZOMBIE MODE

Complete Campaign mode.

CARNIVAL GAMES: MONKEY SEE, MONKEY DO!

AVATAR AWARDS

AWARD	EARNED BY
Barker Bowler	Purchase Barker Bowler Prize.
Barker's Best	Purchase Barker's Best Prize.
Monkey Barker	Purchase Monkey Barker Prize.

CARS 2: THE VIDEO GAME

ALL MODES AND TRACKS

Select Enter Codes from the Options and enter 959595.

LASER GUIDED

Select Enter Codes from the Options and enter 123456. Select Cheats to toggle the cheat on and off.

UNLIMITED ENERGY

Select Enter Codes from the Options and enter 721953. Select Cheats to toggle the cheat on and off.

AVATAR AWARDS

AWARD	EARNED BY
Team Brazil Jumpsuit	Unlock this item by earning the In Your Face Achievement.
Team France Jumpsuit	Unlock this item by earning the Island Hopper Achievement.
Team Spain Jumpsuit	Unlock this item by earning the Smashing Achievement.

CASTLEVANIA: HARMONY OF DESPAIR

HARD MODE

Complete Chapter 6 to unlock Hard Mode for Chapter 1.

ALUCARD GAMERPIC

Complete Chapter 6 in single player.

JAPANESE VOICES

At the character's color select, hold Right Trigger and press A.

CASTLEVANIA: LORDS OF SHADOW

CHEAT MENU

At a loading screen, press Up, Up, Down, Down, Left, Right, Left, Right, B, A. The cheats can be found in the Extra Options. Activating any cheats disables saving and Achievements.

SNAKE OUTFIT

Defeat the game. In the Extras menu, toggle Solid Eye and Bandanna on.

VAMPIRE WARGAME

During Chapter 6-3: Castle Hall, beat the Vampire Wargame to unlock it in the Extras menu.

CATHERINE

NEW RAPUNZEL STAGES

At the title screen, press Up, Down, Down, Up, Up, Up, Down, Down, Down, Down, Right. Re-enter the code to disable.

COMIC JUMPER THE ADVENTURES OF CAPTAIN SMILEY

AVATAR AWARDS

AWARD	EARNED BY
Captain Smiley Giant Head	Complete the whole game
Gerda T-Shirt (female only)	Complete the 1st Level
Star T-Shirt (male only)	Complete the 1st Level

COMMAND & CONQUER 3: TIBERIUM WARS

FREE NOD SHADOW SQUADS

During a NOD game, pause and press Left, Right, Up, Up, Up, Down, RB, LB, LB, B. This code does not work in Skirmish or Career.

CRACKDOWN 2

AVATAR AWARDS

AWARD	EARNED BY
Orb Shirt (Male and Female)	Have First Blood achievement from Crackdown
Freaky Slippers (Male and Female)	Earn First Hurdle achievement
Ruffian Hat	Earn Hope Springs Savior achievement
Level 1 Agent Suit (Male and Female)	Earn Light Bringer achievement
Official Agency Hoodie (Male and Female)	Earn Jack of all Trades achievement

DOWNLOADABLE CONTENT: TOY BOX

AVATAR AWARDS

AWARD	EARNED BY
Green Agent Helmet	Download Toy Box DLC
Green Agent Suit	Earn Rocketeer achievement

CRASH BANDICOOT: MIND OVER MUTANT

A cheat can be deactivated by re-entering the code.

FREEZE ENEMIES WITH TOUCH

Pause the game, hold Right Trigger and press Down, Down, Down, Up.

ENEMIES DROP X4 DAMAGE

Pause the game, hold Right Trigger and press Up, Up, Up, Left.

ENEMIES DROP PURPLE FRUIT

Pause the game, hold Right Trigger and press Up, Down, Down, Up.

ENEMIES DROP SUPER KICK

Pause the game, hold Right Trigger and press Up, Right, Down, Left.

ENEMIES DROP WUMPA FRUIT

Pause the game, hold Right Trigger and press Right, Right, Right, Up.

SHADOW CRASH

Pause the game, hold Right Trigger and press Left, Right, Left, Right.

DEFORMED CRASH

Pause the game, hold Right Trigger and press Left, Left, Left, Down.

CRIMSON ALLIANCE

AVATAR AWARDS

AWARD	EARNED BY
Pocket Shaman	Defeat a Primitive Shaman.
Death Knight Helm	Collect 20 Treasures.

CRIMSON DRAGON

AVATAR AWARDS

AVATAR	EARNED BY
Bloodskin Helmet	Complete the First Mission.
Bloodskin Suit (Top)	Raise the level of Bloodskin.
Bloodskin Suit (Bottom)	Get an S rank five times with Bloodskin.

CRYSIS 2

HIDDEN MINIGAME

At the credits, press Right Trigger five times.

DANCE CENTRAL 2

ANGEL'S DC CLASSIC OUTFIT

Select Gameplay Settings from the Options, choose Enter Cheats and enter Y, Right, Left, Up, X, X, Down, Y.

EMILIA'S DC CLASSIC OUTFIT

Select Gameplay Settings from the Options, choose Enter Cheats and enter Left, Left, Up, Right, Right, X, Down, Y.

MISS AUBREY'S DC CLASSIC OUTFIT

Select Gameplay Settings from the Options, choose Enter Cheats and enter Left, Down, X, X, Down, Right.

TAYE'S DC CLASSIC OUTFIT

Select Gameplay Settings from the Options, choose Enter Cheats and enter Up, Left, Y, X, Left, Up, X, Y.

AVATAR AWARDS

AWARD	EARNED BY
Bring It Tee	Play every song in the game in Perform It mode.
Neon Tee	Get a solo score of at least 2,000,000 points on a song.
Ribbon Tee	Earn Gold Stars on a song.

DARKSIDERS

HARVESTER FOR 0 SOULS

Pause the game and select Enter Code from the Options. Enter The Hollow Lord.

DARKSIDERS II

AVATAR AWARDS

AVATAR	EARNED BY
Game Logo Cap	Show your support for Darksiders II with this Logo Cap.
Death Mask	Don the mask of Death and reap the souls of your enemies as the most feared of the four horsemen.
Darksiders II T-Shirt	A T-Shirt featuring the Joe Mad Darksiders II artwork used to announce the game.

DEAD BLOCK

AVATAR AWARDS

AWARD	EARNED BY
Construction Worker Helmet	Collect the helmet in the tutorial.
Dead Block Shirt	Beat all singleplayer levels.

DEAD OR ALIVE 5

AKIRA YUKI

Defeat Akira in Story mode.

SARAH BRYANT

Defeat Sarah in Story mode.

GEN FU

Complete Eliot's stage in Story mode.

PAI CHAN

Get 100 titles.

ALPHA-152

Get 300 titles

TRUE FIGHTER COURSES

Complete Champ course in Arcade, Survival, or Time Attack.

MASTER COURSE

Complete True Fighter course in Arcade, Survival, or Time Attack.

LEGEND COURSE

Complete Master course in Arcade, Survival, or Time Attack.

CHANGE HAIRSTYLE FOR SOME CHARACTERS

At the costume select, highlight a character, and hold Left Bumper or Right Bumper along with any Hold, Punch, or Kick.

CHANGE ACCESSORY FOR SOME CHARACTERS

At the costume select, highlight a character, and hold any Hold, Punch, or Kick.

CHRISTIE SWIMSUIT

Complete the Legend course in Time Attack (Solo) with Christie, without using a Continue.

LISA SWIMSUIT

Complete the Legend Course in Survival (Solo) with Lisa.

TINA SWIMSUIT

Complete the Legend Course in Arcade (Solo) with Tina, without using a Continue.

KASUMI BLACK SUIT

Complete the True Kasumi stage in Story mode.

KASUMI KIMONO

Complete the Kasumi vs Christie battle in the True Kasumi stage in Story mode.

DEAD RISING 2

KNIGHT ARMOR

Wearing this armor doubles Chuck's health. When his health falls below half, the armor is destroyed.

PIECE OF ARMOR	OBTAINED BY
Full Beard Moustache	In the back of Wave of Style located in Royal Flush Plaza.
Knight Armor	Finish the game with the S ending.
Knight Boots	$2,000,000 at Moe's Maginations pawnshop on the Platinum Strip.
Knight Helmet	Rescue Jack in Meet the Family and then win at poker in Ante Up.

UNLOCKABLE OUTFITS

The following items are unlocked by performing the corresponding task.

ITEM	OBTAINED BY
Bowling Shirt, Diner Waitress, Hunting Jacket, and Overalls	Import a save game from Case Zero.
Champion Jacket	Earn the Win Big! Achievement. Get this by finishing in first place in a TIR Episode.
Dealer Outfit	Earn Chuck Greene: Cross Dresser? Achievement. Get this by changing into all the clothes in the game.
Hockey Mask	Earn the Head Trauma Achievement. Get this by using every type of melee weapon on a zombie.
Orange Prison Outfit	Earn the Judge, Jury, and Executioner Achievement. Get this by killing 10 psychos.
Tattered Clothes	Earn the Zombie Fu Achievement. Get this by killing 1,000 zombies barehanded.
TIR Helmet	Earn $1,000,000 in Terror is Reality.
TIR Outfit	Earn $5,000,000 in Terror is Reality.
Willamette Mall Security Uniform	Earn Hero of Fortune City Achievement. Get this by rescuing 50 survivors.

DEAD SPACE

REFILL STASIS AND KINESIS ENERGY

Pause the game and press X, Y, Y, X, Y.

REFILL OXYGEN

Pause the game and press X, X, Y (x3).

ADD 2 POWER NODES

Pause the game and press Y, X (x3), Y. *This code can only be used once.*

ADD 5 POWER NODES

Pause the game and press Y, X, Y, X, X, Y, X, X, Y, X, X, Y. *This code can only be used once.*

1,000 CREDITS

Pause the game and press X (x3), Y, X. *This code can only be used once.*

2,000 CREDITS

Pause the game and press X (x3), Y, Y. *This code can only be used once.*

5,000 CREDITS

Pause the game and press X (x3), Y, X, Y. *This code can only be used once.*

10,000 CREDITS

Pause the game and press X, Y (x3), X, X, Y. *This code can only be used once.*

DEAD TO RIGHTS: RETRIBUTION

AVATAR AWARDS

AWARD	EARNED BY
GAC Armor	Earn the Best cop this city's ever had Achievement. Get this by completing the game on Officer difficulty.
GAC Helmet	Earn the Boom! Achievement. Get this by getting 30 headshots in any level, on Officer or greater difficulty.
GCPD Shirt	Earn the Brawler Achievement. Get this by completing any level (excluding the Prologue) without firing a shot.
Jack and Shadow Shirt	Earn the Finish him Shadow! Achievement. Get this by combining Jack and Shadow to kill 20 enemies in any level, on Officer or greater.
Logo Shirt	Earn the Protect the Innocent Achievement. Get this by saving the hostages.

DEADLIEST WARRIOR: LEGENDS

AVATAR AWARDS

AWARD	EARNED BY
Sun Tzu's Costume	Complete arcade mode with any warrior on any difficulty level.
Sun Tzu's Helmet	Complete arcade mode as each warrior on the Deadliest difficulty.

KOI WEAPON

Kill 25 enemies in Survival Slice.

DEADLIGHT

AVATAR AWARDS

AVATAR	EARNED BY
Handy Hat	Reach the highway billboard.
Deadlight Ribs T-Shirt	Finish the Game.
Yummy Hat	Discover 100% of the game.

DEATH BY CUBE

LOSS - BLACK ROBOT

At the Upgrade screen, hold Left Trigger and press Right Trigger, Right Trigger, X, Y, X.

SELIS - PINK ROBOT

At the Upgrade screen, hold Right Trigger and press Left Trigger, Y, X, Left Trigger, Start.

DEATHSPANK

AVATAR AWARDS

AWARD	EARNED BY
Dragon Hatchling	Complete Ms. Heybenstances quest to rescue the hatchlings.
Unicorn Poop T-shirt	Kill the twin dragons guarding the artifact.

DEFENSE GRID: THE AWAKENING

The following cheats will disable Achievements.

100,000 RESOURCES
Click and hold the Right Thumbstick and press Right, Right, Right, Right

CORES CANNOT BE TAKEN
Click and hold the Right Thumbstick and press Up, Left, Down, Right

FREE CAMERA MODE
Click and hold the Right Thumbstick and press Down, Up, Down, Down

INSTANT VICTORY
Click and hold the Right Thumbstick and press Up, Up, Up, Up

KILL ALL ALIENS
Click and hold the Right Thumbstick and press Left, Right, Left, Right

KILL ALL ALIENS CARRYING CORES
Click and hold the Right Thumbstick and press Up, Down, Down, Up

LEVEL SELECT
Click and hold the Right Thumbstick and press Up, Up, Down, Down, Left, Right, Left, Right

SELF-DESTRUCT (INSTANT DEFEAT)
Click and hold the Right Thumbstick and press Down, Down, Down, Down

TOGGLE TARGET RETICULE
Click and hold the Right Thumbstick and press Down, Up, Down, Up

UNLOCK ALL TOWER TYPES
Click and hold the Right Thumbstick and press Up, Down, Left, Right

DIRT 2

Win the given events to earn the following cars:

CAR	EVENT
Ford RS200 Evolution	Rally Cross World Tour
Toyota Stadium Truck	Landrush World Tour
Mitsubishi Pajero Dakar 1993	Raid World Tour
Dallenbach Special	Trailblazer World Tour
1995 Subaru Impreza WRX STi	Colin McRae Challenge
Colin McRae R4 [X Games]	X Games Europe
Mitsubishi Lancer Evolution X [X Games]	X Games Asia
Subaru Impreza WRX STi [X Games]	X Games America
Ford Escort MKII and MG Metro 6R4	All X Games events

DIRT 3

AVATAR AWARDS

AVATAR	EARNED BY
Racing Shoes	Reach Fan Level 12.
Racing Gloves	Reach Fan Level 24.
Racing Suit	Complete Season 1.
Rally Helmet	Complete Season 2.

DJ HERO

Select Cheats from Options and enter the following. Some codes will disable high scores and progress. Cheats cannot be used in tutorials and online.

UNLOCK ALL CONTENT
Enter tol0.

ALL CHARACTER ITEMS
Enter uNA2.

ALL VENUES
Enter Wv1u.

ALL DECKS
Enter LAuP.

ALL HEADPHONES
Enter 62Db.

ALL MIXES
Enter 82xl.

AUTO SCRATCH
Enter it6j.

AUTO EFFECTS DIAL
Enter ab1l.

AUTO FADER
Enter sl5d.

AUTO TAPPER
Enter zith.

AUTO WIN EUPHORIA
Enter r3a9.

BLANK PLINTHS
Enter ipr0.

HAMSTER SWITCH
Enter 7geo.

HYPER DECK MODE
Enter 76st.

SHORT DECK
Enter 51uc.

BLACK AND WHITE
Enter b!99.

EDGE EFFECT
Enter 2u4u.

INVISIBLE DJ
Enter oh5t.

MIDAS
Enter 4pe5.

PITCH BLACK OUT
Enter d4kr.

PLAY IN THE BEDROOM
Enter g7nh.

RAINBOW
Enter ?jy!.

ANY DJ, ANY SETLIST
Enter 0jj8.

DAFT PUNK'S CONTENT
Enter d1g?.

DJ AM'S CONTENT
Enter k07u.

DJ JAZZY JEFF'S CONTENT
Enter n1fz.

DJ SHADOW'S CONTENT
Enter omxv.

DJ Z-TRIP'S CONTENT
Enter 5rtg.

GRANDMASTER FLASH'S CONTENT
Enter ami8.

DJ HERO 2

ALL BONUS CONTENT
Select Cheats from the Options. Choose Retail Cheats and enter VIP Pass.

DAVID GUETTA
Select Cheats from the Options. Choose Retail Cheats and enter Guetta Blaster.

DEADMAU5
Select Cheats from the Options. Choose Retail Cheats and enter Open The Trap.

INVISIBLE DJ
Select Cheats from the Options. Choose Retail Cheats and enter Now You See Me.

AUTO CROSSFADE
Select Cheats from the Options. Choose Retail Cheats and enter I Hate Crossfading. This disables Leaderboards.

AUTO SCRATCH
Select Cheats from the Options. Choose Retail Cheats and enter Soothing. This disables Leaderboards.

AUTO TAP
Select Cheats from the Options. Choose Retail Cheats and enter Look No Hands! This disables Leaderboards.

DON KING PRESENTS: PRIZEFIGHTER

Re-enter a code to disable the cheat.

INVULNERABILITY
Select Enter Unlock Code from the Extras menu and enter SHIELDOFSTEEL.

MAXIMUM STATS
Select Enter Unlock Code from the Extras menu and enter BROUSSARDMODE.

INFINITE ADRENALINE
Select Enter Unlock Code from the Extras menu and enter FISTOFTHENORTHSHIELDS.

INFINITE STAMINA
Select Enter Unlock Code from the Extras menu and enter FEELTHEBURN.

SKIP GETUP GAME
Select Enter Unlock Code from the Extras menu and enter NEVERQUIT.

PLAY AS RICARDO MAYORGA
Select Enter Unlock Code from the Extras menu and enter POTSEMAG.

GREAT MOMENTS IN BOXING VIDEO
Select Enter Unlock Code from the Extras menu and enter 1BESTBUYBEST.

DOUBLE DRAGON: NEON

DOUBLE DRAGON 2 BILLY LEE GAMERPIC

As soon as you press Start at the title screen, this gamerpic becomes available.

PLAY AS A RO-BRO

At the stage select, hold Left Trigger + Left Bumper + click left analog stick + Right Trigger + Right Bumper + click right analog stick + Back + Start. Enter again to return to normal.

CONCEPT ART GALLERY

Complete the game to unlock this gallery at the main menu.

DRAGON DIFFICULTY

Defeat the game on Normal difficulty.

DOUBLE DRAGON DIFFICULTY

Defeat the game on Dragon difficulty.

DRAGON'S LAIR

AVATAR AWARDS

AWARD	EARNED BY
Dragon's Lair Logo T-Shirt	Free with your purchase of Dragon's Lair!
Dragon's Lair Castle T-Shirt	Unlock the Secret Achievement.
Dirk the Daring's Helmet	Beat the Game.

DRIVER: SAN FRANCISCO

MOVIE SCENE CHALLENGES

As you collect the 130 Movie Tokens in the game, Movie Scene Challenges are unlocked as shown below.

MOVIE SCENE CHALLENGE	VEHICLE GIVEN	# MOVIE TOKENS
Gone In 60 Seconds	1973 Ford Mustang Mach I	10
Starsky & Hutch	1974 Dodge Monaco Cop	20
Bullitt	1968 Ford Mustang GT Fastback	30
The French Connection	1971 Pontiac LeMans	40
Blues Brothers	1974 Dodge Monaco	50
Cannonball Run	1978 Lamborghini Countach LP400S	60
Dukes of Hazard	1969 Dodge Charger R/T	70
Vanishing Point	1970 Dodge Challenger R/T	80
The Driver	1965 Chevrolet S-10	90
Redline	2011 McLaren MP4-12C	100
Smokey & The Bandit	1977 Pontiac TransAm Firebird	110
Test Drive	1987 RUF CT-R Yellow Bird	120
The Italian Job	1972 Lamborghini Miura	130

DUKE NUKEM FOREVER

CLUB DOOR CODE

Behind the bar in the club, there is a door that requires a code to get in. Enter 4768.

CHEATS

Defeating the game gives you the ability to activate the following cheats in Extras.

- Duke 3D Freeze Ray
- Grayscale Mode
- Head Scale
- Infinite Ammo
- Instagib
- Invincibility
- Mirror Mode

DUNGEON FIGHTER LIVE: FALL OF HENDON MYRE

AVATAR AWARDS

AVATAR	EARNED BY
Goblin Mask	Complete your First Quest.
Slayer Bracelet	Reach Level 20.
Slayer T-Shirt	Clear the final dungeon in under 45 minutes with two or more players in your online party.

DUST: AN ELYSIAN TAIL

AVATAR AWARDS

AVATAR	EARNED BY
Dust Shirt	Wake up in The Glade.
Fidget Shirt	Make Fidget even more powerful.
Ahrah Shirt	Discover the Truth.

EARTH DEFENSE FORCE: INSECT ARMAGEDDON

HIDDEN IMAGES IN GALLERY

Select Gallery from the Extras menu. At the gallery press X, X, Y, X, Left Bumper, Right Bumper.

FABLE HEROES

AVATAR AWARDS

AVATAR	EARNED BY
Heroes T-Shirt	Unlock the Heroes T-Shirt by completing the Millfields level.
Jack of Blades Mask	Unlock the Jack of Blades Mask by purchasing all the abilities for the Jack of Blades puppet.

FABLE: THE JOURNEY

AVATAR AWARDS

AVATAR	EARNED BY
Fable: The Journey T-Shirt	Fable: The Journey T-Shirt can be unlocked by progressing through your Journey.
Mask of the Devourer	Mask of the Devourer can be unlocked by progressing through your Journey.
Theresa's Blindfold	Theresa's Blindfold can be unlocked by progressing through your Journey.

FANTASTIC PETS

AVATAR AWARDS

AWARD	EARNED BY
Fantastic T-Shirt	Reach Fantastic Pet trainer rank 2.
Cute Hat (Female)	Reach Fantastic Pet trainer rank 3.
Fierce Hat (Male)	Reach Fantastic Pet trainer rank 3.
Fantastic Gloves	Reach Fantastic Pet trainer rank 4.
Fantastic Shoes	Reach Fantastic Pet trainer rank 5.
Fantastic Pet	Reach Fantastic Pet trainer rank 6.

FEZ

FLY

In New Game + at any time, press Up, Up, Up, Up + A.

FINAL FANTASY XIII-2

LIGHTNING GAMER PICTURE

This gamer picture is unlocked if you have a save game for Final Fantasy XIII on your console.

ANOTHER LIGHTNING GAMER PICTURE

Earn all of the Achievements.

MOG GAMER PICTURE

Earn the Fair Fighter Achievement.

NOEL GAMER PICTURE

Earn the Chronosavior Achievement.

SERAH GAMER PICTURE

Earn the Defragmented Achievement.

FIRE PRO WRESTLING

AVATAR AWARDS

AVATAR	EARNED BY
Wrestler Mask	Win every match in the Tutorial Series.
Leather Boots	Win every match in the Campion Series.
Bottoms	Obtain every Costume piece.

FLATOUT: ULTIMATE CARNAGE

MOB CAR IN SINGLE EVENTS

Select Enter Code from Extras and enter BIGTRUCK.

PIMPSTER IN SINGLE EVENTS

Select Enter Code from Extras and enter RUTTO.

ROCKET IN SINGLE EVENTS

Select Enter Code from Extras and enter KALJAKOPPA.

FORZA MOTORSPORT 4

AVATAR AWARDS

AVATAR	EARNED BY
Autovista T-Shirt	Fully explore any car in Autovista.
Stopwatch Cap	Post a time in every Rivals Mode Event.

FRACTURE

EXCLUSIVE PRE-ORDER SKIN

Pause the game and press Up, Right, Left, Down, Up, Left, Right, Down.

FROGGER

BIG FROGGER

At the One/Two-Player screen, press Up, Up, Down, Down, Left, Right, Left, Right, B, A.

FROGGER: HYPER ARCADE EDITION

CONTRA STYLE

At the style select, highlight Contra and enter Up, Up, Down, Down, Left, Right, Left, Right, B, A.

FROM DUST

AVATAR AWARDS

AVATAR	EARNED BY
The Tribal Mask	Retrieve this mask by unlocking the complete version of "From Dust".

FRUIT NINJA KINECT

AVATAR AWARDS

AVATAR	EARNED BY
Fruit Ninja T-Shirt	Equip an Item in Sensei's Swag.
Kung Fu Pants	Complete 3 Multplayer Games.
Kung Fu Sensei Shirt	Complete 5 games of Classic, Zen or Arcade.

FULL HOUSE POKER

AVATAR AWARDS

AWARD	EARNED BY
Hoodie	Level up
Bulldog Helmet	Level up to 50

GAME ROOM

SWAP KONAMI AND ASTEROIDS CABINET STYLES

During a game or at a menu, press Up, Up, Down, Down, Left, Right, Left, Right, B, A.

GAMERBOTS: THIRD-ROBOT SHOOTING

300,000 GP

Enter 24162444 as a gift code.

DEMON SWORD

Enter 39121412 as a gift code.

DUAL FLAME

Enter 34094035 as a gift code.

SPIKED CLUB

Enter 56095802 as a gift code.

STAR SLICER

Enter 55122302 as a gift code.

AVATAR AWARDS

AVATAR	EARNED BY
Marcus Doo-Rag	Complete campaign on any difficulty.
Horde Shirt	Earn "Welcome to Horde Mode" achievement.
Locust Drone Mask	Earn "Welcome to Beast Mode" achievement.

MUTATORS

Mutators are special rules that can have…unusual effects on the battlefield. You can enable Mutators for private matches, or watch for playlists from Epic when they turn them on for special events and holidays.

EASY

These Mutators give you an easier time in game.

MUTATOR	DESCRIPTION	HOW TO UNLOCK
Comet	When you Roadie Run, you build up energy until you ignite into a fireball that you can unleash on impacting enemies.	Gold "Shock Trooper" medal. (Versus mode)
Instagib Melee	Melee causes instant death.	Kill 200 enemies while playing a wretch in Beast. (Beast Mode)
Super Reload	Easier active reloads.	Bronze "Master at Arms" Medal. (Versus Mode)
Infinite Ammo	Unlimited clips of ammo, though you still must reload between clips.	Earn 100 "Combat Engineer" Ribbons. (Horde Mode)
Big explosions	Explosions have bigger blast radius.	Earn 100 "Hail Mary" Ribbons. (Arcade, Beast, Horde, Versus Modes)

HARD

These Mutators make the game a little tougher.

MUTATOR	DESCRIPTION	HOW TO UNLOCK
No Ammo Pickups	Gets rid of ammo boxes on map.	Unlocked at start.
Enemies Regeneration	Enemy's health regenerates.	Silver "Afficianado" medal. (Arcade Mode)
Vampire	Health does not regenerate, but every point of damage you inflict heals you in kind.	Earn 100 "Executioner" ribbons. (Versus Mode)
Must Active Reload	You must achieve an Active Reload to reload your weapon.	Silver "Active Reloader" Medal.
Friendly fire	Gunfire hurts your own team.	Complete the campaign in 4-player co-op. (Co-op Campaign)

FUN

These Mutators create fun effects with no effect on gameplay.

MUTATOR	DESCRIPTION	HOW TO UNLOCK
Big Head	Everyone's head (and other key features) are inflated to comical proportrions.	Gold "Horder" Medal (Horde Mode)
Piñata	Special tokens from every kill; collect them to earn points.	Gold "Investor" Medal (Beast Mode)
Flower Blood	Blood looks like flowers.	Silver "King of Cog" medal. (Arcade Mode)
Headless Chicken	Enemies attack each other for several seconds after they lose their heads.	Unlocked at start.
Laugh Track	Play as if your game was filmed before a live studio audience.	Bronze "Tour of Duty", "For the Horde", "I'm a Beast", and "Warmonger" Medals.

MULTIPLAYER CHARACTERS

Unlock the following characters for use in Multiplayer.

LOCUST (23 CHARACTERS)

CHARACTER	HOW TO UNLOCK
Drone	Available from start
Grenadier Elite	Available from start
Savage Drone	Available from start
Savage Grenadier	Available from start
Armored Myrrah	Available from start
Savage Grenadier Elite	Available as preorder from WalMart
Savage Kantus	Available as preorder from Amazon
Miner	Unlocks at XP Level 3
Beast Rider	Unlocks at XP Level 5
Hunter	Unlocks at XP Level 8
Theron Guard	Unlocks at XP Level 12
Spotter	Unlocks at XP Level 20
Flame Grenadier	Unlocks at XP Level 26
Grenadier	Unlocks at XP Level 39
Hunter Elite	Unlocks at XP Level 60
Golden Miner	Unlock with "Rifleman" Gold Medal.
Golden Hunter	Unlock with "Master at Arms" Gold Medal.
Sniper	Unlock with "Headshot" Bronze Medal.
Kantus	Unlock with "Medic" Gold Medal.
Savage Theron Guard	Unlock with Onyx "I'm a Beast" Medal.

COG (33 CHARACTERS)

CHARACTER	HOW TO UNLOCK
Marcus Fenix	Available from start
Dominic Santiago	Available from start
Damon Baird	Available from start
Augustus Cole	Available from start
Anya Stroud	Available from start
Commando Dom	Available as preorder from GameStop
Mechanic Baird	Available as preorder from Best Buy
Soldier Adam	Available as preorder with Gears of War 3 Limited Collector's Edition
COG Gear	Unlocks at XP Level 2
Samantha Byrne	Unlocks at XP Level 4
Dizzy Wallin	Unlocks at XP Level 7
Jace Stratton	Unlocks at XP Level 10
Clayton Carmine	Unlocks at XP Level 14

Classic Dom	Unlocks at XP Level 17
Classic Cole	Unlocks at XP Level 23
Classic Baird	Unlocks at XP Level 30
Benjamin Carmine	Unlocks at XP Level 34
Civilian Anya	Unlocks at XP Level 45
Victor Hoffman	Unlocks at XP Level 50
Anthony Carmine	Unlocks at XP Level 75
Cole Train	Unlocked with participation in Beta.
Classic Marcus	Unlock with "Veteran" Silver Medal.
Superstar Cole	Unlock with "MVP" Gold Medal.
Golden Gear	Unlock with "War Supporter" Bronze Medal.
Aaron Griffin	Unlock with "Big Money" Onyx Medal.
Chairman Prescott	Unlock with "Allfather" Silver Medal.
Underarmor Marcus	Complete the campaign on any difficulty.

THE GODFATHER II

These codes can only be used once every few minutes.

$5,000

While in Don view, press X, Y, X, X, Y, click Left Analog Stick.

FULL HEALTH

While in Don view, press Left, X, Right, Y, Right, click Left Analog Stick.

FULL AMMO

While in Don view, press Y, Left, Y, Right, X, click Right Analog Stick.

GOLDENEYE 007: RELOADED

BLACK MOONRAKER SKIN IN MULTIPLAYER

Select Cheat Codes from the Extras menu and enter las3r3ras3r.

INVISIBILITY AND TAG IN MULTIPLAYER

Select Cheat Codes from the Extras menu and enter f11ypr3load3ed.

PAINTBALL MODE IN MULTIPLAYER

Select Cheat Codes from the Extras menu and enter wr1t1ng1sOnth3wa11.

GRAND THEFT AUTO IV

CHEATS

Call the following phone numbers with Niko's phone to activate the cheats. Some cheats may affect the missions and achievements.

VEHICLE	PHONE NUMBER
Change weather	468-555-0100
Get weapons	486-555-0100
Get different weapons	486-555-0150
Raise wanted level	267-555-0150
Remove wanted level	267-555-0100
Restore armor	362-555-0100
Restore health	482-555-0100
Restore armor, health, and ammo	482-555-0100

SPAWN VEHICLES

Call the following phone numbers with Niko's phone to spawn the corresponding vehicle.

VEHICLE	PHONE NUMBER
Annihilator	359-555-0100
Cognoscenti	227-555-0142
Comet	227-555-0175
FIB Buffalo	227-555-0100
Jetmax	938-555-0100
NRG-900	625-555-0100
Sanchez	625-555-0150
SuperGT	227-555-0168
Turismo	227-555-0147

MAP LOCATIONS

Access a computer in game and enter the following URL: www.whattheydonotwantyoutoknow.com.

GRAND THEFT AUTO IV: THE BALLAD OF GAY TONY

CHEATS

Call the following phone numbers with your phone to activate the cheats. Some cheats may affect the missions and achievements.

CHEAT	PHONE NUMBER
Get weapons	486-555-0100
Get different weapons	486-555-0150
Raise wanted level	267-555-0150
Remove wanted level	267-555-0100
Restore armor	362-555-0100
Restore armor, health, and ammo	482-555-0100
Parachute	359-555-7272
Change Weather	468-555-0100

SPAWN VEHICLES

Call the following phone numbers with your phone to spawn the corresponding vehicle.

VEHICLE	PHONE NUMBER
Akuma	625-555-0200
Annihilator	359-555-0100
APC	272-555-8265
Bullet GT	227-555-9666
Buzzard	359-555-2899
Cognoscenti	227-555-0142
Comet	227-555-0175
FIB Buffalo	227-555-0100

VEHICLE	PHONE NUMBER
Floater	938-555-0150
Jetmax	938-555-0100
NRG-900	625-555-0100
Sanchez	625-555-0150
Super GT	227-555-0168
Turismo	227-555-0147
Vader	625-555-3273

GRAND THEFT AUTO IV: THE LOST AND DAMNED

CHEATS

Call the following phone numbers with your phone to activate the cheats. Some cheats may affect the missions and achievements.

BONUS	PHONE NUMBER
Get weapons	486-555-0100
Get different weapons	486-555-0150
Raise wanted level	267-555-0150
Remove wanted level	267-555-0100
Restore armor	362-555-0100
Restore armor, health, and ammo	482-555-0100

SPAWN VEHICLES

Call the following phone numbers with your phone to spawn the corresponding vehicle.

VEHICLE	PHONE NUMBER
Annihilator	359-555-0100
Burrito	826-555-0150
Double T	245-555-0125
FIB Buffalo	227-555-0100

VEHICLE	PHONE NUMBER
Hakuchou	245-555-0199
Hexer	245-555-0150
Innovation	245-555-0100
Slamvan	826-555-0100

GRID

ALL DRIFT CARS

Select Bonus Codes from the Options. Then choose Enter Code and enter TUN58396.

ALL MUSCLE CARS

Select Bonus Codes from the Options. Then choose Enter Code and enter MUS59279.

BUCHBINDER EMOTIONAL ENGINEERING BMW 320SI

Select Bonus Codes from the Options. Then choose Enter Code and enter F93857372. You can use this in Race Day or in GRID World once you've started your own team.

EBAY

Select Bonus Codes from the Options. Then choose Enter Code and enter DAFJ55E01473M0. You can use this in Race Day or in GRID World once you've started your own team.

GAMESTATION BMW 320SI

Select Bonus Codes from the Options. Then choose Enter Code and enter G29782655. You can use this in Race Day or in GRID World once you've started your own team.

MICROMANIA PAGANI ZONDA R

Select Bonus Codes from the Options. Then choose Enter Code and enter M38572343. You can use this in Race Day or in GRID World once you've started your own team.

PLAY.COM ASTON MARTIN DBR9

Select Bonus Codes from the Options. Then choose Enter Code and enter P47203845. You can use this in Race Day or in GRID World once you've started your own team.

GUARDIAN HEROES

AVATAR AWARDS

AVATAR	EARNED BY
Guardian Heroes Helmet	Scored 360 points in Arcade Mode.
Guardian Heroes T-Shirt	Unlocked at least 30 characters in Story Mode.

GUITAR HERO 5

ALL HOPOS

Select Input Cheats from the Options menu and enter Green, Green, Blue, Green, Green, Green, Yellow, Green.

ALWAYS SLIDE

Select Input Cheats from the Options menu and enter Green, Green, Red, Red, Yellow, Blue, Yellow, Blue.

AUTO KICK

Select Input Cheats from the Options menu and enter Yellow, Green, Red, Blue, Blue, Blue, Blue, Red.

FOCUS MODE

Select Input Cheats from the Options menu and enter Yellow, Green, Red, Green, Yellow, Blue, Green, Green.

HUD FREE MODE

Select Input Cheats from the Options menu and enter Green, Red, Green, Green, Yellow, Green, Green, Green.

PERFORMANCE MODE

Select Input Cheats from the Options menu and enter Yellow, Yellow, Blue, Red, Blue, Green, Red, Red.

AIR INSTRUMENTS

Select Input Cheats from the Options menu and enter Red, Red, Blue, Yellow, Green, Green, Green, Yellow.

INVISIBLE ROCKER

Select Input Cheats from the Options menu and enter Green, Red, Yellow, Yellow, Yellow, Blue, Blue, Green.

ALL CHARACTERS

Select Input Cheats from the Options menu and enter Blue, Blue, Green, Green, Red, Green, Red, Yellow.

CONTEST WINNER 1

Select Input Cheats from the Options menu and enter Green, Green, Red, Red, Yellow, Red, Yellow, Blue.

GUITAR HERO: AEROSMITH

To enter the following cheats, strum the guitar with the given buttons held. For example, if it says Yellow + Orange, hold Yellow and Orange as you strum. Air Guitar, Precision Mode, and Performance Mode can be toggled on and off from the Cheats menu. You can also change between five different levels of Hyperspeed at this menu.

ALL SONGS

Red + Yellow, Green + Red, Green + Red, Red + Yellow, Red + Yellow, Green + Red, Red + Yellow, Red + Yellow, Green + Red, Green + Red, Red + Yellow, Red + Yellow, Green + Red, Red + Yellow, Red + Blue.

AIR GUITAR

Red + Yellow, Green + Red, Red + Yellow, Red + Yellow, Red + Blue, Red + Blue, Red + Blue, Red + Blue, Red + Blue, Yellow + Blue, Yellow + Blue, Yellow + Orange

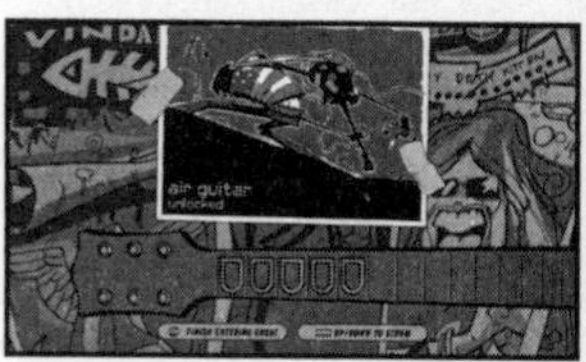

HYPERSPEED

Yellow + Orange, Yellow + Orange, Yellow + Orange, Yellow + Orange, Yellow + Orange, Red + Yellow, Red + Yellow, Red + Yellow, Red + Yellow, Red + Blue, Red + Blue, Red + Blue, Red + Blue, Red + Blue, Yellow + Blue, Yellow + Orange, Yellow + Orange.

NO FAIL

Select Cheats from the Options. Choose Enter Cheat and enter Green + Red, Blue, Green + Red, Green + Yellow, Blue, Green + Yellow, Red + Yellow, Orange, Red + Yellow, Green + Yellow, Yellow, Green + Yellow, Green + Red.

PERFORMANCE MODE

Green + Red, Green + Red, Red + Orange, Red + Blue, Green + Red, Green + Red, Red + Orange, Red + Blue

PRECISION MODE

Red + Yellow, Red + Blue, Red + Blue, Red + Yellow, Red + Yellow, Yellow + Blue, Yellow + Blue, Yellow + Blue, Red + Blue, Red + Yellow, Red + Blue, Red + Blue, Red + Yellow, Red + Yellow, Yellow + Blue, Yellow + Blue, Yellow + Blue, Red + Blue.

GUITAR HERO: METALLICA

Once entered, the cheats must be activated in the Cheats menu.

METALLICA COSTUMES

Select Cheats from Settings and enter Green, Red, Yellow, Blue, Blue, Yellow, Red, Green.

HYPERSPEED

Select Cheats from Settings and enter Green, Blue, Red, Yellow, Yellow, Red, Green, Green.

PERFORMANCE MODE

Select Cheats from Settings and enter Yellow, Yellow, Blue, Red, Blue, Green, Red, Red.

INVISIBLE ROCKER

Select Cheats from Settings and enter Green, Red, Yellow (x3), Blue, Blue, Green.

AIR INSTRUMENTS

Select Cheats from Settings and enter Red, Red, Blue, Yellow, Green (x3), Yellow.

ALWAYS DRUM FILL

Select Cheats from Settings and enter Red (x3), Blue, Blue, Green, Green, Yellow.

AUTO KICK

Select Cheats from Settings and enter Yellow, Green, Red, Blue (x4), Red. With this cheat activated, the bass pedal is automatically hit.

ALWAYS SLIDE
Select Cheats from Settings and enter Green, Green, Red, Red, Yellow, Red, Yellow, Blue. All Guitar Notes Become Touch Pad Sliding Notes.

BLACK HIGHWAY
Select Cheats from Settings and enter Yellow, Red, Green, Red, Green, Red, Red, Blue.

FLAME COLOR
Select Cheats from Settings and enter Green, Red, Green, Blue, Red, Red, Yellow, Blue.

GEM COLOR
Select Cheats from Settings and enter Blue, Red, Red, Green, Red, Green, Red, Yellow.

STAR COLOR
Select Cheats from Settings and enter Press Red, Red, Yellow, Red, Blue, Red, Red, Blue.

ADDITIONAL LINE 6 TONES
Select Cheats from Settings and enter Green, Red, Yellow, Blue, Red, Yellow, Blue, Green.

VOCAL FIREBALL
Select Cheats from Settings and enter Red, Green, Green, Yellow, Blue, Green, Yellow, Green.

GUITAR HERO: SMASH HITS

ALWAYS DRUM FILL
Select Cheats from the Options menu and enter Green, Green, Red, Red, Blue, Blue, Yellow, Yellow.

ALWAYS SLIDE
Select Cheats from the Options menu and enter Blue, Yellow, Red, Green, Blue, Green, Green, Yellow.

AIR INSTRUMENTS
Select Cheats from the Options menu and enter Yellow, Red, Blue, Green, Yellow, Red, Red, Red.

INVISIBLE ROCKER
Select Cheats from the Options menu and enter Blue, Red, Red, Red, Red, Yellow, Blue, Green.

PERFORMANCE MODE
Select Cheats from the Options menu and enter Blue, Red, Yellow, Yellow, Red, Red, Yellow, Yellow.

HYPERSPEED
Select Cheats from the Options menu and enter Red, Green, Blue, Yellow, Green, Yellow, Red, Red. This unlocks the HyperGuitar, HyperBass, and HyperDrums cheats.

AUTO KICK
Select Cheats from the Options menu and enter Blue, Green, Red, Yellow, Red, Yellow, Red, Yellow.

GEM COLOR
Select Cheats from the Options menu and enter Red, Red, Red, Blue, Blue, Blue, Yellow, Green.

FLAME COLOR
Select Cheats from the Options menu and enter Yellow, Blue, Red, Green, Yellow, Red, Green, Blue.

STAR COLOR
Select Cheats from the Options menu and enter Green, Red, Green, Yellow, Green, Blue, Yellow, Red.

VOCAL FIREBALL
Select Cheats from the Options menu and enter Green, Blue, Red, Red, Yellow, Yellow, Blue, Blue.

EXTRA LINE 6 TONES
Select Cheats from the Options menu and enter Green, Red, Yellow, Blue, Red, Yellow, Blue, Green.

GUITAR HERO: VAN HALEN

ALWAYS DRUM FILL
Select Input Cheats from the Options menu and enter Red, Red, Red, Blue, Blue, Green, Green, Yellow.

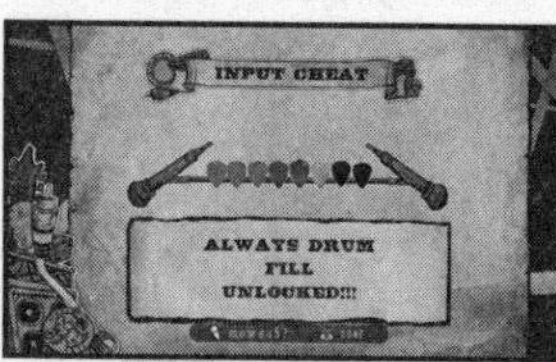

ALWAYS SLIDE
Select Input Cheats from the Options menu and enter Green, Green, Red, Red, Yellow, Red, Yellow, Blue.

AUTO KICK
Select Input Cheats from the Options menu and enter Yellow, Green, Red, Blue, Blue, Blue, Blue, Red.

HYPERSPEED
Select Input Cheats from the Options menu and enter Green, Blue, Red, Yellow, Yellow, Red, Green, Green. This allows you to enable Hyperguitar, Hyperbass, and Hyperdrums.

PERFORMANCE MODE
Select Input Cheats from the Options menu and enter Yellow, Yellow, Blue, Red, Blue, Green, Red, Red.

AIR INSTRUMENTS
Select Input Cheats from the Options menu and enter Red, Red, Blue, Yellow, Green, Green, Green, Yellow.

INVISIBLE ROCKER
Select Input Cheats from the Options menu and enter Green, Red, Yellow, Yellow, Yellow, Blue, Blue, Green.

BLACK HIGHWAY
Select Input Cheats from the Options menu and enter Yellow, Red, Green, Red, Green, Red, Red, Blue.

FLAME COLOR
Select Input Cheats from the Options menu and enter Green, Red, Green, Blue, Red, Red, Yellow, Blue.

GEM COLOR
Select Input Cheats from the Options menu and enter Blue, Red, Red, Green, Red, Green, Red, Yellow.

STAR COLOR
Select Input Cheats from the Options menu and enter Red, Red, Yellow, Red, Blue, Red, Red, Blue.

VOCAL FIREBALL
Select Input Cheats from the Options menu and enter Red, Green, Green, Yellow, Blue, Green, Yellow, Green.

EXTRA LINE 6 TONES
Select Input Cheats from the Options menu and enter Green, Red, Yellow, Blue, Red, Yellow, Blue, Green.

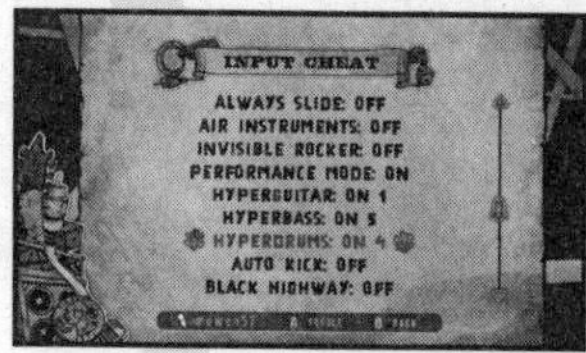

GUITAR HERO: WARRIORS OF ROCK

Select Extras from Options to toggle the following on and off. Some cheats will disable Achievements.

ALL CHARACTERS
Select Cheats from the Options menu and enter Blue, Green, Green, Red, Green, Red, Yellow, Blue.

ALL VENUES
Select Cheats from the Options menu and enter Red, Blue, Blue, Red, Red, Blue, Blue, Red.

ALWAYS SLIDE
Select Cheats from the Options menu and enter Blue, Green, Green, Red, Red, Yellow, Blue, Yellow.

ALL HOPOS
Select Cheats from the Options menu and enter Green (x3), Blue, Green (x3), Yellow. Most notes become hammer-ons or pull-offs.

INVISIBLE ROCKER
Select Cheats from the Options menu and enter Green, Green, Red, Yellow (x3), Blue, Blue.

AIR INSTRUMENTS
Select Cheats from the Options menu and enter Yellow, Red, Red, Blue, Yellow, Green (x3).

FOCUS MODE
Select Cheats from the Options menu and enter Green, Yellow, Green, Red, Green, Yellow, Blue, Green. This removes the busy background.

HUD FREE MODE
Select Cheats from the Options menu and enter Green, Green, Red, Green, Green, Yellow, Green, Green.

PERFORMANCE MODE
Select Cheats from the Options menu and enter Red, Yellow, Yellow, Blue, Red, Blue, Green, Red.

COLOR SHUFFLE
Select Cheats from the Options menu and enter Blue, Green, Blue, Red, Yellow, Green, Red, Yellow.

MIRROR GEMS
Select Cheats from the Options menu and enter Blue, Blue, Red, Blue, Green, Green, Red, Green.

RANDOM GEMS
Select Cheats from the Options menu and enter Green, Green, Red, Red, Yellow, Red, Yellow, Blue.

GUITAR HERO WORLD TOUR

The following cheats can be toggled on and off at the Cheats menu.

QUICKPLAY SONGS
Select Cheats from the Options menu, choose Enter New Cheat and press Blue, Blue, Red, Green, Green, Blue, Blue, Yellow.

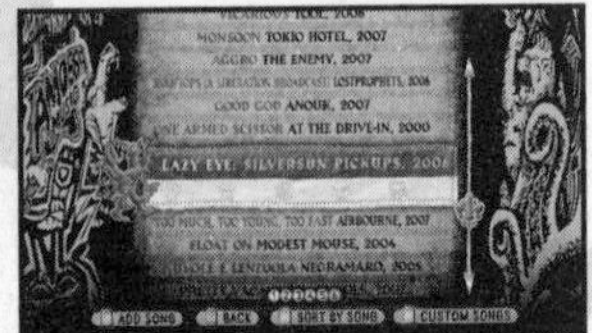

ALWAYS SLIDE
Select Cheats from the Options menu, choose Enter New Cheat and press Green, Green, Red, Red, Yellow, Red, Yellow, Blue.

AT&T BALLPARK
Select Cheats from the Options menu, choose Enter New Cheat and press Yellow, Green, Red, Red, Green, Blue, Red, Yellow.

AUTO KICK
Select Cheats from the Options menu, choose Enter New Cheat and press Yellow, Green, Red, Blue (x4), Red.

EXTRA LINE 6 TONES
Select Cheats from the Options menu, choose Enter New Cheat and press Green, Red, Yellow, Blue, Red, Yellow, Blue, Green.

FLAME COLOR
Select Cheats from the Options menu, choose Enter New Cheat and press Green, Red, Green, Blue, Red, Red, Yellow, Blue.

GEM COLOR
Select Cheats from the Options menu, choose Enter New Cheat and press Blue, Red, Red, Green, Red, Green, Red, Yellow.

STAR COLOR
Select Cheats from the Options menu, choose Enter New Cheat and press Red, Red, Yellow, Red, Blue, Red, Red, Blue.

AIR INSTRUMENTS
Select Cheats from the Options menu, choose Enter New Cheat and press Red, Red, Blue, Yellow, Green (x3), Yellow.

HYPERSPEED

Select Cheats from the Options menu, choose Enter New Cheat and press Green, Blue, Red, Yellow, Yellow, Red, Green, Green. These show up in the menu as HyperGuitar, HyperBass, and HyperDrums.

PERFORMANCE MODE

Select Cheats from the Options menu, choose Enter New Cheat and press Yellow, Yellow, Blue, Red, Blue, Green, Red, Red.

INVISIBLE ROCKER

Select Cheats from the Options menu, choose Enter New Cheat and press Green, Red, Yellow (x3), Blue, Blue, Green.

VOCAL FIREBALL

Select Cheats from the Options menu, choose Enter New Cheat and press Red, Green, Green, Yellow, Blue, Green, Yellow, Green.

AARON STEELE!

Select Cheats from the Options menu, choose Enter New Cheat and press Blue, Red, Yellow (x5), Green.

JONNY VIPER

Select Cheats from the Options menu, choose Enter New Cheat and press Blue, Red, Blue, Blue, Yellow (x3), Green.

NICK

Select Cheats from the Options menu, choose Enter New Cheat and press Green, Red, Blue, Green, Red, Blue, Blue, Green.

RINA

Select Cheats from the Options menu, choose Enter New Cheat and press Blue, Red, Green, Green, Yellow (x3), Green.

HALO 3

TOGGLE HIDE WEAPON

During a local game, hold Left Bumper + Right Bumper + Left Stick + A + Down.

TOGGLE SHOW COORDINATES

During a local game, hold Left Bumper + Right Bumper + Left Stick + A + Up.

TOGGLE BETWEEN PAN-CAM AND NORMAL

During a local game, hold Left Stick + Right Stick and press Left when Show Coordinates is active.

HALO 4

AVATAR AWARDS

AVATAR	EARNED BY
Knight Helmet	Unlock the "Knight in White Assassination" achievement to earn this award.
Platinum Mark VI Helmet	Unlock the "Wake Up, John" achievement to earn this award.
UNSC Infinity Hoodie	Unlock the "Not Some Recruit Anymore" achievement to earn this award.

HALO REACH

AVATAR AWARDS

AWARD	EARNED BY
Carter's Helmet	Clear a Campaign mission on Legendary without dying—Save and quit toward the end of a mission. Resume the game and finish mission without dying to earn this award easily.
Emile's Helmet	Earn a Bulltrue medal in either multiplayer or Firefight Matchmaking
Jorge's Helmet	Earn a Killtacular in multiplayer Matchmaking
Jun's Helmet	Kill 100 enemies in a row without dying in either the Campaign or Firefight
Kat's Helmet	Avenge teammate's death in multiplayer Matchmaking

HARRY POTTER AND THE DEATHLY HALLOWS: PART 1

SUPER STRENGTH POTIONS

Select Unlock Menu from the Options and enter X, Left, Right, A, Right Trigger, Right Bumper.

ELITE CHALLENGES

Select Unlock Menu from the Options and enter Y, Up, X, Left Trigger, Right Trigger, A.

AUGMENTED REALITY CHEAT FROM BOX (PROTEGO TOTALUM)

Select Unlock Menu from the Options and enter Y, B, Up, Left, Right Trigger, Right.

HAUNT

AVATAR AWARDS

AVATAR	EARNED BY
Haunt Hoodie	Unlock the Full Game.
Haunt Jeans	Defeat one of each type of ghost.
Charger Ghost Mask	Successfully avoid 5 Charger ghost attacks.

HOLE IN THE WALL

AVATAR AWARDS

AVATAR	EARNED BY
Spandex Top	Win China Show.
Spandex Trousers	Win Russia Show.
Blue Helmet	Win USA Show.

HYBRID

AVATAR AWARDS

AVATAR	EARNED BY
Hybrid T-Shirt	T-Shirt with Hybrid Logo.
Variant T-Shirt	T-Shirt with Variant Logo.
Paladin T-Shirt	T-Shirt with Paladin Logo.

ILOMILO

ILOMILO SHUFFLE

At the main menu, press Left Trigger, Right Trigger, Left Bumper, Right Bumper.

AVATAR AWARDS

AWARD	EARNED BY
T-Shirt	Complete 3 levels.
Ilo And Milo	Collect enough memory fragments to unlock a full memory.

INSANELY TWISTED SHADOW PLANET

AVATAR AWARDS

AVATAR	EARNED BY
Shadow Planet Tee T-Shirt	Make it from your Homeworld to the Shadow Planet to unlock!
UFO Hero's Ship	Complete the Single-Player Campaign to unlock!

JET SET RADIO

CUBE/COMBO

Complete Chapter 1

PLAY AS GARAM

To unlock Garam simply complete his challenges.

PLAY AS GOJI

To play as Goji, get a JET ranking on all the Grind City levels.

PLAY AS GUM

To unlock Gum simply finish her challenges at the begining of the game.

PLAY AS LOVE SHOCKERS, NOISE TANKS, POISON JAM, AND GOJI

Beat the game with a JET ranking in all stages. This includes regular stages as well as Golden Rhino stages

PLAY AS MEW

Beat all the Benten-Cho (aka City of Night) levels with any ranking. After that, Mew will challenge you. Beat the three of her challenges, and she'll join you, allowing you to pick her as playable character.

PLAY AS POISON JAM

To play as Poison Jam, get a JET ranking on all of the Kogane-cho levels.

TAB

Unlock Gum and complete the challenges Tab gives you afterwards.

UNLOCK POTS, THE DOG!

To get to play as Pots, finish the game with the Jet ranking on every level. Every level, meaning both story mode and the basic areas.

SLATE

Play through the game until Slate challenges you to a race in Kogane-Cho. Beat him to unlock.

YO-YO

Progress through story mode until he challenges you. Beat his challenge to unlock.

AVATAR AWARDS

AVATAR	EARNED BY
Shirt	Unlock Gum and Tab.
Spray Can	Unlock Gum and Tab.

JIMMIE JOHNSON'S ANYTHING WITH AN ENGINE

ALL RACERS

At the main menu, hold R1 + L1 + R2 + L2 and press Up, Right, Down, Left, Up, Left, Down, Right, R3, L3.

XBOX 360

JOE DANGER 2: THE MOVIE

AVATAR AWARDS

AVATAR	EARNED BY
Joe's Cosmic Helmet	Collect a set of D-A-N-G-E-R!
Joe's Jubilant Jetpack	Collect a second set of D-A-N-G-E-R!
Joe's Galactic Trousers	Collect a third set of D-A-N-G-E-R!

JOJO'S BIZARRE ADVENTURE HD VER.

FIGHT DEATH 13

Using one of the original six fighters, do not lose a match. After the fifth fight, Death 13 will challenge your fighter.

JOY RIDE TURBO

AVATAR AWARDS

AVATAR	EARNED BY
JR Turbo T	Win your first race to receive the official T shirt of the unofficial Joy Ride Turbo fan club.
Victory Pants	Purchase your first car in order to strut out of the dealership wearing a victorious pair of slacks.
Cacti Cap	Win a race on every track to unlock this trendy piece of headwear.

JUST CAUSE 2

ISLAND FROM LOST

Grab a plane and fly to the small island in the northwest corner of the map. The plane explodes and falls to the ground as you fly over. There are several references to the show, including a hatch in the southwest corner of the island.

JUST DANCE 3

BARBRA STREISAND SPECIAL CHOREOGRAPHY

At the title screen (Press Start), press Up, Up, Down, Down, Left, Right, Left, Right.

KINECT DISNEYLAND ADVENTURES

AVATAR AWARDS

AVATAR	EARNED BY
Sorcerer Mickey Mouse Hat	Earn the Happiest Place on Earth Achievement.

KINECT PLAYFIT

AVATAR AWARDS

AVATAR	EARNED BY
Muscle Mass	Earn the 150K Ultra-Marathon Achievement.
Power Pants	Earn the Mount Everest Relay Achievement.

OVERLOAD

KINECT SPORTS

AVATAR AWARDS

AWARD	EARNED BY
Classic Kinect Sports Cap	Earn the Amateur Sports Badge.
Classic Kinect Sports Tee	Earn the Professional Sports Badge.
I Heart Kinect Sports Tee	Earn the Champion Sports Badge.
Kinect Sports Champ Trophy	Earn the Legendary Sports Badge.
Kinect Sports Star Tee	Earn the Master Sports Badge.

KINECT SPORTS SEASON TWO

AVATAR AWARDS

AVATAR	EARNED BY
Kinect Sports Darts Top Hat	Stay on target throughout your career with this awesome award for reaching level 5. Woohoo!
Kinect Sports Football Hat	Show your love for all things football with this award for reaching fan level 2. I'm so jealous!
Kinect Sports Golf Green Cap	Impress everyone at the clubhouse with this award for reaching the dizzy heights of fan level 10.

THE KING OF FIGHTERS XIII

ALTERNATE COSTUMES AND COLOR PALETTES

Before selecting the color for the following fighters, press Select to get the alternate outfit.

FIGHTER	OUTFIT
Andy	Ninja Mask
Elisabeth	KOF XI
Joe	Tiger-Striped Boxers
K'	Dual-Colored
Kyo	Orochi Saga
Raiden	Big Bear
Ralf	Camouflage
Takuma	Mr. Karate
Yuri	Braided Ponytail

EXTRA COLORS IN COLOR EDIT

Extra colors become available in color edit mode for every ten times you select a specific character.

BILLY KANE

Successfully pull off 2 target actions in each fight in Arcade Mode until Billy Kane challenges you. Defeat him to unlock him.

SAIKI

Successfully pull off 5 target actions in each fight in Arcade Mode until Saiki challenges you. Defeat him to unlock him.

KINGDOM OF AMALUR: RECKONING

REMOVE STOLEN STATUS FROM ITEM

Find a merchant who buys stolen items and sell the one marked stolen (red hand icon). Without exiting the screen, go to Buy and find the item you just sold. Purchase it and it should no longer be marked as stolen.

L.A. NOIRE

Select Outfits from the Pause menu to change into the following. Some have special bonuses when worn.

SWORD OF JUSTICE OUTFIT
Reach rank 3.

SUNSET STRIP OUTFIT
Reach rank 8.

THE OUTSIDER OUTFIT
Reach rank 13.

HAWKSHAW OUTFIT
Reach rank 18. This outfit adds some resistance to damage.

GOLDEN BOY OUTFIT
Awarded for reaching Traffic Desk

BUTTON MAN OUTFIT
Complete the Badge Pursuit Challenge. This outfit allows you to carry extra ammo.

CHICAGO LIGHTING OUTFIT
Become a member of Rockstar's Social Club. You must reach Detective to wear the outfit. When worn, accuracy with the BAR, Thompson, and shotgun is increased.

THE SHARPSHOOTER OUTFIT
This outfit and the Nickel Plated Pistol were pre-order bonuses from Best Buy. It gives you better accuracy with rifles and pistols.

THE BRODERICK OUTFIT
This outfit was a pre-order bonus from Amazon.com. It increases fist-fighting capabilities and adds resistance to damage.

LARA CROFT AND THE GUARDIAN OF LIGHT

LARA CROFT HEAVY JUNGLE OUTFIT
Complete the game.

LARA CROFT JUNGLE OUTFIT
Score 1,410,000 points.

LARA CROFT BIKER OUTFIT
Score 1,900,000 points.

LARA CROFT LEGEND OUTFIT
Defeat Xolotl.

DOPPELGANGER OUTFIT
Score 2,400,000 points.

LEFT 4 DEAD 2

AVATAR AWARDS

AWARD	EARNED BY
Med Kit	Defeat all campaigns
Left 4 Dead 2 Hat	Play any map in The Passing
Gnome	Play any 6 Mutations
Left 4 Dead 2 Shirt	Win 10 games in Scavenge
Bull Shifters (Ellis) Shirt	Win 10 games in Versus
Depeche Mode (Rochelle) Shirt	Rescue Gnome Chompski from Dark Carnival
Zombie Hand Shirt	Kill 10,000 infected

THE LEGEND OF SPYRO: DAWN OF THE DRAGON

UNLIMITED LIFE
Pause the game, hold Left Bumper and press Right, Right, Down, Down, Left with the Left Control Stick.

UNLIMITED MANA
Pause the game, hold Right Bumper and press Up, Right, Up, Left, Down with the Left Control Stick.

MAXIMUM XP
Pause the game, hold Right Bumper and press Up, Left, Left, Down, Up with the Left Control Stick.

ALL ELEMENTAL UPGRADES
Pause the game, hold Left Bumper and press Left, Up, Down, Up, Right with the Left Control Stick.

LEGENDS OF WRESTLEMANIA

ANIMAL'S SECOND COSTUME

Select Cheat Codes from the Options menu and enter TheRoadWarriorAnimal.

BRUTUS BEEFCAKE'S SECOND COSTUME

Select Cheat Codes from the Options menu and enter BrutusTheBarberShop!.

IRON SHIEK'S SECOND COSTUME

Select Cheat Codes from the Options menu and enter IronSheikCamelClutch.

JIMMY HART'S SECOND COSTUME

Select Cheat Codes from the Options menu and enter WithManagerJimmyHart.

KOKO B WARE'S SECOND COSTUME

Select Cheat Codes from the Options menu and enter TheBirdmanKokoBWare!.

THE ROCK'S SECOND COSTUME

Select Cheat Codes from the Options menu and enter UnlockTheRockBottom!.

SGT. SLAUGHTER'S SECOND COSTUME

Select Cheat Codes from the Options menu and enter CobraClutchSlaughter.

SHAWN MICHAELS'S SECOND COSTUME

Select Cheat Codes from the Options menu and enter ShawnsSweetChinMusic.

UNDERTAKER'S SECOND COSTUME

Select Cheat Codes from the Options menu and enter UndertakersTombstone.

LEGO BATMAN

BATCAVE CODES

Using the computer in the Batcave, select Enter Code and enter the following codes.

CHARACTERS

CHARACTER	CODE
Alfred	ZAQ637
Batgirl	JKR331
Bruce Wayne	BDJ327
Catwoman (Classic)	M1AAWW
Clown Goon	HJK327
Commissioner Gordon	DDP967
Fishmonger	HGY748
Freeze Girl	XVK541
Joker Goon	UTF782
Joker Henchman	YUN924
Mad Hatter	JCA283
Man-Bat	NYU942
Military Policeman	MKL382
Nightwing	MVY759
Penguin Goon	NKA238

CHARACTER	CODE
Penguin Henchman	BJH782
Penguin Minion	KJP748
Poison Ivy Goon	GTB899
Police Marksman	HKG984
Police Officer	JRY983
Riddler Goon	CRY928
Riddler Henchman	XEU824
S.W.A.T.	HTF114
Sailor	NAV592
Scientist	JFL786
Security Guard	PLB946
The Joker (Tropical)	CCB199
Yeti	NJL412
Zoo Sweeper	DWR243

XBOX 360

VEHICLES

VEHICLE	CODE
Bat-Tank	KNTT4B
Bruce Wayne's Private Jet	LEA664
Catwoman's Motorcycle	HPL826
Garbage Truck	DUS483
Goon Helicopter	GCH328
Harbor Helicopter	CHP735
Harley Quinn's Hammer Truck	RDT637
Mad Hatter's Glider	HS000W
Mad Hatter's Steamboat	M4DM4N
Mr. Freeze's Iceberg	ICYICE

VEHICLE	CODE
The Joker's Van	JUK657
Mr. Freeze's Kart	BCT229
Penguin Goon Submarine	BTN248
Police Bike	LJP234
Police Boat	PLC999
Police Car	KJL832
Police Helicopter	CWR732
Police Van	MAC788
Police Watercraft	VJD328
Riddler's Jet	HAHAHA
Robin's Submarine	TTF453
Two-Face's Armored Truck	EFE933

CHEATS

CHEAT	CODE
Always Score Multiply	9LRGNB
Fast Batarangs	JRBDCB
Fast Walk	ZOLM6N
Flame Batarang	D8NYWH
Freeze Batarang	XPN4NG
Extra Hearts	ML3KHP
Fast Build	EVG26J
Immune to Freeze	JXUDY6
Invincibility	WYD5CP
Minikit Detector	ZXGH9J

CHEAT	CODE
More Batarang Targets	XWP645
Piece Detector	KHJ554
Power Brick Detector	MMN786
Regenerate Hearts	HJH7HJ
Score x2	N4NR3E
Score x4	CX9MAT
Score x6	MLVNF2
Score x8	WCCDB9
Score x10	18HW07

LEGO BATMAN 2: DC SUPER HEROES

RED BRICK CODES

Pause the game, select Extras, and then choose Enter Code. Enter the following:

CHEAT	CODE
Attract Studs	MNZER6
Beep Beep	ZHAXFH
Character Studs	TPJ37T
Disguises	BWQ2MS
Extra Hearts	4LGJ7T
Extra Toggle	7TXH5K
Fall Rescue	TPGPG2
Gold Brick Finder	MBXW7V

CHEAT	CODE
Minikit Finder	LRJAG8
Peril Finder	RYD3SJ
Red Brick Finder	5KKQ6G
Regenerate Hearts	ZXEX5D
Studs x2	74EZUT
Super Build	JN2J6V
Vine Grapples	JXN7FJ

CHARACTERS AND VEHICLE

Pause the game, select Extras, and then choose Enter Code. Enter the following:

CHEAT	CODE
Clown Goon	9ZZZBP
LexBot	W49CSJ
Mime Goon	ZQA8MK
Policeman	V9SAGT

CHEAT	CODE
Riddler Goon	Q285LK
Two-Face Goon	95KPYJ
Harley Quinn's Motorbike	C79LVH

OVERLOAD

LEGO HARRY POTTER: YEARS 1-4

RED BRICK EXTRAS

Once you have access to The Leaky Cauldron, enter Wiseacre's Wizarding Supplies from Diagon Alley. Go upstairs to enter the following. Pause the game and select Extras to toggle the cheats on/off.

CHEAT	CODE
Carrot Wands	AUC8EH
Character Studs	H27KGC
Character Token Detector	HA79V8
Christmas	T7PVVN
Disguise	4DMK2R
Fall Rescue	ZEX7MV
Extra Hearts	J9U6Z9
Fast Dig	Z9BFAD
Fast Magic	FA3GQA
Gold Brick Detector	84QNQN
Hogwarts Crest Detector	TTMC6D
Ice Rink	F88VUW

CHEAT	CODE
Invincibility	QQWC6B
Red Brick Detector	7AD7HE
Regenerate Hearts	89ML2W
Score x2	74YKR7
Score x4	J3WHNK
Score x6	XK9ANE
Score x8	HUFV2H
Score x10	H8X69Y
Silhouettes	HZBVX7
Singing Mandrake	BMEU6X
Stud Magnet	67FKWZ

WISEACRE SPELLS

Once you have access to The Leaky Cauldron, enter Wiseacre's Wizarding Supplies from Diagon Alley. Go upstairs to enter the following. You need to learn Wingardium Leviosa before you can use these cheats.

SPELL	CODE
Accio	VE9VV7
Anteoculatia	QFB6NR
Calvorio	6DNR6L
Colovaria	9GJ442
Engorgio Skullus	CD4JLX
Entomorphis	MYN3NB
Flipendo	ND2L7W
Glacius	ERA9DR
Herbifors	H8FTHL
Incarcerous	YEB9Q9

SPELL	CODE
Locomotor Mortis	2M2XJ6
Multicorfors	JK6QRM
Redactum Skullus	UW8LRH
Rictusempra	2UCA3M
Slugulus Eructo	U6EE8X
Stupefy	UWDJ4Y
Tarantallegra	KWWQ44
Trip Jinx	YZNRF6

EEYLOPS GOLD BRICKS

Once you have access to The Leaky Cauldron, enter Wiseacre's Wizarding Supplies from Diagon Alley. Go upstairs to enter the following. To access the LEGO Builder, visit Gringott's Bank at the end of Diagon Alley.

GOLD BRICK	CODE
1	QE4VC7
2	FY8H97
3	3MQT4P
4	PQPM7Z
5	ZY2CPA
6	3GMTP6

GOLD BRICK	CODE
7	XY6VYZ
8	TUNC4W
9	EJ42Q6
10	GFJCV9
11	DZCY6G

LEGO HARRY POTTER: YEARS 5-7

CHEATS

Pause the game and select Extras. Go to Enter Code and enter the following:

CHEAT	CODE
Carrot Wands	AUC8EH
Character Studs	H27KGC
Character Token Detector	HA79V8
Christmas	T7PVVN
Collect Ghost Studs	2FLY6B
Extra Hearts	J9U6Z9
Fall Rescue	ZEX7MV
Fast Dig	Z9BFAD
Ghost Coins	2FLY6B
Gold Brick Detector	84QNQN
Hogwarts Crest Detector	TTMC6D
Invincibility	QQWC6B
Red Brick Detector	7AD7HE
Score x2	74YKR7
Score x6	XK9ANE
Score x8	HUFV2H
Score x10	H8X69Y
Super Strength	BMEU6X

LEGO INDIANA JONES: THE ORIGINAL ADVENTURES

CHARACTERS

Approach the blackboard in the Classroom and enter the following codes.

CHARACTER	CODE
Bandit	12N68W
Bandit Swordsman	1MK4RT
Barranca	04EM94
Bazooka Trooper (Crusade)	MK83R7
Bazooka Trooper (Raiders)	S93Y5R
Belloq	CHN3YU
Belloq (Jungle)	TDR197
Belloq (Robes)	VEO29L
British Commander	B73EUA
British Officer	VJ5TI9
British Soldier	DJ5I2W
Captain Katanga	VJ3TT3
Chatter Lal	ENW936
Chatter Lal (Thuggee)	CNH4RY
Chen	3NK48T
Colonel Dietrich	2K9RKS
Colonel Vogel	8EAL4H
Dancing Girl	C7EJ21
Donovan	3NFTU8
Elsa (Desert)	JSNRT9
Elsa (Officer)	VMJ5US
Enemy Boxer	8246RB
Enemy Butler	VJ48W3
Enemy Guard	VJ7R51
Enemy Guard (Mountains)	YR47WM
Enemy Officer	572E61

CHARACTER	CODE
Enemy Officer (Desert	2MK45O
Enemy Pilot	B84ELP
Enemy Radio Operator	1MF94R
Enemy Soldier (Desert)	4NSU7Q
Fedora	V75YSP
First Mate	0GIN24
Grail Knight	NE6THI
Hovitos Tribesman	H0V1SS
Indiana Jones (Desert Disguise)	4J8S4M
Indiana Jones (Officer)	VJ85OS
Jungle Guide	24PF34
Kao Kan	WMO46L
Kazim	NRH23J
Kazim (Desert)	3M29TJ
Lao Che	2NK479
Maharajah	NFK5N2
Major Toht	13NS01
Masked Bandit	N48SF0
Mola Ram	FJUR31
Monkey Man	3RF6YJ
Pankot Assassin	2NKT72
Pankot Guard	VN28RH
Sherpa Brawler	VJ37WJ
Sherpa Gunner	ND762W
Slave Child	0E3ENW

CHARACTER	CODE
Thuggee	VM683E
Thuggee Acolyte	T2R3F9
Thuggee Slave Driver	VBS7GW
Village Dignitary	KD48TN
Village Elder	4682E1
Willie (Dinner Suit)	VK93R7
Willie (Pajamas)	MEN4IP
Wu Han	3NSLT8

EXTRAS

Approach the blackboard in the Classroom and enter the following codes. Some cheats need to be enabled by selecting Extras from the pause menu.

CHEAT	CODE
Artifact Detector	VIKED7
Beep Beep	VNF59Q
Character Treasure	VIES2R
Disarm Enemies	VKRNS9
Disguises	4ID1N6
Fast Build	V83SLO
Fast Dig	378RS6
Fast Fix	FJ59WS
Fertilizer	B1GW1F
Ice Rink	33GM7J
Parcel Detector	VUT673
Poo Treasure	WWQ1SA
Regenerate Hearts	MDLP69
Secret Characters	3X44AA
Silhouettes	3HE85H
Super Scream	VN3R7S
Super Slap	0P1TA5
Treasure Magnet	H86LA2
Treasure x10	VI3PS8
Treasure x2	VM4TS9
Treasure x4	VLWEN3
Treasure x6	V84RYS
Treasure x8	A72E1M

LEGO INDIANA JONES 2: THE ADVENTURE CONTINUES

Pause the game, select Enter Secret Code from the Extras menu, and enter the following.

CHARACTERS

CHARACTER	CODE
Belloq (Priest)	FTL48S
Dovchenko	WL4T6N
Enemy Boxer	7EQF47
Henry Jones	4CSAKH
Indiana Jones	PGWSEA
Indiana Jones: 2	FGLKYS
Indiana Jones (Collect)	DZFY9S
Indiana Jones (Desert)	M4C34K
Indiana Jones (Desert Disguise)	2W8QR3
Indiana Jones (Dinner Suit)	QUNZUT
Indiana Jones (Kali)	J2XS97
Indiana Jones (Officer)	3FQFKS
Interdimensional Being	PXT4UP
Lao Che	7AWX3J
Mannequin (Boy)	2UJQWC
Mannequin (Girl)	3PGSEL
Mannequin (Man)	QPWDMM
Mannequin (Woman)	U7SMVK
Mola Ram	82RMC2
Mutt	2GKS62
Salah	E88YRP
Willie	94RUAJ

EXTRAS

EFFECT	CODE
Beep Beep	UU3VSC
Disguise	Y9TE98
Fast Build	SNXC2F
Fast Dig	XYAN83
Fast Fix	3Z7PJX
Fearless	TUXNZF
Ice Rink	TY9P4U
Invincibility	6JBB65
Poo Money	SZFAAE
Score x3	PEHHPZ
Score x4	UXGTB3
Score X6	XWLJEY
Score x8	S5UZCP
Score x10	V7JYBU
Silhouettes	FQGPYH
Snake Whip	2U7YCV
Stud Magnet	EGSM5B

LEGO PIRATES OF THE CARIBBEAN: THE VIDEO GAME

CODES

Pause the game and select Extras. Choose Enter Code and enter the following codes:

EFFECT	PASSWORD
Ammand the Corsair	EW8T6T
Angelica (Disguised)	DLRR45
Angry Cannibal	VGF32C
Blackbeard	D3DW0D
Clanker	ZM37GT
Clubba	644THF
Davy Jones	4DJLKR
Govorner Weatherby Swann	LD9454
Gunner	Y611WB

EFFECT	PASSWORD
Hungry Cannibal	64BNHG
Jack Sparrow (Musical)	VDJSPW
Jacoby	BWO656
Jimmy Legs	13GLW5
King George	RKED43
Koehler	RT093G
Mistress Ching	GDETDE
Phillip	WEV040
Quartermaster	RX58HU
The Spaniard	P861JO
Twigg	KDLFKD

LEGO STAR WARS: THE COMPLETE SAGA

The following still need to be purchased after entering the codes.

CHARACTERS

ADMIRAL ACKBAR
At the bar in Mos Eisley Cantina, select Enter Code and enter ACK646.

BATTLE DROID (COMMANDER)
At the bar in Mos Eisley Cantina, select Enter Code and enter KPF958.

BOBA FETT (BOY)
At the bar in Mos Eisley Cantina, select Enter Code and enter GGF539.

BOSS NASS
At the bar in Mos Eisley Cantina, select Enter Code and enter HHY697.

CAPTAIN TARPALS
At the bar in Mos Eisley Cantina, select Enter Code and enter QRN714.

COUNT DOOKU
At the bar in Mos Eisley Cantina, select Enter Code and enter DDD748.

DARTH MAUL
At the bar in Mos Eisley Cantina, select Enter Code and enter EUK421.

EWOK
At the bar in Mos Eisley Cantina, select Enter Code and enter EWK785.

GENERAL GRIEVOUS
At the bar in Mos Eisley Cantina, select Enter Code and enter PMN576.

GREEDO
At the bar in Mos Eisley Cantina, select Enter Code and enter ZZR636.

IG-88
At the bar in Mos Eisley Cantina, select Enter Code and enter GIJ989.

IMPERIAL GUARD
At the bar in Mos Eisley Cantina, select Enter Code and enter GUA850.

JANGO FETT
At the bar in Mos Eisley Cantina, select Enter Code and enter KLJ897.

KI-ADI MUNDI
At the bar in Mos Eisley Cantina, select Enter Code and enter MUN486.

LUMINARA
At the bar in Mos Eisley Cantina, select Enter Code and enter LUM521.

PADMÉ
At the bar in Mos Eisley Cantina, select Enter Code and enter VBJ322.

R2-Q5
At the bar in Mos Eisley Cantina, select Enter Code and enter EVILR2.

STORMTROOPER
At the bar in Mos Eisley Cantina, select Enter Code and enter NBN431.

TAUN WE
At the bar in Mos Eisley Cantina, select Enter Code and enter PRX482.

VULTURE DROID
At the bar in Mos Eisley Cantina, select Enter Code and enter BDC866.

WATTO
At the bar in Mos Eisley Cantina, select Enter Code and enter PLL967.

ZAM WESELL
At the bar in Mos Eisley Cantina, select Enter Code and enter 584HJF.

SKILLS

DISGUISE
At the bar in Mos Eisley Cantina, select Enter Code and enter BRJ437.

FORCE GRAPPLE LEAP
At the bar in Mos Eisley Cantina, select Enter Code and enter CLZ738.

VEHICLES

DROID TRIFIGHTER
At the bar in Mos Eisley Cantina, select Enter Code and enter AAB123.

IMPERIAL SHUTTLE
At the bar in Mos Eisley Cantina, select Enter Code and enter HUT845.

TIE INTERCEPTOR
At the bar in Mos Eisley Cantina, select Enter Code and enter INT729.

TIE FIGHTER
At the bar in Mos Eisley Cantina, select Enter Code and enter DBH897.

ZAM'S AIRSPEEDER
At the bar in Mos Eisley Cantina, select Enter Code and enter UUU875.0

LEGO STAR WARS II: THE ORIGINAL TRILOGY

BEACH TROOPER
At Mos Eisley Canteena, select Enter Code and enter UCK868. You must still select Characters and purchase this character for 20,000 studs.

BEN KENOBI (GHOST)
At Mos Eisley Canteena, select Enter Code and enter BEN917. You must still select Characters and purchase this character for 1,100,000 studs.

BESPIN GUARD
At Mos Eisley Canteena, select Enter Code and enter VHY832. You must still select Characters and purchase this character for 15,000 studs.

BIB FORTUNA
At Mos Eisley Canteena, select Enter Code and enter WTY721. You must still select Characters and purchase this character for 16,000 studs.

BOBA FETT
At Mos Eisley Canteena, select Enter Code and enter HLP221. You must still select Characters and purchase this character for 175,000 studs.

DEATH STAR TROOPER
At Mos Eisley Canteena, select Enter Code and enter BNC332. You must still select Characters and purchase this character for 19,000 studs.

EWOK
At Mos Eisley Canteena, select Enter Code and enter TTT289. You must still select Characters and purchase this character for 34,000 studs.

GAMORREAN GUARD
At Mos Eisley Canteena, select Enter Code and enter YZF999. You must still select Characters and purchase this character for 40,000 studs.

GONK DROID
At Mos Eisley Canteena, select Enter Code and enter NFX582. You must still select Characters and purchase this character for 1,550 studs.

GRAND MOFF TARKIN
At Mos Eisley Canteena, select Enter Code and enter SMG219. You must still select Characters and purchase this character for 38,000 studs.

GREEDO
At Mos Eisley Canteena, select Enter Code and enter NAH118. You must still select Characters and purchase this character for 60,000 studs.

HAN SOLO (HOOD)
At Mos Eisley Canteena, select Enter Code and enter YWM840. You must still select Characters and purchase this character for 20,000 studs.

IG-88
At Mos Eisley Canteena, select Enter Code and enter NXL973. You must still select Characters and purchase this character for 30,000 studs.

IMPERIAL GUARD
At Mos Eisley Canteena, select Enter Code and enter MMM111. You must still select Characters and purchase this character for 45,000 studs.

IMPERIAL OFFICER

At Mos Eisley Canteena, select Enter Code and enter BBV889. You must still select Characters and purchase this character for 28,000 studs.

IMPERIAL SHUTTLE PILOT

At Mos Eisley Canteena, select Enter Code and enter VAP664. You must still select Characters and purchase this character for 29,000 studs.

IMPERIAL SPY

At Mos Eisley Canteena, select Enter Code and enter CVT125. You must still select Characters and purchase this character for 13,500 studs.

JAWA

At Mos Eisley Canteena, select Enter Code and enter JAW499. You must still select Characters and purchase this character for 24,000 studs.

LOBOT

At Mos Eisley Canteena, select Enter Code and enter UUB319. You must still select Characters and purchase this character for 11,000 studs.

PALACE GUARD

At Mos Eisley Canteena, select Enter Code and enter SGE549. You must still select Characters and purchase this character for 14,000 studs.

REBEL PILOT

At Mos Eisley Canteena, select Enter Code and enter CYG336. You must still select Characters and purchase this character for 15,000 studs.

REBEL TROOPER (HOTH)

At Mos Eisley Canteena, select Enter Code and enter EKU849. You must still select Characters and purchase this character for 16,000 studs.

SANDTROOPER

At Mos Eisley Canteena, select Enter Code and enter YDV451. You must still select Characters and purchase this character for 14,000 studs.

SKIFF GUARD

At Mos Eisley Canteena, select Enter Code and enter GBU888. You must still select Characters and purchase this character for 12,000 studs.

SNOWTROOPER

At Mos Eisley Canteena, select Enter Code and enter NYU989. You must still select Characters and purchase this character for 16,000 studs.

STORMTROOPER

At Mos Eisley Canteena, select Enter Code and enter PTR345. You must still select Characters and purchase this character for 10,000 studs.

THE EMPEROR

At Mos Eisley Canteena, select Enter Code and enter HHY382. You must still select Characters and purchase this character for 275,000 studs.

TIE FIGHTER

At Mos Eisley Canteena, select Enter Code and enter HDY739. You must still select Characters and purchase this item for 60,000 studs.

TIE FIGHTER PILOT

At Mos Eisley Canteena, select Enter Code and enter NNZ316. You must still select Characters and purchase this character for 21,000 studs.

TIE INTERCEPTOR

At Mos Eisley Canteena, select Enter Code and enter QYA828. You must still select Characters and purchase this item for 40,000 studs.

TUSKEN RAIDER

At Mos Eisley Canteena, select Enter Code and enter PEJ821. You must still select Characters and purchase this character for 23,000 studs.

UGNAUGHT

At Mos Eisley Canteena, select Enter Code and enter UGN694. You must still select Characters and purchase this character for 36,000 studs.

LEGO STAR WARS III: THE CLONE WARS

Pause the game, select Enter Code from Extras and enter the following:

CHARACTERS

CHARACTER	CODE
Aayla Secura	2VG95B
Adi Gallia	G2BFEN
Admiral Ackbar (Classic)	272Y9Q
Admiral Yularen	NG6PYX
Ahsoka	2VJ9TH
Anakin Skywalker	F9VUYJ
Anakin Skywalker (Geonosian Arena)	9AA4DW
Asajj Ventress	YG9DD7
Aurra Sing	M2V1JV
Bail Organa	GEHX6C
Barriss Offee	BTVTZ5

CHARACTER	CODE
Battle Droid	5Y7MA4
Battle Droid Commander	LSU4LJ
Bib Fortuna	9U4TF3
Boba Fett (Classic)	TY2BYJ
Boil	Q5Q39P
Bossk	2KLW5R
C-3PO	574226
Cad Bane	NHME85
Captain Antilles (Classic)	D8SNGJ
Captain Rex	MW3QYH
Captain Typho	GD6FX3
Chancellor Palpatine	5C62YQ
Chewbacca (Classic)	66UU3T
Clone Pilot	HQ7BVD
Clone Shadow Trooper (Classic)	7GFNCQ
Clone Trooper	NP5GTT
Commander Bly	7CB6NS
Commander Cody	SMN259
Commander Fil	U25HFC
Commander Ponds	JRPR2A
Commander Stone	5XZQSV
Commando Droid	QEGU64
Count Dooku	EWR7WM
Darth Maul (Classic)	QH68AK
Darth Sidious (Classic)	QXY5XN
Darth Vader (Classic)	FM4JB7
Darth Vader Battle Damaged (Classic)	NMJFBL
Destroyer Droid	9MUTS2
Dr. Nuvo Vindi	MB9EMW
Echo	JB9E5S
Eeth Koth	WUFDYA
Gammorean Guard	WSFZZQ
General Grievous	7FNU4T
Geonosian Guard	GAFZUD
Gold Super Battle Droid	2C8NHP
Gonk Droid	C686PK
Grand Moff Tarkin	NH2405
Greedo (Classic)	FUW4C2
Hailfire Droid	T7XF9Z
Han Solo (Classic)	KFDBXF
Heavy Super Battle Droid	G65KJJ
Heavy Weapons Clone Trooper	WXUTWY
HELIOS 3D	4AXTY4
Hevy	EUB8UG
Hondo Ohnaka	5A7XYX
IG-86	EABPCP
Imperial Guard (Classic)	5W6FGD
Jango Fett	5KZQ4D
Jar Jar Binks	MESPTS
Jek	AYREC9
Ki-Adi-Mundi	HGBCTQ
Kit Fitso	PYWJ6N
Lando Calrissian (Classic)	ERAEWE
LEP Servent Droid	SM3Y9B
Lieutenant Thire	3NEUXC
Lok Durd	TKCYUZ
Luke Skywalker (Classic)	PG73HF
Luminara Unduli	MKUYQ8
Lurmen Villager	R35Y7N

CHARACTER	CODE
Luxury Droid	V4WMJN
Mace Windu	8NVRWJ
MagnaGuard	2KEF2D
MSE-6	S6GRNZ
Nahdar Vebb	ZKXG43
Neimoidian	BJB94J
Nute Gunray	QFYXMC
Obi-Wan Kenobi	J9HNF9
Obi-Wan Kenobi (Classic)	FFBU5M
Obi-Wan Kenobi (Geonosian Arena)	5U9FJK
OG-9 Homing Spider Droid	7NEC36
Onaconda Farr	DB7ZQN
Padmé Amidala (Geonosian Arena)	SZ824Q
Padmé Amidala	8X87U6
Pirate Ruffian	BH2EHU
Plo Koon	BUD4VU
Poggle The Lesser	4592WM
Princess Leia (Classic)	2D3D3L
Probe Droid	U2T4SP
Queen Neeyutnee	ZQRN85
Qui-Gon Jinn (Classic)	LKHD3B
R2-D2	RZ5HUV
R3-S6	Z87PAU
R4-P17	5MXSYA
R6-H5	7PMC3C
Rebel Commando (Classic)	PZMQNK
Robonino	2KLW5R
Rys	4PTP53
Savage Oppress	MELL07
Senate Commando	EPBPLK
Senate Commando (Captain)	S4Y7VW
Senator Kharrus	EA4E9S
Senator Philo	9Q7YCT
Shahan Alama	G4N7C2
Sionver Boll	5C62YQ
Stormtrooper (Classic)	HPE7PZ
Super Battle Droid	MJKDV5
Tee Watt Kaa	FYVSHD
Turk Falso	HEBHW5
Tusken Raider (Classic)	GC2XSA
TX-20	PE7FGD
Undead Geonosian	QGENFD
Vader's Apprentice (Classic)	EGQQ4V
Wag Too	VRUVSZ
Wat Tambor	ZP8XVH
Waxer	BNJE79
Wedge Antilles (Classic)	DRGLWS
Whorm Loathsom	4VVYQV
Workout Clone Trooper	MP9DRE
Yoda	CSQTMB

VEHICLES

VEHICLE	CODE
Dwarf Spider Droid	NACMGG
Geonosian Solar Sailor	PJ2U3R
Geonosian Starfighter	EDENEC
Slave I	KDDQVD
The Twilight	T4K5L4
Vulture Droid	7W7K7S

RED BRICKS

CHEAT	CODE
Character Studs	QD2C31
Dark Side	X1V4N2
Dual Wield	C4ES4R
Fast Build	GCHP7S
Glow in the Dark	4GT3VQ
Invincibility	J46P7A
Minikit Detector	CSD5NA
Perfect Deflect	3F5L56
Regenerate Hearts	2D7JNS
Score x2	YZPHUV
Score x4	43T5E5
Score x6	SEBHGR
Score x8	BYFSAQ
Score x10	N1CKR1
Stud Magnet	6MZ5CH
Super Saber Cut	BS828K
Super Speeders	B1D3W3

LOLLIPOP CHAINSAW

VERY HARD DIFFICULTY

Complete the game.

MADAGASCAR 3: THE VIDEO GAME

ALL DISGUISES

Select Promotion from Extras and enter Pineapple, Strawberry, Grapes, Apple.

BANANA DASH MINI-GAME IN LONDON

Select Promotion from Extras and enter Strawberry, Orange, Apple, Grapes.

BANANA DASH MINI-GAME IN PARIS

Select Promotion from Extras and enter Pineapple, Grapes, Pineapple, Banana.

BANANA DASH MINI-GAME IN PISA

Select Promotion from Extras and enter Orange, Banana, Orange, Apple.

BANANA DASH MINI-GAME IN ROME

Select Promotion from Extras and enter Grape, Apple, Grape, Strawberry.

MAGIC: THE GATHERING - DUELS OF THE PLANESWALKERS 2013

BONUS FOIL CARDS

At the Player Status screen, select Magic the Gathering View Promotional Unlocks and then click Enter Code. Enter the following to unlock a bonus foil promo card for each of the original decks.

WMKFGC
KWPMZW
FNMDGP
MWTMJP
FXGJDW
GDZDJC
HTRNPW
NCTFJN
PCNKGR
GPCRSX

AVATAR AWARDS

AVATAR	EARNED BY
Avacynina Breastplate	Planeswalk to Innistard.
Garruk Wildspeaker Helmet	Defeat Garruk Wildspeaker in the Revenge Campaign.
Nicol Bolas Horns	Defeat Nicol Bolas in the Revenge Campaign.

MARS ROVER LANDING

AVATAR AWARDS

AVATAR	EARNED BY
Mars Rover Shirt	Touchdown safely ten times.
Mars Surface Pants	Achieve five stars during the Entry phase five times.
Mars Rover Hat	Achieve a five star Landing rating five times.

MARVEL: ULTIMATE ALLIANCE 2

These codes will disable the ability to save.

GOD MODE

During a game, press Up, Down, Up, Down, Up, Left, Down, Right, Start.

UNLIMITED FUSION

During a game, press Right, Right, Up, Down, Up, Up, Left, Start.

UNLOCK ALL POWERS

During a game, press Left, Right, Up, Down, Up, Down, Start.

UNLOCK ALL HEROES

During a game, press Up, Up, Down, Down, Left, Left, Left, Start.

UNLOCK ALL SKINS

During a game, press Up, Down, Left, Right, Left, Right, Start.

UNLOCK JEAN GREY

During a game, press Left, Left, Right, Right, Up, Down, Up, Down, Start.

UNLOCK HULK

During a game, press Down, Left, Left, Up, Right, Up, Down, Left, Start.

UNLOCK THOR

During a game, press Up, Right, Right, Down, Right, Down, Left, Right, Start.

UNLOCK ALL AUDIO LOGS

At the main menu, press Left, Right, Right, Left, Up, Up, Right, Start.

UNLOCK ALL DOSSIERS

At the main menu, press Down, Down, Down, Right, Right, Left, Down, Start.

UNLOCK ALL MOVIES

At the main menu, press Up, Left, Left, Up, Right, Right, Up, Start.

MARVEL VS. CAPCOM 3: FATE OF TWO WORLDS

CHARACTERS

Gain the following amount of player points to unlock each character.

CHARACTER	GAIN THIS AMOUNT OF PLAYER POINTS
Akuma	2000
Sentinel	4000

CHARACTER	GAIN THIS AMOUNT OF PLAYER POINTS
Hsien-Ko	6000
Taskmaster	8000

MARVEL VS. CAPCOM ORIGINS

MARVEL SUPER HEROES

PLAY AS ANITA
At the characters select, press MP, LP, Left, LK, MK.

PLAY AS DR DOOM
At the characters select, press MK, LP, Down, LK, MP.

PLAY AS THANOS
At the characters select, press HK, MP, MP, Up.

EXTRA POWER
After selecting your character, press player 1 and player 2 start.

USE GEMS
At the versus screen, hold both Starts.

MARVEL VS. CAPCOM: CLASH OF SUPER HEROES

PLAY AS GOLD WAR MACHINE
Highlight Zangief and press Left, Left, Down, Down, Right, Right, Down, Down, Left, Left, Up, Up, Up, Up, Right, Right, Left, Left, Down, Down, Down, Down, Right, Right, Up, Up, Left, Left, Down, Down, Right, Right, Up, Up, Up, Up, Up.

PLAY AS HYPER VENOM
Highlight Chun-Li and press Right, Down, Down, Down, Down, Left, Up, Up, Up, Up, Right, Right, Down, Down, Left, Left, Down, Down, Right, Right, Up, Up, Up, Up, Left, Left, Up.

PLAY AS LILITH
Highlight Zangief and press Left, Left, Down, Down, Right, Right, Up, Up, Down (x4), Left, Left, Up (x4), Right, Left, Down (x4), Right, Right, Up (x4), Left, Left, Down (x4), Right, Down.

PLAY AS ORANGE HULK
Highlight Chun-Li and press Right, Right, Down, Down, Left, Left, Right, Right, Down, Down, Left, Left, Up (x4), Down, Down, Right, Right, Up, Up, Down (x4), Up (x4), Left, Up.

PLAY AS ROLL
Highlight Zangief and press Left, Left, Down, Down, Right, Right, Down, Down, Left, Left, Up, Right, Up, Up, Right, Right.

PLAY AS SHADOW LADY
Highlight Morrigan and press Up, Right, Right, Down (x4), Left, Left, Up (x4), Right, Right, Left, Left, Down, Down, Right, Right, Down, Down, Left, Left, Up, Up, Right, Right, Up, Up, Left, Left, Down (x5).

SELECT PARTNER
Select your two characters, then hold Start and the following buttons:

CHARACTER	CODE
Anita	Light Punch, Medium Punch, Hard Punch
Arthur	Light Punch, Medium Punch
Colossus	Light Punch, Medium Punch, Medium Kick
Cyclops	Light punch, Light Kick, Medium Punch
Devilot	Medium Punch
Iceman	Medium Punch, Medium Kick
Jubilee	Light Kick, Medium Punch, Hard Punch
Juggernaut	Light Punch, Medium Kick
Lou	Medium Punch
Magneo	Light Kick, Hard Punch
Michelle Hart	Light Punch, Light Kick
Psylocke	Medium Kick
Pure and Fur	Light Kick

CHARACTER	CODE
Rogue	Light Punch, Light Kick, Medium Punch, Hard Punch
Saki	Hard Punch
Sentinel	Medium Punch, Medium Kick, Hard Punch
Shadow	Light Punch, Medium Kick, Hard Punch
Storm	Light Punch, Light Kick, Hard Punch
Thor	Light Kick, Medium Punch
Ton-Pooh	Light Punch, Hard Punch
Unknown Soldier	Light Punch
US Agent	Hard Punch, Medium Kick

MASS EFFECT 3

BATTLEFIELD 3 SOLDIER IN MULTIPLAYER

This character is unlocked for multiplayer if you have a Battlefield 3 Online Pass activated on your EA account.

RECKONER KNIGHT ARMOR AND CHAKRAM LAUNCHER

Start the Kingdom of Amalur: Reckoning demo to unlock this armor and weapon in Mass Effect 3.

AVATAR AWARDS

AVATAR	EARNED BY
N7 Helmet	Return to Active Duty.
Omniblade	Kill 25 Enemies with Melee Attacks.

MAX PAYNE 3

NEW YORK MINUTE IN ARCADE MODE

Complete story mode.

CHARACTER SELECT IN ARCADE MODE

Complete story mode on Medium Difficulty.

OLD SCHOOL DIFFICULTY, HARDCORE DIFFICULTY, AND UNLIMITED PAINKILLERS CHEAT

Complete story mode on Hard Difficulty.

MAX PAYNE ADVANCED CHARACTER MODEL

Complete story mode on Old School Difficulty.

The following cheats can be used when replaying a level with the level select:

BULLET CAM ON EVERY KILL

Find all Clues.

ONE HIT KILL CHEAT

Complete story mode on Hardcore difficulty with Free Aim.

UNLIMITED AMMO

Find all Golden Guns.

UNLIMITED BULLET TIME

Earn a Gold Medal on all levels in Arcade Mode.

UNLIMITED PAIN KILLERS

Complete game on Hard difficulty with Free Aim.

MINECRAFT: XBOX 360 EDITION

AVATAR AWARDS

AVATAR	EARNED BY
The Pork-Chop T-Shirt	Earn a Cooked Porkchop.
A Minecraft Watch	Play the game for 100 day to night cycles.
The Creeper Cap	Kill a Creeper with Arrows.

STEVE GAMER PICTURE

Mine redstone for the first time.

CREEPER GAMER PICTURE

Defeat 10 Creepers.

MINECRAFT XBOX 360 EDITION PREMIUM THEME

Pause the game, press Y to grab a shot, and upload the image to Facebook.

MONDAY NIGHT COMBAT

AVATAR AWARDS

AWARD	EARNED BY
Mascot Mask	Meet the Mascot in Monday Night Combat Tutorial-kill the mascot in the tutorial.
Monday Night Combat T-Shirt	Earn the Exhibitor Achievement Get this by completing "Exhibition" Blitz mode.

MORTAL KOMBAT ARCADE KOLLECTION

MORTAL KOMBAT II

NO THROWS OPTION

In a two-player match and before the match begins, hold Down + HP on both controllers.

ULTIMATE MORTAL KOMBAT 3

VS CODES

At the VS screen, each player must use LP, BLK, and LK (A, Right Bumper, B) to enter the following codes:

EFFECT	PLAYER 1	PLAYER 2
Blocking Disabled	020	020
Dark Kombat	688	688
Don't Jump at Me	448	844
Explosive Combat (2 on 2)	227	227
Fast Uppercut Recovery Enabled	688	422
No Fear	282	282
No Powerbars	987	123
Player 1 Half Power	033	N/A
Player 1 Quarter Power	707	N/A
Player 2 Half Power	N/A	033
Player 2 Quarter Power	N/A	707
RandPer Kombat	444	444
Silent Kombat	300	300
Throwing Disabled	100	100
Unikoriv Referri: Sans Power	044	440
Unlimited Run	466	466
Two-Player Mini-Game of Galaga	642	468
Kombat Zone: Bell Tower	910	190
Kombat Zone: The Bridge	077	022
Kombat Zone: The Graveyard	666	333
Kombat Zone: Jade's Desert	330	033
Kombat Zone: Kahn's Kave	004	070
Kombat Zone: Kahn's Tower	880	220
Kombat Zone: Kombat Temple	600	040
Kombat Zone: Noob Saibot Dorfen	050	050
Kombat Zone: The Pit 3	820	028
Kombat Zone: River Kombat	002	003
Kombat Zone: Rooftop	343	343
Kombat Zone: Scislac Busorez	933	933
Kombat Zone: Scorpion's Lair	666	444
Kombat Zone: Soul Chamber	123	901
Kombat Zone: Street	079	035
Kombat Zone: Subway	880	088

EFFECT	PLAYER 1	PLAYER 2
Winner of round fights Motaro	969	141
Winner of round fights Noob Saibot	769	342
Winner of round fights Shao Kahn	033	564
Winner of round fights Smoke	205	205
Revision	999	999
See the Mortal Kombat Live Tour !!	550	550
"Hold Flippers During Casino Run"	987	666
"Rain Can Be Found in the Graveyard"	711	313
"Skunky !!"	122	221
"There Is No Knowledge That Is Not Power"	123	926
"Whatcha Gun Do?"	004	400

UNLOCK CLASSIC SUB-ZERO

Lose a match in arcade mode and let the continue timer run out. Enter the following within 10 seconds on both controllers; HP (x8), LP (x1), BL (x8), LK (x3), HK (x5).

UNLOCK ERMAC

Lose a match in arcade mode and let the continue timer run out. Enter the following within 10 seconds; HP (x1), LP (x2), BL (x3), LK (x4), HK (x4) for player 1 and HP (x4), LP (x4), BL (x3), LK (x2), HK (x1) for player 2.

UNLOCK MILEENA

Lose a match in arcade mode and let the continue timer run out. Enter the following within 10 seconds on both controllers; HP (x2), LP (x2), BL (x2), LK (x6), HK (x4).

HUMAN SMOKE

Select Smoke. For player 1, hold Block + Run + High Punch + High Kick + Left before the fight begins. For player 2, hold Block + Run + High Punch + High Kick + Right before the fight begins.

MORTAL KOMBAT KOMPLETE EDITION

VS CODES

At the VS screen, each player must use LP, BLK, and LK to enter the following codes. The numbers represent how many times you must press each button.

EFFECT	PLAYER 1	PLAYER 2
Armless Kombat	911	911
Blocking Disabled	020	020
Breakers Disabled	090	090
Dark Kombat	022	022
Double Dash	391	193
Dream Kombat	222	555
Enhance Moves Disabled	051	150
Explosive Kombat	227	227
Foreground Objects Disabled	001	001
Headless Kombat	808	808
Health Recovery	012	012
Hyper Fighting	091	091
Invisible Kombat	770	770
Jumping Disabled	831	831
Klassik Music	101	101
Kombos Disabled	931	931
No Blood	900	900
Player 1 Half Health	220	000
Player 1 Quarter Health	110	000
Player 2 Half Health	000	220
Player 2 Quarter Health	000	110
Power Bars Disabled	404	404
Psycho Kombat	707	707

EFFECT	PLAYER 1	PLAYER 2
Quick Uppercut Recovery	303	303
Rainbow Kombat	234	234
Random Phrase 1	717	313
Random Phrase 2	448	844
Random Phrase 3	122	221
Random Phrase 4	009	900
Random Phrase 5	550	055
Random Phrase 6	031	130
Random Phrase 7	282	282
Random Phrase 8	123	926
Sans Power	044	440
Silent Kombat	300	300
Specials Disabled	731	731
Super Recovery	123	123
Throwing Disabled	100	100
Throwing Encouraged	010	010
Tournament Mode	111	111
Unlimited Super Meter	466	466
Vampire Kombat	424	424
XRays Disabled	242	242
Zombie Kombat	666	666

HIDDEN KING OF THE HILL AVATAR ACTIONS

When viewing a fight as a spectator, highlight your avatar and press A to get the action menu. Now enter the following to perform some hidden actions:

EFFECT	CODE
"$%#&!"	Up, Up, B
#1	Down, Up, Y
Big Clap	Right, Up, Y
Cheese	Left, Up, Down, B
Cover Face	Left, Right, B
Devil Horns	Down, Up, X
Diamond	Up, Down, Left, Y
Double Devil Horns	Up, Down, Y
"FATALITY"	Up, Up, Right, Right, X
"FIGHT!	Left, Right, X
"Finish Him!"	Left, Right, Left, Right, Y
Gather Ice	Right, Right, Right, Left, Y
"HA!"	Down, Up, Down, A
Hop	Up, Up, X
"I'm Not Worthy"	Down, Down, Y
Lighter	Down, Down, Up, Up, X
Point	Right, Right, X
Raiden Pose	Left, Left, Right, Right, X
Shake Head	Left, Right, A
Skunk	Left, Right, Up, Up A
Skunk (Stench)	Up, Down, Down, B
Sleep	Down, Down, Down, B
Stink Wave	Right, Left, B
Throw Tomato	Down, Down, Down, Up, A

NARUTO SHIPPUDEN: ULTIMATE NINJA STORM GENERATIONS

9 NARUTO: ULTIMATE NINJA STORM CHARACTERS

As long as you have a save game from the original Naruto: Ultimate Ninja Storm on your system, 9 bonus characters are unlocked. These include: Ino, Shikamaru, Choji, Neji, Tenten, Rock Lee, Kiba, Shino, Hinata, and 50,000 Ryo.

11 NARUTO SHIPPUDEN: ULTIMATE NINJA STORM 2 CHARACTERS

As long as you have a save game from Naruto Shippuden: Ultimate Ninja Storm 2 on your system, 11 bonus characters are unlocked. These include: Ino, Shikamaru, Choji, Neji, Tenten, Rock Lee, Kiba, Shino, Hinata, Asuma, Guy, and 50,000 Ryo.

NINJA CARD PASSWORDS

Select Enter Password from the Collection Screen and enter the following. Each password unlocks one Ninja Info Card.

00HNWGTFV8	BL770WJT70	MKKJMC7CWF
0B7JLNHXA4	BQ7207JT80	MMD4M2BK7K
0CKC96JGVL	BVKHANGBKR	MSJ1BFU4JB
0LP3WPBQ7B	C0DGMFHCCD	MUW7LMT1WG
17769QU0KT	CE8Q9UKG8N	NDD9LG0EV0
1TFLMLP4BE	CJE20EPKWV	PLESLFPVKK
1V8WD29DBJ	CVJVLP6PVS	PQVG0KUCL0
1WQ4WR17VV	D53XB9P4LP	PSA21VB6M2
28G1D0FSBS	DCF515Q8X9	Q8M8P2J295
2DRA0BDFAR	DS1BXA13LD	QCS5D53XBA
2LM5CHLVX1	DX0L0382NT	QEB22X9LNP
2MFFXGNKWL	E23G24EB0B	QTBT1W97M2
39PXPFXEDW	EL52EVS00X	R4C43XB8PD
3ET93PHNNM	ENE5N43M9L	R8JE3QS6QT
3J6R2NS6B4	ERCKGKSN1P	RE6KE7GPCC
3USV86L2HM	F515Q009CE	S5JVSL6DDC
4HB5ELA91R	F6DTQBCXCF	S85PRDRU1T
4LTP2Q6U26	F7T1103JNS	SAUFE2T72U
4RTCRU4BWD	FMBB22KR0J	SKJERP5K15
53HXEB6EQ1	G12P36C5QW	TEP2FTPH4A
5DFQ45CJF0	GB7FS2G8EV	TH9NGBKRFF
5FUU285P1D	GR56DKG1CP	TVQ7HC2PQ5
6PF63C1C35	GWQ8EKCNEG	U3GQH7R65P
6QDPEH0HQL	H3D14HNF2X	U59BHXUEF3
6RQD5KD6GN	HH88SX6Q4P	UCM26NV9TW
6UB06B8FS2	HWR9FKDPFH	UFG3GKQJ5B
794L5RFD5J	HX3CS22CEG	UL4KS3Q2SU
7DEDGW26R1	J22C572J3P	UMK7SHU2QQ
7KXC71MSTS	JFXC608F44	UTG4GWQ65P
8CTCJFSQ6L	JMV3HRHBR7	V9TW64S2JJ
8EJ57XFMJ3	JSB8UFKXHL	VG63VA3W6D
8JPPVC8TUG	JXF97FR2F7	VLGL6FEQSU
8Q1VK79N7B	K1C6VJKXHL	VML7SHV3RR
96XD609G54	KE84GXKREE	W1X6BJWX5C
9FP7L7N1H1	KF4RT7RU4B	W57HWX4B7S
9P8BLJ6FXX	KTS46B3JUP	WH0BJBA5HF
ADUMLGTR7M	L3PAK7BPUM	WV72WQ4B7R
ALNQK2L6VS	L6N0B1XT65	XH5G7ASAHD
AQU0KTTFCB	LMTA6QSEJV	XVN2VPX5TT
B7JHWCTWU3	MB3GA4DK88	XXPF0EMWKV

NASCAR THE GAME 2011

MARK MARTIN PAINT SCHEMES

At the garage main menu, press Down, Down, Up, Up, Right, Left, Right, Left. Enter godaddy.com.

KYLE BUSH NOS ENERGY DRINK CAR

At the garage main menu, press Down, Down, Up, Up, Right, Left, Right, Left. Enter drinknos.

NBA 2K11

MJ: CREATING A LEGEND

In Features, select Codes from the Extras menu. Choose Enter Code and enter icanbe23.

2K CHINA TEAM

In Features, select Codes from the Extras menu. Choose Enter Code and enter 2kchina.

2K SPORTS TEAM

In Features, select Codes from the Extras menu. Choose Enter Code and enter 2Ksports.

NBA 2K TEAM

In Features, select Codes from the Extras menu. Choose Enter Code and enter nba2k.

VC TEAM

In Features, select Codes from the Extras menu. Choose Enter Code and enter vcteam.

ABA BALL

In Features, select Codes from the Extras menu. Choose Enter Code and enter payrespect.

2011 ALL-STAR UNIFORMS

In Features, select Codes from the Extras menu. Choose Enter Code and enter wydololoh.

SECONDARY ROAD UNIFORM

In Features, select Codes from the Extras menu. Choose Enter Code and enter ronoilnm. This unlocks the secondary road uniform for the Hornets, Magic, and Timberwolves.

ORANGE SPLIT DUNK

In Features, select Codes from the Extras menu. Choose Enter Code and enter SPRITEDUNK1. Go to Sprite Slam Dunk Showdown and use the help menu to find out more.

SPIN TOMMY DUNK

In Features, select Codes from the Extras menu. Choose Enter Code and enter SPRITEDUNK2. Go to Sprite Slam Dunk Showdown and use the help menu to find out more.

THE VILLAIN DUNK

In Features, select Codes from the Extras menu. Choose Enter Code and enter SPRITEDUNK3. Go to Sprite Slam Dunk Showdown and use the help menu to find out more.

NBA 2K12

ABA BALL

Select Extras from the Features menu. Choose Codes and enter payrespect. This can be toggled on and off from this Codes menu.

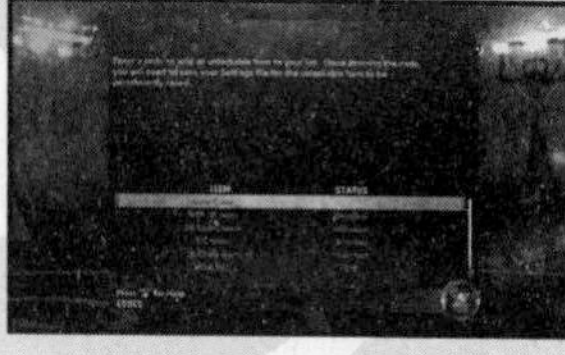

2K CHINA TEAM

Select Extras from the Features menu. Choose Codes and enter 2kchina.

2K SPORTS TEAM

Select Extras from the Features menu. Choose Codes and enter 2ksports.

UNLOCK NBA 2K TEAM

Select Extras from the Features menu. Choose Codes and enter nba2k.

VC TEAM

Select Extras from the Features menu. Choose Codes and enter vcteam.

JORDAN RETRO COLLECTION

Select Extras from the Features menu. Choose Codes and enter 23.

SECONDARY ROAD UNIFORMS

Select Extras from the Features menu. Choose Codes and enter hcsilapadatu. This unlocks uniforms for 76ers, Jazz, Kings, and Mavericks.

CHRISTMAS UNIFORMS

Select Extras from the Features menu. Choose Codes and enter ibyasmliancbhlald. This unlocks uniforms for Bulls, Celtics, Heat, Knicks, Lakers, and Mavericks.

HEAT BACK IN BLACK UNIFORM

Select Extras from the Features menu. Choose Codes and enter albkbinkcca.

RAPTORS MILITARY NIGHT UNIFORM

Select Extras from the Features menu. Choose Codes and enter liyrimta.

NBA 2K13

ABA BALL

Select Features from the main menu and then go to Codes. Enter payrespect.

UA TORCH SHOE

Select Features from the main menu and then go to Codes. Enter underarmour.

SPRITE EFFECT BONUS

Select Features from the main menu and then go to Codes. Enter spriteeffect.ç

NBA JAM

BEASTIE BOYS

At the title screen, press Up, Up, Down, Down, Left, Right, Left, Right, B, A. This team includes Ad Rock, MCA, and Mike D.

J. COLE AND 9TH WONDER

At the title screen, press Up, Left, Down, Right, Up, Left, Down, Right, Circle, A.

DEMOCRATS TEAM

At the title screen, press Left (x13), A. This team includes Barack Obama, Joe Biden, Bill Clinton, and Hillary Clinton.

REPUBLICANS TEAM

At the title screen, press Right (x13), A. The team includes George W. Bush, Sarah Palin, Dick Cheney, and John McCain.

ESPN'S SPORTSNATION

Select Play Now. When entering the initials, enter ESP for P1 and NSN for P2. Advance to the Choose Teams screen to find the team. This team includes the hosts of the show; Colin Cowherd and Michelle Beadle.

NBA MASCOTS

Select Play Now. When entering the initials, enter MAS for P1 and COT for P2.

ORIGINAL GENERATION JAM

Select Play Now. When entering the initials, enter MJT for P1. Advance to the Choose Teams screen to find the team. This team includes Mark Turmell and Tim Kitzrow.

NEED FOR SPEED: THE RUN

AEM CHALLENGE

At the Extras menu enter aemintakes.

NEED FOR SPEED UNDERCOVER

$10,000
Select Secret Codes from the Options menu and enter $EDSOC.

DIE-CAST BMW M3 E92
Select Secret Codes from the Options menu and enter)B7@B=.

DIE-CAST LEXUS IS F
Select Secret Codes from the Options menu and enter 0;5M2;.

NEEDFORSPEED.COM LOTUS ELISE
Select Secret Codes from the Options menu and enter -KJ3=E.

DIE-CAST NISSAN 240SX (S13)
Select Secret Codes from the Options menu and enter ?P:COL.

DIE-CAST PORSCHE 911 TURBO
Select Secret Codes from the Options menu and enter >8P:I;.

SHELBY TERLINGUA
Select Secret Codes from the Options menu and enter NeedForSpeedShelbyTerlingua.

DIE-CAST VOLKSWAGEN R32
Select Secret Codes from the Options menu and enter!2ODBJ:.

NFL BLITZ

Select Cheats from the Blitz Store to purchase the following cheats. They are entered with X, Y, and B. Press these buttons until the three given icons are shown. The number indicates how many times each button is pressed. X is the first number, Y the second, and B is the third.

GAMEPLAY CHEATS
Buy these cheats to change the game to your advantage.

CHEAT	CODE
Tournament Mode	Goalpost, Goalpost, Goalpost (4 4 4)
Faster Passes	Helmet, NFL, NFL (5 1 1)
Speedster	Goalpost, NFL, EA Sports (4 1 0)
Fast Turbo Drain	Helmet, Headset, NFL (5 3 1)
More Fumbles	Helmet, Goalpost, NFL (5 4 1)
No First Downs	Goalpost, Headset, Goalpost (4 3 4)
No Fumbles	Helmet, EA Sports, Headset (5 0 3)
No Interceptions	Helmet, Helmet, EA Sports (5 5 0)
No Onside Kicks	Goalpost, Foam Finger, Foam Finger (4 2 2)
No Punting	Goalpost, Goalpost, EA Sports (4 4 0)
Power Defense	Goalpost, Whistle, Goalpost (4 8 4)
Power Offense	Helmet, Foam Finger, Helmet (5 2 5)
No Stepping out of Bounds	Helmet, EA Sports, EA Sports (5 0 0)
Unlimited Turbo	Helmet, NFL, Goalpost (5 1 4)

VISUAL CHEATS
Your team will get a Blitz makeover after you buy these cheats.

CHEAT	CODE
Big Head Player	Foam Finger, Helmet, EA Sports (2 5 0)
Big Head Team	Foam Finger, NFL, Foam Finger (2 1 2)
Tiny Head Team	Foam Finger, Goalpost, Headset (2 4 3)
Tiny Head Player	Headset, EA Sports, Foam Finger (3 0 2)
Huge Head Team	Headset, NFL, Foam Finger (3 1 2)
Huge Head Player	Foam Finger, EA Sports, NFL (2 0 1)
Super Ball Trail	EA Sports, NFL, Football (0 1 6)
Black & Red Ball	EA Sports, EA Sports, Foam Finger (0 0 2)
Camouflage Ball	EA Sports, EA Sports, Helmet (0 0 5)
Chrome Ball	EA Sports, Foam Finger, EA Sports (0 2 0)
Flames Ball	EA Sports, Goalpost, Foam Finger (0 4 2)
Ice Cream Ball	EA Sports, Foam Finger, Marker (0 2 7)
B-52 Ball	NFL, EA Sports, Goalpost (1 0 4)
Beachball	NFL, EA Sports, NFL (1 0 1)
Glow Ball	EA Sports, Marker, EA Sports (0 7 0)

CHEAT	CODE
Meat Ball	EA Sports, Football, EA Sports (0 6 0)
Pumpkin Ball	Whistle, Headset, NFL (8 3 1)
Soup Can Ball	Marker, NFL, EA Sports (7 1 0)
Blitz Team Ball	NFL, NFL, NFL (1 1 1)
USA Ball	Headset, NFL, Helmet (3 1 5)
Blitz Stadium	EA Sports, NFL, Goalpost (0 1 4)
Cardinals Stadium	EA Sports, Foam Finger, Foam Finger (0 2 2)
Falcons Stadium	EA Sports, Headset, EA Sports (0 3 0)
Ravens Stadium	EA Sports, Headset, Helmet (0 3 5)
Bills Stadium	EA Sports, Headset, Marker (0 3 7)
Panthers Stadium	EA Sports, Goalpost, Goalpost (0 4 4)
Bears Stadium	EA Sports, Goalpost, Football (0 4 6)
Bengals Stadium	EA Sports, Goalpost, Whistle (0 4 8)
Browns Stadium	EA Sports, Helmet, Headset (0 5 3)
Cowboys Stadium	EA Sports, Helmet, Helmet (0 5 5)
Broncos Stadium	EA Sports, EA Sports, Marker (0 0 7)
Lions Stadium	EA Sports, Helmet, Marker (0 5 7)
Packers Stadium	EA Sports, Football, Foam Finger (0 6 2)
Texans Stadium	EA Sports, Football, Goalpost (0 6 4)
Colts Stadium	EA Sports, Football, Football (0 6 6)
Jaguars Stadium	EA Sports, Marker, Foam Finger (0 7 2)
Chiefs Stadium	EA Sports, Whistle, EA Sports (0 8 0)
Dolphins Stadium	EA Sports, Marker, Marker (0 7 7)
Vikings Stadium	NFL, EA Sports, Football (1 0 6)
Patriots Stadium	NFL, NFL, Goalpost (1 1 4)
Saints Stadium	NFL, Foam Finger, Headset (1 2 3)
Giants Stadium	NFL, Headset, EA Sports (1 3 0)
Jets Stadium	NFL, EA Sports, Whistle (1 0 8)
Raiders Stadium	NFL, Foam Finger, Helmet (1 2 5)
Eagles Stadium	NFL, Headset, Headset (1 3 3)
Steelers Stadium	NFL, Headset, Helmet (1 3 5)
Chargers Stadium	NFL, Helmet, EA Sports (1 5 0)
Seahawks Stadium	Foam Finger, Foam Finger, EA Sports (2 2 0)
49ers Stadium	Foam Finger, NFL, EA Sports (2 1 0)
Rams Stadium	Foam Finger, Headset, EA Sports (2 3 0)
Bucs Stadium	Foam Finger, Goalpost, EA Sports (2 4 0)
Titans Stadium	Headset, EA Sports, Headset (3 0 3)
Redskins Stadium	Goalpost, EA Sports, NFL (4 0 1)
Day	EA Sports, Whistle, Foam Finger (0 8 2)
Twilight	NFL, NFL, Marker (1 1 7)
Night	NFL, Whistle, Marker (1 8 7)

SETTINGS CHEATS

Change certain game settings when you buy these cheats.

CHEAT	CODE
Hide Player Name	EA Sports, Foam Finger, Goalpost (0 2 4)
Extra Code Time	Helmet, Helmet, Helmet (5 5 5)
No Ball Target	EA Sports, Helmet, NFL (0 5 1)
Wide Camera	NFL, NFL, Foam Finger (1 1 2)
Show Field Goal Percentage	EA Sports, NFL, Foam Finger (0 1 2)
All-Time QB Coop	Headset, Headset, EA Sports (3 3 0)
All-Time WR Coop	EA Sports, Headset, Headset (0 3 3)
Icon Passing	Headset, Helmet, Headset (3 5 3)
No Player Icon	EA Sports, Goalpost, EA Sports (0 4 0)

FANTASY CHARACTERS

Buy these cheats to play as your favorite characters. Characters must be unlocked by defeating them in Blitz Gauntlet first.

UNLOCKABLE CHARACTERS

CHEAT	CODE
Bigfoot	Headset, Headset, Headset (3 3 3)
Bigfoot Team	Marker, EA Logo, EA Logo (7 0 0)
Cowboy	Headset, Foam Finger, Headset (3 2 3)
Cowboy Team	Goalpost, Marker, Goalpost (4 7 4)
Gladiator	Foam Finger, Whistle, Foam Finger (2 8 2)
Gladiator Team	Helmet, NFL, Marker (5 1 7)
Horse	NFL, Marker, NFL (1 7 1)
Horse Team	Foam Finger, Football, Foam Finger (2 6 2)
Hot Dog	NFL, Football, NFL (1 6 1)
Hot Dog Team	Foam Finger, Headset, Foam Finger (2 3 2)
Lion	Foam Finger, EA Sports, Foam Finger (2 0 2)
Lion Team	Headset, Goalpost, Headset (3 4 3)
Ninja	Foam Finger, Marker, Foam Finger (2 7 2)
Ninja Team	Football, NFL, Football (6 1 6)
Pirate	NFL, Foam Finger, NFL (1 2 1)
Pirate Team	Helmet, Headset, Helmet (5 3 5)

NHL 12

3RD JERSEYS

Select NHL 12 Code Entry from My NHL 12 and enter 2wg3gap9mvrth6kq. This unlocks uniforms for Florida, New York Islanders, Ottawa, and Toronto.

NIGHTS INTO DREAMS

UNLOCK EVERYTHING

At the title screen, press Left, Right, X, B, A, Y, Right Bumper, Right Trigger, Down, Up, Left Bumper, Left Trigger. Achievements, saving, and posting high scores are disabled until the game is restarted.

OPERATION FLASHPOINT: DRAGON RISING

AMBUSH BONUS MISSION

Select Cheats from the Options menu and enter AmbushU454.

CLOSE QUARTERS BONUS MISSION

Select Cheats from the Options menu and enter CloseQ8M3

COASTAL STRONGHOLD BONUS MISSION

Select Cheats from the Options menu and enter StrongM577

DEBRIS FIELD BONUS MISSION

Select Cheats from the Options menu and enter OFPWEB2

ENCAMPMENT BONUS MISSION

Select Cheats from the Options menu and enter OFPWEB1

NIGHT RAID BONUS MISSION

Select Cheats from the Options menu and enter RaidT18Z

THE ORANGE BOX

HALF-LIFE 2

The following codes work for Half-Life 2, Half-Life 2: Episode One, and Half-Life 2: Episode Two.

CHAPTER SELECT

While playing, press Left, Left, Left, Left, Left Bumper, Right, Right, Right, Right, Right Bumper. Pause the game and select New Game to skip to another chapter.

RESTORE HEALTH (25 POINTS)

While playing, press Up, Up, Down, Down, Left, Right, Left, Right, B, A.

RESTORE AMMO FOR CURRENT WEAPON

While playing, press Y, B, A, X, Right Bumper, Y, X, A, B, Right Bumper.

INVINCIBILITY

While playing, press Left Shoulder, Up, Right Shoulder, Up, Left Shoulder, Left Shoulder, Up, Right Shoulder, Right Shoulder, Up.

PORTAL

CHAPTER SELECT

While playing, press Left, Left, Left, Left, Left Bumper, Right, Right, Right, Right, Right Bumper. Pause the game and select New Game to skip to another chapter.

GET A BOX

While playing, press Down, B, A, B, Y, Down, B, A, B, Y.

ENERGY BALL

While playing, press Up, Y, Y, X, X, A, A, B, B, Up.

PORTAL PLACEMENT ANYWHERE

While playing, press Y, A, B, A, B, Y, Y, A, Left, Right.

PORTALGUN ID 0

While playing, press Up, Left, Down, Right, Up, Left, Down, Right, Y, Y.

PORTALGUN ID 1

While playing, press Up, Left, Down, Right, Up, Left, Down, Right, X, X.

PORTALGUN ID 2

While playing, press Up, Left, Down, Right, Up, Left, Down, Right, A, A.

PORTALGUN ID 3

While playing, press Up, Left, Down, Right, Up, Left, Down, Right, B, B.

UPGRADE PORTALGUN

While playing, press X, B, Left Bumper, Right Bumper, Left, Right, Left Bumper, Right Bumper, Left Trigger, Right Trigger.

ORCS MUST DIE!

AVATAR AWARDS

AVATAR	EARNED BY
OMD Logo Tee	Complete Act 1 of Orcs Must Die!
OMD Skull Hat	Kill 1,000 enemies in Orcs Must Dies!

PERFECT DARK

PERFECT DARK ZERO SAVE CHEATS

If you have a save from Perfect Dark Zero on your hard drive, you get the following: All Guns (Solo), Cloaking Device, Hurricane Fists, and Weapon Stash Radar.

PHANTOM BREAKER

FIN

Complete Story Mode with each of the original characters.

INFINITY

Complete Arcade Mode.

KURISU

Win 250 matches.

RIMI

Win 200 matches.

PINBALL FX 2

AVATAR AWARDS

AWARD	EARNED BY
Pinball FX 2 T-Shirt	Achieve 5,000 Wizard Score.
Pinball Sorceress Dress (Female)	Achieve 100,000 Wizard Score.
Pinball Wizard Robe (Male)	Achieve 100,000 Wizard Score.

PLANTS VS. ZOMBIES

During a game, press Left Bumper, Right Bumper, Left Trigger, Right Trigger. Now you can enter the following codes. You must be given a code before it can be used.

MUSTACHES FOR ZOMBIE

Enter mustache.

SHADES FOR ZOMBIES

Enter future.

ZOMBIES DANCE

Enter dance.

CANDY WHEN ZOMBIE DIES

Enter piñata.

DEAD ZOMBIES LEAVE DAISIES

Enter daisies.

ALTERNATE LAWN MOWER

Enter trickedout.

PORTAL 2

AVATAR AWARDS

AWARD	EARNED BY
Companion Cube	Complete Portal 2 Single Player.
Love Shirt	Hug 3 friends in Portal 2 Coop.
Portal 2 Hat	Survive the manual override.
Portal 2 Shirt	Complete Portal 2 Coop
Turret Shirt	Complete Test Chamber 10 in less than 70 seconds.

PRINCE OF PERSIA

SANDS OF TIME PRINCE/FARAH SKINS

Select Skin Manager from the Extras menu. Press Y and enter 52585854. This gives you the Sands of Time skin for the Prince and Farah from Sands of Time for the Princess. Access them from the Skin Manager

PRINCE ALTAIR IBN LA-AHAD SKIN

At the Main menu, press Y for Exclusive Content. Create an Ubisoft account. Then select "Altair Skin for Prince" to unlock.

PROTOTYPE 2

NEW GAME +

Complete every story mission.

AVATAR AWARDS

AVATAR	EARNED BY
James Heller Outfit	With RADNET activated, access the Events Screen for unlock details.
Heller Hoodie	With RADNET activated, access the Events Screen for unlock details.
Alex Mercer Outfit	With RADNET activated, access the Events Screen for unlock details.
Shield	With RADNET activated, access the Events Screen for unlock details.
T-Shirt	With RADNET activated, access the Events Screen for unlock details.

RASKULLS

I HATE YOU SHAPEASAURUS (PLAY AS SHAPEASAURUS)
Pause the game, press Y and enter Right Bumper, Up, Down, Right Bumper, Up, Down.

LE FILS DE I'HOMME (APPLE HEAD)
Pause the game, press Y and enter Up, Up, Up, Down, Down, Down.

EGOMANIACS (BIG HEADS)
Pause the game, press Y and enter Up, Down, Left, Right.

PAPER BAG (PAPER BAG HEAD)
Pause the game, press Y and enter Left, Right, Left, Right, Left.

GET FUNKY (AFRO)
Pause the game, press Y and enter X, X, X, Y, Y, Y.

TRANSIENT MODE (BEARD)
Pause the game, press Y and enter Up, Down, Up, Down, Up.

MOUSTACHE ENGAGE! (MUSTACHE)
Pause the game, press Y and enter Right Bumper, Right Bumper, Right Bumper, Left Bumper, Left Bumper, Left Bumper.

TOO BRIGHT! (SUNGLASSES)
Pause the game, press Y and enter Left Bumper, Right Bumper, Left Bumper, Right Bumper, Left Bumper.

AVATAR AWARDS

AWARD	EARNED BY
Raskulls T-Shirt	Complete a certain Mega-Challenge in Chapter 1.
A Giant King Mask	Complete a certain Mega-Challenge in Chapter 2.

RAVING RABBIDS: ALIVE & KICKING

AVATAR AWARDS

AVATAR	EARNED BY
Rabbids A&K T-Shirt	The official T-Shirt supporting ravingness around the world.
Rabbid Helmet	A Rabbid helmet to stay incognito.
T.V. Helmet	A TV set that acts a stunning piece of headgear.

RED DEAD REDEMPTION

CHEATS

Select Cheats from Options and enter the following codes. Cheats disable Trophies and saving.

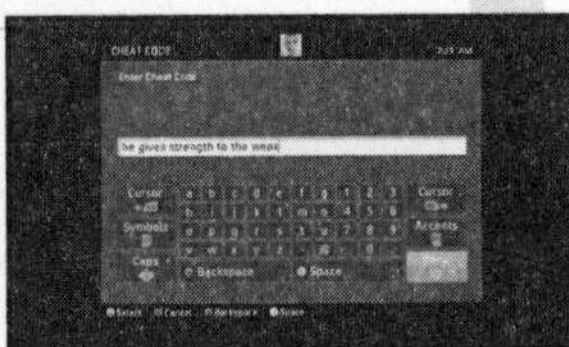

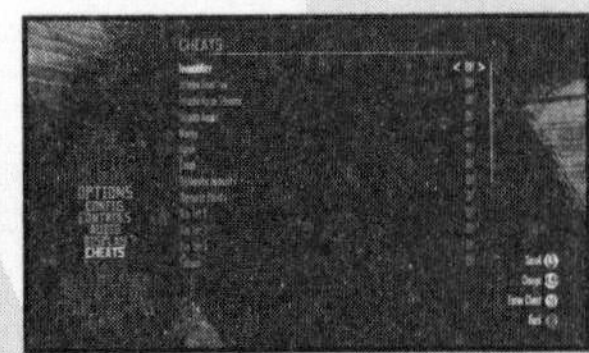

CHEAT	CODE
Invincibility	HE GIVES STRENGTH TO THE WEAK
Infinite Dead Eye	I DON'T UNDERSTAND IMNFINITY
Infinite Horse Stamina	MAKE HAY WHILE THE SUN SHINES
Infinite Ammo	ABUNDANCE IS EVERYWHERE
Money ($500)	THE ROOT OF ALL EVIL, WE THANK YOU!
Coach	NOW WHO PUT THAT THERE?
Horse	BEASTS AND MAN TOGETHER
Good Guy	IT AINT PRIDE. IT'S HONOR
Famous	I AM ONE OF THEM FAMOUS FELLAS
Diplomatic Immunity	I WISH I WORKED FOR UNCLE SAM
Decrease Bounty	THEY SELL SOULS CHEAP HERE

CHEAT	CODE
Gun Set 1	IT'S MY CONSTITUTIONAL RIGHT
Gun Set 2	I'M AN AMERICAN. I NEED GUNS
Who?	HUMILITY BEFORE THE LORD
Old School (Sepia)	THE OLD WAYS IS THE BEST WAYS
Man in Uniform (Bureau, US Army, and US Marshal uniforms)	I LOVE A MAN IN UNIFORM
Sharp Dressed Man (Gentleman's Suit)	DON'T YOU LOOK FINE AND DANDY
Lewis and Clark (All areas)	YOU GOT YOURSELF A FINE PAIR OF EYES
Gang Chic (Treasure Hunter outfit)	YOU THINK YOU TOUGH, MISTER?
Jack Attack (Play as Jack)	OH MY SON, MY BLESSED SON
Hic (Drunk)	I'M DRUNK AS A SKUNK AND TWICE AS SMELLY

AVATAR AWARDS

AWARD	EARNED BY
Sombrero	Shoot the hat off of an enemy.
Black on Red RDR Logo T-Shirt (Male and Female)	Open chest in burnt down house in Riley's Charge.
Yellow Rockstar Logo T-Shirt (Male and Female)	Open the chest in the attic of John Marston's Beechers Hope house.
Gentleman's Attire/Lady's Finest	Complete Skin It To Win It Social Club Challenge
Posse T-Shirt (Male and Female)	High score in Strike It Rich Social Club Challenge

RED FACTION: GUERRILLA

WRECKING CREW MAPS

Select Extras from the Options menu, choose Enter Code, and then enter MAPMAYHEM.

GOLDEN SLEDGEHAMMER, SINGLE PLAYER

Select Extras from the Options menu, choose Enter Code, and then enter HARDHITTER.

RENEGADE OPS

AVATAR AWARDS

AVATAR	EARNED BY
Renegade Ops Hoodie	Engage helicopter in Single Player.

RESIDENT EVIL 6

ADA WONG'S CAMPAIGN

Complete the campaigns for Chris, Jake, and Leon.

ADA WONG IN MERCENARIES

Complete Ada's Campaign.

HELENA HARPER IN MERCENARIES

Complete Urban Chaos with at least a B ranking.

PIERS NIVANS IN MERCENARIES

Complete Steel Beast with at least a B ranking.

SHERRY BIRKIN IN MERCENARIES

Complete Mining the Depths with at least a B ranking.

ALTERNATE COSTUME IN MERCENARIES

Earn an A ranking in Mercenaries on any level to unlock an alternate costume for that character.

CARLA RADAMES IN MERCENARIES

Unlock all other characters and alternate costumes.

RESONANCE OF FATE

Once you have reached Chapter 7, search Leanne's closet. As she speaks her first line, enter the following codes to unlock more outfits.

8-BIT GIRL SHIRT
Up, Up, Down, Down, Left, Right, Left, Right, Y, X

CLUB FAMITSU SHIRT
Y, Y, Up, Up, X, X, Left, Left, Left Bumper, Right Bumper

GEMAGA SHIRT
Right Trigger, Left Trigger, Left Bumper, Right Bumper, Y, Y, Y, X, X, Up

HIRAKOU SHIRT
X, Y, Left Bumper, Left Bumper, Right Bumper, Right Bumper, Click Left Thumbstick, Click Left Thumbstick, Up, Down

PLATFORM LOGO SHIRT
Left, Up, Right, Down, Right Bumper, Right Bumper, Left Bumper, Left Bumper, Y, Click Left Thumbstick

POLITAN SUIT
Click Right Thumbstick (x3), Right, Left, Y, X, Left Trigger, Right Trigger, Left Bumper. This requires you to have the Reindeer Suit first.

RISE OF NIGHTMARES

AVATAR AWARDS

AVATAR	EARNED BY
Nightmarish T-Shirt	Clear Rise Of Nightmares.
Alchemy T-Shirt	Unlock all 50 achievements.

ROBERT LUDLUM'S THE BOURNE CONSPIRACY

LIGHT MACHINE GUNS HAVE SILENCERS
Select Enter Code from the Cheats screen and enter whattheymakeyougive.

EXTRAS UNLOCKED – CONCEPT ART
Select Enter Code from the Cheats screen and enter lastchancemarie. Select Concept Art from the Extras menu.

EXTRAS UNLOCKED – MUSIC TRACKS
Select Enter Code from the Cheats screen and enter jasonbourneisdead. This unlocks Treadstone Appointment and Manheim Suite in the Music Selector found in the Extras menu.

ROCK BAND 2

Most of these codes disable saving, achievements, and Xbox LIVE play.

UNLOCK ALL SONGS
Select Modify Game from the Extras menu, choose Enter Unlock Code and press Red, Yellow, Blue, Red, Red, Blue, Blue, Red, Yellow, Blue or Y, B, X, Y, Y, X, X, Y, B, X. Toggle this cheat on or off from the Modify Game menu.

SELECT VENUE SCREEN
Select Modify Game from the Extras menu, choose Enter Unlock Code and press Blue, Orange, Orange, Blue, Yellow, Blue, Orange, Orange, Blue, Yellow or X, Left Bumper, Left Bumper, X, B, X, Left Bumper, Left Bumper, X, B. Toggle this cheat on or off from the Modify Game menu.

NEW VENUES ONLY
Select Modify Game from the Extras menu, choose Enter Unlock Code and press Red, Red, Red, Red, Yellow, Yellow, Yellow, Yellow or Y (x4), B (x4). Toggle this cheat on or off from the Modify Game menu.

PLAY THE GAME WITHOUT A TRACK

Select Modify Game from the Extras menu, choose Enter Unlock Code and press Blue, Blue, Red, Red, Yellow, Yellow, Blue, Blue or X, X, Y, Y, B, B, X, X. Toggle this cheat on or off from the Modify Game menu.

AWESOMENESS DETECTION

Select Modify Game from the Extras menu, choose Enter Unlock Code and press Yellow, Blue, Orange, Yellow, Blue, Orange, Yellow, Blue, Orange or B, X, Left Bumper, B, X, Left Bumper, B, X, Left Bumper. Toggle this cheat on or off from the Modify Game menu.

STAGE MODE

Select Modify Game from the Extras menu, choose Enter Unlock Code and press Blue, Yellow, Red, Blue, Yellow, Red, Blue, Yellow, Red or X, B, Y, X, B, Y, X, B, Y. Toggle this cheat on or off from the Modify Game menu.

ROCK BAND 3

GUILD X-79 GUITAR

At the main menu, press Blue, Orange, Orange, Blue, Orange, Orange, Blue, Blue.

OVATION D-2010 GUITAR

At the main menu, press Orange, Blue, Orange, Orange, Blue, Blue, Orange, Blue.

STOP! GUITAR

At the main menu, press Orange, Orange, Blue, Blue, Orange, Blue, Blue, Orange.

ROCKET KNIGHT

ALL CHARACTER SKINS

At the title screen, press Up, Up, Down, Down, Left, Right, Left, Right, B, A, Start.

ROCKSMITH

UNLOCKABLE SONGS

As you achieve Double Encores, the following songs are unlocked randomly.

- Boss by Chris Lee
- Jules by Seth Chapla
- Ricochet by Brian Adam McCune
- Six AM Salvation by Versus Them
- Space Ostrich by Disonaur
- The Star Spangled Banner by Seth Chapla

SAINTS ROW 2

CHEAT CODES

Select Dial from the Phone menu and enter these numbers followed by the Call button. Activate the cheats by selecting Cheats from the Phone menu. Enabling a cheat prevents the acquisition of Achievements

PLAYER ABILITY

CHEAT	NUMBER
Give Cash	#2274666399
No Cop Notoriety	#50
No Gang Notoriety	#51
Infinite Sprint	#6
Full Health	#1
Player Pratfalls	#5
Milk Bones	#3

CHEAT	NUMBER
Car Mass Hole	#2
Infinite Ammo	#11
Heaven Bound	#12
Add Police Notoriety	#4
Add Gang Notoriety	#35
Never Die	#36
Unlimited Clip	#9

VEHICLES

CHEAT	NUMBER
Repair Car	#1056
Venom Classic	#1079
Five-0	#1055

CHEAT	NUMBER
Stilwater Municipal	#1072
Baron	#1047
Attrazione	#1043

CHEAT	NUMBER
Zenith	#1081
Vortex	#1080
Phoenix	#1064
Bootlegger	#1049
Raycaster	#1068
Hollywood	#1057
Justice	#1058
Compton	#1052
Eiswolf	#1053
Taxi	#1074
Ambulance	#1040
Backhoe	#1045
Bagboy	#1046
Rampage	#1067
Reaper	#1069
The Job	#1075
Quota	#1066
FBI	#1054
Mag	#1060
Bulldog	#1050
Quasar	#1065
Titan	#1076
Varsity	#1078
Anchor	#1041
Blaze	#1044
Sabretooth	#804

CHEAT	NUMBER
Sandstorm	#805
Kaneda	#801
Widowmaker	#806
Kenshin	#802
Melbourne	#803
Miami	#826
Python	#827
Hurricane	#825
Shark	#828
Skipper	#829
Mongoose	#1062
Superiore	#1073
Tornado	#713
Horizon	#711
Wolverine	#714
Snipes 57	#712
Bear	#1048
Toad	#1077
Kent	#1059
Oring	#1063
Longhauler	#1061
Atlasbreaker	#1042
Septic Avenger	#1070
Shaft	#1071
Bulldozer	#1051

WEAPONS

CHEAT	NUMBER
AR-50	#923
K6	#935
GDHC	#932
NR4	#942
44	#921
Tombstone	#956
T3K	#954
VICE9	#957
AS14 Hammer	#925
12 Gauge	#920
SKR-9	#951
McManus 2010	#938
Baseball Bat	#926
Knife	#936
Molotov	#940
Grenade	#933
Nightstick	#941
Pipebomb	#945
RPG	#946
Crowbar	#955
Pimp Cane	#944

CHEAT	NUMBER
AR200	#922
AR-50/Grenade Launcher	#924
Chainsaw	#927
Fire Extinguisher	#928
Flamethrower	#929
Flashbang	#930
GAL43	#931
Kobra	#934
Machete	#937
Mini-gun	#939
Pepperspray	#943
Annihilator RPG	#947
Samurai Sword	#948
Satchel Charge	#949
Shock Paddles	#950
Sledgehammer	#952
Stungun	#953
XS-2 Ultimax	#958
Pimp Slap	#969

WEATHER

CHEAT	NUMBER
Clear Skies	#78669
Heavy Rain	#78666
Light Rain	#78668
Overcast	#78665

CHEAT	NUMBER
Time Set Midnight	#2400
Time Set Noon	#1200
Wrath Of God	#666

WORLD

CHEAT	NUMBER
Super Saints	#8
Super Explosions	#7
Evil Cars	#16
Pedestrian War	#19

CHEAT	NUMBER
Drunk Pedestrians	#15
Raining Pedestrians	#20
Low Gravity	#18

SAINTS ROW: THE THIRD

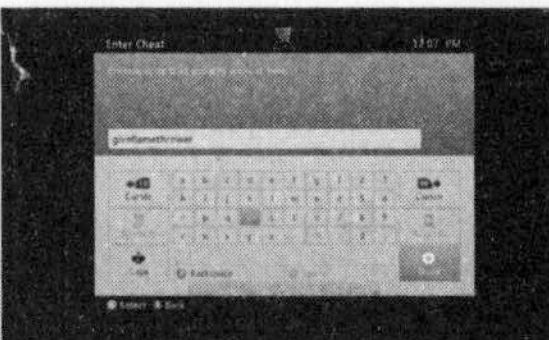

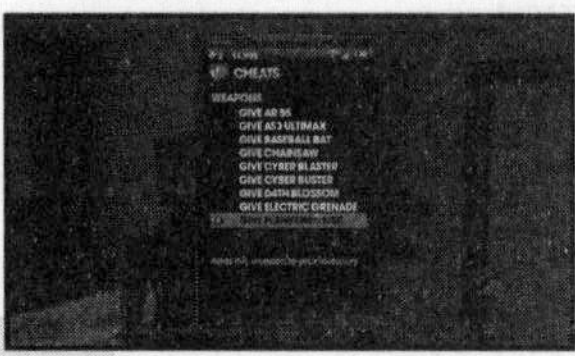

From the cell phone, select Cheats from Extras and enter the following. Using any of these cheats disables autosave and achievements.

GAMEPLAY CHEATS

CHEAT	CODE
Give $100,000	CHEESE
Give Respect	WHATITMEANSTOME
Heavenbound	FRYHOLE
Add Gang Notoriety	LOLZ
Add Police Notoriety	PISSOFPIGS
Infinite Sprint	RUNFAST
No Car Damage	VROOM
No Cop Notoriety	GOODY GOODY
No Gang Notoriety	OOPS
No Gang Notoriety	OOPS
No Police Notoriety	GOODYGOODY
Pedestrians become mascots	MASCOT
Pedestrians become pimps and prostitutes	HOHOHO
Pedestrians become zombies	BRAINS
Repair Car	REPAIRCAR

WORLD CHEATS

CHEAT	CODE
Bloody Mess (Everyone you kill explodes.)	NOTRATED
Drunk pedestrians	DUI

VEHICLES

VEHICLE	CODE
Ambulance	GIVEEMBULANCE
Anchor	GIVEANCHOR
Attrazione	GIVEATTRAZIONE
Bootlegger	GIVEBOOTLEGGER
Challenger	GIVECHALLENGER
Commander	GIVECOMMANDER
Condor	GIVECONDOR
Eagle	GIVEEAGLE
Estrada	GIVEESTRADA
Gatmobile	GIVEGATMOBILE
Kanada	GIVEKANADA
Kenshin	GIVEKENSHIN
Knoxville	GIVEKNOXVILLE
Korbra	GIVEKOBRA

VEHICLE	CODE
Krukov	GIVEKRUKOV
Miami	GIVEMIAMI
Municipal	GIVEMUNICIPAL
Nforcer	GIVENFORCER
Peacemaker	GIVEPEACEMAKER
Phoenix	GIVEPHOENIX
Reaper	GIVEREAPER
Repaircar	REPAIRCAR
RPG	GIVERPG
Sandstorm	GIVESANDSTORM
Satchel Charge	GIVESATCHEL
Shark	GIVESHARK
Sheperd	GIVESHEPERD
Spectre	GIVESPECTRE
Squasar	GIVESQUASAR
Status Quo	GIVESTATUSQUO
Taxi	GIVETAXI
Titan	GIVETITAN
Toad	GIVETOAD
Tornado	GIVETORNADO
Vortex	GIVEVORTEX
VTOL	GIVEVTOL
Vulture	GIVEVULTURE
Widowmaker	GIVEWIDOWMAKER
Woodpecker	GIVEWOODPECKER

WEAPON CHEATS

WEAPON	CODE
45 Sheperd	GIVESHEPERD
Air Strike	GIVEAIRSTRIKE
Apoca-fists	GIVEAPOCA
AR 55	GIVEAR
As3 Ultimax	GIVEULTIMAX
Baseball Bat	GIVEBASEBALL
Chainsaw	GIVECHAINSAW
Cyber Blaster	GIVECYBERSMG
Cyber Buster	GIVECYBER
D4th Blossom	GIVEBLOSSOM
Drone	GIVEDRONE
Electric Grenade	GIVEELECTRIC
Flamethrower	GIVEFLAMETHROWER
Grenade	GIVEGRENADE
Hammer	GIVEHAMMER
K-8 Krukov	GIVEKRUKOV
Minigun	GIVEMINIGUN
Molotov	GIVEMOLOTOV
RPG	GIVERPG
Satchel	GIVESATCHEL
Tek Z-10	GIVETEK

WEATHER CHEATS

WEATHER	CODE
Cloudy	OVERCAST
Rainy	LIGHTRAIN
Sunny	CLEARSKIES
Very Stormy	HEAVYRAIN

AVATAR AWARDS

AVATAR	EARNED BY
Oversized Gat Mask?	Completed the mission "When Good Heists…"
Saints Logo Shirt	Earned the "Flash the Pan" Achievement.
SR:TT Logo Shirt	Created and uploaded your first character to the community site!

SAMURAI SHODOWN 2

PLAY AS KUROKO IN 2-PLAYER

At the character select, press Up, Down, Left, Up, Down, Right + X.

SCOTT PILGRIM VS. THE WORLD: THE GAME

PLAY AS SAME CHARACTER

At the title screen, press Down, Right Bumper, Up, Left Bumper, Y, B.

HEART SWORD

At the title screen, press X, X, X, A, B, A, Y, Y.

BLOOD MODE

At the title screen, press A, B, A, X, A, B, B.

BOSS RUSH MODE

Pause the game on the overworld and press **Right, Right, B, Right Bumper, Right, Right, B, Right Bumper.**

ZOMBIE MODE

At the title screen, press Down, Up, Right, Down, Up, Right, Down, Up, Right, Right, Right.

SOUND CHECK BONUS LEVEL

Pause the game on the overworld and press Left Bumper, Left Bumper, Left Bumper, Right Bumper, Right Bumper, Right Bumper, Left Bumper, Right Bumper.

CHANGE MONEY TO ANIMALS

At the title screen, press Up, Up, Down, Down, Up, Up, Up, Up.

SECTION 8: PREJUDICE

AVATAR AWARDS

AWARD	EARNED BY
T-Shirt	Complete the Answers level of the Campaign.
Gold Helmet	Reach level 20 or earn 46 Stars.

SEGA BASS FISHING

AVATAR AWARDS

AVATAR	EARNED BY
Sega Bass Fishing Tee	Play the game for 5 hours.
Sega Bass Fishing Rod	Play the game for 10 hours.

SEGA VINTAGE COLLECTION: ALEX KIDD & CO.

SUPER HANG-ON

START ARCADE MODE WITH $10,000

Highlight Arcade Mode and press Up, Left, A, B, Start.

THE REVENGE OF SHINOBI

STAGE PRACTICE

At the title screen, hold A + B + C and press Start. This unlocks the mode at the main menu.

SEGA VINTAGE COLLECTION: GOLDEN AXE

A, B, and C refer to the buttons that are mapped to the Sega Genesis A, B, and C.

GOLDEN AXE

27 CREDITS IN ARCADE MODE

At the character select, hold Down-Left + A + C and press Start. At the continue screen, you will have 9 credits instead of 3.

LEVEL SELECT IN ARCADE MODE

At the character select, hold Down-Left + B and press Start. Use the d-pad to change the number in the upper-left corner to the level that you wish to play.

GOLDEN AXE III

LEVEL SELECT

At the character select, press A, A, A, A, Start, C, C, C, C, C, C.

SECRET MESSAGE

At the title screen, press Up, C, Up, C, Up, C, C, C, B, A, Left, Down.

SEGA VINTAGE COLLECTION: STREETS OF RAGE

A, B, and C refer to the buttons that are mapped to the Sega Genesis A, B, and C.

STREETS OF RAGE

EXTRA CONTINUES

At the title screen, press Left, Left, B, B, B, C, C, C, Start.

LEVEL AND LIVES SELECT

At the main menu, hold A + B + C + Right on controller 2 while selecting Options on controller 1.

STREETS OF RAGE 3

9 LIVES

Select Lives from Options, hold Up + A + B + C on controller 2, and press Left or Right on controller 1.

PLAY AS ROO

At the title screen, hold Up + B and press Start.

PLAY AS SHIVA

After defeating Shiva, hold B until the next level begins. When you lose your last life and reach a continue screen, Shiva is selectable.

PLAY AS THE SAME CHARACTER

While select a 2-Player game, hold Down + C on controller 2.

SHANK 2

EVIL IN SURVIVAL MODE

At the character select, press Up, Up, Down, Down, Left, Right, Left, Right. This must be re-entered after quitting the game.

CHARACTERS FOR SURVIVAL MODE

CHARACTER	HOW TO UNLOCK
Boogie	Buy everything in survival mode.
Bubbles	Stay alive for 15 consecutive waves.
Cesar	Kill someone with the kitchen sink.
Chops	60 pistol counter kills.
Classic Shank	Kill a goon by throwing a bomber.
Defender	100 turret kills.
Falcone	Complete Campaign on hard.
Hobo	Complete all 30 waves on any survival map.
Horror	Reach the zombie wave (14) on each survival map.
Junior	50 fire trap kills.
Kats	100 grenade kills.
Rex	Complete campaign on normal.
Rin	Perform 20 bat counter kills.
Sunshine	Purchase any item in survival mode.

SILENT HILL: DOWNPOUR

GREEN LOCKER PASSWORDS

At a green locker enter the following passwords:

WEAPONS	PASSWORD
Nail Gun and Double Axe	171678
Pistol 45 and Baseball Bat	353479
Rifle and Golf Club	911977

SILENT HILL: HOMECOMING

YOUNG ALEX COSTUME

At the Title screen, press Up, Up, Down, Down, Left, Right, Left, Right, B.

THE SIMPSONS ARCADE GAME

ALL EXTRAS

At the title screen, press Up, Up, Down, Down, Left, Right, Left, Right, B, A.

THE SIMS 3

CHEATS

Load your family, press Start, and hold Left Bumper + Left Trigger + Right Bumper + Right Trigger. The game prompts you to save another file before activating the cheats. Spoot the Llama is now available in Misc Décor. Place it in your lot and click it to access the cheats. This disables Achievements and challenges.

THE SIMS 3: PETS

CREATION MODE

Pause the game and press Left Trigger + Left Bumper + Right Trigger + Right Bumper. This disables achievements.

SKATE 2

BIG BLACK

Select Enter Cheat from the Extras menu and enter letsdowork.

3D MODE

Select Enter Cheat from the Extras menu and enter strangeloops. Use glasses to view in 3D.

SKULLGIRLS

COLOR PALETTE 10

At the versus screen in local gameplay, press Down, Right Bumper, Up, Left Bumper, Y, B.

SKYLANDERS GIANTS

SKYLANDERS SPECIFIC QUESTS

Skylanders Giants includes quests specific to each Skylander as a way to improve them. Here we list each Skylander with their quest and tips on how to complete it.

SKYLANDER	QUEST	HOW TO COMPLETE
Bash	On a Roll: Defeat 10 enemies with one roll attack.	If you have trouble completing this quest, opt for the Pulver Dragon upgrade path.
Boomer	On a Troll: Defeat five enemies with one kicked Troll Bomb.	Once you have Troll Bomb Boot, look for a group of tight-knit Chompies. "Chapter 1: Time of the Giants" has several groupings of five Chompies.
Bouncer	Stay on Target!: Target enemies 100 times with laser-guided Shoulder Rockets	You must purchase the Targeting Computer upgrade for Bouncer's Shoulder Rockets.
Camo	Garden Gorger: Eat 10 watermelons.	If you aren't in a rush to complete a level, switch to Camo when a watermelon appears.
Chill	Ice Sore: Defeat six enemies with one Ice Narwhal attack.	Try to find six enemies that are grouped together at a medium distance, such as in an arena.
Chop Chop	Stalwart Defender: Absorb 1,000 damage with your shield.	To complete this quest safely, block attacks from a small group of weaker enemies near a food item (just in case they sneak in some unexpected damage).
Crusher	High Roller: Defeat 100 enemies with boulders.	Use Rockslide defeat enemies until you have completed this quest.
Cynder	On the Haunt: Defeat 50 enemies with your Ghost Ally.	Ghost Ally does not inflict much damage so focus on saving low-health enemies, like Chompies, for the ghost to attack. The Ghost attacks while Cynder is flying, so consider circling an area with Chompies.
Dino-Rang	Fooderang: Pick up 20 food items with boomerangs.	After acquiring Sticky Boomerangs, use it to grab any food found in the area. In the Arena Challenges on Flynn's Ship, the audience throws food items into the arena between rounds.
Double Trouble	Big Bomb Trouble: Defeat 10 enemies with one Magic Bomb attack.	Find a group of 10 or more Chompies and set off a bomb. A good place to earn this is any of of Brock's Arena Challenges with regular Chompies.

SKYLANDER	QUEST	HOW TO COMPLETE
Drill Sergeant	Drill Skill: Defeat Drill-X without changing Skylanders.	Drill Sergeant must defeat Drill-X (the final boss in "Chapter 11: Drill-X's Big Rig") solo. Use Adventure items (like Healing Potion) to survive the battle. You can complete it on Easy difficulty with a fully-upgraded Drill Sergeant.
Drobot	Feed the Burn: Defeat 50 enemies with Afterburners.	It's easiest to hit enemies with Afterburners when Drobot first takes off.
Eruptor	Pizza Burp: Eat 10 Pizzas.	If you want to have a greater chance of encountering a pizza, equip Lucky Wheel of Health in the Luck-O-Tron.
Eye Brawl	Gold Search: Collect 5,000 gold with the eyeball detached	Remember to detach Eye-Brawl's eye before collecting any treasure from chests or enemies.
Flameslinger	Circular Combustion: Defeat 10 enemies with one column of Fire Flame Dash.	There are two upgrades you can get to help you on this quest. The first is Column of Fire. The second is Supernova in the Pyromancer Path.
Flashwing	Let It Shine: Defeat 20 enemies with one Crystal Lighthouse.	Since Crystal Lighthouse is stationary, this is a tricky quest. The best candidate for this is one of the arena maps, particularly Kaos' Royal Flush (the second challenge, Birthday Bash). Set up the Lighthouse in the middle of the birthday cake.
Fright Rider	Delving Throw: Toss 50 enemies into the air	The power to use for this quest is Burrow Bomber. Hit any medium or small enemy with the attack to pop them up in the air and register a toss.
Ghost Roaster	Grave Circumstances: Defeat 100 enemies with Skull Charge.	Repeatedly use Skull Charge to attack enemies and you should complete this quest in no time.
Gill Grunt	Anchors Away!: Defeat six enemies with one Anchor Attack.	Line up a group of Chompies with your Anchor Cannon and let loose to complete the quest. If you have Series 2 Gill Grunt, Anchor's Away! makes completing the quest easier.
Hex	Noggin Knocker: Knock away 100 enemies with your Skull Rain.	Once Hex has Skull Shield, allow enemies to get within melee range while Hex is charging that attack. If they get too close, they get knocked back, tallying a point for this quest.
Hot Dog	Animal Aggravator: Scare away 20 birds.	Look for the small birds pecking at the ground in each level. These birds are the ones you need to scare with Hot Dog for this achievement. Chapter 13: The Oracle and Chapter 1: Time of Giants both have plenty of birds.
Hot Head	Buggy Breakthrough: Destroy 20 walls in Hot Rod mode.	The walls this quest is referring to are the walls that can only be crushed by a Giant or a bomb. Whenever you encounter one of these walls, switch to Hot Head. A good spot with plenty of these types of walls is Chapter 2: Junkyard Isles.
Ignitor	Tinder Trekker: Travel 26,000 feet in Flame Form.	Use Flame Form often and this number will accumulate quickly.

SKYLANDER	QUEST	HOW TO COMPLETE
Jet-Vac	Bird Cleaner: Suck up 50 birds in your Suction Gun.	Look for tiny birds on the ground throughout most levels with green grass. Chapter 13: The Oracle and Chapter 1: Time of Giants both have plenty of birds.
Lightning Rod	Current Event: Defeat 10 enemies with one Grand Lightning strike.	You need to find a group of 10 Chompies in one area and use the Grand Lightning to blast them all. Choosing the Lord of Lightning Path makes this easier since the Grand Lightning attack lasts longer.
Ninjini	Bottle Beatdown: Defeat 5 enemies within five seconds of exiting your bottle.	Transform Ninjini into the bottle and move into a large group of small enemies. Follow up the bottle attack with her swords.
Pop Fizz	Rampage: Do 200 HP of damage in a single run in Beast Form.	Transform into Beast Form in a large group of enemies and destroy everything in sight to complete the quest.
Prism Break	Bifurcation Sensation: Defeat 100 enemies with double refraction.	A beam must pass through two Shards before hitting an enemy to count. Unlock the Chained Refractions upgrade and place plenty of Crystal Shards. Fire an Energy Beam through them to indirectly take out nearby enemies.
Shroomboom	Lunching Launch: Eat a watermelon while performing a Self-Slingshot!	When you find a watermelon, blast Shroomboom through it with the Self-Slingshot power to complete the quest.
Slam Bam	Ice to Meet You: Trap 100 enemies in your Ice Blocks.	You do not need to damage or freeze enemies with Ice Block; it counts if you just hit them with the Ice Block.
Sonic Boom	Sonic Squeak: Babies defeat 50 enemies.	Upgrade Sonic Boom's egg attack powers and keep babies summoned at all times.
Sprocket	Mined Your Step: Defeat 50 enemies using the Landmine Golf attack.	Once you unlock the Landmine Golf ability, use it often. A quick way to complete this quest is to load up one of the easier Arena levels.
Spyro	Full Charge: Collect 3 gold, eat 1 food item, and defeat 2 enemies in 1 Sprint Charge.	Look for two low-health enemies (Chompies are a good choice) as well as some food and gold on the screen. Purchase the Sprint Charge upgrade to increase the distance of Spyro's sprint.
Stealth Elf	Stealth Health: Gain 1,000 HP while stealthed.	You need to first purchase Sylvan Regeneration. Once you do, you get credit towards the 1,000 HP every time you heal while Stealth Elf is in the Stealthier Decoy mode.
Stump Smash	Meganut Bowling: Defeat five enemies with one Meganut.	Meganuts are powerful, and bowling over five Chompies with one is no problem. The upgrade Acorn Croquet makes this much easier to achieve since you can wack the acorn directly at enemies.
Sunburn	Immolation Itinerant: Travel 1 mile using Immolation Teleport	Use Immolation Teleport regularly to tally up the distance towards one full mile. The quickest way to complete this quest is to unlock the Flight of the Phoenix and the Guided Teleportation upgrades.

SKYLANDER	QUEST	HOW TO COMPLETE
Swarm	Swarm Feelings: Defeat 100 enemies in Swarm Form.	While you can complete this quest without pursuing the Wasp Stormer Path, it's extremely difficult, and you must focus on weaker enemies.
Terrafin	Land Lubber: Eat 20 food items while burrowing.	Once you have Surface Feeder, stay underground and collect Food Items as they drop.
Thumpback	Beached Whale: Defeat 8 enemies with one Belly Flop.	Upgrade Thumpback's Belly Flop attack with Slippery Belly. If you are having trouble getting this quest, invest in the Up Close and Personal path to further increase the strength of the Belly Flop attack.
Tree Rex	Timberrrrrl: Defeat 50 enemies by landing on them. Chompies don't count!	Unfortunately, Elbow Drop doesn't work for this quest. Tree Rex must crush enemies by landing on them. The best way to do this is to find a bounce pad in an area with plenty of Chompies.
Trigger Happy	Holding Gold: Save up 50,000 Gold	This is one of the hardest quests any character has in the game. Not because it's difficult, but because it will take some time to collect 50,000 Gold.
Voodood	Trickwire: Defeat six enemies at once with your tripwire.	Find a group of six or more low-health enemies, like Bone Chompies, and set up the Tripwire near them. Chapter 1: Time of the Giants has several good spots to try for this quest.
Warnado	Chompy Catcher: Catch 100 Chompies in tornadoes.	The best place to do this is in the Arena Challenges. Head to any of the early challenges and there are plenty of Chompies. High Winds also helps gather up more Chompies at once.
Wham-Shell	Irate Invertebrate: Defeat 6 enemies with one Poseidon Strike.	To get the most out of Poseidon Strike, invest in the Captain Crustacean path. Once you have unlocked Mace of the Deep, go for this quest by finding a group of Chompies and blasting them.
Whirlwind	What does it mean?: Create 50 double rainbows.	Unlock the Duel Rainbows ability, then fire out a Tempest cloud and following up with a Rainbow of Doom. Rainbows made via the Double Dose of Doom power don't count unless they hit a Tempest Cloud. Triple rainbows created via Triple Tempest count as one double rainbow.
Wrecking Ball	Competitive Eater: Swallow 100 Enemies	Purchase Enemy Slurp and swallow as many enemies as you can. Any medium-sized and smaller enemy can be eaten.
Zap	In the Slimelight: Defeat 50 enemies by electrifying them in Sea Slime	Use Sea Slime to electrify enemies regularly and you'll complete this quest in no time.
Zook	Spore It On: Absorb 1,000 points of damage with a Foliage Barrier	Use Foliage Barrier often and you will complete this quest quickly.

SLEEPING DOGS

RICO'S OUTFIT FROM JUST CAUSE 2

With a Just Cause 2 save game on your system, Rico's outfit can be found in Wei's closet.

SMOOTH OPERATORS

$1 000 000
After loading a call center, select Enter Code and enter dante.

EVERYONE IS HAPPY
After loading a call center, select Enter Code and enter becca.

MAXIMUM BUILD HEIGHT
After loading a call center, select Enter Code and enter gustafsson.

EVERYTHING IS UPGRADABLE
After loading a call center, select Enter Code and enter bengan.

INCREASED WORKLOADS
After loading a call center, select Enter Code and enter kyrksten.

SONIC ADVENTURE 2

AVATAR AWARDS

AVATAR	EARNED BY
2G Vintage Sonic Tee	5 Hours game time in any game mode.
Sonic's 2G Hi-Speed Shoes	10 hours game time in any game mode.

SONIC FREE RIDERS

AVATAR AWARDS

AWARD	EARNED BY
Sonic Free Riders Shirt	Watch the credits in their entirety.
E-10000 G Shirt	Place 1st on every course with E-10000 G.
Jet Shirt	Place 1st on every course with Jet.
Sonic Shirt	Place 1st on every course with Sonic.

CHAOS EMERALD BOARD
Get S-rank on all Story Missions.

PROFESSIONAL BOARD
Complete all Trial Missions.

SONIC GENERATIONS

SECRET STATUE ROOM
In the Collection Room, hold Back for a few seconds. Sonic jumps into the statue room below. Once there, press Back and enter the following.

STATUE	CODE
Aero-Cannon	329 494
Amy Rose	863 358

STATUE	CODE
Big the Cat	353 012
Blaze the Cat	544 873
Booster	495 497
Buzz Bomber	852 363
Capsule	777 921
Chao	629 893
Chaos Emerald	008 140
Charmy Bee	226 454
Chip	309 511
Chopper	639 402
Classic Eggman	103 729
Classic Sonic	171 045
Classic Tails	359 236
Cop Speeder	640 456
Crabmeat	363 911
Cream the Rabbit	332 955
Cucky/Picky/Flicky/Pecky	249 651
Dark Chao	869 292
Dr. Eggman	613 482
E-123 Omega	601 409
Egg Chaser	200 078
Egg Fighter	851 426
Egg Launcher	973 433
Egg Pawn	125 817
Eggrobo	360 031
Espio the Chameleon	894 526
Goal Plate	933 391
Goal Ring	283 015
Grabber	275 843
Gun Beetle	975 073
Gun Hunter	668 250
Hero Chao	507 376
Iblis Biter	872 910
Iblis Taker	513 929
Iblis Worm	711 268
Item Box	209 005
Jet the Hawk	383 870
Knuckles the Echidna	679 417
Metal Sonic	277 087
Miles "Tails" Prower	632 951
Moto Bug	483 990
Omochao	870 580
Ring	390 884
Rouge the Bat	888 200
Sandworm	548 986
Shadow the Hedgehog	262 416
Silver the Hedgehog	688 187
Sonic the Hedgehog	204 390
Spinner	530 741
Spiny	466 913
Spring – Star	537 070
Spring	070 178
Vector the Crocodile	868 377

AVATAR AWARDS

AVATAR	EARNED BY
Classic Eggman Suit (Head)	Defeat the final boss on Hard Mode.
Classic Eggman Suit (Tops)	Defeat all bosses on Hard Mode.
Classic Eggman Suit (Bottoms)	Defeat all rivals on Hard Mode.

SONIC THE HEDGEHOG 4: EPISODE I

AVATAR AWARDS

AWARD	EARNED BY
Sonic Costume (Body)	After collecting the 7 Chaos Emeralds, defeat the final boss 1 more time
Sonic Costume (Head)	Collect all rings during ending after the final stage.

SONIC THE HEDGEHOG 4: EPISODE II

AVATAR AWARDS

AVATAR	EARNED BY
Dr. Eggman Modern Costume (Body)	Defeat the last boss without taking damage.
Dr. Eggman Modern Costume (Legs)	Defeat the "Sylvania Castle Zone" boss without taking damage.

SOULCALIBUR V

ALGOL FEAR AND TOWER OF GLORY: MOST HOLY DICHOTOMY STAGE

Defeat Algol Fear in Legendary Souls or Quick Battle

α PATROKLOS AND ASTRAL CHAOS: PATHWAY STAGE

Defeat Patrolklos in Quick Battle.

EDGE MASTER AND TOWER OF GLORY: SPIRAL OF GOOD AND EVIL

Complete chapter 17 of story mode to unlock Edge Master and his stage. You can also be obtained by defeating him in Arcade, Legendary Souls, or Quick Battle.

ELYSIUM AND UTOPIA OF THE BLESSED

Complete the final chapter of story mode.

KILIK AND THE PENITENTIARY OF DESTINY STAGE

Defeat Kilik in Arcade or Legendary Souls.

PYRRHA Ω AND DENEVER CASTLE: EYE OF CHAOS

Complete chapter 19 of story mode.

DEVIL JIN STYLE ***

Defeat Harada in Quick Battle or Legendary Souls.

Go to Customization and then to Original Characters. Select anyone male or female and enter size. Choose Weapons & Style and then to Style. At bottom of list is Devil Jin (Tekken).

SPACE CHANNEL 5 PART 2

AVATAR AWARDS

AVATAR	EARNED BY
Vintage Space Channel 5 Tee	Play the game for 5 hours.
Morolian's Costume	Play the game for 10 hours.
Ulala's Costume	Play the game for 10 hours.

LET CPU TAKE OVER

Pause the game, hold Left Bumper + Right Bumper and press B, B, Up, Left, A, Left, A, Left, A. The CPU takes over, but achievements are disabled.

SPELUNKY

AVATAR AWARDS

AVATAR	EARNED BY
Spelunky T-Shirt	Play a game of deathmatch to at least 10 wins.
Pith Helmet	Unlock the first shortcut.
Fedora	Beat the first level of the game.

SPIDER-MAN: EDGE OF TIME

SHATTERED DIMENSIONS BONUS SUITS

If you have a saved game data for Spider-Man: Shattered Dimensions on your system, eight new Alternate Suits become available in the Bonus Gallery.

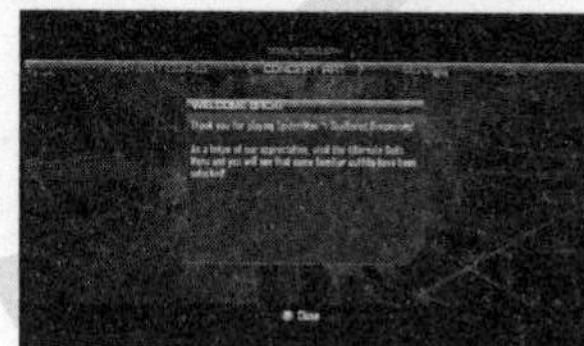

AMAZING SPIDER-MAN #500 SUIT (AMAZING)

Select Enter Code from VIP Unlock Code and enter laststand. Go to the Bonus Gallery to access the alternate suits.

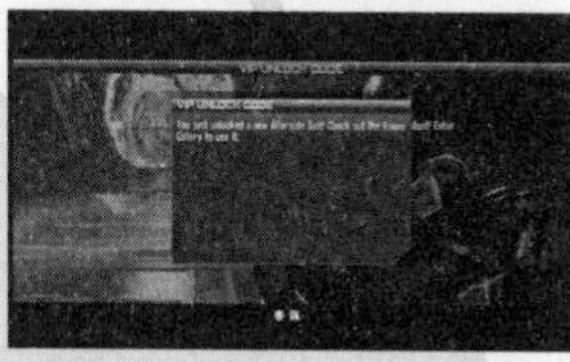

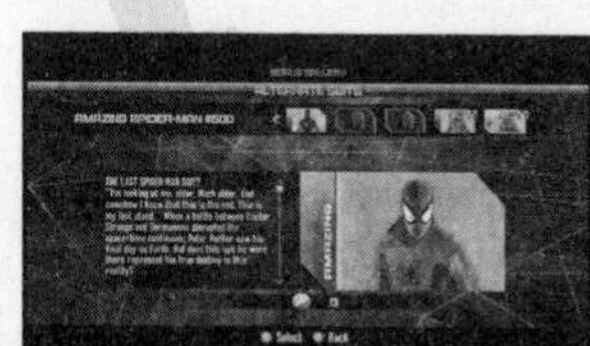

POISON SUIT (2099)

Select Enter Code from VIP Unlock Code and enter innerspider. Go to the Bonus Gallery to access the alternate suits.suits.

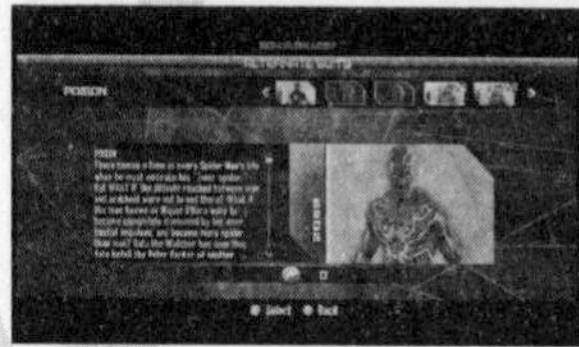

SPIDEY VS WOLVERINE SUIT (AMAZING) – WHAT IF? SPIDERMAN

Select Enter Code from VIP Unlock Code and enter coldhearted. Go to the Bonus Gallery to access the alternate suits.

2099 ARENA CHALLENGE AND AMAZING ARENA CHALLENGE

Select Enter Code from VIP Unlock Code and enter twospidersenter. Select Arenas from the Main Menu.

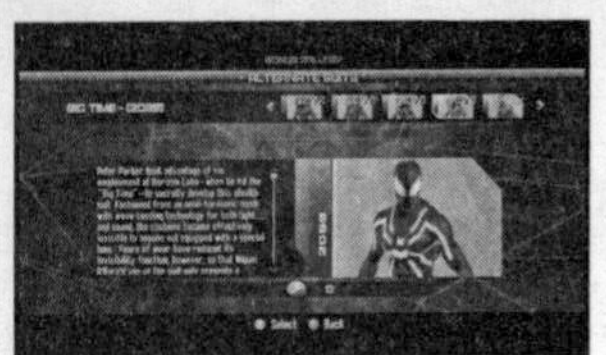

BIG TIME SUIT (2099)
At the main menu, press Right, Down, Down, Up, Left, Down, Down, Right.

FUTURE FOUNDATION SUIT (AMAZING)
At the main menu, press Up, Down, Left, Up, Down, Left, Right, Left.

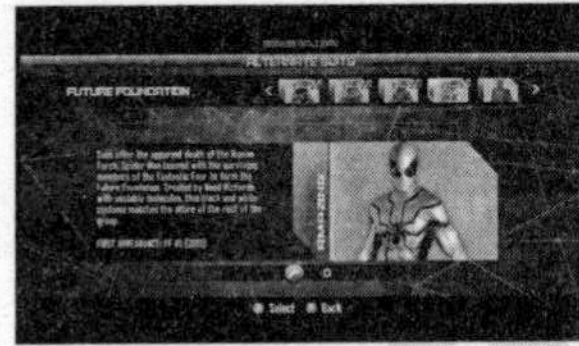

SPIDER-MAN: FRIEND OR FOE

NEW GREEN GOBLIN AS A SIDEKICK
While standing in the Helicarrier between levels, press Left, Down, Right, Right, Down, Left.

SANDMAN AS A SIDEKICK
While standing in the Helicarrier between levels, press Right, Right, Right, Up, Down, Left.

VENOM AS A SIDEKICK
While standing in the Helicarrier between levels, press Left, Left, Right, Up, Down, Down.

5000 TECH TOKENS
While standing in the Helicarrier between levels, press Up, Up, Down, Down, Left, Right.

SPIDER-MAN: SHATTERED DIMENSIONS

The following can be entered after completing the tutorial.

IRON SPIDER SUIT
At the main menu, press Up, Right, Right, Right, Left, Left, Left, Down, Up.

NEGATIVE ZONE SUIT
At the main menu, press Left, Right, Right, Down, Right, Down, Up, Left.

SCARLET SPIDER SUIT
At the main menu, press Right, Up, Left, Right, Up, Left, Right, Up, Left, Right.

THE SPLATTERS

AVATAR AWARDS

AVATAR	EARNED BY
"Die With Style" T-Shirt	Unlock the Air-Strike move to receive this shirt.
"The Splatters" T-Shirt	Unlock the Flip move to receive this shirt.
Splatter-Head	Unlock the Ballistic move to earn this award!

STAR TREK: D-A-C

KOBAYASHI MARU SECRET ACHIEVEMENT
At the start of a solo Death Match, press Start. Then enter Left Trigger, Y, X, X, Y, Right Trigger. This gives you the achievement and improves your ship.

STAR WARS THE CLONE WARS: REPUBLIC HEROES

BIG HEAD MODE
Pause the game, select Shop, and enter Up, Down, Left, Right, Left, Right, Down, Up in Cheats.

MINI-GUN
Pause the game, select Shop, and enter Down, Left, Right, Up, Right, Up, Left, Down in Cheats.

ULTIMATE LIGHTSABER

Pause the game, select Shop, and enter Right, Down, Down, Up, Left, Up, Up, Down in Cheats.

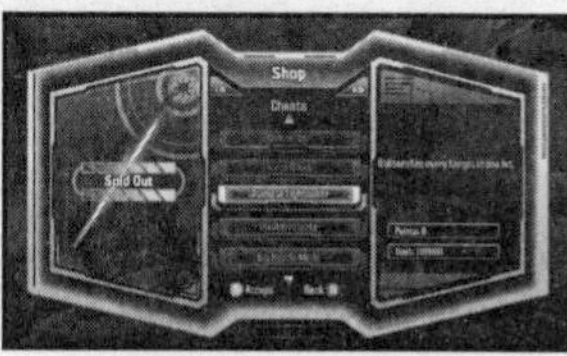

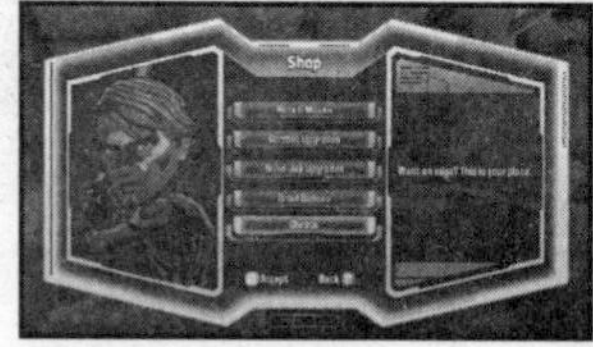

LIGHTSABER THROW UPGRADE

Pause the game, select Shop, and enter Left, Left, Right, Right, Up, Down, Down, Up in Combat Upgrades.

SPIDER DROID UPGRADE

Pause the game, select Shop, and enter Up, Left, Down, Left, Right, Left, Left, Left in Droid-Jak Upgrades.

STAR WARS: THE FORCE UNLEASHED

CHEAT CODES

Pause the game and select Input Code. Here you can enter the following codes. Activating any of the following cheat codes will disable some unlockables, and you will be unable to save your progress.

CHEAT	CODE
All Force Powers at Max Power	KATARN
All Force Push Ranks	EXARKUN
All Saber Throw Ranks	ADEGAN
All Repulse Ranks	DATHOMIR
All Saber Crystals	HURRIKANE
All Talents	JOCASTA
Deadly Saber	LIGHTSABER

COMBOS

Pause the game and select Input Code. Here you can enter the following codes. Activating any of the following cheat codes will disable some unlockables, and you will be unable to save your progress.

COMBO	CODE
All Combos	MOLDYCROW
Aerial Ambush	VENTRESS
Aerial Assault	EETHKOTH
Aerial Blast	YADDLE
Impale	BRUTALSTAB
Lightning Bomb	MASSASSI
Lightning Grenade	RAGNOS
Saber Slam	PLOKOON
Saber Sling	KITFISTO
Sith Saber Flurry	LUMIYA
Sith Slash	DARAGON
Sith Throw	SAZEN
New Combo	FREEDON
New Combo	MARAJADE

ALL DATABANK ENTRIES

Pause the game and select Input Code. Enter OSSUS.

MIRRORED LEVEL

Pause the game and select Input Code. Enter MINDTRICK. Re-enter the code to return level to normal.

SITH MASTER DIFFICULTY

Pause the game and select Input Code. Enter SITHSPAWN.

COSTUMES

Pause the game and select Input Code. Here you can enter the following codes.

COSTUME	CODE
All Costumes	SOHNDANN
Bail Organa	VICEROY
Ceremonial Jedi Robes	DANTOOINE
Drunken Kota	HARDBOILED
Emperor	MASTERMIND
Incinerator Trooper	PHOENIX
Jedi Adventure Robe	HOLOCRON
Kashyyyk Trooper	TK421GREEN
Kota	MANDALORE
Master Kento	WOOKIEE
Proxy	PROTOTYPE
Scout Trooper	FERRAL
Shadow Trooper	BLACKHOLE
Sith Stalker Armor	KORRIBAN
Snowtrooper	SNOWMAN
Stormtrooper	TK421WHITE
Stormtrooper Commander	TK421BLUE

STAR WARS: THE FORCE UNLEASHED II

BOBA FETT COSTUME

Pause the game, select Cheat Codes from the Options, and enter MANDALORE.

DARK APPRENTICE COSTUME

Pause the game, select Cheat Codes from the Options, and enter VENTRESS.

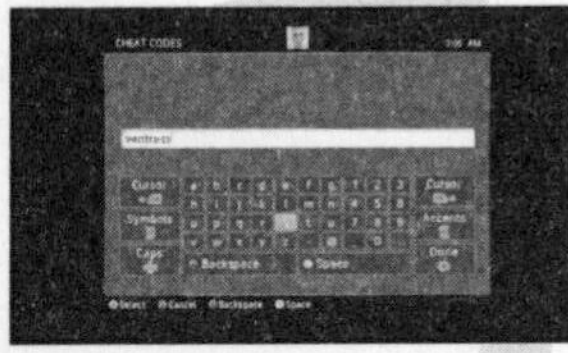

GENERAL KOTA COSTUME

Pause the game, select Cheat Codes from the Options, and enter RAHM.

JUMP TROOPER COSTUME

Pause the game, select Cheat Codes from the Options, and enter AJP400.

NEIMOIDIAN COSTUME

Pause the game, select Cheat Codes from the Options, and enter GUNRAY.

REBEL COMMANDO COSTUME

Pause the game, select Cheat Codes from the Options, and enter SPECFORCE.

REBEL SOLDIER COSTUME

Pause the game, select Cheat Codes from the Options, and enter REBELSCUM.

SABER GUARD COSTUME

Pause the game, select Cheat Codes from the Options, and enter MORGUKAI.

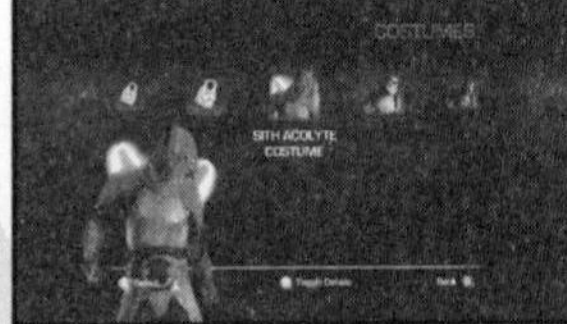

SITH ACOLYTE COSTUME

Pause the game, select Cheat Codes from the Options, and enter HAAZEN.

STORMTROOPER COSTUME
Pause the game, select Cheat Codes from the Options, and enter TK421.

TERROR TROOPER COSTUME
Pause the game, select Cheat Codes from the Options, and enter SHADOW.

TRAINING DROID COSTUME
Pause the game, select Cheat Codes from the Options, and enter HOLODROID.

EXPERIMENTAL JEDI ARMOR
Pause the game, select Cheat Codes from the Options, and enter NOMI.

REPULSE FORCE POWER
Pause the game, select Cheat Codes from the Options, and enter MAREK.

JEDI MIND TRICK
Pause the game, select Cheat Codes from the Options, and enter YARAEL.

SABRE THROW
Pause the game, select Cheat Codes from the Options, and enter TRAYA.

DARK GREEN LIGHTSABER CRYSTAL
Pause the game, select Cheat Codes from the Options, and enter LIBO.

WISDOM LIGHTSABER CRYSTALS
Pause the game, select Cheat Codes from the Options, and enter SOLARI.

OVERLOAD

STREET FIGHTER IV

ALTERNATE STAGES
At the stage select, hold Left Bumper or Right Bumper and select a stage.

SUPER MEAT BOY

PLAY AS BROWNIE
At the character select, press Right Bumper, Right Bumper, Right Bumper, B, B, B, X.

AVATAR AWARDS

AWARD	EARNED BY
Super Meat Boy	Beat the Light World.
Super Meat Boy T-Shirt	Play the first few levels.

SUPER STREET FIGHTER II TURBO HD REMIX

The following codes give you the classic fighters in Classic Arcade Mode. Select the character, quickly enter the given code, and select him/her again.

CLASSIC BALROG
Right, Left, Left, Right

CLASSIC BLANKA
Left, Right (x3)

CLASSIC CAMMY
Up, Up, Down, Down

CLASSIC CHUN-LI
Down (x3), Up

CLASSIC DEE JAY
Down, Down, Up, Up

CLASSIC DHALSIM
Down, Up (x3)

CLASSIC E. HONDA
Up (x3), Down

CLASSIC FEI LONG
Left, Left, Right, Right

CLASSIC GUILE
Up, Down (x3)

CLASSIC KEN
Left (x3), Right

CLASSIC M. BISON
Down, Up, Up, Down

CLASSIC RYU
Right (x3), Left

CLASSIC SAGAT
Up, Down (x3), Up

CLASSIC T. HAWK
Right, Right, Left, Left

CLASSIC VEGA
Left, Right, Right, Left

CLASSIC ZANGIEF
Left, Right (x3)

SUPER STREET FIGHTER IV

BARREL BUSTER AND CAR CRUSHER BONUS STAGES

Beat Arcade Mode in any difficulty

COLORS AND TAUNTS

Colors 1 and 2 plus the first taunt for each fighter are available from the start. For colors 11 & 12, start a game with a Street Fighter IV save game on your system. To earn the rest of the colors and taunts, you need to fight a certain number of matches with that character.

COLOR	# OF MATCHES
3	2
4	4
5	6
6	8
7	10
8	12
9	14
10	16

TAUNT	# OF MATCHES
2	1
3	3
4	5
5	7
6	9
7	11
8	13
9	15
10	16

THE TESTAMENT OF SHERLOCK HOLMES

AVATAR AWARDS

AVATAR	EARNED BY
Sherlock Holmes T-Shirt	Successfully completing the game will earn you this T-Shirt, which is a must for any wardrobe.
Sherlock Holmes Classic Hat	For realising that not all is lost when faced with innumerable dead-ends: this charming Top Hat.

TOM CLANCY'S ENDWAR

EUROPEAN ENFORCER CORPS

Go to Community and Extras, highlight Downloadable Content and press Y. Enter EUCA20.

RUSSIAN SPETZNAZ BATTALION

Go to Community and Extras, highlight Downloadable Content and press Y. Enter SPZT17.

RUSSIAN SPETZNAZ GUARD BRIGADE

Go to Community and Extras, highlight Downloadable Content and press Y. Enter SPZA39.

US JOINT STRIKE FORCE BATTALION

Go to Community and Extras, highlight Downloadable Content and press Y. Enter JSFA35.

TOM CLANCY'S GHOST RECON ADVANCED WARFIGHTER 2

FAMAS IN QUICK MISSION MODE

Create a new campaign with the name: GRAW2QUICKFAMAS.

TOM CLANCY'S HAWX

A-12 AVENGER II

At the hangar, hold Left Trigger and press X, Left Bumper, X, Right Bumper, Y, X.

F-18 HARV

At the hangar, hold Left Trigger and press Left Bumper, Y, Left Bumper, Y, Left Bumper, X.

FB-22 STRIKE RAPTOR

At the hangar, hold Left Trigger and press Right Bumper, X, Right Bumper, X, Right Bumper, Y.

TOM CLANCY'S RAINBOW SIX VEGAS 2

GI JOHN DOE MODE

Pause the game, hold the Right Bumper and press Left Thumbstick, Left Thumbstick, A, Right Thumbstick, Right Thumbstick, B, Left Thumbstick, Left Thumbstick, X, Right Thumbstick, Right Thumbstick, Y.

SUPER RAGDOLL

Pause the game, hold the Right Bumper and press A, A, B, B, X, X, Y, Y, A, B, X, Y.

THIRD-PERSON MODE

Pause the game, hold the Right Bumper and press X, B, X, B, Left Thumbstick, Left Thumbstick, Y, A, Y, A, Right Thumbstick, Right Thumbstick.

TAR-21 ASSAULT RIFLE

At the Character Customization screen, hold Right Bumper and press Down, Down, Up, Up, X, B, X, B, Y, Up, Up, Y.

MULTIPLAYER MAP: COMCAST EVENT

Select Extras from the Main menu. Choose Comcast Gift and enter Comcast Faster.

M468 ASSAULT RIFLE

While customizing your character, hold down RB and press Up, Y, Down, A, Left, X, Right, B, Left, Left, Right, X

TOMB RAIDER: LEGEND

You must unlock the following codes in the game before using them.

BULLETPROOF

During a game, hold Left Trigger and press A, Right Trigger, Y, Right Trigger, X, Left Bumper.

DRAIN ENEMY HEALTH

During a game, hold Left Trigger and press X, B, A, Left Bumper, Right Trigger, Y.

INFINITE ASSAULT RIFLE AMMO

During a game, hold Left Bumper and press A, B, A, Left Trigger, X, Y.

INFINITE GRENADE LAUNCHER AMMO

During a game, hold Left Bumper and press Left Trigger, Y, Right Trigger, B, Left Trigger, X.

INFINITE SHOTGUN AMMO

During a game, hold Left Bumper and press Right Trigger, B, X, Left Trigger, X, A.

INFINITE SMG AMMO

During a game, hold Left Bumper and press B, Y, Left Trigger, Right Trigger, A, B.

EXCALIBUR

During a game, hold Left Bumper and press Y, A, B, Right Trigger, Y, Left Trigger.

SOUL REAVER

During a game, hold Left Bumper and press A, Right Trigger, B, Right Trigger, Left Trigger, X.

1-SHOT KILL

During a game, hold Left Trigger and press Y, A, Y, X, Left Bumper, B.

TEXTURELESS MODE

During a game, hold Left Trigger and press Left Bumper, A, B, A, Y, Right Trigger.

TOMB RAIDER: UNDERWORLD

BULLETPROOF LARA

During a game, hold Left Trigger and press A, Right Trigger, Y, Right Trigger, X, LB.

ONE-SHOT KILL

During a game, hold Left Trigger and press Y, A, Y, X, Left Bumper, B.

SHOW ENEMY HEALTH

During a game, hold Left Trigger and press X, B, A, Left Bumper, Right Trigger, Y.

XBOX 360

TONY HAWK'S PRO SKATER HD

ALL CHEATS
At the skater select, hold Left Trigger and press A, B, Y.

ALL GAME MODES
At the skater select, hold Left Trigger and press A, Y, B.

ALL LEVELS
At the skater select, hold Left Trigger and press Y, X, B.

ALL SKATERS
At the skater select, hold Left Trigger and press Y, B, X.

ALL TRICKS
At the skater select, hold Left Trigger and press A, X, Y.

MAX ALL STATS
At the skater select, hold Left Trigger and press Y, X, A.

MAX MONEY
At the skater select, hold Left Trigger and press Y, B, A. This gives you $999,999,999.

TORCHLIGHT

AVATAR AWARDS

AWARD	EARNED BY
Torchlight Logo Tee	Defeat the Overseer.
Robot Knit Cap	Defeat the game.

DESTROYER GAMERPIC
Earn the Tree Hugger Achievement.

TOY SOLDIERS: COLD WAR

COMMANDO GAMER PICTURE
Buy the game.

RUSSIAN GAMER PICTURE
Complete the game.

AVATAR AWARDS

AVATAR	EARNED BY
Flight Jacket	Complete the first section of Basic Training.
Mullet	Survive until Wave 9 in Basic Training.
Toy Soldiers T-Shirt	Play a survival match to Round 5.

TRANSFORMERS: DARK OF THE MOON

RATCHET IN MULTIPLAYER
At the Unlockables screen, press Up, Right, Down, Left, Up, Start.

TRANSFORMERS: FALL OF CYBERTRON

AVATAR AWARDS

AVATAR	EARNED BY
High Moon T-Shirt	Complete Chapter I.
Optimus Prime Helmet	Complete Chapter XIII as Optimus.
Megatron Helmet	Complete Chapter XIII as Megatron.

ELECTRO BOLTER
Complete the campaign.

GLASS GAS CANNON
Complete the campaign.

TRANSFORMERS REVENGE OF THE FALLEN

LOW GRAVITY MODE
Select Cheat Code and enter A, X, Y, Left Thumbstick, Y, Left Thumbstick.

NO WEAPON OVERHEAT
Select Cheat Code and enter Left Thumbstick, X, A, Left Thumbstick, Y, Left Bumper.

ALWAYS IN OVERDRIVE MODE
Select Cheat Code and enter Left Bumper, B, Left Bumper, A, X, Right Thumbstick.

UNLIMITED TURBO
Select Cheat Code and enter B, Left Thumbstick, X, Right Thumbstick, A, Y.

NO SPECIAL COOLDOWN TIME
Select Cheat Code and enter Right Thumbstick, X, Right Thumbstick, Right Thumbstick, X, A.

INVINCIBILITY
Select Cheat Code and enter Right Thumbstick, A, X, Left Thumbstick, X, X.

4X ENERGON FROM DEFEATED ENEMIES
Select Cheat Code and enter Y, X, B, Right Thumbstick, A, Y.

INCREASED WEAPON DAMAGE, ROBOT FORM
Select Cheat Code and enter Y, Y, Right Thumbstick, A, Left Bumper, Y.

INCREASED WEAPON DAMAGE, VEHICLE FORM
Select Cheat Code and enter Y, B, Right Bumper, X, Right Thumbstick, Left Thumbstick.

MELEE INSTANT KILLS
Select Cheat Code and enter Right Thumbstick, A, Left Bumper, B, Right Thumbstick, Left Bumper.

LOWER ENEMY ACCURACY
Select Cheat Code and enter X, Left Thumbstick, Right Thumbstick, Left Thumbstick, Right Thumbstick, Right Bumper.

INCREASED ENEMY HEALTH
Select Cheat Code and enter B, X, Left Bumper, B, Right Thumbstick, Y.

INCREASED ENEMY DAMAGE
Select Cheat Code and enter Left Bumper, Y, A, Y, Right Thumbstick, Right Thumbstick.

INCREASED ENEMY ACCURACY
Select Cheat Code and enter Y, Y, B, A, X, Left Bumper.

SPECIAL KILLS ONLY MODE
Select Cheat Code and enter B, B, Right Bumper, B, A, Left Thumbstick.

UNLOCK ALL SHANGHAI MISSIONS & ZONES
Select Cheat Code and enter Y, Left Thumbstick, Right Thumbstick, Left Bumper, Y, A.

UNLOCK ALL WEST COAST MISSIONS & ZONES
Select Cheat Code and enter Left Bumper, Right Bumper, Right Thumbstick, Y, Right Thumbstick, B.

UNLOCK ALL DEEP SIX MISSIONS & ZONES
Select Cheat Code and enter X, Right Bumper, Y, B, A, Left Bumper.

UNLOCK ALL EAST COAST MISSIONS & ZONES
Select Cheat Code and enter Right Thumbstick, Left Thumbstick, Right Bumper, A, B, X.

UNLOCK ALL CAIRO MISSIONS & ZONES
Select Cheat Code and enter Right Thumbstick, Y, A, Y, Left Thumbstick, Left Bumper.

UNLOCK AND ACTIVATE ALL UPGRADES
Select Cheat Code and enter Left Bumper, Y, Left Bumper, B, X, X.

TRENCHED

AVATAR AWARDS

AVATAR	EARNED BY
Trenched T-Shirt	Complete Mobile Trench certification.
Trenchie	Wrest control of Europe back from the Northern Pylon.

TWO WORLDS II

UNLOCKABLE ITEMS

Pause the game, select Bonus Code and enter the following:

ITEM	PASSWORD
Anathros Sword	6770-8976-1634-9490
Axe	1775-3623-3298-1928
Elexorien Two-handed Sword	3542-3274-8350-6064
Hammer	6231-1890-4345-5988
Lucienda Sword	9122-5287-3591-0927
Luciendar Sword	6624-0989-0879-6383
Two-handed Hammer	3654-0091-3399-0994
Dragon Scale Armor	4149-3083-9823-6545
Labyrinth Level	1797-3432-7753-9254
Scroll Bonus Map	6972-5760-7685-8477

UFC 2010 UNDISPUTED

BJ PENN (BLACK SHORTS)

At the main menu, press Left Bumper, Right Bumper, Left Trigger, Right Trigger, Right Trigger, Left Trigger, Right Bumper, Left Bumper, Y, X, X, Y, start.

SHAQUILLE O'NEAL

At the main menu, press Right, Up, Left, Right, Down, Left, Up, Right, Down, Left, X, Y, Y, X, Start.

TAPOUT CREW - MASK, PUNKASS, SKYSCRAPE

At the main menu, press Down, Down, Up, Right, Left, Down, Back, Start.

UFC PERSONAL TRAINER: THE ULTIMATE FITNESS SYSTEM

AVATAR AWARDS

AVATAR	EARNED BY
UFC Trainer Gloves	Earn 10 Medals.
UFC Trainer Shorts	Earn 50 Medals.
UFC Trainer Shirt	Earn 150 Medals.

ULTIMATE MARVEL VS. CAPCOM 3

PLAY AS GALACTUS

With a save game from Marvel vs. Capcom 3: Fate of Two Worlds on your system, Galactus becomes available. Otherwise, you need to accumulate 30,000 points on a player card. Now highlight Arcade Mode and press Left Bumper + Back + A.

VIRTUAL ON: ORATORIO TANGRAM VER.5.66

PLAY AS ALPHA RAIDEN

After defeating Arcade Mode with Raiden, do the following at the Character Select screen: highlight Apharmd B, press X, highlight Apharmd S, press X, highlight Dordray, press X, X, highlight Specineff, press X, X, highlight Fei-Yen, press X, X, highlight Cypher, press X (x3).

PLAY AS ALPHA TEMJIN

After defeating Arcade Mode with Temjin, do the following at the Character Select screen: highlight Temjin, press X, highlight Random, press X, highlight Raiden, press X, X, highlight Bal-Bados, press X, X, highlight Angelan, press X, X, highlight Grys-Vok, press X (x3).

VIRTUA TENNIS 4

THERON TENNIEL

At the player select, select Load to access Custom Players. Next, press Left Bumper.

VICKY BARNEY

At the player select, select Load to access Custom Players. Next, press Right Bumper.

VIVA PIÑATA: TROUBLE IN PARADISE

CREDITS

Select Play Garden and name your garden Piñata People. This unlocks the ability to view the credits on the Main menu.

VOLTRON

AVATAR AWARDS

AVATAR	EARNED BY
Voltron Unlock T-Shirt	Purchase the game to unlock.

WARLORDS

AVATAR AWARDS

AVATAR	EARNED BY
Warlords Classic Tee	Complete the Single Player Campaign.
Snoot Fez	Earn 22 coins in the Single Player Campaign's Time Attack Mode.

WIPEOUT: IN THE ZONE

AVATAR AWARDS

AWARD	EARNED BY
Wipeout Life Jacket	At the main menu, press Left, B, Down, Y, A, B, Right, Up.
Wipeout Safety Helmet	At the main menu, press Y, A, B, Up, Down, Left, Y, Right.

WIPEOUT 2

AVATAR AWARDS

AVATAR	EARNED BY
Winter Vest	Complete episode 6 to unlock this sweet avatar item.
Ice Helmet	Complete episode 8 to unlock this stylish avatar item.
Snow Helmet	Complete episode 8 to unlock this stylish avatar item.

A WORLD OF KEFLINGS

AVATAR AWARDS

AWARD	EARNED BY
Baby Dragon	Make friends with the baby dragon released from an egg in the Ice Kingdom.
Winged Hat Of Kefkimo	Talk to the Chief at the great Hall in the Ice Kingdom.

WORMS ULTIMATE MAYHEM

AVATAR AWARDS

AVATAR	EARNED BY
Ultimate Mayhem Tee	Earn any Achievement in Worms: Ultimate Mayhem.
Worm Tee	Locate the 5 hidden Easter Eggs in Worms: Ultimate Mayhem.

WRECKATEER

AVATAR AWARDS

AVATAR	EARNED BY
Wreckateer T-Shirt	Compelte the Tutorials to unlock this Avatar Award.
Wreckateer Hoodie	Complete half the levels to unlock this Avatar Award.
Goblin Hoodie	Beat the game to unlock this Avatar Award.

WWE '12

WWE ATTITUDE ERA HEAVYWEIGHT CHAMPIONSHIP

Select Options from My WWE. Next, choose Cheat Codes and enter OhHellYeah!.

WWE ALL STARS

UNLOCK ARENAS, WRESTLERS, AND ATTIRE

At the main menu, press Left, Y, Down, Left, Y, X, Left, X, Y, Down, Right, X, Left, Up, X, Right.

AUSTIN AND PUNK ATTIRES

At the main menu, press Left, Left, Right, Right, Up, Down, Up, Down.

ROBERTS AND ORTON ATTIRES

At the main menu, press Up, Down, Left, Right, Up, Up, Down, Down.

SAVAGE AND MORRISON ATTIRES

At the main menu, press Down, Left, Up, Right, Right, Up, Left, Down.

WWE SMACKDOWN VS. RAW 2010

THE ROCK

Select Cheat Codes from the Options menu and enter The Great One.

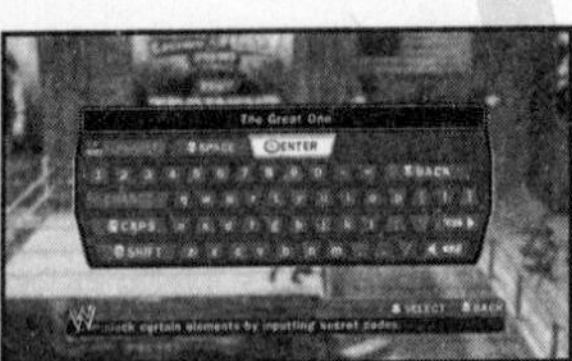

DIRT SHEET BRAWL AND OFFICE STAGE BRAWL

Select Cheat Codes from the Options menu and enter BonusBrawl.

JOHN CENA'S NEW COSTUME

Select Cheat Codes from the Options menu and enter CENATION.

RANDY ORTON'S NEW COSTUME

Select Cheat Codes from the Options menu and enter ViperRKO.

SANTINO MARELLA'S NEW COSTUME

Select Cheat Codes from the Options menu and enter Milan Miracle.

SHAWN MICHAELS' NEW COSTUME

Select Cheat Codes from the Options menu and enter Bow Down.

TRIPLE H'S NEW COSTUME

Select Cheat Codes from the Options menu and enter Suck IT!.

WWE SMACKDOWN VS. RAW 2011

JOHN CENA (ENTRANCE/CIVILIAN)
In My WWE, select Cheat Codes from the Options and enter SLURPEE.

ALL OF RANDY ORTON'S COSTUMES
In My WWE, select Cheat Codes from the Options and enter apexpredator.

TRIBUTE TO THE TROOPS ARENA
In My WWE, select Cheat Codes from the Options and enter 8thannualtribute.

CRUISERWEIGHT TITLE, HARDCORE TITLE, AND MILLION DOLLAR TITLE
In My WWE, select Cheat Codes from the Options and enter Historicalbelts.

XCOM: ENEMY UNKNOWN

Using the following XCOM heroes disables achievements for the rest of the game. They come loaded with abilities and a sweet weapon.

JOE KELLY
Customize your soldier with the name Joe Kelly.

KEN LEVINE
Customize your soldier with the name Ken Levine.

OTTO ZANDER
Customize your soldier with the name Otto Zander.

SID MEIER
Customize your soldier with the name Sid Meier.

X-MEN DESTINY

JUGGERNAUT SUIT
At the title screen, hold Left Bumper + Right Bumper and press Down, Right, Up, Left, Y, B.

EMMA FROST SUIT
At the title screen, hold Left Bumper + Right Bumper and press Up, Down, Right, Left, B, Y.

X-MEN ORIGINS: WOLVERINE

CLASSIC WOLVERINE OUTFIT
During a game, press A, X, B, X, A, Y, A, Y, A, X, B, B, X, R3. This code disables achievements.

DOUBLE ENEMY REFLEX POINTS
During a game, press A, A, X, X, Y, Y, B, B, Y, Y, X, X, A, A, R3. This code disables achievements.

INFINITE RAGE
During a game, press Y, X, X, Y, B, B, Y, A, A, Y, R3. This code disables achievements.

INVINCIBLE
During a game, press X, A, A, X, Y, Y, X, B, B, X, R3. This code disables achievements.

CLASSIC WOLVERINE CHALLENGE/OUTFIT
Find any two Classic Wolverine action figures to unlock this challenge. Defeat Classic Wolverine in combat to unlock the Classic Wolverine outfit.

ORIGINAL WOLVERINE CHALLENGE/OUTFIT
Find any two Original Wolverine action figures to unlock this challenge. Defeat Original Wolverine in combat to unlock the Original Wolverine outfit.

X-FORCE WOLVERINE CHALLENGE/OUTFIT
Find any two X-Force Wolverine action figures to unlock this challenge. Defeat X-Force Wolverine in combat to unlock the X-Force Wolverine outfit.

YOU DON'T KNOW JACK

ALL EPISODES

At the Episode Select, press Left, Left, Right, Left, X.

AVATAR AWARDS

AVATAR	EARNED BY
A Classy Men's T-Shirt	Play any episode and score over $0.
A Trendy Ladies T-Shirt	Play any episode and score over $0.
A Fashionable Men's Pant	Play episode 9 and score over $0.
A Beautiful Ladies Pant	Play episode 9 and score over $0.
A "Bald-Headed" Ski Mask	Play episode 58 score over $0.
Billy O'Brien Replica Dummy	Find the episode 73 wrong answer of the game.

YOU'RE IN THE MOVIES

ALL TRAILERS AND DIRECTOR'S MODE

At the options screen, press Left Bumper, Right Bumper, Left Bumper, Right Bumper, Y.

ZOMBIE APOCALYPSE

7 DAYS OF HELL MODE

Complete Day 55.

CHAINSAW ONLY MODE

Complete a day only using the chainsaw.

HARDCORE MODE

Survive for seven straight days.

TURBO MODE

Get a 100 multiplier.

ZOOMAROOM

ALL COSTUMES, TIERS, & DOUBLE JUMP

At the Title screen, press Left Trigger, Right Trigger, Left Trigger, Right Trigger, X, X, Left Bumper, Right Bumper.

ZUMBA FITNESS RUSH

QUEBRO EXCLUSIVE

At the Song Select, press Left Trigger, X, Right Bumper.

MICROSOFT XBOX 360® ACHIEVEMENTS

GAMES

007 LEGENDS

ACHIEVEMENTS

NAME	GOAL/REQUIREMENT	POINT VALUE
Secret Agent	Complete all levels on 'Agent' difficulty or higher.	50
007	Complete all levels on a 'Classic' difficulty.	50
Goldfinger	Complete the 'Goldfinger' mission.	15
O.H.M.S.S.	Complete the 'O.H.M.S.S.' mission.	15
Licence To Kill	Complete the 'License To Kill' mission.	15
Die Another Day	Complete the 'Die Another Day' mission.	15
Moonraker	Complete the 'Moonraker' mission.	15
People Power	Campaign: Collect 30% of all character bio intel.	10
Making it Personal	Campaign: Collect 100% of all character bio intel.	10
Web of Intrigue	Campaign: Collect 30% of all organization intel.	10
Clandestine	Campaign: Collect 100% of all organization intel.	10
Happy Snapper	Campaign: Take a photograph of the crocodile.	10
Scream if you want to go faster	Campaign: Give someone an exciting training experience.	10
Vodka martini, plenty of ice...	Get 100% collection rating for 'Die Another Day'.	20
I expect you to die	Get 100% collection rating for 'Goldfinger'.	20
Never happened to the other guy	Get 100% collection rating for 'O.H.M.S.S.'	20
You prepare for the unexpected	Get 100% collection rating for 'License To Kill'.	20
Around the world one more time	Get 100% collection rating for 'Moonraker'.	20
Boys with Toys	Campaign: Buy all of the attachments for one weapon class.	10
Very novel Q	Campaign: Upgrade a gadget to its highest level.	10
Standards of Physical Perfection	Campaign: Acquire all of the MI6 training modules.	30
Everything or Nothing	Complete all of the trials on any one level.	5
Extended Operative	Complete eight of the 'Operative' level trials.	20
More Than an Agent	Complete six of the 'Agent' level trials.	25
Above and Beyond a 00	Complete three of the '007' level trials.	30
Spend the money quickly Mr. Bond	Campaign: Be awarded a total of 10,000 XP.	20
Distracting	Distract an enemy.	10
Positively shocking!	Take out two enemies with one shock dart.	12
Master at Arms	Make an elimination with every weapon class.	20
Challenger	Earn a 1 star rating in each mission of the Challenges mode.	20
All That Glitters	Earn a 3 star rating in any mission of the Challenges mode.	10
Shooting Star	Get 30% of all available stars in the Challenges mode.	20
Star Struck	Get 60% of all available stars in the Challenges mode.	40
Fascination with all things gold	Get 100% of all available stars in the Challenges mode.	60
Unlocked and Loaded	Public Match: Reach level 6 (Midshipman).	5
00 Agent	Public Match: Reach level 50 (00 Agent Grade 0).	30
A Farewell to Arms	Multiplayer: Enter 00 Specialization.	50
Laser Eraser	Public Match: Win a match using only laser-based weapons.	15
Midas Touch	Public Match: Win a match on Main Vault, Smelting Room and Loading Bay.	15
Danger! High Voltage	Public Match: Get 25 electrocution kills as Zao or Gustav Graves.	10
Counter-Sniper	Public Match: Kill 50 players while they are aiming down the scope of a sniper rifle.	25

NAME	GOAL/REQUIREMENT	POINT VALUE
Return to Sender	Public Match: In Bomb Defuse disarm the bomb and plant it at enemy base without getting killed.	35
Shaken, but not Stirred	Public Match: Survive 50 explosions while using Reactive Armor.	10
Disarmed and Dangerous	Public Match: In Escalation demote an enemy who is armed with the RPG.	20
Hold the Line	Public Match: Win a Data Miner match without being killed.	30
All the Time in the World	Public Match: Play for more than 24 hours.	40

SECRET ACHIEVEMENTS

NAME	GOAL/REQUIREMENT	POINT VALUE
Signature	Campaign: Reach level three weapon proficiency with the P99.	7
With or Without Q	Reach Grave's plane without using any in-car gadgets.	16
One small step for a man	Experience zero-g.	0
Omega Virus	Public Match: Kill an enemy who has completed the campaign or who already has this Achievement.	15

ARMORED CORE 5

ACHIEVEMENTS

NAME	GOAL/REQUIREMENT	POINT VALUE
Rookie	Awarded for joining a team.	5
Assembler	Awarded for assembling an AC.	5
Color Customizer	Awarded for setting an AC's coloring.	5
Emblem Designer	Awarded for editing an emblem.	5
Communicator	Awarded for editing a message.	5
AC Wrecker	Awarded for winning a battle against an AC.	15
Charge Master	Awarded for destroying an enemy with a boost charge.	5
Complete Custom Part	Awarded for continuing to use an arm unit to maximize its performance.	15
Story 00	Awarded for completing Story Mission 00.	10
Story 01	Awarded for completing Story Mission 01.	10
Story 02	Awarded for completing Story Mission 02.	10
Story 03	Awarded for completing Story Mission 03.	10
Story 04	Awarded for completing Story Mission 04.	10
Story 05	Awarded for completing Story Mission 05.	10
Story 06	Awarded for completing Story Mission 06.	10
Story 07	Awarded for completing Story Mission 07.	10
Story 08	Awarded for completing Story Mission 08.	10
Story 09	Awarded for completing Story Mission 09.	10
Complete Story Missions	Awarded for completing all Story Missions.	50
Story Master	Awarded for completing all Story Missions with Rank S.	50
Order Mission	Awarded for completing at least one Order Mission.	10
Complete Order Missions	Awarded for completing all Order Missions.	40
Subquests 30%	Awarded for completing 30% of all Story Mission and Order Mission subquests.	20
Subquests 50%	Awarded for completing 50% of all Story Mission and Order Mission subquests.	20
Subquest Master	Awarded for completing all Story Mission and Order Mission subquests.	50
Emblem Master	Awarded for getting all emblems and emblem pieces by buying them at the shop and/or destroying ACs.	30
Mercenary	Awarded for accepting and going on a job as a mercenary.	5

NAME	GOAL/REQUIREMENT	POINT VALUE
A Job Well Done	Awarded for successfully completing a job as a mercenary.	10
Team Sortie	Awarded for going on a Conquest Mission or Territory Mission with four or more team members.	15
Operator	Awarded for leading your team to victory on a Conquest Mission or Territory Mission.	15
Territory Mission Sortie	Awarded for going on a Territory Mission.	5
Accomplish Territory Mission	Awarded for claiming victory on a Territory Mission.	10
Territory Mission Victory	Awarded for claiming victory on a Territory Mission in an emergency state.	30
Conquest Mission Sortie	Awarded for going on a Conquest Mission.	5
Conquest Mission Victory	Awarded for claiming victory on a Conquest Mission.	30
Territorial Claim	Awarded for claiming victory on a Conquest Mission as an Invasion Mission.	30
Customize Territory	Awarded for acquiring territory and uploading custom gun battery positions.	10
Perfect Mission	Awarded for completing emergency Territory/Conquest Mission w/four or more members, all surviving.	30
Team Level 10	Awarded for belonging to a team with a team level of 10 or higher.	15
Team Level 50	Awarded for belonging to a team with a team level of 50 or higher.	40
Migrant	Awarded for raising your money to 10 million Au or more.	20
Overlord	Awarded for belonging to a team that holds ten different territories at the same time.	30
Ruler	Awarded for belonging to a team that holds one or more territories in all areas.	50

SECRET ACHIEVEMENTS

NAME	GOAL/REQUIREMENT	POINT VALUE
Blackbird	Awarded for destroying Exusia.	30
Giant Killing	Awarded for destroying LLL.	30
Sea Master	Awarded for destroying St Elmo.	30
Air Master	Awarded for destroying Raijin.	30
Earth Master	Awarded for destroying Type D No. 5.	30
MoH	Awarded for wiping out MoH.	30
Zodiac	Awarded for destroying all Zodiac members.	40

ASSASSIN'S CREED: REVELATIONS

ACHIEVEMENTS

NAME	GOAL/REQUIREMENT	POINT VALUE
Mastering the Art	Earn the INCOGNITO bonus (Multiplayer).	30
Tools of the Templar	Purchase your first ABILITY in the Abstergo Store (Multiplayer).	10
Achiever	Complete a Challenge (Multiplayer).	10
True Templar	Reach level 20 (Multiplayer).	20
Looking Good	Customize a PERSONA (Multiplayer).	10
There Is No I in Team	Win a session of a team mode (Multiplayer).	20
Make the Headlines	Obtain 12 different Accolades (Multiplayer).	30
The Way I Like It	Edit your TEMPLAR PROFILE to change your title, emblem, and patron (Multiplayer).	20
Explorer	Finish a session of each game mode (Multiplayer).	20
Tactician	Score at least 2500 points in a session (Multiplayer).	30
The Early Years	Complete Desmond Sequence 1.	20
Best Served Cold	Complete DNA Sequence 1.	20
The Reluctant Assassin	Complete Desmond Sequence 2.	20

NAME	GOAL/REQUIREMENT	POINT VALUE
Istanbul and Constantinople	Complete DNA Sequence 2.	20
Escape To New York	Complete Desmond Sequence 3.	20
Seal the Deal	Complete DNA Sequence 3.	20
The Prince	Complete DNA Sequence 4.	20
The Plot Thickens	Complete DNA Sequence 5.	20
Successes and Failures	Complete DNA Sequence 6.	20
The Rotten Apple	Complete Desmond Sequence 4.	20
Old Boss, New Boss	Complete DNA Sequence 7.	20
Priorities	Complete DNA Sequence 8.	20
Are You Desmond Miles?	Complete Desmond Sequence 5.	20
Revelations	Complete DNA Sequence 9.	50
Fond Memories	Achieve 100% Synchronization in all Sequences.	20
Holy Wisdom	Complete the Hagia Sofia challenge level.	20
Capped	Collect all animus data fragments.	20
Worth A Thousand Words	Collect all of Ishak Pasha's memoir pages.	20
Pyromaniac	Complete all Bomb Missions.	20
Armchair General	Control all cities (except Rhodes) simultaneously in the Mediterranian Defense game.	20
Iron Curtain	Perform a perfect den defense without using the cannon.	20
Spider Assassin	Climb Hagia Sofia, from the ground to the pinnacle, in under 25 seconds.	20
A Friend Indeed	Complete all Faction Creed Challenges from a single faction.	20
Tax Evasion	Get your money back from a Templar tax collector.	10
The Mentor	Have seven trainees reach the rank of Master Assassin.	20
Lightning Strikes	Kill 5 guards in 5 seconds using only your hidden blades.	20
Overkiller	Assassinate 50 guards with the hidden blade.	20
Show-Off	Parachute onto a zipline.	20
Sage	Collect all available books.	20
Fast Fingers	Loot 50 dead guards with thief looting.	20
Mosh Pit	Have 10 guards poisoned at the same time.	20
Mouse Trap	Kill 5 guards with a scaffold after they have been stunned by caltrops.	20
Craft Maniac	Craft 30 bombs.	20
My Protégé	Have one trainee reach the rank of Master Assassin.	20
Almost Flying	Parachute directly from the top of the Galata Tower to the golden horn.	20
Silent But Deadly	Kill three guards simultaneously with only throwing knives.	20
I can see you	Kill 5 guards while under the cover of a smoke screen bomb.	20
Monster's Dance	Have a guard incapacitate 3 civilians while he's poisoned.	20
Bully	Find and beat up Duccio.	20

THE ANCESTORS CHARACTER PACK ACHIEVEMENTS

NAME	GOAL/REQUIREMENT	POINT VALUE
Stopped Dead	Obtain 3 Hidden Gun kills during a session of Steal The Artifact as The Corsair (Multiplayer).	20
The Vulture	Perform 5 Ground Finish in Manhunt during a session as The Brigand (Multiplayer).	20
Pirate's bravery	Use the Bodyguard against your pursuer as The Privateer (Multiplayer).	30
The Juggernaut	Perform 3 kills using the Charge as The Gladiator (Multiplayer).	20

MEDITERRANEAN TRAVELER MAP PACK

ACHIEVEMENTS

NAME	GOAL/REQUIREMENT	POINT VALUE
Carnival	Stay blended for 3 minutes during a Wanted session in Siena (Multiplayer).	20
Wild Rage	Perform 3 Stuns without dying in Jerusalem (Multiplayer).	30
Restrained Violence	Obtain 5 Kill Assist bonuses during a session of any Team Mode in Dyers (Multiplayer).	20
Straw Hat	Perform 2 kills from haystacks during a session in San Donato (Multiplayer).	30
The Spice of Life	Obtain 2 Variety bonuses during a session in Firenze (Multiplayer).	30
Up and Down	Perform 5 Leaps of Faith during a session of Assassinate in Imperial District (Multiplayer).	20

LOST ARCHIVE

ACHIEVEMENTS

NAME	GOAL/REQUIREMENT	POINT VALUE
Part of the Creed	Take the induction leap of faith	10
Jump they say	Reach the Animus memo	10
Enter the Animus	Enter the Animus simulation	10
Meet your maker	Finish memory five	10
Find all Pieces	Find all decipher fragments	50
Save yourself	Land on a block after falling more than 25 meters	10
Impress Warren Vidic	Complete the Animus testing sequence without failing	50
Cross Styx without dying	Make it across the river Styx without failing	25

SECRET ACHIEVEMENTS

NAME	GOAL/REQUIREMENT	POINT VALUE
The Loop	Experience the loop	25
Breaking the Loop	Break the loop, escape the cycle	50

BATMAN: ARKHAM CITY

ACHIEVEMENTS

NAME	GOAL/REQUIREMENT	POINT VALUE
I'm Batman	Become the Bat	10
Acid Bath	Save the damsel, but is she in distress?	10
Savior	Save the medical volunteers	10
Chimney Sweep	There is only one way in	10
One Armed Bandit	Hammer the point home	10
Communication Breakdown	Clear the airwaves	10
Gladiator	Last man standing	10
Wrecking Ball	Stop the unstoppable	25
Lost And Found	Uncover the secret of Arkham City	10
Sand Storm	We are legion	25
Hide And Seek	A deadly game of hide and seek	25
Ghost Train	Fight for survival	25
Freefall	Don't look down	25
Exit Stage Right	All the world is a stage	50
Forensic Expert	Collect enough evidence to locate the gun for hire	10
Contract Terminated	Stop the contract operative	25
Serial Killer	Track down the serial killer	25
Mystery Stalker	Reveal the mystery watcher	15
Distress Flare	Answer the call for help	5
Broken Toys	Destroy it all	25
Ring Ring	Answer a ringing phone	5

NAME	GOAL/REQUIREMENT	POINT VALUE
Dial Z For Murder	Stop the phone booth killer	25
Stop the Clock	Time is running out	15
Bargaining Chip	Reunite the separated couple	15
AR Knight	Complete all augmented reality training exercises	25
Fully Loaded	Collect all of Batman's gadgets and upgrades	10
Aggravated Assault	Stop all assaults in Arkham City	10
IQ Test	Solve the first riddle	10
Conundrum	Rescue the first hostage from Riddler	20
Mastermind	Rescue the second hostage from Riddler	20
Puzzler	Rescue the third hostage from Riddler	30
Intellectual	Rescue the fourth hostage from Riddler	30
Brainteaser	Rescue the fifth hostage from Riddler	40
Genius	Rescue all the hostages from Riddler	50
Bronze Revenge	Obtain 24 medals on the original Arkham City ranked maps (as Batman)	10
Silver Revenge	Obtain 48 medals on the original Arkham City ranked maps (as Batman)	20
Gold Revenge	Obtain all 72 medals on the original Arkham City ranked maps (as Batman)	40
Campaign Bronze	Obtain 24 medals on the original Arkham City campaigns (as Batman)	10
Campaign Silver	Obtain 72 medals on the original Arkham City campaigns (as Batman)	20
Campaign Gold	Obtain all 108 medals on the original Arkham City campaigns (as Batman)	40
Flawless Freeflow Fighter 2.0	Complete one combat challenge without taking damage (any character)	5
Twice Nightly	Complete New Game Plus	75
Gotham Base Jumper	Jump off the tallest building in Arkham City and glide for 1 minute without touching the ground	5
Pay Your Respects	A moment of remembrance	5
Story Teller	Have 12 murderous dates with Calendar Man	10
Catch	Find someone to play remote Batarang catch with	5
50x Combo	Complete a combo of 50 moves (any play mode, any character)	5
Perfect Freeflow 2.0	Perform a perfect combo including all of Batman's combat moves (any play mode)	5
Gadget Attack	Use 5 different Quickfire gadgets in one fight (any play mode)	5
Perfect Knight - Day 2	Main Story, Side Missions, Upgrades, Collectables, New Game Plus and Riddlers Revenge (as Batman)	75

CATWOMAN BUNDLE PACK ACHIEVEMENTS

NAME	GOAL/REQUIREMENT	POINT VALUE
Sphinx' Riddle	Complete all 40 of the Catwoman Riddler grid items	10
Arkham City Sirens	Drop in on an old friend	25
Pick Pocket	Steal the score of a lifetime	25
Family Jewels	Retrieve your stolen goods	40
Feline Revenge	Obtain all 72 medals on the original Arkham City ranked maps (as Catwoman)	25
Campaign Kitty	Obtain all 108 medals on the original Arkham City campaigns (as Catwoman)	25

ROBIN BUNDLE PACK ACHIEVEMENTS

NAME	GOAL/REQUIREMENT	POINT VALUE
Robin Revenge	Obtain 78 medals on the original Arkham City and Robin Bundle Pack ranked maps (as Robin)	25
Campaign Wonder	Obtain 114 medals on the original Arkham City and Robin Bundle Pack campaigns (as Robin)	25

NIGHTWING BUNDLE PACK

ACHIEVEMENTS

NAME	GOAL/REQUIREMENT	POINT VALUE
Nightwing Revenge	Obtain 78 medals on the original Arkham City and Nightwing Bundle Pack ranked maps (as Nightwing)	25
Campaign Nightwing	Obtain 114 medals on the original Arkham City and Nightwing Bundle Pack campaigns (as Nightwing)	25

HARLEY QUINN'S REVENGE

ACHIEVEMENTS

NAME	GOAL/REQUIREMENT	POINT VALUE
Lost Property	No crimefighter should be without this	20
Breaking and Entering	Find a way into the secret base	20
How's It Hanging?	Clean up the Dry Docks	20
The Last Laugh	The joke's on who?	40
Frequent Flyer	Zip Kick 5 different thugs	10
Battering Ram	Shield Bash 5 different thugs	10
Snap To It	Snap Flash an unarmed thug, an armed thug, an environmental object and a Titan	20
Bomb Squad	Defuse all bombs in 3 minutes or less	40
A Few New Tricks	Use 5 different Quickfire gadgets in one fight as Robin in Harley Quinn's Revenge	20
Party's Over	Destroy all Harley Balloons	50

BATTLEFIELD 3

ACHIEVEMENTS

NAME	GOAL/REQUIREMENT	POINT VALUE
Not on my watch	Protect Chaffin from the soldiers in the street in Operation Swordbreaker	25
Involuntary Euthanasia	Kill the 2 soldiers before the building falls on them in Uprising	25
The Professional	Complete the street chase in Comrades in under 2 minutes 30 seconds without dying	30
Army of Darkness	Shoot out the 4 lights with 4 bullets in Night Shift	30
Practice makes perfect	Headshot each of the targets in the gun range in Kaffarov	15
What the hell *are* you?	Take a russian Dog Tag in the forest ambush in Rock And A Hard Place	20
Roadkill	Kick the car to kill the soldiers in Uprising	20
You can be my wingman anytime	Complete Going Hunting in a perfect run	30
Scrap Metal	Destroy 6 enemy tanks before reaching the fort in Thunder Run	25
Butterfly	Take down the jet in one attempt in Rock And A Hard Place	25
Twofor	Take down 2 enemies with 1 bullet in Night Shift	15
Ooh-rah!	Complete the campaign story	30
Between a rock and a hard place	Beat Solomon, flawlessly, in The Great Destroyer	15
Semper Fidelis	Complete the campaign story on Hard	50
Push On	Reach the garage without going into man-down state in Hit and Run	20
Two-rah!	Complete all co-op missions	30
Lock 'n' Load	Unlock all unique co-op weapons	30
Car Lover	Complete the mission without losing a humvee in Operation Exodus	20
In the nick of time	Disarm the bomb in under 20 seconds in The Eleventh Hour	20
Bullseye	Reach and save the hostages without alerting any enemies in Drop 'em Like Liquid	20
Untouchable	Complete the mission without using the fire extinguisher in Fire From The Sky	20

NAME	GOAL/REQUIREMENT	POINT VALUE
Army of Two	Complete all co-op missions on Hard	50
Ninjas	Reach the VIP without setting off the alarm in Exfiltration	20
Vehicle Warfare	Obtain all 3 vehicle warfare ribbons	30
Infantry Efficiency	Obtain all 4 weapon efficiency ribbons	30
Decorated	Obtain one of each ribbon in the game	50
It's better than nothing!	Finish as 3rd MVP in a ranked match	30
Support Efficiency	Obtain all 4 support efficiency ribbons	30
Colonel	Achieve rank 45	50
1st Loser	Finish as 2nd MVP in a ranked match	30
Most Valuable Player	Finish as MVP in a ranked match	30
M.I.A	Obtain your first enemy Dog Tag	20

SECRET ACHIEVEMENTS

NAME	GOAL/REQUIREMENT	POINT VALUE
This is the end	Failed to prevent the attack	20
Wanted: Dead or Alive	Captured Al Bashir	20
Shock Troop	Survived the quake	15
Where are the other two?	Found the nuke	20
No Escape	Captured Kaffarov	30
FlashForward	Completed Semper Fidelis	10

BATTLEFIELD BAD COMPANY 2

ACHIEVEMENTS

NAME	GOAL/REQUIREMENT	POINT VALUE
I knew we'd make it	Campaign: finish Operation Aurora	15
Retirement just got postponed.	Campaign: finish Cold War	15
It's bad for my karma man!	Campaign: finish Heart of Darkness	15
They got all your intel?	Campaign: finish Upriver	15
Salvage a vehicle.	Campaign: finish Crack the Sky	15
Alright, here it is.	Campaign: finish Snowblind	15
Nobody ever drowned in sweat	Campaign: finish Heavy Metal	15
Ghost rider's here!	Campaign: finish High Value Target	15
Sierra Foxtrot 1079	Campaign: finish Sangre del Toro	15
Thanks for the smokes, brother!	Campaign: finish No One Gets Left Behind	15
Save me some cheerleaders.	Campaign: finish Zero Dark Thirty	15
Turn on a light.	Campaign: finish Force Multiplier	15
P.S. Invasion cancelled, sir.	Campaign: finish Airborne	30
It sucks to be right.	Campaign: finish Airborne on Hard	50
New Shiny Gun	Campaign: find 5 collectable weapons	15
Guns Guns Guns	Campaign: find 15 collectable weapons	50
Link to the Past	Campaign: destroy 1 satellite uplink	15
Communication Issues	Campaign: destroy 15 satellite uplinks	15
Complete Blackout	Campaign: destroy all satellite uplinks	50
Ten Blades	Campaign: 10 melee kills	15
Taxi!	Campaign: drive 5 km in any land vehicle	15
Destruction	Campaign: destroy 100 objects	15
Destruction Part 2	Campaign: destroy 1000 objects	30
Demolish	Campaign: demolish 1 house	15
Demolish Part 2	Campaign: demolish 50 houses	30
Assault Rifle Aggression	Campaign: 50 kills with assault rifles	15
Sub Machine Gun Storm	Campaign: 50 kills with sub machine guns	15

NAME	GOAL/REQUIREMENT	POINT VALUE
Light Machine Gun Lash Out	Campaign: 50 kills with light machine guns	15
Sniper Rifle Strike	Campaign: 50 kills with sniper rifles	15
Wall of Shotgun	Campaign: 50 kills with shotguns	15
Multiplayer Knowledge	Online: reach Rank 10 (Sergeant I)	15
Multiplayer Elite	Online: reach Rank 22 (Warrant Officer I)	50
Assault Expert	Online: unlock 3 weapons in the Assault kit	15
Engineer Expert	Online: unlock 3 weapons in the Engineer kit	15
Medic Expert	Online: unlock 3 weapons in the Medic kit	15
Recon Expert	Online: unlock 3 weapons in the Recon kit	15
Battlefield Expert	Online: obtain all unlocks in any kit or all Vehicle unlocks	50
15 Minutes of Fame	Online: play for 15 minutes	15
Mission... Accomplished.	Online: in a round do one kill with the knife, the M60 and the RPG-7	15
Pistol Man	Online: get 5 kills with every handgun in the game	15
Airkill	Online: roadkill an enemy with any helicopter	15
Et Tu, Brute?	Online: knife 5 friends	15
Demolition Man	Online: get 20 demolish kills	15
Careful Guidence	Online: destroy an enemy helicopter with a stationary RPG	15
The Dentist	Online: do a headshot kill with the repair tool	15
Won Them All	Online: win a round in all online game modes	15
Squad Player	Online: obtain the Gold Squad Pin 5 times	30
Combat Service Support	Online: do 10 resupplies, repairs, heals, revives and motion mine spot assists	15
Award Aware	Online: obtain 10 unique awards	15
Award Addicted	Online: obtain 50 unique awards	30

DOWNLOADABLE CONTENT: WEAPONS PACK 1

NAME	GOAL/REQUIREMENT	POINT VALUE
SPECACT Assault Elite	Get all SPECACT Assault awards	15
SPECACT Engineer Elite	Get all SPECACT Engineer awards	15
SPECACT Medic Elite	Get all SPECACT Medic awards	15
SPECACT Recon Elite	Get all SPECACT Recon awards	15

DOWNLOADABLE CONTENT: ONSLAUGHT

NAME	GOAL/REQUIREMENT	POINT VALUE
Valpariso Conquered	Successfully complete Valpariso in Onslaught mode on any difficulty	10
Valpariso Veteran	Successfully complete Valpariso in Onslaught mode on Hardcore difficulty	20
Isla Inocentes Conquered	Successfully complete Isla Inocentes in Onslaught mode on any difficulty	10
Isla Inocentes Veteran	Successfully complete Isla Inocentes in Onslaught mode on Hardcore difficulty	20
Atacama Desert Conquered	Successfully complete Atacama Desert in Onslaught mode on any difficulty	10
Atacama Desert Veteran	Successfully complete Atacama Desert in Onslaught mode on Hardcore difficulty	20
Nelson Bay Conquered	Successfully complete Nelson Bay in Onslaught mode on any difficulty	10
Nelson Bay Veteran	Successfully complete Nelson Bay in Onslaught mode on Hardcore difficulty	20

BIOSHOCK 2

ACHIEVEMENTS

NAME	GOAL/REQUIREMENT	POINT VALUE
Bought a Slot	Buy one Plasmid or Tonic Slot at a Gatherer's Garden.	5
Max Plasmid Slots	Fully upgrade to the maximum number of Plasmid Slots.	10
Upgraded a Weapon	Upgrade any weapon at a Power to the People Station.	10
Fully Upgraded a Weapon	Install the third and final upgrade to any of your weapons.	10
All Weapon Upgrades	Find all 14 Power to the People weapon upgrades in the game.	20
Prolific Hacker	Successfully hack at least one of every type of machine.	20
Master Hacker	Hack 30 machines at a distance with the Hack Tool.	20
First Research	Research a Splicer with the Research Camera.	5
One Research Track	Max out one Research Track.	20
Research Master	Max out research on all 9 research subjects.	20
Grand Daddy	Defeat 3 Big Daddies without dying during the fight.	25
Master Gatherer	Gather 600 ADAM with Little Sisters.	30
Fully Upgraded a Plasmid	Fully upgrade one of your Plasmids to the level 3 version at a Gatherer's Garden.	10
All Plasmids	Find or purchase all 11 basic Plasmid types.	20
Trap Master	Kill 30 enemies using only Traps.	15
Master Protector	Get through a Gather with no damage and no one getting to the Little Sister.	15
Big Spender	Spend 2000 dollars at Vending Machines.	15
Dealt with Every Little Sister	Either Harvest or Save every Little Sister in the game.	50
Against All Odds	Finish the game on the hardest difficulty level.	30
Big Brass Balls	Finish the game without using Vita-Chambers.	25
Rapture Historian	Find 100 audio diaries.	40
Unnatural Selection	Score your first kill in a non-private match.	10
Welcome to Rapture	Complete your first non-private match.	10
Disgusting Frankenstein	Become a Big Daddy for the first time in a non-private match.	10
"Mr. Bubbles– No!"	Take down your first Big Daddy in a non-private match.	20
Mother Goose	Save your first Little Sister in a non-private match.	20
Two-Bit Heroics	Complete your first trial in a non-private match.	10
Parasite	Achieve Rank 10.	10
Little Moth	Achieve Rank 20.	20
Skin Job	Achieve Rank 30.	20
Choose the Impossible	Achieve Rank 40.	50
Proving Grounds	Win your first non-private match.	20
Man About Town	Play at least one non-private match on each multiplayer map.	10

SECRET ACHIEVEMENTS

NAME	GOAL/REQUIREMENT	POINT VALUE
Daddy's Home	Found your way back into the ruins of Rapture.	10
Protector	Defended yourself against Lamb's assault in the train station.	20
Sinclair's Solution	Joined forces with Sinclair in Ryan Amusements.	20
Confronted Grace	Confronted Lamb's lieutenant in Pauper's Drop.	10
Defeated the Preacher	Defeated the Preacher.	20
Nose for News	Uncovered the secret of Dionysus Park.	20
Found Lamb's Hideout	Gained access to Lamb's stronghold.	20
Reunion	Reunited with your original Little Sister.	50
Heading to the Surface	Headed to the surface on the side of Sinclair's escape pod.	25
Escape	Escaped Rapture.	100
9-Irony	Paid your respects to the founder of Rapture.	5
Distance Hacker	Used the Hack Tool to hack an object at a distance.	5
Unbreakable	Defended yourself against the Big Sister without dying.	20
Look at You, Hacker	Killed 50 enemies using only hacked Security.	15
Adopted a Little Sister	Adopted a new Little Sister for the first time.	5

NAME	GOAL/REQUIREMENT	POINT VALUE
Savior	Saved every Little Sister and spared Grace, Stanley and Gil.	25
Counterattack	Killed an enemy with its own projectile.	5

DOWNLOADABLE CONTENT: RAPTURE METRO PACK

NAME	GOAL/REQUIREMENT	POINT VALUE
Aqua Incognita	Play at least one non-private match on each downloadable content map.	25
Territorial	Win a non-private match in each of the 6 new maps.	25
Reincarnation	Use Rebirth to start again!	100

DOWNLOADABLE CONTENT: THE PROTECTOR TRIALS

NAME	GOAL/REQUIREMENT	POINT VALUE
Litmus Test	Earn 6 stars in the Protector Trials	5
Acid Test	Earn 18 stars in the Protector Trial	10
Trial By Fire	Earn 36 stars in the Protector Trials	15
Enemy of the Family	Earn an A rank in all Protector Trials	15
Perfect Protector	Collect 100% of the ADAM in a single Protector Trial	20
Get a Bigger Bucket	Collect 50% of the ADAM available in all Protector Trials	25

SECRET ACHIEVEMENTS

NAME	GOAL/REQUIREMENT	POINT VALUE
Guardian Angel	Completed all bonus Protector Trials.	10

DOWNLOADABLE CONTENT: MINERVA'S DEN

NAME	GOAL/REQUIREMENT	POINT VALUE
Garbage Collection	Destroy all 10 Vacuum Bots in Minerva's Den	10
Lancer Killer	Kill a Lancer Big Daddy	10
ADAM Addict	Resolve all the Little Sisters in Minerva's Den	10

SECRET ACHIEVEMENTS

NAME	GOAL/REQUIREMENT	POINT VALUE
Login	Reached Rapture Central Computing Operations	20
Root Access Granted	Reached Computer Core Access	20
Logout	Escaped Minerva's Den	50
SUDO	Wrested control of the Thinker from Reed Wahl	20
High Score	Get 9999 points in a single game of spitfire	10

BLADES OF TIME

ACHIEVEMENTS

NAME	GOAL/REQUIREMENT	POINT VALUE
Too Hot For You	Kill Brutal Maul without being frozen by his shockwave.	15
Brutal Kill	Kill 5 enemies at once.	15
Annihilation Kill	Kill 10 enemies at once.	30
Famous Hunter	Kill 1000 enemies in total.	15
Faster Than You!	Use Counterattack 100 times.	15
Grasshopper	Use Dash 30 times without touching the ground.	15
Curious	Find half of the notes.	15
Collector	Find all notes.	30
Ready To Fight	Find all types of equipment.	15
Unstoppable	Win any Outbreak match.	15
Out of My Way	Kill an enemy player in Outbreak match.	15
Outbreak Hero	Kill each Outbreak boss at least once.	30
Experienced	Play 5 Outbreak matches.	10
I'm Rich	Find all the chests in story mode on the Normal difficulty level.	15

NAME	GOAL/REQUIREMENT	POINT VALUE
Treasure Hunter	Find all the chests in story mode on the Hard difficulty level.	30
Double Attack	Kill 25 heavy enemies using the Time Rewind double attack.	15
Angry	Kill 100 enemies during your Time Rewind Berserk buff.	15
Rain of Bullets	Shoot off Magic Armor from 50 enemies using Time Rewind clones.	15

SECRET ACHIEVEMENTS

NAME	GOAL/REQUIREMENT	POINT VALUE
Gather Chi	Get the ability to gather Chi.	15
Rifle	Find the rifle.	15
Coral Dash	Get the ability to dash to corals.	15
Enemy Dash	Get the ability to dash to enemies.	15
Time Rewind	Get the ability to rewind time.	15
Order Spell	Survive Chaos event.	15
Free to go!	Kill Gateguard.	30
Clear the Jungle	Kill Shaman Boss.	30
Your Fire Is Nothing	Kill Shaman Boss without taking damage from his massive fire spell.	15
Old Temple	Reach the Sanctuary.	15
World of Order	Defeat Skyguard Commander.	30
Big Corpse	Defeat Giant Worm.	90
Sky Islands	Leave the Sky Islands.	90
Brutal Lands	Kill the Vicar of Chaos.	90
Dragon	Ayumi gets Dragon form.	15
Keeper Is Dead	Finish game on any difficulty.	90
Hard Times Are Over	Finish game on Hard difficulty.	90

BORDERLANDS 2

ACHIEVEMENTS

NAME	GOAL/REQUIREMENT	POINT VALUE
Best Practices	Beat your high score on a song immediately after practicing it in Rehearse.	15
Master Mimic	Earned "Flawless" on every move your opponent created in Make Your Move.	10
Movin' Up in the World	Earned at least 1,500,000 points in a single round of Make Your Move.	10
Unique Technique	Created a move in Make Your Move that your opponent cannot match.	15
Do It...	Earned 5 stars on "The Hustle."	15
Boogie Woogie Woogie	Earned 5 stars on "Electric Boogie."	15
Que Soy Bueno	Earned 5 stars on "Macarena."	15
Lost in the Shuffle	Earned 5 stars on "Cupid Shuffle."	15
What a Scream	Earned 5 stars on "Scream."	15
OMG Indeed!	Earned 5 stars on "OMG" on Hard difficulty.	100
So Lu$h	Earned 5 stars on all 9 of Lu$h Crew's songs on any difficulty.	30
Hi-Definitely	Earned 5 stars on all 9 of Hi-Def's songs on any difficulty.	30
Flash Back	Earned 5 stars on all 9 of Flash4wrd's songs on any difficulty.	30
DCI's on the Prize	Earned 5 stars on all 9 of DCI's songs on any difficulty.	30
Th3Glitt3rati is online	Completed Story mode and watched through the Credits. Thank you!	20
Let 'Em Know	Flaunted at least 5 scores to your Friends List.	20
Up to the Challenge	Won a Player Challenge.	20
Worth a Thousand Words	Shared a Photo online.	15
First-degree Burn	Burned at least 100 calories in any mode.	15

NAME	GOAL/REQUIREMENT	POINT VALUE
GOOOAAALLL!	Set a weekly fitness goal and achieved that goal.	20
Keep It Old School	Performed a song with both dancers in matching Crew Look outfits.	20
Walk-In Closet	Performed a song with every character in every unlockable outfit.	75
Same Gold Story	Earned Gold stars on a song.	20
Weekend Warrior	Played Dance Central 3 on three weekends in a row.	20
Consistent Performers	Earned the same move rating as your partner 5 times in a row.	15
Top Agent	Deciphered a Craze on your first try in Story mode.	15
Daily Grind	Played Dance Central 3 every day for at least 7 days in a row.	20
Ten Large!	Earned "Flawless" on at least 10,000 moves.	40
Beyond Flaw	Earned "Flawless" on at least 1,000 moves.	20
Really Nice Moves	Earned "Nice" on at least 10,000 moves.	30
Nice Moves	Earned "Nice" on at least 1,000 moves.	20
Go Shorty	Performed "In Da Club" with a character on that character's birthday.	15
Dig In Deep	Changed the sorting options on the Song Select screen.	10
Playing Favorites	Danced with the same character at least 20 times.	25
We're Friends, Right?	Linked Dance Central 3 to your Facebook account.	20
Just Pick Something!	Skipped 5 songs in Party Time.	10
Up All Night	Started a Party before midnight and played 'til morning.	25
Party Planner	Started a Party with a Custom Playlist.	20
Custom-Made	Played through a Custom Playlist at least 15 minutes in length.	15
Beat Down	Earned at least 450,000 points in a single round of Keep the Beat.	10
Minor Skirmish	Finished a Crew Throwdown with two single-player teams competing.	15
Shut 'Em Down	Won every round of a Crew Throwdown.	20
Rematch!	Replayed a Crew Throwdown with the same teams.	15

SECRET ACHIEVEMENTS

NAME	GOAL/REQUIREMENT	POINT VALUE
Rippin' It Up	Earned 5 stars on all 9 of Riptide's songs on any difficulty.	30
Where Have You Been??	Played 10 songs with D-Coy.	20

BRINK

ACHIEVEMENTS

NAME	GOAL/REQUIREMENT	POINT VALUE
That's how you win a match	While on defense, take down an attacker who's completing a Primary Objective	10
Not over till the fat lady sings	Take down an enemy with gunfire while knocked down	10
Cut 'em off at the pass	Close an enemy team's shortcut	10
Oh I'm sorry, was that yours?	Capture an enemy Command Post	10
Not so sneaky now, are you?	Reveal an enemy in disguise	10
You shall not pass!	While on defense, prevent the attackers from completing their first objective	20
Was it the red or the blue wire?	Disarm an HE charge	10
Great shot kid! One in a million	Take down an enemy by shooting a grenade	10
They never knew what hit them	While on offense, win the match in less than 30% of the time limit	20
The story has just begun	Win both story campaigns (not including What-If missions)	100

NAME	GOAL/REQUIREMENT	POINT VALUE
You've escaped the Ark	Win all main missions of the Resistance campaign (not including What-If missions)	75
The start of something big	Win any mission, whether campaign or What-If	20
You've saved the Ark	Win all main missions of the Security campaign (not including What-If missions)	75
Viva la revolution!	Win every Resistance campaign mission, including What-If missions	50
Use the wheel, earn more XP	Complete an objective after first selecting it on the Objective Wheel	10
I think I know a shortcut	Open a shortcut for your team	10
To serve and protect	Win every Security campaign mission, including What-If missions	50
Tough as nails	Win all storyline campaign missions (exc. What-If missions) in either Online Versus, or in Hard mode	80
Well done!	Complete your first 1 Star Challenge	10
Very well done indeed!	Complete your first 3 Star Challenge	20
No I insist, you take it	Use the last of your Supplies to refill a teammate's ammo rather than your own	5
It's a trap!	Take down an enemy with a Satchel Charge	10
Who's bad?	Complete all 1 Star Challenges	25
You're going places, kid!	Reach Rank 2	20
Time to start a new character	Reach Rank 5	100
King of the world!	Complete all 3 Star Challenges	100
Well that was educational	Collect all Audio Logs	50
Smart decisions win battles	Attempt to Revive an objective-class teammate over a non-objective teammate near a Primary Objective	10
I live... again!	Revive yourself	5
You can place another mine now	Take down an enemy with a mine	10
Pump up the volume!	Upgrade your team's Command Post	10
T'is better to give than receive	As a Medic, using the Transfer Supplies ability, give the last of your Supplies away	10
A bit of a headache	Take down an enemy with a Cortex Bomb	5
Boom!	Detonate a HE Charge	10
That mine you found? Disarmed!	Spot a mine which is later defused by another Engineer	10
Brinksmanship	Complete an Operative Primary Objective within 5 seconds of breaking disguise	10

BULLETSTORM

ACHIEVEMENTS

NAME	GOAL/REQUIREMENT	POINT VALUE
Weed Killer	Tidy up the back yard	15
Minced Meat	Take out the Mall's biggest customer	15
Grilled Meat	Prepare a big meal using an improvised electric stove	15
Size Matters	Use your biggest weapon	15
Damsel in Distress	Rescue the princess	15
Destroyer of Worlds	Cause major destruction	15
Disco Inferno	Kill all enemies without leaving the dance floor in the city outskirts	10
Chop-Chopper	Kill the enemy inside the airborne helicopter in the park	30
Red Barrels	Explode all the red barrels on the rooftop while in a helicopter	10
Armed and Dangerous	Grow as a person, experience betrayal. Again.	15
Stowaway	Catch a ride	15
Pointless	Execute at least 10 Headshots before you find the first DropKit	10
All Bow To Heavy Metal	Big head, big headache	15
Blood Symphony	Complete the Campaign on Very Hard Difficulty	50

NAME	GOAL/REQUIREMENT	POINT VALUE
Major Malfunction	Destroy 50% of the Newsbots in the Single Player Campaign	10
Total Malfunction	Destroy all Newsbots in the Single Player Campaign	20
Destructive Beat	Complete the Campaign on Very Easy or Easy Difficulty	20
Violent Melody	Complete the Campaign on Normal Difficulty	30
Brutal Chorus	Complete the Campaign on Hard Difficulty	40
Straight Edge	Destroy at least 20 bottles of Nom Juice in the Single Player Campaign	10
Fits Like a Glove	Meet your new best friend	15
Patched Up	Receive a software update for your leash	15
Insecticide	Destroy 50% of the Electroflies in the Single Player Campaign	10
Pest Control	Destroy all Electroflies in the Single Player Campaign	20
Space Pirate	Drink at least 20 bottles of Nom Juice in the Single Player Campaign	10
Old School	Finish an Echo round without executing a single Skillshot	15
Enforcer	Get at least 15,000 points in one Echo round	20
Star struck	Get 3 Stars on 10 different Echoes	10
Bounty Hunter	Have a total of at least 75,000 points in Echoes Mode's total high score	20
Guerrilla Tactics	Execute at least 25 different Skillshots in one Echo round	10
Halfway There	Get at least 21 stars in Echoes Mode	15
Team Player	Complete 200 team challenges in your career in Anarchy mode	10
Final Echo	Achieve level 65 in Anarchy mode	40
Environment Master	Perform every Anarchy environmental Skillshot	20
Hoarder	Have a total of at least 150,000 points in Echoes Mode's total high score	40
Like A Boss	Defeat a miniboss in Anarchy mode	5
Anarchy Master	Achieve a score of at least 50,000 as a team in Anarchy mode	30
Supernova	Get 3 stars on each of the first 14 Echoes	40
Om Nom Nom!	Feed a flytrap with a Nom parasite	10
Wannabe	Perform 10 different Single Player Skillshots	10
Somebody	Perform 25% of the Single Player Skillshots	20
No Man Left Behind	Kill all enemies while escaping from the collapsed building	20
I might be late	Kill all enemies during the sprint to the jumpship	20
Just one last thing	Kill all enemies before you reach the escape capsule	20
Master of Disaster	Earn 2000 points or more at once	40
Remembrance	Play three different Echoes	10
Shooting Star	Get at least 1 star on each of the first 14 Echoes	10
Big Cheese	Perform 50% of the Single Player Skillshots	30
Celebrity	Perform 75% of the Single Player Skillshots	40
Golden Idol	Perform every Single Player Skillshot in the game	50

DOWNLOADABLE CONTENT: GUN SONATA

NAME	GOAL/REQUIREMENT	POINT VALUE
Last Blood	At the end of Guns of Stygia, kill all the enemies on the walkways before the explosions do	30
Hell Razor	Kill a Burnout using the helicopter that arrives in Crash Site	25
Heart Attack	Kill a Boss using the Hot Dog cart in the Hotel Elysium map	40
Bell End	Kill 5 enemies at the same time using "Dung" in the Villa map	10
Extinguisher	In the Sewer map Kill 5 enemies in 1 wave by setting them on fire then extinguishing them	20

CALL OF DUTY: BLACK OPS II

ACHIEVEMENTS

NAME	GOAL/REQUIREMENT	POINT VALUE
No Man Left Behind	Rescue Woods.	20
Gathering Storm	Investigate the jungle facility.	20
Shifting Sands	Gather intel on Raul Menendez from Mullah Rahmaan.	20
Driven by Rage	Take down Menendez and his operation.	20
Waterlogged	Gather information on Raul Menendez' suspected terrorist plot.	20
What Happens in Colossus...	Find the Karma weapon.	20
False Profit	Capture Manuel Noriega and bring him to justice.	20
Deep Cover	Capture Menendez.	20
Sinking Star	Interrogate Menendez.	20
Late for the Prom	Escort the president to the secure location in downtown LA.	20
Death from Above	Stop Menendez once and for all.	50
Old Fashioned	Complete "Pyrrhic Victory", "Old Wounds", "Time And Fate", and "Suffer With Me" in Veteran.	50
Futurist	Complete all future levels in veteran.	50
Giant Accomplishment	Complete all challenges in Black Ops II.	50
Mission Complete	Complete all challenges in a level.	10
Just Gettin' Started	Complete 1 challenge in any level.	10
Singapore Sling	Successfully neutralize the SDC freighter at Keppel Terminal.	15
Desert Storm	Successfully escort the VIPs to safety.	15
Defender	Successfully defend FOB Spectre from incursion.	15
Black Ops II Master	Complete the campaign on Hardened or Veteran difficulty.	15
Art of War	Successfully assassinate SDC Chairman Tian Zhao.	25
Blind Date	Successfully rescue HVI.	15
Family Reunion	There are two futures.	10
Hey Good Looking	Plastic surgery avoided	10
Showdown	A duel between rivals	15
Dirty Business	Listen and think before you shoot.	15
Ship Shape	Reinforcements on the way.	10
Dead or Alive	Jailor or executioner.	15
Ultimate Sacrifice	Only one can survive.	15
Good Karma	Crack the celerium worm.	20
High IQ	Collect all intel.	20
Back in Time	Use a future weapon in the past.	10
Man of the People	Stop the brutality inflicted by the PDF.	15
Gun Nut	Complete a level with customized loadout.	10
Ten K	Minimum score 10k in every mission	15
Welcome to the Club	Reach Sergeant (Level 10) in multiplayer Public Match.	10
Welcome to the Penthouse	Prestige once in multiplayer Public Match.	50
Big Leagues	Win 5 multiplayer League Play games after being placed in a division.	20
Trained Up	Win 10 multiplayer games while playing in Combat Training playlists.	10
Party Animal	Win 10 multiplayer games while playing in Party Games playlists.	10
Tower of Babble	In TranZit, obey the voices.	75
Don't Fire Until You See	In TranZit, have all doors opened without being set on fire.	30
The Lights Of Their Eyes	In Green Run, pacify at least 10 zombies with 1 EMP.	5
Undead Man's Party Bus	In TranZit, complete all additions to the bus in 1 game.	15
Dance On My Grave	In Green Run, acquire your Tombstone.	5
Standard Equipment May Vary	In TranZit, acquire 4 different equippable items in 1 game.	25
You Have No Power Over Me	You Have No Power Over Me	15

NAME	GOAL/REQUIREMENT	POINT VALUE
I Don't Think They Exist	In TranZit, kill one of the denizens of the forest while it is latched onto you.	10
Fuel Efficient	In TranZit, use an alternative mode of transportation.	10
Happy Hour	In TranZit, buy 2 different perks before turning on the power.	10

CALL OF DUTY: MODERN WARFARE 3

ACHIEVEMENTS

NAME	GOAL/REQUIREMENT	POINT VALUE
Back in the Fight	Start the Single Player Campaign on any difficulty.	5
Too Big to Fail	Destroy the Jamming Tower. Complete "Black Tuesday" on any difficulty.	10
Wet Work	Take back New York Harbor. Complete "Hunter Killer" on any difficulty.	10
Carpe Diem	Escape the mountain safe house. Complete "Persona Non Grata" on any difficulty.	10
Frequent Flyer	Defend the Russian President. Complete "Turbulence" on any difficulty.	10
Up to No Good	Infiltrate the village. Complete "Back on the Grid" on any difficulty.	10
One Way Ticket	Make it to Westminster. Complete "Mind the Gap" on any difficulty.	10
Welcome to WW3	Save the US Vice President. Complete "Goalpost" on any difficulty.	10
Sandstorm!	Assault the shipping company. Complete "Return to Sender" on any difficulty.	10
Back Seat Driver	Track down Volk. Complete "Bag and Drag" on any difficulty.	10
We'll Always Have Paris	Escape Paris with Volk. Complete "Iron Lady" on any difficulty.	10
Vive la Révolution!	Reach the church. Complete "Eye of the Storm" on any difficulty.	10
Requiem	Escape the city. Complete "Blood Brothers" on any difficulty.	10
Storm the Castle	Discover Makarov's next move. Complete "Stronghold" on any difficulty.	10
Bad First Date	Find the girl. Complete "Scorched Earth" on any difficulty.	10
Diamond in the Rough	Rescue the Russian President. Complete "Down the Rabbit Hole" on any difficulty.	10
The Big Apple	Complete "Black Tuesday" and "Hunter Killer" on Veteran difficulty.	25
Out of the Frying Pan…	Complete "Persona Non Grata", "Turbulence", and "Back on the Grid" on Veteran difficulty.	25
Payback	Complete "Mind the Gap", "Goalpost", and "Return to Sender" on Veteran difficulty.	25
City of Lights	Complete "Bag and Drag" and "Iron Lady" on Veteran difficulty.	25
The Darkest Hour	Complete "Eye of the Storm", "Blood Brothers", and "Stronghold" on Veteran difficulty.	25
This is the End	Complete "Scorched Earth", "Down the Rabbit Hole", and "Dust to Dust" on Veteran difficulty.	25
Who Dares Wins	Complete the campaign on any difficulty.	40
The Best of the Best	Complete the campaign on Hardened or Veteran difficulty.	100
Strike!	Kill 5 enemies with a single grenade in Single Player or Special Ops.	20
Jack the Ripper	Melee 5 enemies in a row in Single Player or Special Ops.	20
Informant	Collect 22 Intel Items.	20
Scout Leader	Collect 46 Intel Items.	35
This Is My Boomstick	Kill 30 enemies with the XM25 in "Black Tuesday."	20
What Goes Up[el]	Destroy all the choppers with only the UGV's grenade launcher in "Persona Non Grata."	20

NAME	GOAL/REQUIREMENT	POINT VALUE
For Whom the Shell Tolls	Destroy all targets during the mortar sequence with only 4 shells in "Back on the Grid."	20
Kill Box	Kill 20 enemies with the Chopper Gunner in a single run in "Return to Sender."	20
Danger Close	Take down a chopper with an AC-130 smoke grenade in "Bag and Drag."	20
Ménage à Trois	Destroy 3 tanks with a single 105mm shot in "Iron Lady."	20
Nein	Kill 9 enemies with A-10 strafing runs in "Scorched Earth."	20
50/50	Complete a Special Ops Mission Mode game with the same number of kills as your partner.	20
Birdie	Kill 2 enemy helicopters without getting hit in a Special Ops Survival game.	20
Serrated Edge	Finish a Juggernaut with a knife in Special Ops.	15
Arms Dealer	Buy all items from the Survival Weapon Armory.	20
Danger Zone	Buy all items from the Survival Air Support Armory.	20
Defense Spending	Buy all items from the Survival Equipment Armory.	20
Get Rich or Die Trying	Have $50,000 current balance in a Special Ops Survival game.	25
I Live	Survive 1 wave in a Special Ops Survival game.	10
Survivor	Reach Wave 10 in each mission of Special Ops Survival mode.	20
Unstoppable	Reach Wave 15 in each mission of Special Ops Survival mode.	40
No Assistance Required	Complete a Special Ops Mission Mode game on Hardened or Veteran with no player getting downed.	20
Brag Rags	Earn 1 star in Special Ops Mission Mode.	10
Tactician	Earn 1 star in each mission of Special Ops Mission Mode.	20
Overachiever	Earn 48 stars in Special Ops Mission Mode.	40

SECRET ACHIEVEMENTS

NAME	GOAL/REQUIREMENT	POINT VALUE
Flight Attendant	Kill all 5 enemies during the zero-g sequence in "Turbulence."	20

COLLECTION 1

ACHIEVEMENTS

NAME	GOAL/REQUIREMENT	POINT VALUE
Shotgun Diplomacy	Complete the Special Ops mission "Negotiator" on any difficulty.	15
Not on My Watch	Rescue all the hostages in the Special Ops mission "Negotiator."	35
Skilled Negotiator	Complete the Special Ops mission "Negotiator" on Veteran difficulty.	25
Slippery Slope	Complete the "Black Ice" Special Ops mission on any difficulty.	15
A Baker's Dozen	Run over and kill 13 enemies with the snowmobile in the "Black Ice" Special Ops mission.	35
Ice in Your Veins	Complete the "Black Ice" Special Ops mission on Veteran difficulty.	35

CRYSIS 2

ACHIEVEMENTS

NAME	GOAL/REQUIREMENT	POINT VALUE
Can it run Crysis?	Complete In at the Deep End	10
Foreign Contaminant	Escape the Battery Park evacuation center	10
More than Human	Assimilate alien tissue at the crash site	15
False Prophet	Find Nathan Gould	15
Internal Affairs	Infiltrate the CELL facility at Wall Street	15

NAME	GOAL/REQUIREMENT	POINT VALUE
Into the Abyss	Infiltrate the alien hive	20
Once a Marine, Always a Marine	Assist the Marines in Madison Square	20
Hung Out to Dry	Reach the Hargreave-Rasch building	20
Fire Walker	Assist the evacuation at Bryant Park	25
Dark Night of the Soul	Defend Central Station	25
Crossroads of the World	Complete the evacuation at Times Square	25
Theseus at Last	Locate Jacob Hargreave	25
Home Stretch	Reach Central Park	25
Start Spreading the News	Finish the single player campaign on any difficulty	35
City That Never Sleeps	Complete 6 levels on Veteran difficulty	25
Evolution	Complete 12 levels on Veteran difficulty	25
Heart of Darkness	Complete 6 levels on Supersoldier difficulty	25
Medal of Honor	Complete 12 levels on Supersoldier difficulty	25
Men of Destiny	Complete the single player campaign on Veteran difficulty	45
Supersoldier	Complete the single player campaign on Supersoldier	65
Close Encounters	Single Player: Stealth kill 25 enemies	15
The Tourist	Find all New York Souvenirs	15
Fastball	Kill 10 enemies by throwing an object at them	15
Death Grip	Kill 10 enemies with grab and throw	15
Popcorn	Single Player: Kill 20 enemies with the Microwave cannon	15
Two Heads Are Better Than One	Single Player: Kill two enemies with a single bullet	15
Blast Radius	Single Player: Kill at least 3 enemies with a single grenade	15
Headhunter	Single Player: Kill 4 enemies in a row with headshots	15
Death Slide	Single Player: Kill 5 enemies while sliding	15
Food for thought	Kill a CELL operator with a giant donut in Lower Manhattan	10
Hole in One	Throw an alien down the sinkhole in Dark Heart	10
Band of Brothers	Keep all marines alive during the rescue in Semper Fi or Die	15
Literary Agent	Scan all of Richard Morgan's books in the NY public library	10
Stealth Assassin	Re-route the power in Eye of the Storm without being detected	15
Crysis, What Crysis?	Multiplayer: Reach Rank 50	35
League of Your Own	Multiplayer: Finish top of the Scoreboard	25
Dressed to Kill	Multiplayer: Fully level the Nanosuit	30
Tooled Up	Multiplayer: Unlock all the weapons	30
The Cleaner	Get 1 of each Skill Kill	25
Cry Spy	Multiplayer: Get 30 Spot Assists	25
Jack of all Trades	Multiplayer: Win a match of every game mode	25
Dedication	Play online 6 months after your first time	25
Modern Art	Unlock 150 Dog Tag displays	5
Try Me	Complete 3 Xbox LIVE matches	10
The Collector	Collect 20 Dog Tags	15
Maximum Module	Multiplayer: Fully level a Suit Module	20
Team Player	Be in a squad of at least 3 people and play a full game	10
Nomad	Multiplayer: Play a full game on every map	10
I Am Not A Number	Create your first custom class	10

SECRET ACHIEVEMENTS

NAME	GOAL/REQUIREMENT	POINT VALUE
Speeding Ticket	Break the speed limit in front of 10 speed cameras	10

DANCE CENTRAL 3

ACHIEVEMENTS

NAME	GOAL/REQUIREMENT	POINT VALUE
Best Practices	Beat your high score on a song immediately after practicing it in Rehearse.	15
Master Mimic	Earned "Flawless" on every move your opponent created in Make Your Move.	10
Movin' Up in the World	Earned at least 1,500,000 points in a single round of Make Your Move.	10
Unique Technique	Created a move in Make Your Move that your opponent cannot match.	15
Do It…	Earned 5 stars on "The Hustle."	15
Boogie Woogie Woogie	Earned 5 stars on "Electric Boogie."	15
Que Soy Bueno	Earned 5 stars on "Macarena."	15
Lost in the Shuffle	Earned 5 stars on "Cupid Shuffle."	15
What a Scream	Earned 5 stars on "Scream."	15
OMG Indeed!	Earned 5 stars on "OMG" on Hard difficulty.	100
So Lu$h	Earned 5 stars on all 9 of Lu$h Crew's songs on any difficulty.	30
Hi-Definitely	Earned 5 stars on all 9 of Hi-Def's songs on any difficulty.	30
Flash Back	Earned 5 stars on all 9 of Flash4wrd's songs on any difficulty.	30
DCI's on the Prize	Earned 5 stars on all 9 of DCI's songs on any difficulty.	30
Th3Glitt3rati is online	Completed Story mode and watched through the Credits. Thank you!	20
Let 'Em Know	Flaunted at least 5 scores to your Friends List.	20
Up to the Challenge	Won a Player Challenge.	20
Worth a Thousand Words	Shared a Photo online.	15
First-degree Burn	Burned at least 100 calories in any mode.	15
GOOOAAALLL!	Set a weekly fitness goal and achieved that goal.	20
Keep It Old School	Performed a song with both dancers in matching Crew Look outfits.	20
Walk-In Closet	Performed a song with every character in every unlockable outfit.	75
Same Gold Story	Earned Gold stars on a song.	20
Weekend Warrior	Played Dance Central 3 on three weekends in a row.	20
Consistent Performers	Earned the same move rating as your partner 5 times in a row.	15
Top Agent	Deciphered a Craze on your first try in Story mode.	15
Daily Grind	Played Dance Central 3 every day for at least 7 days in a row.	20
Ten Large!	Earned "Flawless" on at least 10,000 moves.	40
Beyond Flaw	Earned "Flawless" on at least 1,000 moves.	20
Really Nice Moves	Earned "Nice" on at least 10,000 moves.	30
Nice Moves	Earned "Nice" on at least 1,000 moves.	20
Go Shorty	Performed "In Da Club" with a character on that character's birthday.	15
Dig In Deep	Changed the sorting options on the Song Select screen.	10
Playing Favorites	Danced with the same character at least 20 times.	25
We're Friends, Right?	Linked Dance Central 3 to your Facebook account.	20
Just Pick Something!	Skipped 5 songs in Party Time.	10
Up All Night	Started a Party before midnight and played 'til morning.	25
Party Planner	Started a Party with a Custom Playlist.	20
Custom-Made	Played through a Custom Playlist at least 15 minutes in length.	15
Beat Down	Earned at least 450,000 points in a single round of Keep the Beat.	10
Minor Skirmish	Finished a Crew Throwdown with two single-player teams competing.	15
Shut 'Em Down	Won every round of a Crew Throwdown.	20
Rematch!	Replayed a Crew Throwdown with the same teams.	15

SECRET ACHIEVEMENTS

NAME	GOAL/REQUIREMENT	POINT VALUE
Rippin' It Up	Earned 5 stars on all 9 of Riptide's songs on any difficulty.	30
Where Have You Been??	Played 10 songs with D-Coy.	20

DEAD ISLAND

ACHIEVEMENTS

NAME	GOAL/REQUIREMENT	POINT VALUE
Rootin' Tootin' Lootin'	Loot 5 Exceptional Weapons.	30
Tis but a flesh wound!	Sever 100 limbs.	10
There and back again	Explore the entire island.	30
Catch!	Kill an Infected with a grenade blast.	10
Road Trip	Drive a total distance of 10 kilometers.	10
Cardio	Travel a distance of 20 kilometers on foot.	10
Swing them sticks	Kill 150 enemies using Analog Fighting controls.	25
Gesundheit!	Heal yourself with a medkit 100 times.	10
Light my fire	Set 10 zombies on fire simultaneously.	20
10 heads are better than 1	Kill 10 zombies in a row with headshots.	15
A taste of everything	Kill a zombie with 10 different melee weapons.	25
One is all I need	Kill 5 Infected in a row with a single blow.	20
Can't touch this	Use a hammer to kill a series of 15 zombies without taking damage.	20
Humanitarian	Kill 50 human enemies.	15
Tae Kwon Leap	Kill 25 zombies with your bare fists.	25
I want one of those	Customize 25 weapons.	30
Karma-geddon	Kill 50 zombies using a vehicle.	15
To put it bluntly	Kill 250 zombies using blunt melee weapons.	25
Hack & slash	Kill 250 zombies using edged melee weapons.	25
Guns don't kill but they help	Kill 250 zombies using firearms.	25
Need a hand?	Join another player's game.	10
Warranty Void if Used	Create a customized weapon.	10
Gotta find'em all	Find 60 collectibles.	20
Nearly there	Find 120 collectibles.	25
Steam Punk	Create weapons to rival the gods of fire or thunder.	30
Originality	Play in a co-op team of 4 different playable characters.	10
Together in the light	Complete 5 quests in a single co-op game with the same partners.	10
Going steady	Complete 25 quests while playing with at least one co-op partner.	25
Rageman	Kill 100 enemies with Fury attacks.	25
People Person	Play with 10 different co-op partners for at least 15 minutes each.	10
Ménage à trois	Complete 5 quests with 3 co-op partners.	25
Right 4 Life	Complete act I with 4 different characters.	30
A very special day	Kill 250 zombies with modified weapons.	30
School of hard knocks	Reach level 50.	30
Knock, knock	Breach a locked door with the first blow.	15

NAME	GOAL/REQUIREMENT	POINT VALUE
Busy, busy, busy	Finish 75 quests cumulatively.	60
Learning the ropes	Reach level 10.	10
Dedicated student	Reach level 25.	25

SECRET ACHIEVEMENTS

NAME	GOAL/REQUIREMENT	POINT VALUE
Everybody lies	Use a large medkit to heal an injury of 5% or less.	20
Hell in paradise	Complete act I.	30
Ah! Spoiled meat!	Kill a Butcher using an axe.	10
Oh, no you don't	Kill a Ram using tackle skill.	10
Savior	Save 5 people besieged by zombies.	20
How many days exactly?	Play Dead Island at least 28 days after starting it for the first time.	10
No raccoons in here	Complete act II.	30
King of the jungle	Complete act III.	30
Banoi Redemption	Complete act IV.	30
First!	Kill a Suicider with a grenade.	15

DEAD OR ALIVE 5

ACHIEVEMENTS

NAME	GOAL/REQUIREMENT	POINT VALUE
Fighting Entertainment	Have your first fight outside of Training or Versus modes.	10
Rivals	Register 5 fighters in your Fight List.	20
Rival Rumble	Fight online 10 times.	20
Rival Rampage	Fight online 100 times.	30
DOA5 Is My Life	Fight online 1000 times.	50
My Fight, My Rules	Create your own online lobby.	10
Get out there and Fight!	Play a Lobby match.	10
Fighting For Real	Play a Ranked match.	10
Jump In	Play a Simple match.	10
Gesundheit!	Trigger the Special Danger Zone in The Show.	20
Tango Kilo November	Trigger the Special Danger Zone in Hot Zone.	20
You Asked for It!	Fight 10 people through invitations.	20
Anybody, Anytime, Anywhere	Fight 50 people through invitations.	30
First Throwdown	Send a Throwdown Challenge to someone in your Fighter List.	20
Akira Yuki	Unlock Akira.	20
Sarah Bryant	Unlock Sarah.	20
The Ultimate Hyper Clone	Get all titles and unlock Alpha-152.	50
Arcade Cleared	Clear 1 course in Arcade mode.	10
Arcade Master	Clear all courses in Arcade mode.	30
Time Attack Cleared	Clear 1 course in Time Attack mode.	10
Time Attack Master	Clear all courses in Time Attack mode.	30
Survival Cleared	Clear 1 course in Survival mode.	10
Survival Master	Clear all courses in Survival mode.	30
Fledgling Fighter	Fight 10 Versus matches.	20
The Fight Never Ends	Fight 100 Versus matches.	30
Training Hard	Play Training mode for 1 hour.	20
Exercise Newbie	Perform all moves in Command Training.	20
On the Edge of Your Seat	Play Spectator mode.	10
Fighter, Know Thyself	View your results in Fight Record.	10
Ahhh, Memories	View your photos in the Album.	10
Say Cheese!	Take a photo in Spectator mode.	10

NAME	GOAL/REQUIREMENT	POINT VALUE
How Do I Fight?	Display the Move List.	10
How Do I Fight Like a Pro?	Display the Move Details.	10
A Fight to Remember	Save a replay.	10
Safety First	Turn Danger Zones off on the Stage Select screen.	10
Fighting in Style	Unlock all costumes.	50
First Tag Team	Play Tag Battle.	10
The Power of Two	Perform 50 kinds of character-specific tag throws.	30
Blow 'Em Away	Successfully land a Power Blow.	10
Down You Go	Successfully attack during a Cliffhanger.	10
Cliffhanger Comeback	Successfully block an opponent's attack during a Cliffhanger.	10
I Read Every Move	Win without taking any damage.	20
Failure Teaches Success	See all characters' losing poses.	20
Insomniac	Watch all movies in Story mode without skipping any of them.	20
DOA5 Master	Unlock all achievements.	100

SECRET ACHIEVEMENTS

NAME	GOAL/REQUIREMENT	POINT VALUE
The Curtain Rises	Clear the Prologue in Story mode.	10
Ninja Battle	Clear "Kasumi: Part 2" in Story mode.	20
...And Then THIS Happened!	Clear all chapters in Story mode.	30

DEAD SPACE 2

ACHIEVEMENTS

NAME	GOAL/REQUIREMENT	POINT VALUE
Mission Impossible	Complete the game on Zealot setting	50
Romper Stomper	Stomp 10 Containers	25
Vacuum Cleaner	Decompress 20 Necromorphs without getting sucked out yourself	30
Made Us Whole	Complete the game on any difficulty setting	10
Frozen in Time	Kill 50 Necromorphs while they are in Stasis (single player only)	10
First Aid	Use Quick Heal ten times (single player only)	10
Epic Dismemberment	Dismember 2,500 Necromorph Limbs (single player only)	50
...And Stay Down	Kill 25 crawling enemies with Stomp (single player only)	10
Think Fast	Kill 30 Necromorphs with Kinesis objects	15
The Nanny	Kill 30 Crawlers without detonating them	10
C-Section	Knock down an enemy with Contact Beam Alt-Fire then kill it with Primary Fire before it stands up	10
Going for Distance	Impale an enemy and make him fly through the air for 17 meters—it must stick to the surface	20
Taste of your own Medicine	TK Impale a live Slasher to a surface using a Slasher's arm—it must stick to the surface	20
It's a Trap!	Kill 20 enemies with Detonator Mines in a deployed state	20
Necro Flambé	Kill 50 enemies using the Flamethrower	10
Peek a Boo!	Kill a Stalker with the Seeker Rifle while in Zoom Mode	20
Brute Juke	Kill a Brute without taking damage	10
Shoot the Limbs!	Dismember 25 Necromorph Limbs (single player only)	10
Bouncing Betty	Kill a Cyst by catching its Mine and throwing it back	10
Skewered in Space	Impale an enemy into a Decompression Window to cause it to blow out	15
Hard to the Core	Complete the game on Hard Core setting	50
Clean Cut	Sever all three tentacles of a Lurker with one Line Gun Primary Fire shot (single player only)	10
Lawnmower Man	Kill 4 enemies with the same Ripper blade	10

NAME	GOAL/REQUIREMENT	POINT VALUE
Fully Loaded	Simultaneously have four completely upgraded weapons	50
The Sampler Platter	Kill a Necromorph with every Weapon in the game (single player only).	20
Lightspeed de Milo	Dismember the Lightspeed Boy Statue	10
Looking good	Purchase the Advanced Suit	10
Fully Outfitted	Upgrade your RIG and Stasis completely	30
Picking favorites	Upgrade 1 Weapon completely	30
The Engineer	Collect 10 Schematics	10
My Boom Stick	Kill 6 enemies at once with Line Gun's Alt-Fire (single player only)	20
Shock Therapy	Impale an enemy with the Javelin Gun and use its Alt-Fire to shock 3 others (single player only)	10
Collect Peng	Find the Peng treasure	20
The Librarian	Collect 100 logs	10
The Electrician	Collect 10 Semiconductors	10

SECRET ACHIEVEMENTS

NAME	GOAL/REQUIREMENT	POINT VALUE
The Fugitive	Escape the Facility	50
Cross your Heart, Hope to Die	Survive the Eye Poke Machine	30
The Final Sacrifice	Destroy the Marker	50
Clever Girls	Survive your first encounter with Stalkers	10
Torment Me No More	Kill the Tormenter	20
The Graduate	Win the fight at the School	20
Patient on the Loose	Get your first Suit	15
Derailed	Survive the Train Sequence	20
One Small Step	Get through the first Zero-G area	10
Hornet's Nest	Destroy the Tripod Nest	30
Operation!	Snare the Shard with the Ishimura	15
Knock Knock	Complete the Drill Ride	25
Elevator Action	Knock off every Tripod during the Elevator Sequence	15
Shut Down	Defeat the AI	10
Powered Up	Complete the Solar Array Puzzle	15

DOWNLOADABLE CONTENT: SEVERED

NAME	GOAL/REQUIREMENT	POINT VALUE
Grind House	Severed: In the grinder room, cause an enemy to die in the grinders.	20
King of the Hill	Severed: Defend the quarry platform until the door unlocks.	20
Peng Me Again	Severed: Find the Peng treasure in Severed.	20
Remember the Alamo	Severed: Kill 16 or more enemies in the final last stand combat sequence.	20
The Veteran	Severed: Complete on Zealot difficulty.	50

SECRET ACHIEVEMENTS

NAME	GOAL/REQUIREMENT	POINT VALUE
The Betrayal	Severed: Complete Chapter 1.	50
The Sacrifice	Severed: Complete Chapter 2.	50
Ship Shape	Severed: Take out the gunship within 30 seconds.	20

DEUS EX: HUMAN REVOLUTION

ACHIEVEMENTS

NAME	GOAL/REQUIREMENT	POINT VALUE
Cloak & Daggers	Deal with the man in the shadows.	10
Smash the State	Help Officer Nicholas take out the trash.	10
Acquaintances Forgotten	Follow Pritchard's lead to uncover the truth.	10
Doctorate	Read all 29 unique XP books within a single playthrough.	50
Lesser Evil	Deal with Mr. Carella's indiscretion.	10
Motherly Ties	Put a grieving mother's doubts to rest.	10
Corporate Warfare	Protect a client's interests by performing a less-than-hostile takeover.	10
Talion A.D.	Descend into the bowels of an urban jungle and confront a warrior-priest.	10
Gun Nut	Fully upgrade one of your weapons.	20
Bar Tab	Help the Hive Bartender settle a tab.	10
Rotten Business	Help a lady in the oldest of professions clean house.	10
Shanghai Justice	It may take some sleuthing, but justice must be served.	10
Hax0r1!	Successfully hack 50 devices within the same playthrough.	15
Transhumanist	Fully upgrade your first augmentation of choice.	5
Consciousness is Over-rated	Knock out 100 enemies in a single playthrough.	15
First Takedown	Perform your first Takedown. Civilians don't count, so be nice.	5
Opportunist	Perform 50 takedowns within the same playthrough. (Civilians don't count.)	15
First Hack	Perform your first Hack successfully.	5
Deus Ex Machina	Experience all the different endings that Deus Ex: Human Revolution has to offer.	50
Pacifist	Complete Deus Ex: Human Revolution without anyone dying by your hand. (Boss fights don't count.)	100
Foxiest of the Hounds	Complete Deus Ex: Human Revolution without setting off any alarms.	100
Up the Ante!	Upgrade your first weapon of choice.	15
Trooper	Complete Deus Ex: Human Revolution.	50
Legend	Complete Deus Ex: Human Revolution at its hardest setting without ever changing the difficulty.	100

SECRET ACHIEVEMENTS

NAME	GOAL/REQUIREMENT	POINT VALUE
Ghost	You made it through an entire hostile area without so much as a squeak.	15
Sentimental Value	You kept Megan's bracelet for yourself. Apparently, letting go really is the hardest part.	10
The Take	Greedy bastard. You accepted O'Malley's blood money and let him go.	10
Guardian Angel	You paid poor Jaya's debt in full. How very... humane... of you.	10
The D Project	You watched the entire credit list and saw the surprise at the end.	15
Good Soul	Against all odds, you saved Faridah Malik's life.	15
Hangar 18	You found and read the secret message. Now you know too much...	10
Super Sleuth	You really nailed your case against Lee Hong.	10
Ladies Man	You convinced Mengyao to spill the beans on the mysterious Hyron Project.	10
Balls	Seems you like playing with balls, eh?	5
Lucky Guess	Next time, Jacob better use a more complex code to arm his bombs.	10
Kevorkian Complex	You granted a dying man his final request.	10
The Fall	You sent Diamond Chan on the trip of a lifetime.	10
The End	You defeated Zhao Yun Ru and destroyed the Hyron Project.	25

NAME	GOAL/REQUIREMENT	POINT VALUE
Old School Gamer	You found all the hidden story items in Megan's office. Point and Click much?	10
Unforeseen Consequence	You convinced Zeke Sanders to let his hostage go.	15
The Bull	You defeated Lawrence Barrett, elite member of a secret mercenary hit squad.	25
The Mantis	You defeated Yelena Fedorova, elite member of a secret mercenary hit squad.	25
The Snake	You defeated Jaron Namir, Leader of Belltower's Elite Special Operations Unit.	25
The Throwdown	You convinced the smooth-talking politician Bill Taggart to tell the truth in public.	15
The Last Straw	You talked Doctor Isaias Sandoval out of suicide.	15
The Final Countdown	You showed millionaire Hugh Darrow that his logic was flawed.	15
The Desk Job	You convinced Wayne Haas to let you into the morgue.	15
Yes Boss	You had an argument with your boss, David Sarif, and won.	15
Darker Shades	You convinced a fast-talking bartender to let you see Tong Si Hung.	15

DLC: THE MISSING LINK

ACHIEVEMENTS

NAME	GOAL/REQUIREMENT	POINT VALUE
Factory Zero	You survived The Missing Link using no Praxis kits, weapons, or explosives. Whoa.	70
Never Stop Looking	You escaped Rifleman Bank Station. Nothing will stop you from finding Megan now.	20

SECRET ACHIEVEMENTS

NAME	GOAL/REQUIREMENT	POINT VALUE
Good Samaritan	You replaced the power supply on a damaged stasis pod, saving the occupants life.	20
Never Forget	You revisited the site where Belltower discovered and captured you.	20
Out of the Frying Pan	You made it off the boat… but to what end?	20
The learn'd Scholar	When the proofs, the figures, were ranged in columns before me…	20
All of the Above	You managed to save Dr. Kavanagh and all the prisoners, too.	20
Back Stage Pass	You gained access to Quinn's secret store.	20
Apex Predator	You performed a takedown on Burke without being detected.	20
That Old Adage	Apparently, your CASIE augmentation doesn't work on everyone…	20

DISHONORED

ACHIEVEMENTS

NAME	GOAL/REQUIREMENT	POINT VALUE
Thief	You pickpocketed items worth a total of 200 coins	20
Versatile	You killed characters with each weapon and offensive gadget	20
Ghost	You completed all missions after the prologue, alerting or killing no one but key targets	30
Shadow	You completed all missions after the prologue without alerting anyone	30
Mostly Flesh and Steel	You finished the game without purchasing any supernatural powers or enhancements, besides Blink	50
Wall of Sparks	You killed an enemy with the Wall of Light	10
Rogue	You assassinated 10 unaware enemies	10
Specter	After escaping prison, you completed a mission, not alerting anyone and killing less than 5 people	20

NAME	GOAL/REQUIREMENT	POINT VALUE
Faceless	After escaping Coldridge Prison, you completed a mission without alerting anyone	20
Manipulator	You made others kill 5 of their own allies	10
Razor Rain	You killed 5 characters with Drop Assassination	10
Surgical	You played from the first mission through Kaldwin's Bridge killing fewer than 10 characters	30
Clean Hands	You completed the game without killing anyone	100
Harm's Way	You caused 5 unintentional suicides	10
Inhabitant	You stayed in possession of others for most of a 3 minute period	10
Hornets' Nest	You killed 4 enemies in less than 1 second using the crossbow	20
Speed of Darkness	You traveled 30 meters in less than 1 second	10
Tempest	You killed 6 enemies in less than 1 second	20
Merchant of Disorder	You acquired 15 equipment upgrades	20
Art Dealer	You collected all the Sokolov paintings	50
Occultist	You collected 10 bone charms	20
The Escapist	After Coldridge Prison, you eluded 5 pursuers at once without killing them or leaving the map	10
Cleaner	You fought 5 enemies at once and none of them survived	10
Dishonored	You escaped Coldridge Prison	5
Excommunication	You eliminated High Overseer Campbell	5
Child Care	You located Lady Emily Kaldwin, heir to the throne	10
Capturing Genius and Madness	You abducted Anton Sokolov, Royal Physician	10
Regicide	You assassinated the Lord Regent, Hiram Burrows	10
Political Suicide	You brought about the Lord Regent's fall from grace by broadcasting his crimes	10
This Is Mine	You recovered your belongings	10
Resolution	You completed the game	100
Back Home	You grabbed a live grenade and threw it back, killing an attacker	10
Big Boy	You killed a tallboy using only your sword	20

SECRET ACHIEVEMENTS

NAME	GOAL/REQUIREMENT	POINT VALUE
Dunwall in Chaos	You completed the game in high chaos	50
Just Dark Enough	You completed the game in low chaos	50
Vanished	You escaped prison and navigated the sewers undetected	10
Gentleman Caller	You completed all the Granny Rags side missions	10
Street Conspiracy	You completed all the Slackjaw side missions	10
The Art of the Steal	You got the Art Dealer's safe combination for Slackjaw, but robbed the safe first	10
An Unfortunate Accident	You killed Morgan Pendleton with steam	10
Well Mannered	You completed the Boyle Estate mission without spoiling the party	10
King of the World	You reached the top of Kaldwin's Bridge	10
Bodyguard	You protected Callista's uncle, Captain Geoff Curnow	10
Mercy is the Mark	You spared Daud's life	10
Lights Out	You deactivated at least 5 security systems on Kingsparrow Island	10
Long Live the Empress	You saved Empress Emily Kaldwin	10
Poetic Justice	You neutralized all key targets using indirect means	30
Food Chain	You assassinated an assassin	10
Alive Without Breath	You took possession of a fish	10
Creepy Crawly	You used a rat tunnel	10

DOOM 3 BFG EDITION

ACHIEVEMENTS

NAME	GOAL/REQUIREMENT	POINT VALUE
DOOMed Recruit	Complete the DOOM 3 single player campaign on Recruit	5
DOOMed Marine	Complete the DOOM 3 single player campaign on Marine	10
DOOMed Veteran	Complete the DOOM 3 single player campaign on Veteran	15
DOOMed Nightmare	Complete the DOOM 3 single player campaign on Nightmare	20
DOOMed Collector	Collect every PDA in DOOM 3	15
I Like to Watch	Find all video logs in DOOM 3	15
That was Close!	Kill an enemy with 1 health remaining in DOOM 3, RoE, or Lost Mission	15
Goody Finder	Open all storage lockers in DOOM 3	15
Unarmed Badass	Kill 20 enemies with the fists/melee hands in DOOM 3	10
To Be or Not to Be	Kill the scientist trapped next to the Reactor Control Room in DOOM 3	5
Double the Fun!	Kill 2 Imps with one shotgun blast in DOOM 3, RoE, or Lost Mission	10
Killing time	Score 25000 on Super Turbo Turkey Puncher 3 in DOOM 3 or RoE	5
Boomtastic	Blow up 50 barrels in the DOOM 3, RoE, or Lost Mission campaigns	10
Ready for Action!	Get the BFG-9000 from Security Chief's office in DOOM 3	10
Not a Scratch	Complete a level without taking any damage in DOOM 3, RoE, or Lost Mission (except Mars City)	20
RAGE	Find the RAGE logo in the Lost Mission	10
Speed Run	Complete the DOOM 3 single player campaign in 10 hours or less	20
Sticky Situation	Defeat the Vagary boss in DOOM 3	15
Cookie Stealer	Defeat Guardian boss in DOOM 3	15
You're Not My Boss!	Defeat Sabaoth boss in DOOM 3	15
Big Boy	Defeat Cyberdemon boss in DOOM 3	15
Bot Buddy	Keep a Sentry Bot alive to its destination in DOOM 3, RoE, or Lost Mission (except Mars City)	10
Ripped!	Use the chainsaw to kill 20 enemies in DOOM 3	10
All of Us	Find the id logo secret room in DOOM 3	10
You Laugh, It Works	Find the bloody handiwork of Betruger (in Delta 4 Hallway) in DOOM 3	5
Turncoat	Get 2 demons to fight each other in DOOM 3, RoE, or Lost Mission	10
Soulfood	Use the Soul Cube to defeat 20 enemies in DOOM 3	10
Evil Recruit	Complete the RoE campaign on Recruit	5
Evil Marine	Complete the RoE campaign on Marine	10
Evil Veteran	Complete the RoE campaign on Veteran	15
Evil Nightmare	Complete the RoE campaign on Nightmare	20
Evil Collector	Collect every PDA in the RoE campaign	10
Too Slow, Fool!	Kill 5 enemies at once while in Hell Time in RoE	10
Gimme Time!	Defeat the Helltime Hunter in RoE	15
Gimme Power!	Defeat the Berserk Hunter in RoE	15
Shocking!	Defeat the Invulnerability Hunter in RoE	15
Eat This!	Defeat the Maledict boss in RoE	15
Play Catch	Kill 20 enemies with projectiles launched from the Grabber in RoE	10
Fists of Fury	Use the Artifact with Berserk ability to punch out 20 enemies in RoE	10
Lost Recruit	Complete the Lost Mission campaign on Recruit	5
Lost Marine	Complete the Lost Mission campaign on Marine	10
Lost Veteran	Complete the Lost Mission campaign on Veteran	15
Lost Nightmare	Complete the Lost Mission campaign on Nightmare	20
Lost Collector	Collect every PDA in the Lost Mission campaign	10

NAME	GOAL/REQUIREMENT	POINT VALUE
Telefragged!	Kill an enemy player by jumping into a teleporter after them in DOOM 3 Multiplayer	10
Crushed!	Catch an enemy player in the Reactor of Frag Chamber in DOOM 3 Multiplayer	10
Ninja Killer	Kill 5 enemy players while using Invisibility in DOOM 3 Multiplayer	10
Clean Sheet	Complete a DOOM 3 Multiplayer match without dying	15
Berserked!	Use Berserk to kill a player in DOOM 3 Multiplayer	10
2 Deaths - 1 Gun	Kill two enemies in the same room with a rocket in DOOM 3 Multiplayer	10

DRAGON AGE II

ACHIEVEMENTS

NAME	GOAL/REQUIREMENT	POINT VALUE
Master Craftsman	Crafted all of the items from a single crafting tree.	25
Mogul	Had 100 or more sovereigns in your purse.	25
Crowning Glory	Became the viscount of Kirkwall.	25
Dedicated	Reached Level 10.	15
A Friend in Need	Upgraded the armor of one of your party members.	5
Enchanter	Enchanted an item.	5
Immigrant	Became a resident of Kirkwall.	5
Delver of the Deep	Explored the Deep Roads.	10
Birthright	Kicked the slavers out of your ancestral mansion.	15
Specialized	Learned two class specializations.	25
I Got Your Back	Completely upgraded the armor of one of your party members.	25
Legendary	Reached Level 20.	50
Financier	Became a partner in a Deep Roads expedition.	10
Talented	Upgraded a spell or talent.	5
Tag Team	Used teamwork to perform a cross-class combo.	5
That Thing Has Legs	Found and killed a varterral.	25
Weapon Master	Mastered a weapon style.	25
Unstoppable	Completed a full year in Kirkwall without any party member being knocked unconscious.	50
Craftsman	Acquired your first crafting recipe.	5
Dragon Slayer	Found and killed a high dragon.	25
Exorcist	Found and killed the undying Xebenkeck.	25
Demon Slayer	Found and killed the ancient demon, Hybris.	25
Chantry Historian	Found all four chapters of "The History of the Chantry," by Brother Genitivi.	25
A Worthy Rival	Earned the Arishok's respect.	25
Great Minds Think Alike	Earned the friendship or rivalry of four party members.	50
Friend	Earned the friendship of one of your party members.	25
Rival	Earned the rivalry of one of your party members.	25
Romantic	Completed a romance with one of your party members.	25
Epic	Completed Dragon Age II twice, or completed it once with a save imported from Dragon Age Origins.	50
Champion of Kirkwall	Completed Dragon Age II.	20
Mercenary	Allied yourself with the mercenaries upon arriving in Kirkwall.	10
Nefarious	Allied yourself with the smugglers upon arriving in Kirkwall.	10
Flirtatious	Flirted with one of your party members to begin a romance.	5
Mass Exodus	Reached Kirkwall with each character class across multiple playthroughs.	25
Knowledgeable	Unlocked 100 codex entries.	25
Treasure Hunter	Opened 50 chests.	25
Darkness Falls	Toggled the map from day to night.	5
Explorer	Left Kirkwall to explore the outlying regions.	5
Spelunker	Visited 10 caves in Kirkwall and the surrounding area.	25
Full House	Recruited four party members.	10

NAME	GOAL/REQUIREMENT	POINT VALUE
Friends in High Places	Met Grand Cleric Elthina, Viscount Dumar, Knight-Commander Meredith, and First Enchanter Orsino.	15
Gift Giver	Gave a gift to one of your party members.	5
Supplier	Found every variety of crafting resources.	25
Archeologist	During each year in Kirkwall, discovered 3 secret messages from the Band of Three.	50
Tale Within a Tale	Listened to Varric begin his tale of the Champion of Kirkwall.	5

SECRET ACHIEVEMENTS

NAME	GOAL/REQUIREMENT	POINT VALUE
Stone Cold	Defeated the rock wraith on your expedition into the Deep Roads.	5
King of the Hill	Defeated the Arishok.	10
Conqueror	Defeated Meredith, knight-commander of Kirkwall's templars.	15
Arcane Defender	Sided with the mages five times.	25
Mage Hunter	Sided with the templars five times.	25

DOWNLOADABLE CONTENT: THE EXILED PRINCE

NAME	GOAL/REQUIREMENT	POINT VALUE
Avenged	Confront the culprit behind the Vael family's murder.	25
Cloak and Dagger	Meet secretly with the agent of the Divine	25
Loyalty of the Prince	Earn either a friendship or rivalry with Sebastian.	30
Memento	Give Sebastian a family heirloom.	25

SECRET ACHIEVEMENTS

NAME	GOAL/REQUIREMENT	POINT VALUE
Retribution	Dealt with the mercenaries that killed the Vael family.	25

DRAGON'S DOGMA

ACHIEVEMENTS

NAME	GOAL/REQUIREMENT	POINT VALUE
The Patron	Helped Madeleine open her shop.	15
The Coin Collector	Earned a total of 10,000,000G.	30
The Ever-Turning Wheel	Completed the adventure a second time.	50
The Explorer	Visited 150 locations.	35
The Vagabond	Visited 100 locations.	20
The Tourist	Visited 50 locations.	10
Into the Frontier Caverns	Entered the southwestern caves.	15
Into the Manse	Entered the duke's manse.	20
Into Soulflayer Canyon	Entered the Soulflayer Canyon.	15
Into the Ancient Quarry	Entered the ancient quarry.	10
Into Dripstone Cave	Entered the azure caverns.	10
Affinity and Beyond	Raised a person's affinity to the maximum.	10
The Escort	Acted as a reliable travel companion.	10
The Philanthropist	Gave 50 presents.	15
A Queen's Regalia	Dressed a male party member in women's clothing.	20
Well Equipped	Obtained 350 pieces total of weapons and armor.	30
The Artisan	Combined two materials to make an item.	10
The Knave	Obtained a forgery.	15
The Savior	Used a Wakestone to restore the dead to life.	10
Inhuman Resources	Changed your main pawn's vocation.	20
The Captain	Enlisted a large number of pawns.	15
Foreign Recruit	Enlisted a pawn to your party from beyond the rift.	5
Local Recruit	Directly enlisted a pawn to your party.	5
The Veteran	Defeated 3,000 enemies.	35

NAME	GOAL/REQUIREMENT	POINT VALUE
The Specialist	Learned all the skills of a single vocation.	40
Human Resources	Changed your vocation.	20
The Hero	Completed all pre-planned, non-notice board quests.	40
The Laborer	Completed 50 notice board quests.	20

SECRET ACHIEVEMENTS

NAME	GOAL/REQUIREMENT	POINT VALUE
Dragon Forged	Strengthened equipment in wyrmfire.	30
The Messiah	Defeated the Ur-Dragon.	50
Serpents' Bane	Defeated a drake, wyrm, and wyvern.	40
Eye Contact	Defeated an evil eye.	30
Headshunter	Defeated a hydra or archydra.	30
Closure	Put an end to all things.	40
Peace	Took refuge in an illusion.	20
Servitude	Soar unto a new world.	20
Solitude	Obtained the almighty power of sovereignty.	20
Mercy	Dealt the blow of deliverance.	30
Freedom	Escaped the yoke of eternity.	10
Treacherous	Peered into the very depths of the world.	10
Destiny	Accepted the Godsbane blade.	25
Rough Landing	Completed the urgent mission.	10
The Message	Received the duke's commendation.	15
Come Courting	Attended an audience with the duke.	15
Writ Large	Received a writ from the castle.	10
The Courier	Entered Gran Soren.	10
Getting a Head	Earned the approval of the Enlistment Corps.	15
A New Ally	Summoned your own pawn.	10
Onward	Departed from Cassardis.	5
It Begins	Completed the prologue.	5

FABLE HEROES

ACHIEVEMENTS

NAME	GOAL/REQUIREMENT	POINT VALUE
Rolled the Dice	Visit a tile on the Abilities Board. This also unlocks a tile on the Inner Board.	5
Better When Shared	Complete a level as part of a four-player team. This also unlocks a tile on the Inner Board.	5
Cast Party	Unlock all the playable characters. This also unlocks a tile on the Inner Board.	20
Rule the Dice	Purchase all abilities for one puppet. This also unlocks a tile on the Inner Board.	10
Bully	Kick a hobblet, then shoot it out of the air. This also unlocks a tile on the Inner Board.	5
Veg Head	Hit an enemy with its own head. This also unlocks a tile on the Inner Board.	5
Traitor	Kill a Hobbe while disguised as a Hobbe. This also unlocks a tile on the Inner Board.	5
Can't See the Future	Complete a 'Challenging' level in 'No HUD' mode. This also unlocks a tile on the Inner Board.	5
One Down	Buy all abilities on a single tile. This also unlocks a tile on the Inner Board.	5
Puppet Beats Chicken	Complete the Chicken Bomb Mini-Game without getting hurt. This unlocks a tile on the Inner Board.	10
Fast & Furious	Complete the Mine Cart Mini-Game in under 13 seconds. This unlocks a tile on the Inner Board.	5
World Champion	Achieve a Gold Medal in every level. This also unlocks a tile on the Inner Board.	20
Heroes of Millfields	Complete Millfields in the world of Albion.	10
Heroes of Gravestone	Complete Gravestone in the world of Albion.	10
Heroes of Mistpeak	Complete Mistpeak in the world of Albion.	10

NAME	GOAL/REQUIREMENT	POINT VALUE
Ruler of Albion	Complete all levels in the world of Albion.	20
Heroes of Bowerstone	Complete Bowerstone in the world of Albion.	10
Heroes of Aurora	Complete Aurora in the world of Albion.	10
Heroes of The Credits	Complete The Credits in the world of Albion.	10
Ruler of Dark Albion	Complete all levels in the world of Dark Albion.	40
Heroes of The Cloud	Complete The Cloud in the world of Albion.	10
Heroes of Hobbe Caves	Complete Hobbe Caves in the world of Albion.	10
Heroes of Dark Millfields	Complete Millfields in Dark Albion without being hit!	20
Heroes of Dark Gravestone	Complete Gravestone in Dark Albion with Big Heads mode enabled!	20
Heroes of Dark Mistpeak	Complete Mistpeak in Dark Albion with a Perk activated!	20
Heroes of Dark Hobbe Caves	Complete Hobbe Caves in Dark Albion and finish in first place!	20
Heroes of Dark Bowerstone	Complete Bowerstone in Dark Albion on Challenging and without dying!	20
Heroes of Dark Aurora	Complete Aurora in Dark Albion and use at least three Power-Ups!	20
Heroes of The Dark Credits	Complete The Credits in Dark Albion and smash 20 Lionhead developers!	20
Heroes of The Dark Cloud	Complete The Cloud in Dark Albion and make your head POP!	20

FABLE: THE JOURNEY

ACHIEVEMENTS

NAME	GOAL/REQUIREMENT	POINT VALUE
Pest Control	Ten stingers in five seconds. How long for the other 600,000?	10
Hobbe Juggler	You juggled a hobbe. A career in the circus awaits. A pretty odd circus, admittedly.	10
Boom-erang	You killed a hobbe with his own bomb. 'Tis the sport to have the enginer hoist with his own petar.	10
The Whites of Their Eyes	You got cosy with a balverine. You must have nerves of steel[md]and no working olfactory system.	10
Return of the Black Knight	You dismantled a hollow man. It's just a (rotting) flesh-wound!	10
Trollololol	You emerged unscathed from a troll fight. Problem?	20
B-B-Q	Roast chicken is the best smell in the world. Unless you're a chicken.	10
Great Balls of Fire	You killed three enemies with one Fireball. Goodness gracious.	10
Shardly a Problem	You cast Shards with utmost precision. For your next trick, spear an apple off Seren's head.	10
Five Billion Candle Power	You burned the Corruption from three creatures with one spell. Time to break out the factor 40.	10
Mind Your Manas	You dished out a veritable smorgasbord of spell power. Delicious.	20
Toasty	Burning through the sky at 200 degrees. That's why they call him Mr. Pushed-in-the-Lava.	10
Bam!	There it is! You killed ten creatures with explosive barrels.	20
Flail	You killed 500 enemies. The Grim Reaper loves round numbers.	20
Epic Flail	1,000 kills! That's a lot of killing. You should have a lie down. And a shower.	40
Fore!	You killed three enemies with thrown objects. Down in front!	10
Reflectology	You killed 15 enemies with their own attacks. Reflect on your progress, and feel proud.	20
Fear of Flying	You killed 20 enemies in midair. Flying's fine – it's landing that hurts. Also, the magic spells.	30
Hard Shoulder	You dealt with a travelling enemy by making it crash and die. Ben Hur would be proud.	10

NAME	GOAL/REQUIREMENT	POINT VALUE
Roadkill	You ran down an enemy with your cart. Consider investing in a plough.	10
Cartmageddon	A good driver keeps their hands on the reins at all times, apart from when they're killing things.	20
Pimp My Cart	Yo Gabe, we heard you like Heroes so we hung a Hero from your cart so you can Hero while you Hero.	5
Wheeee!	You thrust your arms in the air during the minecart ride. Souvenir photo available in the gift shop.	5
I Used to Be an Adventurer	Then I took an arrow to the horse. She's all better now, though.	10
Happy Camper	You tried your hand at all camp activities. Way to go, cowboy.	20
Why the Long Face?	You healed ten wounds on Seren. If she walked into a bar and bruised herself, you'd heal that too.	10
Long Sustained Attacks	You fully upgraded one of your spells. You'll be able to bring down anything now.	30
Sparrow	You purchased five upgrades. Your Journey has begun.	10
Chicken Chaser	You purchased ten upgrades. Your powers are beginning to soar. Soar like a chicken.	20
Hero	You purchased 15 upgrades. Truly, you are a Hero.	30
For Every Chest, a Consequence	You opened 15 chests. Now on to the greater mystery: Whose stuff have you been stealing?	30
Test Your Medal	You earned your first Medal in Arcade Mode.	10
Heavy Medal	You earned a Bronze Medal in every Arcade Mode challenge.	20
Pedal to the Medal	You earned a Silver Medal in every Arcade Mode challenge.	40
Medal Gear Solid	You earned a Gold Medal in every Arcade Mode challenge.	60
No Claims Bonus	You completed The Last Stand without taking any damage.	20
Off the Chain	You achieved a kill chain of 40 during Arcade Mode.	20
If I Only Had a Brain	You whiled away the hours, conferring with the flowers. And exploding scarecrows' heads.	30
The Open Road	Your story has begun, but where will the road lead you?	20
Saved by the Sun	You escaped the Devourer... for now.	20
In the Palm of Your Hand	The power of the gauntlets is now yours, but so is their burden.	20
Footloose	You rescued Fergus from a spot of Hobbe bother. Your reward? Singing and beans.	20
Shoo!	You made it to the barn and saw off the White Balverine (with a little help from your friends).	20
Off the Menu	The Devourer has been defeated, and Fergus is at rest. There's no turning back now, Hero.	20
Going Underground	You made it out of Bladebarrow. Most don't.	20
Alas, Poor Nodsy!	You laid to rest the spirits of a platoon of morons. They're another dimension's problem now.	20
A Job for Life	You destroyed a man's livelihood and smashed something up while you were at it. You're a true Hero.	10
Mind over Matter	The Temptress is no more. Or was it all just a dream?	20
The Long Road Home	You finally caught up with Katlan. It's you who's needed at the front of the convoy now.	20
Don't Stop Believing	You have completed your Journey. The Spire is no more, and a new dawn awaits Albion.	100

FIFA 12

ACHIEVEMENTS

NAME	GOAL/REQUIREMENT	POINT VALUE
Precision Tackler	Obtain a successful tackle percentage of 80% with a minimum of 5 tackles in a game	15
Megged	Successfully dribble the ball through a defender's legs	30
Riding Bikes	Score with a bicycle kick	50
Legendary	Win a game vs. the CPU on legendary difficulty against a club of the same or higher star level	30

NAME	GOAL/REQUIREMENT	POINT VALUE
Don't Blink	Score within the first 5 minutes of a game in a game vs the CPU	10
Comeback Kid	Win after being down 3 goals in the 2nd half in a game vs. the CPU	15
10 vs 11	Win from a draw or behind while down a man in a game vs the CPU	10
Ruud Boy	Score a goal on a volley	15
Block Party	Manually block 5 shots while defending in a single game	10
Century of Goals	Score 100 goals in FIFA 12 match play	45
All My Own Work	Win a Match with Manual Controls (including Tactical Defending)	10
Warrior	Score a goal after suffering a non-contact injury with a player	20
Quickly Now!	Score shortly after a quick throw-in	20
EAS FC Youth Academy	Reach level 5 in the EA SPORTS Football Club	10
EAS FC Starting 11	Reach level 20 in the EA SPORTS Football Club	30
Challenge Accepted	Complete an EA SPORTS Football Club Game Scenario Challenge	15
Path to the Cup	Win a cup game in Head to Head Seasons	20
Campaign Complete	Complete a Season in Head to Head Seasons	50
Friends now Enemies?	Win an Online Friendlies season	25
Being Social	Play an Online Friendlies Match	10
3 Points	Win a season game in Head to Head Seasons	10
Virtual Debut	Play an online Pro Club or Pro Ranked match with your Virtual Pro	10
New Club in Town	Create your FIFA 12 Ultimate Team club	5
Legends start with Victories	Win a match with your FIFA 12 Ultimate Team club	10
Tournament Victory	Win a tournament in FIFA 12 Ultimate Team	10
I'll have that one	Open your first pack in FIFA 12 Ultimate Team	10
Friendly	Finish a match against a Friend in FIFA 12 Ultimate Team	10
Marquee Signing	Purchase a Gold Player from the trade market for 15,000 or more coins using Buy now	30
Growing Club	Achieve a club value of 85,000,000 in FIFA 12 Ultimate Team	30
Big Cup Squad	Enter an Ultimate Team tournament and finish a match with an overall squad rating of 85 or higher	30
Pack King	Open 100 packs in FIFA 12 Ultimate Team	50
We'll need a larger trophy case	Win your 10th trophy in FIFA 12 Ultimate Team	30
Club Legend	Play 100 matches with any player in FIFA 12 Ultimate Team	15
Trophy Time	Win the league title in any league in Career Mode	50
Procrastinator	Sign a player on Deadline Day in the transfer window in Career Mode	15
Fully Formed	Have three players be in full form at the same time on your club in Career Mode	30
Massive Signing	Sign a player better than anyone else on your club during the transfer window	20
Youth is Served	Sign a player to your youth squad in Career Mode	20
Puppet Master	Talk to the Press in Career Mode	10
Sweet Music	Set up some Custom Audio in FIFA 12	10
Virtual Legend	Play 50 Matches with your Virtual Pro	50
FIFA for Life	Spend 50 hours on the pitch	50
Happy 20th EA SPORTS!	Score 20 match goals in FIFA 12 to celebrate 20 years of EA SPORTS!	20

SECRET ACHIEVEMENTS

NAME	GOAL/REQUIREMENT	POINT VALUE
No Draw for You!	Score a 90th minute winner in a game vs. the CPU	15
How Great is that?	Find a team of the week player in an Ultimate Team pack	20

FIFA 13

ACHIEVEMENTS

NAME	GOAL/REQUIREMENT	POINT VALUE
Bronzed	Complete the Bronze stage of all Skills	30
Skill Legend	Become Legendary on one of the Skill Challenges	50
Road to Mastery	Unlock a Skill Challenge	30
Trolling for Goals	Score on a free kick after running over the ball	15
No Goal for You!	Goal Line Clearance	30
Creeping on the Down Low	Wall creep, free kick is blocked by wall	5
Body Control	Score an off balance shot	5
Cheeky	Chip the Keeper	5
Get In!	Score a Diving Header	15
Brains and Brawn	Shield the ball out of play for a goal kick	15
Road to Promotion	Win a FUT Seasons Match	10
Get Physical	Seal out an attacking player to gain possession of the ball	5
1 week	Win all the EAS FC Match Day Games of the Week in a single week	15
Go Live!	Win an EAS FC Match Day Live Fixture	15
Getting Real	Play 25 EAS FC Match Day Games	30
Division King	Win a Division title in Seasons	50
Filling Cabinets	Win a Cup in Seasons	30
Hello World	Play your first match with your Online Pro	5
On the Rise	Earn a Promotion in Seasons	25
One of the Bros	Be part of a Club win	15
Bros	Play a Seasons game with a Guest	15
Good Start	Unlock 10% of the accomplishments with your Online Pro	30
Well on Your Way	Unlock 25% of the accomplishments with your Online Pro	50
Still Friends?	Win an Online Friendlies Season	30
Mr. Manager	Take Control of your own FIFA Ultimate Team	10
Silverware	Win a Trophy in a FUT Competition	10
Building My Club	Claim your first FUT Pack	10
Press Conference	Purchase a gold player in the Auction House for 15,000 or more coins using buy it now	30
I Love This Club	Achieve a club value of 85,000,000	30
Promoted!	Earn promotion in FUT Seasons	30
Pack King	Open 50 FUT Packs	50
Challenge Accepted	Win a match against the team of the week	30
So Euro	Enable European competition in the first season of Career	5
For Country	Become manager of an international team	20
Way with Words	Successfully request additional funds from your board in Career	5
National Pride	Get called up to the national team as a player	30
Wheeling and Dealing	Complete a Player + cash deal in Career	15
Impressive	Achieve one of your season objectives as a player at any point in your career	50
Nice Form	Achieve your match set objective as player at any point in your career	30
Digi-Me	Start your Player Career with a Created Pro	5
Packing Bags	Go out on loan or transfer to another club with your Pro in Play as Player	15
Master Negotiator	Sell a player by getting your counter offer accepted by the CPU	10
Maxed Out	Reach the daily limit of XP in the EA SPORTS Football Club	10
EASFC Youth Academy	Reach level 5 in the EA SPORTS Football Club	10
EASFC Starting 11	Reach level 20 in the EA SPORTS Football Club	30
Challenging	Complete an EA SPORTS Football Club Challenge	10
Big Spender	Redeem an item with EAS FC Football Club Credits.	10

SECRET ACHIEVEMENTS

NAME	GOAL/REQUIREMENT	POINT VALUE
In Form!	Find a team of the week player in a pack	20

FIFA STREET

ACHIEVEMENTS

NAME	GOAL/REQUIREMENT	POINT VALUE
Got any Nutmeg?	Panna your first Opponent	15
Rush Keepers!	Score a goal while controlling your Goal Keeper	25
Very Entertaining	Earn at least 1500 Style Points without losing possession	25
Sightseer	In any game mode win a match/event in 50% of the venues as the lead profile	25
Globetrotter	In any game mode win a match/event in every venue as the lead profile	95
Geometry was good for something	Score a goal by deflecting the ball off a wall	20
Ultimate Humiliation	Score a goal with a Panna	15
Are we there yet?	Reach the World Tour map screen for the first time as the lead profile	10
New Champion	Win a World Tour Tournament for the first time as the lead profile	15
Regional Street Champion	Win stage 1 of World Tour as the lead profile	20
National Street Champion	Win stage 2 of World Tour as the lead profile	25
European Champion	Win stage 3 of World Tour as the lead profile	50
World Grand Champion	Win stage 4 of World Tour as the lead profile	100
World Tour Around the World	Win any World Tour tournament Online as the lead profile	30
Challenge the pros	Win a street challenge against an authentic club team in stage 4 of world tour as the lead profile	20
Street Legend	Defeat Messi in a street challenge game as the lead profile	20
Local Heroes	Win the final national tournament with at least 8 created players on your team as the lead profile	25
Who brought the snacks?	Win a tournament with a local Co-Op player as the lead profile	15
Mighty Heroes	Have a team with at least 8 created players that are level 50 or higher as the lead profile	40
Career Milestone	Score 100 goals with your created player in any game modes as the lead profile	25
Mister Entertainment	Earn 100,000 Style Points with your created player in any game mode as the lead profile	25
Attributed Success	Upgrade one of your created players attributes to Max as the lead profile	25
It's Tricky	Unlock 10 tricks on a created player as the lead profile	20
5 Tool Player	Upgrade 5 attributes on a created player to maximum as the lead profile	50
Time to Celebrate	Unlock a created player celebration and perform it in game as the lead profile	15
Shopping Spree	Wear an Unlocked item in any game mode as the lead profile	10
Moving on up	In a street season obtain promotion to the next division as the lead profile	25
Online Enthusiast	Win a game of 5 a side, 6 a side and Futsal online as the lead profile	20
Online Cup Champion	Win any Online Cup as the lead profile	25
Online Dominance	Win all 9 online cups as the lead profile	100
Video Proof	Upload a saved video as the lead profile	20
Friendly Publicity	Watch a video posted by one of your Friends as the lead profile	15

NAME	GOAL/REQUIREMENT	POINT VALUE
Making new friends	Add a new Friend using the Friend Recommendation feature as the lead profile	15
Watching Film	Watch a gameplay tutorial video as the lead profile	20

FORZA HORIZON

ACHIEVEMENTS

NAME	GOAL/REQUIREMENT	POINT VALUE
Welcome to Horizon	You arrived at Horizon Festival raring to go.	10
Take Her for a Spin!	You bought a car from the Autoshow. Now take her for a spin!	15
...and across the line!	You competed in your first race at Horizon.	10
First!	You won your first race at Horizon.	20
Born Slippy	You've won your first Mixed-Surface or Dirt Race.	10
WARNING!!! DANGER TO MANIFOLD	You've won 10 Street Races. Ali would be proud.	15
#WINNING!	You've dominated 10 Festival Races.	15
Close Encounters	You've challenged and beaten 10 festival racers on the spot.	20
Lawbreaker	You blasted past 5 speed traps and 5 speed zones.	10
Vendetta	You've beaten a Rival time in 10 events.	20
Been There, Done That!	You've fully explored the Horizon Festival Loop.	10
Rave Paint	You created a paintjob and your ride is looking SWEET!	10
Wheelin' 'n Dealin'	You sold something via your Storefront. KERCHING!	10
May The Forza Be With You	You received free cars for being a loyal Forza fan!	10
One to Watch	You're the 200th most popular driver at Horizon.	10
The Next Big Thing	You're the 100th most popular driver at Horizon.	15
Almost Famous	You're the 50th most popular driver at Horizon.	20
Killer Skills	You're the 10th most popular driver at Horizon.	25
Notorious	You're the most popular driver at Horizon.	30
A Wristed Development	You received your Yellow Wristband.	20
Going Green	You received your Green Wristband.	25
Out of the Blue	You received your Blue Wristband.	30
Racing for Pinks	You received your Pink Wristband.	35
Freshly Squeezed	You received your Orange Wristband.	40
Purple Reign	You received your Purple Wristband.	45
Golden Boy	You received the Golden Wristband.	50
Darius Who?	You owned Darius Flynt and became the Horizon Festival champion.	100
Hard Driving	You finished in first place on HARD? Nice.	10
Gettin' It Done	You rocked every single Festival Event.	30
Win Diesel	You cruised past the competition and won every Street Race.	30
Exhibitionist	You've won every Showcase Event in the game.	20
Domination!	You've sent every Horizon Star packin'.	10
All Your Race Are Belong to Us	You've won every single race in the game!	30
Stuntman	You've completed every Horizon Outpost PR Stunt.	25
Kudos to You	You've completed 5 Sponsorship challenges.	10
Sellout	20 Sponsorship Challenges? Now you're popular and rich!	20
Barn This Way	You found your first barn find.	5
Bargain Shopper	You bagged yourself a nice discount.	10
Black Friday	Never pay for an upgrade again!	20
Road Trip	You've driven along every road in the entire game.	25
Still a Noob...	10 online races complete... not bad!	10
Noob No More	25 online races complete... awesome!	20
Playground Games	You completed each of the Playground game types. How fun was that?	5

NAME	GOAL/REQUIREMENT	POINT VALUE
Swings and Roundabouts	You've completed 3 of each Playground game types.	20
Cruise Club	You've completed 10 free roam challenges online.	20
Ding!	You got to Level 5 online.	5
Just Me and the XP	You've reached level 25 online. Did you win a car yet?	10
OMG	You won your first car online.	5
ZOMG!	You've won 3 cars online.	10
OMGWT*BBQ!?	You got seriously lucky and won 5 cars online.	20

GAME OF THRONES

ACHIEVEMENTS

NAME	GOAL/REQUIREMENT	POINT VALUE
Clever dog	Gain all the skills linked to the dog with Mors	30
Master of light and flame	Gain all the skills linked to R'hllor's fire with Alester	30
Master-at-arms	Learn all skills within a character's stance tree	25
Warlord	Reach the maximum level	30
Great teamwork	Finish the game without a single ally (except Mors and Alester) being KO'd	30
Merciless	Mete out 5 deathblows	20
True warrior	Kill 400 enemies	20
Man's best friend	Kill 10 enemies with Mors' dog in skinchanger mode	20
Golden touch	Acquire 1 golden dragon	30
R'hllor sees all	Find 10 secrets with the vision of R'hllor	30
Fetch!	Use Mors' dog's sense of smell to find 5 secret objects	30
Thorough	Complete all the secondary objectives of the story	40

SECRET ACHIEVEMENTS

NAME	GOAL/REQUIREMENT	POINT VALUE
Devout follower	Find all the statues of the Seven	30
Pimp	Convince Bethany to return to Chataya's brothel with Alester	30
Collector	Seize the three objects of value from the Collector with Alester	30
Endless watch	Send 10 recruits to the Wall with Mors	30
The Greatest	Emerge triumphant in the final arena combat	30
The true face of the Spider	Lose the final battle	10
My darkest hour	Chapter 15: execute the judgement passed down on the Westfords	10
Lesser of two evils	Chapter 14: come to the aid of the Reapers	15
Quiet as a shadow	Chapter 13: reach Jeyne's room without ever being seen	35
Unrivaled strategist	Chapter 12: take back Riverspring with a total victory	35
Swift and deadly	Chapter 11: bring an end to the trial by combat in under 2 minutes	35
'Tis but a scratch !	Chapter 9: suffer all the physical abuse during the torture sequence	20
The butcher comes to dinner	Chapter 9: kill 6 of Lord Harlton's soldiers during the fight at dinner	35
Desecration	Chapter 8: find the key in Alester's father's tomb	15
Am I not merciful?	Chapter 8: save Orys from the City Watch	15
Once more unto the breach	Chapter 7: attack the camp without killing the sentries at the start	35
Bloodhound	Chapter 7: find all the corrupt brothers of the Night's Watch	25
End of the line	Chapter 6: don't lose pursuit of the bastard	20
Man of the people	Chapter 2: protect the people with Alester	15
Know your place	Chapter 2: protect the nobility with Alester	15

NAME	GOAL/REQUIREMENT	POINT VALUE
Disciplinarian	Chapter 1: confront the four recruits during the training session with Mors	10
Sworn brother	Finish Mors' Story	10
Red priest of R'hllor	Finish Alester's story	10
The night is dark[el]	Finish chapter 15	10
Valar morghulis	Finish chapter 14	10
Growing strong	Finish chapter 13	10
As high as honor	Finish chapter 12	10
Come try me	Finish chapter 11	10
Fire and blood	Finish chapter 10	10
Unbowed, unbent, unbroken	Finish chapter 9	10
Family, duty, honor	Finish chapter 8	10
Here we stand	Finish chapter 7	10
Dead men sing no songs	Finish chapter 6	10
Proud to be faithful	Finish chapter 5	10
Hear me roar	Finish chapter 4	10
Dark wings, dark words	Finish chapter 3	10
Family is hope[el]	Finish chapter 2	10
Winter is coming	Finish chapter 1	10

GEARS OF WAR 3

ACHIEVEMENTS

NAME	GOAL/REQUIREMENT	POINT VALUE
Marcus, It's Your Father	Story Progression in Prologue (Standard or Arcade).	5
Swimmin' in Glowie Gravy	Story Progression in Act 1 Chapter 2 (Standard or Arcade).	10
We Struck Gold, Son!	Story Progression in Act 1 Chapter 3 (Standard or Arcade).	10
My Turf! Cougars Territory!	Story Progression in Act 1 Chapter 5 (Standard or Arcade).	10
Putting it Scientifically...	Story Progression in Act 1 Chapter 6 (Standard or Arcade).	10
Okay, Now We Find Hoffman	Story Progression in Act 2 Chapter 1 (Standard or Arcade).	10
Oh Yeah, It's Pirate Time	Story Progression in Act 2 Chapter 5 (Standard or Arcade).	10
Thanks For Flying GasBag Airways	Story Progression in Act 2 Chapter 7 (Standard or Arcade).	10
Anvil Gate's Last Resort	Story Progression in Act 3 Chapter 1 (Standard or Arcade).	10
Was it Good For You?	Story Progression in Act 3 Chapter 2 (Standard or Arcade).	10
Lost Your Good Driver Discount	Story Progression in Act 3 Chapter 3 (Standard or Arcade).	10
Brothers to the End	Story Progression in Act 3 Chapter 5 (Standard or Arcade).	10
Think You Can Handle That?	Story Progression in Act 4 Chapter 3 (Standard or Arcade).	10
Baird's Favorite Kind of Toy	Story Progression in Act 4 Chapter 5 (Standard or Arcade).	10
Welcome To -redacted-	Story Progression in Act 4 Chapter 6 (Standard or Arcade).	10
Look at That, Instant Summer.	Story Progression in Act 5 Chapter 2 (Standard or Arcade).	10
Ok. Faith. Yeah. Got It.	Story Progression in Act 5 Chapter 5 (Standard or Arcade).	10
You're Dead! Now Stay Dead!	Story Progression in Act 5 Chapter 6 (Standard or Arcade).	10
Ready for More	Complete all campaign Acts on Casual or Normal Difficulty (Standard or Arcade).	50
Ain't My First Rodeo	Complete all campaign Acts on Hardcore Difficulty (Standard or Arcade).	50

NAME	GOAL/REQUIREMENT	POINT VALUE
That's Just Crazy	Complete all campaign Acts on Insane Difficulty (Standard or Arcade).	75
Collector	Recover 5 Campaign Collectibles (any difficulty, Standard or Arcade).	5
Pack Rat	Recover 20 Campaign Collectibles (any difficulty, Standard or Arcade).	10
Hoarder	Recover all 42 Campaign Collectibles (any difficulty, Standard or Arcade).	15
Remember the Fallen	Recover all 15 COG Tags during the Campaign (any difficulty, Standard or Arcade).	15
My Fellow Gears	Complete all Campaign Acts in Co-op (any difficulty, Standard or Arcade).	50
We Few, We Happy Few…	Complete all Campaign Acts in 4 player Co-op (any difficulty, Standard or Arcade).	50
Level 5	Reach level 5.	5
Level 10	Reach level 10.	10
Level 15	Reach level 15.	15
Level 25	Reach level 25.	25
Level 50	Reach level 50.	50
Judge, Jury and Executioner	Get a kill with every possible execution finishing move (any mode).	10
Wreaking Locust Vengence	Get a kill with every Locust monster in Beast mode (any difficulty).	10
Enriched and Fortified	Complete all 50 waves of Horde mode (any difficulty, any map).	10
It's All About the Loot!	Earn the Bronze "Loot Courtesan" medal.	25
All for One, One for All	Earn the Bronze "Force Multiplier" medal.	10
First Among Equals	Earn the Silver "Number 1" medal.	25
Award Winning Tactics	Earn at least one Onyx medal.	25
Seriously 3.0	Reach level 100 and earn every Onyx medal.	100
Welcome to Versus	Kill 10 enemies in Team Deathmatch (Standard or Casual).	10
The Versus Sampler Platter	Complete one match of all six Versus game modes (Standard or Casual).	10
Welcome to Horde Mode	Survive the first 10 waves of Horde mode (any difficulty, any map).	10
Welcome to Beast Mode	Survive all 12 waves of Beast mode (any difficulty, any map).	10
Welcome to Arcade Mode	Complete 5 Arcade Campaign chapters in co-op (any difficulty).	10
Welcome to the Big Leagues	Demonstrate your skill in Casual Versus multiplayer.	0
Wait, What Time is it?	Earn the maximum Consecutive Match Bonus in Versus multiplayer (Standard or Casual).	10
Lambency	Execute an Epic employee, or someone who already has Lambency, in Versus multiplayer (any mode).	50
Socialite	Earn the Onyx "War Supporter" medal.	70

SECRET ACHIEVEMENTS

NAME	GOAL/REQUIREMENT	POINT VALUE
Respect for the Dead	Your respect for the dead earned you access to Griffin's special weapons stash.	5

DLC: HORDE COMMAND PACK

NAME	GOAL/REQUIREMENT	POINT VALUE
The Host with the Most	Host a private Horde Match with a party of 5 players on any Horde Command Pack map (any difficulty).	25
Places to See, People to Destroy	Host a private Beast Match with a party of 5 players on any Horde Command Pack map (any difficulty).	25
What Does This Button Do?	Get 500 Silverback rocket kills in Horde (any map, any difficulty).	50
It's Hammer Time!	Achieve Level 4 in Horde Command Center fortifications.	50
Kill Locust (Like a Boss)	Defeat a Boss Wave as 5 Onyx Guards (Hardcore difficulty).	100

GHOST RECON: FUTURE SOLDIER

ACHIEVEMENTS

NAME	GOAL/REQUIREMENT	POINT VALUE
Doing Work	Kill 1000 enemies while in Guerrilla mode	10
Quality Beats Quantity	Defeat all 50 enemy waves on Guerrilla mode (any difficulty, any map)	30
Good Effect on Target	In Guerrilla mode, kill more than 5 enemies with an airstrike	10
Just a Box	While in Guerrilla mode, complete an infiltration sequence without being detected	10
Good Enough for Government Work	Achieve a Ghost skill rating above 80% for all missions	10
Qualified	Achieve a Ghost skill rating of above 90% on one mission	25
Master Tactician	Complete 100% of the Tactical challenges	25
Tactician	Complete 50% of the Tactical challenges	10
Battle Buddies	Complete the campaign in Co-op	30
Future Soldier	Complete the campaign in Elite	50
Advanced Warfighter	Complete the campaign in Veteran	40
Just Another Day at the Office	Complete the campaign for the first time	30
...I Can Do Better	Complete 20 Daily Friend Challenges	5
Anything You Can Do[e]	Complete a Daily Friend Challenge through all return fire volleys	20
Total Domination	Complete all of the Domination achievements	40
Saboteur Domination	Be part of a squad match where your team takes the bomb into the enemy base in under 2 minutes	10
Decoy Domination	In squad matches your team completes the key objective first, five times.	10
Siege Domination	Be part of a squad match where your team captures the objective in under 2 minutes	10
Conflict Domination	Be part of a squad match where your team wins by a margin of 500 points or more	10
Cross-trained	Reach Level 10 on one Rifleman, one Scout, and one Engineer character	10
Backup	Complete 5 Savior Kills in Quick Matches	5
Actionable Intel	Complete 10 Coordinated Kills	10
Mod Pro	Spend 50 Attachment Credits to add attachments to various guns	40
Tuned Up	Customize all the internal parts of one weapon	25
Field Tested	Play 5 MP matches of each game type	5
Counter-Intelligence	Interrupt an enemy's attempt to data hack a teammate 5 times, by killing or stunning the enemy	10
True Ghost	Get 10 consecutive kills in one Quick Match without dying	10
Recon Specialist	Complete 5 Intel Assists in Quick Matches	25
Kitted Out	Customize 1 weapon with an external attachment at every attachment point	25
Mod Rookie	Add an attachment to any gun	5
High-Value Target	Kill a member of the dev team, or kill someone who has	5
Coordinated Assault	Use the Coordination System to reach an objective	5
Armorer	Spend 25 Attachment Credits with each role	35
High Speed, Low Drag	Reach Level 50 on any character	50
Call, Answered	Complete all Tours of Duty	35
Tour of Duty: North Sea	Win 3 MP matches of any game type on each: Harbor, Cargo, and Rig maps	25
Tour of Duty: Arctic	Win 3 MP matches of any game type on each: Underground, Mill, and Alpha maps	25
Tour of Duty: Nigeria	Win 3 MP of any game type on each: Pipeline, Market, Sand Storm, and Overpass maps	25

SECRET ACHIEVEMENTS

NAME	GOAL/REQUIREMENT	POINT VALUE
No Loose Ends	Eliminate the leader of the Raven's Rock faction	20
Relieved of Command	Kill the general commanding the Moscow defenses	20

NAME	GOAL/REQUIREMENT	POINT VALUE
Special Election	Rescue Russian President Volodin from the prison camp	20
Breathing Room	Destroy the second piece of enemy artillery	20
Fuel for the Fire	Secure the drilling ships and complete the mission	20
Blood Brother	Rescue the Georgian Spec Ops	20
[el]Must Come Down.	Destroy the plane with the weapons system on board while it is in flight	20
EOD	Destroy the Russian weapons transfer station	20
Source Control	Secure the VIP and transfer them to the exfiltration team	20
Precious Cargo	Secure the VIP and transfer him to the exfiltration team	20
What Goes Up[el]	Shoot down the cargo plane	20
Loose Thread	Secure Gabriel Paez	20

GOLDENEYE 007: RELOADED

ACHIEVEMENTS

NAME	GOAL/REQUIREMENT	POINT VALUE
MI6 Ops Recruit	Earn 10 stars in MI6 Ops.	10
MI6 Ops Specialist	Earn 25 stars in MI6 Ops.	25
MI6 Ops Elite	Earn 44 stars in MI6 Ops.	45
Operative	Complete all objectives for every mission on Operative difficulty.	10
Agent	Complete all objectives for every mission on Agent difficulty.	15
007	Complete all objectives for every mission on 007 difficulty.	25
Classic	Complete all objectives for every mission on 007 Classic difficulty.	40
Arkhangelsk Dossier	Complete all objectives in Arkhangelsk on 007 difficulty or higher.	40
Barcelona Dossier	Complete all objectives in Barcelona on 007 difficulty or higher.	15
Dubai Dossier	Complete all objectives in Dubai on 007 difficulty or higher.	15
Severnaya Dossier	Complete all objectives in Severnaya on 007 difficulty or higher.	30
St. Petersburg Dossier	Complete all objectives in St. Petersburg on 007 difficulty or higher.	40
Nigeria Dossier	Complete all objectives in Nigeria on 007 difficulty or higher.	40
Phone a Friend	Get 20 kills with hacked drone guns in 'Jungle'.	15
Bullet Dance	Get 40 kills with the Wolfe .44 in 'Nightclub'.	20
Emblem Hunter	Single Player: Find and destroy a Janus emblem.	5
Emblem Marksman	Single Player: Find and destroy 20 Janus emblems.	10
Emblem Elite	Single Player: Find and destroy 50 Janus emblems.	15
I am INVINCIBLE!	Single Player: Complete any mission without taking any damage.	25
Dressed to Kill	Single Player: Complete any mission without collecting any body armor on 007 Classic difficulty.	20
Going Dark	Get to master engineering in 'Facility' without reinforcements getting called in.	15
Choppers Down	Shoot down 15 helicopters in 'Tank'.	15
Invisible Descent	Get to the server room in 'Bunker' without reinforcements getting called in.	15
Secret Servers	Destroy all the servers in 'Archives' within 40 secs of the first being damaged.	10
Haven't Got Nine Minutes	Complete 'Airfield' in under 4:35 (007 Classic difficulty).	15
Made you feel it, did he?	Single Player: Silently subdue 30 enemies.	10
Master at Arms	Single Player: Make a kill with every weapon.	10
Get to the Chopper	Complete 'Carrier' in under 11:00 (007 difficulty or higher).	15
Russian Escape	Complete 'Archives' in under 15:10 (Agent difficulty or higher).	15

NAME	GOAL/REQUIREMENT	POINT VALUE
Solar Agitated	Complete 'Solar' in under 13:00 (007 Classic difficulty).	15
Orbis Non Sufficit	Public Match: Complete a match on every map.	15
Butter Hook	Public Match: As Tee Hee, get the most kills with a melee strike (min 3 melee kills).	15
Au-ned	Public Match: Achieve 79 kills with the Golden Gun in Golden Gun mode.	30
Clobbering	Public Match: Achieve 64 melee kills with the KL-033 Mk2.	30
Hat Trick	Public Match: In one life, make three kills with Oddjob's hat.	20
Braced for Impact	Public Match: As Jaws, survive a shot to the head which would otherwise have killed you.	15
The Man Who Cannot Die	Public Match: As Baron Samedi, survive a bullet which would otherwise have killed you.	15
Console Compliancy	Public Match: Capture and defend the most consoles in one match of GoldenEye mode.	30
For England, Alec	Public Match: As Bond, kill 006 with an explosive device.	20
The Other Cheek	Public Match: As Bond, kill Zukovsky with a melee strike.	20
Full Deck	Public Match: Play at least one complete match of Classic Conflict with every character.	15
Boys with Toys	Public Match: Kill 50 enemies with Proximity Mines.	50
Lucky Seven	Public Match: Defuse a planted bomb which has exactly 0:07 seconds remaining on its fuse.	40
Boxing Clever	Public Match: Earn all accolades specific to Black Box.	30
Had Your Six	Public Match: Kill six enemies with the Wolfe .44 or Gold Plated Revolver without reloading.	30

SECRET ACHIEVEMENTS

NAME	GOAL/REQUIREMENT	POINT VALUE
Rocket Man	Kill an enemy with the RPG in 'Dam'.	15
Royal Flush	In 'Facility', successfully kill the enemy in the toilet cubicle without any shots being fired.	2
Dance Commander	Surrender to the music in 'Nightclub'.	5
Welcome to Russia	Make the initial rendezvous with 006 in 'Dam'.	5
Cheated	Public Match: Get killed the most times by Oddjob's hat (min 3 deaths).	3

GUITAR HERO: WARRIORS OF ROCK

ACHIEVEMENTS

NAME	GOAL/REQUIREMENT	POINT VALUE
Tracker of Deeds	Follow any five Hero Feed items (Xbox LIVE only)	10
Anthemic Archivist	Expand your song library to at least 115 songs of any type. Be creative!	10
Stellar Centurion	Deploy Star Power a total of 100 times (Quest)	20
Gem Collector	Hit a cumulative total of 75,000 notes (Quest)	20
Gem Hoarder	Hit a cumulative total of 150,000 notes (Quest)	30
Champion of Challenges	Target another person's score on any Challenge and earn a higher grade than they did (Local QP+)	20
Self Improver	Target your own score on a Challenge and earn a higher grade than you did previously (Local QP+)	10
Ultimate Answerer	Earn all Stars from any one song (excluding the Power Challenge) (QP+)	30
Scions of Excess	Earn an 11x Band multiplier with any 4-player Band configuration (QP+)	20
Player of the Ear Worm	Play any one non-GH(tm)Tracks song 10 or more times (QP+, Quest, Competitive)	10
Patron of the Arts	5-Star any GH(tm)Tracks song containing at least 200 notes (QP+)	10
Apostates of Orthodoxy	5-Star any song as a 4-player Non-Standard Band, with all players on Medium or higher (QP+)	10

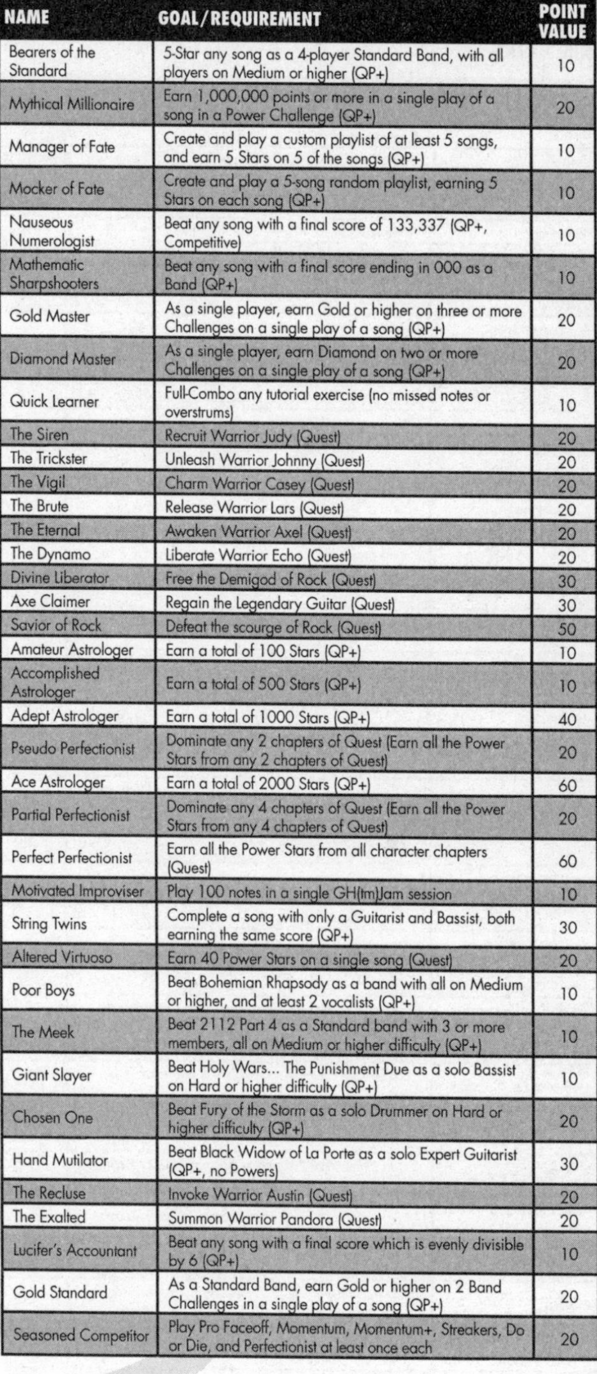

NAME	GOAL/REQUIREMENT	POINT VALUE
Bearers of the Standard	5-Star any song as a 4-player Standard Band, with all players on Medium or higher (QP+)	10
Mythical Millionaire	Earn 1,000,000 points or more in a single play of a song in a Power Challenge (QP+)	20
Manager of Fate	Create and play a custom playlist of at least 5 songs, and earn 5 Stars on 5 of the songs (QP+)	10
Mocker of Fate	Create and play a 5-song random playlist, earning 5 Stars on each song (QP+)	10
Nauseous Numerologist	Beat any song with a final score of 133,337 (QP+, Competitive)	10
Mathematic Sharpshooters	Beat any song with a final score ending in 000 as a Band (QP+)	10
Gold Master	As a single player, earn Gold or higher on three or more Challenges on a single play of a song (QP+)	20
Diamond Master	As a single player, earn Diamond on two or more Challenges on a single play of a song (QP+)	20
Quick Learner	Full-Combo any tutorial exercise (no missed notes or overstrums)	10
The Siren	Recruit Warrior Judy (Quest)	20
The Trickster	Unleash Warrior Johnny (Quest)	20
The Vigil	Charm Warrior Casey (Quest)	20
The Brute	Release Warrior Lars (Quest)	20
The Eternal	Awaken Warrior Axel (Quest)	20
The Dynamo	Liberate Warrior Echo (Quest)	20
Divine Liberator	Free the Demigod of Rock (Quest)	30
Axe Claimer	Regain the Legendary Guitar (Quest)	30
Savior of Rock	Defeat the scourge of Rock (Quest)	50
Amateur Astrologer	Earn a total of 100 Stars (QP+)	10
Accomplished Astrologer	Earn a total of 500 Stars (QP+)	10
Adept Astrologer	Earn a total of 1000 Stars (QP+)	40
Pseudo Perfectionist	Dominate any 2 chapters of Quest (Earn all the Power Stars from any 2 chapters of Quest)	20
Ace Astrologer	Earn a total of 2000 Stars (QP+)	60
Partial Perfectionist	Dominate any 4 chapters of Quest (Earn all the Power Stars from any 4 chapters of Quest)	20
Perfect Perfectionist	Earn all the Power Stars from all character chapters (Quest)	60
Motivated Improviser	Play 100 notes in a single GH(tm)Jam session	10
String Twins	Complete a song with only a Guitarist and Bassist, both earning the same score (QP+)	30
Altered Virtuoso	Earn 40 Power Stars on a single song (Quest)	20
Poor Boys	Beat Bohemian Rhapsody as a band with all on Medium or higher, and at least 2 vocalists (QP+)	10
The Meek	Beat 2112 Part 4 as a Standard band with 3 or more members, all on Medium or higher difficulty (QP+)	10
Giant Slayer	Beat Holy Wars... The Punishment Due as a solo Bassist on Hard or higher difficulty (QP+)	10
Chosen One	Beat Fury of the Storm as a solo Drummer on Hard or higher difficulty (QP+)	20
Hand Mutilator	Beat Black Widow of La Porte as a solo Expert Guitarist (QP+, no Powers)	30
The Recluse	Invoke Warrior Austin (Quest)	20
The Exalted	Summon Warrior Pandora (Quest)	20
Lucifer's Accountant	Beat any song with a final score which is evenly divisible by 6 (QP+)	10
Gold Standard	As a Standard Band, earn Gold or higher on 2 Band Challenges in a single play of a song (QP+)	20
Seasoned Competitor	Play Pro Faceoff, Momentum, Momentum+, Streakers, Do or Die, and Perfectionist at least once each	20

HALO 4

ACHIEVEMENTS

NAME	GOAL/REQUIREMENT	POINT VALUE
Dawn	Completed mission 1 on any difficulty.	10
Requiem	Completed mission 2 on any difficulty.	10
Forerunner	Completed mission 3 on any difficulty.	10
Infinity	Completed mission 4 on any difficulty.	10
Reclaimer	Completed mission 5 on any difficulty.	10
Shutdown	Completed mission 6 on any difficulty.	10
Composer	Completed mission 7 on any difficulty.	10
Midnight	Completed mission 8 on any difficulty.	10
Wake Up, John	Completed the Campaign on Normal or harder.	20
I Need a Hero	Completed the Campaign on Heroic or harder.	40
The Legend of 117	Completed the Campaign on Legendary difficulty.	70
Lone Wolf Legend	Completed the Campaign solo on Legendary difficulty.	90
Skullduggery	Completed any Campaign mission with 3 or more Skulls on Heroic or harder.	15
Bropocalypse	Completed any Campaign mission cooperatively on Heroic or harder.	10
Contact the Domain	Found a Terminal in the Campaign.	10
Terminus	Found all of the Terminals in the Campaign.	50
Digging up the Past	Found and accessed Chief's record in mission 1.	20
Midnight Launch	Got significant air in the Warthog at midnight in mission 2.	20
This is my Rifle, This is my Gun	Carried a UNSC weapon all the way through mission 3 on Heroic or harder.	20
Bros to the Close	Completed mission 4 without one preventable Marine death on Heroic or harder.	20
Mortardom	Hijacked a Wraith and used it to kill at least four enemy Wraiths in mission 5 on Heroic or harder.	20
Explore the Floor	Tricked or forced a Hunter to fall to his demise in mission 6.	20
Give Him the Stick	Took out both Hunters using only the Sticky Detonator in mission 7.	20
Chief, Smash!	Killed 3 Crawlers in one hit with the Gravity Hammer in mission 8.	20
Not Some Recruit Anymore	Ranked up your Spartan-IV to SR-5.	15
Movin' On Up	Ranked up your Spartan-IV to SR-20.	25
I <3 Red vs Blue	Won 5 War Games matchmaking matches.	15
Hanging on the Combat Deck	Won 20 War Games matchmaking matches.	30
Operation Completion	Completed a Spartan Ops Mission on any difficulty.	15
A Legendary Episode	Completed all chapters in Spartan Ops Episode 1 on Legendary difficulty.	40
Dedicated to Crimson	Completed all chapters in the first 5 episodes of Spartan Ops on any difficulty.	80
Crimson Alone	Completed a Spartan Ops chapter solo on Legendary.	20
Roses vs Violets	Found one of the RvB Easter Eggs in Spartan Ops.	20
No One Left Behind	Saved at least one Marine in Chapter 3 of Episode 2 of Spartan Ops on Heroic or harder.	20
Knight in White Assassination	Assassinated a Knight in any Spartan Ops mission.	20
What Power Outage?	Completed Chapter 4, Episode 5 of Spartan Ops without losing a generator on Heroic or harder.	20
No Easy Way Out	In Ch 1, Ep 5 of Spartan Ops survived the enemy assault during the defense on Normal or harder.	20
The Challenged	Completed a Challenge.	10
The Challenger	Completed 25 Challenges.	20
Armorer	Changed your Spartan's armor in the Spartan Armor card.	5
Badge	Changed your Emblem in the Spartan ID card.	5
PWND	Changed your Service Tag in the Spartan ID card.	5
What a Poser!	Changed your Spartan's pose in the Spartan ID card.	5
The Cartographer	Created and saved a Custom Map in Forge.	5
Game Changer	Created and saved a Custom Game type in War Games.	5

NAME	GOAL/REQUIREMENT	POINT VALUE
Snapshot!	Saved a Screenshot from the Theater.	5
The Director	Saved a Film Clip from the Theater.	5
Sharing is Caring	Uploaded a File to your File Share.	5
Bromageddon	Completed the Campaign cooperatively on Heroic or harder.	40

HALO: COMBAT EVOLVED ANNIVERSARY

ACHIEVEMENTS

NAME	GOAL/REQUIREMENT	POINT VALUE
The Silent Cartographer	Complete the level "The Silent Cartographer" on any difficulty.	25
Assault on the Control Room	Complete the level "Assault on the Control Room" on any difficulty.	25
Pillar of Autumn	Complete the level "Pillar of Autumn" on any difficulty.	25
Halo	Complete the level "Halo" on any difficulty.	25
Truth and Reconciliation	Complete the level "Truth and Reconciliation" on any difficulty.	25
343 Guilty Spark	Complete the level "343 Guilty Spark" on any difficulty.	25
The Library	Complete the level "The Library" on any difficulty.	25
Two Betrayals	Complete the level "Two Betrayals" on any difficulty.	25
Keyes	Complete the level "Keyes" on any difficulty.	25
The Maw	Complete the level "The Maw" on any difficulty.	25
Tsantsa	Complete any level with at least three skulls active on Heroic difficulty or higher.	50
What have we here?	Read a terminal.	10
Heavy Reading	Read half the terminals hidden throughout the campaign.	25
Dear Diary…	Read all of the terminals hidden throughout the campaign.	50
Looks like the Oddball	Find your first campaign skull.	10
Skulls Taken!	Locate half of the skulls hidden throughout the campaign.	25
Headhunter	Locate all the skulls hidden throughout the campaign.	50
Birth of a Spartan	Complete every level of the game on Normal difficulty.	10
Believe in a Hero	Complete every level of the game on Heroic difficulty.	20
Living Legend	Complete every level of the game on Legendary difficulty.	50
Standard Operating Brocedure	Complete any level on Normal difficulty cooperatively.	10
Brovershield	Complete any level on Heroic difficulty cooperatively.	20
Bro Hammer	Complete any level on Legendary difficulty cooperatively.	50
He's Unstoppable!	Complete any level on Heroic difficulty or higher without taking health damage.	20
Overshields are for Sissies	Complete the level "Pillar of Autumn" on Legendary without picking up an Overshield.	10
Walk it Off	Complete the level "Pillar of Autumn" on Legendary without picking up a health kit.	25
No-Fly Zone	Destroy three of the four Banshees on "Halo" on any difficulty during a single play-through.	10
How Pedestrian	Complete the level "Halo" on any difficulty without entering a vehicle.	25
Close Quarters Combat	Complete the level "Truth and Reconciliation" with at least four rounds left in your Sniper Rifle.	25
I'll Be Taking That!	Pilot a Banshee on the level "Assault on the Control Room."	25
This One's for Jenkins!	Kill 50 Flood Combat Forms on the level "343 Guilty Spark" on Heroic difficulty or higher.	10
That Just Happened	Complete the level "The Library" on Heroic difficulty or higher without dying.	10
Speed Reader	Complete the level "The Library" on Legendary difficulty in 30 minutes or less.	25
Look Out for the Little Guys	Complete the level "Two Betrayals" on Heroic difficulty or higher without killing any Grunts.	10

NAME	GOAL/REQUIREMENT	POINT VALUE
Leave It Where It Lay	Complete the level "Two Betrayals" on Legendary difficulty without picking up a new weapon.	25
Popcorn.gif	Kill 100 Flood Infection Forms on the level "Keyes" on Heroic difficulty or above.	25
All According to Plan...	Kill all the enemies in the first encounter of "Truth and Reconciliation" without being detected.	10
Beachhead	Storm the beach of "The Silent Cartographer" with no marine casualties on Heroic or Legendary.	10
Grenadier	Escape the map room in "The Silent Cartographer" without firing a shot on Heroic or Legendary.	25
Wraith Hunter	Destroy four Wraith tanks in "Assault on the Control Room" with the Scorpion tank, in a single play.	10
Breaking Quarantine	Escape the Forerunner facility on the level "343 Guilty Spark" in 21 minutes or less.	25
Tying Up Loose Ends	Kill every Elite on the level "Keyes" on Heroic difficulty or above.	10
This Side Up	Complete the Warthog ride on the level "The Maw" without being forcibly ejected from your vehicle.	10
Never Tell Me the Odds	Escape "The Maw" on Legendary with at least a minute left on the count down.	25

HALO REACH

ACHIEVEMENTS

NAME	GOAL/REQUIREMENT	POINT VALUE
The Soldier We Need You To Be	Completed the Campaign on Normal difficulty.	25
Folks Need Heroes...	Completed the Campaign on Heroic difficulty.	50
Gods Must Be Strong	Completed the Campaign on Legendary difficulty.	125
A Monument To All Your Sins	Completed every mission in Halo: Reach alone, on Legendary.	150
We're Just Getting Started	Completed the 2nd mission on Normal or harder.	10
Protocol Dictates Action	Completed the 3rd mission on Normal or harder.	10
I Need A Weapon	Completed the 4th mission on Normal or harder.	10
To War	Completed the 5th mission on Normal or harder.	10
You Flew Pretty Good	Completed the 6th mission on Normal or harder.	10
Into The Howling Dark	Completed the 7th mission on Normal or harder.	10
Dust And Echoes	Completed the 8th mission on Normal or harder.	10
This Is Not Your Grave	Completed the 9th mission on Normal or harder.	10
Send Me Out...With A Bang	Completed the 10th mission on Normal or harder.	10
They've Always Been Faster	Cleared the 2nd mission without setting foot in a drivable vehicle.	25
Two Corpses In One Grave	Killed 2 vehicles at once with the Target Locator in the 3rd mission.	25
Banshees, Fast And Low	Hijacked a Banshee during the Reach Campaign.	25
Your Heresy Will Stay Your Feet	Killed the Elite Zealot before he escaped during the 5th mission.	25
If They Came To Hear Me Beg	Performed an Assassination against an Elite to survive a fall that would've been fatal.	25
Wake Up Buttercup	Destroyed the Corvette's engines & escort in under 3 minutes in the 6th mission on Heroic or harder.	25
Tank Beats Everything	Finished the 9th mission on Legendary with the Scorpion intact.	25
Lucky Me	Earned a Triple Kill while Jetpacking in Campaign, Firefight or Matchmaking.	25
KEEP IT CLEAN	Killed 7 Moa during the 2nd mission of the Campaign.	5
I Didn't Train To Be A Pilot	Killed 3 of the anti-aircraft batteries during the 8th mission.	10
Doctor, Doctor	Used a Health Pack to replenish life after taking body damage.	5
That's A Knife	Performed an Assassination on an enemy.	10
I See You Favour A .45	Killed 10 enemies in a Firefight or Campaign session with the M6G pistol.	10

NAME	GOAL/REQUIREMENT	POINT VALUE
An Elegant Weapon	Killed 10 enemies in a Firefight or Campaign session with the DMR.	10
Swap Meet	Traded weapons with an AI ally in Campaign.	10
A Spoonful Of Blamite	Killed 10 enemies in Firefight or Campaign with a supercombine explosion.	10
Be My Wingman Anytime	Let a teammate spawn on you 5 times in an Invasion Matchmaking game.	5
Yes, Sensei	Earned a First Strike Medal in a Matchmaking game.	10
Skunked	Won a game of Invasion in the 1st phase.	10
What's A Killing Spree?	Earned a Killing Spree in multiplayer Matchmaking.	5
Crowd Control	Earned a Killionaire medal in Firefight.	10
Knife To A Gun Fight	As an Elite, killed 5 Spartan players in Matchmaking.	5
Score Attack	Scored 15,000 points in Score Attack Firefight Matchmaking.	10
Firestarter	Scored 50,000 points in a Firefight game.	10
Blaze Of Glory	Scored 200,000 points in a Firefight game.	25
Heat In The Pipe	Scored 1,000,000 points in a Firefight game.	75
Game, Set, Match	Completed a Firefight set on Legendary without dying.	25
Make It Rain	Purchased an item from the Armory that required the rank of Lt. Colonel.	10
The Start Of Something	Reached the rank of Corporal in the UNSC.	15
An Honor Serving	Reached the rank of Captain in the UNSC.	25
A Storage Solution	Used the File Browser to upload a file to your File Share.	5
A New Challenger	Completed all of the Daily Challenges in a given day.	10
Make It Drizzle	Purchased an item from the Armory.	10
Cool File, Bro	Recommended a file to someone.	5
Lemme Upgrade Ya	Advanced a Commendation to a Silver state.	10
One Down, 51 To Go	Completed a Weekly Challenge.	10

HOMEFRONT

ACHIEVEMENTS

NAME	GOAL/REQUIREMENT	POINT VALUE
Why We Fight	Complete chapter 1 in the Single Player Campaign	10
Freedom	Complete chapter 2 in the Single Player Campaign	10
Fire Sale	Complete chapter 3 in the Single Player Campaign	10
The Wall	Complete chapter 4 in the Single Player Campaign	10
Heartland	Complete chapter 5 in the Single Player Campaign	10
Overwatch	Complete chapter 6 in the Single Player Campaign	10
Why We Fight - Guerrilla	Complete chapter 1 on the Hardest Difficulty in the Single Player Campaign	25
Freedom - Guerrilla	Complete chapter 2 on the Hardest Difficulty in the Single Player Campaign	25
Fire Sale - Guerrilla	Complete chapter 3 on the Hardest Difficulty in the Single Player Campaign	25
The Wall - Guerrilla	Complete chapter 4 on the Hardest Difficulty in the Single Player Campaign	25
Heartland - Guerrilla	Complete chapter 5 on the Hardest Difficulty in the Single Player Campaign	25
Overwatch - Guerrilla	Complete chapter 6 on the Hardest Difficulty in the Single Player Campaign	25
Weapon Expert	Complete an expert challenge for any weapon in Xbox LIVE	25
Drone Expert	Complete an expert challenge for any drone in Xbox LIVE	25
Vehicle Expert	Complete an expert challenge for any vehicle in Xbox LIVE	25
Expert Of War	Complete all challenges for weapons, drones, vehicles, and modes in Xbox LIVE	100
Over the Hill	Reach experience level 50 in Xbox LIVE	50
Squad Commander	Enter an Xbox LIVE Ranked match as the Party Leader of a 4-Player Minimum Party	20

NAME	GOAL/REQUIREMENT	POINT VALUE
Medal of Honor	Win an Xbox LIVE Ranked match as the Party Leader of a Party	20
Full Boat	Enter an Xbox LIVE Ranked match in a Party with 16 players	30
3-Star Threat	Become a 3-Star threat in a Battle Commander Xbox LIVE Ranked match	30
5-Star Threat	Become a 5-Star threat in a Battle Commander Xbox LIVE Ranked match	75
Iron Man - Why We Fight	Complete chapter 1 in the Single Player Campaign without dying or restarting a checkpoint	25
Iron Man - Freedom	Complete chapter 2 in the Single Player Campaign without dying or restarting a checkpoint	25
Iron Man - Fire Sale	Complete chapter 3 in the Single Player Campaign without dying or restarting a checkpoint	25
Iron Man - The Wall	Complete chapter 4 in the Single Player Campaign without dying or restarting a checkpoint	25
Iron Man - Heartland	Complete chapter 5 in the Single Player Campaign without dying or restarting a checkpoint	25
Iron Man - Overwatch	Complete chapter 6 in the Single Player Campaign without dying or restarting a checkpoint	25
Archivist	Find 30 of 61 News Pickups in the Single Player Campaign	10
Historian	Find all 61 News Pickups in the Single Player Campaign	30
Pistol Whipped	Kill 25 enemies with a pistol in Chapter 1: Why We Fight	10
Give Him the Stick	Kill 25 enemies with melee attacks in Chapter 1: Why We Fight	10
Welcome to Freedom	Talk at least once to each inhabitant of Oasis in Chapter 2: Freedom	10
Good Use of Cover	Destroy the first sentry without taking any damage in Chapter 2: Freedom	10
Mercy	Kill 5 enemies while they are on fire in Chapter 3: Fire Sale	10
Let 'em Burn	Don't kill any of the enemies that are on fire in Chapter 3: Fire Sale	10
Chronicler	Find the first of 61 news pickups	10
Stairway to Heaven	From the front door of the church, make it to the crow's nest in 240 seconds in Chapter 5: Heartland	10
Speed Demon	Hijack the tankers in less than 8 minutes in one life in Chapter 6: Overwatch	10
Safer Skies	Destroy all the SAM trucks in the level in Chapter 6: Overwatch	10

SECRET ACHIEVEMENTS

NAME	GOAL/REQUIREMENT	POINT VALUE
Golden Gate	Complete chapter 7 in the Single Player Campaign	10
Golden Gate - Guerrilla	Complete chapter 7 on the Hardest Difficulty in the Single Player Campaign	25
Iron Man - Golden Gate	Complete chapter 7 in the Single Player Campaign without dying or restarting a checkpoint	25
David Rejected	Complete the street section without Goliath taking any damage in Chapter 4: The Wall	10
Fatal and Tragic	Jump off the Golden Gate Bridge in Chapter 7: Golden Gate	10
Wilhelm's Nightmare	Knock 10 enemies off of the scaffolding during the helicopter fly-in in Chapter 7: Golden Gate	10
Soft Targets	Destroy all vehicles using the UAV in Chapter 7: Golden Gate	10

JUST DANCE 4

ACHIEVEMENTS

NAME	GOAL/REQUIREMENT	POINT VALUE
First Dance	Complete your First Song	10
3 Star Performance	Get 3 Stars on a Song	15
Highway to the Stars	Get 3 Stars on 5 Songs	20
5 Star Performance	Get 5 Stars on a Song	20
Rising Star	Get 5 Stars on 5 Songs	30
Golden!	Perform all Gold Moves in a Song	15
Solid Gold Baby!	Perform all Gold Moves in 5 Songs	25
Looking Good	Perform only Good Moves or better in a Song	25
You got the Moves!	Perform only Good Moves or better in 5 Songs	40
Perfect Finish	Get a Perfect on the Last Move of a Song	10
Streaker!	Get 10 Perfect Moves in a row in any Song	20
Reflection of Perfection	Complete a Song with 80% or more Perfect Moves	30
There's no I in Dance	In any Dance Crew Song, All Four Players Get 3 Stars or better (Four Coaches)	20
In-Sync	In any Dance Crew Song, All Four Players Get 5 Stars (Four Coaches)	35
Dynamic Duo	Finish a Duet with 2 players getting 5 Stars on both choreographies	25
Mixing it up	Get 5 Stars on any Mash-Up	20
On a Quest	Complete 5 Dance Quests	20
Superstar!	Get 3 Stars on All Songs (No Alternate Versions, Mash-Ups or Battles)	30
Megastar!	Get 5 Stars on All Songs (No Alternate Versions, Mash-Ups or Battles)	50
Winning!	Win a Battle	20
Epic Winning!	Win each Battle Once	30
Wheel... of... Gifts!	Unlock an Item from the Wheel of Gifts	10
Just Sweatin'	Complete a Sweat Class	5
I Work Out	Complete a full 10 Minute Sweat Class	10
Bring it on!	Complete a full 25 Minute Sweat Class	20
Spartan	Complete a full 45 Minute Sweat Class	45
Getting Warmed Up	Burn 500 Calories in Sweat Mode	25
Feel the Burn	Burn 1000 Calories in Sweat Mode	50
Burn Baby Burn!	Burn 2000 Calories in Sweat Mode	100
The Complete Package	Complete at least one Class from each of the 5 Sweat Programs	50
Stuck on Replay	Dance to the Same song 3 times in a row	15
Blind Ambition	Get 5 Stars on a Song with Pictograms Disabled	25
New Sheriff in Town	Get 5 Stars on the Extreme Version of Wild Wild West	25
Baby is in the Corner	Dance to (I've Had) The Time of my Life Alone	20
Dancing Friends!	Dance to We No Speak Americano with 3 Others	20
Let's do the Time Warp Again	Dance to Time Warp Twice in a Row	15
RickRoll'd	Win a Battle as the Never Gonna Give You Up Coach	15
Musical Statues	In any Dance Crew Song, All Four Players Stay Still for 30 seconds	30

SECRET ACHIEVEMENTS

NAME	GOAL/REQUIREMENT	POINT VALUE
Spin me Right Round	Spin the Carousel at its Maximum Speed	5
Look Ma, Both Hands!	Use Each hand at least Once to Navigate the Menus	5

OVERLOAD

KINGDOMS OF AMALUR: RECKONING

ACHIEVEMENTS

NAME	GOAL/REQUIREMENT	POINT VALUE
House of Ballads	Complete the House of Ballads storyline quests.	20
House of Sorrows	Complete the House of Sorrows storyline quests.	20
Scholia Arcana	Complete the Scholia Arcana storyline quests.	20
Travelers	Complete the Travelers storyline quests.	20
Warsworn	Complete the Warsworn storyline quests.	20
Reckoning Rampage	Kill 5 enemies with a single Fateshift.	20
Niskaru Slayer	Kill 25 Niskaru.	20
Out of Your League	Kill an enemy 4 levels higher than you.	20
Cleaning Up the Streets	Kill 50 bandits.	20
Blades of Glory	Acquire 10 Unique weapons (Special Delivery weapons excluded).	15
Foiled Again!	Parry 100 times.	15
Trapper	Kill 25 enemies with traps.	15
Riposte!	Land 25 special attacks out of Parry.	10
Would You Like Fries with that?	Land 100 complete attack chains.	15
Shock and Awe	Kill 100 enemies with abilities.	15
And Then There Were None	Kill 500 enemies with abilities.	20
Juggler	Land 5 consecutive hits on a launched enemy.	20
Elixir of Fate	Make a potion with the Essence of Fate.	20
It Didn't Explode!	Make a stable potion by experimenting.	10
Green Thumb	Harvest 10 of each type of reagent.	15
Good as New	Repair a piece of equipment.	10
Shop Class	Craft a piece of equipment with Blacksmithing.	10
Master of the Forge	Craft an item that uses all 5 forge component slots.	20
Romancing the Gem	Craft an Epic Gem.	15
Diamond in the Rough	Craft a Pristine Shard.	10
They Never Saw it Coming	Backstab 20 enemies.	10
Cartographer	Discover 100 locations.	20
The Great Detective	Detect 25 hidden things.	10
Loremaster	Discover all Lorestones.	20
Bookworm	Read 50 books.	15
Big Spender	Spend 200,000 gold.	15
Five Finger Discount	Steal and fence an item.	10
Where's My Wallet?	Pickpocket 20 times.	15
Jailbreak	Break out of jail.	10
A Life of Crime	Get caught committing a crime 25 times.	15
Crime Doesn't Pay	Spend over 10,000 gold in crime bribes.	10
Some of This, Some of That	Unlock a two-class hybrid destiny.	10
It is Your Destiny	Unlock a top tier destiny.	50
Jack of All Trades	Unlock a Jack of All Trades destiny.	10
Breaking and Entering	Pick 50 locks.	15
Open Sesame	Dispel 50 wards.	15
A Wink and a Smile	Succeed at 50 Persuasion attempts.	15
Bull in a China Shop	Smash 1,000 objects.	15

SECRET ACHIEVEMENTS

NAME	GOAL/REQUIREMENT	POINT VALUE
Reborn	You were reborn from the Well of Souls, and have escaped Allestar Tower.	10
No Destiny, All Determination	You have met High King Titarion, and have been confronted with the true scope of your powers.	15
Turning the Tide	A ruse has baited Octienne into betraying the necromantic nature of his experiments.	20
Hero of Mel Senshir	You have defeated the great Balor.	75
Destiny Defiant	You have defeated Tirnoch, and defied destiny.	75

NAME	GOAL/REQUIREMENT	POINT VALUE
Destiny Dominated	You have won the game on Hard difficulty.	100
Streaker	You spoke to someone while not wearing clothes.	10

THE LEGEND OF DEAD KEL

ACHIEVEMENTS

NAME	GOAL/REQUIREMENT	POINT VALUE
Message in a Bottle	Locate all eight message bottles in Gallows End.	25
Keep on Rising	Fully restore Gravehal Keep.	50
Exterminator	Kill 50 Scavs.	25

SECRET ACHIEVEMENTS

NAME	GOAL/REQUIREMENT	POINT VALUE
Give Her a Hand	Found Aubrey Gilcrest's severed hand.	25
Manic Pixie Dream Elf	Wooed Rast Brattigan.	25

TEETH OF NAROS

ACHIEVEMENTS

NAME	GOAL/REQUIREMENT	POINT VALUE
Murder Most Fowl	Kill 50 Pteryx.	25

SECRET ACHIEVEMENTS

NAME	GOAL/REQUIREMENT	POINT VALUE
The Harder They Fall	You've bested Kahrunk without killing his attendants.	20
We Built this City	You helped the Kollossae in the Teeth of Naros break free from their fate.	50
Mistaken Identity	You've found a strange Almain who has been hiding in the sewers of Idylla.	25
Beam Me Up	Used the Henge to enter Idylla.	25
I Regret Nothing	Fell to your death from the Idylla Concourse.	5

L.A. NOIRE

ACHIEVEMENTS

NAME	GOAL/REQUIREMENT	POINT VALUE
Asphalt Jungle	Chase down and tackle a fleeing suspect on foot as an LAPD Detective.	15
Traffic Stop	Disable a suspect vehicle with help from your partner.	15
Not So Hasty	Stop a fleeing suspect with a warning shot as an LAPD Detective.	15
Shamus To The Stars	Complete all story cases with a five star rating.	80
The Brass	Achieve maximum rank.	30
The Plot Thickens	Find and solve an inspection puzzle.	15
Golden Boy	Clear a case finding every clue as an LAPD Detective or Investigator.	15
The Straight Dope	Use evidence to prove a lie as an LAPD Detective or Investigator.	15
One For The File	Find and inspect a clue as an LAPD Detective or Investigator.	15
The City Of The Angels	Reach 100% Game Complete.	80
The Up And Up	Complete a story case with a five star rating.	30
The Long Arm Of The Law	Complete all street crime cases.	30
A Cop On Every Corner	Complete a single street crime case.	15
Johnny On The Spot	Respond to 20 street crime cases.	30
Public Menace	Rack up $47,000 in penalties during a single story case.	30

NAME	GOAL/REQUIREMENT	POINT VALUE
The Moose	Follow Candy Edwards without using cover or incognito, except when starting or picking up the tail.	15
Star Map	Discover all landmark locations around the city.	15
The Third Degree	Correctly branch every question in every interview in a single story case.	30
The Hunch	Use four intuition points in a single interview session, correctly branching each question.	30
Auto Fanatic	Drive every vehicle in the city.	30
Hollywoodland	Find and inspect all gold film reels.	30
Auto Collector	Drive 40 different vehicles.	15
Keep A Lid On	Complete a brawl without losing your hat as an LAPD Detective or Investigator.	15
Auto Enthusiast	Drive 5 different vehicles.	15
Lead Foot	Keep the needle above 80mph for more than ten seconds while driving.	15
Miles On The Clock	Drive more than 194.7 miles.	15
Magpie	Find and inspect 95% of all clues.	80

LEFT 4 DEAD 2

ACHIEVEMENTS

NAME	GOAL/REQUIREMENT	POINT VALUE
PRICE CHOPPER	Survive the Dead Center campaign.	20
MIDNIGHT RIDER	Survive the Dark Carnival campaign.	20
RAGIN' CAJUN	Survive the Swamp Fever campaign.	20
WEATHERMAN	Survive the Hard Rain campaign.	20
BRIDGE BURNER	Survive the Parish campaign.	20
STILL SOMETHING TO PROVE	Survive all campaigns on Expert.	35
THE REAL DEAL	Survive a campaign on Expert skill with Realism mode enabled.	35
CONFEDERACY OF CRUNCHES	Finish a campaign using only melee weapons.	30
HEAD HONCHO	Decapitate 200 Infected with a melee weapon.	15
CLUB DEAD	Use every melee weapon to kill Common Infected.	15
CHAIN OF COMMAND	Kill 100 Common Infected with the chainsaw.	15
TANK BURGER	Kill a Tank with melee weapons.	30
SHOCK JOCK	Revive 10 dead Survivors with the defibrillator.	30
THE QUICK AND THE DEAD	Revive 10 incapacitated Survivors while under the speed-boosting effects of adrenaline.	30
ARMORY OF ONE	Deploy an ammo upgrade and have your team use it.	15
BURNING SENSATION	Ignite 50 Common Infected with incendiary ammo.	15
DISMEMBERMENT PLAN	Kill 15 Infected with a single grenade launcher blast.	20
SEPTIC TANK	Use a bile bomb on a Tank.	15
CRASS MENAGERIE	Kill one of each Uncommon Infected.	20
DEAD IN THE WATER	Kill 10 swampy Mudmen while they are in the water.	20
ROBBED ZOMBIE	Collect 10 vials of Boomer vomit from infected CEDA agents you have killed.	15
CL0WND	Honk the noses of 10 Clowns.	15
FRIED PIPER	Using a Molotov, burn a Clown leading at least 10 Common Infected.	15
LEVEL A CHARGE	Kill a Charger with a melee weapon while they are charging.	15
ACID REFLEX	Kill a Spitter before she is able to spit.	15
A RIDE DENIED	Kill a Jockey within 2 seconds of it jumping on a Survivor.	15
STACHE WHACKER	Prove you are faster than Moustachio.	15
GONG SHOW	Prove you are stronger than Moustachio.	15
GUARDIN' GNOME	Rescue Gnome Chompski from the Carnival.	30
WING AND A PRAYER	Defend yourself at the crashed airliner without taking damage.	30

NAME	GOAL/REQUIREMENT	POINT VALUE
SOB STORY	Navigate the sugar mill and reach the safe room without killing any Witches.	30
VIOLENCE IN SILENCE	Navigate the impound lot and reach the cemetery safe room without tripping any alarms.	30
BRIDGE OVER TREBLED SLAUGHTER	Cross the bridge finale in less than three minutes.	30
HEARTWARMER	In a Versus round, leave the saferoom to defibrillate a dead teammate.	20
STRENGTH IN NUMBERS	Form a team and beat an enemy team in 4v4 Versus or Scavenge.	15
QUALIFIED RIDE	As the Jockey, ride a Survivor for more than 12 seconds.	15
BACK IN THE SADDLE	As the Jockey, ride the Survivors twice in a single life.	15
RODE HARD, PUT AWAY WET	As the Jockey, ride a Survivor and steer them into a Spitter's acid patch.	20
GREAT EXPECTORATIONS	As the Spitter, hit every Survivor with a single acid patch.	15
A SPITTLE HELP FROM MY FRIENDS	As the Spitter, spit on a Survivor being choked by a Smoker.	15
SCATTERING RAM	As the Charger, bowl through the entire enemy team in a single charge.	20
MEAT TENDERIZER	As the Charger, grab a Survivor and smash them into the ground for a solid 15 seconds.	20
LONG DISTANCE CARRIER	As the Charger, grab a Survivor and carry them over 80 feet.	15
BEAT THE RUSH	In a Survival round, get a medal only using melee weapons.	15
HUNTING PARTY	Win a game of Scavenge.	15
GAS GUZZLER	Collect 100 gas cans in Scavenge.	20
CACHE AND CARRY	Collect 15 gas cans in a single Scavenge round.	20
SCAVENGE HUNT	Stop the enemy team from collecting any gas cans during a Scavenge round.	15
FUEL CRISIS	Make a Survivor drop a gas can during overtime.	15
GAS SHORTAGE	Cause 25 gas can drops as a Special Infected.	20

DOWNLOADABLE CONTENT: THE PASSING

ACHIEVEMENTS

NAME	GOAL/REQUIREMENT	POINT VALUE
TORCH BEARER	Survive The Passing Campaign.	20
WEDDING CRASHER	As the Charger, grab a Survivor and crash them through 8 chairs at the wedding.	30
TIL IT GOES CLICK	Using the M60, kill 25 infected without letting go of the trigger.	20
GRAVE ROBBER	Collect 10 items dropped by a Fallen Survivor.	25
MUTANT OVERLORD	Play 6 Mutations.	30
FORE!	Knock off the heads of 18 infected with the golf club.	25
KILLING 'EM SWIFTLY TO THIS SONG	Play the new Midnight Riders song on a jukebox.	20
KITE LIKE A MAN	Kill a Tank only with damage from the original Survivors.	30
CACHE GRAB	Open 5 foot lockers.	20
PORT OF SCAVENGE	Play 5 full games of Scavenge on The Port.	30

LEGO BATMAN 2: DC SUPER HEROES

ACHIEVEMENTS

NAME	GOAL/REQUIREMENT	POINT VALUE
Gorilla Thriller	Climb to the top of Wayne tower while riding a Gorilla and playing as a female character.	20
Kal-El Last Son of Krypton	Defeat Zod as Superman	20
Green Lantern's Light	Defeat Sinestro as Green Lantern	20

NAME	GOAL/REQUIREMENT	POINT VALUE
It's A Bird... It's A Plane...	Fly with Superman	20
Inferior Machines	With Brainiac, defeat any LexBot	20
Girl Power	Unlock all female heroes and villains. (Single Player Only)	20
The House of Luthor	Obtain more than 10,100,000,000 Studs (Single Player Only)	20
Combo Hero	Do a finishing move	20
Subway Hero	Use the Gotham City Metro	20
Super-Villain	Unlock all the Bosses (Single Player Only)	20
Toy Gotham	Complete the Bonus level	20
Justice League	Unlock all Justice League characters (Single Player Only)	20
Dynamic Duo	Play a level in co-op	20
My Hero	Rescue all Citizens in Peril (Single Player Only)	50
Super Hero	Get Super Hero in all levels (Single Player Only)	50
Team Building	Unlock all characters (Single Player Only)	50
Minikit Hero	Use all the Minikit vehicles	20
Test Hero	Test a custom character	20
Extra! Extra!	Collect all the red bricks (Single Player Only)	20
The End	Get 100% (Single Player Only)	70
Halfway Through	Get 50% (Single Player Only)	50
City Slicker	Collect all the gold bricks (Single Player Only)	35
Heroes Unite	Complete story level 15	25
Tower Defiance	Complete story level 14	25
Core Instability	Complete story level 13	25
The Next President	Complete story level 12	25
Underground Retreat	Complete story level 11	25
Down to Earth	Complete story level 10	25
Research and Development	Complete story level 9	25
Destination Metropolis	Complete story level 8	25
Unwelcome Guests	Complete story level 7	25
Chemical Signature	Complete story level 6	25
Chemical Crisis	Complete story level 5	25
Asylum Assignment	Complete story level 4	25
Arkham Asylum Antics	Complete story level 3	25
Harboring a Criminal	Complete story level 2	25
Theatrical Pursuits	Complete story level 1	25

LEGO HARRY POTTER: YEARS 5-7

ACHIEVEMENTS

NAME	GOAL/REQUIREMENT	POINT VALUE
Albus Percival Wulfric Brian	Complete "Dark Times"	10
Off the Beaten Track	Complete "Dumbledore's Army"	10
Attempt to Resist	Complete "Focus!"	10
Did Santa Eat That Cake?	Complete "Kreacher Discomforts"	10
Accordion to Grawp	Complete "A Giant Virtuoso"	10
He's Back!	Complete "A Veiled Threat"	10
Phoenix Rising	Complete Year 5	25
Chair-ismatic	Complete "Out of Retirement"	10
The Slug Club	Complete "Just Desserts"	10
Weasleys' Wizard Woes	Complete "A Not So Merry Christmas"	10
Sectumsempra	Complete "Love Hurts"	10
A Riddle Revealed	Complete "Felix Felicis"	10
Dumbledore's Demise	Complete "Horcrux and the Hand"	10
I am the Half-Blood Prince	Complete Year 6	25

NAME	GOAL/REQUIREMENT	POINT VALUE
Cake or Death Eater?	Complete "The Seven Harrys"	10
A Wise Disguise	Complete "Magic is Might"	10
Shedding Skin	Complete "In Grave Danger"	10
Soul Searching	Complete "Sword and Locket"	10
The Tale of the Three Brothers	Complete "Lovegood's Lunacy"	10
Here Lies a Free Elf	Complete "DOBBY!"	10
To Be Continued	Complete Year 7	25
That's Unfortunate	Complete "The Thief's Downfall"	10
Undesirable No. 1	Complete "Back to School"	10
You and Whose Army?	Complete "Burning Bridges"	10
Wit Beyond Measure...	Complete "Fiendfyre Frenzy"	10
Kick the Bucket	Complete "Snape's Tears"	10
Voldemort's Demise	Complete "The Flaw in the Plan"	10
All Was Well	Complete Year 8	50
Collector's dream	Complete the Bonus Level	25
But... I Am The Chosen One	Complete the game to 100% (Single Player Only)	100
Hogwarts has Changed	Visit the Hogwarts Foyer in Year 7	30
Halfway There	Unlocked on hitting 50% game completion (Single Player Only)	30
Avid Reader	Use a Quibbler dispenser 25 times	25
Idling	Stand still with no controller input for 5 minutes	20
Lessons Learned	Complete all lessons (Single Player Only)	30
We are the D.A.	Unlock all of the members of Dumbledore's Army (Single Player Only)	30
Weasley Does It	Use a Weasley box with every Weasley	25
O Children	Complete the scene where Hermione and Harry dance in the tent	20
Knuts and Vaults	Collect 1 billion studs (Single Player Only)	50
What if?	Defeat every Harry freeplay variant as Lord Voldemort	20
Tall Order	Unlock ALL of the Order of the Phoenix character variants (Single Player Only)	40
A Minifig's Best Friend	Unlock every character with a pet (Single Player Only)	30
Witch!	Unlock all witch characters (Single Player Only)	50
Pyjama Drama	Unlock every pyjama character variant (Single Player Only)	20
A Dish Best Served Cold	Defeat Bellatrix with Neville (Waiter) in a duel	20
Not "Fun Guys"	Defeat 30 Red Caps	15
Dark Times Ahead	Unlock every bad wizard (Single Player Only)	25
Lighten Up	Use the Deluminator	10
A Sirius Family Issue	Defeat Bellatrix as any Sirius Black character variant in a duel	20

LEGO PIRATES OF THE CARIBBEAN

ACHIEVEMENTS

NAME	GOAL/REQUIREMENT	POINT VALUE
Welcome to the Caribbean!	Complete Port Royal	12
Hello, poppet!	Unlock all Elizabeth characters (Single Player Only)	15
The Green Flash	Watch a sunset	15
You may throw my hat	Collect all the red hats (Single Player Only)	40
A weather eye on the horizon	Use a spyglass	15
More what you'd call guidelines	Complete the Brethren Court	15
A pirate's life for me	Test any custom character	15
The worst pirate I've ever seen	Complete Port Royal in Story with zero studs	15
The Brethren Court	Unlock all the Pirate Lord characters (Single Player Only)	25

NAME	GOAL/REQUIREMENT	POINT VALUE
The best pirate I've ever seen	Complete Port Royal in Story without dying	15
On Stranger Tides	Complete the Film 4 story	20
Take what you can	Collect all Gold bricks (Single Player Only)	65
At World's End	Complete the Film 3 story	20
The Curse of the Black Pearl	Complete the Film 1 story	20
Dead Man's Chest	Complete the Film 2 story	20
Do you fear death?	Unlock all the Flying Dutchman crew characters (Single Player Only)	25
The pirate all pirates fear	Unlock all the Queen Anne's Revenge crew characters (Single Player Only)	25
Believing in ghost stories	Unlock all the cursed Black Pearl crew characters (Single Player Only)	25
Now bring me that horizon	Complete the game to 100% (Single Player Only)	100
Here there be monsters	Get eaten by a creature in deadly water	15
Gents, take a walk	Walk on the sea bed with all possible characters	20
I am a bad man	Play a level with all Extras turned on (Single Player Only)	15
Sea turtles, mate	Ride on all types of animal in the game	25
There's the Jack I know	Get True Pirate in all levels (Single Player Only)	25
Aye-aye, captain!	Play a level in co-op	15
You're off the edge of the map	Highlight the secret 6th point on all 4 level select maps (Single Player Only)	15
Hello, beastie	Get eaten by the Kraken 10 times	25
Fire!	Fire 100 cannonballs	15
Fight to the bitter end!	Defeat 100 enemies	20
Five lashes be owed	As Jimmy Legs, whip Will Turner 5 times	15
Hoist the colours!	Sail all the minikits in the hub	50
Parley!	Unlock all characters (Single Player Only)	25
What do you want most?	In any level use only the compass to find all its secrets in one go, alone.	25
You filthy, slimy, mangy cur!	Complete all the Guard Dog levels	15
Try wearing a corset	Do 5 lady backflips in a row	15
Pieces of Eight	Reach 888,888,888 studs	88
Did everybody see that?	High dive into the Maelstrom	20
Wind in your sails!	Hit a flying parrot on Smuggler's Den	15
And really bad eggs	Play as all the Extra Toggle characters	25
Savvy?	Unlock all the Jack Sparrow characters (Single Player Only)	15

LOLLIPOP CHAINSAW

ACHIEVEMENTS

NAME	GOAL/REQUIREMENT	POINT VALUE
Zombie Hunter Apprentice	Buy a combo at Chop2Shop.Zom and use it.	5
Unclean and Uncool	Defeated Hazmat in Prologue.	15
Zed's Dead, Baby, Zed's Dead	Defeated Zed.	15
Viking Metal Rules!	Defeated Vikke.	15
Dirty Hippy	Defeated Mariska.	15
Disco's Dead	Defeated Josey.	15
Leapfrog Girl	Leapfrogged 10 times in a row.	10
I Swear! I Did It By Mistake!	Peeped under Juliet's skirt once.	10
Endorsed by Cordelia	Get 30 headshots.	10
Sparkle Hunting Master	Succeed in 7 zombie Sparkle Hunting.	10
Gunn Struck	Struck by lightning 10 times.	10
Super Shopper	Spend 10,000 medals at Chop2Shop.Zom.	15

NAME	GOAL/REQUIREMENT	POINT VALUE
Love Nick	Kissed Nick 100 times.	15
JULIET51	51 successful dropkicks.	15
International Zombie Hunter	Registered in world leaderboards for all stages.	15
Groovy Hunter	Kill 500 zombies.	10
Zombie Slayer?!	Kill 3,000 zombies.	30
Rich Hunter	Pick up 1,000 zombie medals.	10
Millionaire Hunter	Pick up 10,000 zombie medals.	30
San Romero Knights Savior	Rescued All Classmates.	30
Lollipop Addict	Collected all lollipop wrappers.	30
Always On The Phone	Collected all telephone messages.	30
Zombie Fancier	Completed the zombie album.	30
OMG, Music Is Soooo Coooool	Collected all BGM.	30
Perfect Body	Completely level up Juliet.	30
Master Sushi Chef	Collected all combos.	30
Watch Out For The Balls	Dodge & Counter Zed's Electric Balls 15 times.	10
Cheerleader Overboard!	Succeed in QTE at edge of Vikke's ship.	10
Third Eye	Dodge all balloon attacks in Mariska battle.	10
Critical UFO Finish	Funk Josey in the last 10 seconds.	10
Elephant Tamer	Counter Lewis' attack 10 times.	10
Fingered	Cut off 20 fingers during Killabilly's fight!	10
Life Guard	Rescued all classmates in Prologue.	15
Accidental Vandalism	Destroyed 300 objects in the game.	15
Go, Medal Racer, Go!	Picked up all zombie medals on the rooftop with Chainsaw Dash.	15
Legendary harvester	Harvested all crops in the 1st field with the combine in Stage 3.	15
No Fear Of Heights	Beat the Gondola game without shooting.	15
Little Sisters Are The Worst!	Do not get hit by Rosalind's wrecking ball.	15
Aced Auto-shop Class	Clear all the Kill Car QTE's in a row.	15
n00b Zombie Hunter	Clear Prologue, surpassing Dad's score.	30
Beginner Zombie Hunter	Clear Stage 1, surpassing Dad's score.	30
Intermediate Zombie Hunter	Clear Stage 2, surpassing Dad's score.	30
Advanced Zombie Hunter	Clear Stage 3, surpassing Dad's score.	30
Super Zombie Hunter	Clear Stage 4, surpassing Dad's score.	30
Excellent Zombie Hunter	Clear Stage 5, surpassing Dad's score.	30
Master Zombie Hunter	Clear Stage 6, surpassing Dad's score.	30
Congratulations! Happy Birthday!	Watched the happy ending.	100
Horrid Birthday	Watched the bad ending.	15
Rock'n Roll Isn't Here Anymore	Defeated Lewis LEGEND.	15
I Came, I Saw, I Kicked Its Ass	Defeated Killabilly.	15

LORD OF THE RINGS: WAR IN THE NORTH

ACHIEVEMENTS

NAME	GOAL/REQUIREMENT	POINT VALUE
Where there's life, there's hope	Revive a fallen ally.	10
Foe-hammer	Kill 200 enemies in a single playthrough.	10
Sudden Fury	Perform 3 critical hits within 10 seconds.	10
Strength of Our Alliance	Slay one enemy together with 2 other players.	25
Seeker	Discover 25 secrets in a single playthrough.	20
Gem-studded	Slot an elfstone into an item.	10
Relentless	While in Hero Mode, perform a streak of 50 hits.	20
Now for wrath, now for ruin!	Kill 4 enemies simultaneously.	20
Troll's Bane	Slay the wild snow trolls.	10
Battle-master	Unlock every active-cast ability in one character's skill tree.	20
War-hardened	Achieve at least 1 rank in a tier 3 skill.	10
Like a Thunderbolt	Deal 3000 damage with a single ranged strike.	20
Fell-handed	Deal 1500 damage in a single melee strike.	20
Living Shield	Absorb 25,000 total damage during the course of 1 level.	20
Many deeds, great and small	Complete 15 quests in a single playthrough.	20
War-machinist	Kill 150 enemies with war machines in a single playthrough.	20
Well-arrayed	Equip a complete magical armor set.	25
Keen-eyed Marksman	Kill 50 enemies with headshots in a single playthrough.	20
Swift-winged Warrior	Summon Beleram 10 times in a single playthrough.	20
Warrior Exemplar	For one character unlock every skill that provides a modification to War Cry, Sanctuary or Evasion.	25
Defender of the North	Achieve level 10.	10
Champion of the North	Achieve level 20.	20
Herb-master	Create 15 potions in a single playthrough.	10
Bane of Mordor	Kill 600 enemies in a single playthrough.	25
Dragon-hoard	Amass 25,000 coins.	20
Expert Treasure-hunter.	Locate 5 gilded treasure chests in a single playthrough.	25
Victorious in Battle	Complete a playthrough on at least Normal difficulty.	25
Against All Odds	Complete a playthrough on Legendary difficulty.	80
The Lidless Eye	Complete the investigation of the Cult of the Lidless Eye.	25
Hero of Legend	Complete a playthrough on Heroic difficulty.	50

SECRET ACHIEVEMENTS

NAME	GOAL/REQUIREMENT	POINT VALUE
Giant-slayer	Slay Bargrisar the stone giant.	20
Begone, lord of carrion!	Defeat the Barrow Wight Lord.	20
Trusted with the Secret	Learn of the Ring of Power and the plan for its destruction.	10
In the Dragon's Den	Meet a dragon and survive.	20
Friend of the Woodland Realm	Free the elf from his captors in Mirkwood Marsh.	10
Eagle Savior	Defeat Agandaûr without the aid of Beleram.	20
Friend to the Ring-bearer	Speak with Frodo in Rivendell.	10
Tharzog's Bane	Defeat Agandaûr's lieutenant Tharzog.	20
Mountain-breaker	Help destroy the citadel within Mount Gundabad.	25
Wulfrun's Bane	Defeat the Sorceror Wulfrun.	20
Tracker	Discover what happened to the missing Rangers.	10
Spider-slayer	Slay Saenathra.	25
Elf-friend	Join forces with the sons of Elrond.	10
Friend to the Eagles	Help free the Great Eagle Beleram.	20
Siege-breaker	Help weather the siege of Nordinbad.	35
Hero of the North	Defeat Sauron's Lieutenant Agandaûr.	80

MADDEN NFL 13

ACHIEVEMENTS

NAME	GOAL/REQUIREMENT	POINT VALUE
Single Riders Only	Play a MUT game against the CPU.	5
MUT Maniac	Complete 20 MUT games.	20
This One is Hard 2.0	Build an 85 rated MUT team.	15
This One is Easy. We Promise	Create a MUT team.	5
Hall Of Famer	As a created player or coach, get inducted into the Hall of Fame in Connected Careers.	100
All Madden	As a created coach, win 100 games in your first 10 seasons in Connected Careers.	100
Montana's Mountain	As a created QB, win 4 Super Bowls in Connected Careers.	20
Vince Lombardi Award	As a created coach, surpass Vince Lombardi on Legacy Score in Connected Careers.	30
Deion Sanders Award	As a created DB, surpass Deion Sanders on Legacy Score in Connected Careers.	30
Lawrence Taylor Award	As a created LB, surpass Lawrence Taylor on Legacy Score in Connected Careers.	30
Reggie White Award	As a created DL, surpass Reggie White on Legacy Score in Connected Careers.	30
Shannon Sharpe Award	As a created TE, surpass Shannon Sharpe on Legacy Score in Connected Careers.	30
Jerry Rice Award	As a created WR, surpass Jerry Rice on Legacy Score in Connected Careers.	30
Emmitt Smith Award	As a created RB, surpass Emmitt Smith on Legacy Score in Connected Careers.	30
Joe Montana Award	As a created QB, surpass Joe Montana on Legacy Score in Connected Careers.	30
Peak Performance	As a created player, achieve a player rating of 99 overall in Connected Careers.	30
Overall 90	As a created player, achieve a player rating of 90 overall in Connected Careers.	20
85 Overall	As a created player, achieve a player rating of 85 overall in Connected Careers.	15
80 Overall	As a created player, achieve a player rating of 80 overall in Connected Careers.	10
MVP! MVP! MVP!	Complete the Level 4 season goals in one season in Connected Careers.	30
Welcome to the Community	Join an Online Community.	5
Battle Tested	Score 600 points in Online Ranked Head to Head Games.	20
Online Level 9	Score 500 points in Online Ranked Head to Head Games.	15
Online Level 8	Score 400 points in Online Ranked Head to Head Games.	15
Online Level 7	Score 300 points in Online Ranked Head to Head Games.	15
Online Level 6	Score 250 points in Online Ranked Head to Head Games.	10
Online Level 5	Score 200 points in Online Ranked Head to Head Games.	10
Online Level 4	Score 150 points in Online Ranked Head to Head Games.	10
Online Level 3	Score 100 points in Online Ranked Head to Head Games.	5
Online Level 2	Score 50 points in Online Ranked Head to Head Games.	5
Online Level 1	Score 25 points in Online Ranked Head to Head Games.	5
Tebowing	Tebow Time! Throw a TD with Tim Tebow on the first play in overtime (no SuperSim, OTP or co-op).	25
Gronk Spike	Score a TD with Rob Gronkowski (no SuperSim, OTP or co-op).	25
Pass The Salsa	Score a TD with Victor Cruz (no SuperSim, OTP or co-op).	25

NAME	GOAL/REQUIREMENT	POINT VALUE
Verizon Scoreboard Overload	Score 50 points in one game (no SuperSim, OTP or co-op).	50
Matt Flynn's Arcade	Score 6 touchdowns with your backup quarterback (no SuperSim, OTP or co-op).	55
Let's Get Physical	Tackle an opponent using the Hit Stick (no SuperSim, OTP or co-op).	5
Made Ya Look	Abort the play action and complete a pass for a TD (no SuperSim, OTP or co-op).	10
Smart Mouth	Complete a successful pre-play adjustment using Kinect (no SuperSim, OTP or co-op).	25
Belting	Complete a Madden Moments Live situation.	25
The Penitent Man Shall Pass	As a QB, win the game with 4 or fewer completed passes (no SuperSim, OTP or co-op).	20
You're In the Game	Download A Game Face in Create-a-Player or in Connected Careers.	10

MAGNA CARTA 2

ACHIEVEMENTS

NAME	GOAL/REQUIREMENT	POINT VALUE
Battle of Highwind Island	Complete the battle of Highwind Island.	10
Battle of Oldfox Canyon	Complete the battle of Oldfox Canyon.	20
Battle of Cota Mare	Complete the battle of Cota Mare.	30
Battle of Dunan Hill	Complete the battle of Dunan Hill.	40
Battle of Ruhalt Basin	Complete the battle of Ruhalt Basin.	50
First Quest Cleared	Clear the first quest.	5
10 Quests Cleared	Clear 10 quests.	5
50 Quests Cleared	Clear 50 quests.	10
80 Quests Cleared	Clear 80 quests.	20
All Quests Cleared	Clear all quests.	30
Co-op Technique: Juto & Zephie	Learn Co-op Technique for Juto & Zephie.	10
Style Master: 1 Handed Sword	Master Juto's 1 Handed Sword skill tree.	30
Style Master: 2 Handed Sword	Master Juto's 2 Handed Sword skill tree.	30
Style Master: Hammer	Master Argo's Hammer skill tree.	30
Style Master: Axe	Master Argo's Axe skill tree.	30
Style Master: Rod	Master Zephie's Rod skill tree.	30
Style Master: Fan	Master Zephie's Fan skill tree.	30
Style Master: Fireball	Master Crocell's Fireball skill tree.	30
Style Master: Knuckles	Master Crocell's Knuckle skill tree.	30
Style Master: Aroma	Master Celestine's Aroma skill tree.	30
Style Master: Bow	Master Celestine's Bow skill tree.	30
Style Master: Katana	Master Rue's Katana skill tree.	30
Style Master: Shuriken	Master Rue's Shuriken skill tree.	30
Weapon Enhanced	Use Enhancements on a weapon.	5
Obtained Item Recipe	Obtain an item recipe.	5
Obtained 6 Item Recipes	Obtain 6 item recipes.	10
Obtained All Item Recipes	Obtain all item recipes.	30
100 Chain Breaks	Complete 100 chain breaks.	10
300 Chain Breaks	Complete 300 chain breaks.	30
500 Chain Breaks	Complete 500 chain breaks.	50
Viewed Live Drama 1	View Live Drama 1	20
Viewed Live Drama 2	View Live Drama 2	20
Viewed Live Drama 3	View Live Drama 3	20
Weapon Collector: Juto	Collect all of Juto's weapons, including downloadable content.	30
Weapon Collector: Zephie	Collect all of Zephie's weapons, including downloadable content.	30

NAME	GOAL/REQUIREMENT	POINT VALUE
Weapon Collector: Argo	Collect all of Argo's weapons, including downloadable content.	30
Weapon Collector: Crocell	Collect all of Crocell's weapons, including downloadable content.	30
Weapon Collector: Celestine	Collect all of Celestine's weapons, including downloadable content.	30
Weapon Collector: Rue	Collect all of Rue's weapons, including downloadable content.	30

SECRET ACHIEVEMENTS

NAME	GOAL/REQUIREMENT	POINT VALUE
Escape from Belfort	Successfully escaped from Belfort.	60
Assault on Ruhalt Plateau	Completed the assault on Ruhalt Plateau.	70
Game Completed	Completed the game's main story.	80
Co-op Technique: Argo&Celestine	Learned Co-op Technique for Argo & Celestine.	10
Co-op Technique: Zephie & Rue	Learned Co-op Technique for Zephie & Rue.	10
Co-op Technique: Juto & Crocell	Learned Co-op Technique for Juto & Crocell.	20
Co-op Technique: Celestine & Rue	Learned Co-op Technique for Celestine & Rue.	20

MAJOR LEAGUE BASEBALL 2K12

ACHIEVEMENTS

NAME	GOAL/REQUIREMENT	POINT VALUE
Home, Sweet Home	Score 193 runs with your user profile.	10
Chicks Dig It	Hit 74 home runs with your user profile.	10
Almost There	Hit 37 triples with your user profile.	10
Fanning the Flames	Strike out 514 batters with your user profile.	10
Set the Table	Hit 68 doubles with your user profile.	15
Productivity	Get 263 hits with your user profile.	20
Domination	Save 63 games with your user profile.	20
Production	Drive in 192 RBI with your user profile.	20
You Make Your Own Destiny	Steal 139 bases with your user profile.	20
As Good as a Hit	Walk 233 times with your user profile.	40
Down But Not Out	Get a hit with 2 strikes in a non-simulated game.	5
Grab Some Pine	Get a strikeout to end the inning in a non-simulated game.	5
A Pitcher's Best Friend	Turn a double play in a non-simulated game.	10
To the Rescue	Get a save with the tying run on base in a non-simulated game.	10
Don't Call it a Comeback	Win after being down by 4 after the 6th inning in a non-simulated game.	10
The Start of Something Special	Lead off an inning by hitting a triple in a non-simulated game.	10
Stooges	Strikeout all three hitters in the inning in a non-simulated game.	10
No Hole too Deep	Battle Back: Down 0-2, get walked in a non-simulated game.	10
Throw First and Aim Later	Miss your throw to first base with 2 outs in a non-simulated game.	10
Take That	Get an RBI after getting brushed back off the plate in a non-simulated game.	15
My Main Squeeze	Bunt the man home in a non-simulated game.	15
Dual Threat	Steal base with pitcher in a non-simulated game.	20
I Came, I Saw...	Hit a Walk-off Home Run in a non-simulated game.	20
He Taketh Away	Rob a Home Run in a non-simulated game.	20
State Farm®: The Road to Victory	Get 3 consecutive batters on base in a non-simulated game.	20
Mr. Consistency	Get a hit in all 9 innings in a non-simulated game.	20

NAME	GOAL/REQUIREMENT	POINT VALUE
A Virtue	Face 10 pitches as the batter in a non-simulated game.	20
One Man Show	Throw a No-Hitter in a 9 inning, non-simulated game.	80
The Goal	Accomplish a Team Season Goal in My Player Mode.	10
Back to the Cage	Get a Golden Sombrero (strikeout 4 times in 1 game) in My Player Mode.	10
Payback	Hit a home run off a former team in My Player Mode.	15
Your Day	Win player of the game in an MLB game in My Player Mode.	15
This is Why I'm Here	Be successful in a major league clutch moment in My Player Mode.	15
The Call	Get called up to the Majors in My Player Mode.	20
A Job Well Done	Win 100+ games in a season in My Player Mode.	25
2-Peat	Win Back to Back World Series® in My Player Mode.	25
The Top	Become the #1 ranked player in your My Player organization.	30
The Star	Make the All-Star team in My Player Mode.	40
The Hall	Make the Hall of Fame in My Player Mode.	75
What's Your Ring Size?	Win a World Series® in My Player Mode.	80
You're Special	Win a Season award in Franchise Mode. (play at least 20 games)	20
Remember Me	Break a record in Franchise Mode. (play at least 20 games)	20
The Champs	Win a World Series® in Franchise Mode. (play at least 20 games)	20
King of the Hill	Get to the top of the Best of the Best ladder in Home Run Derby® Mode.	20
My Fellow Man	Complete and win an online league game.	10
Count it	Complete and win a ranked match.	10
Upset Alert	Use the Houston Astros in a completed ranked match.	10
The Spice of Life	Play 10 ranked matches using 10 different teams.	10
The Team to Beat	Beat the St. Louis Cardinals in a completed online match.	15
The Road to Greatness	Complete and win 3 ranked matches in a row.	20

MARVEL VS. CAPCOM: ORIGINS

ACHIEVEMENTS

NAME	GOAL/REQUIREMENT	POINT VALUE
Marvel Legend	Finish arcade mode without losing a round (Marvel Super Heroes)	30
Pocketful Of Gems	Finish arcade mode (Marvel Super Heroes)	5
Crossover Legend	Finish arcade mode without losing a round (Marvel vs. Capcom)	30
Pocketful Of Partners	Finish arcade mode (Marvel vs. Capcom)	5
Super Heroes Unite	Finish arcade mode with each hero (Marvel Super Heroes)	15
Villains Unite	Finish arcade mode with each villain (Marvel Super Heroes)	15
Capcom Unite	Finish arcade mode with each Capcom character (Marvel vs. Capcom)	10
Marvel Unite	Finish arcade mode with each Marvel character (Marvel vs. Capcom)	10
From the Shadows	Finish arcade mode with each Hidden character (Marvel vs. Capcom)	10
Another Notch	Complete the third tier of the challenge "Another Notch"	10
Big Finish	Complete the fourth tier of the challenge "Big Finish"	10
Hyper Artist	Complete the third tier of the challenge "Hyper Artist"	10
Going Streaking	Complete the third tier of the challenge "Going Streaking"	10
Grinder	Complete the third tier of the challenge "Grinder"	25
Hip Tosser	Complete the third tier of the challenge "Hip Tosser"	10
Powers Combined	Complete the third tier of the challenge "Powers Combined" (Marvel vs. Capcom)	10

NAME	GOAL/REQUIREMENT	POINT VALUE
Duo of Heroes	Complete the third tier of the challenge "Duo of Heroes" (Marvel vs. Capcom)	10
War of the Gems	Complete the third tier of the challenge "War of the Gems" (Marvel Super Heroes)	10
It's Not Over	Complete the third tier of the challenge "It's Not Over"	10
Your Turn	Complete the third tier of the challenge "Your Turn" (Marvel vs. Capcom)	10
Not a Scratch	Complete the second tier of the challenge "Not a Scratch"	15
Fast Fingers	Complete the second tier of the challenge "Fast Fingers"	10
Chain Reaction	Complete the second tier of the challenge "Chain Reaction"	10
Aerial Rave	Complete the second tier of the challenge "Aerial Rave"	10
Looking Cross	Complete the second tier of the challenge "Looking Cross"	10
Around The Universe	Win a match with every normally selectable character (Marvel Super Heroes)	30
Around The Multiverse	Win a match with every character (Marvel vs. Capcom)	30
Heroic Banter	Complete the second tier of the challenge "Heroic Banter"	10
Level Up	Complete the second tier of the challenge "Level Up"	10
Uatu the Watcher	Complete the first tier of the challenge "Uatu the Watcher"	10

MASS EFFECT 3

ACHIEVEMENTS

NAME	GOAL/REQUIREMENT	POINT VALUE
Driven	Return to active duty.	5
Bringer of War	Chase down an assassin.	10
Mobilizer	Bring a veteran officer aboard.	15
World Shaker	Destroy an Atlas dropped from orbit.	15
Pathfinder	Explore a lost city.	15
Tunnel Rat	Survive the swarm.	15
Party Crasher	Sabotage a dreadnought.	15
Hard Target	Call down an orbital strike.	15
Saboteur	Disable a group of fighter squadrons.	15
Arbiter	Win a political stand-off.	25
Last Witness	Extract ancient technology.	25
Executioner	Defeat an old adversary.	25
Well Connected	Send a warning across the galaxy.	15
Fact Finder	Discover an enemy's monstrous origin.	15
Liberator	Stop a Cerberus kidnapping.	15
Problem Solver	Evacuate a scientific facility.	15
Patriot	Make the final assault.	25
Legend	Mission accomplished.	50
Shopaholic	Visit a store in the single-player campaign.	10
Master and Commander	Deliver most of the Galaxy at War assets to the final conflict.	50
Lost and Found	Dispatch 10 probes to retrieve people or resources in Reaper territory.	25
Long Service Medal	Complete Mass Effect 3 twice, or once with a Mass Effect 2 import.	50
Insanity	Finish the game on Insanity without changing difficulty after leaving Earth.	75
A Personal Touch	Modify a weapon.	10
Paramour	Establish or rekindle a romantic relationship.	25
Combined Arms	Perform any combination of 50 biotic combos or tech bursts.	25
Focused	Evolve any of your powers to rank 6.	25
Recruit	Kill 250 enemies.	10

NAME	GOAL/REQUIREMENT	POINT VALUE
Soldier	Kill 1,000 enemies.	15
Veteran	Kill 5,000 enemies.	25
Bruiser	Kill 100 enemies with melee attacks.	10
Untouchable	Escape a Reaper in the galaxy map.	10
Defender	Attain the highest level of readiness in each theater of war.	25
Overload Specialist	Overload the shields of 100 enemies.	15
Sky High	Lift 100 enemies off the ground with powers.	15
Pyromaniac	Set 100 enemies on fire with powers.	15
Eye of the Hurricane	Kill a brute while it's charging you.	10
Mail Slot	Kill 10 guardians with headshots from the front while their shields are raised.	10
Hijacker	Hijack an Atlas mech.	10
Giant Killer	Defeat a harvester.	10
Enlisted	Start a character in multiplayer or customize a character in single-player.	5
Tour of Duty	Finish all multiplayer maps or all N7 missions in single-player.	20
Always Prepared	Obtain two non-customizable suits of armor.	10
Tourist	Complete one multiplayer match or two N7 missions.	5
Explorer	Complete three multiplayer matches or five N7 missions.	15
Gunsmith	Upgrade any weapon to level 10.	25
Almost There	Reach level 15 in multiplayer or level 50 in single-player.	15
Peak Condition	Reach level 20 in multiplayer or level 60 in single-player.	25
Battle Scarred	Promote a multiplayer character to the Galaxy at War or import an ME3 character.	25
Unwavering	Finish all multiplayer maps on Gold or all single-player missions on Insanity.	50

FROM ASHES

ACHIEVEMENTS

NAME	GOAL/REQUIREMENT	POINT VALUE
Freedom Fighter	Find all required intel to help Eden Prime's colonists.	25
Prothean Expert	Learn more about the Prothean Empire.	25

MAX PAYNE 3

ACHIEVEMENTS

NAME	GOAL/REQUIREMENT	POINT VALUE
Feel The Payne	Story Complete [MEDIUM]	30
Serious Payne	Story Complete [HARD]	50
Maximum Payne	Story Complete [OLD SCHOOL]	80
Payne In The Ass	Story Complete [HARDCORE]	20
Part I Complete	Complete Part I Of The Story	20
Part II Complete	Complete Part II Of The Story	20
Part III Complete	Complete Part III Of The Story	20
A New York Minute	Finish In A New York Minute	100
The Shadows Rushed Me	Unlock And Complete New York Minute Hardcore	10
Out The Window	Get 6 Kills While Diving Through The VIP Window [FREE AIM]	10
The One Eyed Man Is King	Cover Passos With Perfect Aim	10
Something Wicked This Way Comes	Get 7 Kills While Jumping From The Rickety Boat [FREE AIM]	10
That Old Familiar Feeling	Clear The Hallway Of Lasers	10
Amidst The Wreckage	Destroy All The Models In The Boardroom	5

NAME	GOAL/REQUIREMENT	POINT VALUE
So Much For Being Subtle	Get 9 Kills While Being Pulled By A Chain [FREE AIM]	10
The Only Choice Given	Get 8 Kills While Dangling From A Chain [FREE AIM]	10
Trouble Had Come To Me	Clear Everyone On The Bus Ride	15
Along For The Ride	Trigger A Bullet Cam On The Zipline [FREE AIM]	10
Sometimes You Get Lucky	Get A Headshot During The Rooftop Tremors	5
It Was Chaos And Luck	Get 6 Kills While Riding The Push Cart [FREE AIM]	10
The Road-Kill Behind Me	Total Everything On The Runway	10
The Fear Of Losing It	Survive A Level Without Painkillers	20
It's Fear That Gives Men Wings	10 Bullet Time® Kills In A Row	20
You Might Hurt Someone With That	Shoot 10 Airborne Grenades	20
One Bullet At A Time	300 Headshots	20
You Play, You Pay, You Bastard	100 Kills With Melee	20
With Practiced Bravado	100 Kills During Shootdodge.	20
Colder Than The Devil's Heart	Kill 30 Enemies In 2 Minutes	15
A Few Hundred Bullets Back	Use Every Weapon In The Game	20
Past The Point Of No Return	Take 100 Painkillers	10
An Echo Of The Past	Find All Clues	35
Sure Know How To Pick A Place	Discover All Tourist Locations	10
A License To Kill	Collect All Golden Guns	40
All Of The Above	Finish All Single Player Grinds	100
Full Monty	Complete One Of Each Game Mode Including All Gang Wars	10
Payne Bringer	Kill 100 Other Players	30
Max Payne Invitational	Invite someone to play through the in-game contact list	5
Man Of Many Weapons	Unlock All Weapons	25
Man Of Many Faces	Unlock All Faction Characters	25
Deathmatch Challenge	Winner In Any Public Deathmatch	20
Grave Robber	Looted A Body	5
The Gambler	Won A Wager	15
Training Complete	Achieve Level Rank 50	25
Dearest Of All My Friends	Kill Someone On Your Friends List	10

SECRET ACHIEVEMENTS

NAME	GOAL/REQUIREMENT	POINT VALUE
Sweep	Flawless Team Gang Wars Victory	10
You Push A Man Too Far	Don't Shoot The Dis-Armed Man	5

MINECRAFT (XBOX 360 EDITION)

ACHIEVEMENTS

NAME	GOAL/REQUIREMENT	POINT VALUE
Into The Nether	Construct a Nether Portal.	40
Dispense With This	Construct a Dispenser.	20
MOAR Tools	Construct one type of each tool (one pickaxe, one spade, one axe and one hoe).	15
Leader Of The Pack	Befriend five wolves.	30
When Pigs Fly	Use a saddle to ride a pig, then have the pig get hurt from fall damage while riding it.	40

NAME	GOAL/REQUIREMENT	POINT VALUE
Cow Tipper	Harvest some leather.	15
Monster Hunter	Attack and destroy a monster.	20
Time to Strike!	Use planks and sticks to make a sword.	10
On A Rail	Travel by minecart to a point at least 500m in a single direction from where you started.	40
Delicious Fish	Catch and cook a fish!	15
Getting an Upgrade	Construct a better pickaxe.	15
The Lie	Bake a cake using wheat, sugar, milk and eggs!	40
Bake Bread	Turn wheat into bread.	20
Time to Farm!	Use planks and sticks to make a hoe.	10
Acquire Hardware	Smelt an iron ingot.	15
Hot Topic	Construct a furnace out of eight cobblestone blocks.	15
Time to Mine!	Use planks and sticks to make a pickaxe.	10
Benchmarking	Craft a workbench with four blocks of wooden planks.	10
Getting Wood	Punch a tree until the block of wood pops out.	10
Taking Inventory	Open your inventory.	10

MORTAL KOMBAT

ACHIEVEMENTS

NAME	GOAL/REQUIREMENT	POINT VALUE
Cyber Challenger	Complete 100 Online Matches	20
Wavenet...	Win 100 total Online Matches	80
Humiliation	Get a Flawless Victory in an Online Match	10
Tough Guy!	Win an Online Match	10
Robots Rule!	Win Arcade Tag Ladder with robot Sektor and Cyrax	10
Outstanding!	Win 10 Ranked Online Matches in a row	60
There Will Be Blood!	Spill 10000 pints of blood	40
License to Kill	Complete Fatality Trainer	20
Ultimate Respect!	Earn 2500 Respect Points via King of the Hill Matches	20
You Will Learn Respect!	Earn 1000 Respect Points via King of the Hill Matches	10
Undertaker	Unlock 50% of the Krypt	20
The Krypt Keeper	Unlock 100% of the Krypt	20
What Does This Button Do??	Complete Arcade Ladder without blocking (allowed to continue)	10
Fatality!	Perform a Fatality!	5
Block This!	Perform a 10-hit combo with any fighter	10
The Grappler	Perform every fighter's forward and backwards throws	10
Halfway There!	Complete Story Mode 50%	5
Back In Time...	Complete Story Mode 100%	20
A For Effort	Complete Tutorial Mode	10
The Competitor	Complete 200 Versus matches (online OR offline)	30
Ladder Master	Complete Arcade Ladder on max difficulty without using a continue	20
Don't Jump!	Win A Ranked Online Match without jumping	10
Where's The Arcade?	Complete Arcade Ladder with Any Fighter	10
Arcade Champion	Complete Arcade Ladder with All Fighters	40
Finish What You Start!	Perform a Fatality with all playable fighters	60
Tag, You're It!	Perform and land a Tag Combo	10
These Aren't My Glasses!	Complete all Test Your Sight mini-game challenges	20
Tower Apprentice	Complete 25 Tower missions	10
Tower Master	Complete all Tower missions	20
Dim Mak!	Complete all Test Your Strike mini-game challenges	20
I'm Not Dead Yet!	Comeback with under 10% health in an Online Ranked Match	20
e-X-cellent!	Successfully land every playable fighter's X-Ray attack	10
There Can Be Only One!	Win 10 King of the Hill Matches in a row	20
Throws Are For Champs	Perform 8 throws in an Online Ranked Match	20

NAME	GOAL/REQUIREMENT	POINT VALUE
Turtle!	Win both rounds with timer running out in an Online Ranked Match	20
My Kung Fu Is Strong	Gain Mastery of 1 Fighter	20
My Kung Fu Is Stronger	Gain Mastery of All Fighters	60
I "Might" Be the Strongest	Complete all Test Your Might mini-game challenges	20
Luck Be A Lady	Get all MK Dragons in Test Your Luck	10
You've Got Style!	Unlock all Alternate Costumes	20

SECRET ACHIEVEMENTS

NAME	GOAL/REQUIREMENT	POINT VALUE
Complet-ality	Perform 1 of each type of "-ality"	10
Finish Him?	Perform any fighter's hidden finishing move	10
Hide and Seek	Discover and fight Hidden Kombatant 2 in Arcade Ladder	10
Pit Master	Discover and fight Hidden Kombatant 3 in Arcade Ladder	10
Brotherhood of Shadow	Discover and fight Hidden Kombatant 4 in Arcade Ladder	20
Ultimate Humiliation	Perform every fighter's hidden finishing move	20
Quan-Tease	Unlock Hidden Fighter "Quan Chi"	20
You Found Me!	Discover and fight Hidden Kombatant 1 in Arcade Ladder	10
Cold Fusion	Unlock Hidden Fighter "Cyber Sub-Zero"	20
Best...Alternate...Ever!	Unlock Mileena's 3rd Alternate Costume	10

NARUTO SHIPPUDEN: ULTIMATE NINJA STORM GENERATIONS

ACHIEVEMENTS

NAME	GOAL/REQUIREMENT	POINT VALUE
Tale of Naruto Uzumaki complete	Completed Tale of Naruto Uzumaki.	15
Tale of Sasuke Uchiha complete	Completed Tale of Sasuke Uchiha.	15
Tale of Young Naruto complete	Completed Tale of Young Naruto.	15
Substitution Jutsu Master	Substitution Jutsu collected: 80%	15
Ninja Info Card Collector	Ninja Info Card images collected: 50%	5
Ninja Tool Master	Ninja Tools collected: 80%	15
Image Master	Images collected: 80%	15
Ultimate Jutsu Movie Master	Ultimate Jutsu scenes collected: 80%	15
First S Rank!	You've earned your first S Rank in a battle.	5
Introductory Stage Survivor!	You've completed all of Introductory Survival.	15
Beginner Survivor!	You've completed all of Beginner Survival.	15
Intermediate Survivor!	You've completed all of Intermediate Survival.	15
Advanced Survivor!	You've completed all of Advanced Survival.	15
10 Down	You've defeated 10 opponents in Ultimate Survival.	30
Team Seven Tournament Champ!	You've completed the Team Seven Tournament.	15
Sand Genin Tournament Champ!	You've completed the Sand Genin Tournament.	15
Leaf Genin Tournament Champ!	You've completed all Leaf Genin Tournament battles.	15
Boy's Life Tournament Champ!	You've completed the Boy's Life Tournament.	15
New Team Seven Tournament Champ!	You've completed the New Team Seven Tournament.	15
Leaf Chunin Tournament Champ!	You've completed the Leaf Chunin Tournament.	15

NAME	GOAL/REQUIREMENT	POINT VALUE
Ultimate Ninja Tournament Champ!	You've completed the Ultimate Ninja Tournament.	15
Leaf Higher-Up Tournament Champ!	You've completed the Leaf Higher-Up Tournament.	15
Shippuden Tournament Champ!	You've completed the Shippuden Tournament.	15
Peerless Ninja Tournament Champ!	You've completed the Peerless Ninja Tournament.	15
Akatsuki Tournament Champ!	You've completed the Akatsuki Tournament.	15
Five Kage Tournament Champ!	You've completed the Five Kage Tournament.	15
First Shopping!	You've done your first shopping.	5
First Ninja Tool Edit!	You've edited a ninja tool set for the first time.	5
Wealthy Ninja	You've earned a total of 1,000,000 Ryo.	50
I'm the greatest ninja!	You've unlocked all achievements.	0

SECRET ACHIEVEMENTS

NAME	GOAL/REQUIREMENT	POINT VALUE
Tale of Minato Namikaze complete	Completed Tale of Minato Namikaze.	15
Tale of Itachi Uchiha complete	Completed Tale of Itachi Uchiha.	15
Tale of Madara Uchiha complete	Completed Tale of Madara Uchiha.	15
Tale of Zabuza and Haku complete	Completed Tale of Zabuza Momochi and Haku.	15
Tale of Jiraiya complete	Completed Tale of Jiraiya.	15
Tale of Gaara complete	Completed Tale of Gaara.	15
Tale of Kakashi Hatake complete	Completed Tale of Kakashi Hatake.	15
Tale of Killer Bee complete	Completed Tale of Killer Bee.	15
Card Collection Master	Ninja Info Card images collected: 80%	100
Alias Master	Titles collected: 80%	100
Gimme a hand!	You can now use all support characters.	5
Master Survivor!	You've completed all of Survival Mode.	30
Five Kage Summit	All Kage at the Five Kage Summit can now be used.	5
Past Hokages	You can now use all past Hokages.	5
Younger Version	You can use all the characters of the Young Version.	15
Shippuden	You can use all the characters from Shippuden.	15
Game Master!	You've played for a total of over 30 hours.	30
Ninja Lover!	You've used all leader characters.	50
Ultimate Ninja Gathering	You can now use all characters.	50
Tournament Champ!	You've completed all Challenge Tournaments.	30

NASCAR 2011: THE GAME

ACHIEVEMENTS

NAME	GOAL/REQUIREMENT	POINT VALUE
"Let's Go Racin Boys"	You took part in your first online race.	10
Hotrod	You created a custom tuning setup.	20
Up on the Wheel	You lead 5 consecutive laps in an online race.	10
Pedal to the Metal	You achieved the fastest lap of the race during an online race.	10
Rubbin is Racin!	You raced online at every track.	20
Run the Gauntlet	You won a Gauntlet Invitational Event.	10
Last Man Standing	You survived a 43 car eliminator race to the end.	10
The Champ is here!	You won the Championship Showdown Invitational Event.	20
Give me 4	You performed your first 4-tire pit stop in a race.	20
Finishing in First!	You won a race crossing the line in first gear.	10

NAME	GOAL/REQUIREMENT	POINT VALUE
Win on Sunday, Sell on Monday	You won a race in all brands of car.	10
Boy Scout	You unlocked every NASCAR Pin in the game.	70
Name to Remember	You unlocked every Gold Legends Coin in the game.	50
Kingly	You defeated Richard Petty's race win record of 200 wins.	50
Pit Perfection	You performed a 4-tire pit stop, and went on to win an online race.	20
Styling 'N' Profiling	You won a race with a personalized Paint Scheme.	10
Ride in Style	You've collected 88 Paint Schemes by completing all Invitational Events and reaching rank 29	40
Surfin' USA	You mastered every track in the game.	40
Groovy	You mastered a track by completing all the objectives on a Master the Track card.	20
Victory Lane	You have won a race at every circuit in the game.	20
Saddle Up & Hang On	You have qualified in pole position at every circuit in the game in Career Mode.	50
Race Rivalry	You achieved 20 rival victories.	30
Star of Tomorrow	You achieved a total of 100 fastest laps.	50
NXP Challenge	You have achieved over 6,666 NXP in a single race.	20
Now ya Talkin'	You reached Rank 10.	20
One for the Road	You ranked up for the first time.	20
NASCAR Legend	You reached Rank 30.	70
Decorated Driver	You reached Rank 20.	30
Keep Diggin'	You have driven 500 miles.	10
VIP	You completed all three objectives for a single sponsor in Career Mode.	20
Any Place, Any Time	You competed in every Invitational Event.	20
Car Stylist	You entered the Create New Paint Scheme Menu	10
MVP	You received full sponsorship status for your driver in Career Mode.	20
Cup Contender	You achieved a top 10 finish in every Career Mode race.	40
Sprint to the Finish	You won a race in Career Mode and got the full 195 points.	10
Tailgating	You performed a draft of 500 yards.	10
Series Champion	You finished top of the Career Mode standings and became the Sprint Cup series champion.	70
Race to the Chase	You achieved enough points in Career Mode to move into The Chase, as one of the top 12 drivers.	20

SECRET ACHIEVEMENTS

NAME	GOAL/REQUIREMENT	POINT VALUE
Celebration Shot	You photographed the driver celebrating on the car after a Career Mode race win.	10
Rookie Mistake	You received a drive through or speeding penalty.	0

NBA 2K13

ACHIEVEMENTS

NAME	GOAL/REQUIREMENT	POINT VALUE
Dawn of an Era	Get drafted as a lottery pick in the NBA draft in MyCAREER mode.	15
Serving Notice	Get 250,000 fans in MyCAREER mode.	15
I'm Here to Stay	Get 1,000,000 fans in MyCAREER mode.	25
Man of the People	Get 2,000,000 fans in MyCAREER mode.	40
Everyone is Special	Purchase and equip 1 Special Ability in MyCAREER mode.	15
Some more Special than Others	Purchase and equip 5 Special Abilities simultaneously in MyCAREER mode.	30
Now Playing	Purchase a pre-game ritual in MyCAREER mode.	15
Both Feet on the Ground	Sign an endorsement contract with either Nike® or Jordan in MyCAREER mode.	30

NAME	GOAL/REQUIREMENT	POINT VALUE
Come Fly with Me	Purchase Michael Jordan's dunk package (Historic Jordan) in MyCAREER mode.	15
NBA Cares	Make a donation to the NBA Cares global community outreach initiative in MyCAREER mode.	15
MyPLAYER of the Game	Be named Player of the Game (in an NBA game) in MyCAREER mode.	20
My Every Day Player	Become a starter in the NBA in MyCAREER Mode.	20
My All-Star	Be named an NBA All-Star in MyCAREER mode.	25
Immortality	Make the Hall of Fame in MyCAREER mode.	30
Runneth Over	Obtain a balance of 20,000 VC.	30
Buzzer Beater	Make a game winning shot with no time left on the clock in a non-simulated game.	20
Trip-Dub	Record a triple double with any player in a non-simulated game.	20
Dub-Dub	Record two double doubles with any teammates in the same non-simulated game.	20
Five by Five	Record 5 or more in 5 different stats with any player in a non-simulated game.	20
It's Raining	Make 15 or more 3-pointers with any team in a non-simulated game.	20
Block Party	Record 10 or more blocks with any team in a non-simulated game.	20
Men of Steal	Record 10 or more steals with any team in a non-simulated game.	20
Swat and Swipe	Record at least 5 blocks and 5 steals with any team in a non-simulated game.	20
Smothering	Hold the opposing team's FG% below 40% with any team in a non-simulated game.	20
Giveth and Taketh Away	Record 10 or more rebounds and assists with any player in a non-simulated game.	20
Hold the Fat Lady	Start the 4th period losing by 10 or more points and win with any team in a non-simulated game.	20
Wire to Wire	Do not allow your opponent to lead the game at any point with any team in a non-simulated game.	20
The Closer	Hold the opposing team to zero points in the final two minutes of a non-simulated game.	20
The Here and Now	Begin a "Today" Association.	15
Puppet Master	Adjust your "Total Sim Control" strategy in The Association or Season mode.	10
Not Your Father's Association	Join an Online Association.	10
Another Day, Another Win	Win 5 NBA Today matchups.	20
Don't Hate the Player	Win the championship in an Online Association.	30
Streaking	Win 5 non-simulated games in a row in The Association mode.	25
Ticker Tape	Win an NBA Championship in The Association mode (playing every playoff game).	30
Shooting Star	Win the MVP award in NBA: Creating a Legend mode.	30
Hey Mr. DJ	Create a 2K Beats Playlist.	10
Maestro	Create a shoe in the 2K Shoe Creator.	15
Raining 3's	Make at least 9 three-pointers in one game with Brandon Jennings to set a new career-high.	20
KD Unlimited	Score at least 52 points in one game with Kevin Durant to set a new career-high.	20
From the Ground Up	Purchase 15 Boosters in MyTEAM mode.	20
To Good Use	Play a MyTEAM game online.	15
On the Road Again	Play a MyPLAYER Blacktop game online.	15
Remaking History	Play with an historic team online.	15
This One Counts	Win one online Versus match.	15
Back to Back to Back	Win 3 Versus matches in a row.	15
You're Officially Hot	Win 5 Versus matches in a row.	20
Lincoln	Win 5 Versus matches total.	15
Hamilton	Win 10 Versus matches total.	20
The Sum of Its Parts	Play a Team-Up Game.	15

ALL-STAR WEEKEND

ACHIEVEMENTS

NAME	GOAL/REQUIREMENT	POINT VALUE
The Future is Now	Win the Rising Stars Challenge.	20
All The Sprite® Moves	Win the Sprite® Slam Dunk Contest with at least one AI opponent.	20
Home, Home on Long Range	Win the Three-Point Contest with at least one AI opponent.	20
Starry, Starry Night	Win the All-Star Game.	30
I Came, I Saw...	Win all 4 All-Star events.	60

NINJA GAIDEN 3

ACHIEVEMENTS

NAME	GOAL/REQUIREMENT	POINT VALUE
Falcon Dive	Learn the Falcon Dive.	10
Sliding	Learn how to slide.	10
Kunai Climb	Learn the Kunai Climb.	10
Wall Run	Learn the Wall Run.	10
Flying Bird Flip	Learn the Flying Bird Flip.	10
Rope Crossing	Learn how to cross a rope.	10
Izuna Drop	Learn the Izuna Drop.	10
Ultimate Technique	Learn the Ultimate Technique.	10
Steel on Bone	Cut down 100 enemies with Steel on Bone attacks.	10
I Got Your Back	Play a Co-op Ninja Trial with a partner.	10
Initiation	Play a Clan Battle.	10
Teamwork	Win 10 team battles.	10
One Against the World	Win a battle royale match.	10
Shady	Perform a betrayal.	10
Sneaky	Perform a ghost kill.	10
An Honorable Death	Perform harakiri.	10
Snowman	Play the Snowfield stage 10 times.	10
Guardian of the Village	Play the Hidden Village stage 10 times.	10
Observer	Play the Watchtower stage 10 times.	10
The Spice of Life	Get 10 customization parts.	10
Walking Dictionary	Get 100 kanji.	50

SECRET ACHIEVEMENTS

NAME	GOAL/REQUIREMENT	POINT VALUE
Inferno	Learned Ninpo.	10
Steel on Steel	Destroyed the Steel Spider.	10
The Grip of Murder	Finish Day 1.	10
Mind the Gap	Escaped from the monorail.	10
Bumpy Ride	Finish Day 2.	10
Beyond the Flames	Made it through the fire.	15
Antediluvian Slumber	Finish Day 3.	15
Abysmal Creations	Escaped from the Chimera Disposal Facility.	15
The Great Escape	Finish Day 4.	15
The Acolyte	Successfully responded to Sanji's ambush.	15
The Karma of a Shinobi	Finish Day 5.	15
Evil Twin	Defeated the Epigonos.	15
Waiting	Finish Day 6.	15
Ahab	Land on the Black Narwhal.	15
Advent of the Goddess	Finish Day 7.	15
Brothers	Defeated Cliff.	15
Atonement	Defeated Theodore.	15
Hero	Cleared the game on Hero.	50
Shinobi	Cleared the game on Normal.	50
Mentor	Cleared the game on Hard.	60

NAME	GOAL/REQUIREMENT	POINT VALUE
Master Ninja	Cleared the game on Master Ninja.	100
Initiate	Cleared 10 Acolyte Trials.	10
Veteran	Cleared 10 Mentor Trials.	10
Prestige	Cleared 5 Leader Trials.	10
Overlord	Cleared 5 Master Ninja Trials.	50
Ultimate Ninja	Cleared 3 Ultimate Ninja Trials.	100
Master of the Katana	Raised the katana to level 10.	15
Hayabusa Style Grand Master	Reached level 50.	15
Lone Ninja	Cleared 10 Solo Ninja Trials.	50

NINJA PACK 1

SECRET ACHIEVEMENTS

NAME	GOAL/REQUIREMENT	POINT VALUE
Bloodied Talons		
15		
Defeat 100 opponents in Clan Battles with the Metal Claws.		
Warrior		
45		
Clear all Ninja Trials included in Ninja Pack 1.		

NINJA PACK 2

SECRET ACHIEVEMENTS

NAME	GOAL/REQUIREMENT	POINT VALUE
Grim Reaper	Defeat 100 opponents in Clan Battles with the Great Scythe.	15
Sage	Clear all Ninja Trials included in Ninja Pack 2.	45

OF ORCS AND MEN

ACHIEVEMENTS

NAME	GOAL/REQUIREMENT	POINT VALUE
Back to business	You support the local weapon trade. That's... well, nice of you.	5
King of the arena	You fought like a lion and ended up victorious in the Row.	10
Nobody's perfect	The Imperial officer in the Monastery seemed to be of good faith. Just to be safe, you offed him.	15
Warrior	You have valiantly dealt with all the trials in Of Orcs and Men	50
I'm a killer	You slit 47 throats and they never saw it coming. So you dig?	30
You crack me up	You have a delicate tendency to break the bones of people who get in your way, so congratulations.	30
Big chest lover	So you went digging around in every corner to find at least twenty chests to empty, huh?	75
Jack of all blades	You hit eight enemies with a single blow. Huh, not bad.	30
Guidance counselor	You were able to find the best people for your squad for the assault on the Pillar.	15
Smart and smarter	You chose to improve one of your Skills before you learned another one. Kudos for that.	5
Poisoner	You don't like wasting perfectly good poison, so you cleaned your blade off on 3 different enemies.	10
Go bling-bling	You only wear upgraded equipment. It's a matter of reputation.	15
I know a shortcut	The good thing with shortcuts is that they are faster. It would seem you got that right.	5

OVERLOAD

NAME	GOAL/REQUIREMENT	POINT VALUE
Deratizator	You cut short the Goblin invasion in the shantytown. Pretty violently.	15
A hair too late	You pulled your girlfriend Brune out of trouble. She owes you a massage for that.	15
Well trained	You got even with the Trainer. And he got dead.	15
One less nutcase	You avenged your friend and killed the mad Shaman. He'll guide the dead himself.	15
Hand shake	You showed those Black Hands who's the boss.	15
Off the Wall	You finally got past that damn Wall ! Well done !	50
Class struggle	You avoided a miners' revolt. Thanks to you, they will be able to die for a nobler cause.	15
Throat-slitter	You sent Styx to introduce his daggers to the sentinels of the Mire. He thanks you.	15
I don't like chit-chat	You didn't feel like letting Gorkash bore you with his bull, so you cut him off.	5
No quarter	You have imposed your authority by taking out all opposing Orcs. An age-old method that still works.	15
Samaritan	In a spirit of forgiveness as heroic as it was delusional, you decided to spare Dakath the traitor.	15
All this for that	You had to put up with a pile of enraged Goblins, but you got your flask of water!	15
The beast and the beast	Garok is now your friend for life. Now that's a sign of upcoming great conversations!	5
You mythed!	You showed that big-mouth Braggart that when he blows his own horn he's talking to the wrong guy!	5
Team spirit	You made sure to put together a special team to assault the Pillar from the Mire.	15
In open air	You managed to escape the Mire. With the chick, too.	50
Slicer-Dicer	You decided to forget your past to devote yourself to a career as an Assassin. Enjoy.	10
Into the shadow	You decided that black magic isn't so bad, especially when you're the only one who knows it.	10
Inner rage	You turned Arkail into a berserk monster. More than before, that is. And it went well. For some.	10
Anger management	You helped Arkail control his rage. Those of his friends and family who are still alive thank you.	10
I've got my friends in my head	You've gone through nightmares, but now you're finally setting off for the Island of Laments.	50
Regicide the first	You've killed Emperor Damocles. Which is nice to hear, 'cause that was the idea in the first place.	10
Your sister too	You have taken on the most formidable warriors in the Empire. Apart from you, of course.	50
Repeat offender	You killed the Emperor again, and set fire to the Tower. Maybe you should stop now.	50
Rakash	You have smoothly dealt with all the trials in Of Orcs and Men	20
Mercenary	You have bravely dealt with all the trials in Of Orcs and Men	30
Bloodjaw	You dealt with all the trials in Of Orcs and Men like a berserker.	100
The hard way	You handled your first quarrel like... an Orc. Well, you sure got into your character!	5
Talk it out	You allowed Styx to calm things down before Arkail went berserk. Literally.	5
Manual worker	Nice move, you sliced up a boss without a single auto attack!	5
To each his branch	As a good specialist, you've decided to learn every skill in a single tree.	10
My house!	As a good master, you've decided to learn and perfect each Skill in a single tree.	50

PORTAL 2

ACHIEVEMENTS

NAME	GOAL/REQUIREMENT	POINT VALUE
Pit Boss	Show that pit who's boss	30
Preservation of Mass	Break the rules in Test Chamber 07	20
Pturretdactyl	Use an Aerial Faith Plate to launch a turret	5
Lunacy	That just happened	20
Drop Box	Place a cube on a button without touching the cube	20
Overclocker	Complete Test Chamber 10 in 70 seconds	30
No Hard Feelings	Save a turret from redemption	10
Schrodinger's Catch	Catch a blue-painted box before it touches the ground	20
Ship Overboard	Discover the missing experiment	10
Final Transmission	Find the hidden signal in one of the Rat Man's dens	20
Good Listener	Take GLaDOS' escape advice	5
Scanned Alone	Stand in a defective turret detector	5
The Part Where He Kills You	This is that part	20
Bridge Over Troubling Water	Complete the first Hard Light Bridge test	10
SaBOTour	Make a break for it	10
Stalemate Associate	Press the button!	15
Wake Up Call	Survive the manual override	5
You Monster	Reunite with GLaDOS	5
Undiscouraged	Complete the first Thermal Discouragement Beam test	10
White Out	Complete the first Conversion Gel test	15
Tunnel of Funnel	Master the Excursion Funnel	15
Dual Pit Experiment	Do the same test twice	15
Tater Tote	Carry science forward	15
Vertically Unchallenged	Master the Repulsion Gel	15
Stranger Than Friction	Master the Propulsion Gel	15
Professor Portal	After completing co-op, complete Calibration Course online with a friend who hasn't played before	75
Air Show	Perform 2 aerial gestures before touching the ground in co-op	20
Portal Conservation Society	Complete Chamber 3 in the Hard-Light Surfaces co-op course using only 5 total portal placements	20
Empty Gesture	Drop your co-op partner in goo while they are gesturing by removing the bridge under them	25
Party of Three	Find the hidden companion cube in co-op test chamber	25
Narbacular Drop	Place a portal under your co-op partner while they are gesturing	25
Asking for Trouble	Taunt GLaDOS in front of a camera in each of the five co-op courses	10
Rock Portal Scissors	Win 3 co-op games of rock-paper-scissors in a row	20
Friends List With Benefits	While playing co-op, hug 3 different people on your friends list	50
Four Ring Circus	Enter 4 different portals without touching the ground in co-op	25
Triple Crown	Solve 3 co-op chambers in the Mass and Velocity course in under 60 seconds each	15
Still Alive	Complete Course 4 with neither you nor your co-op partner dying	15
Can't Touch This	Dance in front of a turret blocked by a hard light bridge in co-op	10
Smash TV	Break 11 test chamber monitors	75
High Five	Celebrate your cooperative calibration success	5
Team Building	Complete all test chambers in the Team Building co-op course	10
Door Prize	Examine all the vitrified test chamber doors	20
Portrait of a Lady	Find a hidden portrait	10
You Made Your Point	Refuse to solve the first test in Chapter 8	10
You Saved Science	Complete all test chambers in all courses of co-op	100
Iron Grip	Never lose a cube in Chamber 6 of the Mass and Velocity co-op course	20
Gesticul-8	Perform all 8 gestures of your own volition in co-op	15

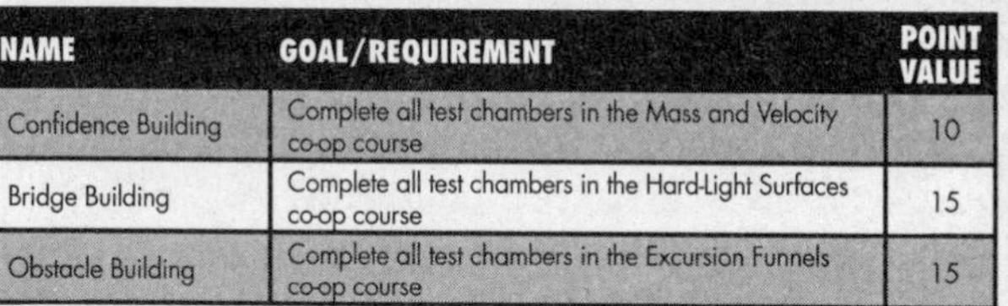

NAME	GOAL/REQUIREMENT	POINT VALUE
Confidence Building	Complete all test chambers in the Mass and Velocity co-op course	10
Bridge Building	Complete all test chambers in the Hard-Light Surfaces co-op course	15
Obstacle Building	Complete all test chambers in the Excursion Funnels co-op course	15

PROTOTYPE 2

ACHIEVEMENTS

NAME	GOAL/REQUIREMENT	POINT VALUE
Anger Management	Destroyed 5 vehicles using a Finisher.	20
So Above It All	Spend at least 25 consecutive seconds in the air (helicopters don't count).	20
Vitamin B-rains	Acquired 10 upgrades through Consumes.	10
Eating Your Way to the Top	Acquired 30 upgrades through Consumes.	30
Finally Full	Acquired all 46 upgrades through Consumes.	50
Icarus	Reached the highest point in the world.	15
Spindler's Search	Destroyed all Lairs.	40
//BLACKNET Hacker	Completed all //BLACKNET dossiers.	40
One by One	Stealth Consumed 50 Blackwatch troopers.	20
Wanted Man	Triggered 50 alerts.	20
All Growed Up	Fully upgraded Heller.	50
Master Prototype	Completed the game on HARD difficulty.	50
It's an Epidemic	Complete MEET YOUR MAKER.	10
I Want Some More	Complete RESURRECTION.	10
Religious Experience	Meet Father Guerra.	10
This is a Knife	First Prototype Power aquired.	20
Project Closed	Completed a //BLACKNET mission.	20
The Mad Scientist	Complete NATURAL SELECTION.	30
Something to Live For	Complete FALL FROM GRACE.	30
What a Bitch	Complete LABOR OF LOVE.	30
Murder your Maker?	Complete the game.	100
Follow Your Nose	Found all BlackBoxes.	30
Up to No Good	Defeated all Field Ops teams.	30
Strike, You're Out.	Destroyed a Strike Team in 15 seconds or less.	10
Compulsive Eater	5 consumes in 10 seconds or less.	10
Do the Evolution	Acquired 5 Mutations.	20
Just a Flesh Wound	Dismembered a Brawler.	10
All Together Now	10 or more kills with a single Black Hole attack.	20
Back Atcha!	Deflected 5 missiles at enemies using Shield Block.	20
Two for the Price of One	Simultaneously killed 2 Brawlers using a single Devastator.	20
Lair to Rest	Destroyed a single Lair.	15
Hijack Be Nimble	Stealth hijacked 5 tanks or APCs.	15
Road Rage	Destroyed 10 Blackwatch tanks, APCs or helicopters using a single hijacked tank or APC.	20
Who Watches the Watchers?	Consumed 10 //BLACKNET targets.	20
Hard to Please	Acquired a Mutation in each of the 5 categories.	20
The Floor is Lava	Traveled a half mile using only Wall Run, Glide, Jump and Air Dash.	15
Cannonball!	20 or more kills with a single Hammerfist dive attack.	10
You're the Bomb	10 or more kills using a single Bio-Bomb.	10
Sic 'em!	Destroyed 5 helicopters using Pack Leader.	20
Over-Equipped	Weaponized 10 vehicles.	20
The Best Offense	Countered enemy attacks 20 times using Shield.	20
Arcade Action	Karate kicked a helicopter.	10
I Caught a Big One!	Mounted a helicopter using Whipfist.	10

RAGE

ACHIEVEMENTS

NAME	GOAL/REQUIREMENT	POINT VALUE
Arts and Crafts	Construct 10 Engineering Items	10
Tinkerer	Construct 50 Engineering Items	20
Passive Aggressive	Get 3 kills with a single Sentry Bot	30
Three Birds, One Bomb Car	Kill 3 Enemies with one RC Bomb Car	30
Keep 'Em Coming	Get 5 kills with one deployed Sentry Turret	30
Mechanocide	Kill 100 Enemies with Sentry Bots, Sentry Turrets, or RC Bomb Cars	50
Jetpacker	Kill an Authority Enforcer during Jetpack descent	20
Silent But Deadly	Stealth kill 10 Enemies with the Striker Crossbow	15
Hat Trick	Kill at least 3 Enemies with a single Mind Controlled Enemy	15
Decapathon	Get 10 Headshot kills with the Wingstick	15
Open Minded	Get 10 Headshot kills with the Sniper Rifle	15
Jumper	Perform all 18 Vehicle Jumps	20
Gotta Have 'Em All	Collect all Playing Cards on one play-through	20
Master Chef	Collect all Recipes and Schematics in one play-through	20
Hardest Deck	Beat Teague's hardest Deck	25
JACKPOT!	Roll 4 Targets in the first round of Tombstones	15
Just a Flesh Wound	Complete the final round of 5 Finger Filet	15
Deliverance	Complete the final round of Strum	15
Minigamer	Win all Minigames	15
Lead Foot	Win a Race in the Campaign	10
Rage Cup	Win all Races in the Campaign	50
Demolition Man	Destroy 100 Enemy Cars	20
It's Good!	Score each of the 3 Field Goals from the ATV	15
Roadkill	Run over 10 Mutants	15
Ghost Buster	Complete Ghost Hideout in the Campaign	10
Waste Management	Complete Wasted Garage in the Campaign	10
Gladiator	Complete Mutant Bash TV in the Campaign	10
It's Alive!	Complete Dead City in the Campaign	10
Wellness Plan	Complete The Well in the Campaign	10
Debunked	Complete Shrouded Bunker in the Campaign	10
ytiC daeD	Complete Dead City Reverse in the Campaign	10
Jail Break	Complete Authority Prison in the Campaign	10
Vault Assault	Complete Gearhead Vault in the Campaign	10
Power Struggle	Complete Power Plant in the Campaign	10
Decrypted	Complete Jackal Canyon in the Campaign	10
Mutie Blues	Complete Blue Line Station in the Campaign	10
Bringin' Home the Bacon	Earn 750 Dollars in one episode of Bash TV in the Campaign	20
Mr. Oddjob	Complete 5 Job Board Quests in one play-through	40
Dev Graffiti	Find the secret Developer Graffiti Room	15
Hey, not too rough	Finish the Campaign on any difficulty	50
Hurt me plenty	Finish the Campaign on at least Normal difficulty	25
Ultra-violence	Finish the Campaign on at least Hard difficulty	25
RAGE Nightmare	Finish the Campaign on Nightmare difficulty	25
Obsessive Compulsive	Reach 100% Completion in the Campaign	75
The Legend Begins...	Complete a Legend of the Wasteland	10
Anthology	Complete all Legends of the Wasteland	20
A True Legend	Complete a Legend of the Wasteland on Nightmare difficulty	25
No Room for Sidekicks	Complete a Legend of the Wasteland without any player(s) becoming incapacitated	15
Fresh Meat	Complete a public Road RAGE match	10
MVP	Get first place in a public Road RAGE match	20

RED DEAD REDEMPTION

ACHIEVEMENTS

NAME	GOAL/REQUIREMENT	POINT VALUE
High Roller	Win over 2000 chips in a hand of Poker.	10
No Dice	Complete a game of Liar's Dice without losing a single die.	10
What About Hand Grenades?	Get a ringer in a game of Horseshoes.	10
Austin Overpowered	Complete Twin Rocks, Pike's Basin, and Gaptooth Breach Hideouts in Single Player.	25
Evil Spirits	Complete Tumbleweed and Tesoro Azul Hideouts in Single Player.	25
Instinto Asesino	Complete Fort Mercer and Nosalida Hideouts in Single Player.	25
Fightin' Around the World	Knock someone out in melee in every saloon in the game in Single Player.	5
Strange Things are Afoot	Complete a task for a Stranger.	10
People are Still Strange	Complete 15 tasks for Strangers.	25
Buckin' Awesome	Break the Kentucky Saddler, the American Standard-bred, and the Hungarian Half-bred.	10
Clemency Pays	Capture a bounty alive.	10
Exquisite Taste	Purchase a rare weapon from a gunsmith.	10
Bearly Legal	Kill and skin 18 grizzly bears.	5
He Cleans Up Well!	Obtain the Elegant Suit.	10
More than a Fistful	Earn $10,000 in Single Player.	10
Frontiersman	Obtain Legendary rank in any Single Player Ambient Challenge.	20
The Gunslinger	Score a headshot on any enemy using Expert targeting mode.	5
Man of Honor / Chivalry's Dead	Attain highest Fame rank and either highest Honor rank or lowest Honor rank.	25
Gold Medal	Earn a Gold Medal Rank for a combat mission in Single Player.	25
On the Trail of de Vaca	Uncover every location on the map in Single Player.	10
Friends in High Places	Use a pardon letter with more than $5000 bounty in Single Player.	10
Redeemed	Attain 100% in the Single Player Game Completion stat.	100
Mowing Them Down	Kill 500 enemies with a mounted weapon in any game mode.	20
In a Hail of Bullets	Kill 500 enemies with any pistol or revolver in any game mode.	20
Long Arm of Marston	Kill 500 enemies with any rifle, repeater, or shotgun in any game mode.	20
Bullseye	Get 250 headshots in any game mode.	20
Unnatural Selection	Kill one of every animal species in the game in any game mode.	20
Have Gun Will Travel	Complete all Hideouts in a single public Free Roam session.	20
Slow on the Draw	Get 10 assists in a single Hideout in a public Free Roam session.	10
Hit the Trail	Get from Blackwater to Escalera before sundown in a public Free Roam session.	10
Posse Up!	Create a posse and get the maximum number of members.	10
The Quick and Everyone Else...	Be the top scoring player in any three consecutive FFA games in public matches.	20
How the West Was Won	Reach the top rank for multiplayer experience.	20
Go Team!	Be on the winning team for four consecutive victories in any team based game in public matches.	20
Most Wanted	Become a Public Enemy for 10 minutes and escape alive in a public Free Roam session.	10
Red Dead Rockstar	Kill a Rockstar or someone with this achievement in a public multiplayer match.	10

SECRET ACHIEVEMENTS

NAME	GOAL/REQUIREMENT	POINT VALUE
That Government Boy	Complete "Exodus in America".	10
Land of Opportunity	Complete "The Assault on Fort Mercer".	30
Sons of Mexico	Complete "The Gates of El Presidio".	40
No More Fancy Words	Complete "An Appointed Time".	20
A Savage Soul	Complete "At Home with Dutch".	10
The Benefits of Civilization	Complete "And the Truth Will Set You Free".	90
Into the Sunset	Complete "The Last Enemy That Shall Be Destroyed".	100
Nurture or Nature?	Complete "Remember My Family".	50
Dastardly	Place a hogtied woman on the train tracks, and witness her death by train.	5
Spurred to Victory	Complete 20 story missions without switching to a new horse at a hitching post.	10
Heading South on a White Bronco	Evade the US Marshals while riding the Hungarian Half-Bred horse in Single Player.	5
Manifest Destiny	Kill the last buffalo in the Great Plains in Single Player.	5

DOWNLOADABLE CONTENT: OUTLAWS TO THE END

NAME	GOAL/REQUIREMENT	POINT VALUE
Well done	Complete a Co-Op mission.	5
Have posse, will travel	Complete all Co-Op missions.	15
2 guys, 1 Coop	Complete a Co-Op mission with just 2 people.	10
Stake a claim	Gold medal any Co-Op mission.	5
Struck gold	Gold medal all Co-Ops missions.	10
Friends indeed	Complete a Co-Op mission without anyone dying.	5
You rule!	Complete all Advanced Co-Op missions.	15
The mother lode	Gold medal all Advanced Co-Op missions.	20
Dodge this	Achieve a kill chain of 10 or more in any Advanced Co-Op mission.	10
Bulletproof	Complete a Co-Op mission without dying.	5

DOWNLOADABLE CONTENT: LEGENDS AND KILLERS

NAME	GOAL/REQUIREMENT	POINT VALUE
Call it a Comeback!	Come back from a 2-0 deficit and win a Hold Your Own game.	10
Who needs Deadeye?	Kill 3 or more players in a standoff or showdown.	10
Stick and Move	Get 3 kills with knives or throwing knives in a single competitive match.	10
Double bagger	Double capture 3 times in a single Gold Rush map.	10
Headhunter	Kill 5 players via headshot in a single Shootout or Gang Shootout.	10
Legendary	Reach level 50 and pass into Legend.	10
Hail Mary	Get a kill greater than 35 yards with a Tomahawk.	10
Axe Master	Complete all Tomahawk challenges in Single Player.	10
Original Gunslinger	Get 25 Deadeye kills with Red.	10
Reeeeal Good	Get 25 Dynamite kills with Pig Josh.	10

DOWNLOADABLE CONTENT: LIARS & CHEATS

NAME	GOAL/REQUIREMENT	POINT VALUE
Master Exploder	Complete the Explosive Rifle Single Player Challenge	10
Pa-Pa-Pa-Poker Ace	In a full Multiplayer Poker game, beat the table when blinds are at maximum	10
The Big Bluff	In a Multiplayer Poker game, win a hand by forcing someone with a better hand to fold	5
In A Van Down By The River	In a Multiplayer Poker game, win a hand on the last card when you were losing prior	5
Compulsive Liar	In a full Multiplayer Liar's Dice game, win without losing a single die	10

NAME	GOAL/REQUIREMENT	POINT VALUE
Good Call	In a single Multiplayer Liar's Dice game, successfully make a spot-on call	5
One Die to Rule Them All	In a Multiplayer Liar's Dice game, win with only one die left	5
Triple Crown	Get first place in all races in any Grand Prix	10
Peacewalker	Finish a single race without getting shot or killed, and without shooting a bullet	5
From Glue to Mon Dieu!	During a Grand Prix, finish a race in first after placing last in the previous race.	5
We Must Protect This House!	While on defense, do not allow the attacking team to capture any of their objectives	10
Avatar of Death	Successfully complete either round of a Stronghold map without dying	5
Legion of Boom	Get a triple kill while on the attacking team in Stronghold	5
Over 9001	Attain over 9,001 points in a single Free Roam session	5
Put the Posse on a Pedestal	Attain over 50,000 posse points in a single Free Roam session	5

RED FACTION: GUERRILLA

ACHIEVEMENTS

NAME	GOAL/REQUIREMENT	POINT VALUE
Welcoming Committee	Complete the Tutorial mission.	10
Martian Tea Party	Complete 2 missions for the Red Faction.	10
Spread the Word	Liberate Parker Sector.	10
Death From Above	Liberate Dust Sector.	20
Friendly Skies	Liberate Badlands Sector.	30
Don't Tread On Me	Liberate Oasis Sector.	40
Coup D'etat	Liberate Eos Sector.	50
Red Dawn	Liberate Mars.	100
Insurgent	Complete 5 Guerrilla Actions.	5
Guerrilla	Complete 25 Guerrilla Actions.	10
Freedom Fighter	Complete 50 Guerrilla Actions.	15
Revolutionary	Complete all Guerrilla Actions.	25
Clean and Righteous!	Destroy 5 High Importance targets.	15
Warp Speed	Beat all Transporter Pro times.	15
Got Any Fingers Left?	Beat all Pro times in Demolitions Master.	15
Lost Memories	Locate all missing radio tags.	25
Working the Land	Mine all ore locations.	25
Free Your Mind	Destroy all instances of propaganda.	25
One Man Army	Complete 25 killing sprees during the Campaign.	25
Disaster Area	Destroy 1 billion credits worth of EDF property.	50
Broken Supply Line	Destroy 250 EDF supply crates.	10
Power to the People	Raise the Morale of 3 sectors to 100%.	10
Tank Buster	Blow up 100 small hydrogen tanks.	10
Best Friends Forever	Kill 100 EDF with the sledgehammer during the Campaign.	10
Coming Down!	Destroy 50 EDF owned buildings.	10
Freed Space	Destroy 50 EDF flyers.	10
Just the Beginning	Win a Matchmaking match.	5
Start of Something Special	Play 5 Matchmaking matches.	5
Doing Your Part	Kill 10 enemies in a Matchmaking Match.	10
Juggernaut	Destroy a Siege target.	5
Doozer	Reconstruct a Damage Control target.	5
Grab Some Popcorn	Enter Spectator mode and enjoy the show!	5
Try Anything Once	Finish a match in every mode.	10
Check Your Map	Finish a match on every map in Multiplayer.	10
Tools of the Trade	Score a kill with every weapon in Multiplayer.	10
Field Tested	Earn 1,000 XP in Multiplayer.	10
Battle Scarred	Earn 10,000 XP in Multiplayer.	25

NAME	GOAL/REQUIREMENT	POINT VALUE
War Veteran	Earn 100,000 XP in Multiplayer.	50
A Winner is You!	Win 250 matchmaking games.	20
Topher Would Be Proud	Play 250 matchmaking games.	20
Courier of Pain	Score 5,000 kills in Multiplayer.	20
Experimenter	Complete 4 hidden challenges in Multiplayer.	10
Detective	Complete 8 hidden challenges in Multiplayer.	20
Mad Genius	Complete 16 hidden challenges in Multiplayer.	40
Jack of all Trades	Score 10 kills while wearing each backpack.	10
The High and Mighty	Kill a flying opponent using a remote charge stuck to them.	10
Party Time	Play all Wrecking Crew modes once.	10
Can't Get Enough	Play every mode on all maps in Wrecking Crew.	20
Wrecking Ball	Score 25 million points worth of destruction in Wrecking Crew.	40
Red Faction Member	Play online with another player who has completed the Campaign.	50
Bound By Blood	Complete Rescue.	30
Family Vengeance	Complete Retribution.	40
A Greater Purpose	Complete Redemption.	50
Deliverance Defender	Complete Marauder Actions.	20
Tumbling Down	Beat all Pro times in Mariner Valley Demo Masters and Transporters.	10
Mobile Bombs	Destroy 100 EDF vehicles.	10
Structural Integrity	Destroy all Medium and High Priority Targets in Mariner Valley.	20
Purge the Valley	Break the EDF Control of the Mariner Valley.	30
Ares' Bloodlust	Destroy the 4 Marauder War Totems.	20
The Power of One	Collect 75 Marauder Power Cells.	20

RESIDENT EVIL 6

ACHIEVEMENTS

NAME	GOAL/REQUIREMENT	POINT VALUE
The Longest Night	Complete the tutorial.	10
Gone to Hell	Complete Chapter 1 in Leon's campaign.	15
Buried Secrets	Complete Chapter 2 in Leon's campaign.	15
Get on the Plane	Complete Chapter 3 in Leon's campaign.	15
Big Trouble in China	Complete Chapter 4 in Leon's campaign.	15
The Trouble with Women	Complete Chapter 5 in Leon's campaign.	15
Rescue the Hostages	Complete Chapter 1 in Chris' campaign.	15
Tragedy in Europe	Complete Chapter 2 in Chris' campaign.	15
After Her!	Complete Chapter 3 in Chris' campaign.	15
There's Always Hope	Complete Chapter 4 in Chris' campaign.	15
Duty Calls	Complete Chapter 5 in Chris' campaign.	15
Money Talks	Complete Chapter 1 in Jake's campaign.	15
A Revolting Development	Complete Chapter 2 in Jake's campaign.	15
Let's Blow This Joint	Complete Chapter 3 in Jake's campaign.	15
Still on the Run	Complete Chapter 4 in Jake's campaign.	15
See You Around	Complete Chapter 5 in Jake's campaign.	15
Green around the Ears	Complete the entire game on Amateur.	15
Normal Is Good	Complete the entire game on Normal.	30
Back in My Day	Complete the entire game on Veteran.	30
Leave It to the Pro	Complete the entire game on Professional.	90
Check Out My Dogs	Customize your dog tags.	15
Titular Achievement	Earn 10 different titles.	15
One Is Better Than None	Purchase one skill.	15
Mad Skillz	Max out all the skills that allow you to level up.	90
Silent Killer	Use a stealth attack to take down five enemies.	15
Finish What You Start	Perform a coup de grâce on ten enemies.	15

NAME	GOAL/REQUIREMENT	POINT VALUE
Bob and Weave	Counter an enemy's attack three times in row.	15
Down, Not Out	Defeat an enemy while dying, then recover without any help.	15
Lifesaver	Help or rescue your partner ten times.	15
Weapons Master	Use all the weapons in the game and kill ten enemies with each of them.	30
Give a Little Push	Knock ten enemies off a high place.	15
Rising Up	Earn a level-four title.	30
They're ACTION Figures!	Collect 3 figures.	15
Stuntman	Defeat 20 enemies with the Hydra using a quick shot.	15
Bring the Heat	Take down an enemy from 50 meters away with a headshot using the thermal scope.	15
High Voltage	Defeat ten enemies with a stun rod charge attack.	15
Zombie Massacre	Defeat 500 zombies.	15
J'avo Genocide	Defeat 500 J'avo.	15
B.O.W.s Are Ugly	Defeat 100 enemies that have come out of a chrysalid.	30
I Prefer Them Alive	Rescue two female survivors at the cathedral.	15
Flying Ace	Pilot the VTOL without getting a scratch on it.	15
Hard Choice	Shoot the helicopter pilot with a Magnum at point-blank range.	15
Covered in Brass	Earn 150 different medals.	30
Heirlooms	Collect all the serpent emblems.	30

SECRET ACHIEVEMENTS

NAME	GOAL/REQUIREMENT	POINT VALUE
I Spy	Complete Chapter 1 in Ada's campaign.	15
Counterintelligence	Complete Chapter 2 in Ada's campaign.	15
This Takes Me Back	Complete Chapter 3 in Ada's campaign.	15
Ada's Demise	Complete Chapter 4 in Ada's campaign.	15
What's Next?	Complete Chapter 5 in Ada's campaign.	15
Sneaking Around	Get through the aircraft carrier's bridge area without being noticed.	15

RESIDENT EVIL: OPERATION RACCOON CITY

ACHIEVEMENTS

NAME	GOAL/REQUIREMENT	POINT VALUE
Witness	Witness the beginning of the Raccoon City outbreak.	20
Corrupted	Complete the second mission of the USS campaign.	20
Danger, High Voltage!	Complete the third mission of the USS campaign.	20
Rogue's Gallery	Complete the fourth mission of the USS campaign.	20
Betrayal	Complete the fifth mission of the USS campaign.	20
Down in the Labs	Complete the sixth mission of the USS campaign.	20
Outbreak Survivalist	Complete all U.S.S. missions on Veteran.	25
Raccoon City Cleanser	Complete all U.S.S. missions on Professional.	35
Success	Complete all U.S.S. missions with an S Rank.	30
Great Success	Gain S+ on all U.S.S. mission on Professional/Veteran difficulty	45
On A Roll	Achieve a 5 kill streak in a Versus match.	15
Skill[el] Or Luck?	Achieve a 10 kill streak in a Versus match.	25
Now That's G	Collect 3 G-Virus Samples in one Biohazard match.	15
No Sample For You	Force 25 enemies to drop G-Virus Samples in Biohazard (lifetime).	30
Supreme Survivors	In Survivors mode, have all 4 players on your team Survive the game.	20
Fallen Idols	In Heroes mode, eliminate 4 Heroes in one game.	30
Sampler	Play at least one match in every Versus game type	20
You Love to Hate my 98	Complete 98 Versus games	50
Tongue Tied	Kill a Licker that is grappling a Teammate.	10

NAME	GOAL/REQUIREMENT	POINT VALUE
Like a Butterfly	Kill 100 zombies with CQC (lifetime)	15
Green Thumb	Heal with 101 Green Herbs (lifetime)	25
Down Boy	Kill 13 zombie dogs (lifetime)	15
These Will Do	Purchase 5 weapons.	10
Choices Aplenty	Purchase 15 weapons.	15
Quite The Collection	Purchase all available weapons.	30
One Trick Pony	Purchase an ability.	10
Feelin' Stronger Every Day	Fully upgrade an ability.	15
Look What I Can Do	Purchase all abilities for one character class.	20
Ready To Dominate	Fully upgrade all abilities for one character class.	20
So Many Choices	Purchase all abilities for all character classes.	30
Epic Standards	Upgrade all abilities for all characters to its maximum level.	40
Organic Shield	Kill 5 enemies consecutively while using a zombie as a shield.	20
Baker's Dozen	Kill 13 zombified teammates.	30
So Hot Right Now	Kill 103 enemies with incendiary rounds (lifetime)	15
Bloody Good Time	Kill 5 enemies by causing Blood Frenzy in a single campaign game or multiplayer match.	20
Up Close and Personal	Kill 5 players in one multiplayer game with CQC Kills.	10
Chaos Averted	Kill an infected teammate with a headshot before they become a zombie in any mode.	5
Like a Bee	Kill 10 enemy players in one Versus game with CQC.	20
A Gun by Any Other Name	Kill an enemy with each weapon type including special weapons.	15
Raccoon City Mascot	Collect all 7 Raccoons.	15

SECRET ACHIEVEMENTS

NAME	GOAL/REQUIREMENT	POINT VALUE
Died Trying	Attempt "The Rescue" and fail.	15
A Hero Spared!	Attempt "The Rescue" and survive.	15
The Loyalists	Follow orders and defeat all liabilities	15
Stop Squirming	17 Hunters Killed (lifetime)	10
This Place Crawls	31 Parasites killed (lifetime)	15
By Trail Of Dead	50 Versus opponents killed (lifetime)	10
Hat Trick	3 Tyrants Killed (lifetime)	15
Only Hurts For A While	Infected 13 times (lifetime)	10
Clingy	13 Parasite Zombies killed (lifetime)	10
Revival	Revive 31 team mates (lifetime)	20

ECHO SIX EXPANSION PACK 1 ACHIEVEMENTS

NAME	GOAL/REQUIREMENT	POINT VALUE
Happy Trails	Complete By the Trail of Our Dead	20
Hot Pants	Complete I Now Know Why You Cry	20
Oh Yeah!!!	Complete Nothing is as it Seems	20
Boom Worse than Bite	13 Bomb Dogs Detonated	30
Ticket to the Gun Show	As Tweed, use C4 to open door in Foundry	25
Ladies Night	Beat an Echo Six Expansion Pack mission with the 3 female characters in your party.	30
Who needs guns?	Complete an Echo Six Expansion mission without killing anything with a gun.	30
Leave no Dead Man Behind	Kill every zombie in the Park before leaving.	25
Burning Inside	Kill another player with Crucible in a Foundry Versus Match	15

SECRET ACHIEVEMENTS

NAME	GOAL/REQUIREMENT	POINT VALUE
Let Lounging Lickers Lie	Do not wake up Lickers in the Atrium encounter in By the Trail of Our Dead	35

ECHO SIX EXPANSION PACK 2

ACHIEVEMENTS

NAME	GOAL/REQUIREMENT	POINT VALUE
Rocket Socket	Kill 5 enemies with Rocket Launcher	15
Bigger They Are	Complete Longest Yard	20
Birth of An Abomination	Complete Root of All Evil	20
Derailed	Complete The Places We're Meant to Die	20
Tyranical	5 Tyrants Slain	15
Delivery Specialist	Deliver all 5 virus samples for your team in Dispatch's Biohazard Mode	50
Turrets Syndrome	Shut Down or Destroy 5 Turrets	20
Boys Club	Beat an Echo Six Expansion Pack mission with 3 male characters in your party.	30
Supernaut	3 Super Tyrants Slain	30
Divided We Fall	Complete an Echo Six Expansion mission with no human player incapacitated from death or infection.	30

ROCK BAND 3

ACHIEVEMENTS

NAME	GOAL/REQUIREMENT	POINT VALUE
Tune Up	Calibrate your audio/video setup for the optimal Rock Band 3 experience.	4
Self-Made Dude or Lady	Create a Character.	5
Best. Name. Ever.	Rename your band.	5
Well Connected	Connect your Rock Band 3 Band with rockband.com at http://www.rockband.com.	6
You Ain't Seen Nothing Yet	Maintain overdrive for 60 seconds.	20
Millionaire Club	Get 1,000,000 on one song.	25
Rock Band Master	5 Star on Medium (or 3 Star on a higher difficulty) any 50 Rock Band 3 songs.	25
Rock Band Legend	5 Star every song in Rock Band 3 on Hard.	30
Rock Band Immortal	5 Star every song in Rock Band 3 on Expert.	50
Alex's Luggage Combination	Beat a Rock Band 3 score of 12,345,678.	30
Hometown Threwdown	Complete the "Hometown Throwdown" Road Challenge.	20
Real Nor'easter	Complete "The Wicked Awesome Tour".	20
Hell Defrosted	Win all rewards on the "Hell Freezes Over" Road Challenge.	25
Wilderness Survival	Complete the "Through the Wilderness, Eh?" Road Challenge.	20
Major Mileage	Get 90 or more spades on "The Long Drive South" Road Challenge.	25
Party Animal	Completed the "Total Debauchery" Road Challenge.	20
The Connoisseur's Connoisseur	Get 90 or more spades on "The European Connoisseur" Road Challenge.	25
Mile High Club	Complete the "Really Frequent Flyers" Road Challenge.	25
Ultimate Road Warrior	Win all awards on the "Really Frequent Flyers" Road Challenge.	30
HOPO-cidal Maniac	Kill 53,596 Hammer-ons and Pull-offs.	25
Bleeding Fingers	Get 85% on all Guitar Solos in Rock Band 3 on Hard or Expert.	30
Guitar Perfectionist	Get 100% accuracy on Expert Guitar.	25

NAME	GOAL/REQUIREMENT	POINT VALUE
Guitar Apprentice	5 Star on Easy Guitar (or 3 Star on a higher difficulty) any 25 Rock Band 3 songs.	20
Bass Streaker	Get a streak of 500 notes on Bass.	10
Most Authentic Strummer	Hit 100% of the notes, only strumming up, on Hard Bass.	10
Bass Apprentice	5 Starred on Easy Bass (or 3 Starred on a higher difficulty) 25 Rock Band 3 songs.	20
Drum Roll, Please!	Nail a drum roll.	10
Fastest Feet	Hit 90% of the Kick notes in a song on Hard Drums.	15
Drums Apprentice	5 Star on Easy Drums (or 3 Star on a higher difficulty) any 25 Rock Band 3 songs.	20
Keys Streaker	Get a streak of 350 notes on Keys.	15
Keys Apprentice	5 Star on Easy Keys (or 3 Star on a higher difficulty) any 25 Rock Band 3 songs.	20
Pro Bass Apprentice	5 Star on Easy Pro Bass (or 3 Star on a higher difficulty) any 25 Rock Band 3 songs.	20
Drum Trainer Initiate	Complete the introductory Pro Drum Trainer lessons.	15
Drum Trainer Graduate	Complete the final Pro Drum Trainer lessons.	30
Play a Real Guitar Already!	Play "The Hardest Button to Button" on Pro Guitar.	15
Pro Guitar to the Max	Max out your Score Multiplier meter on Pro Guitar.	15
Power Chords	Complete the "Power Chords" lessons in the Pro Guitar trainer.	15
Complex Chords	Complete the "More Chord Holding and Arpeggiation" Pro Guitar lessons.	25
Pro Guitar Apprentice	5 Star on Easy Pro Guitar (or 3 Star on a higher difficulty) any 25 Rock Band 3 songs.	20
Pro Keyboardist	Hit at least 90% of the notes in 3 songs on Expert Pro Keys.	15
Pro Keys Graduate	Complete the final Pro Keys trainers.	25
Pro Keys to the Max	Max out your Score Multiplier meter on Pro Keys.	15
Pro Keys Apprentice	5 Star on Easy Pro Keys (or 3 Star on a higher difficulty) any 25 Rock Band 3 songs.	20
Triple Awesome	Get a Triple Awesome while playing with Vocal Harmonies.	10
Is This Just Fantasy?	Hit all triple awesomes in "Bohemian Rhapsody" on Medium or a higher difficulty.	25
Vocals Showmanship	Deploy overdrive four times in a single song as a vocalist.	10
Tambourine Master	Hit 100% of the notes in a percussion section.	10
Vocal Virtuoso	Earn an Awesome rating on at least 90% of the phrases in 6 songs on Hard Vocals.	15
Vocal Apprentice	5 Star on Easy Vocals (or 3 Star on a higher difficulty) any 25 Rock Band 3 songs.	20
The Endless Setlist III	Successfully complete "The Endless Setlist III!"	50
Downloader	Play a downloaded song.	20
Mercurial Vocalist	Earn 5 stars on Vocals on a downloaded Queen song.	30
Live Free or Die	Beat all of the free downloadable songs for Rock Band.	25
Fistful of Awesome	Beat 5 downloaded songs.	15
Accountant's Dozen	Beat 12 downloaded songs.	15
Decent Collection	Beat 20 downloaded songs.	15
I Want It All	Play a downloaded Queen song.	15
Shameless Self-Promotion	Download and play three songs from a band that has Harmonix team members in it.	15
Just Another Band Out of Boston	5 Star any Boston song.	15
Face Melter	Melt faces by beating any three '80s Metal songs.	25
Dave Grohl Band	Beat 5 songs from any band that has had Dave Grohl as a member.	30
The Perfect Drug	Get a 200 note streak on "The Perfect Drug".	30

ROCKSMITH

ACHIEVEMENTS

NAME	GOAL/REQUIREMENT	POINT VALUE
Duck Hunter	Play the Guitarcade game: Ducks	5
Fret Fast	Beat 10,000,000 points in the Guitarcade game: Ducks	20
Ducks x 6	Play the Guitarcade game: Super Ducks	5
Just Super!	Beat 150,000,000 points in the Guitarcade game: Super Ducks	20
Solo Foundations	Play the Guitarcade game: Scale Runner	5
Scales Owned	Beat 50,000,000 points in the Guitarcade game: Scale Runner	20
Challenge Harmonics	Play the Guitarcade game: Harmonically Challenged	5
Beat Harmonics	Beat 1,000,000 points in the Guitarcade game: Harmonically Challenged	20
Batter Up	Play the Guitarcade game: Big Swing Baseball	5
Giant!	Beat 2,000,000 points in the Guitarcade game: Big Swing Baseball	20
Slide Puzzle	Play the Guitarcade game: Super Slider	5
Slide to Victory	Beat 15,000,000 points in the Guitarcade game: Super Slider	20
Where Rainbows Come From	Play the Guitarcade game: Quick Pick Dash	5
Furious Plucker	Beat 5,000,000 points in the Guitarcade game: Quick Pick Dash	20
The One With Zombies	Play the Guitarcade game: Dawn of the Chordead	5
Guitardead	Beat 1,000,000 points in the Guitarcade game: Dawn of the Chordead	20
Happy Shopper	Visit the shop	5
Singles Rock	Beat 100,000 points in a Single Note Arrangement	20
Chordinated	Beat 100,000 points in a Chord Arrangement	20
All Rounder	Beat 100,000 points in a Combo Arrangement	20
The Basics	Complete Soundcheck (Reach Rank 1)	5
New Act	Reach Rank 2	5
Local Support Act	Reach Rank 3	10
Local Headliner	Reach Rank 4	10
National Support Act	Reach Rank 5	20
National Headliner	Reach Rank 6	20
International Support Act	Reach Rank 7	40
International Headliner	Reach Rank 8	40
Elite Guitarist	Reach Rank 9	60
Super Elite Guitarist	Reach Rank 10	60
Rocksmith	Reach Rank 11	100
My 1st Gig	Play an Event	5
My 1st Encore	Qualify for an Encore	10
Better Than An Encore?	Qualify for a Double Encore	20
The Rocksmith Method	Earn all Bronze Technique Medals	20
Tutorials My Axe	Earn all Gold Technique Medals	30
Tone is My Avatar	Create and save a custom tone	10
Hear Me Now	Use the Amp	10
D-licious	Use the Tuner to tune to Drop-D	10
Cente-beater	Beat a 100 Note Streak	10
Just Awesome	Beat a 750 Note Streak	40
Strummer	Beat a 5 Chord Streak	5
No Dischord	Beat a 25 Chord Streak	20
Half-K	Beat a 500 Note Streak	25
Art + Functionality	Collect all guitars	30
Tone Peddler	Collect 50 effects pedals	30
OK, I Learned	Beat 200,000 points in Master Mode	20
Stage Ready	Complete a Master Event	40
Beneficial Friends	Play multiplayer with 2 guitars	20
Just Singing?	Using a mic, sing along and achieve Nice Singing	10

SAINTS ROW: THE THIRD

ACHIEVEMENTS

NAME	GOAL/REQUIREMENT	POINT VALUE
Dead Presidents	Complete 'When Good Heists[el]'.	10
The Welcome Wagon	Complete 'I'm Free - Free Falling'.	15
We're Takin' Over	Complete 'We've Only Just Begun'.	20
Tower Defense	Complete Act 1 in one way.	20
Kuh, Boom.	Complete Act 1 in another way.	20
Gotta Break Em In	Complete 'The Ho Boat'.	25
I Heart Nyte Blayde	Complete 'STAG Party'.	25
kill-deckers.exe	Complete 'http://deckers.die'.	25
Titanic Effort	Complete Act 2.	40
Once Bitten[el] Braaaaaaains	Complete 'Zombie Attack'.	25
Murderbrawl 31	Complete 'Murderbrawl XXXI'.	25
Mr. Fury Would Be Proud	Complete Act 3 in one way.	30
Gangstas[el] In Space!	Complete Act 3 in another way.	30
Hanging With Mr. Pierce	Complete all City Takeover gameplay in the Downtown district.	25
Mourning Stars	Complete all City Takeover gameplay in the New Colvin district.	25
Hack the Planet	Complete all City Takeover gameplay in the Stanfield district.	25
You're the Best[el]	Complete all City Takeover gameplay in the Carver Island district.	25
Bright Lights, Big City	Complete all City Takeover gameplay in the entire city of Steelport.	80
Ouch.	Complete all instances of Insurance Fraud.	20
Tune In, Drop Off	Complete all instances of Trafficking.	20
And Boom Goes the Dynamite	Complete all instances of Heli Assault.	20
Fence Killa 2011	Complete all instances of Mayhem.	20
Your Backseat Smells Funny	Complete all instances of Escort.	20
Double Dose of Pimping	Complete all instances of Snatch.	20
Porkchop Sandwiches	Complete all instances of Trail Blazing.	20
Go Into the Light	Complete all instances of Guardian Angel.	20
Tank You Very Much	Complete all instances of Tank Mayhem.	20
Have A Reality Climax	Complete all instances of Professor Genki's Super Ethical Reality Climax.	20
Everything is Permitted	Kill all of the hitman Assassination targets.	10
Hi-Jack It	Steal and deliver all Vehicle Theft targets.	10
Getting the Goods	Find 25% of all Collectibles.	10
Life of the Party	Find 100% of all Collectibles.	20
Shake and Bake	Complete your first Challenge.	10
You're My Hero!	Complete ALL Challenges.	30
Ow My Balls!	Do your first nutshot AND testicle assault.	10
Gender Equality	Play for at least 2 hours as a male character AND 2 hours as a female character.	10
Bo-Duke-En	Hijack 50 vehicles - Dukes style.	10
Love/Hate Relationship	Taunt AND/OR Compliment 50 gang members.	10
Gellin' Like Magellan	Explore every hood in Steelport.	20
Who Loves Ya Baby	Kill 50 brutes.	10
A Better Person	Buy your first Upgrade from the Upgrade Store.	15
Haters Gonna Hate	Kill 1000 Gang Members.	15
Cowboy Up	Fully upgrade one Weapon in each slot.	10
Pimped Out Pad	Upgrade one Stronghold to its full glory.	10
Flash the Pan	Destroy all Gang Operations in Steelport.	10
Third and 30	Spend over 30 hours in Steelport.	40
Jumped In	Create and share a character online.	10
Opulence, You Has It	Complete 'Party Time'.	20

NAME	GOAL/REQUIREMENT	POINT VALUE
Stay Classy Steelport	Kill 25 Gang Members each with 'the Penetrator' AND the Fart in a Jar.	10
The American Dream	Customize 10 vehicles.	10

GENKIBOWL VII ACHIEVEMENTS

NAME	GOAL/REQUIREMENT	POINT VALUE
Cooked To Perfection	Roast 50 peds with the car's flamethrower (in a single instance of Super Ethical PR Opportunity).	10
Get off My Back	Destroy 5 chase vehicles (in a single instance of Super Ethical PR Opportunity).	5
Stick the Landing	Land on Magarac Island (in Sad Panda Skyblazing).	5
Cat on a Hot Tin Roof	Kill all of the rooftop mascots (in a single instance of Sad Panda Skyblazing).	10
Flame On	Fly through all of the rings (in a single instance of Sad Panda Skyblazing).	10
Feeding Time	Throw 5 mascots into the water (in a single instance of Apocalypse Genki).	10
Murder in the Jungle	Finish both instances of Apocalypse Genki.	10
Storm the Yarn	Destroy a mouse ATV during Sexy Kitten Yarngasm.	10
C-C-C-Combo Breaker	Cause $150,000 worth of damage in a single Sexy Kitten Yarngasm combo.	10
Genki Bowl Champ	Complete all activity instances in Genki Bowl VII.	20

GANGSTAS IN SPACE ACHIEVEMENTS

NAME	GOAL/REQUIREMENT	POINT VALUE
C-List Celebrity	Complete all missions for Gangstas in Space.	20
Do a Barrel Roll!	Perform all vehicle stunts with the Aegean.	10
Revenge of the Navigator	Destroy 10 enemy spacecraft with the Aegean while filming.	10
Warrior Princess	Kill 7 Space Amazons with melee attacks.	10
Pew! Pew! Pew!	Kill 35 Space Amazons with the Laser Pistol.	10
Lights! Camera! Action!	Collect all 6 hidden clapboards.	5
Xenaphobe	Kill Space Brutina.	10
Union Buster	Kill 15 cameramen.	10
First Contact	Destroy all enemy spacecraft during the chase scene.	10
I Do My Own Stunts	Land on the Parachute Target during the rescue scene.	5

THE TROUBLE WITH CLONES ACHIEVEMENTS

NAME	GOAL/REQUIREMENT	POINT VALUE
B.A.M.F.	Defeat 15 enemies at Technically Legal using only melee attacks.	10
Public Enemy #1	Destroy 45 Police and Swat Vehicles while protecting Jimmy's car.	10
Weird Science	Complete mission 'Weird Science'.	10
Eye of the Bee-Holder	Spray 25 rabid fans with the Swarmitron.	10
Sting Operation	Destroy 5 Steelport Guard vehicles during mission 'Tour de Farce'.	5
Tour de Farce	Complete mission 'Tour de Farce'.	10
Supaa-Excellent!	Shoot down a helicopter with a Saints Flow fireball.	10
Send in the Clones	Kill a Brute using only melee damage while under the influence of Saints Flow.	5
The Johnnyguard	Prevent Johnny Tag from taking damage on the Magarac Bridge.	10
My Pet, Monster	Complete all missions for "The Trouble With Clones[el]"	20

SERIOUS SAM 3: BFE

ACHIEVEMENTS

NAME	GOAL/REQUIREMENT	POINT VALUE
Serious Beginner	Complete any level in single player.	5
Serious Sam	Complete the single player campaign.	20
Are You Serious!?	Complete the game in single player on unmodified serious difficulty.	30
Kung-fu Fighter	Perform all possible finishing moves in the game.	10
Wanted Dead or Alive	Rescue professor Stein. So to say.	10
Get the hell off my ride!	Secure the bird.	10
Problem solver	Solve the riddle of the Sphynx.	10
Mission completed	Power up the Timelock.	10
The doorman should wear a suit	Awake the Guardian of Time.	10
Look, it's a secret	Find at least 50 secrets in single player.	15
Co-op Master	Complete the campaign in cooperative with at least 2 players.	10
Killer Jewelry	Kill an enemy using the Mutilator.	5
Headsman	Decapitate a Khnum.	10
Chain Explosion	Kill at least 5 headless kamikazes in one explosion.	10
Bone Crusher	Smash 20 Kleers with the Sledgehammer.	5
Maintenance time	Blow a Major Biomechanoid into pieces.	5
Trick Shot	Kill the kicked enemy while it is still in the air.	5
Load of Scrap	Rip Scrapjack's head off.	5
Wall of Bullets	Kill 20 enemies with the Minigun without releasing the trigger.	5
Classic Outfit	Find Sam's classic outfit.	10

JEWEL OF THE NILE

ACHIEVEMENTS

NAME	GOAL/REQUIREMENT	POINT VALUE
Jewel of the Nile	Complete the Jewel of The Nile single player campaign.	20
Look Ma, I won!	Win a versus match.	5
Deathmatch Master	Win 10 deathmatch games.	10
Flag Thief	Score a total of 10 points in CTF matches.	10
Instant Killer	Make at least 3 kills in one Instant Kill match.	5

SHIFT 2: UNLEASHED

ACHIEVEMENTS

NAME	GOAL/REQUIREMENT	POINT VALUE
Semi-Pro	Reached Driver Level 10	10
Veteran	Reached Driver Level 20	75
Road to Glory	Beaten your first Rival	10
Proving Grounds	Won JR's GTR Challenge	10
Recommended	Completed an event recommended by a friend	5
Cub Scout	Won your first Event Set badge	10
The Driver's battle	Completed an event purely from helmet cam	5
Dominator	Beaten all the Rivals	100
Works Champion	Beat Mad Mike Whiddett and won the Works Championship	50
Going the extra mile	Completed 250 Event Objectives	25
GT3 Champion	Beat Patrick Soderlund and won the FIA GT3 European Championship	50
I. Am. Iron Man.	Placed 1st in 5 consecutive Online events	10
GT1 Champion	Beat Jamie Campbell-Walter and won the FIA GT1 World Championship	100
Amateur	Reached Driver Level 5	5

NAME	GOAL/REQUIREMENT	POINT VALUE
Day Walker	Mastered every location in day or dusk	50
Night Rider	Mastered every location at night	100
Pro	Reached Driver Level 15	50
Bounty Hunter	Earned $10,000,000 total during your career	20
King of the Hill	Won your first Driver Duel Championship crown	10
Leno would be proud	Have at least one car from each manufacturer in your garage	10
Badge Hunter	Earned 50 Badges	10
Badge Collector	Earned 100 Badges	50
Badge Earner	Earned 10 Badges	5
Workaholic	Upgraded 3 vehicles to Works spec	10
Grass Roots	Completed JR's Grass Roots event	10
In The Zone	Won an Online event from helmet cam	10
Notorious	Played Online for over 10 hours total	25
Intercept & Pursue	Completed an Online Catchup Pack and Online Catchup Duel event	10
I'm Going To Hollywood!	Got through the Qualifying round in the Driver Duel Championship	10
Paparazzi	Shared a photo or replay with others	5
Race License	Won 75 Career events on Hard difficulty	50
Sizzlin'	Beaten the 1st Target Time in a Hot Lap event	10
Competition License	Won 50 Career events on Medium difficulty or higher	10
Elitist	Placed 1st in an event using Elite handling model	10
Sports License	Won 25 Career events on Easy difficulty or higher	10
Tic Tac Toe	Own a Modern, Retro, and Muscle car	10
Dialled In	Used On-Track Tuning to save a Tuning Setup for a car	10
Globetrotter	Competed at every location in the game	20
The World is my Oyster	Unlocked the FIA GT1 Branch	10
Nailed It	Track Mastered your first location	10

DOWNLOADABLE CONTENT: LEGENDS PACK

NAME	GOAL/REQUIREMENT	POINT VALUE
Mattley Crue	Beat Matt Powers and win the Legends Championship	25
Rock Hard	Win an Online event in a car from the Legends Pack	10

DOWNLOADABLE CONTENT: SPEED HUNTERS

NAME	GOAL/REQUIREMENT	POINT VALUE
250 Club	Reach over 250mph in a Standing Mile event	10
8 Second Club	Run a Quarter Mile in less than 9 seconds	10
Ready To Rock	Win an Online event in a Speedhunters Edition car	10
Grim Reaper	Beat Chris Rado and win the 1320 Outlaws Championship	20
Monster Dog	Beat Koz and win the Standing Mile World Championship	20
Speedhunter	Complete a Career event in each of the Speedhunters Edition Cars	10

SILENT HILL: DOWNPOUR

ACHIEVEMENTS

NAME	GOAL/REQUIREMENT	POINT VALUE
Capital Punishment	Completed the game on the hard game difficulty setting, any ending.	100
Good Behavior	Completed the game on any difficulty without killing any monsters.	50
Silent Hill Tour Guide	Completed all side quests.	100
Useless Trinkets	Completed the "Digging up the Past" side quest.	5
Birdman	Completed the "Bird Cage" side quest.	5
Calling All Cars	Completed the "All Points Bulletin" side quest.	5
Neighborhood Watch	Completed the "Stolen Goods" side quest.	5

NAME	GOAL/REQUIREMENT	POINT VALUE
Art Appreciation	Completed "The Art Collector" side quest.	5
Silent Alarm	Completed "The Bank" side quest.	5
Will Work For Food	Completed the "Homeless" side quest.	5
Cutting Room Floor	Completed the "Cinéma Vérité" side quest.	5
Turn Back Time	Completed "The Gramophone" side quest.	5
What's Your Sign?	Completed the "Shadow Play" side quest.	5
Telltale Heart	Completed the "Dead Man's Hand" side quest.	5
Dust to Dust	Completed the "Ashes to Ashes" side quest.	5
Long Walk, Short Pier	Completed the "Ribbons" side quest.	5
Spot the Difference	Completed the "Mirror, Mirror" side quest.	5
Silence is Golden	Killed or incapacitated 10 Screamers.	20
Shadow Boxer	Killed or incapacitated 10 Dolls.	20
Piñata Party	Killed or incapacitated 10 Weeping Bats.	20
Lockdown	Killed or incapacitated 10 Prisoner Minions.	20
The Bigger They Are...	Killed or incapacitated 10 Prisoner Juggernauts.	20
Fight or Flight?	Escaped from 20 monsters.	20
Silent Hill Historic Society	Completed Murphy's Journal with all Mysteries.	50
Stay of Execution	Incapacitated 20 monsters without killing them.	25
Gun Control	Killed 25 monsters with the Pistol or Shotgun.	25
Hypochondriac	Used 20 First Aid Kits.	10
Puzzle Master	Completed the game on the hard puzzle difficulty setting, any ending.	100

SECRET ACHIEVEMENTS

NAME	GOAL/REQUIREMENT	POINT VALUE
Now You're Cooking...	Survived the Diner Otherworld.	10
Out of the Frying Pan	Rode the Sky Tram to Devil's Pit.	10
Going off the Rails	Escaped from Devil's Pit.	10
Found a Friend!	Met DJ Ricks in the Radio Station.	10
Whatever Doesn't Kill You...	Escaped the Radio Station Otherworld.	10
Ashes, Ashes	Collected 3 pages of the rhyme book.	10
Broken Cycle	Defeated The Bogeyman.	10
No Turning Back	Reached Overlook Penitentiary.	10
Ending A	Achieved "Forgiveness" ending.	50
Ending C	Achieved "Full Circle" ending.	50
Ending B	Achieved "Truth & Justice" ending.	50
Ending D	Achieved "Execution" ending.	50
Ending E	Achieved "Surprise!" ending.	70

SKYLANDERS GIANTS

ACHIEVEMENTS

NAME	GOAL/REQUIREMENT	POINT VALUE
Rumbletown Ranger	Complete Chapter 3	10
Skystones Superstar	Complete Chapter 4	10
Glacier Great	Complete Chapter 5	10
Vault Victor	Complete Chapter 6	10
Wilikin Winner	Complete Chapter 7	10
Security Breacher	Complete Chapter 8	10
King of the Castle	Complete Chapter 9	10
Sky Survivor	Complete Chapter 10	10
Drill-X Defeator	Complete Chapter 11	10
Molekin Liberator	Complete Chapter 12	10
Trial Taker	Complete Chapter 13	10
Copter Captain	Complete Chapter 14	10
Arkus Adventurer	Complete Chapter 15	10
Savior of Skylands!	Complete the Story Mode by recovering the Iron Fist of Arkus and defeating Kaos on any difficulty	150

NAME	GOAL/REQUIREMENT	POINT VALUE
Nightmare Avenger	Complete the Story Mode on Nightmare difficulty	100
Completionist	Earn 3 Stars on any Adventure Level	40
Elemental Explorer	Unlock your first Elemental area	10
A New Hero	Complete 1 Heroic Challenge	10
1 and 0	Complete your first arena challenge	10
Great Gladiator!	Complete all 21 Arena Challenges	100
Elemental Enthusiast	Chapter 1 - Open all the Elemental areas	10
Chain Champ	Chapter 2 - Complete the Chain Pull Feat of Strength	10
Log Lifter	Chapter 3 - Complete the Log Lift Feat of Strength	10
Skystone Sampler	Chapter 4 - Collect all of the Skystones	10
Snowman Slammer	Chapter 5 - Destroy 7 snowmen	10
Autogyro Pyrotechnician	Chapter 6 - Destroy all the Arkeyan Autogyros	10
Talker in a Strange Land	Chapter 7 - Talk to all of the Wilikins	40
Cannon Confounder	Chapter 8 - Complete the level without getting directly hit by a cannon	10
Kaos Buster	Chapter 9 - Destroy 10 Kaos Bust Statues	10
Mine Menace	Chapter 10 - Shoot down 10 mines	10
Pipe Petard	Chapter 11 - Damage Drill-X by throwing a pipe at him	10
Hut Wrecker	Chapter 12 - Destroy 3 enemy huts with boulders Giants can lift	10
Column Crusher	Chapter 13 - Destroy all the columns in the second trial	10
Pedal to the Metal	Chapter 14 - Collect all 16 speed boosts in "The Long Hall" section	40
Freebot Isn't Free	Chapter 15 - Defeat Freebot in a game of Skystones	10
Keepin' Cool	Chapter 16 - Complete the chapter without taking damage from fire traps	10
Skystones Strategist	SkyStones - Capture 2 stones with 1 single stone	20
Clean Jersey	Don't take any damage from Kaos' rockets during the mini-game on the Dread-Yacht	10
Soul Surfer	Collect soul gems for Tree Rex and Jet-Vac	20
Seeker Adept	Collect 10 Legendary Ship Parts	20
Hint Scholar	Collect 10 Story Scrolls	20
Fashionista	Collect 10 Hats	20
To the Max	Level up any Skylander to level 15	40
Upgrade Uniter	Purchase all upgrades for any one Skylander	40
Spend That Loot!	Amass 65,000 Treasure with any one Skylander	40

SLEEPING DOGS

ACHIEVEMENTS

NAME	GOAL/REQUIREMENT	POINT VALUE
Chief Inspector	Complete 100% of all missions, cases, favors, events, jobs and races.	75
Detective	Complete 50% of all missions, cases, favors, events, jobs and races.	35
Officer	Complete 25% of all missions, cases, favors, events, jobs and races.	15
Rookie	Complete 10% of all missions, cases, favors, events, jobs and races.	10
Pure Gold	Achieve 30 Gold Stat Awards.	60
Golden Touch	Achieve 15 Gold Stat Awards.	30
Gold Rush	Achieve 5 Gold Stat Awards.	10
Strike Gold	Achieve 1 Gold Stat Award.	5
Solid Silver	Achieve 30 Silver Stat Awards.	35
Substantial Silver	Achieve 15 Silver Stat Awards.	15
Slight Silver	Achieve 5 Silver Stat Awards.	5
Auto Enthusiast	Purchase all vehicles.	10
Spiritual Healing	Pray at all of the Health Shrines.	15
Fashion Victim	Purchase all clothing.	15
Hong Kong Super Hacker	Hack every Security Camera in the game.	15

NAME	GOAL/REQUIREMENT	POINT VALUE
Karaoke Superstar	Achieving 90% and above for all songs at the Karaoke Bars in HK.	10
Bounty Hunter	Complete all of Roland's Jobs.	20
West End Scavenger	Unlock every lockbox in Kennedy Town and Aberdeen.	20
Central Scavenger	Unlock every lockbox in Central.	20
North Point Scavenger	Unlock every lockbox in North Point.	20
Super Cop	Unlock ten Cop Upgrades.	15
Ultimate Fighter	Unlock ten Triad Upgrades.	15
Wei of the Road	Complete all Street Races.	15
Event Planner	Complete all of the open world Events.	15
Event Driven	Complete half of the open world events.	20
Mr. Nice Guy	Complete all Favors.	30
Case Closed	Complete all cases.	30
Sharpshooter	Shoot out a cop's tires while fleeing in a police chase.	25
Kleptomaniac	Hijack 5 trucks and collect their cargo.	15
Infowlable	Win 50,000 on a single cockfight.	15
Tourist	Win a bet on a cockfight.	10
Whatever's Handy	Use 10 different melee weapons to defeat enemies.	15
Gun Nut	Use 10 different firearms to defeat enemies.	15
Safe Driver	Cruise for 2 minutes straight without damaging your car.	20
Gadgetman	Pick a lock, plant a bug, trace a phone, crack a safe, and take over a spy camera.	20
Environmentalist	Perform 5 unique environmental kills.	15
Foodie	Try 10 different foods or drinks.	10
Man Around Town	Visit Aberdeen, Central, Kennedy Town and North Point.	20
Take A Bite Out Of Crime	Complete a Case.	10
A Slap in the Face	Kill someone with a fish.	10
Stuntman	Successfully perform an action hijack.	5
Fashion Statement	Change all your clothes in your wardrobe or a clothing store.	10
Great Face	Achieve Face Level 10.	50
Gaining Face	Achieve Face Level 5.	25
Minor Face	Achieve Face Level 2.	5

SECRET ACHIEVEMENTS

NAME	GOAL/REQUIREMENT	POINT VALUE
Martial Law	Defeat all 4 Martial Arts Clubs	15
Big Smiles All Around	Complete Big Smile Lee.	50
A Big Betrayal	Complete Dockyard Heist.	35
That'll Show 'em	Complete Payback.	20
In With the Gang	Complete Night Market Chase.	5

SNIPER ELITE V2

ACHIEVEMENTS

NAME	GOAL/REQUIREMENT	POINT VALUE
Can Do!	Complete all co-op Overwatch Missions	20
Detonator	Career total of 50 shots on explosives	20
Bomb Happy	Survive 10 Games of bombing run	20
Bedpan Commando	Resuscitate your partner in coop 10 times	20
Target Eliminated!	As a sniper in Overwatch, snipe 50 enemies tagged by your partner	30
Target Spotted!	As a spotter in Overwatch, tag 50 enemies	30
Kilroy was Here	Make it through the tower to the winch room without being spotted	15
Fish Tank	Send the tank into the river by blowing up the bridge	15
High and Mighty	Wipe out the Elite Russian Sniper Team from the rooftops	15

NAME	GOAL/REQUIREMENT	POINT VALUE
Get Off the ground	Kill everyone in the convoy from ground level, except for Kreidl	15
Sniper Elite	Complete all missions on highest difficulty	100
Legendary Sniper	Prevent Wolff from escaping	65
Feared Sniper	Destroy the V2 rocket	20
Veteran Sniper	Discover the location of the V2 launch site	20
Master Sniper	Uncover Wolff's plan	20
Expert Sniper	Eliminate Müller	20
Pro Sniper	Collect intel from the church and make it out alive	20
Skilled Sniper	Stop the execution	20
Journeyman Sniper	Hold off the Russian advance	20
Apprentice Sniper	Destroy the V2 Facility and escape to safety	20
Novice Sniper	Stop the convoy	20
Trainee Sniper	Escape the German assault	20
Hide and Hope	Complete a level without being shot a single time	50
Make Every Bullet Count	Complete a level with 100% accuracy, using only rifles	25
Cooking Off	Snipe a grenade on an enemy's webbing from 100m	20
Double Dose	Snipe 2 people with one shot	20
Pass the Buck	Get a sniped ricochet headshot	30
Gold Rush	Find and retrieve all the stolen gold bars	50
Jungle Juice	Find and snipe all the hidden bottles throughout the game	50
Head Honcho	Get 100 sniped headshots	20
Gung Ho	Snipe 100 moving targets	20
World Record	Get 506 cumulative sniper kills	30
Potato Masher	Kill 100 enemies with explosives	20
Iron Lung	Hold your breath for a cumulative time of half an hour	20
Go the Distance	Get a cumulative sniped kill distance of a marathon	20
Deadeye	Snipe an enemy through his eye	10
Silent but deadly	Covertly kill 25 unaware enemies	10
Fuel Tank	Destroy a tank by sniping the fuel supply	10
Ear Plugs	Snipe an enemy while your rifle fire is masked by a loud sound	10
Mousetrap Fuse	Use a trip mine to kill an enemy who is trying to assault your position	10
Front and Center	Get a scoped headshot over 150m	10

SONIC GENERATIONS

ACHIEVEMENTS

NAME	GOAL/REQUIREMENT	POINT VALUE
The Opening Act	Race through the first stage.	10
All Stages Cleared!	Clear Sonic Generations.	50
Greased Lightning	Clear GREEN HILL Act 1 within one minute.	10
Bright Star	Get Rank S in an Act.	15
Shooting Star	Get Rank S in three Acts.	20
Blazing Meteor	Get Rank S in seven Acts.	30
Blue Comet	Get Rank S in twelve Acts.	40
Big Bang	Get Rank S in all Acts.	50
Trickstar	Pull off a seven or more trick combo or six trick combo ending in a finishing trick.	10
Eradicator	Defeat 100 enemies.	15
Ring King	Reach the goal without dropping any of the rings you collected in GREEN HILL Act 1.	15
Action Hero	Perform all of Sonic's moves in Act 2.	10
Bonds of Friendship	Complete all Challenge Acts featuring Sonic's friends.	10
Walkie Talkie	Chat with each of Sonic's friends you have saved.	10
Join the Ranks	Join the rankings.	20
A 30-Second Test	Participate in a 30 Second Trial.	20
Mad Skillz	Get all Skills.	30

NAME	GOAL/REQUIREMENT	POINT VALUE
(Hedge)Hogging It All Up!	Get all collectibles.	50
Time Attacker	Play Ranking Attack on all stages.	30
Red Ring Collector	Get all Red Star Rings.	30
Halfway Point	Clear half the Challenge Acts.	30
Mission Accomplished!	Clear all the Challenge Acts.	30

SECRET ACHIEVEMENTS

NAME	GOAL/REQUIREMENT	POINT VALUE
SKY SANCTUARY Restored!	Restored the SKY SANCTUARY Stage Gate.	15
SPEED HIGHWAY Restored!	Restored the SPEED HIGHWAY Stage Gate.	15
CITY ESCAPE Restored!	Restored the CITY ESCAPE Stage Gate.	15
GREEN HILL Restored!	Restored the GREEN HILL Stage Gate.	15
CHEMICAL PLANT Restored!	Restored the CHEMICAL PLANT Stage Gate.	15
PLANET WISP Restored!	Restored the PLANET WISP Stage Gate.	15
SEASIDE HILL Restored!	Restored the SEASIDE HILL Stage Gate.	15
CRISIS CITY Restored!	Restored the CRISIS CITY Stage Gate.	15
ROOFTOP RUN Restored!	Restored the ROOFTOP RUN Stage Gate.	15
Treasure Hunter	Collected all the Chaos Emeralds.	20
Shadow Boxing	Defeated Shadow.	25
Silver Got Served	Defeated Silver.	30
Scrap Metal	Defeated Metal Sonic.	20
Perfect Punisher	Defeated Perfect Chaos.	25
Boom Boom Dragoon	Defeated Egg Dragoon.	30
Sunny Side Up	Defeated Death Egg Robot.	20
Can't Touch This	Took no damage from the final boss and cleared the stage.	30
A Quick Breather	Got the Red Star Ring atop the highest spot in ROOFTOP RUN Act 2 and reached the goal.	10
Color Power!	Got the Red Star Ring by using an Orange Wisp in PLANET WISP Act 2 and reached the goal.	10
Supersonic!	Cleared a regular stage as Super Sonic.	20
Walk on Air	Cleared SKY SANCTUARY Act 1 without falling and losing a life.	20
Demolition Derby	Wrecked 30 or more cars in CITY ESCAPE Act 2.	10
Secret Sleuth	Got the Red Star Ring located in the hidden room in SEASIDE HILL Act 1 and reached the goal.	10
Look Both Ways	Reached the goal in CRISIS CITY Act 2 without being hit by a tornado-carried cars or rocks.	10
Walk on Water	Cleared CHEMICAL PLANT Act 2 without entering the water.	10
Jump for Joy!	Found the spring hidden in GREEN HILL Act 1 and reached the goal with a Red Star Ring.	10
The Byway or the Highway	Got the Red Star Ring located on the shortcut route in SPEED HIGHWAY Act 2 and reached the goal.	20

SONIC & SEGA ALL-STARS RACING

ACHIEVEMENTS

NAME	GOAL/REQUIREMENT	POINT VALUE
True Blue	Earn your BLUE SEGA License.	10
Amber De Amigo	Earn your AMBER SEGA License.	10
Red Out	Earn your RED SEGA License.	15
Virtual Bronze	Earn your BRONZE SEGA License.	20
Captain Silver	Earn your SILVER SEGA License.	30
Golden Acts	Earn your GOLD SEGA License.	80
Now There Are No Limits!	Win your first Grand Prix Cup.	10

NAME	GOAL/REQUIREMENT	POINT VALUE
Welcome to the Next Level!	Win every race within a Grand Prix Cup.	15
To be this good takes AGES!	Win every Grand Prix Cup.	30
Fighters Megamix	Take out an opponent with each character's All-Star Move.	30
Time Stalker	Set a Personal Best Time on any Time Trial course.	10
Clock Work	Set a Personal Best Time on every Time Trial course.	30
Shadow Dancing	Defeat a Staff Ghost on any Time Trial course.	10
Ghost Master	Defeat a Staff Ghost on every Time Trial course.	30
Mega Driver	Score AAA on any mission.	10
Crazy Box	Pass every mission.	15
Magical Sound Shower	Race to every piece of music.	30
Top of the Class	Score AAA on every mission.	30
Dreamarena	Play a friend over Xbox LIVE.	10
Racing Hero	Win any race over Xbox LIVE.	15
Outrunner	Lap a trailing player in a race over Xbox LIVE.	30
Death Adder	Take out opponents with items one hundred times over Xbox LIVE.	30
Lucky Dime	Purchase any item from the shopping menu.	10
High Roller	Purchase every item from the shopping menu.	15
Classic Collection	Win a race as each racer.	15
SEGA World	Complete a race on each course in Grand Prix, Single Race or Time Trial mode.	30
Power Drift	Perform a fifteen second Drift.	15
Turbo	Perform twenty Turbo-Boosts within a single lap of any event.	15
Triple Trouble	Perform three Tricks in one jump and make the landing.	15
Gaining Ground	Get a Turbo-Boost Start in any event.	10
Wheels of Fire	Perform a Turbo-Boost Start across 3 consecutive events.	15
Rolling Start	Complete Sonic's Test Drive.	15
Road Rampage	Take out three opponents with one All-Star Move.	15
After Burner	Take out three opponents with one triple-weapon.	15
Up 'N' Down	Take out a racer by manually directing an item.	10
Streets of Rage	Ram an opponent off the course without using a Weapon or Power-Up.	15
Wonder Boy	Win a race by crossing the finish line in reverse.	15
Altered Beast	Win a race while using an All-Star Move.	10
Last Survivor	Finish the first lap in last position and go on to win the race.	15
Super Hang-On	Win the race holding first place on each lap.	15
Project Rub	Complete any Race event without collisions.	15
Enduro Racer	Play one hundred events including any race, mission or time trial in any mode.	15
Ultimate Collection	Earn every achievement in the game.	100

SECRET ACHIEVEMENTS

NAME	GOAL/REQUIREMENT	POINT VALUE
Sonic Unleashed	Use Sonic's All-Star Move to take out Dr. Eggman and show him who's boss!	15
Feel the Magic	Use Amy's All-Star Move to send Sonic dizzy with love!	15
Working Man	Use Ryo's All-Star Move to take out Jacky and Akira and show them who's the ultimate martial artist!	15
Giant Egg	Use Billy's All-Star Move to squash the Crows!	15
Top Skater	Perform three tricks in one jump with Beat on Tokyo-to - Shibuya Downtown.	15
The Chariot	Use Zobio and Zobiko to send one hundred Curien Mansion Creatures back to the grave.	15
Cat Mania	Summon the giant KapuKapu and gobble up Big the Cat for mouse revenge!	15

SPLATTERHOUSE

ACHIEVEMENTS

NAME	GOAL/REQUIREMENT	POINT VALUE
The Berserker	Complete Phase 2: The Doll that Bled.	10
Be Garbage of Cesspool	Complete Phase 4: The Meat Factory.	20
Experiment 765	Complete Phase 6: Beast with a Human Heart.	30
Shattered Narcissus	Complete Phase 8: Reflections in Blood.	40
Pyre for the Damned	Complete Phase 10: The Wicker Bride.	50
Bride of the Corrupted	Complete the game on any difficulty.	100
I Walk with Death	Complete the game on "Savage" difficulty (or harder).	110
Dreams of the Dead	Complete the game on "Brutal" Difficulty.	120
Death Came Ripping	Kill an enemy with a Splatter Slash.	5
Razor of Hell	Get 100 kills with Splatter Slash.	5
Must Kill	Kill an enemy with Splatter Smash.	5
Downpour of Blood	Get 100 kills with Splatter Smash.	5
Flesh Re-animation!	Regenerate with Splatter Siphon.	5
One Who Slays	Get 300 kills in Berserker Mode.	5
Heavy Frikkin' Metal!	Get 50 kills with non-fleshy weapons.	5
Triumph of Iron	Get 500 kills with non-fleshy weapons.	15
See you at the Party	Kill an enemy with an enemy's arm.	5
None More Dead	Get 150 kills with enemy arms.	10
Tongue in Cheek	Kill an enemy with an enemy's head.	5
Head on Arrival	Get 50 kills with enemy heads.	10
You Got Red on You	Splat an enemy on a wall with a weapon.	5
Blood and Lightning	Splat 100 enemies on a wall with a weapon.	5
The Blackest of Sundays	Splat 200 enemies on a wall with a weapon.	10
The Business of Killing	Perform a Splatterkill.	5
South of Hell	Perform 75 Splatterkills.	5
Vigorous Vengeance	Perform 150 Splatterkills.	10
Morbid Dismemberment	Kill an enemy with your own dismembered arm.	5
Brain Dead	Tackle an enemy and pummel it 20 times.	5
Bad Taste	Impale an enemy on a spike.	5
Army of Dead Evil	Kill 6 enemies within one second.	5
Headlong into Monsters	Kill 6 enemies in one ram attack.	5
POW!	Launch an enemy straight up with "No Head Room".	5
Barrels of Blood	Get 2000 or more BLOOD Points in one chain of attacks.	5
Audiophile	Listen to all of Dr. West's gramophone records.	5
Boreworm Massacre	Stomp on 1000 Boreworms.	10
Killer of Killers	Get an S-rank in Survival Arena mode.	5
Anvil Horror	Get three S-ranks in Survival Arena mode.	15
Jason Schmason	Get six S-ranks in Survival Arena mode.	50
Dead on the Rise	Accomplish 5 Secret Missions in a single Survival Arena attempt.	5
Too much Horror business	Accomplish all 10 Secret Missions in a single Survival Arena attempt.	10
Hunger Pangs	Purchase a skill.	5
Blood Lust	Unlock 25 skills.	25
Lust for After Life	Unlock all skills.	50
Call of the Thule	Unlock 5% of Dr. West's journal.	10
Nightmare in Arkham	Unlock 25% of Dr. West's journal.	20
Lovecraft Baby	Unlock 50% of Dr. West's journal.	20
The House that West Built	Unlock all pages of Dr. West's journal.	100
Jen Smells of Rot…of the Grave	Re-assemble one of Jen's sexy photos.	5
Creepy Show	Re-assemble 8 of Jen's photos.	10
Happy Ending?	Re-assemble all of Jen's photos.	20

SSX

ACHIEVEMENTS

NAME	GOAL/REQUIREMENT	POINT VALUE
This Gear Is Bronze	Collect all Bronze Gear Badges	10
This Gear Is Silver	Collect all Silver Gear Badges	25
This Gear Is Golden	Collect all Gold Gear Badges	50
The Bronze Campaign	Collect all Bronze World Tour Badges	10
The Silver Campaign	Collect all Silver World Tour Badges	25
The Silver Survival Guide	Collect all Silver Survive Badges	25
The Golden Survival Guide	Collect all Gold Survive Badges	50
Team SSX	Unlock every member of Team SSX through World Tour (or purchase in Explore or Global Events)	10
Tree Hugger	Survive Trees Deadly Descent without equipping armor (in World Tour)	25
The Apple Theory	Survive Gravity Deadly Descent without equipping a wingsuit (in World Tour)	25
Do You See What I See	Survive Darkness Deadly Descent without equipping a headlamp or pulse goggles (in World Tour)	25
Ice To See You	Survive Ice Deadly Descent without equipping ice axes (in World Tour)	25
Buried Alive	Survive Avalanche Deadly Descent without equipping armor (in World Tour)	25
Playing Favorites	Reach level 10 with any character	25
It's Cold Out Here	Survive Cold Deadly Descent without equipping a solar panel (in World Tour)	25
Rocky Road	Survive Rock Deadly Descent without equipping armor (in World Tour)	25
Caution Low Visibility	Survive Whiteout Deadly Descent without equipping pulse goggles (in World Tour)	25
That Was Easy	Unlock all Game Modes	5
I Am A Ghost	Upload your first personal ghost	5
Grindage	Grind your first rail (not achievable in Tutorial)	5
Around The World	Ride with all three Pilots with each member of Team SSX	10
I Ain't Afraid of Snow Ghost	Beat a Friend's Rival Ghost in every Range (in Explore)	10
The Golden Trick It	Earn your 1st Gold in a Trick Event (in Explore)	10
The Gold Standard	Earn your 1st Gold in a Race Event (in Explore)	10
Heart Of Gold	Earn your 1st Gold in a Survive Event (in Explore)	10
Peak-A-Boo	Participate in a Global Event in every Peak	10
Tag Team	Earn a Bronze in a Trick Event with every member of Team SSX (in Explore)	10
Pass The Baton	Earn a Bronze in a Race Event with every member of Team SSX (in Explore)	10
Leave No One Behind	Earn a Bronze in a Survive Event with every member of Team SSX (in Explore)	10
Überlesscious	Earn a Bronze Medal on a Trick Event in Explore without landing any Super Übers	20
Who Needs Boost	Earn a Bronze Medal on a Race Event in Explore without using any boost	20
I'm Alive!	Rewind out of Death for the First Time (not achievable in Tutorial)	5
I'm Flying!	Deploy your wingsuit for the first time (not achievable in Tutorial)	5
Gear Up!	Make your first Gear Purchase	5
Pass The Board Wax	Make your first Board Purchase	5
I Need A Boost	Make your first Mod Purchase	5
The Golden Campaign	Collect all Gold World Tour Badges	50
The Bronze Miner	Collect all Bronze Explore Badges	10
The Silver Miner	Collect all Silver Explore Badges	25
The Gold Miner	Collect all Gold Explore Badges	50
The Bronze Spender	Collect all Bronze Global Events Badges	10
The Silver Spender	Collect all Silver Global Events Badges	25
The Gold Spender	Collect all Gold Global Events Badges	50

NAME	GOAL/REQUIREMENT	POINT VALUE
The Bronze Badger	Collect all Bronze Tricky Badges	10
The Silver Boarder	Collect all Silver Tricky Badges	25
The Golden Tricker	Collect all Gold Tricky Badges	50
The Bronze Finish	Collect all Bronze Race Badges	10
The Silver Finish	Collect all Silver Race Badges	25
The Gold Finish	Collect all Gold Race Badges	50
The Bronze Survival Guide	Collect all Bronze Survive Badges	10

STAR TREK: D-A-C

ACHIEVEMENTS

NAME	GOAL/REQUIREMENT	POINT VALUE
Academy Graduate	Earn 1 kill with each ship class	5
Red Shirt	Be the first to die in a Versus multiplayer match	5
Imperial Instincts	Earn 25 cumulative point captures in Conquest	10
Bridge Commander	Earn 250 cumulative kills in Team Deathmatch	15
Mirror, Mirror	Capture a point with the aid of your own wingman	10
Born Leader	Capture all 4 points in a single Assault match	15
NCC-1701	Earn 250,000 points as the Flagship class in one Team Deathmatch game	20
No Mercy	Earn 50 cumulative Escape Pod kills	20
Starfleet Medal of Honor	No deaths or ejections, plus at least 15 kills, in a single match	30
Vulcan Wisdom	Don't die or shoot, yet capture 3 points (including the enemy base) in a Conquest match	25
Nero's Rage	Destroy 3 enemies while using a single invulnerability powerup	25

SECRET ACHIEVEMENTS

NAME	GOAL/REQUIREMENT	POINT VALUE
Kobayashi Maru	Some achievements are unachievable... unless you cheat	20

DELUXE EDITION ACHIEVEMENTS

NAME	GOAL/REQUIREMENT	POINT VALUE
Dreadnought	Destroy all 5 ship classes plus 1 escape pod using the Missile Cruiser in Versus.	15
Captain on the Bridge	Earn the Captain rank in Survival Mode	20

SUPER STREET FIGHTER IV

ACHIEVEMENTS

NAME	GOAL/REQUIREMENT	POINT VALUE
Overachiever	Attain all the Achievements! The path of the warrior demands this from those who walk on it!	0
Fashion Plate	Even a top rate fighter needs to coordinate properly! You gotta get all of the Colors first!	10
Dan the Man	Mastery of the Saikyo arts requires mastery of the Personal Action! Collect 'em all, punk!	10
Entitled	A Title does not tell all of a man, sir, but if I were to see one Title, I'd want them all...	50
Iconoclast	Oh my gosh, those Icons are so adorable! I gotta find Don-chan and catch 'em all!	50
Special Movement	Do a Special Move 100 times! If you're a true student of the Rindo-kan dojo, it's your duty!	10

NAME	GOAL/REQUIREMENT	POINT VALUE
EXtra! EXtra!	Battle requires courage! Train by using your EX Gauge to successfully land 100 EX Moves!	10
Super, Man!	To battle is to win a fight with overwhelming strength! Show me you can do 100 Super Combos!	10
Ultra, Man!	If yer gonna fight, give it your all, pal. Performing 100 Ultra Combos oughta do it, eh?	10
It Takes Focus	Your mission, should you wish to join Delta Red, is to connect with 100 Focus Attacks!	10
Superior Super	Trust your instincts and winning will come easy. Let's begin with 50 Super Combo finishes!	10
Ultimate Ultra	Candy always says you gotta win with style, so go out there and perform 50 Ultra Combo finishes!	10
Sunspotter	Amigo, perform 365 Super or Ultra Combo finishes against your opponents! The dawn is coming!	10
Absolute Perfection	Lauren's waiting, so how about you finish your fights quickly and get 30 Perfects. Sound good?	20
Clear Headed	Hey! Got time to kill? Try to clear Arcade Mode on Medium or higher! That's all you gotta do!	10
All Clear	To get strong takes lots of fighting! Clear Arcade Mode on Medium or higher with all characters!	10
Herculean Effort	Can you finish Arcade Mode on Medium or higher without using a continue? Show me you can!	10
Hard Times	To escape death is to beat the strongest of the strong. Finish Arcade Mode on Hardest, kid!	20
Long Time No See	Do you wish for defeat? If so, complete Arcade Mode on Hardest difficulty and beat Gouken!	50
Rival Schooled	See your future by clearing every Rival Battle on Medium or higher with every character.	20
Speed Freak	Finish each round in Arcade Mode on Medium or higher in 20 seconds or less. Too easy.	30
Good Start	All of nature must withstand a trial. You must clear 10 trials in Trial Mode to succeed.	10
Trail of Trials	There is no shortcut in the art of Yoga. Aim to clear any character's Trial Mode trials!	20
Trial Athlete	I shall assimilate all and be all-powerful! Clear all Trial Mode challenges, and so can you!	50
Oh! My Car!	Hee hee, destruction is so much fun! Score 80,000 points or more in the Car Crusher bonus stage!	10
Barrel of Laughs	No need for barrels without oil! Score 110,000 points or more in the Barrel Buster bonus stage!	10
It Begins	The fight starts here! Set your Title and Icon, and begin fighting on Xbox Live!	10
First Timer	I'll never forget my first time for Ryu's sake! Win one Ranked Match! Gotta aim for the top!	10
Threepeat	You think being this good is easy? Let's see you win 3 Ranked Matches in a row, champ!	20
Fivepeat	This is your real power, child? Show me it's not luck by winning 5 Ranked Matches in a row!	30
Tenpeat	Don't hold back your true potential! Win 10 Ranked Matches in a row!	50
Moving On Up	Ya need to do anything to reach the top of the food chain! Let's see a Rank Up via Ranked Match!	10
Now You C Me...	I wrestle only the strong! You shall rank up to C Rank if you wanna face me, comrade!	20
From C to Shining C	You think you're good, don't you? Prove it by ranking up all characters to C Rank!	50
Road to Victory	You wanna get that fight money? You're gonna have to win 10 Xbox LIVE matches first, sucka!	10
Battle Master	Only winners can attain such beauty. Win 30 Xbox LIVE matches and I may share my beauty secrets.	20
Legendary Fighter	I shall make you the right hand of Shadaloo if you can win 100 Xbox LIVE matches!	50
Worldly Warrior	Let's do this, amigo! Fight 50 Xbox LIVE matches, because that's the only way to become strong!	10
Bring it on!	No comrade, this will not do! We must become stronger, for our fans! Fight 100 Xbox LIVE matches!	20
This is Madness!	Fighting is fun, huh? Well then, let's aim for 300 Xbox LIVE matches fought, OK buddy?	50

NAME	GOAL/REQUIREMENT	POINT VALUE
Team Player	A 1-on-1 fight is fun, but it's more fun with friends! Try fighting in a Team Battle!	10
Team Mate	Win 1 Team Battle match, and you will learn that teamwork can help you become stronger!	10
Teamworker	A pro can win with any team. Win 10 Team Battles but don't forget, you have to win too!	30
Keep on Truckin'	If you want to focus on nothing but the fight, entering an Endless Battle is for you!	10
Three For The Road	In the pursuit of strength, one must have a goal! In Endless Battle win 3 matches in a row.	20
Endless Ten	Throw away your fears and focus on the fight! Win 10 fights in a row in Endless Battle!	50
Replayer	Watch 30 Replays via the Replay Channel! Isn't it fun watching people go at it tooth and nail!?	10
Endless Lobbyist	It's only natural for warriors to seek fights! Create 30 Endless Battle lobbies!	10
Team Lobbyist	Hey mon, battlin' is fun, no? Go out and create 30 Team Battle lobbies and enjoy the rhythm!	10
Quarter Up	Fight 30 opponents via Arcade Fight Request. It'd be easy with the right bait, he he.	10

SUPREME COMMANDER 2

ACHIEVEMENTS

NAME	GOAL/REQUIREMENT	POINT VALUE
Start Here	Complete both parts of the tutorial	10
Easy Going	Complete all three campaigns on 'Easy' difficulty	25
A Winner is You	Complete all three campaigns 'Normal' difficulty	75
Supremest Commander	Complete all three campaigns on 'Hard' difficulty	100
Knows it All	Complete all primary and secondary campaign objectives	25
Completist	Complete all hidden campaign objectives	25
Score Hoarder	Get a complete campaign score over 150,000	50
Replayer	Improve your score on any operation	5
Cakewalk	Win a skirmish or online match against any AI opponent	5
Good Game	Win a skirmish or online match against all AI opponents	20
Luddite	Win a skirmish or online match without building any Experimentals	10
To the Victor...	Win 25 skirmish or online matches	25
Rushin' Front	Win a skirmish or online match in less than five minutes	10
Sampling	Win a skirmish or online match with each faction	10
Dating	Play 10 skirmish or online matches with one faction	15
Committed Relationship	Play 25 skirmish or online matches with one faction	25
Sightseer	Win a skirmish or online match on every multiplayer map	20
Sharp Shooter	Destroy 10,000 units	25
Masster	Extract 1,000,000 mass	25
Master Builder	Build 10,000 units	25
Time Cruncher	Play the game for over 24 hours in total	50
Internet Commander	Win an online match	10
Friends	Win a co-op match vs AI	10
Ranker	Win a Ranked Match	10
Supreme Online Commander	Win 25 Ranked Matches	50
Good Friends	Win 10 co-op matches vs AI	20

SECRET ACHIEVEMENTS

NAME	GOAL/REQUIREMENT	POINT VALUE
Communication Breakdown	Complete the 'Prime Target' operation	10
Second Target	Complete the 'Off Base' operation	10

NAME	GOAL/REQUIREMENT	POINT VALUE
Deep Freeze	Complete the 'Strike While Cold' operation	10
Fatboy Parade	Complete the 'Titans of Industry' operation	15
Nuclear Strike	Complete the 'Factions or Family Plan' operation	15
Rodgers is Relievedis	Complete the 'End of an Alliance' operation	25
Barge Ahead	Complete the 'Delta Force' operationthe	10
Alarming	Complete the 'Lethal Weapons' operation	10
Prison Break	Complete the 'Back on the Chain Gang' operation	15
Hole in the Ground	Complete the 'Steamed' operation	15
Gorged	Complete the 'Cliff Diving' operation	20
Reunited	Complete the 'Prime Time' operation	25
Downloading	Complete the 'Fact Finder' operation	10
Bugs in the Systemthe	Complete the 'The Trouble With Technology' operation	20
Animal Magnetism	Complete the 'The Great Leap Forward' operation	10
Class Reunion	Complete the 'Gatekeeper' operation	20
Well Stocked	Complete the 'Surface Tension' operation	15
Terra Firma	Complete the 'The Final Countdown' operation	25
Survivor	Don't lose any units during the first attack in 'Prime Target'	10
Bot Lord	Complete 'Prime Time' with an army made up entirely of Assault Bots	15
Survivalist	Survive multiple waves after the download completes in 'Fact Finder'	15

TEKKEN 6

ACHIEVEMENTS

NAME	GOAL/REQUIREMENT	POINT VALUE
Give Your Fists a Rest	Defeat an enemy using a weapon in Scenario Campaign Mode.	15
Night at the Movies	Unlock a movie in Scenario Campaign Mode.	15
Item Connoisseur	Obtain a Rank S Item in Scenario Campaign Mode.	30
Treasure Amateur	Collect 50 treasures in Scenario Campaign Mode.	10
Treasure Enthusiast	Collect 100 treasures in Scenario Campaign Mode.	20
Treasure Master	Collect 200 treasures in Scenario Campaign Mode.	30
Enemy Hunting Amateur	Defeat 300 enemies in Scenario Campaign Mode.	10
Enemy Hunting Enthusiast	Defeat 1000 enemies in Scenario Campaign Mode.	20
Enemy Hunting Master	Defeat 2000 enemies in Scenario Campaign Mode.	30
Playing With Fire	Defeat 100 enemies with the Flamethrower in Scenario Campaign Mode.	15
Heavy Artillery	Defeat 100 enemies with the Gatling Gun in Scenario Campaign Mode.	15
Ready for Action	Pick up 300 health recovery items in Scenario Campaign Mode.	15
Brute Force	Defeat 100 enemies with the Lead Pipe in Scenario Campaign Mode.	15
Thirsty Fighter	Pick up 50 drink items in Scenario Campaign Mode.	15
Crate Breaker	Destroy 100 wooden crates in Scenario Campaign Mode.	15
Alien Hunter	Defeat 10 aliens in Scenario Campaign Mode.	20
Scenario Expert	Clear all of the stages in Scenario Campaign Mode.	30
King of the Hill	Knock 10 enemies in the water in Scenario Campaign Mode.	20
A Friend in Need	Rescue your downed partner 3 times in Scenario Campaign Mode (single player).	15
Combo Amateur	Perform a 10 chain combo in Scenario Campaign Mode.	10
Combo Enthusiast	Perform a 30 chain combo in Scenario Campaign Mode.	20
Combo Master	Perform a 50 chain combo in Scenario Campaign Mode.	30
Upgraded Assistant	Upgrade Alisa to the highest possible level.	15

NAME	GOAL/REQUIREMENT	POINT VALUE
What's So Special About It?	Obtain the Special Flag in Scenario Campaign Mode.	20
No Key For Me	Clear the Millennium Tower stage without the boot-up key in Scenario Campaign Mode.	45
Learning is Fun	Clear the tutorial stage in Scenario Campaign Mode.	15
Moving On Up	Win a Ranked Match in Online Mode.	20
No Pressure	Win a Player Match in Online Mode.	20
Fighting Amateur	Play 3 matches in Online Mode.	10
Fighting Enthusiast	Play 10 matches in Online Mode.	20
Fighting Master	Play 30 matches in Online Mode.	30
Arcade Addict	Clear the Arcade Battle in Offline Mode.	15
Team Toppler	Defeat 3 teams in Team Battle in Offline Mode.	15
Survival of the Fittest	Earn 10 consecutive wins in Survival in Offline Mode.	15
Practice Makes Perfect	Inflict a total of 1000 damage in Practice in Offline Mode.	15
Gallery Completionist	Complete the Gallery.	45
Ghost Vanquisher	Defeat 30 Ghosts.	20
Love That Money	Collect more than 5,000,000 G.	15
Machine Crusher	Defeat NANCY-MI847J.	30

SECRET ACHIEVEMENTS

NAME	GOAL/REQUIREMENT	POINT VALUE
Tekken Fanatic	Complete all other objectives.	10
Friend or Foe?	Reunite with your ally in Scenario Campaign Mode.	15
Locate the Target	Learn the whereabouts of Heihachi Mishima in Scenario Campaign Mode.	15
It's All Coming Back to Me	Recover your memory in Scenario Campaign Mode.	15
The Key to Victory	Obtain the boot-up key in Scenario Campaign Mode.	15
That's No Hero	Defeat the Hero in Scenario Campaign Mode.	15
The Destroyer Has Fallen	Defeat the Destroyer of Worlds in Scenario Campaign Mode.	15
Showdown	Win the final battle in Scenario Campaign Mode.	30
What a Nightmare	Clear the Nightmare Train stage in Scenario Campaign Mode.	30
Wooden Warrior	Clear the Subterranean Pavilion stage in Scenario Campaign Mode.	30
Eastern Explorer	Clear the Kigan Island stage in Scenario Campaign Mode.	30

TEST DRIVE UNLIMITED 2

ACHIEVEMENTS

NAME	GOAL/REQUIREMENT	POINT VALUE
Small Collection	Own 3 different cars	5
One of each	Own a car from each category (A7-A6-A5-A4-A3-A2-A1, C4-C3, B4-B3)	30
God of Cars	Own all purchasable cars	50
Mummy	Complete 20 multiplayer challenges with bandages	10
My Beautiful Caravan	Own 1 house (caravan)	5
Subprime crisis?	Own one house from each level	30
Fashion Victim	Change your clothes or hairstyle 40 times	10
Hard earned money	Bank the maximum level of F.R.I.M. (10)	10
Kangaroo	Make a 100 m (109 yd) jump (any game mode)	20
Cruising	Drive 200 km (124 miles)	5
Easy Money	Earn $100,000 with F.R.I.M.	10
Car-tist	Decorate 5 different cars	15
Big Spender	Spend 1 million dollars	50
Reckless Driver	Drive around and hit 100 AI controlled cars and destructible objects	10
The Beginner	Win a championship	5
King of Ibiza	Win Ibiza Cup, area 1	25

NAME	GOAL/REQUIREMENT	POINT VALUE
Coronation	Win all championships & cups	75
Racing School Master	Obtain all licenses	20
Level 60	Reach level 60	100
Aloha!	Make it to Hawaii	20
Learning	Obtain The C4 license	5
Fast and Luxurious	Drive at 400 km/h (249 mph) for 5 sec. (any game mode)	10
Say "Cheese!"	Get clocked by the radar 100 times (Speedtrap game mode)	10
Tuning Addict	Tune a car to the max level	5
Cockpit Addict	Drive 500 km (311 miles) using the cockpit view (any game mode)	20
Get rich or try driving	Possess 1 million dollars	25
Multi-Challenger	Win 5 challenges in each multiplayer mode (Race, Speed, Speedtrap)	25
Instant challenge, easy cash!	Earn $10,000 in Instant Challenges	20
Road Eater	Drive 1000 km (621 miles)	10
Fugitive Wanted	Outrun the police 30 times in Online Chase Mode	10
My Club and Me	Drive 150 km (93 miles) in intra-Club challenges	15
Club Basher	Win 30 Club vs. Club challenges	25
Marshall	Arrest 30 outlaws in Online Chase Mode	10
Reporter	Find all viewpoints (photographer)	30
Hey! What's this car?!	Own 1 bonus car (treasure hunt)	5
Tyrannosaurus wrecks	Own all 6 bonus cars (treasure hunt)	25
Ibiza Photographer	Find 5 viewpoints on Ibiza (photographer)	10
The Explorer	Drive 5000 km (3107 miles)	50
Helping hand	Succeed in 10 missions	15
Events Accomplished	Achieve all missions	40
Keep your distance	Drive for 15 sec. above 100 km/h (62 mph) with 8 players in "Keep Your Distance" mode	30
Exclusive Car	Drive a Club car	10
Exclusive CarS	Drive all Club cars	30
Co-op Challenger	Drive 150 km (93 miles) in "Keep Your Distance" and "Follow the Leader" modes	15
Me against all of you	Play 40 challenges in the Community Racing Center	25
Social Butterfly	Join and invite friends 100 times (any game mode)	10
Better than a GPS	Invite 10 players to drive with you in your car.	10

DOWNLOADABLE CONTENT: CASINO ONLINE

NAME	GOAL/REQUIREMENT	POINT VALUE
Risk Taker	Casino: Give up a Three of a Kind while playing Video Poker and win the next hand	10
Island Caretaker	Casino: Wake up the Island caretaker	10
Drinks	Casino: Have 10 cocktails at once at a poker table	10
Casino Fashion Victim	Casino: Buy all clothes available in the Casino Clothes Shop	25
Socializing	Casino: Unlock all cocktails and emotes	25
V.I.P.	Casino: Become VIP of the Casino by reaching level 5	35
Ready to play TDU2?	Casino: Win the luxury car displayed in the entrance hall	20
Western	Casino: Play the "duel" emote at the same time as your rival at a poker table for two	15
Wanted	Casino: Get the right look to get the reward	25
1-in-38 Chance	Casino: Win a straight-up bet at Roulette	20

TIGER WOODS PGA TOUR 13

ACHIEVEMENTS

NAME	GOAL/REQUIREMENT	POINT VALUE
Going Green with a Hybrid	Land on the green from over 175 yards away using a Hybrid	30
Live from your couch	Play in a Live Tournament	25
Tigers have FIR	Complete an 18 hole round with a 100 percent FIR. FIR = Fairway in Regulation	30
That was GIRrrreat!	Complete an 18 hole round with a 100 percent GIR. GIR = Green in Regulation	15
No Handouts Please	Actually get a hole in 1 in the 1982 First Hole in One event in Tiger Legacy Challenge	10
Shouting at Amen Corner	Complete Amen Corner (Augusta 11,12,13) with a birdie or better on each in a single round.	10
It's a Start	Master 1 Course	15
Now we're talking	Master 8 Courses	30
Like a Boss	Master 16 Courses	60
So Much Easier than Putting	Make a hole in one	30
From the Ladies Tees	Complete an 18 hole round using the Red Tees	15
When do we get paid?	Compete in an amateur championship	15
Never leave home without it	Earn PGA TOUR card	15
Top 50 Countdown	Break the top 50 in EA SPORTS Golf Rankings	15
Top 10 Hits	Break the top 10 in EA SPORTS Golf Rankings	30
King of the Hill	Become #1 in the EA SPORTS Golf Rankings	50
Don't quit your day job	Win the Masters as an amateur	15
It's all in the Hips	Sink a 40ft putt	15
Like a Homing Pigeon	From the Fairway, land within 1 yard of the flagstick from 150 yards out	15
I Own this Place	Defend your title in any Major	25
Small Tiger, Big Bite	Complete an 18 hole online head-to-head match with toddler Tiger	15
Play Date	Play a Four Player online match with all players using toddlers	15
Can you give me a Boost?	Play an 18 hole round with Boost Pins equipped	15
Toddler Years	Complete Toddler Years in Tiger Legacy Challenge	15
Early Years	Complete the Early Years in Tiger Legacy Challenge	15
Junior Years	Complete the Junior Years in Tiger Legacy Challenge	15
Amateur Years	Complete the Amateur Years in Tiger Legacy Challenge	15
Rookie Years	Complete the Rookie Years in Tiger Legacy Challenge	15
Tiger Slam	Complete the Tiger Slam in Tiger Legacy Challenge	20
Pro Years	Complete the Pro Years in Tiger Legacy Challenge	20
Present Day	Complete the Present Day in Tiger Legacy Challenge	30
The Future	Complete the Future in Tiger Legacy Challenge	30
Dig Deep	Land within 1 yard of the flagstick from a bunker	15
He's going the distance	Hit a drive over 400 yards	30
Like a Metronome	Complete 10 perfect Tempo Swings with TOUR Pro Difficulty or better	15
Check out my Custom Settings	Complete an 18 hole round using a Custom Difficulty	15
I Finally Belong!	Create or Join a Country Club in Game	15
Members Only	Play in a Country Club Tournament	15
I Need a Commitment	Earn a Four Day loyalty Bonus	15
Internal Conflict	Compete with a teammate in a head-to-head match launched from the Clubhouse lobby	15
Putt from the rough	Make a putt from the rough	15
One Small Step for Mankind	Win the Green Jacket in Career Mode	35
Unstoppable!	Win the Green Jacket for a Record 7 times in Career Mode	75

SECRET ACHIEVEMENTS

NAME	GOAL/REQUIREMENT	POINT VALUE
Swing and a miss	Whiff the ball	10
Child's Play	Complete an 18 hole round with toddler Ricky	15
That was Easy	Beat the course record of 63 at the Masters (In Career Mode)	30

TOM CLANCY'S GHOST RECON: FUTURE SOLDIER

ACHIEVEMENTS

NAME	GOAL/REQUIREMENT	POINT VALUE
Doing Work	Kill 1000 enemies while in Guerrilla mode	10
Quality Beats Quantity	Defeat all 50 enemy waves on Guerrilla mode (any difficulty, any map)	30
Good Effect on Target	In Guerrilla mode, kill more than 5 enemies with an airstrike	10
Just a Box	While in Guerrilla mode, complete an infiltration sequence without being detected	10
Good Enough for Government Work	Achieve a Ghost skill rating above 80% for all missions	10
Qualified	Achieve a Ghost skill rating of above 90% on one mission	25
Master Tactician	Complete 100% of the Tactical challenges	25
Tactician	Complete 50% of the Tactical challenges	10
Battle Buddies	Complete the campaign in Co-op	30
Future Soldier	Complete the campaign in Elite	50
Advanced Warfighter	Complete the campaign in Veteran	40
Just Another Day at the Office	Complete the campaign for the first time	30
...I Can Do Better	Complete 20 Daily Friend Challenges	5
Anything You Can Do...	Complete a Daily Friend Challenge through all return fire volleys	20
Total Domination	Complete all of the Domination achievements	40
Saboteur Domination	Be part of a squad match where your team takes the bomb into the enemy base in under 2 minutes	10
Decoy Domination	In squad matches your team completes the key objective first, five times.	10
Siege Domination	Be part of a squad match where your team captures the objective in under 2 minutes	10
Conflict Domination	Be part of a squad match where your team wins by a margin of 500 points or more	10
Cross-trained	Reach Level 10 on one Rifleman, one Scout, and one Engineer character	10
Backup	Complete 5 Savior Kills in Quick Matches	5
Actionable Intel	Complete 10 Coordinated Kills	10
Mod Pro	Spend 50 Attachment Credits to add attachments to various guns	40
Tuned Up	Customize all the internal parts of one weapon	25
Field Tested	Play 5 MP matches of each game type	5
Counter-Intelligence	Interrupt an enemy's attempt to data hack a teammate 5 times, by killing or stunning the enemy	10
True Ghost	Get 10 consecutive kills in one Quick Match without dying	10
Recon Specialist	Complete 5 Intel Assists in Quick Matches	25
Kitted Out	Customize 1 weapon with an external attachment at every attachment point	25
Mod Rookie	Add an attachment to any gun	5
High-Value Target	Kill a member of the dev team, or kill someone who has	5
Coordinated Assault	Use the Coordination System to reach an objective	5
Armorer	Spend 25 Attachment Credits with each role	35
High Speed, Low Drag	Reach Level 50 on any character	50
Call, Answered	Complete all Tours of Duty	35

NAME	GOAL/REQUIREMENT	POINT VALUE
Tour of Duty: North Sea	Win 3 MP matches of any game type on each: Harbor, Cargo, and Rig maps	25
Tour of Duty: Arctic	Win 3 MP matches of any game type on each: Underground, Mill, and Alpha maps	25
Tour of Duty: Nigeria	Win 3 MP of any game type on each: Pipeline, Market, Sand Storm, and Overpass maps	25

SECRET ACHIEVEMENTS

NAME	GOAL/REQUIREMENT	POINT VALUE
No Loose Ends	Eliminate the leader of the Raven's Rock faction	20
Relieved of Command	Kill the general commanding the Moscow defenses	20
Special Election	Rescue Russian President Volodin from the prison camp	20
Breathing Room	Destroy the second piece of enemy artillery	20
Fuel for the Fire	Secure the drilling ships and complete the mission	20
Blood Brother	Rescue the Georgian Spec Ops	20
...Must Come Down.	Destroy the plane with the weapons system on board while it is in flight	20
EOD	Destroy the Russian weapons transfer station	20
Source Control	Secure the VIP and transfer them to the exfiltration team	20
Precious Cargo	Secure the VIP and transfer him to the exfiltration team	20
What Goes Up...	Shoot down the cargo plane	20
Loose Thread	Secure Gabriel Paez	20

TOM CLANCY'S SPLINTER CELL: CONVICTION

ACHIEVEMENTS

NAME	GOAL/REQUIREMENT	POINT VALUE
Realistic Difficulty	Complete single player story on "Realistic" difficulty	50
Co-op Realistic Difficulty	Complete the co-op story on "Realistic" difficulty	50
Quality Time	Invite a friend to join and participate in a co-op story or game mode session	20
Hunter	Complete any 1 map in "Hunter" game mode in co-op	10
Last Stand	Complete any 1 map in "Last Stand" game mode in co-op	10
Hunter Completionist	Complete all maps in "Hunter" game mode on rookie or normal difficulty	20
Hunter Master	Complete all maps in "Hunter" game mode on realistic difficulty	50
Last Stand Completionist	Complete all maps in "Last Stand" game mode on rookie or normal difficulty	20
Last Stand Master	Complete all maps in "Last Stand" game mode on realistic difficulty	50
Face-Off Completionist	Complete all maps in "Face-Off" game mode using any connection type	20
Face Off	Win one match in "Face-Off" game mode on any difficulty	10
Preparation Master	Complete all prepare & execute challenges	30
Stealth Master	Complete all vanish challenges	30
Best Of The Best	Complete all Splinter Cell challenges	30
Well-Rounded	Complete all challenges	50
Weapon Upgraded	Purchase all 3 upgrades for any 1 weapon	10
Gadget Upgraded	Purchase all 3 upgrades for any 1 gadget	10
Weapons Expert	Purchase all 3 upgrades for all weapons	20
Gadgets Expert	Purchase both upgrades for all gadgets	20
Weapons Collector	Unlock all weapons in the weapon vault	20
Variety	Purchase any 1 uniform	10
Accessorizing	Purchase any 1 accessory for any 1 uniform	10
Ready For Anything	Purchase all 9 accessories for all uniforms	20
Fashionable	Purchase all 6 texture variants for all uniforms	20
Perfect Hunter	Complete any map in Hunter without ever having been detected on realistic difficulty	20

NAME	GOAL/REQUIREMENT	POINT VALUE
Last Man Standing	In Last Stand, survive all enemy waves of any map in one session without failing on any difficulty	50
Revelations	Discover Anna Grimsdottir's dark secret	10

SECRET ACHIEVEMENTS

NAME	GOAL/REQUIREMENT	POINT VALUE
Merchant's Street Market	Complete Single Player Story "Merchant's Street Market" on any difficulty	20
Kobin's Mansion	Complete Single Player Story "Kobin's Mansion" on any difficulty	20
Price Airfield	Complete Single Player Story "Price Airfield" on any difficulty	20
Diwaniya, Iraq	Complete Single Player Story "Diwaniya, Iraq" on any difficulty	20
Washington Monument	Complete Single Player Story "Washington Monument" on any difficulty	20
White Box Laboratories	Complete Single Player Story "White Box Laboratories" on any difficulty	20
Lincoln Memorial	Complete Single Player Story "Lincoln Memorial" on any difficulty	20
Third Echelon HQ	Complete Single Player Story "Third Echelon HQ" on any difficulty	20
Michigan Ave. Reservoir	Complete Single Player Story "Michigan Ave. Reservoir" on any difficulty	20
Downtown District	Complete Single Player Story "Downtown District" on any difficulty	20
White House	Complete Single Player Story "White House" on any difficulty	20
St. Petersburg Banya	Complete CO-OP Story "St. Petersburg Banya" on any difficulty	20
Russian Embassy	Complete CO-OP Story "Russian Embassy" on any difficulty	20
Yastreb Complex	Complete CO-OP Story "Yastreb Complex" on any difficulty	20
Modzok Proving Grounds	Complete CO-OP Story "Modzok Proving Grounds" on any difficulty	20
Judge, Jury and Executioner	Take down Tom Reed	10
Man of Conviction	Allow Tom Reed to live	10
Survivor	Battle your CO-OP teammate and survive	10

TRANSFORMERS: REVENGE OF THE FALLEN

ACHIEVEMENTS

NAME	GOAL/REQUIREMENT	POINT VALUE
Down to Chinatown	Medal in all Autobot Shanghai Missions	20
West Side	Medal in all Autobot West Coast Missions	20
Aerialbot Assault	Medal in all Autobot Deep Six Missions	20
East Side	Medal in all Autobot East Coast Missions	20
The Dagger's Tip	Medal in all Autobot Cairo Missions	20
One Shall Stand	Defeat Megatron—Autobot Campaign	25
Now I've Seen It All	Unlock all Autobot Unlockables	50
Power to the People	Purchase All Autobot Upgrades	25
Awesome Achievement!	Eliminate 250 Decepticons—Autobot Campaign	25
Do the Math	Acquire 2,000,000 Energon in the Autobot Campaign	20
A True Autobot	Earn Platinum Medals on ALL Autobot Missions	75
Shanghai'd	Medal in all Decepticon Shanghai Missions	25
West Coast For The Win!	Medal in all Decepticon West Coast Missions	25
Rise of The Fallen	Medal in all Decepticon Deep Six Missions	25
Coast to Coast	Medal in all Decepticon East Coast Missions	25
Lies	Medal in all Decepticon Cairo Missions	25
One Shall Fall	Defeat Optimus Prime—Decepticon Campaign	25

NAME	GOAL/REQUIREMENT	POINT VALUE
Now I've Really Seen It All	Unlock all Decepticon Unlockables	50
Spoils of War	Purchase All Decepticon Upgrades	25
Bad Boys	Eliminate 350 Autobots—Decepticon Campaign	25
Break the Bank	Acquire 3,000,000 Energon in the Decepticon Campaign	25
A True Decepticon	Earn Platinum Medals on ALL Decepticon Missions	75
Platty For The Win!	Earn a Platinum Medal—Either Campaign	20
Golden Boy	Earn a Gold Medal—Either Campaign	15
Not Gold Enough	Earn a Silver Medal—Either Campaign	10
Cast in Bronze	Earn a Bronze Medal—Either Campaign	5
On the Board	Make it into the Top 100000 on SP Leaderboards—Either Campaign	15
Good Mojo	Make it into the Top 10000 on SP Leaderboards—Either Campaign	25
Bonecrusher	Make it into the Top 1000 on SP Leaderboards—Either Campaign	25
And So It Begins...	Unlock a Single Unlockable—Either Campaign	5
Grind On	Purchase an Upgrade—Either Campaign	5
Choices...	Unlock a New Zone—Either Campaign	5
You've Got The Touch	Fill OVERDRIVE Meter—Either Campaign	25
Choose a Side	Win one RANKED/PLAYER MATCH game as Autobots and one as Decepticons	15
Hold!	Win a Control Point round without losing a control point in a RANKED/PLAYER MATCH game	15
Follow the Leader	While playing One Shall Stand, as the leader, kill the opposing leader in a RANKED/PLAYER MATCH game	15
Life of the Party	Host one game of each game type in a PLAYER MATCH game	15
Smells Like Victory	Win a Match as Each of the 15 Default Characters	50

ULTIMATE MARVEL VS. CAPCOM 3

ACHIEVEMENTS

NAME	GOAL/REQUIREMENT	POINT VALUE
The Ultimate	Unlock all achievements.	50
Waiting for the Trade	View all endings in Arcade mode.	50
The Best There Is	Beat Arcade mode on the hardest difficulty.	10
Saving My Quarters	Beat Arcade mode without using any continues.	10
The Points Do Matter	Earn 400,000 points in Arcade mode.	20
High-Score Hero	Earn 500,000 points in Arcade mode.	30
Missions? Possible.	Clear 120 missions in Mission mode.	20
Up To The Challenge	Clear 240 missions in Mission mode.	30
Master of Tasks	Clear 480 missions in Mission mode.	40
Above Average Joe	Land a Viewtiful Combo. (Arcade/Xbox LIVE)	10
Mutant Master	Land an Uncanny Combo. (Arcade/Xbox LIVE)	10
Mega Buster	Use 1,000 Hyper Combo Gauge bars. (Arcade/Xbox LIVE)	20
Defender	Block 100 times. (Arcade/Xbox LIVE)	10
Advancing Guardian	Perform 100 Advancing Guards. (Arcade/Xbox LIVE)	10
A Friend in Need	Perform 100 Crossover Assists. (Arcade/Xbox LIVE)	20
First Strike	Land 50 First Attacks. (Arcade/Xbox LIVE)	10
Savage Playing	Perform 50 Snap Backs. (Arcade/Xbox LIVE)	10
Quick Change-Up	Perform 50 Crossover Counters. (Arcade/Xbox LIVE)	10
Perfect X-ample	Use X-Factor 50 times. (Arcade/Xbox LIVE)	10
Gravity? Please...	Land 50 Team Aerial Combos. (Arcade/Xbox LIVE)	10
Mighty Teamwork	Land 30 Team Aerial Counters. (Arcade/Xbox LIVE)	10
Big Bang Theory	Perform 30 Hyper Combo Finishes. (Arcade/Xbox LIVE)	15
Hard Corps	Perform 30 Crossover Combination Finishes. (Arcade/Xbox LIVE)	15
Training Montage	Play in Offline Mode for over 5 hours.	20

NAME	GOAL/REQUIREMENT	POINT VALUE
Training in Isolation	Play in Offline Mode for over 30 hours.	30
Seductive Embrace	Play on Xbox LIVE for over 5 hours.	20
Rivals Welcome	Play on Xbox LIVE for over 30 hours.	30
Brave New World	Participate in any mode over Xbox LIVE.	10
Hellbent	Participate in 100 matches in Xbox LIVE.	20
Dreaded Opponent	Participate in 200 matches in Xbox LIVE.	20
Forged From Steel	Participate in 300 matches in Xbox LIVE.	30
Full Roster	Battle against all characters over Xbox LIVE.	30
Incredible	Win without calling your partners or switching out in a Xbox LIVE match.	20
Need a Healing Factor	Win without blocking in an Xbox LIVE match.	20
Crazy Good	Surpass the rank of Fighter.	10
Mega Good	Surpass the 6th rank of any class.	40
Hotshot	Win 10 battles in Ranked Match.	15
Slam Master	Win 50 battles in Ranked Match.	20
Fighting Machine	Win 100 battles in Ranked Match.	40
Noble Effort	Get a 5-game win streak in Ranked Match.	15
Assemble!	Participate in an 8 player Lobby over Xbox LIVE.	15
Dominator	Collect 100 titles.	30
A Warrior Born	Earn 5,000 Player Points (PP).	10
Devil with a Blue Coat	Earn 30,000 Player Points (PP).	15
Divine Brawler	Earn 100,000 Player Points (PP).	50
Comic Collector	Unlock all items in the Gallery.	50
Passport to Beatdown Country	Fight in all of the stages.	10

VANQUISH

ACHIEVEMENTS

NAME	GOAL/REQUIREMENT	POINT VALUE
One Day at DARPA	Complete all DARPA training exercises.	10
Space Normandy	Complete Act 1.	15
Storming Grand Hill	Complete Act 2.	15
I Don't Speak Kreon!	Complete Act 3.	15
My Way	Complete Act 4.	15
End to Major Combat Operations	Complete Act 5.	15
Survivor	Complete all Acts.	30
Operation Overlord II	Complete Act 1 on Hard difficulty or above.	25
Ain't Life Grand?	Complete Act 2 on Hard difficulty or above.	25
Cry on, Kreon!	Complete Act 3 on Hard difficulty or above.	25
The High Way	Complete Act 4 on Hard difficulty or above.	25
Mission Accomplished	Complete Act 5 on Hard difficulty or above.	25
ARS Operator	Complete all Acts on Hard difficulty or above.	50
Gun Runner	Scan and acquire all weapons.	10
King of the Hill	Level a weapon up to maximum operational capability.	20
Fight or Flight	Manually trigger AR Mode and destroy an enemy robot.	10
Adrenaline Rush	Manually trigger AR Mode and destroy three enemy robots in a row.	20
Going in for the Kill	Destroy ten enemy robots with melee attacks.	10
A Heartbreaker and Lifetaker	Destroy 100 enemy robots with melee attacks.	30
Helloooo, Nurse	Revive a friendly troop.	5
Knight in Shining White Armor	Revive 20 friendly troops.	15
Death Wish	Destroy three enemy robots while in damage-triggered AR Mode.	20
40 Yard Dash	Maintain a Boost dash to the limit of the ARS reactor without overheating.	30
Home Run	Destroy an incoming missile or grenade.	10
Home Run God	Destroy ten incoming missiles or grenades.	10

NAME	GOAL/REQUIREMENT	POINT VALUE
Brutality Bonus	Destroy a Romanov's arms and legs, then finish it with a melee attack.	10
Romanov This!	Destroy a Romanov with a melee attack.	20
The Hand of God	Destroy two Romanovs in a row using only melee attacks.	30
Robots Tend to Blow Up	Destroy three enemy robots at once with one hand grenade.	10
Hole-in-One	Destroy a Chicane with a hand grenade.	5
Short Circuit	Destroy ten enemy robots that have been disabled with an EMP emitter.	20
Two Birds with One Stone	Destroy two or more enemy robots at once with the LFE gun.	20
Trick Shot	Destroy three enemy robots at once with rocket launcher splash damage.	20
Flash! King of the Impossible	Destroy four enemies simultaneously with the Lock-on Laser.	30
Piece by Piece	Destroy the arms, head, and back of an KNRB-0 Argus robot.	20
That Ended Up Working Out Nicely	After taking control of the enemy transport in Act 2-2, do not let a single enemy escape.	10
Failure Breeds Success	Destroy two Argus robots in Act 2-3 while they are in bipedal mode.	15
Leibniz Defense Agency	Defend the Pangloss statue in Act 3-2.	10
Tightrope Walker	Destroy two cannons in Act 3-3 and complete the mission.	10
Fisher is the Other Sam	Proceed on the monorail in Act 3-4 without being spotted by the enemy troops or searchlights.	15
Flyswatter	Destroy all the floating turrets in Act 3-4.	20
Guardian	Do not allow any friendly armor to be destroyed during Act 3-5.	10
Hurry the #@$% Up!	Destroy five or more enemy transports from atop the Kreon in Act 3-7.	10
Civil Disobedience	Ignore the elevator start order in Act 4-1. Instead, hold position and destroy all reinforcements.	30
Buzzard Beater	Destroy the Buzzard without allowing it to reach ground level in Act 5-1.	30
Smoke 'em if ya got 'em!	Destroy 10 enemies distracted by cigarettes during one mission.	30
Auld Lang Syne	Destroy two enemy robots who have been distracted by a cigarette.	15
The Best of All Possible Worlds	Find and fire upon all of the Pangloss statues hidden on the colony.	30
Living Legend	Complete the game without dying, regardless of difficulty level.	50

SECRET ACHIEVEMENTS

NAME	GOAL/REQUIREMENT	POINT VALUE
Tactical Challenges	Complete all of the Tactical Challenges in VANQUISH	50

THE WITCHER 2: ASSASSINS OF KINGS

ACHIEVEMENTS

NAME	GOAL/REQUIREMENT	POINT VALUE
To Aedirn!	Complete Chapter 1.	5
Alea Iacta Est	Complete Chapter 2.	10
Once Ain't Enough	Complete Chapter 3.	15
Apprentice	Use alchemy to brew five potions or oils.	10
Master Alchemist	Acquire the Mutant ability.	10
The Butcher of Blaviken	Kill 500 foes.	30
Miser	Collect 10000 orens.	10
Focus	Perform three successful ripostes in a row.	30
Craftsman	Hire a craftsman to create an item.	10
Pest Control	Finish all quests involing the destruction of monster nests.	20

NAME	GOAL/REQUIREMENT	POINT VALUE
Torn Asunder!	Kill more than one opponent using a single exploding bomb.	15
Gambler	Win an arm wrestling match, a dice poker game and a fist fight.	15
Gladiator	Defeat all opponents in the Kaedweni arena.	15
Madman	Finish the game while playing at the Dark difficulty level.	100
Journeyman	Achieve character level 10.	10
Guru	Achieve character level 35.	50
Master of Magic	Acquire the Sense of Magic ability.	10
Mutant!	Enhance abilities using mutagens at least five times.	30
Last Man Standing	Survive your 30th fight in the Arena	15
Perfectionist	Kill 10 foes in a row without losing any Vitality.	15
Poker!	Roll five-of-a-kind at dice poker.	30
Tried-and-True	Survive your 5th fight in the Arena	10
The Fugitive	Complete the Prologue.	5
Ricochet	Kill a foe by deflecting his own arrow at him.	10
Swordmaster	Acquire the Combat Acumen ability.	10
To Be Continued...	Finish the game at any difficulty level.	50
Threesome	Kill three foes at once by performing a group finisher.	15

SECRET ACHIEVEMENTS

NAME	GOAL/REQUIREMENT	POINT VALUE
Avenger	Finish the game by killing Letho.	30
Backbone	Craft a suit of armor from elements of the kayran's carapace.	20
Being Witcher George	Kill the dragon.	20
Fat Man	Kill the draug.	15
Eagle Eye	Hit Count Etcheverry using the ballista.	10
Heartbreaker	Seduce Ves.	10
Kingmaker	Help Roche rescue Anais from the Kaedweni camp.	15
Dragonheart	Spare or save Saskia.	20
Librarian	Find all additional information about the insane asylum's history.	30
Necromancer	Relive all of Auckes's memories in Dethmold's vision.	50
Old Friends	Finish the game by sparing Letho.	30
Sensitive Guy	Save Síle from dying in the unstable portal.	10
Intimidator	Intimidate someone.	15
Man of the Shadows	Successfully sneak through Loredo's garden and find the component of the kayran trap.	15
Black Ops	Sneak through the lower camp without raising the alarm.	20
Spellbreaker	Help Iorveth find the dagger needed to free Saskia from the spell that holds her.	15
Reasons of State	Stop Roche from killing Henselt.	15
Kayranslayer	Kill the kayran.	10
Artful Dodger	Cut off a tentacle using the kayran trap.	30
Tourist	Tour the camp with Zyvik.	10
Friend of Trolls	Spare all trolls in the game.	15
Trollslayer	Kill all the trolls in the game.	30
Witch Hunter	Leave Síle to die in the unstable portal.	10

WOLFENSTEIN

ACHIEVEMENTS

NAME	GOAL/REQUIREMENT	POINT VALUE
Safe Keeping	Finish a match on Bank, spending the majority of your time on the winning team. (1 min minimum)	10
Route Canal	Finish a match on Canals, spending the majority of your time on the winning team. (1 min minimum)	10
Chemical Burn	Finish a match on Chemical, spending the majority of your time on the winning team. (1 min minimum)	10

NAME	GOAL/REQUIREMENT	POINT VALUE
Facilitated	Finish a match on Facility, spending the majority of your time on the winning team. (1 min minimum)	10
Hospitalized	Finish a match on Hospital, spending the majority of your time on the winning team. (1 min minimum)	10
Mind your Manors	Finish a match on Manor, spending the majority of your time on the winning team. (1 min minimum)	10
Pirate Radio	Finish a match on Rooftops, spending the majority of your time on the winning team. (1 min minimum)	10
Shock and Awe	Finish a match on Tesla, spending the majority of your time on the winning team. (1 min minimum)	10
Test Subject	Use every Veil ability once in multiplayer.	10
Veilophile	Spend 5 minutes in the Veil in multiplayer.	10
Ley Vacuum	Suck up 5 Veil Pools' worth of Veil energy in multiplayer.	10
Surgical Striker	Kill 200 enemy players using the Veil Strike in multiplayer.	30
Sneaky Pete	Kill 100 enemy players with the Satchel Charge in multiplayer.	30
Unholy Lifeline	Revive 250 teammates, including 10 revives in a single match in multiplayer.	30
Focal Point	Restore 5000 points of health to teammates using the Healing Aura in multiplayer.	30
Quartermaster	Give 100 Health Packs to teammates in multiplayer.	30
Run-gineer	Use Veil Speed for 30 minutes in multiplayer.	30
Engineering Corps	Complete 30 primary objectives and 50 secondary objectives in multiplayer.	30
Beatdown	Kill 50 enemies with melee attacks in a single player campaign.	30
Bubble Boy	Block 1000 shots with Shield power in a single player campaign.	20
Buster	Destroy 1000 breakable objects in a single player campaign.	20
Conservationist	Complete a story mission in the single player campaign without reloading a gun.	30
Endgame	Finish the single player campaign on any difficulty.	10
Gadget Freak	Purchase all the upgrades for one of your weapons in the single player campaign.	20
Game Hunter	Kill an enemy of every type in a single player campaign.	10
Gold Digger	Collect all the valuables in a single player campaign.	30
Gun Nut	Collect all the weapons in a single player campaign.	10
Honorary Geist	Spend two hours in the Veil in a single player campaign.	20
Nerd Rage	Complete the single player campaign on Hard or Über difficulty.	20
Librarian	Collect all the Tomes of Power in a single player campaign.	20
Man About Town	Complete all the Downtown missions in a single player campaign.	20
Blitzkrieg	Complete the single player campaign in under 12 hours.	30
Master Spy	Collect all the Intel in a single player campaign.	20
Monitor Tan	Collect every collectible in a single player campaign.	30
Newbie	Complete the Train Station mission in a single player campaign.	10
Rampage	Kill 200 enemies with Empower in a single player campaign.	20
Single Quarter	Complete the single player campaign with less than three deaths.	30
Slumming	Complete all the Midtown missions in a single player campaign.	10
Super Soldier	Complete the single player campaign on Über difficulty.	30
Time Out	Use the Mire power for more than an hour in a single player campaign.	20
Warchest	Collect more than $30,000 in a single player campaign.	20
Enemies in a Barrel	Kill 3 floating enemies.	20

NAME	GOAL/REQUIREMENT	POINT VALUE
Career Soldier	Reach Rank 25 in multiplayer.	15
Das Big Man	Reach Rank 50 in multiplayer.	15
Boot Camp	Get a kill with each Soldier weapon, the Satchel Charge and Veil Strike in multiplayer.	30
Heavy-Handed	Kill 200 enemy players with either the Panzerschreck or the Flammenwerfer in multiplayer.	30
Med School	Revive a player, supply a Health Pack, and heal someone using Healing Aura in multiplayer.	30
Basic Training	Complete a primary objective, supply an Ammo Pack, and use Veil Speed once in multiplayer.	30
Johnny-on-the-spot	Give 100 Ammo Packs to teammates in multiplayer.	30

WWE ALL STARS

ACHIEVEMENTS

NAME	GOAL/REQUIREMENT	POINT VALUE
Running Wild	Performed 50 successful finishers in any mode over the course of the game.	20
Born to Fly	Performed 10 successful regular aerial moves in a single match.	20
Five Moves of Doom	Executed five signature moves in a single match.	20
Dominating	Won a match against the CPU without losing any health.	20
Layeth the Smacketh Down!	Won a match in under 2 minutes.	20
Punch Drunk	Landed at least 100 strikes in a single match in any mode.	20
Man of 1000 Holds	Won a match without using any strikes.	25
Slobberknocker	Won a match without using any grapples.	25
Make Them Humble	Won 25 matches by knockout.	25
Five Star Rating	Achieved a five star rating while facing the CPU.	20
Mark of Excellence	Earned a gold medal while facing the CPU.	20
The Apex Predator	Completed the Superstars Path of Champions.	20
Breaking the Rules	Completed the Tag Team Path of Champions.	20
Facing the Deadman	Completed the Legends Path of Champions.	20
The New Generation	Defeated a Legend with a Superstar.	10
Showing Them How It's Done	Defeated a Superstar with a Legend.	10
Rising Star	Completed Path of Champions with a created Superstar.	20
Reversal of Fortune	Performed at least 5 grapple reversals during a match.	15
Chain Gang	Performed a combo at least 5 moves in length.	15
The Next WWE Superstar	Made a created Superstar.	10
Old School	Completed all Fantasy Warfare matches as a WWE Legend.	15
Legend Killer	Completed all Fantasy Warfare matches as a WWE Superstar.	15
Over the Top	Won a Steel Cage match.	15
Suck It	Won a Tornado Tag Team match as Triple H and Shawn Michaels.	20
Mega Powers	Won a Tornado Tag Team match as Hulk Hogan and Randy Savage.	20
The New Face of Cyberspace	Defeated a created Superstar in an Xbox LIVE match with your own created Superstar.	20
Main Eventer	Won 50 Xbox LIVE matches.	50
You Can't See Me!	Won 10 consecutive Xbox LIVE matches.	50
Comeback of the Year	Won a match when your Superstar is at zero health.	20
Beating the Odds	Won a Handicap match.	15
Totally Extreme!	Won an Extreme Rules match.	15
He's Got a Chair!	Landed at least 10 successful strikes with an object in a single match.	20
In the Spotlight	Won an Xbox LIVE match.	15
Last Man Standing	Won a Fatal 4 Way Elimination match.	15

NAME	GOAL/REQUIREMENT	POINT VALUE
The Champ is Here!	Completed all three Path of Champions as John Cena.	50
Enhancement Talent	Won 10 Xbox LIVE matches.	20
Mid Carder	Won 25 Xbox LIVE matches.	25
The Bottom Line	Defeated the entire WWE All Stars roster with a single created Superstar.	50
The King of Kings	Defeated the entire WWE All Stars roster as Triple H.	50
The Ultimate Achievement	Defeated the entire Roster and all three Path of Champions as The Ultimate Warrior.	75

SECRET ACHIEVEMENTS

NAME	GOAL/REQUIREMENT	POINT VALUE
Winner by Default	Won an Xbox LIVE match due to opponent's disqualification.	10
Attitude Problem	Got disqualified in three consecutive matches.	10
Booyaka Booyaka	Defeated Andre the Giant and Big Show in a Handicap Match as Rey Mysterio.	10
I'm Your Papi!	Defeated Rey Mysterio in a Steel Cage match as Eddie Guerrero.	10
The Pride of Scotland	Won a Tornado Tag Team match as Roddy Piper and Drew McIntyre.	10

XCOM: ENEMY UNKNOWN

ACHIEVEMENTS

NAME	GOAL/REQUIREMENT	POINT VALUE
No Looking Back	Beat the game in Ironman mode on Classic or Impossible difficulty.	100
Humanity's Savior	Beat the game on any difficulty.	30
Earth First	Beat the game on Classic difficulty.	60
Our Finest Hour	Beat the game on Impossible difficulty.	90
Lone Wolf	Clear a UFO crash site with one soldier on Classic or Impossible difficulty.	20
Bada Boom	Kill 50 aliens with explosive weapons.	10
Welcoming Committee	Kill 150 aliens.	20
Pale Horse	Kill 500 aliens.	50
Shooting Stars	Shoot down 40 UFOs.	35
Ain't No Cavalry Comin'	Have a soldier survive every mission in a full game.	50
As A Scalpel	Earn the "Excellent" rating in every performance category on a terror mission.	25
Edison	In a single game, complete every Research Project.	25
All Employees Must Wash Hands...	In a single game, complete every Autopsy.	10
Eye in the Sky	Launch a Satellite.	5
All Together Now	Get satellite coverage over every country on one continent.	10
Hunter/Killer	In a single game, shoot down one of each alien craft.	15
Man No More	Build a suit of powered armor.	10
We Happy Few	Complete a mission without losing a soldier.	10
The Hardest Road	Advance one of your soldiers to Colonel rank.	10
Worth Every Penny	Acquire 1000 credits in one month.	20
Oppenheimer	Staff the Research Labs with 80 scientists.	20
One Gun at a Time	Staff the Engineering Department with 80 engineers	20
Skunkworks	In a single game, complete every Foundry project.	20
You Have 5 Seconds to Comply	Build a S.H.I.V.	10
Theory...	Build a Laboratory.	10
...and Practice	Build a Workshop.	10
Wet Work	Complete a Very Hard abduction mission in five turns or less on Classic or Impossible difficulty.	10
A Continental Fellow	Win the game from each of the 5 starting locations.	50
What Wonders Await	Complete a Research Project.	5

NAME	GOAL/REQUIREMENT	POINT VALUE
Up and Running	Build a base facility.	5
Combat Ready	Build an item.	5
Drums in the Deep	Gain access to the lowest level in your base.	10
Happy to Oblige	Fulfill a Council request.	15
Tables Turned	Shoot down a UFO.	10
And So It Begins...	Complete the tutorial mission.	15

SECRET ACHIEVEMENTS

NAME	GOAL/REQUIREMENT	POINT VALUE
Meet New People. Then Kill Them.	Win a multiplayer match.	25
Xavier	Mind Control an Ethereal. Single player only.	10
Angel of Death	Kill an alien while flying. Single player only.	10
Beyond the Veil	Find a soldier with the Gift.	10
Prisoner of War	Capture a live alien.	10
The Gatekeeper	Stun an Outsider.	10
X Marks the Spot	Uncover the alien base's location.	10
See All, Know All	Build the Hyperwave Relay.	10
On the Shoulders of Giants	Build the Gollop Chamber.	10
Ride the Lightning	Build a Firestorm.	10
Poison Control	Cure poison on five soldiers in a single mission. Single player only.	10
And Hell's Coming With Me	Successfully assault an Overseer UFO.	10
Off My Planet	Recover the Hyperwave Beacon.	25
The Volunteer	Make contact with the Ethereal hive mind.	10
Flight of the Valkyries	Win a mission with an all-female squad. Single player only	10.

NINTENDO Wii™

GAMES

2010 FIFA WORLD CUP SOUTH AFRICA

WORLD CLASSIC XI TEAM

Earn at least Bronze against each team in Kazumi's Dream Team to play the World Classic XI Team. Defeat them in a best of three match to play as the team in Hit the Pitch.

THE AMAZING SPIDER-MAN

CLASSIC SPIDER-MAN SUIT

Complete all petty crimes.

ASTRO BOY: THE VIDEO GAME

INVULNERABLE

Pause the game and press Up, Down, Down, Up, 1, 2.

MAX STATS

Pause the game and press Left, Left, 2, Down, Down, 1.

INFINITE SUPERS

Pause the game and press Left, 1, Right, 1, Up, Down.

INFINITE DASHES

Pause the game and press 2, 2, 1, 2, Left, Up.

DISABLE SUPERS

Pause the game and press 1, 1, 2, 2, 1, Left.

COSTUME SWAP (ARENA AND CLASSIC COSTUMES)

Pause the game and press 2, Up, 1, Up, Down, 2.

UNLOCK LEVELS

Pause the game and press Up, 1, Right, 1, Down, 1. This allows you to travel to any level from the Story menu.

AVATAR: THE LAST AIRBENDER— INTO THE INFERNO

After you have defeated the first level, The Awakening, go to Ember Island. Walk to the left, past the volleyball net, to a red and yellow door. Select Game Secrets and then Code Entry. Now you can enter the following cheats:

MAX COINS
Enter 66639224.

ALL ITEMS AVAILABLE FROM SHOP
Enter 34737253.

ALL CHAPTERS
Enter 52993833.

UNLOCK CONCEPT ART IN GALLERY
Enter 27858343.

BAKUGAN BATTLE BRAWLERS

1,000 BP
Enter 33204429 as your name.

5,000 BP
Enter 42348294 as your name.

10,000 BP
Enter 46836478 as your name.

100,000 BP
Enter 18499753 as your name.

500,000 BP
Enter 26037947 as your name.

BRONZE WARIUS
Enter 44982493 as your name.

BAKUGAN: DEFENDERS OF THE CORE

HIDDEN ITEMS
Select Unlock Codes from Collection and enter HXV6Y7BF. Now you can enter up to 8 of your unique Bakugan Dimensions codes.
The codes unlock the following:

10,000 Core Energy
Ten Vexos Passes
Earthen Armor
Fire Spirit
Light Arrow
Tornado Vortex
Water Pillar
Zorch Thunder
Here are 8 codes:
2FKRRMNCDQ
82D77YK6P8
HUUH8ST7AR
JJUZDEACXX
QY8CLD5NJE
TD4UMFSRW3
YJ7RGG7WGZ
YQLHBBSMDC

BAND HERO

MOST CHARACTERS UNLOCKED
Select Input Cheats from the options and enter Blue, Yellow, Green, Yellow, Red, Green, Red, Yellow.

ELECTRIKA STEEL UNLOCKED
Select Input Cheats from the options and enter Blue, Blue, Red, Yellow, Red, Yellow, Blue, Blue.

ALL HOPO MODE
Select Input Cheats from the options and enter Red, Green, Blue, Green, Blue, Green, Red, Green.

ALWAYS SLIDE
Select Input Cheats from the options and enter Yellow, Green, Yellow, Yellow, Yellow, Red, Blue, Red.

AUTO KICK
Select Input Cheats from the options and enter Yellow, Green, Yellow, Blue, Blue, Red, Blue, Red.

FOCUS MODE
Select Input Cheats from the options and enter Yellow, Yellow, Green, Green, Red, Red, Blue, Blue.

HUD FREE MODE
Select Input Cheats from the options and enter Green, Red, Green, Red, Yellow, Blue, Green, Red.

PERFORMANCE MODE
Select Input Cheats from the options and enter Yellow, Yellow, Blue, Green, Blue, Red, Red, Red.

AIR INSTRUMENTS
Select Input Cheats from the options and enter Blue, Yellow, Blue, Red, Red, Yellow, Green, Yellow.

INVISIBLE ROCKER
Select Input Cheats from the options and enter Green, Red, Yellow, Green, Yellow, Blue, Yellow, Green.

BATMAN: THE BRAVE AND THE BOLD - THE VIDEOGAME

Access the terminal on the left side of the Batcave and enter the following:

BATMAN COSTUMES

COSTUME	CODE
Dark Batsuit	3756448
Medieval Batsuit	5644863
Rainbow Suit	7629863

CHALLENGE MAPS

CHALLENGE MAP	CODE
Gotham 1 & 2	4846348
Proto Sparring	6677686
Science Island 1 & 2	7262348

WEAPONS

WEAPON	CODE
Barrier	2525655
Belt Sword	2587973
Flashbangs	3527463
Smoke Pellets	7665336

BATTLE OF GIANTS: DINOSAURS STRIKE

ARMORED

DINOSAUR	PASSWORD
Cassosaurus	09182
Gastonia	69281
Hillierosaurus	27139
NeoAnkylosaurus	13579
NeoDacentrurus	81726
NeoEdmontonia	90817
NeoMiragaia	23071
NeoScolosaurus	86420
NeoStegosaurus	84570
Wuerhosaurus	18963

PREDATORS

DINOSAUR	PASSWORD
Neo Baryonyx	75139
NeoCarcharodon	37452
NeoCarnotaurus	4629
NeoCeratosaur	20135
NeoDilophosaurus	43782
NeoTrex	73096
Suchominus	03275

HORNED

DINOSAUR	PASSWORD
Chasmosaurus	46135
Naxocertops	16948
NeoEiniosaurus	31946
NeoStyracosaurus	25378
NeoTriceratops	18275

RAPTORS

DINOSAUR	PASSWORD
Allosaurus	35274
Gorgoraptor	23587
NeoJuravenator	74312
NeoOviraptor	93245
NeoVelociraptor	10927
Trodon	51274

BEN 10: ALIEN FORCE VILGAX ATTACKS

LEVEL SKIP
Pause the game and enter Portal in the Cheats menu.

UNLOCK ALL SPECIAL ATTACKS (ALL FORMS)
Pause the game and enter Everythingproof in the Cheats menu.

UNLOCK ALL ALIEN FORMS
Pause the game and enter Primus in the Cheats menu.

TOGGLE INVULNERABILITY ON AND OFF
Pause the game and enter Xlmrsmoothy in the Cheats menu.

FULL HEALTH
Pause the game and enter Herotime in the Cheats menu.

QUICK ENERGY REGENERATION
Pause the game and enter Generator in the Cheats menu.

BEN 10 ULTIMATE ALIEN: COSMIC DESTRUCTION

To remove the following cheats, you must start a new game.

1,000,000 DNA
Pause the game, select Cheats, and enter Cash.

REGENERATE HEALTH
Pause the game, select Cheats, and enter Health.

REGENERATE ENERGY
Pause the game, select Cheats, and enter Energy.

UPGRADE EVERYTHING
Pause the game, select Cheats, and enter Upgrade.

ALL LEVELS
Pause the game, select Cheats, and enter Levels.

DAMAGE
Pause the game, select Cheats, and enter Hard. With this code, enemies cause double damage while you cause half damage.

BOOM BLOX

ALL TOYS IN CREATE MODE
At the Title screen, press Up, Right, Down, Left to bring up a cheats menu. Enter Tool Pool.

SLOW-MO IN SINGLE PLAYER
At the Title screen, press Up, Right, Down, Left to bring up a cheats menu. Enter Blox Time.

CHEERLEADERS BECOME PROFILE CHARACTER
At the Title screen, press Up, Right, Down, Left to bring up a cheats menu. Enter My Team.

FLOWER EXPLOSIONS
At the Title screen, press Up, Right, Down, Left to bring up a cheats menu. Enter Flower Power.

JINGLE BLOCKS
At the Title screen, press Up, Right, Down, Left to bring up a cheats menu. Enter Maestro.

BOOM BLOX BASH PARTY

At the title screen, press Up, Right, Down, Left. Now you can enter the following codes:

UNLOCK EVERYTHING
Enter Nothing But Hope.

1 MILLION BOOM BUX
Enter Bailout.

TURN ON BLOX TIME
Enter Freeze Frame.

TURNS ALL SOUND EFFECTS INTO VIRUS BLOX SOUND EFFECTS
Enter Musical Fruit.

ALL COLORED BLOX
Enter Rainbow Blox.

CALL OF DUTY: BLACK OPS

ACCESS TERMINAL
At the main menu, alternately press aim and fire until you break free of the restraints. Find the terminal behind the chair. Here you can enter the following.

TERMINAL COMMANDS

EFFECT	COMMAND
List Commands	Help
Root directory (use ls to list codes)	cd .. [enter] cd .. [enter] cd bin [enter]
List directory	ls
List audio files and pictures	DIR
Open file	CAT [filename found from DIR command]
View a file	TYPE (filename.extension)
List CIA e-mail	mail
List login names (does not give passwords)	WHO
FI FIE FOE	FOOBAR
All Intel	3ARC INTEL
Dead Ops Arcade	DOA
Dead Ops Arcade and Presidential Zombie Mode	3ARC UNLOCK
Virtual Therapist Software	Alicia
Zork I: The Great Underground Adventure	ZORK

CIA DATA SYSTEM LOGINS
Use the following IDs and Passwords to access users' files and mail.

USER ACCOUNT	ID	PASSWORD
Alex Mason	amason	PASSWORD
Bruce Harris	bharris	GOSKINS
D. King	dking	MFK
Dr. Adrienne Smith	asmith	ROXY
Dr. Vannevar Bush	vbush	MANHATTAN
Frank Woods	fwoods	PHILLY
Grigori "Greg" Weaver	gweaver	GEDEON
J. Turner	jturner	CONDOR75
Jason Hudson	jhudson	BRYANT1950
John McCone	jmccone	BERKLEY22
Joseph Bowman	jbowman	UWD
President John Fitzgerald Kennedy	jfkennedy	LANCER
President Lyndon Baines Johnson	lbjohnson	LADYBIRD
President Richard Nixon	rnixon	CHECKERS
Richard Helms	rhelms	LEROSEY
Richard Kain	rkain	SUNWU
Ryan Jackson	rjackson	SAINTBRIDGET
T. Walker	twalker	RADIO
Terrance Brooks	tbrooks	LAUREN
William Raborn	wraborn	BROMLOW

CALL OF DUTY: MODERN WARFARE 3

NAME COLOR FOR PROFILE

When entering your name for your Multiplayer Profile, click Shift and then ^. Now enter the number as given below to change the color. The ^ will be removed and the text that you enter will be the color you chose.

FONT COLOR	NUMBER
Black	0
Red	1
Green	2
Yellow	3
Blue	4
Dark Blue	5
Pink	6
Orange	7
Grey	8
Dark Grey	9

CARS 2: THE VIDEO GAME

ALL MODES AND TRACKS

Select Enter Codes from the Options and enter 959595.

UNLIMITED ENERGY

Select Enter Codes from the Options and enter 721953. Select Cheats to toggle the cheat on and off.

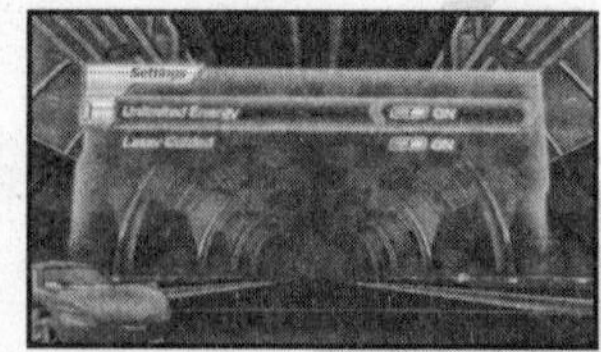

LASER GUIDED

Select Enter Codes from the Options and enter 123456. Select Cheats to toggle the cheat on and off.

CASTLEVANIA THE ADVENTURE REBIRTH

LEVEL SELECT

Select Game Start and hold Right for a few seconds. You can play any level you have already played.

THE CONDUIT

SECRET AGENT MODEL, MULTIPLAYER

Enter SuitMP13 at the Cheat menu.

SPECIAL ASE TEXTURE

Enter NewASE11 at the Cheat menu.

PLAY AS DRONE, SINGLE PLAYER

Enter Drone4SP at the Cheat menu.

CONDUIT 2

EYE OF RA ASE
Select Promotional Codes from the Extras menu and enter EYEOFRA.

GOLDEN DESTROYER ARMOR (ONLINE ONLY)
Select Promotional Codes from the Extras menu and enter 14KARMOR.

CONTRA REBIRTH

DEBUG MENU
At the title screen, press Plus + 1 + 2.

CORALINE

UNLIMITED LEVEL SKIP
Select Cheats from the Options menu and enter beldam.

UNLIMITED HEALTH
Select Cheats from the Options menu and enter beets.

UNLIMITED FIREFLIES
Select Cheats from the Options menu and enter garden.

FREE HALL PASSES
Select Cheats from the Options menu and enter well.

BUTTON EYE CORALINE
Select Cheats from the Options menu and enter cheese.

CRASH: MIND OVER MUTANT

FREEZE ENEMIES WITH TOUCH
Pause the game, hold guard and press Down, Down, Down, Up.

ENEMIES DROP X4 DAMAGE
Pause the game, hold guard and press Up, Up, Up, Left.

ENEMIES DROP PURPLE FRUIT
Pause the game, hold guard and press Up, Down, Down, Up.

ENEMIES DROP SUPER KICK
Pause the game, hold guard and press Up, Right, Down, Left.

ENEMIES DROP WUMPA FRUIT
Pause the game, hold guard and press Right, Right, Right, Up.

SHADOW CRASH
Pause the game, hold guard and press Left, Right, Left, Right.

DEFORMED CRASH
Pause the game, hold guard and press Left, Left, Left, Down.

COSTUMES
Complete all of the following character's mini-games to unlock each costume.

COSTUME	CHARACTER
Magmadon	Little Bear
Ratcicle	Ratcicle Kid
Skeleton	Sludge Brother
Snipe	Crunch
Spike	Uka Uka

DE BLOB

INVULNERABILITY
During a game, hold C and press 1, 1, 1, 1. Re-enter the code to disable.

LIFE UP
During a game, hold C and press 1, 1, 2, 2.

TIME BONUS
During a game, hold C and press 1, 2, 1, 2. This adds 10 minutes to your time.

ALL MOODS
At the Main menu, hold C and press B, B, 1, 2, 1, 2, B, B.

ALL MULTIPLAYER LEVELS
At the Main menu, hold C and press 2, 2, B, B, 1, 1, B, B.

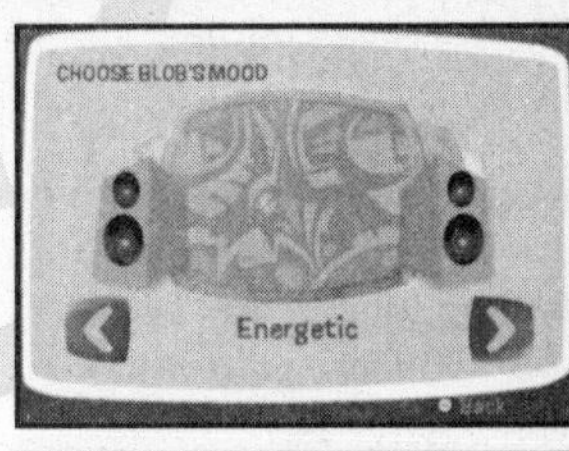

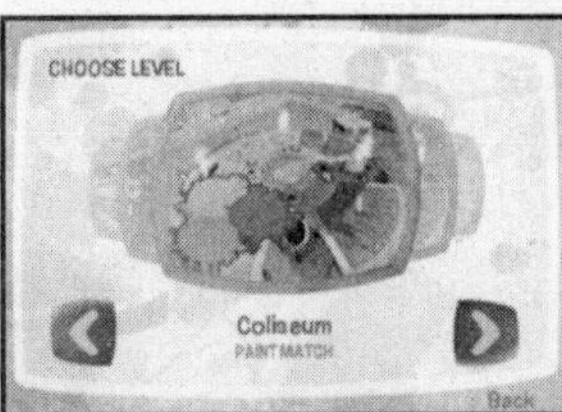

DEAD SPACE EXTRACTION

4 CHALLENGE MODE LEVELS

At the title screen, press Down, Up, Left, Right, Right, Left.

DEADLY CREATURES

ALL CHAPTERS

At the chapter select, press Right, Right, Up, Down, 2, 1, 1, 2. When you jump to a later chapter, you get any move upgrades you would have, but not health upgrades.

DEFEND YOUR CASTLE

GIANT ENEMIES

Select Credits and click SMB3W4 when it appears.

TINY UNITS

Select Credits and click Chuck Norris when it appears.

EASY LEVEL COMPLETE

Pause the game and wait for the sun to set. Unpause to complete the level.

DESTROY ALL HUMANS! BIG WILLY UNLEASHED

Pause the game and go to the Unlockables screen. Hold the analog stick Up until a Enter Unlock Code window appears. You can now enter the following cheats with the directional-pad. Press A after entering a code.

Use this menu to toggle cheats on and off.

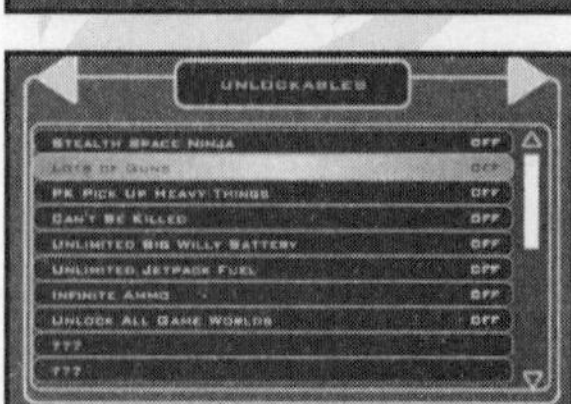

UNLOCK ALL GAME WORLDS

Up, Right, Down, Right, Up

CAN'T BE KILLED

Left, Down, Up, Right, Up

LOTS OF GUNS

Right, Left, Down, Left, Up

INFINITE AMMO

Right, Up, Up, Left, Right

UNLIMITED BIG WILLY BATTERY

Left, Left, Up, Right, Down

UNLIMITED JETPACK FUEL

Right, Right, Up, Left, Left

PICK UP HEAVY THINGS

Down, Up, Left, Up, Right

STEALTH SPACE NINJA

Up, Right, Down, Down, Left

CRYPTO DANCE FEVER SKIN

Right, Left, Right, Left, Up

KLUCKIN'S CHICKEN BLIMP SKIN

Left, Up, Down, Up, Down

LEISURE SUIT SKIN

Left, Down, Right, Left, Right

PIMP MY BLIMP SKIN

Down, Up, Right, Down, Right

DJ HERO

Select Cheats from Options and enter the following. Some codes will disable high scores and progress. Cheats cannot be used in tutorials and online.

UNLOCK ALL CONTENT
Enter tol0.

ALL CHARACTER ITEMS
Enter uNA2.

ALL VENUES
Enter Wv1u.

ALL DECKS
Enter LAuP.

ALL HEADPHONES
Enter 62Db.

ALL MIXES
Enter 82xl.

AUTO SCRATCH
Enter IT6j.

AUTO EFFECTS DIAL
Enter ab1L.

AUTO FADER
Enter SL5d.

AUTO TAPPER
Enter ZitH.

AUTO WIN EUPHORIA
Enter r3a9.

BLANK PLINTHS
Enter ipr0.

HAMSTER SWITCH
Enter 7geo.

HYPER DECK MODE
Enter 76st.

SHORT DECK
Enter 51uC.

INVISIBLE DJ
Enter oh5T.

PITCH BLACK OUT
Enter d4kR.

PLAY IN THE BEDROOM
Enter g7nH.

ANY DJ, ANY SETLIST
Enter 0jj8.

DAFT PUNK'S CONTENT
Enter d1g?.

DJ AM'S CONTENT
Enter k07u.

DJ JAZZY JEFF'S CONTENT
Enter n1fz.

DJ SHADOW'S CONTENT
Enter oMxV.

DJ Z-TRIP'S CONTENT
Enter 5rtg.

GRANDMASTER FLASH'S CONTENT
Enter ami8.

DOKAPON KINGDOM

DOUBLE THE TAXES FROM A TOWN
After saving a town, hold the controller sideways and press A, A + 2.

DRAGON BLADE: WRATH OF FIRE

ALL LEVELS
At the Title screen, hold Plus + Minus and select New Game or Load game. Hold the buttons until the stage select appears.

EASY DIFFICULTY
At the Title screen, hold Z + 2 when selecting "New Game."

HARD DIFFICULTY
At the Title screen, hold C + 2 when selecting "New Game."

To clear the following codes, hold Z at the stage select.

DRAGON HEAD
At the stage select, hold Z and press Plus. Immediately Swing Wii-mote Right, swing Wii-mote Down, swing Nunchuck Left, swing Nunchuck Right.

DRAGON WINGS
At the stage select, hold Z and press Plus. Immediately Swing Nunchuck Up + Wii-mote Up, swing Nunchuck Down + Wii-mote Down, swing Nunchuck Right + Wii-mote Left, swing Nunchuck Left + Wii-mote Right.

TAIL POWER
At the stage select, hold Z and press Plus. Immediately Swing your Wii-mote Down, Up, Left, and Right

DOUBLE FIST POWER
At the stage select, hold Z and press Plus. Immediately swing your Nunchuck Right, swing your Wii-mote left, swing your Nunchuck right while swinging your Wii-mote left, then swing both Wii-mote and Nunchuck down

EARTHWORM JIM

CHEAT MENU

Pause the game and press Y + Left, B, B, Y, Y + Right, B, B, Y. Notes that these are the button presses for the classic controller.

EA SPORTS NBA JAM

Hold the Wii Remote vertically when entering the following codes. To access the teams, press + at the Team Select screen.

BEASTIE BOYS

At the Title screen, press Up, Up, Down, Down, Left, Right, Left, Right, B, +. This team includes Ad Rock, MCA, and Mike D.

J.COLE & 9TH WONDER

At the Title screen, press Up, Left, Down, Right, Up, Left, Down, Right, 1, 2.

DEMOCRAT TEAM

At the Title screen, press Left (x13), +. This team includes Barack Obama, Joe Biden, Bill Clinton, and Hillary Clinton.

REPUBLICAN TEAM

At the Title screen, press Right (x13), +. The team includes George W. Bush, Sarah Palin, and John McCain.

ESPN'S SPORTSNATION

Select Play Now. When entering the initials, enter ESP for P1 and NSN for P2. Advance to the Choose Teams screen and use + to find the team. This team includes the hosts of the show, Colin Cowherd and Michelle Beadle.

NBA MASCOTS

Select Play Now. When entering the initials, enter MAS for P1 and COT for P2. Advance to the Choose Teams screen and use + to find the team.

ORIGINAL JAM

Select Play Now. When entering the initials, enter MJT for P1. Advance to the Choose Teams screen and use + to find the team. This team includes Mark Turmell and Tim Kitzrow.

FAST - RACING LEAGUE

NEUTRON SIBERIA LEAGUE

Complete Neutron Shima League.

NEUTRON SUNAHARA LEAGUE

Complete Neutron Siberia League.

PROTON SHIMA LEAGUE

Complete Neutron Sunahara League.

PROTON SIBERIA LEAGUE

Complete Proton Shima League.

PROTON SUNAHARA LEAGUE

Complete Proton Siberia League.

FAIA VM SHIP

Place in the Neutron Shima league.

DT BOSUTON SHIP

Place in the Neutron Siberia league.

DENKOU QX SHIP

Place in the Proton Siberia league.

KAN Y SHIP

Place in the Proton Sunahara league.

BOOST AT START OF RACE

Right when the announcers says Go, press the accelerator.

FIGHTING STREET

+4 CREDITS, SIMPLIFIED SPECIAL MOVES, AND STAGE SELECT

After getting a high score, enter .SD as your initials. Then, at the title screen, hold Left + 1 + 2, and press Minus.

+4 CREDITS

After getting a high score, enter .HU as your initials. Then, at the title screen, hold Left + 1 + 2, and press Minus.

SIMPLIFIED SPECIAL MOVES

After getting a high score, enter .LK as your initials. Then, at the title screen, hold Left + 1 + 2, and press Minus.

STAGE SELECT

After getting a high score, enter .AS as your initials. Then, at the title screen, hold Left + 1 + 2, and press Minus.

FROGGER: HYPER ARCADE EDITION

CONTRA STYLE

At the style select, highlight Contra and enter Up, Up, Down, Down, Left, Right, Left, Right, 1, 2.

GHOUL PATROL

PASSWORDS

LEVEL	PASSWORD
5	CP4V
9	7LBR

LEVEL	PASSWORD
13	KVCY

G.I. JOE: THE RISE OF COBRA

CLASSIC DUKE

At the Title screen, press Left, Up, Minus, Up, Right, Plus.

CLASSIC SCARLETT

At the Title screen, press Right, Up, Down, Down, Plus.

GOLDENEYE 007

BIG HEADS IN LOCAL MULTIPLAYER

Select Cheat Codes from the Extras menu and enter <477MYFR13NDS4R3SP13S>.

INVISIBILITY MODIFIER IN LOCAL MULTIPLAYER

Select Cheat Codes from the Extras menu and enter Inv1s1bleEv3ryth1ng.

TAG MODIFIER IN LOCAL MULTIPLAYER

Select Cheat Codes from the Extras menu and enter NotIt!!!11.

GRADIUS REBIRTH

4 OPTIONS

Pause the game and press Up, Up, Down, Down, Left, Right, Left, Right, Fire, Powerup. This code can be used once for each stage you have attempted.

GRAVITRONIX

VERSUS OPTIONS AND LEVEL SELECT

At the Options menu, press 1, 2, 2, 2, 1.

GREG HASTINGS PAINTBALL 2

PRO & NEW GUN

Select Career, hold C, and press Up, Up, Down, Right, Left, Left, Right, Up.

GUITAR HERO 5

ALL HOPOS

Select Input Cheats from the Options menu and enter Green, Green, Blue, Green, Green, Green, Yellow, Green.

ALWAYS SLIDE

Select Input Cheats from the Options menu and enter Green, Green, Red, Red, Yellow, Blue, Yellow, Blue.

AUTO KICK

Select Input Cheats from the Options menu and enter Yellow, Green, Red, Blue, Blue, Blue, Blue, Red.

FOCUS MODE

Select Input Cheats from the Options menu and enter Yellow, Green, Red, Green, Yellow, Blue, Green, Green.

HUD FREE MODE
Select Input Cheats from the Options menu and enter Green, Red, Green, Green, Yellow, Green, Green, Green.

PERFORMANCE MODE
Select Input Cheats from the Options menu and enter Yellow, Yellow, Blue, Red, Blue, Green, Red, Red.

AIR INSTRUMENTS
Select Input Cheats from the Options menu and enter Red, Red, Blue, Yellow, Green, Green, Green, Yellow.

INVISIBLE ROCKER
Select Input Cheats from the Options menu and enter Green, Red, Yellow, Yellow, Yellow, Blue, Blue, Green.

ALL CHARACTERS
Select Input Cheats from the Options menu and enter Blue, Blue, Green, Green, Red, Green, Red, Yellow.

CONTEST WINNER 1
Select Input Cheats from the Options menu and enter Green, Green, Red, Red, Yellow, Red, Yellow, Blue.

GUITAR HERO: METALLICA

METALLICA COSTUMES
Select Cheats from Settings and enter Green, Red, Yellow, Blue, Blue, Yellow, Red, Green.

HYPERSPEED
Select Cheats from Settings and enter Green, Blue, Red, Yellow, Yellow, Red, Green, Green.

PERFORMANCE MODE
Select Cheats from Settings and enter Yellow, Yellow, Blue, Red, Blue, Green, Red, Red.

INVISIBLE ROCKER
Select Cheats from Settings and enter Green, Red, Yellow (x3), Blue, Blue, Green.

AIR INSTRUMENTS
Select Cheats from Settings and enter Red, Red, Blue, Yellow, Green (x3), Yellow.

ALWAYS DRUM FILL
Select Cheats from Settings and enter Red (x3), Blue, Blue, Green, Green, Yellow.

AUTO KICK
Select Cheats from Settings and enter Yellow, Green, Red, Blue (x4), Red. With this cheat activated, the bass pedal is automatically hit.

ALWAYS SLIDE
Select Cheats from Settings and enter Green, Green, Red, Red, Yellow, Red, Yellow, Blue. All Guitar Notes Become Touch Pad Sliding Notes.

BLACK HIGHWAY
Select Cheats from Settings and enter Yellow, Red, Green, Red, Green, Red, Red, Blue.

FLAME COLOR
Select Cheats from Settings and enter Green, Red, Green, Blue, Red, Red, Yellow, Blue.

GEM COLOR
Select Cheats from Settings and enter Blue, Red, Red, Green, Red, Green, Red, Yellow.

STAR COLOR
Select Cheats from Settings and enter Press Red, Red, Yellow, Red, Blue, Red, Red, Blue.

ADDITIONAL LINE 6 TONES
Select Cheats from Settings and enter Green, Red, Yellow, Blue, Red, Yellow, Blue, Green.

VOCAL FIREBALL
Select Cheats from Settings and enter Red, Green, Green, Yellow, Blue, Green, Yellow, Green.

GUITAR HERO: SMASH HITS

ALWAYS DRUM FILL
Select Cheats from the Options menu and enter Green, Green, Red, Red, Blue, Blue, Yellow, Yellow.

ALWAYS SLIDE
Select Cheats from the Options menu and enter Blue, Yellow, Red, Green, Blue, Green, Green, Yellow.

AIR INSTRUMENTS
Select Cheats from the Options menu and enter Yellow, Red, Blue, Green, Yellow, Red, Red, Red.

INVISIBLE ROCKER
Select Cheats from the Options menu and enter Blue, Red, Red, Red, Red, Yellow, Blue, Green.

PERFORMANCE MODE
Select Cheats from the Options menu and enter Blue, Red, Yellow, Yellow, Red, Red, Yellow, Yellow.

HYPERSPEED
Select Cheats from the Options menu and enter Red, Green, Blue, Yellow, Green, Yellow, Red, Red. This unlocks the HyperGuitar, HyperBass, and HyperDrums cheats.

AUTO KICK
Select Cheats from the Options menu and enter Blue, Green, Red, Yellow, Red, Yellow, Red, Yellow.

GEM COLOR
Select Cheats from the Options menu and enter Red, Red, Red, Blue, Blue, Blue, Yellow, Green.

FLAME COLOR
Select Cheats from the Options menu and enter Yellow, Blue, Red, Green, Yellow, Red, Green, Blue.

STAR COLOR
Select Cheats from the Options menu and enter Green, Red, Green, Yellow, Green, Blue, Yellow, Red.

VOCAL FIREBALL
Select Cheats from the Options menu and enter Green, Blue, Red, Red, Yellow, Yellow, Blue, Blue.

GUITAR HERO: WARRIORS OF ROCK

Select Extras from the Options menu to toggle the following on and off.

ALL CHARACTERS
Select Cheats from the Options menu and enter Blue, Green, Green, Red, Green, Red, Yellow, Blue.

ALL VENUES
Select Cheats from the Options menu and enter Red, Blue, Blue, Red, Red, Blue, Blue, Red.

ALWAYS SLIDE
Select Cheats from the Options menu and enter Blue, Green, Green, Red, Red, Yellow, Blue, Yellow.

ALL HOPOS
Select Cheats from the Options menu and enter Green (x3), Blue, Green (x3), Yellow. Most notes become hammer-ons or pull-offs.

INVISIBLE ROCKER
Select Cheats from the Options menu and enter Green, Green, Red, Yellow (x3), Blue, Blue.

AIR INSTRUMENTS
Select Cheats from the Options menu and enter Yellow, Red, Red, Blue, Yellow, Green (x3).

FOCUS MODE
Select Cheats from the Options menu and enter Green, Yellow, Green, Red, Green, Yellow, Blue, Green. This removes the busy background.

NO HUD MODE
Select Cheats from the Options menu and enter Green, Green, Red, Green, Green, Yellow, Green, Green.

PERFORMANCE MODE
Select Cheats from the Options menu and enter Red, Yellow, Yellow, Blue, Red, Blue, Green, Red.

COLOR SHUFFLE
Select Cheats from the Options menu and enter Blue, Green, Blue, Red, Yellow, Green, Red, Yellow.

MIRROR GEMS
Select Cheats from the Options menu and enter Blue, Blue, Red, Blue, Green, Green, Red, Green.

RANDOM GEMS
Select Cheats from the Options menu and enter Green, Green, Red, Red, Yellow, Red, Yellow, Blue.

GUITAR HERO WORLD TOUR

The following cheats can be toggled on and off at the Cheats menu.

QUICKPLAY SONGS
Select Cheats from the Options menu, choose Enter New Cheat and press Blue, Blue, Red, Green, Green, Blue, Blue, Yellow.

ALWAYS SLIDE
Select Cheats from the Options menu, choose Enter New Cheat and press Green, Green, Red, Red, Yellow, Red, Yellow, Blue.

AT&T BALLPARK
Select Cheats from the Options menu, choose Enter New Cheat and press Yellow, Green, Red, Red, Green, Blue, Red, Yellow.

AUTO KICK
Select Cheats from the Options menu, choose Enter New Cheat and press Yellow, Green, Red, Blue (x4), Red.

EXTRA LINE 6 TONES
Select Cheats from the Options menu, choose Enter New Cheat and press Green, Red, Yellow, Blue, Red, Yellow, Blue, Green.

FLAME COLOR
Select Cheats from the Options menu, choose Enter New Cheat and press Green, Red, Green, Blue, Red, Red, Yellow, Blue.

GEM COLOR
Select Cheats from the Options menu, choose Enter New Cheat and press Blue, Red, Red, Green, Red, Green, Red, Yellow.

STAR COLOR
Select Cheats from the Options menu, choose Enter New Cheat and press Red, Red, Yellow, Red, Blue, Red, Red, Blue.

AIR INSTRUMENTS
Select Cheats from the Options menu, choose Enter New Cheat and press Red, Red, Blue, Yellow, Green (x3), Yellow.

HYPERSPEED
Select Cheats from the Options menu, choose Enter New Cheat and press Green, Blue, Red, Yellow, Yellow, Red, Green, Green. These show up in the menu as HyperGuitar, HyperBass, and HyperDrums.

PERFORMANCE MODE
Select Cheats from the Options menu, choose Enter New Cheat and press Yellow, Yellow, Blue, Red, Blue, Green, Red, Red.

INVISIBLE ROCKER
Select Cheats from the Options menu, choose Enter New Cheat and press Green, Red, Yellow (x3), Blue, Blue, Green.

VOCAL FIREBALL
Select Cheats from the Options menu, choose Enter New Cheat and press Red, Green, Green, Yellow, Blue, Green, Yellow, Green.

AARON STEELE!
Select Cheats from the Options menu, choose Enter New Cheat and press Blue, Red, Yellow (x5), Green.

JONNY VIPER
Select Cheats from the Options menu, choose Enter New Cheat and press Blue, Red, Blue, Blue, Yellow (x3), Green.

NICK
Select Cheats from the Options menu, choose Enter New Cheat and press Green, Red, Blue, Green, Red, Blue, Blue, Green.

RINA
Select Cheats from the Options menu, choose Enter New Cheat and press Blue, Red, Green, Green, Yellow (x3), Green.

HARRY POTTER AND THE HALF-BLOOD PRINCE

BONUS TWO-PLAYER DUELING ARENA CASTLE GATES
At the Rewards menu, press Right, Right, Down, Down, Left, Right, Left, Right, Left, Right, +.

INDIANA JONES AND THE STAFF OF KINGS

FATE OF ATLANTIS GAME
At the Extras menu, hold Z and press A, Up, Up, B, Down, Down, Left, Right, Left, B.

JERRY RICE & NITUS' DOG FOOTBALL

3 OF ALL TREATS AND GAME BALLS
At the player select, press Down, A, +, A.

B BUTTON FOR BOOST
At the player select, press Up, Left, +, Right, A.

CPU VS. CPU
At the player select, hold 2 as you select Play.

FIRST PERSON VIEW
At the player select, press Down, A, Right, +.

GENERIC FIELD
While selecting a field, hold 2.

CREDITS
At the title screen, press A, -, -, A.

JUST DANCE 3

BARBRA STREISAND SPECIAL CHOREOGRAPHY
At the title screen (Press Start), press Up, Up, Down, Down, Left, Right, Left, Right.

KARAOKE REVOLUTION GLEE: VOLUME 2

ICE ICE BABY

Select Unlockables from the Options and enter A64112.

PINK HOUSES

Select Unlockables from the Options and enter DD6C62.

KARAOKE REVOLUTION GLEE: VOLUME 3

BORN THIS WAY

Select Unlockables from the Options and enter 60328B.

FIREWORK

Select Unlockables from the Options and enter 41025F.

TOXIC

Select Unlockables from the Options and enter B81120.

KIRBY'S DREAM COLLECTION: SPECIAL EDITION

KIRBY 64: THE CRYSTAL SHARDS CHEATS

SOUND CHECK

Defeat Miracle Matter.

DARK STAR LEVEL

Collect 100 shards and defeat Miracle Matter.

BOSS BATTLES

Defeat O2.

MINI-GAME DIFFICULTIES

COMPLETE MINI-GAME ON[EL]	UNLOCK DIFFICULTY
Easy	Normal
Normal	Hard
Hard	Intense

KIRBY'S ADVENTURE

EXTRA GAME

Defeat the game with 100%.

SOUND TEST

Defeat Extra Game with 100%.

KIRBY'S DREAM LAND

CONFIGURATION MODE

At the title screen, hold Down + Select + B.

BONUS GAME

At the title screen, hold Up + Select+ A.

KIRBY'S DREAM LAND 2

OPTION MODE

Complete the game with 100% and then load up your file. Select Option to get a Sound Test, Boss Battle, and Bonus Game.

KIRBY'S DREAM LAND 3

J OPTION

Complete the M Option to get this Jumping mini-game.

B OPTION

Defeat the final boss to unlock this option. It allows you to face all of the bosses with one life and no healing.

? OPTION

Beat all other options to view all videos.

KIRBY SUPER STAR

REVENGE OF META-KNIGHT

Defeat DynaBlade.

MILKY WAY WISHES

Defeat Great Cave Offensive and Revenge of Meta-Knight.

THE ARENA

Defeat all other levels.

SOUND TEST

Defeat The Arena.

THE LEGEND OF SPYRO: DAWN OF THE DRAGON

INFINITE HEALTH

Pause the game, hold Z and move the Nunchuk Right, Right, Down, Down, Left.

INFINITE MANA

Pause the game, hold Z and move the Nunchuk Up, Right, Up, Left, Down.

MAX XP

Pause the game, hold Z and move the Nunchuk Up, Left, Left, Down, Up.

ALL ELEMENTAL UPGRADES

Pause the game, hold Z and move the Nunchuk Left, Up, Down, Up, Right.

THE LEGEND OF ZELDA: SKYWARD SWORD

HERO MODE

After completing the main quest, you can choose to play Hero Mode, which is a tougher version of the regular game. Defeat the game on this mode to unlock a Tri-force next to the save.

GRATITUDE CRYSTAL REWARDS

There are 80 Gratitude Crystals that can be found and received throughout the game[md]65 come from completing side quests and the rest must be found. The following lists the rewards you gain by returning these Gratitude Crystals to Batreaux.

REWARD	NUMBER OF GRATITUDE CRYSTALS
Medium Wallet (500 Rupees)	5
Heart Piece	10
Big Wallet (1000 Rupees) and Cursed Medal	30
Gold Rupee	40
Giant Wallet (5,000 Rupees)	50
2 Gold Rupees	70
Tycoon Wallet (9,000 Rupees)	80

LEGO BATMAN

BATCAVE CODES

Using the computer in the Batcave, select Enter Code and enter the following codes.

CHARACTERS

CHARACTER	CODE
Alfred	ZAQ637
Batgirl	JKR331
Bruce Wayne	BDJ327
Catwoman (Classic)	M1AAWW
Clown Goon	HJK327
Commissioner Gordon	DDP967
Fishmonger	HGY748
Freeze Girl	XVK541
Joker Goon	UTF782
Joker Henchman	YUN924
Mad Hatter	JCA283
Man-Bat	NYU942
Military Policeman	MKL382
Nightwing	MVY759
Penguin Goon	NKA238

CHARACTER	CODE
Penguin Henchman	BJH782
Penguin Minion	KJP748
Poison Ivy Goon	GTB899
Police Marksman	HKG984
Police Officer	JRY983
Riddler Goon	CRY928
Riddler Henchman	XEU824
S.W.A.T.	HTF114
Sailor	NAV592
Scientist	JFL786
Security Guard	PLB946
The Joker (Tropical)	CCB199
Yeti	NJL412
Zoo Sweeper	DWR243

VEHICLES

VEHICLE	CODE
Bat-Tank	KNTT4B
Bruce Wayne's Private Jet	LEA664
Catwoman's Motorcycle	HPL826
Garbage Truck	DUS483
Goon Helicopter	GCH328
Harbor Helicopter	CHP735
Harley Quinn's Hammer Truck	RDT637
Mad Hatter's Glider	HS000W
Mad Hatter's Steamboat	M4DM4N
Mr. Freeze's Iceberg	ICYICE
The Joker's Van	JUK657
Mr. Freeze's Kart	BCT229
Penguin Goon Submarine	BTN248
Police Bike	LJP234
Police Boat	PLC999
Police Car	KJL832
Police Helicopter	CWR732
Police Van	MAC788
Police Watercraft	VJD328
Riddler's Jet	HAHAHA
Robin's Submarine	TTF453
Two-Face's Armored Truck	EFE933

CHEATS

CHEAT	CODE
Always Score Multiply	9LRGNB
Fast Batarangs	JRBDCB
Fast Walk	ZOLM6N
Flame Batarang	D8NYWH
Freeze Batarang	XPN4NG
Extra Hearts	ML3KHP
Fast Build	EVG26J
Immune to Freeze	JXUDY6
Invincibility	WYD5CP
Minikit Detector	ZXGH9J
More Batarang Targets	XWP645
Piece Detector	KHJ554
Power Brick Detector	MMN786
Regenerate Hearts	HJH7HJ
Score x2	N4NR3E
Score x4	CX9MAT
Score x6	MLVNF2
Score x8	WCCDB9
Score x10	18HW07

LEGO BATMAN 2: DC SUPER HEROES

RED BRICK CODES

Pause the game, select Extras, and then choose Enter Code. Enter the following:

CHEAT	CODE
Attract Studs	MNZER6
Beep Beep	ZHAXFH
Character Studs	TPJ37T
Disguises	BWQ2MS
Extra Hearts	4LGJ7T
Extra Toggle	7TXH5K
Fall Rescue	TPGPG2
Gold Brick Finder	MBXW7V
Minikit Finder	LRJAG8
Peril Finder	RYD3SJ
Red Brick Finder	5KKQ6G
Regenerate Hearts	ZXEX5D
Studs x 2	74EZUT
Super Build	JN2J6V
Vine Grapples	JXN7FJ

CHARACTERS AND VEHICLE

Pause the game, select Extras, and then choose Enter Code. Enter the following:

CHEAT	CODE
Clown Goon	9ZZZBP
LexBot	W49CSJ
Mime Goon	ZQA8MK
Policeman	V9SAGT
Riddler Goon	Q285LK
Two-Face Goon	95KPYJ
Harley Quinn's Motorbike	C79LVH

NINTENDO Wii

LEGO HARRY POTTER: YEARS 1-4

RED BRICK EXTRAS

After gaining access to The Leaky Cauldron, enter Wiseacre's Wizarding Supplies from Diagon Alley. Go upstairs to enter the following codes. Pause the game and select Extras to toggle the cheats on/off.

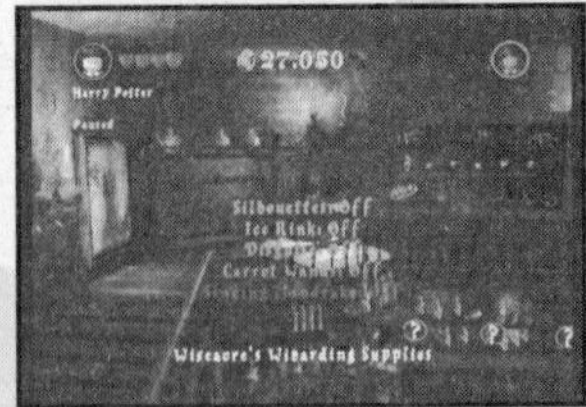

CODE	ENTER
Carrot Wands	AUC8EH
Character Studs	H27KGC
Character Token Detector	HA79V8
Christmas	T7PVVN
Disguise	4DMK2R
Fall Rescue	ZEX7MV
Extra Hearts	J9U6Z9
Fast Dig	Z9BFAD
Fast Magic	FA3GQA
Gold Brick Detector	84QNQN
Hogwarts Crest Detector	TTMC6D

CODE	ENTER
Ice Rink	F88VUW
Invincibility	QQWC6B
Red Brick Detector	7AD7HE
Regenerate Hearts	89ML2W
Score x2	74YKR7
Score x4	J3WHNK
Score x6	XK9ANE
Score x8	HUFV2H
Score x10	H8X69Y
Silhouettes	HZBVX7
Singing Mandrake	BMEU6X
Stud Magnet	67FKWZ

WISEACRE SPELLS

After gaining access to The Leaky Cauldron, enter Wiseacre's Wizarding Supplies from Diagon Alley. Go upstairs to enter the following codes. You need to learn Wingardium Leviosa before you can use these cheats.

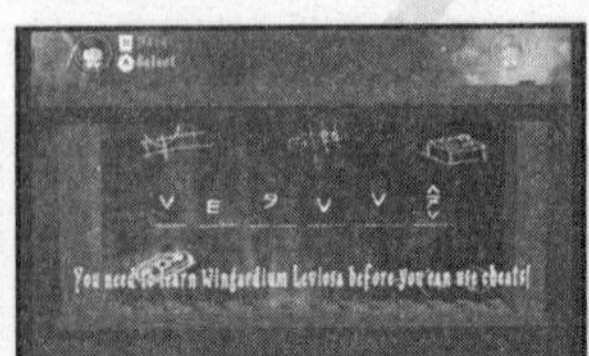

SPELL	ENTER
Accio	VE9VV7
Anteoculatia	QFB6NR
Calvorio	6DNR6L
Colovaria	9GJ442
Engorgio Skullus	CD4JLX
Entomorphis	MYN3NB
Flipendo	ND2L7W
Glacius	ERA9DR
Herbifors	H8FTHL
Incarcerous	YEB9Q9
Locomotor Mortis	2M2XJ6
Multicorfors	JK6QRM
Redactum Skullus	UW8LRH

SPELL	ENTER
Rictusempra	2UCA3M
Slugulus Eructo	U6EE8X
Stupefy	UWDJ4Y
Tarantallegra	KWWQ44
Trip Jinx	YZNRF6

OVERLOAD

EEYLOPS GOLD BRICKS

After gaining access to The Leaky Cauldron, enter Wiseacre's Wizarding Supplies from Diagon Alley. Go upstairs to enter the following codes. To access the LEGO Builder, visit Gringott's Bank at the end of Diagon Alley.

GOLD BRICK	ENTER
1	QE4VC7
2	FY8H97
3	3MQT4P
4	PQPM7Z
5	ZY2CPA
6	3GMTP6

GOLD BRICK	ENTER
7	XY6VYZ
8	TUNC4W
9	EJ42Q6
10	GFJCV9
11	DZCY6G

LEGO HARRY POTTER: YEARS 5-7

CHEATS

Pause the game and select Extras. Go to Enter Code and enter the following:

CHEAT	CODE
Carrot Wands	AUC8EH
Character Studs	H27KGC
Character Token Detector	HA79V8
Christmas	T7PVVN
Collect Ghost Studs	2FLY6B
Extra Hearts	J9U6Z9
Fall Rescue	ZEX7MV
Fast Dig	Z9BFAD
Ghost Coins	2FLY6B
Gold Brick Detector	84QNQN
Hogwarts Crest Detector	TTMC6D
Invincibility	QQWC6B
Red Brick Detector	7AD7HE
Score x2	74YKR7
Score x6	XK9ANE
Score x8	HUFV2H
Score x10	H8X69Y
Super Strength	BMEU6X

LEGO INDIANA JONES: THE ORIGINAL ADVENTURES

EXTRAS

Approach the blackboard in the Classroom and enter the following codes. Pause the game and select Extras. Here you can enable the cheat.

EXTRA	CODE
Artifact Detector	VIKED7
Beep Beep	VNF59Q
Character Treasure	VIES2R
Disarm Enemies	VKRNS9
Disguises	4ID1N6
Fast Build	V83SLO
Fast Dig	378RS6
Fast Fix	FJ59WS
Fertilizer	B1GW1F

EXTRA	CODE
Ice Rink	33GM7J
Parcel Detector	VUT673
Poo Treasure	WWQ1SA
Regenerate Hearts	MDLP69
Secret Characters	3X44AA
Silhouettes	3HE85H
Super Scream	VN3R7S
Super Slap	0P1TA5
Treasure Magnet	H86LA2

EXTRA	CODE
Treasure x2	VM4TS9
Treasure x4	VLWEN3
Treasure x6	V84RYS
Treasure x8	A72E1M
Treasure x10	VI3PS8

CHARACTERS

Approach the blackboard in the Classroom and enter the following codes.

CHARACTER	CODE
Bandit	12N68W
Bandit Swordsman	1MK4RT
Barranca	04EM94
Bazooka Trooper (Crusade)	MK83R7
Bazooka Trooper (Raiders)	S93Y5R
Belloq	CHN3YU
Belloq (Jungle)	TDR197
Belloq (Robes)	VEO29L
British Commander	B73EUA
British Officer	VJ5TI9
British Soldier	DJ5I2W
Captain Katanga	VJ3TT3
Chatter Lal	ENW936
Chatter Lal (Thuggee)	CNH4RY
Chen	3NK48T
Colonel Dietrich	2K9RKS
Colonel Vogel	8EAL4H
Dancing Girl	C7EJ21
Donovan	3NFTU8
Elsa (Desert)	JSNRT9
Elsa (Officer)	VMJ5US
Enemy Boxer	8246RB
Enemy Butler	VJ48W3
Enemy Guard	VJ7R51
Enemy Guard (Mountains)	YR47WM
Enemy Officer	572E61
Enemy Officer (Desert	2MK450
Enemy Pilot	B84ELP
Enemy Radio Operator	1MF94R
Enemy Soldier (Desert)	4NSU7Q
Fedora	V75YSP
First Mate	0GIN24
Grail Knight	NE6THI
Hovitos Tribesman	H0V1SS
Indiana Jones (Desert Disguise)	4J8S4M
Indiana Jones (Officer)	VJ85OS
Jungle Guide	24PF34
Kao Kan	WMO46L
Kazim	NRH23J
Kazim (Desert)	3M29TJ
Lao Che	2NK479
Maharajah	NFK5N2
Major Toht	13NS01
Masked Bandit	N48SF0
Mola Ram	FJUR31
Monkey Man	3RF6YJ
Pankot Assassin	2NKT72
Pankot Guard	VN28RH
Sherpa Brawler	VJ37WJ
Sherpa Gunner	ND762W
Slave Child	0E3ENW
Thuggee	VM683E
Thuggee Acolyte	T2R3F9
Thuggee Slave Driver	VBS7GW
Village Dignitary	KD48TN
Village Elder	4682E1
Willie (Dinner Suit)	VK93R7
Willie (Pajamas)	MEN4IP
Wu Han	3NSLT8

EXTRAS

Approach the blackboard in the Classroom and enter the following codes. Some cheats must be enabled by selecting Extras from the Pause menu.

CHEAT	CODE
Artifact Detector	VIKED7
Beep Beep	VNF59Q
Character Treasure	VIES2R
Disarm Enemies	VKRNS9
Disguises	4ID1N6
Fast Build	V83SLO
Fast Dig	378RS6
Fast Fix	FJ59WS
Fertilizer	B1GW1F
Ice Rink	33GM7J
Parcel Detector	VUT673
Poo Treasure	WWQ1SA
Regenerate Hearts	MDLP69
Secret Characters	3X44AA
Silhouettes	3HE85H
Super Scream	VN3R7S
Super Slap	0P1TA5
Treasure Magnet	H86LA2
Treasure x10	VI3PS8
Treasure x2	VM4TS9
Treasure x4	VLWEN3
Treasure x6	V84RYS
Treasure x8	A72E1M

LEGO INDIANA JONES 2: THE ADVENTURE CONTINUES

Pause the game, select Enter Secret Code from the Extras menu, and enter the following.

CHARACTERS

CHARACTER	CODE
Belloq (Priest)	FTL48S
Dovchenko	WL4T6N
Enemy Boxer	7EQF47
Henry Jones	4CSAKH
Indiana Jones	PGWSEA
Indiana Jones: 2	FGLKYS
Indiana Jones (Collect)	DZFY9S
Indiana Jones (Desert)	M4C34K
Indiana Jones (Desert Disquise)	2W8QR3
Indiana Jones (Dinner Suit)	QUNZUT
Indiana Jones (Kali)	J2XS97
Indiana Jones (Officer)	3FQFKS
Interdimensional Being	PXT4UP
Lao Che	7AWX3J

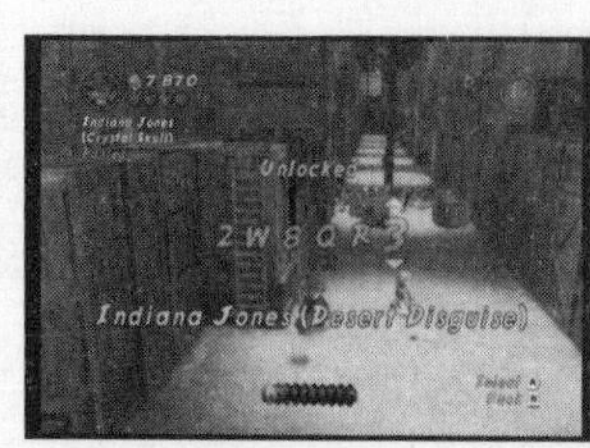

CHARACTER	CODE
Mannequin (Boy)	2UJQWC
Mannequin (Girl)	3PGSEL
Mannequin (Man)	QPWDMM
Mannequin (Woman)	U7SMVK
Mola Ram	82RMC2
Mutt	2GKS62
Salah	E88YRP
Willie	94RUAJ

EXTRAS

EFFECT	CODE
Beep Beep	UU3VSC
Disguise	Y9TE98
Fast Build	SNXC2F
Fast Dig	XYAN83
Fast Fix	3Z7PJX
Fearless	TUXNZF
Ice Rink	TY9P4U
Invincibility	6JBB65
Poo Money	SZFAAE
Score x3	PEHHPZ
Score x4	UXGTB3
Score X6	XWLJEY

EFFECT	CODE
Score x8	S5UZCP
Score x10	V7JYBU
Silhouettes	FQGPYH
Snake Whip	2U7YCV
Stud Magnet	EGSM5B

LEGO PIRATES OF THE CARIBBEAN: THE VIDEO GAME

CODES

Pause the game and select Extras. Choose Enter Code and enter the following codes:

EFFECT	PASSWORD
Ammand the Corsair	EW8T6T
Blackbeard	D3DW0D
Clubba	644THF
Davy Jones	4DJLKR
Governor Weatherby Swann	LD9454
Gunner	Y611WB

Hungry Cannibal	64BNHG
Jack Sparrow	VDJSPW
Jacoby	BWO656
Jimmy Legs	13GLW5
Koehler	RT093G
Mistress Ching	GDETDE
Philip	WEV040
Quartermaster	RX58HU
The Spaniard	P861JO
Twigg	KDLFKD

LEGO STAR WARS: THE COMPLETE SAGA

The following must still be purchased after entering the codes.

CHARACTERS

ADMIRAL ACKBAR
At the bar in Mos Eisley Cantina, select Enter Code and enter ACK646.

BATTLE DROID (COMMANDER)
At the bar in Mos Eisley Cantina, select Enter Code and enter KPF958.

BOBA FETT (BOY)
At the bar in Mos Eisley Cantina, select Enter Code and enter GGF539.

BOSS NASS
At the bar in Mos Eisley Cantina, select Enter Code and enter HHY697.

CAPTAIN TARPALS
At the bar in Mos Eisley Cantina, select Enter Code and enter QRN714.

COUNT DOOKU
At the bar in Mos Eisley Cantina, select Enter Code and enter DDD748.

DARTH MAUL
At the bar in Mos Eisley Cantina, select Enter Code and enter EUK421.

EWOK
At the bar in Mos Eisley Cantina, select Enter Code and enter EWK785.

GENERAL GRIEVOUS
At the bar in Mos Eisley Cantina, select Enter Code and enter PMN576.

GREEDO
At the bar in Mos Eisley Cantina, select Enter Code and enter ZZR636.

IG-88
At the bar in Mos Eisley Cantina, select Enter Code and enter GIJ989.

IMPERIAL GUARD
At the bar in Mos Eisley Cantina, select Enter Code and enter GUA850.

JANGO FETT
At the bar in Mos Eisley Cantina, select Enter Code and enter KLJ897.

KI-ADI MUNDI
At the bar in Mos Eisley Cantina, select Enter Code and enter MUN486.

LUMINARA
At the bar in Mos Eisley Cantina, select Enter Code and enter LUM521.

PADMÉ
At the bar in Mos Eisley Cantina, select Enter Code and enter VBJ322.

R2-Q5
At the bar in Mos Eisley Cantina, select Enter Code and enter EVILR2.

STORMTROOPER
At the bar in Mos Eisley Cantina, select Enter Code and enter NBN431.

TAUN WE
At the bar in Mos Eisley Cantina, select Enter Code and enter PRX482.

VULTURE DROID
At the bar in Mos Eisley Cantina, select Enter Code and enter BDC866.

WATTO
At the bar in Mos Eisley Cantina, select Enter Code and enter PLL967.

ZAM WESELL
At the bar in Mos Eisley Cantina, select Enter Code and enter 584HJF.

VEHICLES

DROID TRIFIGHTER
At the bar in Mos Eisley Cantina, select Enter Code and enter AAB123.

IMPERIAL SHUTTLE
At the bar in Mos Eisley Cantina, select Enter Code and enter HUT845.

TIE INTERCEPTOR
At the bar in Mos Eisley Cantina, select Enter Code and enter INT729.

TIE FIGHTER
At the bar in Mos Eisley Cantina, select Enter Code and enter DBH897.

ZAM'S AIRSPEEDER
At the bar in Mos Eisley Cantina, select Enter Code and enter UUU875.

SKILLS

DISGUISE

At the bar in Mos Eisley Cantina, select Enter Code and enter BRJ437.

FORCE GRAPPLE LEAP

At the bar in Mos Eisley Cantina, select Enter Code and enter CLZ738.

LEGO STAR WARS III: THE CLONE WARS

Pause the game, select Enter Code from Extras and enter the following:

CHARACTERS

CHARACTER	CODE
Aayla Secura	2VG95B
Adi Gallia	G2BFEN
Admiral Ackbar (Classic)	272Y9Q
Admiral Yularen	NG6PYX
Ahsoka	2VJ9TH
Anakin Skywalker	F9VUYJ
Anakin Skywalker (Geonosian Arena)	9AA4DW
Asajj Ventress	YG9DD7
Aurra Sing	M2V1JV
Bail Organa	GEHX6C
Barriss Offee	BTVTZ5
Battle Droid	5Y7MA4
Battle Droid Commander	LSU4LJ
Bib Fortuna	9U4TF3
Boba Fett (Classic)	TY2BYJ
Boil	Q5Q39P
Bossk	2KLW5R
C-3PO	574226
Cad Bane	NHME85
Captain Antilles (Classic)	D8SNGJ
Captain Rex	MW3QYH
Captain Typho	GD6FX3
Chancellor Palpatine	5C62YQ
Chewbacca (Classic)	66UU3T
Clone Pilot	HQ7BVD
Clone Shadow Trooper (Classic)	7GFNCQ
Clone Trooper	NP5GTT
Commander Bly	7CB6NS
Commander Cody	SMN259
Commander Fil	U25HFC
Commander Ponds	JRPR2A
Commander Stone	5XZQSV
Commando Droid	QEGU64
Count Dooku	EWR7WM
Darth Maul (Classic)	QH68AK
Darth Sidious (Classic)	QXY5XN
Darth Vader (Classic)	FM4JB7
Darth Vader Battle Damaged (Classic)	NMJFBL

CHARACTER	CODE
Destroyer Droid	9MUTS2
Dr. Nuvo Vindi	MB9EMW
Echo	JB9E5S
Eeth Koth	WUFDYA
Gammorean Guard	WSFZZQ
General Grievous	7FNU4T
Geonosian Guard	GAFZUD
Gold Super Battle Droid	2C8NHP
Gonk Droid	C686PK
Grand Moff Tarkin	NH2405
Greedo (Classic)	FUW4C2
Hailfire Droid	T7XF9Z
Han Solo (Classic)	KFDBXF
Heavy Super Battle Droid	G65KJJ
Heavy Weapons Clone Trooper	WXUTWY
Helios 3D	4AXTY4
Hevy	EUB8UG
Hondo Ohnaka	5A7XYX
IG-86	EABPCP
Imperial Guard (Classic)	5W6FGD
Jango Fett	5KZQ4D
Jar Jar Binks	MESPTS
Jek	AYREC9
Ki-Adi-Mundi	HGBCTQ
Kit Fitso	PYWJ6N
Lando Calrissian (Classic)	ERAEWE
LEP Servent Droid	SM3Y9B
Lieutenant Thire	3NEUXC
Lok Durd	TKCYUZ
Luke Skywalker (Classic)	PG73HF
Luminara Unduli	MKUYQ8
Lurmen Villager	R35Y7N
Luxury Droid	V4WMJN
Mace Windu	8NVRWJ
MagnaGuard	2KEF2D
MSE-6	S6GRNZ
Nahdar Vebb	ZKXG43
Neimoidian	BJB94J
Nute Gunray	QFYXMC
Obi-Wan Kenobi	J9HNF9
Obi-Wan Kenobi (Classic)	FFBU5M

CHARACTER	CODE
Obi-Wan Kenobi (Geonosian Arena)	5U9FJK
OG-9 Homing Spider Droid	7NEC36
Onaconda Farr	DB7ZQN
Padmé Amidala (Geonosian Arena)	SZ824Q
Padmé Amidala	8X87U6
Pirate Ruffian	BH2EHU
Plo Koon	BUD4VU
Poggle The Lesser	4592WM
Princess Leia (Classic)	2D3D3L
Probe Droid	U2T4SP
Queen Neeyutnee	ZQRN85
Qui-Gon Jinn (Classic)	LKHD3B
R2-D2	RZ5HUV
R3-S6	Z87PAU
R4-P17	5MXSYA
R6-H5	7PMC3C
Rebel Commando (Classic)	PZMQNK
Robonino	2KLW5R
Rys	4PTP53
Savage Oppress	MELL07
Senate Commando	EPBPLK
Senate Commando (Captain)	S4Y7VW
Senator Kharrus	EA4E9S
Senator Philo	9Q7YCT
Shahan Alama	G4N7C2
Sionver Boll	5C62YQ
Stormtrooper (Classic)	HPE7PZ
Super Battle Droid	MJKDV5
Tee Watt Kaa	FYVSHD
Turk Falso	HEBHW5
Tusken Raider (Classic)	GC2XSA
TX-20	PE7FGD
Undead Geonosian	QGENFD
Vader's Apprentice (Classic)	EGQQ4V
Wag Too	VRUVSZ
Wat Tambor	ZP8XVH
Waxer	BNJE79
Wedge Antilles (Classic)	DRGLWS
Whorm Loathsom	4VVYQV
Workout Clone Trooper	MP9DRE
Yoda	CSQTMB

VEHICLES

VEHICLE	CODE
Dwarf Spider Droid	NACMGG
Geonosian Solar Sailor	PJ2U3R
Geonosian Starfighter	EDENEC
Slave I	KDDQVD
The Twilight	T4K5L4
Vulture Droid	7W7K7S

RED BRICKS

CHEAT	CODE
Character Studs	QD2C31
Dark Side	X1V4N2
Dual Wield	C4ES4R
Fast Build	GCHP7S
Glow in the Dark	4GT3VQ
Invincibility	J46P7A
Minikit Detector	CSD5NA
Perfect Deflect	3F5L56
Regenerate Hearts	2D7JNS
Score x2	YZPHUV
Score x4	43T5E5
Score x6	SEBHGR
Score x8	BYFSAQ
Score x10	N1CKR1
Stud Magnet	6MZ5CH
Super Saber Cut	BS828K
Super Speeders	B1D3W3

LOST IN SHADOW

GOBLIN HAND

While the game is loading, press and hold Z.

KNIFE

While the game is loading, press and hold C.

MADAGASCAR 3: THE VIDEO GAME

ALL DISGUISES
Select Promotion from Extras and enter Pineapple, Strawberry, Grapes, Apple.

BANANA DASH MINI-GAME IN LONDON
Select Promotion from Extras and enter Strawberry, Orange, Apple, Grapes.

BANANA DASH MINI-GAME IN PARIS
Select Promotion from Extras and enter Pineapple, Grapes, Pineapple, Banana.

BANANA DASH MINI-GAME IN PISA
Select Promotion from Extras and enter Orange, Banana, Orange, Apple.

BANANA DASH MINI-GAME IN ROME
Select Promotion from Extras and enter Grape, Apple, Grape, Strawberry.

MADDEN NFL 10

UNLOCK EVERYTHING
Select Enter Game Code from the Extras menu and enter THEWORKS.

FRANCHISE MODE
Select Enter Game Code from the Extras menu and enter TEAMPLAYER.

SITUATION MODE
Select Enter Game Code from the Extras menu and enter YOUCALLIT.

SUPERSTAR MODE
Select Enter Game Code from the Extras menu and enter EGOBOOST.

PRO BOWL STADIUM
Select Enter Game Code from the Extras menu and enter ALLSTARS.

SUPER BOWL STADIUM
Select Enter Game Code from the Extras menu and enter THEBIGSHOW.

MADSTONE

HIGH GRAVITY
At the Main menu, press Down, Down, Down, Down, Right, Left, Right, Left.

LOW GRAVITY
At the Main menu, press Up, Up, Left, Left, Up, Up, Right, Right.

PLAYER SKULLS, ARCADE MODE
At the Difficulty Select screen, press Up, Right, Down, Left, Up, Right, Down, Left.

SAVANT MODE, ARCADE MODE
At the Difficulty Select screen, press Down (x10).

MARBLE SAGA: KORORINPA

MASTER HIGGINS BALL
Select ??? from the Options. Press A on the right lamp, the left lamp twice, and the right lamp again. Now select the right icon and enter TV, Car, Sunflower, Bike, Helicopter, Strawberry.

MIRROR MODE
Select ??? from the Options. Press A on the right lamp, the left lamp twice, and the right lamp again. Now select the right icon and enter Beetle, Clover, Boy, Plane, Car, Bike.

MARIO & SONIC AT THE OLYMPIC GAMES

UNLOCK 4X100M RELAY EVENT
Medal in Mercury, Venus, Jupiter, and Saturn.

UNLOCK SINGLE SCULLS EVENT
Medal in Mercury, Venus, Jupiter, and Saturn.

UNLOCK DREAM RACE EVENT
Medal in Mercury, Venus, Jupiter, and Saturn.

UNLOCK ARCHERY EVENT
Medal in Moonlight Circuit.

UNLOCK HIGH JUMP EVENT
Medal in Stardust Circuit.

UNLOCK 400M EVENT
Medal in Planet Circuit.

UNLOCK DREAM FENCING EVENT
Medal in Comet Circuit.

UNLOCK DREAM TABLE TENNIS EVENT
Medal in Satellite Circuit.

UNLOCK 400M HURDLES EVENT
Medal in Sunlight Circuit.

UNLOCK POLE VAULT EVENT
Medal in Meteorite Circuit.

UNLOCK VAULT EVENT
Medal in Meteorite Circuit.

UNLOCK DREAM PLATFORM EVENT
Medal in Cosmos Circuit.

CROWNS
Get all gold medals in all events with a character to unlock their crown.

MARVEL SUPER HERO SQUAD

IRON MAN BONUS COSTUME
Select Enter Code from the Options menu and enter 111111. This unlocks the bonus costume "War Machine."

HULK BONUS COSTUMES
Select Enter Code from the Options menu and enter 222222. This unlocks the bonus costumes "Grey Hulk and "Red Hulk."

WOLVERINE BONUS COSTUMES
Select Enter Code from the Options menu and enter 333333. This unlocks the bonus costumes "Wolverine (Brown Costume)" and "Feral Wolverine."

THOR BONUS COSTUMES
Select Enter Code from the Options menu and enter 444444. This unlocks the bonus costumes "Thor (Chain Armor)" and "Loki-Thor."

SILVER SURFER BONUS COSTUMES
Select Enter Code from the Options menu and enter 555555. This unlocks the bonus costumes "Anti-Surfer" and "Gold Surfer."

FALCON BONUS COSTUME
Select Enter Code from the Options menu and enter 666666. This unlocks the bonus costume "Ultimates Falcon."

DOCTOR DOOM BONUS COSTUMES
Select Enter Code from the Options menu and enter 999999. This unlocks the bonus costumes "Ultimates Doctor Doom" and "Professor Doom."

CAPTAIN AMERICA BONUS COSTUME
Select Enter Code from the Options menu and enter 177674. This unlocks the bonus costume "Ultimate Captain America."

A.I.M. AGENT BONUS COSTUME
Select Enter Code from the Options menu and enter 246246. This unlocks the bonus costume "Blue Suit A.I.M."

SUPER KNOCKBACK
Select Enter Code from the Options menu and enter 777777.

NO BLOCK MODE
Select Enter Code from the Options menu and enter 888888.

GROUNDED
Select Enter Code from the Options menu and enter 476863

ONE-HIT TAKEDOWN
Select Enter Code from the Options menu and enter 663448

INFINITE SHARD DURATION
Select Enter Code from the Options menu and enter 742737

THROWN OBJECT TAKEDOWN
Select Enter Code from the Options menu and enter 847936

MARVEL: ULTIMATE ALLIANCE 2

GOD MODE
At any point during a game, press Up, Up, Down, Down, Left, Right, Down.

GIVE MONEY
At the Team Select or Hero Details screen press Up, Up, Down, Down, Up, Up, Up, Down.

UNLOCK ALL POWERS
At the Team Select or Hero Details screen press Up, Up, Down, Down, Left, Right, Right, Left.

ADVANCE ALL CHARACTERS TO L99
At the Hero Details screen press Down, Up, Left, Up, Right, Up, Left, Down.

UNLOCK ALL BONUS MISSIONS

While using the Bonus Mission Simulator, press Up, Right, Down, Left, Left, Right, Up, Up.

ADD 1 CHARACTER LEVEL

During a game, press Down, Up, Right, Up, Right, Up, Right, Down.

ADD 10 CHARACTER LEVELS

During a game, press Down, Up, Left, Up, Left, Up, Left, Down.

MEGA MAN 5

ALL WEAPONS AND ITEMS PASSWORD

Enter Blue B4 D6 F1 and Red C1 D4 F6 as a password.

METROID OTHER M

HARD MODE

Finish the game with all items.

CHAPTERS	HOW TO UNLOCK
Unlock Chapters 1-26	Defeat the final boss.
Unlock Chapters 27-30	After the credits, finish the bonus area and defeat the boss.

THEATER MODE

Defeat the final boss.

GALLERY MODE

Defeat the final boss.

GALLERY PAGES	HOW TO UNLOCK
1-4	Defeat the final boss.
5-7	After the credits, finish the bonus area and defeat the boss.
8	Finish the game with all items.

MONSTER LAIR

CONTINUE

At the Game Over screen, press Left, Right, Down, Up, Select + Left.

UNLIMITED CONTINUES

Enter 68K as your initials.

SOUND TEST

At the Title screen, press and hold 1 + 2 and then press Run.

MONSTER WORLD IV

SOUND TEST

Highlight New Game and press Up, Down, Up, Down, Left, Left, Right, Right.

MYSIMS AGENTS

ASTRONAUT SUIT

At the Create-a-Sim screen, press Up, Down, Up, Down, Left, Right, Left, Right.

BLACK NINJA OUTFIT

At the Create-a-Sim screen, press Right, Up, Right, Up, Down, Left, Down, Left.

STEALTH SUIT

At the Create-a-Sim screen, press Left, Right, Left, Right, Up, Down, Up, Down.

MYSIMS KINGDOM

DETECTIVE OUTFIT

Pause the game and press Left, Right, Left, Right, Left, Right.

SWORDSMAN OUTFIT

Pause the game and press Down, Up, Down, Up, Down, Up, Down, Up.

TATTOO VEST OUTFIT

Pause the game and press C, Z, C, Z, B, A, B, A.

NARUTO SHIPPUDEN: CLASH OF NINJA REVOLUTION III

RYO BONUS

A 50,00 starting Ryo bonus is given if you have a saved data from Naruto Shippuden: Clash of Ninja Revolution 1 or 2 on your Nintendo Wii.

NASCAR KART RACING

JOEY LOGANO

Select Enter Cheat from the Profile Info menu and enter 426378.

NBA 2K12

ABA BALL

Select Extras from the Features menu. Choose Codes and enter payrespect. This can be toggled on and off from this Codes menu.

2K CHINA TEAM

Select Extras from the Features menu. Choose Codes and enter 2kchina.

2K SPORTS TEAM

Select Extras from the Features menu. Choose Codes and enter 2ksports.

UNLOCK NBA 2K TEAM

Select Extras from the Features menu. Choose Codes and enter nba2k.

VC TEAM

Select Extras from the Features menu. Choose Codes and enter vcteam.

JORDAN RETRO COLLECTION

Select Extras from the Features menu. Choose Codes and enter 23.

SECONDARY ROAD UNIFORMS

Select Extras from the Features menu. Choose Codes and enter hcsilapadatu. This unlocks uniforms for 76ers, Jazz, Kings, and Mavericks.

CHRISTMAS UNIFORMS

Select Extras from the Features menu. Choose Codes and enter ibyasmliancbhlald. This unlocks uniforms for Bulls, Celtics, Heat, Knicks, Lakers, and Mavericks.

HEAT BACK IN BLACK UNIFORM

Select Extras from the Features menu. Choose Codes and enter albkbinkcca.

RAPTORS MILITARY NIGHT UNIFORM

Select Extras from the Features menu. Choose Codes and enter liyrimta.

NEED FOR SPEED PROSTREET

$2,000

Select Career and then choose Code Entry. Enter 1MA9X99.

$4,000

Select Career and then choose Code Entry. Enter W2IOLL01.

$8,000

Select Career and then choose Code Entry. Enter L1IS97A1.

$10,000

Select Career and then choose Code Entry. Enter 1MI9K7E1.

$10,000

Select Career and then choose Code Entry. Enter CASHMONEY.

$10,000

Select Career and then choose Code Entry. Enter REGGAME.

AUDI TT
Select Career and then choose Code Entry. Enter ITSABOUTYOU.

CHEVELLE SS
Select Career and then choose Code Entry. Enter HORSEPOWER.

COKE ZERO GOLF GTI
Select Career and then choose Code Entry. Enter COKEZERO.

DODGE VIPER
Select Career and then choose Code Entry. Enter WORLDSLONGESTLASTING.

MITSUBISHI LANCER EVOLUTION
Select Career and then choose Code Entry. Enter MITSUBISHIGOFAR.

UNLOCK ALL BONUSES
Select Career and then choose Code Entry. Enter UNLOCKALLTHINGS.

5 REPAIR MARKERS
Select Career and then choose Code Entry. Enter SAFETYNET.

ENERGIZER VINYL
Select Career and then choose Code Entry. Enter ENERGIZERLITHIUM.

CASTROL SYNTEC VINYL
Select Career and then choose Code Entry. Enter CASTROLSYNTEC. This also gives you $10,000.

NERF: N-STRIKE

BLACK HEART VENGEANCE
Select Codes from the Main menu and enter BHDETA8.

CRUSHER SAD-G
Select Codes from the Main menu and enter CRUSH14.

FIREFLY ELITE
Select Codes from the Main menu and enter HELIOX6.

GOLIATHAN NITRO
Select Codes from the Main menu and enter FIERO2.

HABANERO
Select Codes from the Main menu and enter 24KGCON4.

HYDRA
Select Codes from the Main menu and enter HRANGEL3.

LONGSHOT STREET
Select Codes from the Main menu and enter LONGST5.

MAVERICK CRYSTAL
Select Codes from the Main menu and enter CRISTOL10.

MAVERICK MIDNIGHT
Select Codes from the Main menu and enter MAVMID7.

MERCURIO
Select Codes from the Main menu and enter RSMERC9.

SEMPER FIRE ULTRA
Select Codes from the Main menu and enter CROMO1.

SPARTAN NCS-12
Select Codes from the Main menu and enter THISIS12.

STAMPEDE
Select Codes from the Main menu and enter DOGIE15.

VULCAN MAGMA
Select Codes from the Main menu and enter MAGMA3.

NERF: N-STRIKE ELITE

Select Codebook and enter the following codes.

10 CANISTERS
Enter NERF.

UNLIMITED AMMO
Enter DART. This can be toggled on and off.

CERBERUS CS-12
Enter DUDE.

CRUSHER SAD-G
Enter RUSH.

GOLITHAN UB-1
Enter ROCK.

HAMMERHEAD GL-1
Enter PONG.

HYDRA SG-7
Enter WIDE.

ICARUS HM-7
Enter DOOM.

LONGSHOT CS-6
Enter IDOL.

LONGSTRIKE CS-6
Enter PING.

RECON CS-6
Enter DIRT.

SEMPERFIRE RF-100
Enter FLEX.

SPARTAN NCS-12
Enter ICON.

VULCAN EBF-25
Enter LOTS.

NINTENDO Wii

NICKTOONS: ATTACK OF THE TOYBOTS

DAMAGE BOOST
Select Cheats from the Extras menu. Choose Enter Cheat Code and enter 456645.

INVULNERABILITY
Select Cheats from the Extras menu. Choose Enter Cheat Code and enter 313456.

UNLOCK EXO-HUGGLES 9000
Select Cheats from the Extras menu. Choose Enter Cheat Code and enter 691427.

UNLOCK MR. HUGGLES
Select Cheats from the Extras menu. Choose Enter Cheat Code and enter 654168.

UNLIMITED LOBBER GOO
Select Cheats from the Extras menu. Choose Enter Cheat Code and enter 118147.

UNLIMITED SCATTER GOO
Select Cheats from the Extras menu. Choose Enter Cheat Code and enter 971238.

UNLIMITED SPLITTER GOO
Select Cheats from the Extras menu. Choose Enter Cheat Code and enter 854511.

PHINEAS AND FERB: ACROSS THE 2ND DIMENSION

SKIN FOR AGENT P: PERRY THE PLATYBORG
During a game, press the Minus button to bring up the pause menu. Select Enter Code from Extras and enter BAB121.

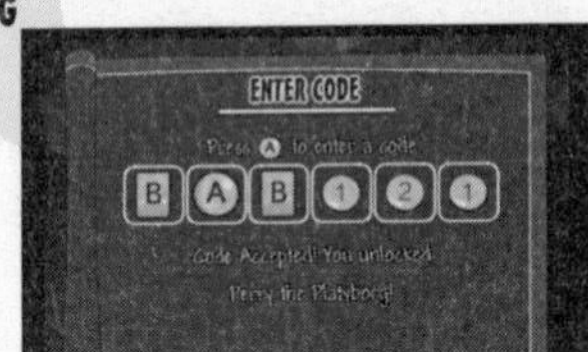

PINBALL HALL OF FAME - THE GOTTLIEB COLLECTION

UNLOCK TABLES IN FREEPLAY, EXTRA OPTIONS, AND PAYOUT MODE
Select Enter Code from the Main Menu and enter the following:

EFFECTS	CODE
Aces High Freeplay	UNO
Big Shot Freeplay	UJP
Black Hole Freeplay	LIS
Central Park Freeplay	NYC
Goin' Nuts Freeplay	PHF
Love Machine Freeplay	HOT
Playboy Freeplay	HEF

EFFECTS	CODE
Strikes 'N Spares Freeplay	PBA
Tee'd Off Freeplay	PGA
Xolten Freeplay	BIG
Custom Balls in Options	CKF
Optional Tilt in Options	BZZ
Payout Mode	WGR

PIRATES PLUNDARRR

CHEAT MENU
Press + to pause the game. Press Up, Up, Down, Down, Left, Right, Left, Right, 2, 1 to make a new Cheat option appear at the bottom of the menu.

AMAZON
Defeat Tecciztecatl, Witch Doctor.

SPECTRAL
Defeat Nanauatl, Hero of the Sun.

OVERLOAD

POKEMON RUMBLE

POKÉMON PASSWORDS

Go to the recruitment building in the terminal and enter the following passwords to get the corresponding Pokémon.

POKÉMON	PASSWORD
Blastoise	9580-1423
Charizard	7968-4528
Charmander	7927-6161
Cherrim Positive Forme	7540-5667
Chimchar	8109-8384
Eevee	0511-0403
Giratina (Origin Form)	8322-3706

POKÉMON	PASSWORD
Mew	9561-8808
Piplup	9900-2455
Shaymin (Sky Form)	5468-6284
Shiny Bidoof	5575-2435
Shiny Rattata	9849-3731
Squirtle	6824-2045
Turtwig	8672-1076
Venusaur	1589-3955

POKÉPARK 2: WONDERS BEYOND

KECLEON'S AWARDS

Befriend Kecleon by using Snivy to clear the southeastern buildings in Cove Town. Examine the red stripe to gain access to Kecleon. Here you can check your Records and the following Awards.

AWARD	EARNED BY
Ace Strikers	Score 100 goals.
Attraction Elite	Score first place in the four Attractions at Wish Park.
Battle Experts	Win all battles, including the Battle Tournament.
Battle Tournament Champs	Win the Battle Tournament after finishing the game.
Berry Rich	Collect 50,000 Berries.
Camera Czars	Take 100 Photos.
Chase Champions	Beat every Pokémon that plays Chase.
Collectors	Collect all Collection items.
Epic Explorers	Explore the Lighthouse, Stump, Cave, and Lab a lot.
Friendly Folk	Greet Pokémon 100 times.
Friends with Everyone	Befriend all 194 Pokémon.
Landscapers	Scatter plants 100 times.
Max Power	Get maximum Power Up for Pikachu and all his Pals.
Mighty Smashers	Hit Pokémon with Dash 500 times.
Portal Pros (Arbor)	Get 50,000 points when opening the Wish Park portal in Windmill Way.
Portal Pros (Cove)	Get 50,000 points when opening the Wish Park portal on Seaside Beach.
Portal Pros (Crag)	Get 50,000 points when opening the Wish Park portal in the Colosseum building.
Portal Pros (Tech)	Get 50,000 points when opening the Wish Park portal in the Scientorium.
Quillseekers	Collect all 40 Vast White Quills.
Sure Shots	Hit Pokémon 100 with objects.
Wrecking Crew	Destroy 100 objects in PokéPark.

POKEPARK WII: PIKACHU'S ADVENTURE

CELEBI APPEARS
Enter 58068773 as a password.

DARKRAI APPEARS
Enter 65967413 as a password.

GROUDON APPEARS
Enter 49446209 as a password.

JIRACHI APPEARS
Enter 73938790 as a password.

PIKACHU'S BALLOONS
Enter 99930457 as a password.

PIKACHU'S SNOWBOARD
Enter 67446162 as a password.

PIKACHU'S SURFBOARD
Enter 02970626 as a password.

POWER RANGER SAMURAI

ALL RANGERS IN EVERY LEVEL
Complete Mission 15 and go through the credits.

PRESS YOUR LUCK 2010 EDITION

WARDROBE PIECES FOR AVATAR
Select the lock tab from the Wardrobe screen and enter SECRET.

THE PRICE IS RIGHT 2010 EDITION

AVATAR UPGRADES
Select the lock tab from the Wardrobe screen and enter PRIZES.

PRINCE OF PERSIA RIVAL SWORDS

BABY TOY WEAPON
Pause the game and enter the following code. Use the D-pad for the directions.
Left, Left, Right, Right, Z, Nunchuck down, Nunchuck down, Z, Up, Down

CHAINSAW
Pause the game and enter the following code. Use the D-pad for the directions.
Up, Up, Down, Down, Left, Right, Left, Right, Z, Nunchuck down, Z, Nunchuck down

SWORDFISH
Pause the game and enter the following code. Use the D-pad for the directions.
Up, Down, Up, Down, Left, Right, Left, Right, Z, Nunchuck down, Z, Nunchuck down

TELEPHONE SWORD
Pause the game and enter the following code. Use the D-pad for the directions.
Right, Left, Right, Left, Down, Down, Up, Up, Z, Nunchuck Down, Z, Z, Nunchuck Down, Nunchuck Down

PRINCESS TOMATO IN THE SALAD KINGDOM

DEBUG BATTLE PASSWORD
Enter GG62 as a password.

PUNCH-OUT!!

REGAIN HEALTH IN BETWEEN ROUNDS
Press the Minus button between rounds to regain health at the start of the next round.

DONKEY KONG, EXHIBITION MODE
Fight Donkey Kong in Last Stand mode.

CHAMPIONS MODE
Win 10 bouts in Mac's Last Stand.

ASSASSIN RABBID

Finish Nick of Time to unlock the Rabbid customization option. Enter this option and select a Rabbid. Go to the menu and select Manage Figurines from the Figurines screen. Hold C + Z and press 2, 2, 1, 1, A, A, 1, 1.

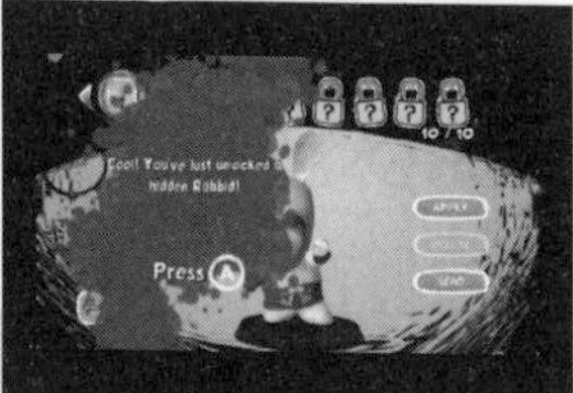

BEST BUY RABBID

Finish Nick of Time to unlock the Rabbid customization option. Enter this option and select a Rabbid. Go to the menu and select Manage Figurines from the Figurines screen. Hold C + Z and press B, 1, 1, B, A, 2, 2, A.

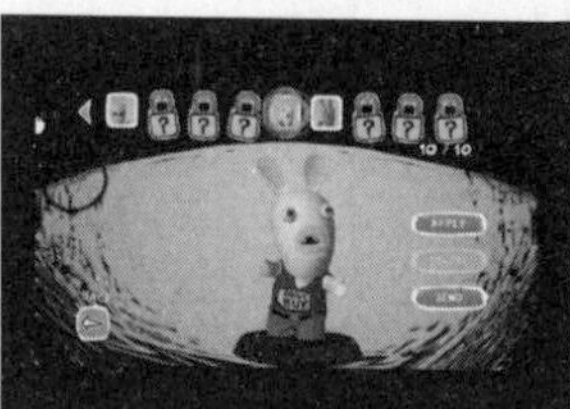

GEEK SQUAD RABBID

Finish Nick of Time to unlock the Rabbid customization option. Enter this option and select a Rabbid. Go to the menu and select Manage Figurines from the Figurines screen. Hold C + Z and press A, A, 1, 1, 1, 1, 2, 2.

KANGAROO RABBID

Finish Nick of Time to unlock the Rabbid customization option. Enter this option and select a Rabbid. Go to the menu and select Manage Figurines from the Figurines screen. Hold C + Z and press 1, 1, 1, 1, 1, 2, 1, 2.

LEONARDO RABBID

Finish Nick of Time to unlock the Rabbid customization option. Enter this option and select a Rabbid. Go to the menu and select Manage Figurines from the Figurines screen. Hold C + Z and press 1, 1, 2, 2, A, A, 1, 1.

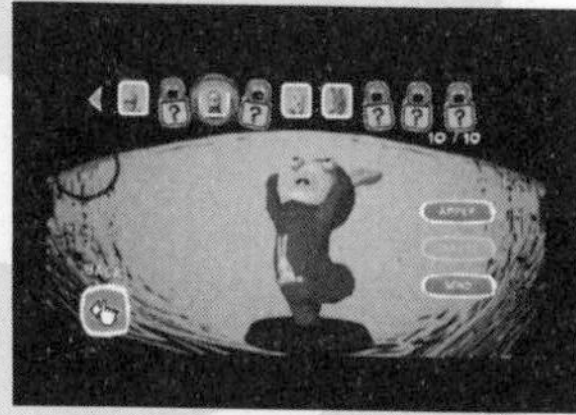

PRINCE RABBID

Finish Nick of Time to unlock the Rabbid customization option. Enter this option and select a Rabbid. Go to the menu and select Manage Figurines from the Figurines screen. Hold C + Z and press 1, 2, 1, 2, 1, 2, A, A.

SPLINTER CELL RABBID

Finish Nick of Time to unlock the Rabbid customization option. Enter this option and select a Rabbid. Go to the menu and select Manage Figurines from the Figurines screen. Hold C + Z and press B, B, B, B, A, A, A, A.

RATATOUILLE

Select Gusteau's Shop from the Extras menu. Choose Secrets, select the appropriate code number, and then enter the code. Once the code is entered, select the cheat you want to activate it.

CODE NUMBER	CODE	EFFECT
1	Pieceocake	Very Easy difficulty mode
2	Myhero	No impact and no damage from enemies
3	Shielded	No damage from enemies
4	Spyagent	Move undetected by any enemy
5	Ilikeonions	Fart every time Remy jumps
6	Hardfeelings	Head butt when attacking instead of tailswipe
7	Slumberparty	Multiplayer mode
8	Gusteauart	All Concept Art
9	Gusteauship	All four championship modes
10	Mattelme	All single player and multiplayer minigames
11	Gusteauvid	All Videos
12	Gusteaures	All Bonus Artworks
13	Gusteaudream	All Dream Worlds in Gusteau's Shop
14	Gusteauslide	All Slides in Gusteau's Shop
15	Gusteaulevel	All single player minigames
16	Gusteaucombo	All items in Gusteau's Shop
17	Gusteaupot	5,000 Gusteau points
18	Gusteaujack	10,000 Gusteau points
19	Gusteauomni	50,000 Gusteau points

RED STEEL 2

.357 MAGNUM, THE TATARO

Select Preorder from Extras and enter 370402.

BARRACUDA

Select Preorder from Extras and enter 3582880.

THE LOST BLADE OF THE KUSAGARI CLAN

Select Preorder from Extras and enter 360378.

NIHONTO HANA SWORD

Select Preorder from Extras and enter 58855558.

SORA KATANA OF THE KATAKARA CLAN

Select Preorder from Extras and enter 360152.

RUBIK'S PUZZLE WORLD

ALL LEVELS AND CUBIES

At the Main menu, press A, B, B, A, A.

RUGBY LEAGUE 3

$100,000,000 SALARY CAP

Go to Create a Player and enter SOMBRERO as the name.

UNLIMITED FUNDING

Go to Create a Player and enter Sugar Daddy as the name.

HUGE MUSCLES

Go to Create a Player and enter i'll be back as the name.

PRESS Z FOR MAX SPEED

Go to Create a Player and enter RSI as the name.

STRONG WIND

Go to Create a Player and enter Beans & Eggs as the name.

ONE TACKLE THEN HANDOVER

Go to Create a Player and enter Force Back as the name.

RHYTHM HEAVEN FEVER

THE CLAPPY TRIO GAME
Earn 35 Medals. Select the samurai head to play this game.

SNEAKY SPIRITS GAME
Earn 38 Medals. Select the samurai head to play this game.

POWER CALLIGRAPHY GAME
Earn 41 Medals. Select the samurai head to play this game.

TAP TRIAL GAME
Earn 44 Medals. Select the samurai head to play this game.

MR. UPBEAT ENDLESS GAME
Earn 3 Medals. Select the purple A button to play the game.

WAKE-UP CALLER ENDLESS GAME
Earn 11 Medals. Select the purple A button to play the game.

MUNCHY MONK ENDLESS GAME
Earn 23 Medals. Select the purple A button to play the game.

LADY CUPID ENDLESS GAME
Earn 32 Medals. Select the purple A button to play the game.

ENDLESS REMIX ENDLESS GAME
Earn a Perfect on all 50 games. Select the purple A button to play the game.

CLAP TRAP 2-PLAYER ENDLESS GAME
Earn 1 Duo Medal. Select the purple AA button to play the game.

MOCHI POUNDING 2-PLAYER ENDLESS GAME
Earn 2 Duo Medals. Select the purple AA button to play the game.

KUNG FU BALL 2-PLAYER ENDLESS GAME
Earn 4 Duo Medals. Select the purple AA button to play the game.

PIRATE CREW 2-PLAYER ENDLESS GAME
Earn 6 Duo Medals. Select the purple AA button to play the game.

BOSSA NOVA 2-PLAYER ENDLESS GAME
Earn 8 Duo Medals. Select the purple AA button to play the game.

TOY CAR RHYTHM TOY
Earn 1 Medal. Select the yellow smiley face to play around with it.

POLICE CALL RHYTHM TOY
Earn 7 Medals. Select the yellow smiley face to play around with it.

HI-HAT RHYTHM TOY
Earn 14 Medals. Select the yellow smiley face to play around with it.

RHYTHM FIGHTER RHYTHM TOY
Earn 21 Medals. Select the yellow smiley face to play around with it.

POLICE CALL RHYTHM TOY CODES
After unlocking the Police Call Rhythm Toy, the following can be entered for different effects:

BIRDS
BOUTS
GOLFHERO
MATCH
SEESAW
STAFF

SAKURA WARS: SO LONG, MY LOVE

ALL 3 EVENTS
In Free & Easy Day in N.Y., visit Romando and enter 928993363528 as a password.

ALL 30 PHOTOS
In Free & Easy Day in N.Y., visit Romando and enter 837871465578 as a password.

ALL 6 RINGTONES
In Free & Easy Day in N.Y., visit Romando and enter 924005530128 as a password.

PASSWORDS IN FREE & EASY DAY IN N.Y.
In Free & Easy Day in N.Y., visit Romando and enter the following as a password.

NAME	PASSWORD
Photograph 1	945476282278
Photograph 2	909316867958
Photograph 3	511006563288
Photograph 4	510846764928
Photograph 5	574728027208
Photograph 6	596268228578
Photograph 7	558588824458
Photograph 8	535038549588
Photograph 9	589858748428
Photograph 10	567793040508
Photograph 11	560273209078
Photograph 12	524513806358
Photograph 13	546403500088

NAME	PASSWORD
Photograph 14	508343915328
Photograph 15	313123116008
Photograph 16	379665471878
Photograph 17	397985673158
Photograph 18	390435372888
Photograph 19	354355997128
Photograph 20	332195193808
Photograph 21	388679494778
Photograph 22	363919657658
Photograph 23	329209358788
Photograph 24	347549954628
Photograph 25	340029139708
Photograph 26	304867438278

NAME	PASSWORD
Photograph 27	812787630958
Photograph 28	878237389288
Photograph 29	893557986928
Photograph 30	859097180208
Ringtone: Gemini	922566130958
Ringtone: Cheiron	926906817278
Ringtone: Rosita	928267292088
Ringtone: Diana	928935668428

NAME	PASSWORD
Ringtone: Subaru	928974804588
Ringtone: Ratchet	928993468958
Special Event 1	928996495658
Special Event 2	928993482128
Special Event 3	928996609188
Unlock Shinjiro's Girl Costume	928996605128

SCOOBY-DOO! FIRST FRIGHTS

DAPHNE'S SECRET COSTUME

Select Codes from the Extras menu and enter 2839.

FRED'S SECRET COSTUME

Select Codes from the Extras menu and enter 4826.

SCOOBY DOO'S SECRET COSTUME

Select Codes from the Extras menu and enter 1585.

SHAGGY'S SECRET COSTUME

Select Codes from the Extras menu and enter 3726.

VELMA'S SECRET COSTUME

Select Codes from the Extras menu and enter 6588.

SCOOBY-DOO! AND THE SPOOKY SWAMP

BIG HEAD

Enter the clubhouse and select Codes from the Extras menu. Enter 2654.

CHIPMUNK TALK

Enter the clubhouse and select Codes from the Extras menu. Enter 3293.

DOUBLE DAMAGE

Enter the clubhouse and select Codes from the Extras menu. Enter 9991.

SLOW MOTION

Enter the clubhouse and select Codes from the Extras menu. Enter 1954.

THE SECRET SATURDAYS: BEASTS OF THE 5TH SUN

ALL LEVELS

Select Enter Secret Code from the Secrets menu and input Zon, Zon, Zon, Zon.

UNLOCK AMAROK TO BE SCANNED IN LEVEL 2

Select Enter Secret Code from the Secrets menu and input Fiskerton, Zak, Zon, Komodo.

UNLOCK BISHOPVILLE LIZARDMAN TO BE SCANNED IN LEVEL 3

Select Enter Secret Code from the Secrets menu and input Komodo, Zon, Zak, Komodo.

UNLOCK NAGA TO BE SCANNED IN LEVEL 7

Select Enter Secret Code from the Secrets menu and input Zak, Zak, Zon, Fiskerton.

UNLOCK RAKSHASA TO BE SCANNED IN LEVEL 8

Select Enter Secret Code from the Secrets menu and input Zak, Komodo, Fiskerton, Fiskerton.

UNLOCK BILOKO TO BE SCANNED IN LEVEL 9

Select Enter Secret Code from the Secrets menu and input Zon, Zak, Zon, Fiskerton.

SHOCKMAN

REFILL ENERGY

Pause the game and press Left + Select + 2

SOUND TEST

After completing the game and at the To Be Continued screen, hold Select and press Up or Down.

SIMANIMALS

FERRET

Begin a game in an unlocked forest area, press 2 to pause, and select Enter Codes. Enter Ferret.

PANDA

Begin a game in an unlocked forest area, press 2 to pause, and select Enter Codes. Enter PANDA.

RED PANDA

Begin a game in an unlocked forest area, press 2 to pause, and select Enter Codes. Enter Red Panda.

SIMCITY CREATOR

EGYPTIAN BUILDING SET

Name your city Mummy's desert.

GREEK BUILDING SET

Name your city Ancient culture.

JUNGLE BUILDING SET

Name your city Become wild.

SCI-FI BUILDING SET

Name your city Future picture.

SKYLANDERS GIANTS

SKYLANDERS SPECIFIC QUESTS

Skylanders Giants includes quests specific to each Skylander as a way to improve them. Here we list each Skylander with their quest and tips on how to complete it.

SKYLANDER	QUEST	HOW TO COMPLETE
Bash	On a Roll: Defeat 10 enemies with one roll attack.	If you have trouble completing this quest, opt for the Pulver Dragon upgrade path.
Boomer	On a Troll: Defeat five enemies with one kicked Troll Bomb.	Once you have Troll Bomb Boot, look for a group of tight-knit Chompies. "Chapter 1: Time of the Giants" has several groupings of five Chompies.
Bouncer	Stay on Target!: Target enemies 100 times with laser-guided Shoulder Rockets	You must purchase the Targeting Computer upgrade for Bouncer's Shoulder Rockets.
Camo	Garden Gorger: Eat 10 watermelons.	If you aren't in a rush to complete a level, switch to Camo when a watermelon appears.
Chill	Ice Sore: Defeat six enemies with one Ice Narwhal attack.	Try to find six enemies that are grouped together at a medium distance, such as in an arena.
Chop Chop	Stalwart Defender: Absorb 1,000 damage with your shield.	To complete this quest safely, block attacks from a small group of weaker enemies near a food item (just in case they sneak in some unexpected damage).
Crusher	High Roller: Defeat 100 enemies with boulders.	Use Rockslide defeat enemies until you have completed this quest.
Cynder	On the Haunt: Defeat 50 enemies with your Ghost Ally.	Ghost Ally does not inflict much damage so focus on saving low-health enemies, like Chompies, for the ghost to attack. The Ghost attacks while Cynder is flying, so consider circling an area with Chompies.
Dino-Rang	Fooderang: Pick up 20 food items with boomerangs.	After acquiring Sticky Boomerangs, use it to grab any food found in the area. In the Arena Challenges on Flynn's Ship, the audience throws food items into the arena between rounds.
Double Trouble	Big Bomb Trouble: Defeat 10 enemies with one Magic Bomb attack.	Find a group of 10 or more Chompies and set off a bomb. A good place to earn this is any of of Brock's Arena Challenges with regular Chompies.
Drill Sergeant	Drill Skill: Defeat Drill-X without changing Skylanders.	Drill Sergeant must defeat Drill-X (the final boss in Chapter 11: Drill-X's Big Rig) solo. Use Adventure items (like Healing Potion) to survive the battle. You can complete it on Easy difficulty with a fully-upgraded Drill Sergeant.
Drobot	Feed the Burn: Defeat 50 enemies with Afterburners.	It's easiest to hit enemies with Afterburners when Drobot first takes off.
Eruptor	Pizza Burp: Eat 10 Pizzas.	If you want to have a greater chance of encountering a pizza, equip Lucky Wheel of Health in the Luck-O-Tron.
Eye Brawl	Gold Search: Collect 5,000 gold with the eyeball detached	Remember to detach Eye-Brawl's eye before collecting any treasure from chests or enemies.

SKYLANDER	QUEST	HOW TO COMPLETE
Flameslinger	Circular Combustion: Defeat 10 enemies with one column of Fire Flame Dash.	There are two upgrades you can get to help you on this quest. The first is Column of Fire. The second is Supernova in the Pyromancer Path.
Flashwing	Let It Shine: Defeat 20 enemies with one Crystal Lighthouse.	Since Crystal Lighthouse is stationary, this is a tricky quest. The best candidate for this is one of the arena maps, particularly Kaos' Royal Flush (the second challenge, Birthday Bash). Set up the Lighthouse in the middle of the birthday cake.
Fright Rider	Delving Throw: Toss 50 enemies into the air	The power to use for this quest is Burrow Bomber. Hit any medium or small enemy with the attack to pop them up in the air and register a toss.
Ghost Roaster	Grave Circumstances: Defeat 100 enemies with Skull Charge.	Repeatedly use Skull Charge to attack enemies and you should complete this quest in no time.
Gill Grunt	Anchors Away!: Defeat six enemies with one Anchor Attack.	Line up a group of Chompies with your Anchor Cannon and let loose to complete the quest. If you have Series 2 Gill Grunt, Anchor's Away! makes completing the quest easier.
Hex	Noggin Knocker: Knock away 100 enemies with your Skull Rain.	Once Hex has Skull Shield, allow enemies to get within melee range while Hex is charging that attack. If they get too close, they get knocked back, tallying a point for this quest.
Hot Dog	Animal Aggravator: Scare away 20 birds.	Look for the small birds pecking at the ground in each level. These birds are the ones you need to scare with Hot Dog for this achievement. Chapter 13: The Oracle and Chapter 1: Time of Giants both have plenty of birds.
Hot Head	Buggy Breakthrough: Destroy 20 walls in Hot Rod mode.	The walls this quest is referring to are the walls that can only be crushed by a Giant or a bomb. Whenever you encounter one of these walls, switch to Hot Head. A good spot with plenty of these types of walls is Chapter 2: Junkyard Isles.
Ignitor	Tinder Trekker: Travel 26,000 feet in Flame Form.	Use Flame Form often and this number will accumulate quickly.
Jet-Vac	Bird Cleaner: Suck up 50 birds in your Suction Gun.	Look for tiny birds on the ground throughout most levels with green grass. Chapter 13: The Oracle and Chapter 1: Time of Giants both have plenty of birds.
Lightning Rod	Current Event: Defeat 10 enemies with one Grand Lightning strike.	You need to find a group of 10 Chompies in one area and use the Grand Lightning to blast them all. Choosing the Lord of Lightning Path makes this easier since the Grand Lightning attack lasts longer.
Ninjini	Bottle Beatdown: Defeat 5 enemies within five seconds of exiting your bottle.	Transform Ninjini into the bottle and move into a large group of small enemies. Follow up the bottle attack with her swords.
Pop Fizz	Rampage: Do 200 HP of damage in a single run in Beast Form.	Transform into Beast Form in a large group of enemies and destroy everything in sight to complete the quest.

SKYLANDER	QUEST	HOW TO COMPLETE
Prism Break	Bifurcation Sensation: Defeat 100 enemies with double refraction.	A beam must pass through two Shards before hitting an enemy to count. Unlock the Chained Refractions upgrade and place plenty of Crystal Shards. Fire an Energy Beam through them to indirectly take out nearby enemies.
Shroomboom	Lunching Launch: Eat a watermelon while performing a Self-Slingshot!	When you find a watermelon, blast Shroomboom through it with the Self-Slingshot power to complete the quest.
Slam Bam	Ice to Meet You: Trap 100 enemies in your Ice Blocks.	You do not need to damage or freeze enemies with Ice Block; it counts if you just hit them with the Ice Block.
Sonic Boom	Sonic Squeak: Babies defeat 50 enemies.	Upgrade Sonic Boom's egg attack powers and keep babies summoned at all times.
Sprocket	Mined Your Step: Defeat 50 enemies using the Landmine Golf attack.	Once you unlock the Landmine Golf ability, use it often. A quick way to complete this quest is to load up one of the easier Arena levels.
Spyro	Full Charge: Collect 3 gold, eat 1 food item, and defeat 2 enemies in 1 Sprint Charge.	Look for two low-health enemies (Chompies are a good choice) as well as some food and gold on the screen. Purchase the Sprint Charge upgrade to increase the distance of Spyro's sprint.
Stealth Elf	Stealth Health: Gain 1,000 HP while stealthed.	You need to first purchase Sylvan Regeneration. Once you do, you get credit towards the 1,000 HP every time you heal while Stealth Elf is in the Stealthier Decoy mode.
Stump Smash	Meganut Bowling: Defeat five enemies with one Meganut.	Meganuts are powerful, and bowling over five Chompies with one is no problem. The upgrade Acorn Croquet makes this much easier to achieve since you can wack the acorn directly at enemies.
Sunburn	Immolation Itinerant: Travel 1 mile using Immolation Teleport	Use Immolation Teleport regularly to tally up the distance towards one full mile. The quickest way to complete this quest is to unlock the Flight of the Phoenix and the Guided Teleportation upgrades.
Swarm	Swarm Feelings: Defeat 100 enemies in Swarm Form.	While you can complete this quest without pursuing the Wasp Stormer Path, it's extremely difficult, and you must focus on weaker enemies.
Terrafin	Land Lubber: Eat 20 food items while burrowing.	Once you have Surface Feeder, stay underground and collect Food Items as they drop.
Thumpback	Beached Whale: Defeat 8 enemies with one Belly Flop.	Upgrade Thumpback's Belly Flop attack with Slippery Belly. If you are having trouble getting this quest, invest in the Up Close and Personal path to further increase the strength of the Belly Flop attack.
Tree Rex	Timberrrrr!: Defeat 50 enemies by landing on them. Chompies don't count!	Unfortunately, Elbow Drop doesn't work for this quest. Tree Rex must crush enemies by landing on them. The best way to do this is to find a bounce pad in an area with plenty of Chompies.

SKYLANDER	QUEST	HOW TO COMPLETE
Trigger Happy	Holding Gold: Save up 50,000 Gold	This is one of the hardest quests any character has in the game. Not because it's difficult, but because it will take some time to collect 50,000 Gold.
Voodood	Trickwire: Defeat six enemies at once with your tripwire.	Find a group of six or more low-health enemies, like Bone Chompies, and set up the Tripwire near them. Chapter 1: Time of the Giants has several good spots to try for this quest.
Warnado	Chompy Catcher: Catch 100 Chompies in tornadoes.	The best place to do this is in the Arena Challenges. Head to any of the early challenges and there are plenty of Chompies. High Winds also helps gather up more Chompies at once.
Wham-Shell	Irate Invertebrate: Defeat 6 enemies with one Poseidon Strike.	To get the most out of Poseidon Strike, invest in the Captain Crustacean path. Once you have unlocked Mace of the Deep, go for this quest by finding a group of Chompies and blasting them.
Whirlwind	What does it mean?: Create 50 double rainbows.	Unlock the Duel Rainbows ability, then fire out a Tempest cloud and following up with a Rainbow of Doom. Rainbows made via the Double Dose of Doom power don't count unless they hit a Tempest Cloud. Triple rainbows created via Triple Tempest count as one double rainbow.
Wrecking Ball	Competitive Eater: Swallow 100 Enemies	Purchase Enemy Slurp and swallow as many enemies as you can. Any medium-sized and smaller enemy can be eaten.
Zap	In the Slimelight: Defeat 50 enemies by electrifying them in Sea Slime	Use Sea Slime to electrify enemies regularly and you'll complete this quest in no time.
Zook	Spore It On: Absorb 1,000 points of damage with a Foliage Barrier	Use Foliage Barrier often and you will complete this quest quickly.

SONIC COLORS

EXTRA LIVES

After completing a level, the results screen shows how well you did. Jump through the numbers until they break apart revealing gold rings and extra lives.

SPACE HARRIER

CONTINUE AFTER GAME OVER

At the Game Over screen, press Up, Up, Down, Down, Left, Right, Left, Right, Down, Up, Down, Up.

SPECTROBES: ORIGINS

METALLIC LEO AND RYZA

At the Title screen and before creating a game save, press Up, Down, Left, Right, A.

SPIDER-MAN: EDGE OF TIME

SHATTERED DIMENSIONS BONUS SUITS

If you have a saved game data for Spider-Man: Shattered Dimensions on your system, new Alternate Suits become available in the Bonus Gallery.

BIG TIME SUIT (2099)

At the main menu, press Right, Down, Down, Up, Left, Down, Down, Right.

FUTURE FOUNDATION SUIT (AMAZING)

At the main menu, press Up, Down, Left, Up, Down, Left, Right, Left.

SPIDER-MAN: SHATTERED DIMENSIONS

The following can be entered after completing the tutorial.

IRON SPIDER SUIT

After completing the tutorial and at the Main menu, press Up, Right, Right, Right, Left, Left, Left, Down, Up.

NEGATIVE ZONE SUIT

After completing the tutorial and at the Main menu, press Left, Right, Right, Down, Right, Down, Up, Left.

SCARLET SPIDER SUIT

After completing the tutorial and at the Main menu, press Right, Up, Left, Right, Up, Left, Right, Up, Left, Right.

SPONGEBOB SQUAREPANTS FEATURING NICKTOONS: GLOBS OF DOOM

When entering the following codes, the order of the characters going down is: SpongeBob SquarePants, Nicolai Technus, Danny Phantom, Dib, Zim, Tlaloc, Tak, Beautiful Gorgeous, Jimmy Neutron, Plankton. These names are shortened to the first name in the following.

ATTRACT COINS

Using the Upgrade Machine on the bottom level of the lair, select "Input cheat codes here". Enter Tlaloc, Plankton, Danny, Plankton, Tak. Coins are attracted to you making them much easier to collect.

DON'T LOSE COINS

Using the Upgrade Machine on the bottom level of the lair, select "Input cheat codes here." Enter Plankton, Jimmy, Beautiful, Jimmy, Plankton. You don't lose coins when you get knocked out.

GOO HAS NO EFFECT

Using the Upgrade Machine on the bottom level of the lair, select "Input cheat codes here". Enter Danny, Danny, Danny, Nicolai, Nicolai. Goo does not slow you down.

MORE GADGET COMBO TIME

Using the Upgrade Machine on the bottom level of the lair, select "Input cheat codes here". Enter SpongeBob, Beautiful, Danny, Plankton, Nicolai. You have more time to perform gadget combos.

STAR WARS THE CLONE WARS: LIGHTSABER DUELS

COUNT DOOKU
Select Cheats from Extras and press 2, 2, +, 2, 2, +, 2, 2, -, A, -, C, -, Z, +, Z.

GENERAL GRIEVOUS
Select Cheats from Extras and press 2, 2, +, 2, 2, +, 2, 2, -, Z, -, A, -, C, +, C.

ALL STORY MODE STAGES
Select Cheats from Extras and press A, +, 2, 2, +, C, +, 2, 2, +, Z, +, 2, 2.

MUSTAFAR STAGE
Select Cheats from Extras and press Z (x5), +, Z (x5), +, 1.

RAXUS PRIME STAGE
Select Cheats from Extras and press A (x5), +, A (x5), +, , 2.

SEPARATIST DROID FACTORY STAGE
Select Cheats from Extras and press C (x5), +, C (x5), +, 1.

CREDITS
Select Cheats from Extras and press 1, 2, +, 1.

GALLERY ONE
Select Cheats from Extras and press -, A, +, 1.

GALLERY TWO
Select Cheats from Extras and press -, A, +, 2.

GALLERY THREE
Select Cheats from Extras and press +, A, +, 1, +, 2.

GALLERY FOUR
Select Cheats from Extras and press +, A, +, 2, +, 2.

STAR WARS: THE FORCE UNLEASHED

CHEATS
Once you have accessed the Rogue Shadow, select Enter Code from the Extras menu. Now you can enter the following codes:

CHEAT	CODE
Invincibility	CORTOSIS
Unlimited Force	VERGENCE
1,000,000 Force Points	SPEEDER
All Force Powers	TYRANUS
Max Force Power Level	KATARN
Max Combo Level	COUNTDOOKU
Stronger Lightsaber	LIGHTSABER

COSTUMES
Once you have accessed the Rogue Shadow, select Enter Code from the Extras menu. Now you can enter the following codes:

COSTUME	CODE
All Costumes	GRANDMOFF
501st Legion	LEGION
Aayla Secura	AAYLA
Admiral Ackbar	ITSATWAP
Anakin Skywalker	CHOSENONE
Asajj Ventress	ACOLYTE
Ceremonial Jedi Robes	DANTOOINE
Chop'aa Notimo	NOTIMO
Classic stormtrooper	TK421
Count Dooku	SERENNO
Darth Desolous	PAUAN
Darth Maul	ZABRAK
Darth Phobos	HIDDENFEAR
Darth Vader	SITHLORD
Drexl Roosh	DREXLROOSH
Emperor Palpatine	PALPATINE
General Rahm Kota	MANDALORE
Han Solo	NERFHERDER

COSTUME	CODE
Heavy trooper	SHOCKTROOP
Juno Eclipse	ECLIPSE
Kento's Robe	WOOKIEE
Kleef	KLEEF
Lando Calrissian	SCOUNDREL
Luke Skywalker	T16WOMPRAT
Luke Skywalker (Yavin)	YELLOWJCKT
Mace Windu	JEDIMASTER
Mara Jade	MARAJADE
Maris Brook	MARISBROOD
Navy commando	STORMTROOP
Obi Wan Kenobi	BENKENOBI
Proxy	HOLOGRAM
Qui Gon Jinn	MAVERICK
Shaak Ti	TOGRUTA
Shadow trooper	INTHEDARK
Sith Robes	HOLOCRON
Sith Stalker Armor	KORRIBAN
Twi'lek	SECURA

STAR WARS: THE FORCE UNLEASHED II

ALL COSTUMES

Select Story Mode and then choose Costumes from the Profile. Hold Z until you hear a sound and then press Left, Right, C, Left, Right, C, Up, Down.

STREET FIGHTER ALPHA 2

AUSTRALIA STAGE

In versus mode, highlight Sagat, hold Start, and press any button.

CHUN-LI'S HIDDEN COSTUME

At the character select, highlight Chun-li, hold Start and press any button.

STRONG BAD'S COOL GAME FOR ATTRACTIVE PEOPLE EPISODE 1: HOMESTAR RUINER

COBRA MODE IN SNAKE BOXER 5

At the Snake Boxer 5 title screen, press Up, Up, Down, Up, Plus.

SUPER C

RETAIN LIVES AND SCORE ON NEW GAME

After defeating the game, press A and then Start.

RETAIN SCORE ON NEW GAME

After defeating the game, press A, B, and then Start.

10 LIVES

At the Title screen, press Right, Left, Down, Up, A, B, Start.

SOUND TEST

At the Title screen, hold A + B and press Start.

SUPER MARIO GALAXY 2

ALL LUIGI GHOSTS

Collect 9999 coins.

BANKER TOAD

Depositing star bits with Banker Toad changes his outfit as indicated in the following table.

ITEM	# OF STAR BITS
Glasses	1000
Spear/Shield	2000
Pickaxe	4000
Scuba Suit	6000
Explorer Outfit	8000

GREEN STARS

Collect 120 stars to unlock 120 green stars.

WORLD S

After completing the game and watching the game ending, you'll unlock World S.

GRANDMASTER GALAXY

Collect 120 stars and 120 green stars.

GRANDMASTER GALAXY COMET—T HE PERFECT RUN

Deposit 9999 star bits with Banker Toad.

TENCHU: SHADOW ASSASSINS

ALL NORMAL ITEMS

At the Title screen, hold C + Z and quickly press Up, Left, Down, Right, Up, Left, Down, Right, Right, 1, 2.

ALL SECRET ITEMS

At the Title screen, hold C + Z and quickly press Up, Right, Down, Left, Up, Right, Down, Left, Left, 1, 2.

MAX ITEMS

At the Title screen, hold C + Z and quickly press Down, Up, Down, Up, Right, Left, Right, Left, Left, 1.

ALL MISSIONS/ASSIGNMENTS

At the Title screen, hold C + Z and quickly press Left, Left, Left, Left, Right, Right, Right, Right, 1, 2.

FULL SWORD GAUGE

At the Title screen, hold C + Z and quickly press Up, Down, Up, Down, Left, Right, Left, Right, Right, 1, 2.

TIGER WOODS PGA TOUR 12: THE MASTERS

ALL BALLS AVAILABLE AT SHOP
Select Passwords from the Options and enter tour proving.

ALL CLUBS AVAILABLE AT SHOP
Select Passwords from the Options and enter clubsoda.

ADIDAS EQUIPMENT
Select Passwords from the Options and enter ClimaCool.

FOOTJOY EQUIPMENT
Select Passwords from the Options and enter Dry Joys.

ALL PING CLUBS
Select Passwords from the Options and enter rapture.

TIGER WOODS APPAREL
Select Passwords from the Options and enter gearoftheTiger.

JEWELRY
Select Passwords from the Options and enter Platinum.

TONY HAWK RIDE

RYAN SHECKLER
Select Cheats from the Options menu and enter SHECKLERSIG.

QUICKSILVER 80S LEVEL
Select Cheats from the Options menu and enter FEELINGEIGHTIES.

ULTIMATE SHOOTING COLLECTION

ROTATE DISPLAY ON SIDE IN TATE MODE
At the Main menu, press Left, Right, Left, Right, Up, Up, 1, 2.

VIRTUA TENNIS 4

THERON TENNIEL
At the player select, select Load to access Custom Players. Next, press -.

VICKY BARNEY
At the player select, select Load to access Custom Players. Next, press +.

WII PARTY

SPOT THE SNEAK IN MINI-GAMES
Play all of the 4-player mini-games.

WII SPORTS

BOWLING BALL COLOR
After selecting your Mii, hold the following direction on the D-pad and press A at the warning screen:

DIRECTION	COLOR
Up	Blue
Right	Gold
Down	Green
Left	Red

NO HUD IN GOLF
Hold 2 as you select a course to disable the power meter, map, and wind speed meter.

BLUE TENNIS COURT
After selecting your Mii, hold 2 and press A at the warning screen.

WII SPORTS RESORT

MODIFY EVENTS

At the Select a Mii screen, hold 2 while pressing A while on "OK." This will make the following modifications to each event.

EVENT	MODIFICATION
Air Sports Island Flyover	No balloons or I points
Air Sports Skydiving	Play intro event
Archery	More difficult; no aiming reticule
Basketball Pickup Game	Nighttime
Frisbee Golf	No wind display or distance
Golf	No wind display or distance
Swordplay Duel	Evening
Table Tennis Match	11-point match

WIPEOUT: THE GAME

JOHN ANDERSON ALTERNATE OUTFIT

Play a single player game.

MAD COWGIRL, VALLEY GIRL (SECOND OUTFIT) AND GRASSHOPPER

Play a multiplayer game.

CHEF MUTTEN

Defeat Wipeout Zone within 1:00.

WWE '12

WWE ATTITUDE ERA HEAVYWEIGHT CHAMPIONSHIP

Select Options from My WWE. Next, choose Cheat Codes and enter OhHellYeah!.

WWE ALL STARS

UNLOCK EVERYTHING

At the main menu, press Left, Right, Left, Down, Up, Left, Right, Up on the d-pad. This code does not save, so it must be entered again after resetting the game.

WWE SMACKDOWN VS. RAW 2010

THE ROCK

Select Cheat Codes from the Options and enter The Great One.

VINCE'S OFFICE AND DIRT SHEET FOR BACKSTAGE BRAWL

Select Cheat Codes from the Options menu and enter BonusBrawl.

HBK/SHAWN MICHAEL'S ALTERNATE COSTUME

Select Cheat Codes from the Options menu and enter Bow Down.

JOHN CENA'S ALTERNATE COSTUME

Select Cheat Codes from the Options menu and enter CENATION.

RANDY ORTON'S ALTERNATE COSTUME

Select Cheat Codes from the Options menu and enter ViperRKO.

SANTINO MARELLA'S ALTERNATE COSTUME

Select Cheat Codes from the Options menu and enter Milan Miracle.

TRIPLE H'S ALTERNATE COSTUME

Select Cheat Codes from the Options menu and enter Suck IT!.

WWE SMACKDOWN VS. RAW 2011

JOHN CENA (ENTRANCE/CIVILIAN)

In My WWE, select Cheat Codes from the Options and enter SLURPEE.

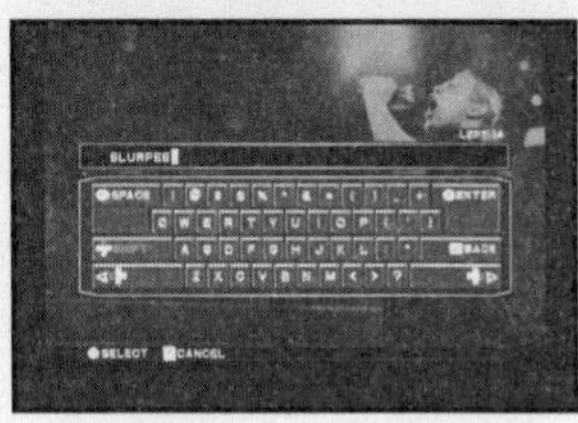

ALL OF RANDY ORTON'S COSTUMES

In My WWE, select Cheat Codes from the Options and enter apexpredator.

TRIBUTE TO THE TROOPS ARENA

In My WWE, select Cheat Codes from the Options and enter 8thannualtribute.

CRUISERWEIGHT TITLE, HARDCORE TITLE, AND MILLION DOLLAR TITLE

In My WWE, select Cheat Codes from the Options and enter Historicalbelts.

SONY PLAYSTATION® 3

GAMES

3D DOT GAME HEROES

HIDE SHIELD

Pause the game and press Up, Up, Down, Down, Left, Right, Left, Right, ■, ▲. Re-enter the code to reveal the shield again.

TOGGLE SWAY IN WALKING

Pause the game and press L1, R1, L1, R1, L1, L1, R1, R1, ■. Re-enter to turn the code back on.

SPELUNKER MODE

Enter your name as SPELUNKER. In this mode, you will die with one hit.

ALICE: MADNESS RETURNS

DRESSES

Completing each chapter unlocks a new dress—each with a special ability.

DRESS	COMPLETE THIS CHAPTER	DRESS ABILITY
Steamdress	Chapter 1	Breakables drop more Teeth and Roses.
Siren	Chapter 2	Enemies drop twice as many Roses.
Silk Maiden	Chapter 3	Enemies drop twice as many Teeth.
Royal Suit	Chapter 4	Health limited to 4 Roses total.
Misstitched	Chapter 5	Shrink Sense duration is doubled.
Classic	Chapter 6	Regain health while shrunk.

ASSASSIN'S CREED: BROTHERHOOD

CAPES

Equip capes in the Inventory screen.

CAPE	HOW TO OBTAIN
Auditore Cape	100% Rebuilding Rome
Borgia Cape	Collect 100 Borgia Flags
Medici and Venetian Capes	Complete Auditore Trail Mnemonic in Assassin's Creed: Project Legacy

CHEATS

The following cheats can only be used when replaying memories.

CHEAT	OBTAIN 100% SYNC IN THIS SEQUENCE
Ride the Unicorn	1
Buns of Steel	2
Killing Spree	3
Sisterhood	4
Ultimate Guild	5
Unlimited Assassins Signals	6
Desmond	8

ASSASSIN'S CREED: REVELATIONS

100% SYNC CHEATS

The following cheats can be used when replaying a memory. They are accessed through the Options.

CHEAT	COMPLETE SEQUENCE WITH 100% SYNC
Buns of Steel	2
Calling All Assassins	5
Infinite Ammunition	7
Killing Spree	3
Permanent Secrecy	6
The Old Eagle Outfit	8
Ultimate Guild	4

BAJA: EDGE OF CONTROL

CAREER COMPLETE 100%

Select Cheat Codes from the Options menu and enter SHOWTIME.

INSTALL ALL PARTS

Select Cheat Codes from the Options menu and enter SUPERMAX.

BAKUGAN BATTLE BRAWLERS

1,000 BP
Enter 33204429 as your name.

10,000 BP
Enter 46836478 as your name.

100,000 BP
Enter 18499753 as your name.

5,000 BP
Enter 42348294 as your name.

500,000 BP
Enter 26037947 as your name.

BAKUGAN: DEFENDERS OF THE CORE

HIDDEN ITEMS
Select Unlock Codes from Collection and enter HXV6Y7BF. Now you can enter up to 8 of your unique Bakugan Dimensions codes.

The codes unlock the following:

- 10,000 Core Energy
- Ten Vexos Passes
- Earthen Armor
- Fire Spirit
- Light Arrow
- Tornado Vortex
- Water Pillar
- Zorch Thunder

Here are 8 codes:

- 2FKRRMNCDQ
- 82D77YK6P8
- HUUH8ST7AR
- JJUZDEACXX
- QY8CLD5NJE
- TD4UMFSRW3
- YJ7RGG7WGZ
- YQLHBBSMDC

BATMAN: ARKHAM CITY

ALL BATMAN SKINS
This code allows you to start the campaign with all of the skins that you have downloaded, purchased, or unlocked. After selecting your save slot, press Left, Left, Down, Down, Left, Left, Right, Up, Up, Down at the main menu. You are then given the opportunity to select a skin.

BIG HEAD MODE
In the game, select the Cryptographic Sequencer. Hold L2 and then hold R2 to get Batman to use the device. Next, rotate the right analog stick clockwise while rotating the left analog stick counter-clockwise. Eventually, you notice Batman's head enlarge. Enemies and other characters' heads are also big. This works in Normal, Hard, and New Game +.

BATTLE: LOS ANGELES

HOLLYWOOD MODE (BIG HEADS)
Complete Campaign mode on easy difficulty.

DOUBLE-PHYSICS (INCREASES EXPLOSIONS)
Complete Campaign mode on medium difficulty.

TOUGH GUYS (INCREASES ENEMY HEALTH)
Complete Campaign mode on hard difficulty.

BATTLEFIELD: BAD COMPANY

M60
Select Unlocks from the Multiplayer menu, press Start and enter try4ndrunf0rcov3r.

QBU88
Select Unlocks from the Multiplayer menu, press Start and enter your3mynextt4rget.

UZI
Select Unlocks from the Multiplayer menu, press Start and enter cov3r1ngthecorn3r.

BAYONETTA

In Chapter 2 after Verse 3, find the phones in the plaza area. Stand in front of the appropriate phone and enter the following codes. The left phone is used for Weapons, the right phone is for Accessories, and the far phone is for Characters.

These codes require a certain amount of halos to be used. You will lose these halos immediately after entering the code.

WEAPONS

BAZILLIONS
Required Halos: 1 Million
Up, Up, Up, Up, Down, Down, Down, Down, Left, Right, Left, Right, △

PILLOW TALK
Required Halos: 1 Million
Up, Up, Up, Up, Down, Down, Down, Down, Left, Right, Left, Right, X

RODIN
Required Halos: 5 Million
Up, Up, Up, Up, Down, Down, Down, Down, Left, Right, Left, Right, L1

ACCESSORIES

BANGLE OF TIME
Required Halos: 3 Million
Up, Up, Up, Up, Down, Down, Down, Down, Left, Right, Left, Right, L2

CLIMAX BRACELET
Required Halos: 5 Million
Up, Up, Up, Up, Down, Down, Down, Down, Left, Right, Left, Right, R2

ETERNAL TESTIMONY
Required Halos: 2 Million
Up, Up, Up, Up, Down, Down, Down, Down, Left, Right, Left, Right, R1

CHARACTERS

JEANNE
Required Halos: 1 Million
Up, Up, Up, Up, Down, Down, Down, Down, Left, Right, Left, Right, ○

LITTLE ZERO
Required Halos: 5 Million
Up, Up, Up, Up, Down, Down, Down, Down, Left, Right, Left, Right, □

BEJEWELED 3

BUTTERFLIES MODE
Reach Level 5 in Zen Mode.

DIAMOND MINE MODE
In Quest Mode, unlock the second relic by completing four challenges of the first.

ICE STORM MODE
Score over 100,000 points in Lightning Mode.

POKER MODE
Reach Level 5 in Classic Mode.

BEN 10 GALACTIC RACING

KINECELARATOR
Select Promotional Codes from Extras and enter Ben, Spidermonkey, Kevin Levin, Ultimate Echo Echo.

BEN 10 ULTIMATE ALIEN: COSMIC DESTRUCTION

Note that these cheats will disable Trophies! To remove the cheats, you will need to start a new game.

1,000,000 DNA
Pause the game, select Cheats, and enter Cash.

REGENERATE HEALTH
Pause the game, select Cheats, and enter Health.

REGENERATE ENERGY
Pause the game, select Cheats, and enter Energy.

UPGRADE EVERYTHING
Pause the game, select Cheats, and enter Upgrade.

ALL LEVELS
Pause the game, select Cheats, and enter Levels.

DAMAGE

Pause the game, select Cheats, and enter Hard. When entered, the enemies cause double damage while the player inflicts about half damage.

UNLOCK FOUR ARMS

Pause the game, select Cheats, and enter Classic.

THE BIGS

START A ROOKIE WITH HIGHER STATS

When you create a rookie, name him HOT DOG. His stats will be higher than when you normally start.

BIONIC COMMANDO REARMED

The following challenge rooms can be found in the Challenge Room list. Only one code can be active at a time.

AARON SEDILLO'S CHALLENGE ROOM (CONTEST WINNER)

At the Title screen, Right, Down, Left, Up, L1, R1, ▲, ▲, ✖, ✖, Start.

EUROGAMER CHALLENGE ROOM

At the Title screen, press Down, Up, Down, Up, Left, L1, ■, L1, ■, ▲, Start.

GAMESRADAR CHALLENGE ROOM

At the Title screen, R1, ▲, ■, ■, Up, Down, L1, L1, Up, Down, Start.

IGN CHALLENGE ROOM

At the Title screen, Up, Down, ▲, ■, ■, ▲, Down, Up, L1, L1, Start.

BLACKLIGHT: TANGO DOWN

UNLOCK CODES

Select Unlock Code from the Help & Options menu, then enter the following. These tags can be used on your customized weapons.

TAG	UNLOCK CODE
Alienware Black	Alienwarec8pestU
Alienware	Al13nwa4re5acasE
AMD VISION	4MDB4quprex
AMD VISION	AMD3afrUnap
ATi	AT1hAqup7Su
Australian Flag	AUS9eT5edru
Austria Flag	AUTF6crAS5u
Belgium Flag	BELS7utHAsP
Blacklight	R41nB0wu7p3
Blacklight	Ch1pBLuS9PR
Canada Flag	CANfeprUtr5
Denmark Flag	DENdathe8HU
E3 Dog Tags	E3F6crAS5u
Famitsu Magazine	Fam1tsuprusWe2e
Finland Flag	FINw3uthEfe
France Flag	FRApRUyUT4a
Germany Flag	GERtRE4a4eS
Holland Flag	HOLb8e6UWuh
Hong Kong Flag	HOKYeQuKuw3
India Flag	INDs4u8RApr
Ireland Flag	IRE8ruGejec
Italy Flag	ITAQ7Swu9re
Jace Hall Show	J4ceH4llstuFaCh4
Japan Flag	JPNj7fazebR
Korea Flag	KORpaphA9uK
Mexico Flag	MEX5Usw2YAd
New Zealand Flag	NZLxut32eSA
Norway Flag	NOR3Waga8wa
Orange Scorpion	Ch1pMMRSc0rp

TAG	UNLOCK CODE
Order Logo Chip	Ch1p0RD3Ru02
Pink Brass Knuckles	H4rtBr34kerio4u
Portugal Flag	PORQ54aFrEY
Razer	R4z3erzu8habuC
Russia Flag	RUS7rusteXe
Singapore Flag	SINvuS8E2aC
Spain Flag	ESPChE4At5p
Storm Lion Comics	StormLion9rAVaZ2
Storm Lion Comics	St0rmLi0nB4qupre
Sweden Flag	SWEt2aPHutr
Switzerland Flag	SWIsTE8tafU
Taiwan Flag	TAW8udukUP2
United Kingdom Flag	UKv4D3phed
United States Flag	USAM3spudre
Upper Playground	UPGr0undv2FUDame
Upper Playground	UPGr0undWupraf4u
UTV Lightning Logo chip	Ch1p1GN1u0S
Yellow Teddy Bear	Denek1Ju3aceH7
Zombie Studios Logo Chip	Ch1pZ0MB1Et7

BLUR

CONCEPT 1 SERIES TII CHROME

In the Multiplayer Showroom, highlight the BMW Concept 1 Series tii and press L2, R2, L2, R2.

FORD BRONCO FULLY UPGRADED

In the Multiplayer Showroom, highlight the Ford Bronco and press L2, R2, L2, R2.

BOLT

Many of the following cheats can be toggled on/off by pausing the game and selecting Cheats.

LEVEL SELECT

Select Cheats from the Extras menu and enter Right, Up, Left, Right, Up, Right.

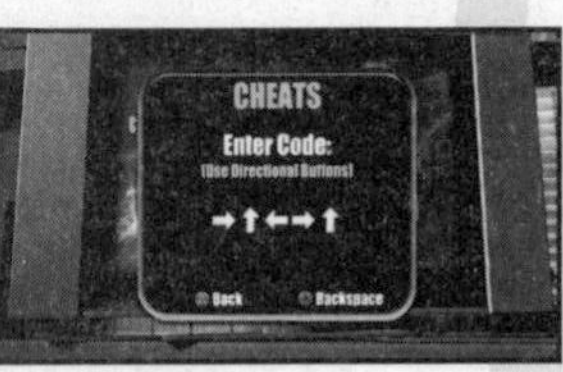

ALL MINIGAMES

Select Cheats from the Extras menu and enter Right, Up, Right, Right.

UNLIMITED ENHANCED VISION

Select Cheats from the Extras menu and enter Left, Right, Up, Down.

UNLIMITED GROUND POUND

Select Cheats from the Extras menu and enter Right, Up, Right, Up, Left, Down.

UNLIMITED INVULNERABILITY

Select Cheats from the Extras menu and enter Down, Down, Up, Left.

UNLIMITED GAS MINES

Select Cheats from the Extras menu and enter Right, Left, Left, Up, Down, Right.

UNLIMITED LASER EYES

Select Cheats from the Extras menu and enter Left, Left, Up, Right.

UNLIMITED STEALTH CAMO

Select Cheats from the Extras menu and enter Left, Down (x3).

UNLIMITED SUPERBARK

Select Cheats from the Extras menu and enter Right, Left, Left, Up, Down, Up.

BORDERLANDS 2

BORDERLANDS 1 SKIN

With a Borderlands save game on your system, veteran skins from the first game is unlocked. Find them in the Extras menu.

MINECRAFT SKINS

Go to Caustic Caverns, which is reached by cutting through Sanctuary Hole. Find the train tracks to the northwest and follow them to a big door. Move around it, turn right and hop over the blocks. Move along the left wall until you find Minecraft dirt. Break through them until a Badass Creeper appears. Defeat it to unlock the skins.

EXTRA WUBS

At the title screen, press Up, Up, Down, Down, Left, Right, Left, Right, ◉, ⊗, Start. This is a pretty useless code as Wubs do not do anything.

BROTHERS IN ARMS: HELL'S HIGHWAY

ALL CHAPTERS

Select Enter Code from the Options and enter gimmechapters.

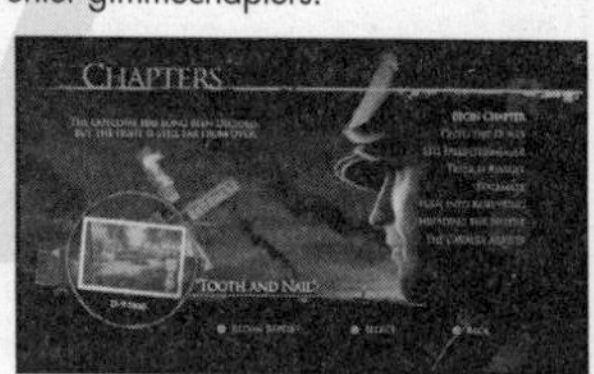

ALL RECON POINTS

Select Enter Code from the Options and enter 0zndrbicra.

KILROY DETECTOR

Select Enter Code from the Options and enter sh2vyivnzf.

TWO MULTIPLAYER SKINS

Select Enter Code from the Options and enter hi9wtpxsuk.

CALL OF DUTY: MODERN WARFARE 3

ARCADE MODE

After a complete playthrough of the game, Arcade Mode becomes available from the Main menu.

UNLOCKABLE CHEATS

After completing the game, cheats are unlocked based on how many intelligence pieces were gathered. These cheats cannot be used during Arcade Mode. These cheats may also disable the ability to earn Achievements.

CHEAT	INTEL ITEMS	DESCRIPTION
CoD Noir	2	Black and white
Photo-Negative	4	Inverses colors
Super Contrast	6	Increases contrast
Ragtime Warfare	8	Black and white, scratches fill screen, double speed, piano music
Cluster Bombs	10	Four extra grenade explosions after frag grenade explodes.
A Bad Year	15	Enemies explode into a bunch of old tires when killed.
Slow-Mo Ability	20	Melee button enables/disables slow-motion mode.
Infinite Ammo	30	Unlimited ammo and no need to reload. Doesn't work for single-shot weapons such as RPG.

CALL OF DUTY: BLACK OPS

ACCESS TERMINAL

At the main menu, alternately press aim and fire until you break free of the restraints. Find the terminal behind the chair. Here you can enter the following.

TERMINAL COMMANDS

EFFECT	COMMAND
List Commands	Help
Root directory (use ls to list codes)	cd .. [enter] cd .. [enter] cd bin [enter]
List directory	ls
List audio files and pictures	DIR
Open file	CAT [filename found from DIR command]
View a file	TYPE (filename.extension)
List CIA e-mail	mail
List login names (does not give passwords)	WHO
FI FIE FOE	FOOBAR
All Intel	3ARC INTEL
Dead Ops Arcade	DOA
Dead Ops Arcade and Presidential Zombie Mode	3ARC UNLOCK
Virtual Therapist Software	Alicia
Zork I: The Great Underground Adventure	ZORK

CIA DATA SYSTEM LOGINS

Use the following IDs and Passwords to access users' files and mail.

USER ACCOUNT	ID	PASSWORD
Alex Mason	amason	PASSWORD
Bruce Harris	bharris	GOSKINS
D. King	dking	MFK
Dr. Adrienne Smith	asmith	ROXY
Dr. Vannevar Bush	vbush	MANHATTAN
Frank Woods	fwoods	PHILLY
Grigori "Greg" Weaver	gweaver	GEDEON
J. Turner	jturner	CONDOR75
Jason Hudson	jhudson	BRYANT1950
John McCone	jmccone	BERKLEY22
Joseph Bowman	jbowman	UWD

CALL OF DUTY: WORLD AT WAR

ZOMBIE MODE

Complete Campaign mode.

USER ACCOUNT	ID	PASSWORD
President John Fitzgerald Kennedy	jfkennedy	LANCER
President Lyndon Baines Johnson	lbjohnson	LADYBIRD
President Richard Nixon	rnixon	CHECKERS
Richard Helms	rhelms	LEROSEY
Richard Kain	rkain	SUNWU
Ryan Jackson	rjackson	SAINTBRIDGET
T. Walker	twalker	RADI0
Terrance Brooks	tbrooks	LAUREN
William Raborn	wraborn	BROMLOW

CARS 2: THE VIDEO GAME

ALL MODES AND TRACKS

Select Enter Codes from the Options and enter 959595.

LASER GUIDED

Select Enter Codes from the Options and enter 123456. Select Cheats to toggle the cheat on and off.

UNLIMITED ENERGY

Select Enter Codes from the Options and enter 721953. Select Cheats to toggle the cheat on and off.

CASTLEVANIA: LORDS OF SHADOW

CHEAT MENU

At a loading screen, press Up, Up, Down, Down, Left, Right, Left, Right, Circle, X. The cheats can be found in the Extra Options. Activating any cheats disables saving and Trophies.

SNAKE OUTFIT

After completing the game, go to the Extras menu and toggle on Solid Eye and Bandanna.

VAMPIRE WARGAME

During Chapter 6-3, Castle Hall, complete the Vampire Wargame to unlock this mini-game in the Extras menu.

CATHERINE

NEW RAPUNZEL STAGES

At the title screen, press Up, Down, Down, Up, Up, Up, Down, Down, Down, Down, Right. Re-enter the code to disable.

CONAN

PROMOTIONAL UNLOCKABLE #1 CONCEPT ART

Go to the Concept Art menu in Extras and press Up, Down, Up, Down, Left, Right, Left, Right, Square, Triangle.

PROMOTIONAL UNLOCKABLE #2 CONCEPT ART

Go to the Concept Art menu in Extras and press Up, Down, Left, Left, Square, Square, Square.

PROMOTIONAL UNLOCKABLE #3 CONCEPT ART

Go to the Concept Art menu in Extras and press L3, L3, Triangle, Triangle, Square, R3.

PROMOTIONAL UNLOCKABLE #4 CONCEPT ART

Go to the Concept Art menu in Extras and press Left, Square, Left, Triangle, Down, R3, R3.

PROMOTIONAL UNLOCKABLE #5 CONCEPT ART

Go to the Concept Art menu in Extras and press Right, Right, Left, Left, Up, Down, Up, Down, Square, Square.

PROMOTIONAL UNLOCKABLE #6 CONCEPT ART

Go to the Concept Art menu in Extras and press Triangle, Triangle, L3, Square, Square, R3, Up, Down.

CRYSIS 2

HIDDEN MINIGAME

At the credits, press R2 five times.

DAMNATION

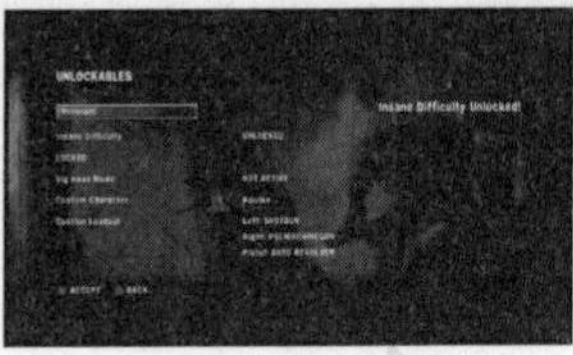

INSANE DIFFICULTY
Select Enter Code from Unlockables and enter Revenant.

VORPAL MECHANICAL REPEATER
Select Enter Code from Unlockables and enter BlowOffSomeSteam.

BIG HEAD MODE
Select Enter Code from Unlockables and enter LincolnsTopHat.

CUSTOM CHARACTERS
Select Enter Code from Unlockables and enter PeoplePerson.

CUSTOM LOADOUT
Select Enter Code from Unlockables and enter LockNLoad.

DARKSIDERS

HARVESTER FOR 0 SOULS
Pause the game and select Enter Code from the Options. Enter The Hollow Lord.

DEAD OR ALIVE 5

AKIRA YUKI
Defeat Akira in Story mode.

SARAH BRYANT
Defeat Sarah in Story mode.

GEN FU
Complete Eliot's stage in Story mode.

PAI CHAN
Get 100 titles.

ALPHA-152
Get 300 titles

TRUE FIGHTER COURSES
Complete Champ course in Arcade, Survival, or Time Attack.

MASTER COURSE
Complete True Fighter course in Arcade, Survival, or Time Attack.

LEGEND COURSE
Complete Master course in Arcade, Survival, or Time Attack.

CHANGE HAIRSTYLE FOR SOME CHARACTERS
At the costume select, highlight a character, hold L1 or R1 along with any Hold, Punch, or Kick.

CHANGE ACCESSORY FOR SOME CHARACTERS
At the costume select, highlight a character, and hold any Hold, Punch, or Kick.

CHRISTIE SWIMSUIT
Complete the Legend course in Time Attack (Solo) with Christie, without using a Continue.

LISA SWIMSUIT
Complete the Legend Course in Survival (Solo) with Lisa.

TINA SWIMSUIT
Complete the Legend Course in Arcade (Solo) with Tina, without using a Continue.

KASUMI BLACK SUIT
Complete the True Kasumi stage in Story mode.

KASUMI KIMONO
Complete the Kasumi vs Christie battle in the True Kasumi stage in Story mode.

DEAD RISING 2

KNIGHT ARMOR
Wearing this armor doubles Chuck's health. When his health falls below half, though, the armor is destroyed.

ARMOR NAME	OBTAIN
Full Beard Moustache	Found in the back of Wave of Style, located in Royal Flush Plaza.
Knight Armor	Finish the game with an "S" ending.

Knight Boots	Purchase for $2,000,000 at Moe's Maginations pawnshop on the Platinum Strip.
Knight Helmet	Rescue Jack in "Meet the Family" and win at poker in "Ante Up."

UNLOCKABLE OUTFITS

The following items are unlocked by performing the corresponding task.

ITEM	OBTAINED BY
Bowling Shirt, Diner Waitress, Hunting Jacket, and Overalls	Import a save game from Case Zero.
Champion Jacket	Earn the Win Big! Trophy. Get this by finishing in first place in a TIR Episode.
Dealer Outfit	Earn Chuck Greene: Cross Dresser? Trophy. Get this by changing into all the clothes in the game.
Hockey Mask	Earn the Head Trauma Trophy. Get this by using every type of melee weapon on a zombie.
Orange Prison Outfit	Earn the Judge, Jury and Executioner Trophy. Get this by killing 10 psychos.
Tattered Clothes	Earn the Zombie Fu Trophy. Get this by killing 1000 zombies barehanded.
TIR Helmet	Earn $1,000,000 in Terror is Reality.
TIR Outfit	Earn $5,000,000 in Terror is Reality.
Willamette Mall Security Uniform	Earn Hero of Fortune City Trophy. Get this by rescuing 50 survivors.

DEAD SPACE

REFILL STASIS AND KINESIS ENERGY

Pause the game and press ■, ▲, ▲, ■, ▲.

REFILL OXYGEN

Pause the game and press ■, ■, ▲ (x3).

ADD 2 POWER NODES

Pause the game and press ▲, ■ (x3), ▲. This code can only be used once.

ADD 5 POWER NODES

Pause the game and press ▲, ■, ▲, ■, ■, ▲, ■, ■, ▲, ■, ■, ▲. This code can only be used once.

1,000 CREDITS

Pause the game and press ■ (x3), ▲, ■. This code can only be used once.

2,000 CREDITS

Pause the game and press ■ (x3), ▲, ▲. This code can only be used once.

5,000 CREDITS

Pause the game and press ■ (x3), ▲, ■, ▲. This code can only be used once.

10,000 CREDITS

Pause the game and press ■, ▲ (x3), ■, ■, ▲. This code can only be used once.

DEAD SPACE IGNITION

HACKER SUIT

Complete the game in single-player mode.

DIRT 2

Win the given events to earn the following cars:

VEHICLE	EVENT
Ford RS200 Evolution	Rally Cross World Tour
Toyota Stadium Truck	Landrush World Tour
Mitsubishi Pajero Dakar 1993	Raid World Tour
Dallenbach Special	Trailblazer World Tour
1995 Subaru Impreza WRX STi	Colin McRae Challenge
Colin McRae R4 [X Games]	X Games Europe
Mitsubishi Lancer Evolution X [X Games]	X Games Asia
Subaru Impreza WRX STi [X Games]	X Games America
Ford Escort MKII and MG Metro 6R4	All X Games events

DISGAEA 4: A PROMISE UNFORGOTTEN

EXTRA CHARACTERS

After completing the story, extra battles become available from the Senate. Clear these to unlock the following characters.

CHARACTER	CLEAR EXTRA BATTLE
Axel	1
Flonne	2
Raspberyl	3
Etna	4
Laharl	5
Asagi	6
Kurtis	7
Zetta	9

DJ HERO

Select Cheats from Options and enter the following. Some codes will disable high scores and progress. Cheats cannot be used in tutorials and online.

UNLOCK ALL CONTENT
Enter tol0.

ALL CHARACTER ITEMS
Enter uNA2.

ALL VENUES
Enter Wv1u.

ALL DECKS
Enter LAuP.

ALL HEADPHONES
Enter 62Db.

ALL MIXES
Enter 82xl.

AUTO SCRATCH
Enter it6j.

AUTO EFFECTS DIAL
Enter ab1l.

AUTO FADER
Enter sl5d.

AUTO TAPPER
Enter zith.

AUTO WIN EUPHORIA
Enter r3a9.

BLANK PLINTHS
Enter ipr0.

HAMSTER SWITCH
Enter 7geo.

HYPER DECK MODE
Enter 76st.

SHORT DECK
Enter 51uc.

BLACK AND WHITE
Enter b!99.

EDGE EFFECT
Enter 2u4u.

INVISIBLE DJ
Enter oh5t.

MIDAS
Enter 4pe5.

PITCH BLACK OUT
Enter d4kr.

PLAY IN THE BEDROOM
Enter g7nh.

RAINBOW
Enter ?jy!.

ANY DJ, ANY SETLIST
Enter 0jj8.

DAFT PUNK'S CONTENT
Enter d1g?.

DJ AM'S CONTENT
Enter k07u.

DJ JAZZY JEFF'S CONTENT
Enter n1fz.

DJ SHADOW'S CONTENT
Enter omxv.

DJ Z-TRIP'S CONTENT
Enter 5rtg.

GRANDMASTER FLASH'S CONTENT
Enter ami8.

DJ HERO 2

ALL BONUS CONTENT
Select Cheats from the Options. Choose Retail Cheats and enter VIP Pass.

DAVID GUETTA
Select Cheats from the Options. Choose Retail Cheats and enter Guetta Blaster.

DEADMAU5
Select Cheats from the Options. Choose Retail Cheats and enter Open The Trap.

INVISIBLE DJ
Select Cheats from the Options. Choose Retail Cheats and enter Now You See Me.

AUTO CROSSFADE
Select Cheats from the Options. Choose Retail Cheats and enter I Hate Crossfading. This disables Leaderboards.

AUTO SCRATCH
Select Cheats from the Options. Choose Retail Cheats and enter Soothing. This disables Leaderboards.

AUTO TAP
Select Cheats from the Options. Choose Retail Cheats and enter Look No Hands! This disables Leaderboards.

DOUBLE DRAGON: NEON

PLAY AS A RO-BRO

At the stage select, hold L1 + L2 + L3 + R1 + R2 + R3 + Select + Start. Enter again to return to normal.

CONCEPT ART GALLERY

Complete the game to unlock this gallery at the main menu.

DRAGON DIFFICULTY

Defeat the game on Normal difficulty.

DOUBLE DRAGON DIFFICULTY

Defeat the game on Dragon difficulty.

DRAGON AGE II

STAFF OF PARTHALAN

Create a BioWare Social account and sign up for the newsletter.

HAYDER'S RAZOR

Complete the Dragon Age II demo while logged in to your EA Account.

HINDSIGHT

Visit the Penny Arcade page from the Dragon Age 2 website and click on "Get your DAII Penny Arcade Belt."

SER ISAAC'S ARMOR

Put in Dead Space 2, sign in with your EA Account and then insert Dragon Age II and sign in with that same EA Account.

BLOOD DRAGON ARMOR

Have a save game from Dragon Age Origins with the Blood Dragon Armor unlocked on your hard drive.

DRIVER: SAN FRANCISCO

MOVIE SCENE CHALLENGES

As you collect the 130 Movie Tokens in the game, Movie Scene Challenges are unlocked as shown below.

MOVIE SCENE CHALLENGE	VEHICLE GIVEN	# MOVIE TOKENS
Gone In 60 Seconds	1973 Ford Mustang Mach I	10
Starsky & Hutch	1974 Dodge Monaco Cop	20
Bullitt	1968 Ford Mustang GT Fastback	30
The French Connection	1971 Pontiac LeMans	40
Blues Brothers	1974 Dodge Monaco	50
Cannonball Run	1978 Lamborghini Countach LP400S	60
Dukes of Hazard	1969 Dodge Charger R/T	70
Vanishing Point	1970 Dodge Challenger R/T	80
The Driver	1965 Chevrolet S-10	90
Redline	2011 McLaren MP4-12C	100
Smokey & The Bandit	1977 Pontiac TransAm Firebird	110
Test Drive	1987 RUF CT-R Yellow Bird	120
The Italian Job	1972 Lamborghini Miura	130

DUKE NUKEM FOREVER

CLUB DOOR CODE

Behind the bar in the club, there is a door that requires a code to get in. Enter 4768.

CHEATS

Defeating the game on at least Normal Difficulty gives you the ability to activate the following cheats in Extras.

- Duke 3D Freeze Ray
- Grayscale Mode
- Head Scale
- Infinite Ammo
- Instagib
- Invincibility
- Mirror Mode

EARTH DEFENSE FORCE: INSECT ARMAGEDDON

HIDDEN IMAGES IN GALLERY

Select Gallery from the Extras menu. At the gallery press ■, ■, ▲, ■, L1, R1.

FINAL FANTASY XIII-2

LIGHTNING THEME

This theme is unlocked if you have a save game for Final Fantasy XIII on your console.

ANOTHER LIGHTNING THEME

Earn the Master of Time Trophy.

MOG THEME

Earn the Fair Fighter Trophy.

NOEL THEME

Earn the Chronosavior Trophy.

SERAH THEME

Earn the Defragmented Trophy.

FROGGER: HYPER ARCADE EDITION

CONTRA STYLE

At the style select, highlight Contra and enter Up, Up, Down, Down, Left, Right, Left, Right, ●, ✕.

GOD OF WAR III

TREASURES OF THE GODS

These items can be turned on and off after you've completed the game. Note, however, that using these items disables Trophies.

TREASURE	DESCRIPTION	LOCATION
Zeus' Eagle	Grants infinite Rage of Sparta.	Climb the vines on the wall east of Gaia's heart. The treasure is located beneath an ancient mural.
Hades' Helm	Maxes Health, Magic, and Item Meters.	After defeating Hades and diving into the River Styx, search the bottom for this treasure.
Helios' Shield	Triples the number on the Hits Counter.	After defeating Helios, search the area to the right.
Hermes' Coin	Kratos collects 10 times the amount of Red Orbs.	After Kratos and Hermes fall and land in the damaged room, search behind the head of the demolished Athena Statue.
Hercules' Shoulder Guard	Decreases damage taken by one-third.	After defeating Hercules, search the bottom of the pool beneath his body.
Poseidon's Conch Shell	Grants infinite Magic.	After freeing the frightened Princess, this treasure is near an item chest.
Aphrodite's Garter	Lets Kratos continue to use Athena's Blades.	Fly behind Aphrodite's bed to find this rare treasure.
Hephaestus' Ring	Kratos automatically wins all context-sensitive attacks.	Finish off Hephaestus and search his cooling pool for the ring.

TREASURE	DESCRIPTION	LOCATION
Daedalus' Schematics	Grants infinite item use.	Found in Daedalus' Workshop after lowering two item chests with a pull of a lever.
Hera's Chalice	Causes your Health Meter to slowly drain over time; it never completely empites.	It's located to the left of where Kratos enters Hera's Garden and a Save Altair.

CHAOS DIFFICULTY, CHALLENGES OF OLYMPUS, & FEAR KRATOS COSTUME

Complete the game on any difficulty.

COMBAT ARENA

Complete the Challenges of Olympus.

GOD OF WAR SAGA

GOD OF WAR III

CHALLENGES OF OLYMPUS

Defeat the game.

COMBAT ARENA

Defeat the challenges.

GOD OF WAR: CHAINS OF OLYMPUS

CHALLENGE OF HADES AND GOD MODE

Complete the game.

THE LOST LEVELS

Complete the Challenge of Hades.

Unlockable Costumes

Costumes can selected only when selecting a new game, (must beat God mode to use costumes in God mode)

SPUD OF WAR COSTUME

Complete the game. Select this costume when starting a new game. The skill for this costume is Magic.

MCKRATOS COSTUME

Complete the Challenge of Hades. Select this costume when starting a new game. The skill for this costume is Attack.

MIME OF WAR COSTUME

Complete the game on God Mode. Select this costume when starting a new game. The skill for this costume is Red Orbs.

GOD OF WAR: GHOST OF SPARTA

THE TEMPLE OF ZEUS, COMBAT ARENA, AND GOD MODE

Complete the game.

DEIMOS AND GOD ARMOR COSTUMES

Complete the game.

GRAVE DIGGER COSTUME

Complete the Temple of Zeus.

ROBOTOS COSTUME

Purchase in the Temple of Zeus for 250,000 Red Orbs.

GHOST OF SPARTA COSTUME

Complete the game on God Mode.

GOLDENEYE 007: RELOADED

BLACK MOONRAKER SKIN IN MULTIPLAYER

Select Cheat Codes from the Extras menu and enter las3r3ras3r.

INVISIBILITY AND TAG IN MULTIPLAYER

Select Cheat Codes from the Extras menu and enter f11ypr3load3ed.

PAINTBALL MODE IN MULTIPLAYER

Select Cheat Codes from the Extras menu and enter wr1t1ng1s0nth3wa11.

ALL MI6 OPS WITH 4-STAR RATINGS

Select Cheat Codes from the Extras menu and enter Quimbecile. Then, play one of the missions. Any missions you had already play will remain the rating that you earned.

GRAND THEFT AUTO IV

CHEATS

Call the following phone numbers with Niko's phone to activate the cheats. Some cheats may affect the missions and achievements.

VEHICLE	PHONE NUMBER
Change weather	468-555-0100
Get weapons	486-555-0100
Get different weapons	486-555-0150
Raise wanted level	267-555-0150
Remove wanted level	267-555-0100
Restore armor	362-555-0100
Restore health	482-555-0100
Restore armor, health, and ammo	482-555-0100

SPAWN VEHICLES

Call the following phone numbers with Niko's phone to spawn the corresponding vehicle.

VEHICLE	PHONE NUMBER
Annihilator	359-555-0100
Cognoscenti	227-555-0142
Comet	227-555-0175
FIB Buffalo	227-555-0100

VEHICLE	PHONE NUMBER
Jetmax	938-555-0100
NRG-900	625-555-0100
Sanchez	625-555-0150
SuperGT	227-555-0168

VEHICLE	PHONE NUMBER
Turismo	227-555-0147

MAP LOCATIONS

Access a computer in-game and enter the following URL: www.whattheydonotwantyoutoknow.com.

GRAND THEFT AUTO IV: THE BALLAD OF GAY TONY

CHEATS

Call the following phone numbers with your phone to activate the cheats. Some cheats may affect the missions and achievements.

CHEAT	PHONE NUMBER
Get weapons	486-555-0100
Get different weapons	486-555-0150
Raise wanted level	267-555-0150
Remove wanted level	267-555-0100
Restore armor	362-555-0100

CHEAT	PHONE NUMBER
Restore armor, health, and ammo	482-555-0100
Sniper uses exploding bullets	486-555-2526
Super Punch	276-555-2666
Parachute	359-555-7272
Change Weather	468-555-0100

SPAWN VEHICLES

Call the following phone numbers with your phone to spawn the corresponding vehicle.

VEHICLE	PHONE NUMBER
Akuma	625-555-0200
Annihilator	359-555-0100
APC	272-555-8265
Bullet GT	227-555-9666
Buzzard	359-555-2899
Cognoscenti	227-555-0142
Comet	227-555-0175
FIB Buffalo	227-555-0100

VEHICLE	PHONE NUMBER
Floater	938-555-0150
Jetmax	938-555-0100
NRG-900	625-555-0100
Sanchez	625-555-0150
Super GT	227-555-0168
Turismo	227-555-0147
Vader	625-555-3273

GRAND THEFT AUTO IV: THE LOST AND DAMNED

SPAWN VEHICLES

Call the following phone numbers with your phone to spawn the corresponding vehicle.

VEHICLE	PHONE NUMBER
Annihilator	359-555-0100
Burrito	826-555-0150
Cognoscenti	227-555-0142
Comet	227-555-0175
Double T	245-555-0125
FIB Buffalo	227-555-0100
Hakuchou	245-555-0199

VEHICLE	PHONE NUMBER
Hexer	245-555-0150
Innovation	245-555-0100
Jetmax	938-555-0100
NRG-900	625-555-0100
Sanchez	625-555-0150
Slamvan	826-555-0100
Turismo	227-555-0147

GRAN TURISMO 5

B LICENSE TESTS

Buy a car.

A LICENSE TESTS

Reach Level 3 and complete the B License Tests.

INTERNATIONAL C LICENSE TESTS

Reach Level 6 and complete the A License Tests.

INTERNATIONAL B LICENSE TESTS

Reach Level 9 and complete the International C License Tests.

INTERNATIONAL A LICENSE TESTS

Reach Level 12 and complete the International B License Tests.

S LICENSE TESTS

Reach Level 15 and complete the International A License Tests.

TOP GEAR TEST TRACK

Complete Top Gear Challenge Beginner with gold.

NÜRBURGRING NORDSCHLEIFE

Complete all AMG Challenge Intermediate with at least bronze.

NÜRBURGRING NORDSCHLEIFE 4-HOUR CIRCUIT WITHOUT TIME AND WEATHER CHANGE

Complete all AMG Challenge Intermediate with at least silver.

NÜRBURGRING NORDSCHLEIFE 24-HOUR CIRCUIT WITH TIME AND WEATHER CHANGE

Complete all AMG Challenge Intermediate with gold.

GREG HASTINGS PAINTBALL 2

GUN AND PRO PLAYER

At any time, hold R2 and press Up, Up, Down, Right, Left, Left, Right, Up.

GRID

ALL DRIFT CARS
Select Bonus Codes from the Options. Then choose Enter Code and enter TUN58396.

ALL MUSCLE CARS
Select Bonus Codes from the Options. Then choose Enter Code and enter MUS59279.

BUCHBINDER EMOTIONAL ENGINEERING BMW 320SI
Select Bonus Codes from the Options. Then choose Enter Code and enter F93857372. You can use this in Race Day or in GRID World once you've started your own team.

EBAY MOTORS MUSTANG
Select Bonus Codes from the Options. Then choose Enter Code and enter DAFJ55E01473M0. You can use this in Race Day or in GRID World once you've started your own team.

GAMESTATION BMW 320SI
Select Bonus Codes from the Options. Then choose Enter Code and enter G29782655. You can use this in Race Day or in GRID World once you've started your own team.

MICROMANIA PAGANI ZONDA R
Select Bonus Codes from the Options. Then choose Enter Code and enter M38572343. You can use this in Race Day or in GRID World once you've started your own team.

PLAY.COM ASTON MARTIN DBR9
Select Bonus Codes from the Options. Then choose Enter Code and enter P47203845. You can use this in Race Day or in GRID World once you've started your own team.

GUITAR HERO 5

ALL HOPOS
Select Input Cheats from the Options menu and enter Green, Green, Blue, Green, Green, Green, Yellow, Green.

ALWAYS SLIDE
Select Input Cheats from the Options menu and enter Green, Green, Red, Red, Yellow, Blue, Yellow, Blue.

AUTO KICK
Select Input Cheats from the Options menu and enter Yellow, Green, Red, Blue, Blue, Blue, Blue, Red.

FOCUS MODE
Select Input Cheats from the Options menu and enter Yellow, Green, Red, Green, Yellow, Blue, Green, Green.

HUD FREE MODE
Select Input Cheats from the Options menu and enter Green, Red, Green, Green, Yellow, Green, Green, Green.

PERFORMANCE MODE
Select Input Cheats from the Options menu and enter Yellow, Yellow, Blue, Red, Blue, Green, Red, Red.

AIR INSTRUMENTS
Select Input Cheats from the Options menu and enter Red, Red, Blue, Yellow, Green, Green, Green, Yellow.

INVISIBLE ROCKER
Select Input Cheats from the Options menu and enter Green, Red, Yellow, Yellow, Yellow, Blue, Blue, Green.

ALL CHARACTERS
Select Input Cheats from the Options menu and enter Blue, Blue, Green, Green, Red, Green, Red, Yellow.

CONTEST WINNER 1
Select Input Cheats from the Options menu and enter Green, Green, Red, Red, Yellow, Red, Yellow, Blue.

GUITAR HERO: AEROSMITH

Select Cheats from the Options menu and enter the following. To do this, strum the guitar with the given buttons held. For example, if it says Yellow + Orange, hold Yellow and Orange as you strum. Air Guitar, Precision Mode, and Performance Mode can be toggled on and off from the Cheats menu. You can also change between five different levels of Hyperspeed at this menu.

ALL SONGS
Red + Yellow, Green + Red, Green + Red, Red + Yellow, Red + Yellow, Green + Red, Red + Yellow, Red + Yellow, Green + Red, Green + Red, Red + Yellow, Red + Yellow, Green + Red, Red + Yellow, Red + Blue. This code does not unlock Pandora's Box.

AIR GUITAR
Red + Yellow, Green + Red, Red + Yellow, Red + Yellow, Red + Blue, Red + Blue, Red + Blue, Red + Blue, Red + Blue, Yellow + Blue, Yellow + Blue, Yellow + Orange

HYPERSPEED

Yellow + Orange, Yellow + Orange, Yellow + Orange, Yellow + Orange, Yellow + Orange, Red + Yellow, Red + Yellow, Red + Yellow, Red + Yellow, Red + Blue, Red + Blue, Red + Blue, Red + Blue, Red + Blue, Yellow + Blue, Yellow + Orange, Yellow + Orange.

NO FAIL

Select Cheats from the Options. Choose Enter Cheat and enter Green + Red, Blue, Green + Red, Green + Yellow, Blue, Green + Yellow, Red + Yellow, Orange, Red + Yellow, Green + Yellow, Yellow, Green + Yellow, Green + Red.

PERFORMANCE MODE

Green + Red, Green + Red, Red + Orange, Red + Blue, Green + Red, Green + Red, Red + Orange, Red + Blue.

PRECISION MODE

Red + Yellow, Red + Blue, Red + Blue, Red + Yellow, Red + Yellow, Yellow + Blue, Yellow + Blue, Yellow + Blue, Red + Blue, Red + Yellow, Red + Blue, Red + Blue, Red + Yellow, Red + Yellow, Yellow + Blue, Yellow + Blue, Yellow + Blue, Red + Blue.

GUITAR HERO: METALLICA

Once entered, the cheats must be activated in the Cheats menu.

METALLICA COSTUMES

Select Cheats from Settings and enter Green, Red, Yellow, Blue, Blue, Yellow, Red, Green.

HYPERSPEED

Select Cheats from Settings and enter Green, Blue, Red, Yellow, Yellow, Red, Green, Green.

PERFORMANCE MODE

Select Cheats from Settings and enter Yellow, Yellow, Blue, Red, Blue, Green, Red, Red.

INVISIBLE ROCKER

Select Cheats from Settings and enter Green, Red, Yellow (x3), Blue, Blue, Green.

AIR INSTRUMENTS

Select Cheats from Settings and enter Red, Red, Blue, Yellow, Green (x3), Yellow.

ALWAYS DRUM FILL

Select Cheats from Settings and enter Red (x3), Blue, Blue, Green, Green, Yellow.

AUTO KICK

Select Cheats from Settings and enter Yellow, Green, Red, Blue (x4), Red. With this cheat activated, the bass pedal is automatically hit.

ALWAYS SLIDE

Select Cheats from Settings and enter Green, Green, Red, Red, Yellow, Red, Yellow, Blue. All Guitar Notes Become Touch Pad Sliding Notes.

BLACK HIGHWAY

Select Cheats from Settings and enter Yellow, Red, Green, Red, Green, Red, Red, Blue.

FLAME COLOR

Select Cheats from Settings and enter Green, Red, Green, Blue, Red, Red, Yellow, Blue.

GEM COLOR

Select Cheats from Settings and enter Blue, Red, Red, Green, Red, Green, Red, Yellow.

STAR COLOR

Select Cheats from Settings and enter Press Red, Red, Yellow, Red, Blue, Red, Red, Blue.

ADDITIONAL LINE 6 TONES

Select Cheats from Settings and enter Green, Red, Yellow, Blue, Red, Yellow, Blue, Green.

VOCAL FIREBALL

Select Cheats from Settings and enter Red, Green, Green, Yellow, Blue, Green, Yellow, Green.

GUITAR HERO: SMASH HITS

ALWAYS DRUM FILL

Select Cheats from the Options menu and enter Green, Green, Red, Red, Blue, Blue, Yellow, Yellow.

ALWAYS SLIDE

Select Cheats from the Options menu and enter Blue, Yellow, Red, Green, Blue, Green, Green, Yellow.

AIR INSTRUMENTS

Select Cheats from the Options menu and enter Yellow, Red, Blue, Green, Yellow, Red, Red, Red.

INVISIBLE ROCKER

Select Cheats from the Options menu and enter Blue, Red, Red, Red, Red, Yellow, Blue, Green.

PERFORMANCE MODE
Select Cheats from the Options menu and enter Blue, Red, Yellow, Yellow, Red, Red, Yellow, Yellow.

HYPERSPEED
Select Cheats from the Options menu and enter Red, Green, Blue, Yellow, Green, Yellow, Red, Red. This unlocks the Hyperguitar, Hyperbass, and Hyperdrums cheats.

AUTO KICK
Select Cheats from the Options menu and enter Blue, Green, Red, Yellow, Red, Yellow, Red, Yellow.

GEM COLOR
Select Cheats from the Options menu and enter Red, Red, Red, Blue, Blue, Blue, Yellow, Green.

FLAME COLOR
Select Cheats from the Options menu and enter Yellow, Blue, Red, Green, Yellow, Red, Green, Blue.

STAR COLOR
Select Cheats from the Options menu and enter Green, Red, Green, Yellow, Green, Blue, Yellow, Red.

VOCAL FIREBALL
Select Cheats from the Options menu and enter Green, Blue, Red, Red, Yellow, Yellow, Blue, Blue.

EXTRA LINE 6 TONES
Select Cheats from the Options menu and enter Green, Red, Yellow, Blue, Red, Yellow, Blue, Green.

GUITAR HERO: WARRIORS OF ROCK

Select Extras from Options menu to toggle the following on and off. Note, however, that some cheats will disable Trophies.

ALL CHARACTERS
Select Cheats from the Options menu and enter Blue, Green, Green, Red, Green, Red, Yellow, Blue.

ALL VENUES
Select Cheats from the Options menu and enter Red, Blue, Blue, Red, Red, Blue, Blue, Red.

ALWAYS SLIDE
Select Cheats from the Options menu and enter Blue, Green, Green, Red, Red, Yellow, Blue, Yellow.

ALL HOPOS
Select Cheats from the Options menu and enter Green (x3), Blue, Green (x3), Yellow. With this code, most notes become hammer-ons (HO) or pull-offs (PO).

INVISIBLE ROCKER
Select Cheats from the Options menu and enter Green, Green, Red, Yellow (x3), Blue, Blue.

AIR INSTRUMENTS
Select Cheats from the Options menu and enter Yellow, Red, Red, Blue, Yellow, Green (x3).

FOCUS MODE
Select Cheats from the Options menu and enter Green, Yellow, Green, Red, Green, Yellow, Blue, Green. This code removes the busy background.

NO HUD MODE
Select Cheats from the Options menu and enter Green, Green, Red, Green, Green, Yellow, Green, Green.

PERFORMANCE MODE
Select Cheats from the Options menu and enter Red, Yellow, Yellow, Blue, Red, Blue, Green, Red.

COLOR SHUFFLE
Select Cheats from the Options menu and enter Blue, Green, Blue, Red, Yellow, Green, Red, Yellow.

MIRROR GEMS
Select Cheats from the Options menu and enter Blue, Blue, Red, Blue, Green, Green, Red, Green.

RANDOM GEMS
Select Cheats from the Options menu and enter Green, Green, Red, Red, Yellow, Red, Yellow, Blue.

GUITAR HERO WORLD TOUR

The following cheats can be toggled on and off at the Cheats menu.

QUICKPLAY SONGS
Select Cheats from the Options menu, choose Enter New Cheat and press Blue, Blue, Red, Green, Green, Blue, Blue, Yellow.

ALWAYS SLIDE
Select Cheats from the Options menu, choose Enter New Cheat and press Green, Green, Red, Red, Yellow, Red, Yellow, Blue.

\AT&T BALLPARK
Select Cheats from the Options menu, choose Enter New Cheat and press Yellow, Green, Red, Red, Green, Blue, Red, Yellow.

AUTO KICK
Select Cheats from the Options menu, choose Enter New Cheat and press Yellow, Green, Red, Blue (x4), Red.

EXTRA LINE 6 TONES

Select Cheats from the Options menu, choose Enter New Cheat and press Green, Red, Yellow, Blue, Red, Yellow, Blue, Green.

FLAME COLOR

Select Cheats from the Options menu, choose Enter New Cheat and press Green, Red, Green, Blue, Red, Red, Yellow, Blue.

GEM COLOR

Select Cheats from the Options menu, choose Enter New Cheat and press Blue, Red, Red, Green, Red, Green, Red, Yellow.

STAR COLOR

Select Cheats from the Options menu, choose Enter New Cheat and press Red, Red, Yellow, Red, Blue, Red, Red, Blue.

AIR INSTRUMENTS

Select Cheats from the Options menu, choose Enter New Cheat and press Red, Red, Blue, Yellow, Green (x3), Yellow.

HYPERSPEED

Select Cheats from the Options menu, choose Enter New Cheat and press Green, Blue, Red, Yellow, Yellow, Red, Green, Green. These show up in the menu as HyperGuitar, HyperBass, and HyperDrums.

PERFORMANCE MODE

Select Cheats from the Options menu, choose Enter New Cheat and press Yellow, Yellow, Blue, Red, Blue, Green, Red, Red.

INVISIBLE ROCKER

Select Cheats from the Options menu, choose Enter New Cheat and press Green, Red, Yellow (x3), Blue, Blue, Green.

VOCAL FIREBALL

Select Cheats from the Options menu, choose Enter New Cheat and press Red, Green, Green, Yellow, Blue, Green, Yellow, Green.

AARON STEELE!

Select Cheats from the Options menu, choose Enter New Cheat and press Blue, Red, Yellow (x5), Green.

JONNY VIPER

Select Cheats from the Options menu, choose Enter New Cheat and press Blue, Red, Blue, Blue, Yellow (x3), Green.

NICK

Select Cheats from the Options menu, choose Enter New Cheat and press Green, Red, Blue, Green, Red, Blue, Blue, Green.

RINA

Select Cheats from the Options menu, choose Enter New Cheat and press Blue, Red, Green, Green, Yellow (x3), Green.

HARRY POTTER AND THE DEATHLY HALLOWS: PART 1

SUPER STRENGTH POTIONS

Select Unlock Menu from the Options and enter ✕, Left, Right, ✕, R2, R1.

ELITE CHALLENGES

Select Unlock Menu from the Options and enter △, Up, ✕, L2, R2, ✕.

AUGMENTED REALITY CHEAT FROM BOX (PROTEGO TOTALUM)

Select Unlock Menu from the Options and enter △, ○, Up, Left, R2, and Right

HEROES OVER EUROPE

Cheats disable saving and Trophies.

CHEAT MODE

At the main menu, press △, L2, Left on d-pad, R2, Right on d-pad, L1.

ALL MISSIONS

At the main menu, press Up on right analog stick, Down on right analog stick, L1, R1, Left on right analog stick, Right on right analog stick.

ALL PLANES

At the main menu, press L2, Left on right analog stick, R2, Right on right analog stick, L1, △.

BF109 G10

At the main menu, press Left on left analog stick, Right on left analog stick, L2, R2, Left on right analog stick, Right on right analog stick.

SPITFIRE MK IX-C

At the main menu, press Up on left analog stick, Down on left analog stick, L2, R2, Up on right analog stick, Down on right analog stick.

JIMMIE JOHNSON'S ANYTHING WITH AN ENGINE

ALL RACERS

At the main menu, hold Right Trigger + Left Trigger + Right Bumper + Left Bumper and press Up, Right, Down, Left, Up, Left, Down, Right, click the Right Thumbstick, click the Left Thumbstick.

JUST DANCE 3

BARBRA STREISAND SPECIAL CHOREOGRAPHY

At the title screen (Press Start), press Up, Up, Down, Down, Left, Right, Left, Right.

THE KING OF FIGHTERS XIII

ALTERNATE COSTUMES AND COLOR PALETTES

Before selecting the color for the following fighters, press Select to get the alternate outfit.

FIGHTER	OUTFIT
Andy	Ninja Mask
Elisabeth	KOF XI
Joe	Tiger-Striped Boxers
K'	Dual-Colored
Kyo	Orochi Saga
Raiden	Big Bear
Ralf	Camouflage
Takuma	Mr. Karate
Yuri	Braided Ponytail

EXTRA COLORS IN COLOR EDIT

Extra colors become available in color edit mode for every ten times you select a specific character.

BILLY KANE

Successfully pull off 2 target actions in each fight in Arcade Mode until Billy Kane challenges you. Defeat him to unlock him.

SAIKI

Successfully pull off 5 target actions in each fight in Arcade Mode until Saiki challenges you. Defeat him to unlock him.

L.A. NOIRE

Select Outfits from the Pause menu to change into the following. Some have special bonuses when worn.

SWORD OF JUSTICE OUTFIT

Reach rank 3.

SUNSET STRIP OUTFIT

Reach rank 8.

THE OUTSIDER OUTFIT

Reach rank 13.

HAWKSHAW OUTFIT

Reach rank 18. This outfit adds some resistance to damage.

GOLDEN BOY OUTFIT

Awarded for reaching Traffic Desk

BUTTON MAN OUTFIT

Complete the Badge Pursuit Challenge. This outfit allows you to carry extra ammo.

CHICAGO LIGHTING OUTFIT

Become a member of Rockstar's Social Club. You must reach Detective to wear the outfit. When worn, accuracy with the BAR, Thompson, and shotgun is increased.

THE SHARPSHOOTER OUTFIT

This outfit and the Nickel Plated Pistol were pre-order bonuses from Best Buy. It gives you better accuracy with rifles and pistols.

THE BRODERICK OUTFIT

This outfit was a pre-order bonus from Amazon.com. It increases fist-fighting capabilities and adds resistance to damage.

LARA CROFT AND THE GUARDIAN OF LIGHT

HEAVY JUNGLE OUTFIT
Complete the game.

JUNGLE OUTFIT
Score 1,410,000 points.

BIKER OUTFIT
Score 1,900,000 points.

LEGEND OUTFIT
Defeat Xolotl.

DOPPELGANGER OUTFIT
Score 2,400,000 points.

THE LEGEND OF SPYRO: DAWN OF THE DRAGON

UNLIMITED LIFE
Pause the game, hold L1 and press Right, Right, Down, Down, Left with the Left Analog Stick.

UNLIMITED MANA
Pause the game, hold R1 and press Up, Right, Up, Left, Down with the Left Analog Stick.

MAXIMUM XP
Pause the game, hold R1 and press Left, Right, Right, Up, Up with the Left Analog Stick.

ALL ELEMENTAL UPGRADES
Pause the game, hold L1 and press Left, Up, Down, Up, Right with the Left Analog Stick.

LEGO BATMAN

BATCAVE CODES
Using the computer in the Batcave, select Enter Code and enter the following:

CHARACTERS

CHARACTER	CODE
Alfred	ZAQ637
Batgirl	JKR331
Bruce Wayne	BDJ327
Catwoman (Classic)	M1AAWW
Clown Goon	HJK327
Commissioner Gordon	DDP967
Fishmonger	HGY748
Freeze Girl	XVK541
Joker Goon	UTF782
Joker Henchman	YUN924
Mad Hatter	JCA283
Man-Bat	NYU942
Military Policeman	MKL382
Nightwing	MVY759
Penguin Goon	NKA238

CHARACTER	CODE
Penguin Henchman	BJH782
Penguin Minion	KJP748
Poison Ivy Goon	GTB899
Police Marksman	HKG984
Police Officer	JRY983
Riddler Goon	CRY928
Riddler Henchman	XEU824
S.W.A.T.	HTF114
Sailor	NAV592
Scientist	JFL786
Security Guard	PLB946
The Joker (Tropical)	CCB199
Yeti	NJL412
Zoo Sweeper	DWR243

VEHICLES

VEHICLE	CODE
Bat-Tank	KNTT4B
Bruce Wayne's Private Jet	LEA664
Catwoman's Motorcycle	HPL826
Garbage Truck	DUS483
Goon Helicopter	GCH328
Harbor Helicopter	CHP735
Harley Quinn's Hammer Truck	RDT637
Mad Hatter's Glider	HS000W
Mad Hatter's Steamboat	M4DM4N
Mr. Freeze's Iceberg	ICYICE

VEHICLE	CODE
The Joker's Van	JUK657
Mr. Freeze's Kart	BCT229
Penguin Goon Submarine	BTN248
Police Bike	LJP234
Police Boat	PLC999
Police Car	KJL832
Police Helicopter	CWR732
Police Van	MAC788
Police Watercraft	VJD328
Riddler's Jet	HAHAHA
Robin's Submarine	TTF453
Two-Face's Armored Truck	EFE933

CHEATS

CHEAT	CODE
Always Score Multiply	9LRGNB
Fast Batarangs	JRBDCB
Fast Walk	ZOLM6N
Flame Batarang	D8NYWH
Freeze Batarang	XPN4NG
Extra Hearts	ML3KHP
Fast Build	EVG26J
Immune to Freeze	JXUDY6
Invincibility	WYD5CP
Minikit Detector	ZXGH9J

CHEAT	CODE
More Batarang Targets	XWP645
Piece Detector	KHJ554
Power Brick Detector	MMN786
Regenerate Hearts	HJH7HJ
Score x2	N4NR3E
Score x4	CX9MAT
Score x6	MLVNF2
Score x8	WCCDB9
Score x10	18HW07

LEGO BATMAN 2: DC SUPER HEROES

RED BRICK CODES

Pause the game, select Extras, and then choose Enter Code. Enter the following:

CHEAT	CODE
Attract Studs	MNZER6
Beep Beep	ZHAXFH
Character Studs	TPJ37T
Disguises	BWQ2MS
Extra Hearts	4LGJ7T
Extra Toggle	7TXH5K
Fall Rescue	TPGPG2
Gold Brick Finder	MBXW7V

CHEAT	CODE
Minikit Finder	LRJAG8
Peril Finder	RYD3SJ
Red Brick Finder	5KKQ6G
Regenerate Hearts	ZXEX5D
Studs x 2	74EZUT
Super Build	JN2J6V
Vine Grapples	JXN7FJ

CHARACTERS AND VEHICLE

Pause the game, select Extras, and then choose Enter Code. Enter the following:

CHEAT	CODE
Clown Goon	9ZZZBP
LexBot	W49CSJ
Mime Goon	ZQA8MK
Policeman	V9SAGT

CHEAT	CODE
Riddler Goon	Q285LK
Two-Face Goon	95KPYJ
Harley Quinn's Motorbike	C79LVH

LEGO HARRY POTTER: YEARS 1-4

RED BRICK EXTRAS

After gaining access to the Leaky Cauldron, enter Wiseacre's Wizarding Supplies from Diagon Alley. Go upstairs to enter the following. Pause the game and select Extras to toggle the cheats on and off.

NAME	ENTER
Carrot Wands	AUC8EH
Character Studs	H27KGC
Character Token Detector	HA79V8
Christmas	T7PVVN
Disguise	4DMK2R
Fall Rescue	ZEX7MV
Extra Hearts	J9U6Z9
Fast Dig	Z9BFAD
Fast Magic	FA3GQA
Gold Brick Detector	84QNQN
Hogwarts Crest Detector	TTMC6D

NAME	ENTER
Ice Rink	F88VUW
Invincibility	QQWC6B
Red Brick Detector	7AD7HE
Regenerate Hearts	89ML2W
Score x2	74YKR7
Score x4	J3WHNK
Score x6	XK9ANE
Score x8	HUFV2H
Score x10	H8X69Y
Silhouettes	HZBVX7
Singing Mandrake	BMEU6X
Stud Magnet	67FKWZ

WISEACRE SPELLS

After gaining access to the Leaky Cauldron, enter Wiseacre's Wizarding Supplies from Diagon Alley. Go upstairs to enter the following. Note that you must learn Wingardium Leviosa before you can use these cheats.

NAME	ENTER
Accio	VE9VV7
Anteoculatia	QFB6NR
Calvorio	6DNR6L
Colovaria	9GJ442
Engorgio Skullus	CD4JLX
Entomorphis	MYN3NB
Flipendo	ND2L7W
Glacius	ERA9DR
Herbifors	H8FTHL
Incarcerous	YEB9Q9
Locomotor Mortis	2M2XJ6
Multicorfors	JK6QRM
Redactum Skullus	UW8LRH
Rictusempra	2UCA3M
Slugulus Eructo	U6EE8X
Stupefy	UWDJ4Y
Tarantallegra	KWWQ44
Trip Jinx	YZNRF6

EEYLOPS GOLD BRICKS

After gaining access to the Leaky Cauldron, enter Wiseacre's Wizarding Supplies from Diagon Alley. Go upstairs to enter the following. To access the LEGO Builder, visit Gringott's Bank at the end of Diagon Alley.

GOLD BRICK	ENTER
1	QE4VC7
2	FY8H97
3	3MQT4P
4	PQPM7Z
5	ZY2CPA
6	3GMTP6
7	XY6VYZ
8	TUNC4W
9	EJ42Q6
10	GFJCV9
11	DZCY6G

LEGO HARRY POTTER: YEARS 5-7

CHEATS

Pause the game and select Extras. Go to Enter Code and enter the following:

CHEAT	CODE
Carrot Wands	AUC8EH
Character Studs	H27KGC
Character Token Detector	HA79V8
Christmas	T7PVVN
Collect Ghost Studs	2FLY6B
Extra Hearts	J9U6Z9
Fall Rescue	ZEX7MV
Fast Dig	Z9BFAD
Ghost Coins	2FLY6B
Gold Brick Detector	84QNQN
Hogwarts Crest Detector	TTMC6D
Invincibility	QQWC6B
Red Brick Detector	7AD7HE
Score x2	74YKR7
Score x6	XK9ANE
Score x8	HUFV2H

LEGO INDIANA JONES 2: THE ADVENTURE CONTINUES

Pause the game, select Enter Secret Code from the Extras menu, and enter the following.

CHARACTER

CHARACTER	CODE
Belloq (Priest)	FTL48S
Dovchenko	WL4T6N
Enemy Boxer	7EQF47
Henry Jones	4CSAKH
Indiana Jones	PGWSEA
Indiana Jones: 2	FGLKYS
Indiana Jones (Collect)	DZFY9S
Indiana Jones (Desert)	M4C34K
Indiana Jones (Desert Disguise)	2W8QR3
Indiana Jones (Dinner Suit)	QUNZUT

CHARACTER	CODE
Indiana Jones (Kali)	J2XS97
Indiana Jones (Officer)	3FQFKS
Interdimensional Being	PXT4UP
Lao Che	7AWX3J
Mannequin (Boy)	2UJQWC
Mannequin (Girl)	3PGSEL
Mannequin (Man)	QPWDMM
Mannequin (Woman)	U7SMVK
Mola Ram	82RMC2
Mutt	2GKS62
Salah	E88YRP
Willie	94RUAJ

EXTRAS

EFFECT	CODE
Beep Beep	UU3VSC
Disguise	Y9TE98
Fast Build	SNXC2F
Fast Dig	XYAN83
Fast Fix	3Z7PJX
Fearless	TUXNZF
Ice Rink	TY9P4U
Invincibility	6JBB65
Poo Money	SZFAAE

EFFECT	CODE
Score x3	PEHHPZ
Score x4	UXGTB3
Score X6	XWLJEY
Score x8	S5UZCP
Score x10	V7JYBU
Silhouettes	FQGPYH
Snake Whip	2U7YCV
Stud Magnet	EGSM5B

LEGO PIRATES OF THE CARIBBEAN: THE VIDEO GAME

CODES

Pause the game and select Extras. Choose Enter Code and enter the following codes:

EFFECT	PASSWORD
Ammand the Corsair	EW8T6T
Angelica (Disguised)	DLRR45
Angry Cannibal	VGF32C
Blackbeard	D3DW0D
Clanker	ZM37GT
Clubba	644THF
Davy Jones	4DJLKR
Govorner Weatherby Swann	LD9454
Gunner	Y611WB
Hungry Cannibal	64BNHG
Jack Sparrow (Musical)	VDJSPW
Jacoby	BWO656
Jimmy Legs	13GLW5
King George	RKED43
Koehler	RT093G
Mistress Ching	GDETDE
Phillip	WEV040
Quartermaster	RX58HU
The Spaniard	P861JO
Twigg	KDLFKD

LEGO STAR WARS III: THE CLONE WARS

Pause the game and select the Extras menu to enter the following:

CHARACTERS

CHARACTER	CODE
Aayla Secura	2VG95B
Adi Gallia	G2BFEN
Admiral Ackbar (Classic)	272Y9Q
Admiral Yularen	NG6PYX
Ahsoka	2VJ9TH
Anakin Skywalker	F9VUYJ
Anakin Skywalker (Geonosian Arena)	9AA4DW
Asajj Ventress	YG9DD7
Aurra Sing	M2V1JV
Bail Organa	GEHX6C
Barriss Offee	BTVTZ5
Battle Droid	5Y7MA4
Battle Droid Commander	LSU4LJ
Bib Fortuna	9U4TF3
Boba Fett (Classic)	TY2BYJ
Boil	Q5Q39P
Bossk	2KLW5R
C-3PO	574226
Cad Bane	NHME85
Captain Antilles (Classic)	D8SNGJ
Captain Rex	MW3QYH
Captain Typho	GD6FX3
Chancellor Palpatine	5C62YQ
Chewbacca (Classic)	66UU3T
Clone Pilot	HQ7BVD
Clone Shadow Trooper (Classic)	7GFNCQ
Clone Trooper	NP5GTT
Commander Bly	7CB6NS
Commander Cody	SMN259
Commander Fil	U25HFC
Commander Ponds	JRPR2A
Commander Stone	5XZQSV
Commando Droid	QEGU64
Count Dooku	EWR7WM
Darth Maul (Classic)	QH68AK
Darth Sidious (Classic)	QXY5XN
Darth Vader (Classic)	FM4JB7
Darth Vader Battle Damaged (Classic)	NMJFBL
Destroyer Droid	9MUTS2
Dr. Nuvo Vindi	MB9EMW
Echo	JB9E5S
Eeth Koth	WUFDYA
Gammorean Guard	WSFZZQ
General Grievous	7FNU4T
Geonosian Guard	GAFZUD
Gold Super Battle Droid	2C8NHP
Gonk Droid	C686PK
Grand Moff Tarkin	NH2405
Greedo (Classic)	FUW4C2
Hailfire Droid	T7XF9Z
Han Solo (Classic)	KFDBXF
Heavy Super Battle Droid	G65KJJ
Heavy Weapons Clone Trooper	WXUTWY
HELIOS 3D	4AXTY4
Hevy	EUB8UG
Hondo Ohnaka	5A7XYX
IG-86	EABPCP
Imperial Guard (Classic)	5W6FGD

CHARACTER	CODE
Jango Fett	5KZQ4D
Jar Jar Binks	MESPTS
Jek	AYREC9
Ki-Adi-Mundi	HGBCTQ
Kit Fitso	PYWJ6N
Lando Calrissian (Classic)	ERAEWE
LEP Servent Droid	SM3Y9B
Lieutenant Thire	3NEUXC
Lok Durd	TKCYUZ
Luke Skywalker (Classic)	PG73HF
Luminara Unduli	MKUYQ8
Lurmen Villager	R35Y7N
Luxury Droid	V4WMJN
Mace Windu	8NVRWJ
MagnaGuard	2KEF2D
MSE-6	S6GRNZ
Nahdar Vebb	ZKXG43
Neimoidian	BJB94J
Nute Gunray	QFYXMC
Obi-Wan Kenobi	J9HNF9
Obi-Wan Kenobi (Classic)	FFBU5M
Obi-Wan Kenobi (Geonosian Arena)	5U9FJK
OG-9 Homing Spider Droid	7NEC36
Onaconda Farr	DB7ZQN
Padmé Amidala (Geonosian Arena)	SZ824Q
Padmé Amidala	8X87U6
Pirate Ruffian	BH2EHU
Plo Koon	BUD4VU
Poggle The Lesser	4592WM
Princess Leia (Classic)	2D3D3L
Probe Droid	U2T4SP
Queen Neeyutnee	ZQRN85
Qui-Gon Jinn (Classic)	LKHD3B
R2-D2	RZ5HUV
R3-S6	Z87PAU
R4-P17	5MXSYA
R6-H5	7PMC3C
Rebel Commando (Classic)	PZMQNK
Robonino	2KLW5R
Rys	4PTP53
Savage Oppress	MELL07
Senate Commando	EPBPLK
Senate Commando (Captain)	S4Y7VW
Senator Kharrus	EA4E9S
Senator Philo	9Q7YCT
Shahan Alama	G4N7C2
Sionver Boll	5C62YQ
Stormtrooper (Classic)	HPE7PZ
Super Battle Droid	MJKDV5
Tee Watt Kaa	FYVSHD
Turk Falso	HEBHW5
Tusken Raider (Classic)	GC2XSA
TX-20	PE7FGD
Undead Geonosian	QGENFD
Vader's Apprentice (Classic)	EGQQ4V
Wag Too	VRUVSZ
Wat Tambor	ZP8XVH
Waxer	BNJE79
Wedge Antilles (Classic)	DRGLWS
Whorm Loathsom	4VVYQV
Workout Clone Trooper	MP9DRE
Yoda	CSQTMB

VEHICLES

VEHICLE	CODE
Dwarf Spider Droid	NACMGG
Geonosian Solar Sailor	PJ2U3R
Geonosian Starfighter	EDENEC
Slave I	KDDQVD
The Twilight	T4K5L4
Vulture Droid	7W7K7S

RED BRICKS

CHEAT	CODE
Character Studs	QD2C31
Dark Side	X1V4N2
Dual Wield	C4ES4R
Fast Build	GCHP7S
Glow in the Dark	4GT3VQ
Invincibility	J46P7A
Minikit Detector	CSD5NA
Perfect Deflect	3F5L56
Red Brick Detector	N3R01A
Regenerate Hearts	2D7JNS
Score x2	YZPHUV
Score x4	43T5E5
Score x6	SEBHGR
Score x8	BYFSAQ
Score x10	N1CKR1
Stud Magnet	6MZ5CH
Super Saber Cut	BS828K
Super Speeders	B1D3W3

LOST PLANET 2

Go to the Customization screen from My Page and select Character Parts. Press ▲ to access the LP2 Slot Machine and then press ■ to enter the following passwords.

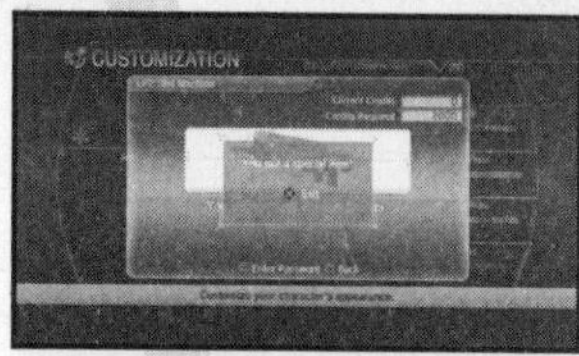

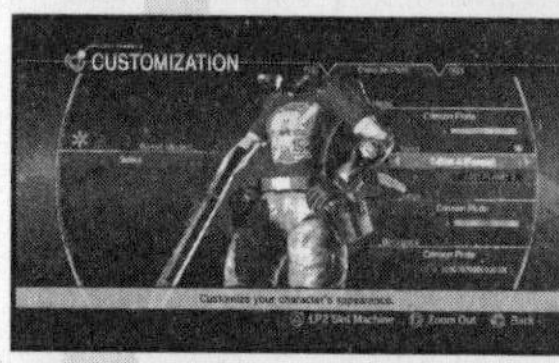

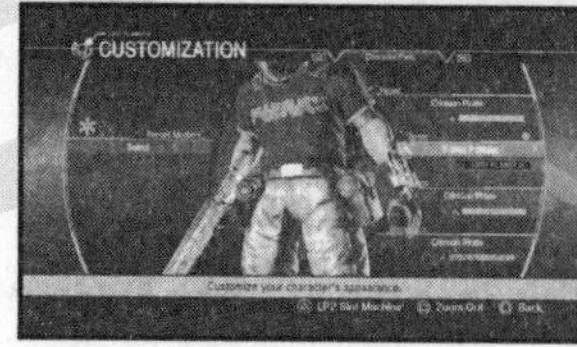

T-SHIRT 1
Enter 73154986.

T-SHIRT 4
Enter 40358056.

T-SHIRT 5
Enter 96725729.

T-SHIRT 6
Enter 21899787.

T-SHIRT 7
Enter 52352345.

T-SHIRT 8
Enter 63152256.

T-SHIRT 9
Enter 34297758.

T-SHIRT 10
Enter 88020223.

PLAYSTATION 3

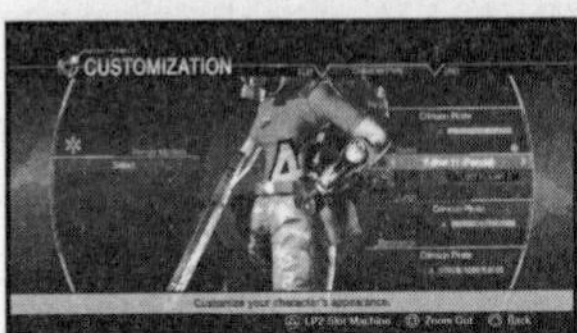

T-SHIRT 11
Enter 25060016.

T-SHIRT 12
Enter 65162980.

T-SHIRT 13
Enter 56428338.

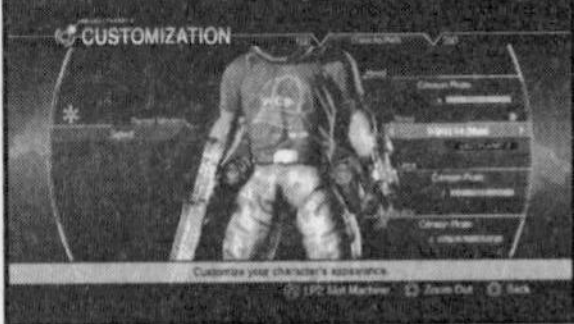

T-SHIRT 14
Enter 18213092.

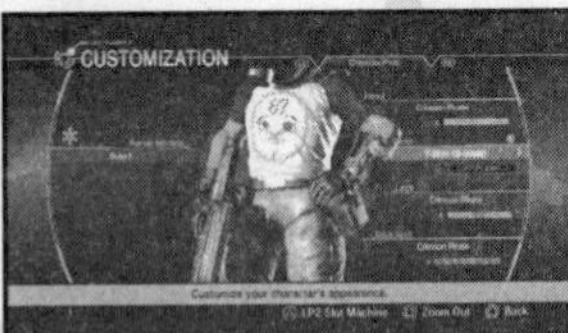

T-SHIRT 15
Enter 26797358.

T-SHIRT 16
Enter 71556463.

T-SHIRT 17
Enter 31354816.

T-SHIRT 18
Enter 12887439.

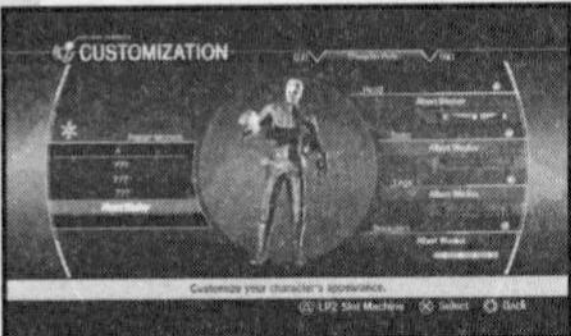

ALBERT WESKER
To unlock Albert Wesker, you need a save game from Resident Evil 5. Alternately, you can unlock him from the LP2 Slot Machine by entering 72962792. This character model can be found in Customization under Preset Models.

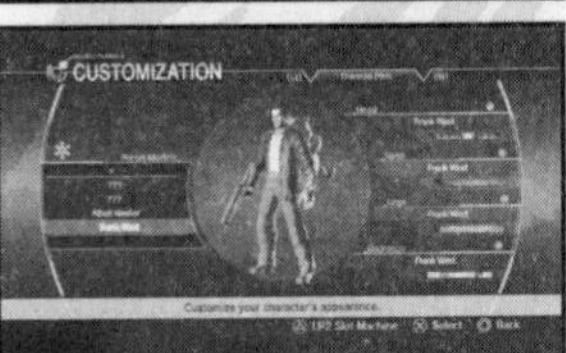

FRANK WEST
To unlock Frank West, you need a save game from Lost Planet. Alternately, you can unlock him from the LP2 Slot Machine by entering 83561942. This character model can be found in Customization under Preset Models.

MADAGASCAR 3: THE VIDEO GAME

ALL DISGUISES
Select Promotion from Extras and enter Pineapple, Strawberry, Grapes, Apple.

BANANA DASH MINI-GAME IN LONDON
Select Promotion from Extras and enter Strawberry, Orange, Apple, Grapes.

BANANA DASH MINI-GAME IN PARIS
Select Promotion from Extras and enter Pineapple, Grapes, Pineapple, Banana.

BANANA DASH MINI-GAME IN PISA
Select Promotion from Extras and enter Orange, Banana, Orange, Apple.

BANANA DASH MINI-GAME IN ROME
Select Promotion from Extras and enter Grape, Apple, Grape, Strawberry.

MADDEN NFL 12

MADDEN NFL 12 DEVELOPERS TEAM IN EXHIBITION
Select Exhibition from Play Now. At the team select, press the Random Team button, L2, until the Developers team shows up. Once you have entered a game as the team, they will always be on the list.

MARVEL: ULTIMATE ALLIANCE 2

These codes will disable the ability to save.

GOD MODE

During a game, press Up, Down, Up, Down, Up, Left, Down, Right, Start.

UNLIMITED FUSION

During a game, press Right, Right, Up, Down, Up, Up, Left, Start.

UNLOCK ALL POWERS

During a game, press Left, Right, Up, Down, Up, Down, Start.

UNLOCK ALL HEROES

During a game, press Up, Up, Down, Down, Left, Left, Left, Start.

UNLOCK ALL SKINS

During a game, press Up, Down, Left, Right, Left, Right, Start.

UNLOCK JEAN GREY

During a game, press Left, Left, Right, Right, Up, Down, Up, Down, Start.

UNLOCK HULK

During a game, press Down, Left, Left, Up, Right, Up, Down, Left, Start.

UNLOCK THOR

During a game, press Up, Right, Right, Down, Right, Down, Left, Right, Start.

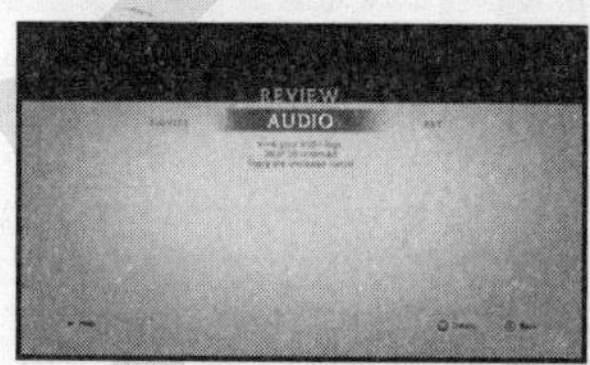

UNLOCK ALL AUDIO LOGS

At the main menu, press Left, Right, Right, Left, Up, Up, Right, Start.

UNLOCK ALL DOSSIERS

At the main menu, press Down, Down, Down, Right, Right, Left, Down, Start.

UNLOCK ALL MOVIES

At the main menu, press Up, Left, Left, Up, Right, Right, Up, Start.

MARVEL VS. CAPCOM ORIGINS

MARVEL SUPER HEROES

PLAY AS ANITA

At the characters select, press MP, LP, Left, LK, MK.

PLAY AS DR DOOM

At the characters select, press MK, LP, Down, LK, MP.

PLAY AS THANOS

At the characters select, press HK, MP, MP, Up.

EXTRA POWER

After selecting your character, press player 1 and player 2 start.

USE GEMS

At the versus screen, hold both Starts.

MARVEL VS. CAPCOM: CLASH OF SUPER HEROES

PLAY AS GOLD WAR MACHINE

Highlight Zangief and press Left, Left, Down, Down, Right, Right, Down, Down, Left, Left, Up, Up, Up, Up, Right, Right, Left, Left, Down, Down, Down, Down, Right, Right, Up, Up, Left, Left, Down, Down, Right, Right, Up, Up, Up, Up, Up.

PLAY AS HYPER VENOM

Highlight Chun-Li and press Right, Down, Down, Down, Down, Left, Up, Up, Up, Up, Right, Right, Down, Down, Left, Left, Down, Down, Right, Right, Up, Up, Up, Up, Left, Left, Up.

PLAY AS LILITH

Highlight Zangief and press Left, Left, Down, Down, Right, Right, Up, Up, Down (x4), Left, Left, Up (x4), Right, Left, Down (x4), Right, Right, Up (x4), Left, Left, Down (x4), Right, Down.

PLAY AS ORANGE HULK

Highlight Chun-Li and press Right, Right, Down, Down, Left, Left, Right, Right, Down, Down, Left, Left, Up (x4), Down, Down, Right, Right, Up, Up, Down (x4), Up (x4), Left, Up.

PLAY AS ROLL

Highlight Zangief and press Left, Left, Down, Down, Right, Right, Down, Down, Left, Left, Up, Right, Up, Up, Right, Right.

PLAY AS SHADOW LADY

Highlight Morrigan and press Up, Right, Right, Down (x4), Left, Left, Up (x4), Right, Right, Left, Left, Down, Down, Right, Right, Down, Down, Left, Left, Up, Up, Right, Right, Up, Up, Left, Left, Down (x5).

SELECT PARTNER

Select your two characters then hold Start and the following buttons:

CHARACTER	CODE
Anita	Weak Punch, Medium Punch, High Punch
Arthur	Weak Punch, Medium Punch
Colossus	Weak Punch, Medium Punch, Medium Kick
Cyclops	Weak punch, Weak Kick, Medium Punch
Devilot	Medium Punch
Iceman	Medium Punch, Medium Kick
Jubilee	Weak Kick, Medium Punch, High Punch
Juggernaut	Weak Punch, Medium Kick
Lou	Medium Punch
Magneo	Weak Kick, High Punch
Michelle Hart	Weak Punch, Weak Kick
Psylocke	Medium Kick
Pure and Fur	Weak Kick
Rogue	Weak Punch, Weak Kick, Medium Punch, High Punch
Saki	High Punch
Sentinel	Medium Punch, Medium Kick, High Punch
Shadow	Weak Punch, Medium Kick, High Punch
Storm	Weak Punch, Weak Kick, High Punch
Thor	Weak Kick, Medium Punch
Ton-Pooh	Weak Punch, High Punch
Unknown Soldier	Weak Punch
US Agent	High Punch, Medium Kick

MASS EFFECT 3

BATTLEFIELD 3 SOLDIER IN MULTIPLAYER

This character is unlocked for multiplayer if you have a Battlefield 3 Online Pass activated on your EA account.

RECKONER KNIGHT ARMOR AND CHAKRAM LAUNCHER

Start the Kingdom of Amalur: Reckoning demo to unlock this armor and weapon in Mass Effect 3.

MAX PAYNE 3

NEW YORK MINUTE IN ARCADE MODE
Complete story mode.

CHARACTER SELECT IN ARCADE MODE
Complete story mode on Medium Difficulty.

OLD SCHOOL DIFFICULTY, HARDCORE DIFFICULTY, AND UNLIMITED PAINKILLERS CHEAT
Complete story mode on Hard Difficulty.

MAX PAYNE ADVANCED CHARACTER MODEL
Complete story mode on Old School Difficulty.

The following cheats can be used when replaying a level with the level select:

BULLET CAM ON EVERY KILL
Find all Clues.

ONE HIT KILL CHEAT
Complete story mode on Hardcore difficulty with Free Aim.

UNLIMITED AMMO
Find all Golden Guns.

UNLIMITED BULLET TIME
Earn a Gold Medal on all levels in Arcade Mode.

UNLIMITED PAIN KILLERS
Complete game on Hard difficulty with Free Aim.

MERCENARIES 2: WORLD IN FLAMES

To use Cheat Mode, you must update the game by being online when the game is started. The cheats will keep you from earning trophies, but anything earned up to that point remains. You can still save with the cheats, but be careful if you want to earn trophies. Quit the game without saving to return to normal.

CHEAT MODE
Access your PDA by pressing Select. Press L2, R2, R2, L2, R2, L2, L2, R2, R2, R2, L2 and close the PDA. You then need to accept the agreement that says trophies are disabled. Now you can enter the following cheats.

INVINCIBILITY
Access your PDA and press Up, Down, Left, Down, Right, Right. This activates invincibility for you and anyone that joins your game.

INFINITE AMMO
Access your PDA and press Up, Down, Left, Right, Left, Left.

GIVE ALL VEHICLES
Access your PDA and press Up, Down, Left, Right, Right, Left.

GIVE ALL SUPPLIES
Access your PDA and press Left, Right, Right, Left, Up, Up, Left, Up.

GIVE ALL AIRSTRIKES (EXCEPT NUKE)
Access your PDA and press Right, Left, Down, Up, Right, Left, Down, Up.

GIVE NUKE
Access your PDA and press Up, Up, Down, Down, Left, Right, Left, Right.

FILL FUEL
Access your PDA and press Up, Up, Up, Down, Down, Down.

ALL COSTUMES
Access your PDA and press Up, Right, Down, Left, Up.

GRAPPLING HOOK
Access your PDA and press Up, Left, Down, Right, Up.

METAL GEAR SOLID 4 GUNS OF THE PATRIOTS

100,000 DREBIN POINTS
At Otacon's computer in Shadow Moses, enter 14893.

OPENING – OLD L.A. 2040 IPOD SONG
At Otacon's computer in Shadow Moses, enter 78925.

POLICENAUTS END TITLE IPOD SONG
At Otacon's computer in Shadow Moses, enter 13462.

You must first defeat the game to use the following passwords.

DESPERATE CHASE IPOD SONG
Select password from the Extras menu and enter thomas.

GEKKO IPOD SONG
Select password from the Extras menu and enter george.

MIDNIGHT SHADOW IPOD SONG
Select password from the Extras menu and enter theodore.

MOBS ALIVE IPOD SONG
Select password from the Extras menu and enter abraham.

DESERT EAGLE—LONG BARREL
Select password from the Extras menu and enter deskyhstyl.

MK. 23 SOCOM PISTOL
Select password from the Extras menu and enter mekakorkkk.

MOSIN NAGANT
Select password from the Extras menu and enter mnsoymsyhn.

TYPE 17 PISTOL
Select password from the Extras menu and enter jmsotsynrn.

ALTAIR COSTUME
Select password from the Extras menu and enter aottrykmyn.

MONSTER WORLD IV

SOUND TEST
Highlight New Game and press Up, Down, Up, Down, Left, Left, Right, Right.

MORTAL KOMBAT ARCADE KOLLECTION

MORTAL KOMBAT II

NO THROWS OPTION
In a two-player match and before the match begins, hold Down + HP on both controllers.

ULTIMATE MORTAL KOMBAT 3

VS CODES
At the VS screen, each player must use LP, BLK, and LK to enter the following codes:

EFFECT	PLAYER 1	PLAYER 2
Blocking Disabled	020	020
Dark Kombat	688	688
Don't Jump at Me	448	844
Explosive Combat (2 on 2)	227	227
Fast Uppercut Recovery Enabled	688	422
No Fear	282	282
No Powerbars	987	123
Player 1 Half Power	033	N/A
Player 1 Quarter Power	707	N/A
Player 2 Half Power	N/A	033
Player 2 Quarter Power	N/A	707
RandPer Kombat	444	444
Silent Kombat	300	300
Throwing Disabled	100	100
Unikoriv Referri: Sans Power	044	440
Unlimited Run	466	466
Two-Player Mini-Game of Galaga	642	468
Kombat Zone: Bell Tower	910	190
Kombat Zone: The Bridge	077	022
Kombat Zone: The Graveyard	666	333
Kombat Zone: Jade's Desert	330	033
Kombat Zone: Kahn's Kave	004	070
Kombat Zone: Kahn's Tower	880	220
Kombat Zone: Kombat Temple	600	040
Kombat Zone: Noob Saibot Dorfen	050	050
Kombat Zone: The Pit 3	820	028
Kombat Zone: River Kombat	002	003
Kombat Zone: Rooftop	343	343
Kombat Zone: Scislac Busorez	933	933

EFFECT	PLAYER 1	PLAYER 2
Kombat Zone: Scorpion's Lair	666	444
Kombat Zone: Soul Chamber	123	901
Kombat Zone: Street	079	035
Kombat Zone: Subway	880	088
Winner of round fights Motaro	969	141
Winner of round fights Noob Saibot	769	342
Winner of round fights Shao Kahn	033	564
Winner of round fights Smoke	205	205
Revision	999	999
See the Mortal Kombat Live Tour !!	550	550
"Hold Flippers During Casino Run"	987	666
"Rain Can Be Found in the Graveyard"	711	313
"Skunky !!"	122	221
"There Is No Knowledge That Is Not Power"	123	926
"Whatcha Gun Do?"	004	400

UNLOCK CLASSIC SUB-ZERO

Lose a match in arcade mode and let the continue timer run out. Enter the following within 10 seconds on both controllers; HP (x8), LP (x1), BL (x8), LK (x3), HK (x5).

UNLOCK ERMAC

Lose a match in arcade mode and let the continue timer run out. Enter the following within 10 seconds; HP (x1), LP (x2), BL (x3), LK (x4), HK (x4) for player 1 and HP (x4), LP (x4), BL (x3), LK (x2), HK (x1) for player 2.

UNLOCK MILEENA

Lose a match in arcade mode and let the continue timer run out. Enter the following within 10 seconds on both controllers; HP (x2), LP (x2), BL (x2), LK (x6), HK (x4).

HUMAN SMOKE

Select Smoke. For player 1, hold Block + Run + High Punch + High Kick + Left before the fight begins. For player 2, hold Block + Run + High Punch + High Kick + Right before the fight begins

MORTAL KOMBAT KOMPLETE EDITION

VS CODES

At the VS screen, each player must use LP, BLK, and LK to enter the following codes. The numbers represent how many times you must press each button.

EFFECT	PLAYER 1	PLAYER 2
Armless Kombat	911	911
Blocking Disabled	020	020
Breakers Disabled	090	090
Dark Kombat	022	022
Double Dash	391	193
Dream Kombat	222	555
Enhance Moves Disabled	051	150
Explosive Kombat	227	227
Foreground Objects Disabled	001	001
Headless Kombat	808	808
Health Recovery	012	012
Hyper Fighting	091	091
Invisible Kombat	770	770
Jumping Disabled	831	831
Klassik Music	101	101
Kombos Disabled	931	931
No Blood	900	900
Player 1 Half Health	220	000
Player 1 Quarter Health	110	000

EFFECT	PLAYER 1	PLAYER 2
Player 2 Half Health	000	220
Player 2 Quarter Health	000	110
Power Bars Disabled	404	404
Psycho Kombat	707	707
Quick Uppercut Recovery	303	303
Rainbow Kombat	234	234
Random Phrase 1	717	313
Random Phrase 2	448	844
Random Phrase 3	122	221
Random Phrase 4	009	900
Random Phrase 5	550	055
Random Phrase 6	031	130
Random Phrase 7	282	282
Random Phrase 8	123	926
Sans Power	044	440
Silent Kombat	300	300
Specials Disabled	731	731
Super Recovery	123	123
Throwing Disabled	100	100
Throwing Encouraged	010	010
Tournament Mode	111	111
Unlimited Super Meter	466	466
Vampire Kombat	424	424
XRays Disabled	242	242
Zombie Kombat	666	666

HIDDEN KING OF THE HILL AVATAR ACTIONS

When viewing a fight as a spectator, highlight your avatar and press ✕ to get the action menu. Now enter the following to perform some hidden actions:

EFFECT	CODE
"$%#&!"	Up, Up, ○
#1	Down, Up, △
Big Clap	Right, Up, △
Cheese	Left, Up, Down, ○
Cover Face	Left, Right, ○
Devil Horns	Down, Up, □
Diamond	Up, Down, Left, △
Double Devil Horns	Up, Down, △
"FATALITY"	Up, Up, Right, Right, □
"FIGHT!	Left, Right, □
"Finish Him!"	Left, Right, Left, Right, △
Gather Ice	Right, Right, Right, Left, △
"HA!"	Down, Up, Down, ✕
Hop	Up, Up, □
"I'm Not Worthy"	Down, Down, △
Lighter	Down, Down, Up, Up, □
Point	Right, Right, □
Raiden Pose	Left, Left, Right, Right, □
Shake Head	Left, Right, ✕
Skunk	Left, Right, Up, Up ✕
Skunk (Stench)	Up, Down, Down, ○
Sleep	Down, Down, Down, ○
Stink Wave	Right, Left, ○
Throw Tomato	Down, Down, Down, Up, ✕

MX VS. ATV REFLEX

MX VEHICLES FOR PURCHASE

Select Enter Cheat Code from the Options and enter brapbrap.

JUSTIN BRAYTON, KTM MX BIKES AND ATVS IN ARCADE MODE

Select Enter Cheat Code from the Options and enter readytorace.

ALL EVENT LOCATIONS IN ARCADE MODE

Select Enter Cheat Code from the Options and enter whereto.

ALL AI OPPONENTS

Select Enter Cheat Code from the Options and enter allai.

ATV VEHICLES FOR PURCHASE

Select Enter Cheat Code from the Options and enter couches.

ALL AVAILABLE RIDER GEAR

Select Enter Cheat Code from the Options and enter gearedup.

ALL AVAILABLE HELMETS

Select Enter Cheat Code from the Options and enter skullcap.

ALL AVAILABLE BOOTS

Select Enter Cheat Code from the Options and enter kicks.

ALL AVAILABLE GOGGLES

Select Enter Cheat Code from the Options and enter windows.

NARUTO SHIPPUDEN: ULTIMATE NINJA STORM GENERATIONS

NINJA CARD PASSWORDS

Select Enter Password from the Collection Screen and enter the following. Each password unlocks one Ninja Info Card.

00HNWGTFV8	BL770WJT70	MKKJMC7CWF
0B7JLNHXA4	BQ7207JT80	MMD4M2BK7K
0CKC96JGVL	BVKHANGBKR	MSJ1BFU4JB
0LP3WPBQ7B	C0DGMFHCCD	MUW7LMT1WG
17769QU0KT	CE8Q9UKG8N	NDD9LG0EV0
1TFLMLP4BE	CJE20EPKWV	PLESLFPVKK
1V8WD29DBJ	CVJVLP6PVS	PQVG0KUCL0
1WQ4WR17VV	D53XB9P4LP	PSA21VB6M2
28G1D0FSBS	DCF515Q8X9	Q8M8P2J295
2DRA0BDFAR	DS1BXA13LD	QCS5D53XBA
2LM5CHLVX1	DX0L0382NT	QEB22X9LNP
2MFFXGNKWL	E23G24EB0B	QTBT1W97M2
39PXPFXEDW	EL52EVS00X	R4C43XB8PD
3ET93PHNNM	ENE5N43M9L	R8JE3QS6QT
3J6R2NS6B4	ERCKGKSN1P	RE6KE7GPCC
3USV86L2HM	F515Q009CE	S5JVSL6DDC
4HB5ELA91R	F6DTQBCXCF	S85PRDRU1T
4LTP2Q6U26	F7T1103JNS	SAUFE2T72U
4RTCRU4BWD	FMBB22KR0J	SKJERP5K15
53HXEB6EQ1	G12P36C5QW	TEP2FTPH4A
5DFQ45CJF0	GB7FS2G8EV	TH9NGBKRFF
5FUU285P1D	GR56DKG1CP	TVQ7HC2PQ5
6PF63C1C35	GWQ8EKCNEG	U3GQH7R65P
6QDPEH0HQL	H3D14HNF2X	U59BHXUEF3
6RQD5KD6GN	HH88SX6Q4P	UCM26NV9TW
6UB06B8FS2	HWR9FKDPFH	UFG3GKQJ5B
794L5RFD5J	HX3CS22CEG	UL4KS3Q2SU
7DEDGW26R1	J22C572J3P	UMK7SHU2QQ
7KXC71MSTS	JFXC608F44	UTG4GWQ65P
8CTCJFSQ6L	JMV3HRHBR7	V9TW64S2JJ
8EJ57XFMJ3	JSB8UFKXHL	VG63VA3W6D
8JPPVC8TUG	JXF97FR2F7	VLGL6FEQSU
8Q1VK79N7B	K1C6VJKXHL	VML7SHV3RR
96XD609G54	KE84GXKREE	W1X6BJWX5C
9FP7L7N1H1	KF4RT7RU4B	W57HWX4B7S
9P8BLJ6FXX	KTS46B3JUP	WH0BJBA5HF

ADUMLGTR7M	L3PAK7BPUM	WV72WQ4B7R
ALNQK2L6VS	L6N0B1XT65	XH5G7ASAHD
AQU0KTTFCB	LMTA6QSEJV	XVN2VPX5TT
B7JHWCTWU3	MB3GA4DK88	XXPF0EMWKV

NASCAR THE GAME 2011

MARK MARTIN PAINT SCHEMES

At the garage main menu, press Down, Down, Up, Up, Right, Left, Right, Left. Enter godaddy.com.

KYLE BUSH NOS ENERGY DRINK CAR

At the garage main menu, press Down, Down, Up, Up, Right, Left, Right, Left. Enter drinknos.

NBA 2K11

MJ: CREATING A LEGEND

In Features, select Codes from the Extras menu. Choose Enter Code and enter icanbe23.

2K CHINA TEAM

In Features, select Codes from the Extras menu. Choose Enter Code and enter 2kchina.

2K SPORTS TEAM

In Features, select Codes from the Extras menu. Choose Enter Code and enter 2Ksports.

NBA 2K TEAM

In Features, select Codes from the Extras menu. Choose Enter Code and enter nba2k.

VC TEAM

In Features, select Codes from the Extras menu. Choose Enter Code and enter vcteam.

ABA BALL

In Features, select Codes from the Extras menu. Choose Enter Code and enter payrespect.

2011 ALL-STAR UNIFORMS

In Features, select Codes from the Extras menu. Choose Enter Code and enter wydololoh.

SECONDARY ROAD UNIFORM

In Features, select Codes from the Extras menu. Choose Enter Code and enter ronoilnm. This unlocks the secondary road uniform for the Hornets, Magic, and Timberwolves.

ORANGE SPLIT DUNK

In Features, select Codes from the Extras menu. Choose Enter Code and enter SPRITEDUNK1. Go to Sprite Slam Dunk Showdown and use the help menu to find out more.

SPIN TOMMY DUNK

In Features, select Codes from the Extras menu. Choose Enter Code and enter SPRITEDUNK2. Go to Sprite Slam Dunk Showdown and use the help menu to find out more.

THE VILLAIN DUNK

In Features, select Codes from the Extras menu. Choose Enter Code and enter SPRITEDUNK3. Go to Sprite Slam Dunk Showdown and use the help menu to find out more.

NBA 2K12

ABA BALL

Select Extras from the Features menu. Choose Codes and enter payrespect. This can be toggled on and off from this Codes menu.

2K CHINA TEAM

Select Extras from the Features menu. Choose Codes and enter 2kchina.

2K SPORTS TEAM

Select Extras from the Features menu. Choose Codes and enter 2ksports.

UNLOCK NBA 2K TEAM

Select Extras from the Features menu. Choose Codes and enter nba2k.

VC TEAM

Select Extras from the Features menu. Choose Codes and enter vcteam.

JORDAN RETRO COLLECTION

Select Extras from the Features menu. Choose Codes and enter 23.

SECONDARY ROAD UNIFORMS

Select Extras from the Features menu. Choose Codes and enter hcsilapadatu. This unlocks uniforms for 76ers, Jazz, Kings, and Mavericks.

CHRISTMAS UNIFORMS

Select Extras from the Features menu. Choose Codes and enter ibyasmliancbhlald. This unlocks uniforms for Bulls, Celtics, Heat, Knicks, Lakers, and Mavericks.

HEAT BACK IN BLACK UNIFORM

Select Extras from the Features menu. Choose Codes and enter albkbinkcca.

RAPTORS MILITARY NIGHT UNIFORM

Select Extras from the Features menu. Choose Codes and enter liyrimta.

NBA 2K13

ABA BALL

Select Features from the main menu and then go to Codes. Enter payrespect.

UA TORCH SHOE

Select Features from the main menu and then go to Codes. Enter underarmour.

SPRITE EFFECT BONUS

Select Features from the main menu and then go to Codes. Enter spriteeffect. This adds +3 to Ball handling.

NBA JAM

BEASTIE BOYS

At the title screen, press Up, Up, Down, Down, Left, Right, Left, Right, ◉, ⊗. This team includes Ad Rock, MCA, and Mike D.

J. COLE AND 9TH WONDER

At the title screen, press Up, Left, Down, Right, Up, Left, Down, Right, ◉, ⊗.

DEMOCRATS TEAM

At the title screen, press Left (x13), ⊗. This team includes Barack Obama, Joe Biden, Bill Clinton, and Hillary Clinton.

REPUBLICANS TEAM

At the title screen, press Right (x13), ⊗. The team includes George W. Bush, Sarah Palin, Dick Cheney, and John McCain.

ESPN'S SPORTSNATION

Select Play Now. When entering the initials, enter ESP for P1 and NSN for P2. Advance to the Choose Teams screen to find the team. This team includes the hosts of the show; Colin Cowherd and Michelle Beadle.

NBA MASCOTS

Select Play Now. When entering the initials, enter MAS for P1 and COT for P2.

ORIGINAL GENERATION JAM

Select Play Now. When entering the initials, enter MJT for P1. Advance to the Choose Teams screen to find the team. This team includes Mark Turmell and Tim Kitzrow.

NBA LIVE 10

CHARLOTTE BOBCATS' 2009/2010 RACE DAY ALTERNATE JERSEYS

Select Options from My NBA Live and go to Select Codes. Enter ceobdabacarstcy.

NEW ORLEANS HORNETS' 2009/2010 MARDI GRAS ALTERNATE JERSEYS

Select Options from My NBA Live and go to Select Codes. Enter nishrag1rosmad0.

ALTERNATE JERSEYS

Select Options from My NBA Live and go to Select Codes. Enter ndnba1rooaesdc0. This unlocks alternate jerseys for Atlanta Hawks, Dallas Mavericks, Houston Rockets, and Memphis Grizzlies.

MORE HARDWOOD CLASSICS NIGHTS JERSEYS

Select Options from My NBA Live and go to Select Codes. Enter hdogdrawhoticns. This unlocks Hardwood Classics Nights jerseys for Cleveland Cavaliers, Golden State Warriors, Minnesota Timberwolves, Orlando Magic, Philadelphia 76ers.

ADIDAS EQUATIONS

Select Options from My NBA Live and go to Select Codes. Enter adaodqauieints1.

ADIDAS TS CREATORS WITH ANKLE BRACES

Select Options from My NBA Live and go to Select Codes. Enter atciadsstsdhecf.

ADIDAS TS SUPERNATURAL COMMANDERS

Select Options from My NBA Live and go to Select Codes. Enter andsicdsmatdnsr.

ADIDAS TS SUPERNATURAL CREATORS

Select Options from My NBA Live and go to Select Codes. Enter ard8siscdnatstr.

AIR MAX LEBRON VII

Select Options from My NBA Live and go to Select Codes. Enter ere1nbvlaoeknii, 2ovnaebnkrielei, 3rioabeneikenvl, ri4boenanekilve, ivl5brieekaeonn, or n6ieirvalkeeobn.

KOBE V

Select Options from My NBA Live and go to Select Codes. Enter ovze1bimenkoko0, m0kveokoiebozn2, eev0nbimokk3ozo, or bmo4inozeeo0kvk.

JORDAN CP3 IIIS

Select Options from My NBA Live and go to Select Codes. Enter iaporcdian3ejis.

JORDAN MELO M6S

Select Options from My NBA Live and go to Select Codes. Enter emlarmeoo6ajdsn.

JORDAN SIXTY PLUSES

Select Options from My NBA Live and go to Select Codes. Enter aondsuilyjrspxt.

NIKE HUARACHE LEGIONS

Select Options from My NBA Live and go to Select Codes. Enter aoieuchrahelgn.

NIKE KD 2S

Select Options from My NBA Live and go to Select Codes. Enter kk2tesaosepinrd.

NIKE ZOOM FLIP'NS

Select Options from My NBA Live and go to Select Codes. Enter epfnozaeminolki.

NEED FOR SPEED: THE RUN

AEM INTAKE CHALLENGE SERIES

Select Enter Cheat Code from Extras and enter aemintakes.

NEED FOR SPEED UNDERCOVER

$10,000

Select Secret Codes from the Options menu and enter %%$3/".

DIE-CAST BMW M3 E92

Select Secret Codes from the Options menu and enter)B7@B=.

DIE-CAST LEXUS IS F

Select Secret Codes from the Options menu and enter 0;5M2;.

NEEDFORSPEED.COM LOTUS ELISE

Select Secret Codes from the Options menu and enter -KJ3=E.

DIE-CAST NISSAN 240SX (S13)

Select Secret Codes from the Options menu and enter ?P:COL.

DIE-CAST PORSCHE 911 TURBO

Select Secret Codes from the Options menu and enter >8P:I;.

SHELBY TERLINGUA

Select Secret Codes from the Options menu and enter NeedForSpeedShelbyTerlingua.

DIE-CAST VOLKSWAGEN R32

Select Secret Codes from the Options menu and enter!2ODBJ:.

NFL BLITZ

Select Cheats from the Blitz Store to purchase the following cheats. They are entered with ■, ▲, ●. Press these buttons until the three given icons are shown. The number indicates how many times each button is pressed. ■ is the first number, ▲ the second, and ● is the third.

GAMEPLAY CHEATS

Buy these cheats to change the game to your advantage.

CHEAT	CODE
Tournament Mode	Goalpost, Goalpost, Goalpost (4 4 4)
Faster Passes	Helmet, NFL, NFL (5 1 1)
Speedster	Goalpost, NFL, EA Sports (4 1 0)
Fast Turbo Drain	Helmet, Headset, NFL (5 3 1)
More Fumbles	Helmet, Goalpost, NFL (5 4 1)
No First Downs	Goalpost, Headset, Goalpost (4 3 4)
No Fumbles	Helmet, EA Sports, Headset (5 0 3)
No Interceptions	Helmet, Helmet, EA Sports (5 5 0)
No Onside Kicks	Goalpost, Foam Finger, Foam Finger (4 2 2)
No Punting	Goalpost, Goalpost, EA Sports (4 4 0)
Power Defense	Goalpost, Whistle, Goalpost (4 8 4)
Power Offense	Helmet, Foam Finger, Helmet (5 2 5)
No Stepping out of Bounds	Helmet, EA Sports, EA Sports (5 0 0)
Unlimited Turbo	Helmet, NFL, Goalpost (5 1 4)

VISUAL CHEATS

Your team will get a Blitz makeover after you buy these cheats.

CHEAT	CODE
Big Head Player	Foam Finger, Helmet, EA Sports (2 5 0)
Big Head Team	Foam Finger, NFL, Foam Finger (2 1 2)
Tiny Head Team	Foam Finger, Goalpost, Headset (2 4 3)
Tiny Head Player	Headset, EA Sports, Foam Finger (3 0 2)
Huge Head Team	Headset, NFL, Foam Finger (3 1 2)
Huge Head Player	Foam Finger, EA Sports, NFL (2 0 1)
Super Ball Trail	EA Sports, NFL, Football (0 1 6)
Black & Red Ball	EA Sports, EA Sports, Foam Finger (0 0 2)
Camouflage Ball	EA Sports, EA Sports, Helmet (0 0 5)
Chrome Ball	EA Sports, Foam Finger, EA Sports (0 2 0)
Flames Ball	EA Sports, Goalpost, Foam Finger (0 4 2)
Ice Cream Ball	EA Sports, Foam Finger, Marker (0 2 7)
B-52 Ball	NFL, EA Sports, Goalpost (1 0 4)
Beachball	NFL, EA Sports, NFL (1 0 1)
Glow Ball	EA Sports, Marker, EA Sports (0 7 0)
Meat Ball	EA Sports, Football, EA Sports (0 6 0)
Pumpkin Ball	Whistle, Headset, NFL (8 3 1)
Soup Can Ball	Marker, NFL, EA Sports (7 1 0)
Blitz Team Ball	NFL, NFL, NFL (1 1 1)
USA Ball	Headset, NFL, Helmet (3 1 5)
Blitz Stadium	EA Sports, NFL, Goalpost (0 1 4)
Cardinals Stadium	EA Sports, Foam Finger, Foam Finger (0 2 2)
Falcons Stadium	EA Sports, Headset, EA Sports (0 3 0)
Ravens Stadium	EA Sports, Headset, Helmet (0 3 5)
Bills Stadium	EA Sports, Headset, Marker (0 3 7)
Panthers Stadium	EA Sports, Goalpost, Goalpost (0 4 4)
Bears Stadium	EA Sports, Goalpost, Football (0 4 6)
Bengals Stadium	EA Sports, Goalpost, Whistle (0 4 8)
Browns Stadium	EA Sports, Helmet, Headset (0 5 3)
Cowboys Stadium	EA Sports, Helmet, Helmet (0 5 5)
Broncos Stadium	EA Sports, EA Sports, Marker (0 0 7)
Lions Stadium	EA Sports, Helmet, Marker (0 5 7)
Packers Stadium	EA Sports, Football, Foam Finger (0 6 2)
Texans Stadium	EA Sports, Football, Goalpost (0 6 4)
Colts Stadium	EA Sports, Football, Football (0 6 6)
Jaguars Stadium	EA Sports, Marker, Foam Finger (0 7 2)
Chiefs Stadium	EA Sports, Whistle, EA Sports (0 8 0)
Dolphins Stadium	EA Sports, Marker, Marker (0 7 7)
Vikings Stadium	NFL, EA Sports, Football (1 0 6)
Patriots Stadium	NFL, NFL, Goalpost (1 1 4)
Saints Stadium	NFL, Foam Finger, Headset (1 2 3)
Giants Stadium	NFL, Headset, EA Sports (1 3 0)
Jets Stadium	NFL, EA Sports, Whistle (1 0 8)
Raiders Stadium	NFL, Foam Finger, Helmet (1 2 5)
Eagles Stadium	NFL, Headset, Headset (1 3 3)
Steelers Stadium	NFL, Headset, Helmet (1 3 5)
Chargers Stadium	NFL, Helmet, EA Sports (1 5 0)
Seahawks Stadium	Foam Finger, Foam Finger, EA Sports (2 2 0)
49ers Stadium	Foam Finger, NFL, EA Sports (2 1 0)
Rams Stadium	Foam Finger, Headset, EA Sports (2 3 0)
Bucs Stadium	Foam Finger, Goalpost, EA Sports (2 4 0)
Titans Stadium	Headset, EA Sports, Headset (3 0 3)
Redskins Stadium	Goalpost, EA Sports, NFL (4 0 1)
Day	EA Sports, Whistle, Foam Finger (0 8 2)
Twilight	NFL, NFL, Marker (1 1 7)
Night	NFL, Whistle, Marker (1 8 7)

SETTINGS CHEATS

Change certain game settings when you buy these cheats.

CHEAT	CODE
Hide Player Name	EA Sports, Foam Finger, Goalpost (0 2 4)
Extra Code Time	Helmet, Helmet, Helmet (5 5 5)
No Ball Target	EA Sports, Helmet, NFL (0 5 1)
Wide Camera	NFL, NFL, Foam Finger (1 1 2)
Show Field Goal Percentage	EA Sports, NFL, Foam Finger (0 1 2)
All-Time QB Coop	Headset, Headset, EA Sports (3 3 0)
All-Time WR Coop	EA Sports, Headset, Headset (0 3 3)
Icon Passing	Headset, Helmet, Headset (3 5 3)
No Player Icon	EA Sports, Goalpost, EA Sports (0 4 0)

FANTASY CHARACTERS

Buy these cheats to play as your favorite characters. Characters must be unlocked by defeating them in Blitz Gauntlet first.

UNLOCKABLE CHARACTERS

CHEAT	CODE
Bigfoot	Headset, Headset, Headset (3 3 3)
Bigfoot Team	Marker, EA Logo, EA Logo (7 0 0)
Cowboy	Headset, Foam Finger, Headset (3 2 3)
Cowboy Team	Goalpost, Marker, Goalpost (4 7 4)
Gladiator	Foam Finger, Whistle, Foam Finger (2 8 2)
Gladiator Team	Helmet, NFL, Marker (5 1 7)
Horse	NFL, Marker, NFL (1 7 1)
Horse Team	Foam Finger, Football, Foam Finger (2 6 2)
Hot Dog	NFL, Football, NFL (1 6 1)
Hot Dog Team	Foam Finger, Headset, Foam Finger (2 3 2)
Lion	Foam Finger, EA Sports, Foam Finger (2 0 2)
Lion Team	Headset, Goalpost, Headset (3 4 3)
Ninja	Foam Finger, Marker, Foam Finger (2 7 2)
Ninja Team	Football, NFL, Football (6 1 6)
Pirate	NFL, Foam Finger, NFL (1 2 1)
Pirate Team	Helmet, Headset, Helmet (5 3 5)

NHL 12

3RD JERSEYS

Select NHL 12 Code Entry from My NHL 12 and enter 2wg3gap9mvrth6kq. This unlocks uniforms for Florida, New York Islanders, Ottawa, and Toronto.

NIGHTS INTO DREAMS

UNLOCK EVERYTHING

At the title screen, press Left, Right, ■, ●, ✖, ▲, R1, R2, Down, Up, L1, L2. Trophies, saving, and posting high scores are disabled until the game is restarted.

ONE PIECE: PIRATE WARRIORS

SEVEN LUFFY COSTUMES

Complete the main log.

SANJI'S NEW WORLD COSTUME

Complete Sanji's Another Log

ZORO'S NEW WORLD COSTUME

Complete Zoro's Another Log.

OPERATION FLASHPOINT: DRAGON RISING

AMBUSH BONUS MISSION
Select Cheats from the Options menu and enter AmbushU454.

CLOSE QUARTERS BONUS MISSION
Select Cheats from the Options menu and enter CloseQ8M3

COASTAL STRONGHOLD BONUS MISSION
Select Cheats from the Options menu and enter StrongM577

DEBRIS FIELD BONUS MISSION
Select Cheats from the Options menu and enter OFPWEB2

ENCAMPMENT BONUS MISSION
Select Cheats from the Options menu and enter OFPWEB1

NIGHT RAID BONUS MISSION
Select Cheats from the Options menu and enter RaidT18Z

PHINEAS AND FERB: ACROSS THE 2ND DIMENSION

SKIN FOR AGENT P: PERRY THE PLATTYBORG
Pause the game, select Enter Code from Extras, and enter Circle, X, Circle, Triangle, Square, Triangle.

PLANTS VS. ZOMBIES

If a code does not work, your Tree of Wisdom may not be tall enough. Try again later.

ALTERNATE LAWN MOWER
During a game, press R1 + R2 + L1 + L2 and enter trickedout.

ZOMBIE SHADES
During a game, press R1 + R2 + L1 + L2 and enter future.

ZOMBIES HAVE A MUSTACHE
During a game, press R1 + R2 + L1 + L2 and enter mustache.

ZOMBIES DANCE
During a game, press R1 + R2 + L1 + L2 and enter dance.

DEAD ZOMBIES LEAVE DAISIES BEHIND
During a game, press R1 + R2 + L1 + L2 and enter daisies.

CANDY SHOWER WHEN ZOMBIE DIES
During a game, press R1 + R2 + L1 + L2 and enter piñata.

CHANGES ZOMBIES SOUND
During a game, press R1 + R2 + L1 + L2 and enter sukhbir.

PRINCE OF PERSIA: THE SANDS OF TIME

CLASSIC PRINCE OF PERSIA
Start a new game and while on the balcony, hold L3 and enter X, Square, Triangle, Circle, Triangle, X, Square, Circle.

CLASSIC PASSWORDS

LEVEL	PASSWORD
2	KIEJSC
3	DMKERC
4	ACCVQC
5	XRTLQC
6	UHLCQC
7	RXCTPC
8	KBJOOC
9	DFPJNC
10	SWJJLC
11	LAQEKC
12	ZMBTOC

PROTOTYPE 2

NEW GAME +
Complete every story mission.

RATCHET & CLANK

The following cheats can be activated only after defeating Drek. After getting the Cheat Enabled message, go to Cheats in the Goodies Menu and toggle it on/off.

CLANK BIG HEAD

During a game, perform the following: Flip Back, Hyper-Strike, Comet-Strike, Double Jump, Hyper-Strike, Flip Left, Flip Right, Full Second Crouch.

RATCHET BIG HEAD

During a game, perform the following: Flip Back (X3), Full Second Crouch, Stretch Jump, Full Second Glide.

ENEMY BIG HEAD

During a game, perform the following: Stretch Jump, Flip Back (x3), Stretch Jump, Flip Back (x3), Stretch Jump, Flip Back (x3), Full Second Crouch.

NPC BIG HEAD

During a game, perform the following: Flip Left, Flip Right, Flip Back (x3), Comet-Strike, Double Jump, Comet-Strike, Hyper-Strike.

INVINCIBILITY

During a game, perform the following: Comet-Strike (x4), Flip Back, Full Second Crouch, Flip Back, Full Second Crouch, Comet-Strike (x4).

MIRRORED LEVELS

During a game, perform the following: Flip Left (x4), Multi-Strike, Hyper-Strike, Flip Right, Flip Right, Double Jump, Flip Right, Flip Right, Double Jump, Full Second Crouch.

TRIPPY CONTRAILS

During a game, perform the following: Wall Jump (x10), Double Jump, Hyper-Strike. This adds effect behind Ratchet during rail slide.

THE RATCHET & CLANK COLLECTION

RATCHET & CLANK

The following cheats can be activated only after defeating Drek. After getting the Cheat Enabled message, go to Cheats in the Goodies Menu and toggle it on/off.

CLANK BIG HEAD

During a game, perform the following: Flip Back, Hyper-Strike, Comet-Strike, Double Jump, Hyper-Strike, Flip Left, Flip Right, Full Second Crouch.

RATCHET BIG HEAD

During a game, perform the following: Flip Back (X3), Full Second Crouch, Stretch Jump, Full Second Glide.

ENEMY BIG HEAD

During a game, perform the following: Stretch Jump, Flip Back (x3), Stretch Jump, Flip Back (x3), Stretch Jump, Flip Back (x3), Full Second Crouch.

NPC BIG HEAD

During a game, perform the following: Flip Left, Flip Right, Flip Back (x3), Comet-Strike, Double Jump, Comet-Strike, Hyper-Strike.

INVINCIBILITY

During a game, perform the following: Comet-Strike (x4), Flip Back, Full Second Crouch, Flip Back, Full Second Crouch, Comet-Strike (x4).

MIRRORED LEVELS

During a game, perform the following: Flip Left (x4), Multi-Strike, Hyper-Strike, Flip Right, Flip Right, Double Jump, Flip Right, Flip Right, Double Jump, Full Second Crouch.

TRIPPY CONTRAILS

During a game, perform the following: Wall Jump (x10), Double Jump, Hyper-Strike. This adds effect behind Ratchet during rail slide.

RATCHET & CLANK: UP YOUR ARSENAL

DUAL BLADE LASER SWORD

Pause the game and press Circle, Square, Circle, Square, Up, Down, Left, Left.

QWARK'S ALTERNATE COSTUME

Start a game of Qwark Vid-Comic and press Up, Up, Down, Down, Left, Right, Circle, Square, Square.

SQUAT STATS

At the online menu, highlight Stats and press Up, Down, Left, Right, Square.

PIRATE VS NINJA MINI-GAME

At the Qwark Comics Issue select, press Square to bring up a password screen. Enter _MEGHAN_ as a password.

RATCHET & CLANK FUTURE: A CRACK IN TIME

DISCOUNT AT WEAPON VENDORS

Have a save game for Ratchet and Clank Future: Tools of Destruction.

PIRATE HAT SKIN

Have a save game for Ratchet and Clank Future: Quest for Booty.

BANCHO RATCHET SKIN

Pause the game and enter Up, Right, Down, Left, Triangle, Square, X, Circle, R3.

RED DEAD REDEMPTION

CHEATS

Select Cheats from Options menu and enter the following codes. Note, though, that entering cheats will disable Trophies and saving.

NAME	ENTER
Invincibility	HE GIVES STRENGTH TO THE WEAK
Infinite Dead Eye	I DON'T UNDERSTAND IMNFINITY
Infinite Horse Stamina	MAKE HAY WHILE THE SUN SHINES
Infinite Ammo	ABUNDANCE IS EVERYWHERE
Money ($500)	THE ROOT OF ALL EVIL, WE THANK YOU!
Coach	NOW WHO PUT THAT THERE?
Horse	BEASTS AND MAN TOGETHER
Good Guy	IT AINT PRIDE. IT'S HONOR
Famous	I AM ONE OF THEM FAMOUS FELLAS
Diplomatic Immunity	I WISH I WORKED FOR UNCLE SAM
Decrease Bounty	THEY SELL SOULS CHEAP HERE
Gun Set 1	IT'S MY CONSTITUTIONAL RIGHT
Gun Set 2	I'M AN AMERICAN. I NEED GUNS
Who?	HUMILITY BEFORE THE LORD
Old School (Sepia)	THE OLD WAYS IS THE BEST WAYS
Man in Uniform (Bureau, US Army, and US Marshal uniforms)	I LOVE A MAN IN UNIFORM
Sharp Dressed Man (Gentleman's Suit)	DON'T YOU LOOK FINE AND DANDY
Lewis and Clark (All areas)	YOU GOT YOURSELF A FINE PAIR OF EYES
Gang Chic (Treasure Hunter outfit)	YOU THINK YOU TOUGH, MISTER?
Jack Attack (Play as Jack)	OH MY SON, MY BLESSED SON
Hic (Drunk)	I'M DRUNK AS A SKUNK AND TWICE AS SMELLY

PLAYSTATION HOME AVATAR ITEMS

ITEM	EARNED BY
Sombrero	Shooting the hat off an enemy.
Black on red RDR logo T-shirt (male & female)	Opening the chest in the burned out house in Riley's Charge.
Yellow Rockstar logo T-shirt (male & female)	Opening the chest in the attic of John Marston's Beechers Hope house.
Gentleman's attire/lady's finest	Completing Skin It To Win It Social Club Challenge
Posse T-shirt (male & female)	Getting the high score in Strike It Rich Social Club Challenge

RED FACTION: GUERRILLA

WRECKING CREW MAPS

Select Extras from the Options menu, choose Enter Code, and enter MAPMAYHEM.

GOLDEN SLEDGEHAMMER, SINGLE-PLAYER MODE

Select Extras from the Options menu, choose Enter Code, and enter HARDHITTER.

RESIDENT EVIL 5

MERCENARY CHARACTERS

Complete the following stages in The Mercenaries with at least an A-rank to unlock the corresponding character.

CHARACTER (OUTFIT)	STAGE
Jill (BSAA)	Public Assembly
Wesker (Midnight)	The Mines
Chris (Safari)	The Village
Sheva (Clubbin')	Ancient Ruins
Chris (S.T.A.R.S.)	Experimental Facility
Sheva (Tribal)	Missile Area
Jill (Battle Suit)	Ship Deck
Wesker (S.T.A.R.S.)	Prison

RESIDENT EVIL 6

ADA WONG'S CAMPAIGN

Complete the campaigns for Chris, Jake, and Leon.

ADA WONG IN MERCENARIES

Complete Ada's Campaign.

HELENA HARPER IN MERCENARIES

Complete Urban Chaos with at least a B ranking.

PIERS NIVANS IN MERCENARIES

Complete Steel Beast with at least a B ranking.

SHERRY BIRKIN IN MERCENARIES

Complete Mining the Depths with at least a B ranking.

ALTERNATE COSTUME IN MERCENARIES

Earn an A ranking in Mercenaries on any level to unlock an alternate costume for that character.

CARLA RADAMES IN MERCENARIES

Unlock all other characters and alternate costumes.

RESONANCE OF FATE

Once you have reached Chapter 7, search Leanne's closet. As she speaks her first line enter the following codes to unlock more outfits.

8-BIT GIRL SHIRT
Up, Up, Down, Down, Left, Right, Left, Right, △, □

CLUB FAMITSU SHIRT
△, △, Up, Up, □, □, Left, Left, L1, R1

GEMAGA SHIRT
R2, L2, L1, R1, △, △, △, □, □, Up

HIRAKOU SHIRT
□, △, L1, L1, R1, R1, L3, L3, Up, Down

PLATFORM LOGO SHIRT
R2, R1, R3, L3, L1, L2, Right, Left, □, △

POLITAN SUIT
R3, R3, R3, Right, Left, △, □, L2, R2, L1. This requires you to have the Reindeer Suit first.

RETRO CITY RAMPAGE

Be careful as saving, trophies, and leaderboards are disabled until you restart the game.

$100,000
During a game, press Left, Right, Left, Right, Up, Up, Down, Down, R, ○.

ALL STAGES
During a game, press △, △, ✕, △, △, ✕, △, △, ✕, ○, ○.

ALL STYLES
During a game, press Left, Left, Right, Right, Up, Down, Up, Down, ✕, ○.

ALL WEAPONS
During a game, press Up, Up, Down, Down, Left, Right, Left, Right, ✕, ○.

GAWD MODE
During a game, press Up, Up, Left, Right, Left, Right, Down, Down, R, ✕.

GAWD MODE OFF
During a game, press Down, Down, Left, Right, Left, Right, Up, Up, R, ✕.

RED SWEAT MODE
During a game, press ✕, ○, ✕, △, ✕, ○, ○.

SPEED SHOES
During a game, press Right, Right, Up, Down, Left, Left, Up, Down, R, ✕.

DESTRUCTOID STAFF PLAYABLE CHARACTERS
Go to MJ's Face-R-Us and enter DTOID as a coupon code.

MOJANG STAFF PLAYABLE CHARACTERS
Go to MJ's Face-R-Us and enter MOJANG as a coupon code.

THE REVENGE OF SHINOBI

STAGE PRACTICE
At the title screen, hold A + B + C and press Start. This unlocks the mode at the main menu.

ROBERT LUDLUM'S THE BOURNE CONSPIRACY

AUTOMATIC SHOTGUNS REPLACE SIMI-AUTOS
Select Cheats from the Main menu, press □, and then enter alwaysanobjective.

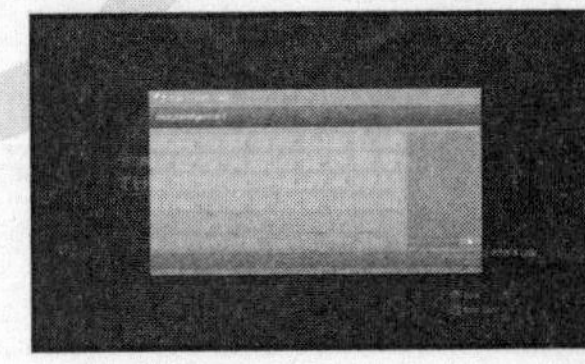

LIGHT MACHINE GUNS HAVE SILENCERS
Select Enter Code from the Cheats screen and enter whattheymakeyougive.

EXTRAS UNLOCKED – CONCEPT ART

Select Enter Code from the Cheats screen and enter lastchancemarie. Select Concept Art from the Extras menu.

EXTRAS UNLOCKED – MUSIC TRACKS

Select Enter Code from the Cheats screen and enter jasonbourneisdead. This unlocks Treadstone Appointment and Manheim Suite in the Music Selector found in the Extras menu.

ROCK BAND 3

GUILD X-79 GUITAR

At the main menu, press Blue, Orange, Orange, Blue, Orange, Orange, Blue, Blue.

OVATION D-2010 GUITAR

At the main menu, press Orange, Blue, Orange, Orange, Blue, Blue, Orange, Blue.

STOP! GUITAR

At the main menu, press Orange, Orange, Blue, Blue, Orange, Blue, Blue, Orange.

ROCK REVOLUTION

ALL CHARACTERS

At the Main menu, press Circle, Square, Circle, Square, Circle, Square, Circle, Triangle, Square.

ALL VENUES

At the Main menu, press Square, Circle, Triangle, Circle, Square, Circle, Triangle, Square, Triangle.

ROCKET KNIGHT

ALL CHARACTER SKINS

At the Title screen, press Up, Up, Down, Down, Left, Right, Left, Right, Circle, X, Start.

ROCKSMITH

UNLOCKABLE SONGS

As you achieve Double Encores, the following songs are unlocked randomly.

Boss by Chris Lee
Jules by Seth Chapla
Ricochet by Brian Adam McCune
Six AM Salvation by Versus Them
Space Ostrich by Disonaur
The Star Spangled Banner by Seth Chapla

SAINTS ROW: THE THIRD

From the cell phone, select Cheats from Extras and enter the following. Using any of these cheats disables autosave and achievements.

GAMEPLAY CHEATS

CHEAT	CODE
Give $100,000	CHEESE
Give Respect	WHATITMEANSTOME
Heavenbound	FRYHOLE
Add Gang Notoriety	LOLZ
Add Police Notoriety	PISSOFPIGS
Infinite Sprint	RUNFAST
No Car Damage	VROOM
No Cop Notoriety	GOODY GOODY
No Gang Notoriety	OOPS
No Gang Notoriety	OOPS
No Police Notoriety	GOODYGOODY
Pedestrians become mascots	MASCOT
Pedestrians become pimps and prostitutes	HOHOHO
Pedestrians become zombies	BRAINS
Repair Car	REPAIRCAR

WORLD CHEATS

CHEAT	CODE
Bloody Mess (Everyone you kill explodes.)	NOTRATED
Drunk pedestrians	DUI

VEHICLES

VEHICLE	CODE
Ambulance	GIVEEMBULANCE
Anchor	GIVEANCHOR
Attrazione	GIVEATTRAZIONE
Bootlegger	GIVEBOOTLEGGER
Challenger	GIVECHALLENGER
Commander	GIVECOMMANDER
Condor	GIVECONDOR
Eagle	GIVEEAGLE
Estrada	GIVEESTRADA
Gatmobile	GIVEGATMOBILE
Kanada	GIVEKANADA
Kenshin	GIVEKENSHIN
Knoxville	GIVEKNOXVILLE
Korbra	GIVEKOBRA
Krukov	GIVEKRUKOV
Miami	GIVEMIAMI
Municipal	GIVEMUNICIPAL
Nforcer	GIVENFORCER
Peacemaker	GIVEPEACEMAKER
Phoenix	GIVEPHOENIX
Reaper	GIVEREAPER
Repaircar	REPAIRCAR
RPG	GIVERPG
Sandstorm	GIVESANDSTORM
Satchel Charge	GIVESATCHEL
Shark	GIVESHARK
Sheperd	GIVESHEPERD
Spectre	GIVESPECTRE
Squasar	GIVESQUASAR
Status Quo	GIVESTATUSQUO
Taxi	GIVETAXI
Titan	GIVETITAN
Toad	GIVETOAD
Tornado	GIVETORNADO
Vortex	GIVEVORTEX
VTOL	GIVEVTOL
Vulture	GIVEVULTURE
Widowmaker	GIVEWIDOWMAKER
Woodpecker	GIVEWOODPECKER

WEAPON CHEATS

WEAPON	CODE
45 Sheperd	GIVESHEPERD
Air Strike	GIVEAIRSTRIKE
Apoca-fists	GIVEAPOCA
AR 55	GIVEAR
As3 Ultimax	GIVEULTIMAX
Baseball Bat	GIVEBASEBALL
Chainsaw	GIVECHAINSAW
Cyber Blaster	GIVECYBERSMG
Cyber Buster	GIVECYBER

WEAPON	CODE
D4th Blossom	GIVEBLOSSOM
Drone	GIVEDRONE
Electric Grenade	GIVEELECTRIC
Flamethrower	GIVEFLAMETHROWER
Grenade	GIVEGRENADE
Hammer	GIVEHAMMER
K-8 Krukov	GIVEKRUKOV
Minigun	GIVEMINIGUN
Molotov	GIVEMOLOTOV
RPG	GIVERPG
Satchel	GIVESATCHEL
Tek Z-10	GIVETEK

WEATHER CHEATS

WEATHER	CODE
Cloudy	OVERCAST
Rainy	LIGHTRAIN
Sunny	CLEARSKIES
Very Stormy	HEAVYRAIN

SCOTT PILGRIM VS. THE WORLD: THE GAME

PLAY AS SAME CHARACTER

At the title screen, press Down, R1, Up, L1, △, ○.

POWER OF LOVE SWORD

At the title screen, press □, □, □, ✕, ○, ✕, △

HEARTS WHEN HITTING OPPONENT

At the title screen, press ✕, ○, ✕, ○, □, ✕, ○, ○.

BLOOD MODE

At the title screen, press ✕, ○, ✕, □, ✕, ○, ○.

BOSS RUSH MODE

Pause the game on the overworld and press Right, Right, ○, R1, Right, Right, ○, R1.

ZOMBIE MODE

At the title screen, press Down, Up, Right, Down, Up, Right, Down, Up, Right, Right, Right.

SOUND CHECK BONUS LEVEL

Pause the game on the overworld and press L1, L1, R1, R1, L1, L1, L1, R1, R1, R1, L1, R1.

CHANGE MONEY TO ANIMALS

At the title screen, press Up, Up, Down, Down, Up, Up, Up, Up.

SHANK

KUNG FU SHANK

Reach 1000 kills. Press Start to view your tally.

SHANK THE GIMP

Kill 500 creatures.

HORROR SHANK

Get 100 kills with the Chainsaw.

WHITE PAJAMAS SHANK

Perform a 100-hit combo.

RED PAJAMAS SHANK

Perform a 150-hit combo.

DANCE SHANK

Complete the single-player campaign on Normal mode.

WILDMAN SHANK

Complete the single-player campaign on Hard mode.

SHANK THE SPARTAN

Complete the Backstory Co-op mode.

ANY-S

After completing the single-player campaign, pause a game and press Up, Up, Down, Down, Left, Right, Left, Right, ○, ✕.

DEATHSPANK

After completing the single-player campaign, pause a game and press Up, □, Down, ○, Left, △, Right, ✕

SHANK 2

EVIL IN SURVIVAL MODE

At the character select, press Up, Up, Down, Down, Left, Right, Left, Right. This must be re-entered after quitting the game.

CHARACTERS FOR SURVIVAL MODE

CHARACTER	HOW TO UNLOCK
Boogie	Buy everything in survival mode.
Bubbles	Stay alive for 15 consecutive waves.
Cesar	Kill someone with the kitchen sink.
Chop Chop	60 pistol counter kills.
Classic Shank	Kill a goon by throwing a bomber.
Defender	100 turret kills.
Falcone	Complete Campaign on hard.
Hobo	Complete all 30 waves on any survival map.
Horror	Reach the zombie wave (14) on each survival map.
Junior	50 fire trap kills.
Kats	100 grenade kills.
Rex	Complete campaign on normal.
Rin	Perform 20 bat counter kills.
Sunshine	Purchase any item in survival mode.

SILENT HILL: DOWNPOUR

GREEN LOCKER PASSWORDS

At a green locker enter the following passwords:

WEAPONS	PASSWORD
Nail Gun and Double Axe	171678
Pistol 45 and Baseball Bat	353479
Rifle and Golf Club	911977

THE SIMPSONS ARCADE GAME

ALL EXTRAS

At the title screen, press Up, Up, Down, Down, Left, Right, Left, Right, ●, ⊗.

THE SIMS 3

CHEATS

Load your family, press Start, and hold L1 + L2 + R1 + R2. The game will then prompt you to save another file before activating the cheats. After doing so, Spoot the Llama will be available in Misc Décor. Place it in your lot and click it to access the cheats. Note, however, that this disables Trophies and challenges.

THE SIMS 3: PETS

CREATION MODE

Pause the game and press L2 + L1 + R2 + R1. This disables trophies.

SKATE 3

HOVERBOARD MODE

In Free Play, select Extras from the Options menu. Choose Enter Cheat Code and input mcfly.

MINI SKATER MODE

In Free Play, select Extras from the Options menu. Choose Enter Cheat Code and input miniskaters.

ZOMBIE MODE

In Free Play, select Extras from the Options menu. Choose Enter Cheat Code and input zombie.

ISAAC CLARK FROM DEADSPACE

In Free Play, select Extras from the Options menu. Choose Enter Cheat Code and input deadspacetoo.

DEM BONES

Defeat most of the Hall of Meat Challenges.

MEAT MAN

Complete all Hall of Meat Challenges.

RESET OBJECTS TO ORIGINAL POSITIONS

In Free Play, select Extras from the Options menu. Choose Enter Cheat Code and input streetsweeper.

SKULLGIRLS

COLOR PALETTE 10

At the versus screen in local gameplay, press Down, R1, Up, L1, ■, ✖.

SKYLANDERS GIANTS

SKYLANDERS SPECIFIC QUESTS

Skylanders Giants includes quests specific to each Skylander as a way to improve them. Here we list each Skylander with their quest and tips on how to complete it.

SKYLANDER	QUEST	HOW TO COMPLETE
Bash	On a Roll: Defeat 10 enemies with one roll attack.	If you have trouble completing this quest, opt for the Pulver Dragon upgrade path.
Boomer	On a Troll: Defeat five enemies with one kicked Troll Bomb.	Once you have Troll Bomb Boot, look for a group of tight-knit Chompies. "Chapter 1: Time of the Giants" has several groupings of five Chompies.
Bouncer	Stay on Target!: Target enemies 100 times with laser-guided Shoulder Rockets	You must purchase the Targeting Computer upgrade for Bouncer's Shoulder Rockets.
Camo	Garden Gorger: Eat 10 watermelons.	If you aren't in a rush to complete a level, switch to Camo when a watermelon appears.
Chill	Ice Sore: Defeat six enemies with one Ice Narwhal attack.	Try to find six enemies that are grouped together at a medium distance, such as in an arena.
Chop Chop	Stalwart Defender: Absorb 1,000 damage with your shield.	To complete this quest safely, block attacks from a small group of weaker enemies near a food item (just in case they sneak in some unexpected damage).
Crusher	High Roller: Defeat 100 enemies with boulders.	Use Rockslide defeat enemies until you have completed this quest.
Cynder	On the Haunt: Defeat 50 enemies with your Ghost Ally.	Ghost Ally does not inflict much damage so focus on saving low-health enemies, like Chompies, for the ghost to attack. The Ghost attacks while Cynder is flying, so consider circling an area with Chompies.

SKYLANDER	QUEST	HOW TO COMPLETE
Dino-Rang	Fooderang: Pick up 20 food items with boomerangs.	After acquiring Sticky Boomerangs, use it to grab any food found in the area. In the Arena Challenges on Flynn's Ship, the audience throws food items into the arena between rounds.
Double Trouble	Big Bomb Trouble: Defeat 10 enemies with one Magic Bomb attack.	Find a group of 10 or more Chompies and set off a bomb. A good place to earn this is any of of Brock's Arena Challenges with regular Chompies.
Drill Sergeant	Drill Skill: Defeat Drill-X without changing Skylanders.	Drill Sergeant must defeat Drill-X (the final boss in Chapter 11: Drill-X's Big Rig) solo. Use Adventure items (like Healing Potion) to survive the battle. You can complete it on Easy difficulty with a fully-upgraded Drill Sergeant.
Drobot	Feed the Burn: Defeat 50 enemies with Afterburners.	It's easiest to hit enemies with Afterburners when Drobot first takes off.
Eruptor	Pizza Burp: Eat 10 Pizzas.	If you want to have a greater chance of encountering a pizza, equip Lucky Wheel of Health in the Luck-O-Tron.
Eye Brawl	Gold Search: Collect 5,000 gold with the eyeball detached	Remember to detach Eye-Brawl's eye before collecting any treasure from chests or enemies.
Flameslinger	Circular Combustion: Defeat 10 enemies with one column of Fire Flame Dash.	There are two upgrades you can get to help you on this quest. The first is Column of Fire. The second is Supernova in the Pyromancer Path.
Flashwing	Let It Shine: Defeat 20 enemies with one Crystal Lighthouse.	Since Crystal Lighthouse is stationary, this is a tricky quest. The best candidate for this is one of the arena maps, particularly Kaos' Royal Flush (the second challenge, Birthday Bash). Set up the Lighthouse in the middle of the birthday cake.
Fright Rider	Delving Throw: Toss 50 enemies into the air	The power to use for this quest is Burrow Bomber. Hit any medium or small enemy with the attack to pop them up in the air and register a toss.
Ghost Roaster	Grave Circumstances: Defeat 100 enemies with Skull Charge.	Repeatedly use Skull Charge to attack enemies and you should complete this quest in no time.
Gill Grunt	Anchors Away!: Defeat six enemies with one Anchor Attack.	Line up a group of Chompies with your Anchor Cannon and let loose to complete the quest. If you have Series 2 Gill Grunt, Anchor's Away! makes completing the quest easier.
Hex	Noggin Knocker: Knock away 100 enemies with your Skull Rain.	Once Hex has Skull Shield, allow enemies to get within melee range while Hex is charging that attack. If they get too close, they get knocked back, tallying a point for this quest.
Hot Dog	Animal Aggravator: Scare away 20 birds.	Look for the small birds pecking at the ground in each level. These birds are the ones you need to scare with Hot Dog for this achievement. Chapter 13: The Oracle and Chapter 1: Time of Giants both have plenty of birds.

SKYLANDER	QUEST	HOW TO COMPLETE
Hot Head	Buggy Breakthrough: Destroy 20 walls in Hot Rod mode.	The walls this quest is referring to are the walls that can only be crushed by a Giant or a bomb. Whenever you encounter one of these walls, switch to Hot Head. A good spot with plenty of these types of walls is Chapter 2: Junkyard Isles.
Ignitor	Tinder Trekker: Travel 26,000 feet in Flame Form.	Use Flame Form often and this number will accumulate quickly.
Jet-Vac	Bird Cleaner: Suck up 50 birds in your Suction Gun.	Look for tiny birds on the ground throughout most levels with green grass. Chapter 13: The Oracle and Chapter 1: Time of Giants both have plenty of birds.
Lightning Rod	Current Event: Defeat 10 enemies with one Grand Lightning strike.	You need to find a group of 10 Chompies in one area and use the Grand Lightning to blast them all. Choosing the Lord of Lightning Path makes this easier since the Grand Lightning attack lasts longer.
Ninjini	Bottle Beatdown: Defeat 5 enemies within five seconds of exiting your bottle.	Transform Ninjini into the bottle and move into a large group of small enemies. Follow up the bottle attack with her swords.
Pop Fizz	Rampage: Do 200 HP of damage in a single run in Beast Form.	Transform into Beast Form in a large group of enemies and destroy everything in sight to complete the quest.
Prism Break	Bifurcation Sensation: Defeat 100 enemies with double refraction.	A beam must pass through two Shards before hitting an enemy to count. Unlock the Chained Refractions upgrade and place plenty of Crystal Shards. Fire an Energy Beam through them to indirectly take out nearby enemies.
Shroomboom	Lunching Launch: Eat a watermelon while performing a Self-Slingshot!	When you find a watermelon, blast Shroomboom through it with the Self-Slingshot power to complete the quest.
Slam Bam	Ice to Meet You: Trap 100 enemies in your Ice Blocks.	You do not need to damage or freeze enemies with Ice Block; it counts if you just hit them with the Ice Block.
Sonic Boom	Sonic Squeak: Babies defeat 50 enemies.	Upgrade Sonic Boom's egg attack powers and keep babies summoned at all times.
Sprocket	Mined Your Step: Defeat 50 enemies using the Landmine Golf attack.	Once you unlock the Landmine Golf ability, use it often. A quick way to complete this quest is to load up one of the easier Arena levels.
Spyro	Full Charge: Collect 3 gold, eat 1 food item, and defeat 2 enemies in 1 Sprint Charge.	Look for two low-health enemies (Chompies are a good choice) as well as some food and gold on the screen. Purchase the Sprint Charge upgrade to increase the distance of Spyro's sprint.
Stealth Elf	Stealth Health: Gain 1,000 HP while stealthed.	You need to first purchase Sylvan Regeneration. Once you do, you get credit towards the 1,000 HP every time you heal while Stealth Elf is in the Stealthier Decoy mode.
Stump Smash	Meganut Bowling: Defeat five enemies with one Meganut.	Meganuts are powerful, and bowling over five Chompies with one is no problem. The upgrade Acorn Croquet makes this much easier to achieve since you can wack the acorn directly at enemies.

SKYLANDER	QUEST	HOW TO COMPLETE
Sunburn	Immolation Itinerant: Travel 1 mile using Immolation Teleport	Use Immolation Teleport regularly to tally up the distance towards one full mile. The quickest way to complete this quest is to unlock the Flight of the Phoenix and the Guided Teleportation upgrades.
Swarm	Swarm Feelings: Defeat 100 enemies in Swarm Form.	While you can complete this quest without pursuing the Wasp Stormer Path, it's extremely difficult, and you must focus on weaker enemies.
Terrafin	Land Lubber: Eat 20 food items while burrowing.	Once you have Surface Feeder, stay underground and collect Food Items as they drop.
Thumpback	Beached Whale: Defeat 8 enemies with one Belly Flop.	Upgrade Thumpback's Belly Flop attack with Slippery Belly. If you are having trouble getting this quest, invest in the Up Close and Personal path to further increase the strength of the Belly Flop attack.
Tree Rex	Timberrrrr!: Defeat 50 enemies by landing on them. Chompies don't count!	Unfortunately, Elbow Drop doesn't work for this quest. Tree Rex must crush enemies by landing on them. The best way to do this is to find a bounce pad in an area with plenty of Chompies.
Trigger Happy	Holding Gold: Save up 50,000 Gold	This is one of the hardest quests any character has in the game. Not because it's difficult, but because it will take some time to collect 50,000 Gold.
Voodood	Trickwire: Defeat six enemies at once with your tripwire.	Find a group of six or more low-health enemies, like Bone Chompies, and set up the Tripwire near them. Chapter 1: Time of the Giants has several good spots to try for this quest.
Warnado	Chompy Catcher: Catch 100 Chompies in tornadoes.	The best place to do this is in the Arena Challenges. Head to any of the early challenges and there are plenty of Chompies. High Winds also helps gather up more Chompies at once.
Wham-Shell	Irate Invertebrate: Defeat 6 enemies with one Poseidon Strike.	To get the most out of Poseidon Strike, invest in the Captain Crustacean path. Once you have unlocked Mace of the Deep, go for this quest by finding a group of Chompies and blasting them.
Whirlwind	What does it mean?: Create 50 double rainbows.	Unlock the Duel Rainbows ability, then fire out a Tempest cloud and following up with a Rainbow of Doom. Rainbows made via the Double Dose of Doom power don't count unless they hit a Tempest Cloud. Triple rainbows created via Triple Tempest count as one double rainbow.
Wrecking Ball	Competitive Eater: Swallow 100 Enemies	Purchase Enemy Slurp and swallow as many enemies as you can. Any medium-sized and smaller enemy can be eaten.
Zap	In the Slimelight: Defeat 50 enemies by electrifying them in Sea Slime	Use Sea Slime to electrify enemies regularly and you'll complete this quest in no time.
Zook	Spore It On: Absorb 1,000 points of damage with a Foliage Barrier	Use Foliage Barrier often and you will complete this quest quickly.

SLEEPING DOGS

RICO'S OUTFIT FROM JUST CAUSE 2

With a Just Cause 2 save game on system, Rico's outfit can be found in Wei's closet.

THE SLY COLLECTION

SLY 2: BAND OF THIEVES

RESTART CURRENT EPISODE

Pause the game and press Left, R1, Up, Down, Up, Left.

TUTORIAL

Pause the game and press Right, Left, Up, Up, Up, R1.

SKIP TO EPISODE 1

Pause the game and press Down, R1, Left, Right, R1, Down.

SKIP TO EPISODE 2

Pause the game and press R1, Left, Right, R1, Left, Down.

SKIP TO EPISODE 3

Pause the game and press Up, Left, Right, Left, Down, Up.

SKIP TO EPISODE 4

Pause the game and press Up, Right, Right, Up, Left, Left.

SKIP TO EPISODE 5

Pause the game and press Left, R1, Down, Down, Up, Right.

SKIP TO EPISODE 6

Pause the game and press Down, Up, R1, R1, Left, Down.

SKIP TO EPISODE 7

Pause the game and press Left, Left, Left, Down, Down, R1.

SKIP TO EPSIODE 8

Pause the game and press Down Up, Left, Left, R1, Right.

UNLOCK TOM GADGET

Pause the game and press Left, Left, Down, Right, Left, Right.

TIME RUSH ABILITY

Pause the game and press Down, Down, Up, Down, Right, Left.

SLY 3: HONOR AMONG THIEVES

FLY THE TOONAMI PLANE

While in the regular plane, pause the game and press R1, R1, Right, Down, Down, Right.

RESTART MISSIONS

Pause the game and enter the following codes to restart the corresponding missions:

RESTART THIS MISSION	ENTER THIS CODE
Episode 1, Day 1	Left, R2, Right, L1, R2, L1
Episode 1, Day 2	Down, L2, Up, Left, R2, L2
Episode 2, Day 1	Right, L2, Left, Up, Right, Down
Episode 2, Day 2	Down, Up, R1, Up, R2, L2
Episode 3, Day 1	R2, R1, L1, Left, L1, Down
Episode 3, Day 2	L2, R1, R2, L2, L1, Up
Episode 4, Day 1	Left, Right, L1, R2, Right, R2
Episode 4, Day 2	L1, Left, L2, Left, Up, L1
Episode 5, Day 1	Left, R2, Right, Up, L1, R2

Episode 5, Day 2	R2, R1, L1, R1, R2, R1
Operation Laptop Retrieval	L2, Left, R1, L2, L1, Down
Operation Moon Crash	L2, Up, Left, L1, L2, L1
Operation Reverse Double Cross	Right, Left, Up, Left, R2, Left
Operation Tar Be-Gone	Down, L2, R1, L2, R1, Right
Operation Turbo Dominant Eagle	Down, Right, Left, L2, R1, Right
Operation Wedding Crasher	L2, R2, Right, Down, L1, R2

SOCOM: U.S. NAVY SEALS CONFRONTATION

AMELI MACHINE GUN

Select Spain as your clan country.

FAMAS G2 ASSAULT RIFLE

Select France as your clan country.

GMP SUBMACHINE GUN

Select Germany as your clan country.

IW-80 A2 ASSAULT RIFLE

Select U.K. as your clan country.

SCFR-LW ASSAULT RIFLE

Select U.S. as your clan country.

SONIC GENERATIONS

SECRET STATUE ROOM

In the Collection Room, hold Select for a few seconds. Sonic jumps into the statue room below. Once there, press Select and enter the following.

STATUE	CODE
Aero-Cannon	329 494
Amy Rose	863 358
Big the Cat	353 012
Blaze the Cat	544 873
Booster	495 497
Buzz Bomber	852 363
Capsule	777 921
Chao	629 893
Chaos Emerald	008 140
Charmy Bee	226 454
Chip	309 511
Chopper	639 402
Classic Eggman	103 729
Classic Sonic	171 045
Classic Tails	359 236
Cop Speeder	640 456
Crabmeat	363 911
Cream the Rabbit	332 955
Cucky/Picky/Flicky/Pecky	249 651
Dark Chao	869 292
Dr. Eggman	613 482
E-123 Omega	601 409
Egg Chaser	200 078
Egg Fighter	851 426
Egg Launcher	973 433
Egg Pawn	125 817
Eggrobo	360 031
Espio the Chameleon	894 526

STATUE	CODE
Goal Plate	933 391
Goal Ring	283 015
Grabber	275 843
Gun Beetle	975 073
Gun Hunter	668 250
Hero Chao	507 376
Iblis Biter	872 910
Iblis Taker	513 929
Iblis Worm	711 268
Item Box	209 005
Jet the Hawk	383 870
Knuckles the Echidna	679 417
Metal Sonic	277 087
Miles "Tails" Prower	632 951
Moto Bug	483 990
Omochao	870 580
Ring	390 884
Rouge the Bat	888 200
Sandworm	548 986
Shadow the Hedgehog	262 416
Silver the Hedgehog	688 187
Sonic the Hedgehog	204 390
Spinner	530 741
Spiny	466 913
Spring – Star	537 070
Spring	070 178
Vector the Crocodile	868 377

SOULCALIBUR V

ALGOL FEAR AND TOWER OF GLORY: MOST HOLY DICHOTOMY STAGE

Defeat Algol Fear in Legendary Souls or Quick Battle

ALPHA PATROKLOS AND ASTRAL CHAOS: PATHWAY STAGE

Defeat Patrolklos in Quick Battle.

EDGE MASTER AND TOWER OF GLORY: SPIRAL OF GOOD AND EVIL

Complete chapter 17 of story mode to unlock Edge Master and his stage. You can also be obtained by defeating him in Arcade, Legendary Souls, or Quick Battle.

ELYSIUM AND UTOPIA OF THE BLESSED

Complete the final chapter of story mode.

KILIK AND THE PENITENTIARY OF DESTINY STAGE

Defeat Kilik in Arcade or Legendary Souls.

PYRRHA OMEGA AND DENEVER CASTLE: EYE OF CHAOS

Complete chapter 19 of story mode.

DEVIL JIN STYLE

***

Defeat Harada in Quick Battle or Legendary Souls.

Go to Customization and then to Original Characters. Select anyone male or female and enter size. Choose Weapons & Style and then to Style. At bottom of list is Devil Jin (Tekken).

SPIDER-MAN: EDGE OF TIME

SHATTERED DIMENSIONS BONUS SUITS

If you have a saved game data for Spider-Man: Shattered Dimensions on your system, eight new Alternate Suits become available in the Bonus Gallery.

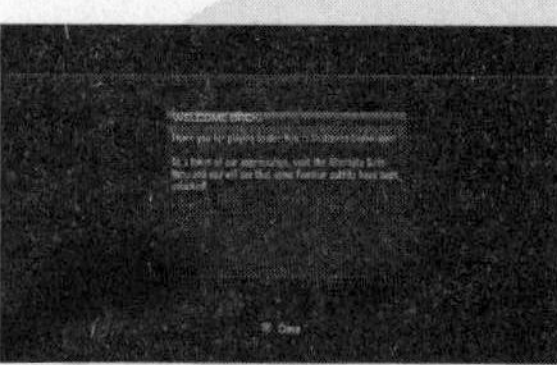

AMAZING SPIDER-MAN #500 SUIT (AMAZING)

Select Enter Code from VIP Unlock Code and enter laststand. Go to the Bonus Gallery to access the alternate suits.

POISON SUIT (2099)

Select Enter Code from VIP Unlock Code and enter innerspider. Go to the Bonus Gallery to access the alternate suits.

SPIDEY VS WOLVERINE SUIT (AMAZING) – WHAT IF? SPIDERMAN

Select Enter Code from VIP Unlock Code and enter coldhearted. Go to the Bonus Gallery to access the alternate suits.

2099 ARENA CHALLENGE AND AMAZING ARENA CHALLENGE

Select Enter Code from VIP Unlock Code and enter twospidersenter. Select Arenas from the Main Menu.

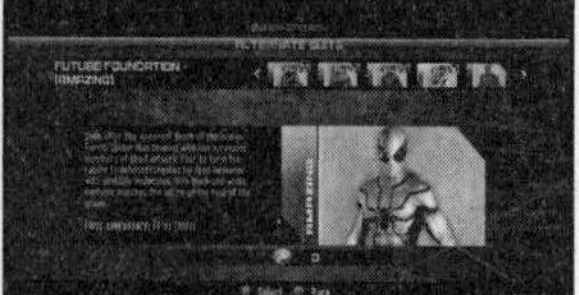

BIG TIME SUIT (2099)

At the main menu, press Right, Down, Down, Up, Left, Down, Down, Right.

FUTURE FOUNDATION SUIT (AMAZING)

At the main menu, press Up, Down, Left, Up, Down, Left, Right, Left.

SPIDER-MAN: SHATTERED DIMENSIONS

The following codes can be entered after completing the tutorial. All the suits are found in the Bonus Gallery under Alternate Suits.

IRON SPIDER SUIT

At the Main menu, press Up, Right, Right, Right, Left, Left, Left, Down, Up.

NEGATIVE ZONE SUIT

At the Main menu, press Left, Right, Right, Down, Right, Down, Up, Left.

SCARLET SPIDER SUIT

At the Main menu, press Right, Up, Left, Right, Up, Left, Right, Up, Left, Right.

STAR TREK: D-A-C

KOBAYASHI MARU SECRET ACHIEVEMENT

At the start of a solo Death Match, press Start. Then enter R2, L2, R1, L1, △, □. This gives you the achievement and improves your ship.

STAR WARS THE CLONE WARS: REPUBLIC HEROES

BIG HEAD MODE

Pause the game, select Shop, and enter the following in Cheats: Up, Down, Left, Right, Left, Right, Down, Up.

MINI-GUN

Pause the game, select Shop, and enter the following in Cheats: Down, Left, Right, Up, Right, Up, Left, Down.

ULTIMATE LIGHTSABER

Pause the game, select Shop, and enter the following in Cheats: Right, Down, Down, Up, Left, Up, Up, Down.

LIGHTSABER THROW UPGRADE

Pause the game, select Shop, and enter the following in Combat Upgrades: Left, Left, Right, Right, Up, Down, Down, Up.

SPIDER DROID UPGRADE

Pause the game, select Shop, and enter the following in Droid-Jak Upgrades: Up, Left, Down, Left, Right, Left, Left, Left.

STAR WARS THE FORCE UNLEASHED: ULTIMATE SITH EDITION

CHEAT CODES

Pause the game and select Input Code. Here you can enter the following codes. Activating any of the following cheat codes will disable some unlockables, and you will be unable to save your progress.

CHEAT	CODE
All Force Powers at Max Power	KATARN
All Force Push Ranks	EXARKUN
All Saber Throw Ranks	ADEGAN

CHEAT	CODE
All Repulse Ranks	DATHOMIR
All Saber Crystals	HURRIKANE
All Talents	JOCASTA
Deadly Saber	LIGHTSABER

COMBOS

Pause the game and select Input Code. Here you can enter the following codes. Activating any of the following cheat codes will disable some unlockables, and you will be unable to save your progress.

COMBO	CODE
All Combos	MOLDYCROW
Aerial Ambush	VENTRESS
Aerial Assault	EETHKOTH
Aerial Blast	YADDLE
Impale	BRUTALSTAB

COMBO	CODE
Lightning Bomb	MASSASSI
Lightning Grenade	RAGNOS
Saber Slam	PLOKOON
Saber Sling	KITFISTO
Sith Saber Flurry	LUMIYA

COMBO	CODE
Sith Slash	DARAGON
Sith Throw	SAZEN

COMBO	CODE
New Combo	FREEDON
New Combo	MARAJADE

ALL DATABANK ENTRIES
Pause the game and select Input Code. Enter OSSUS.

MIRRORED LEVEL
Pause the game and select Input Code. Enter MINDTRICK. Re-enter the code to return level to normal.

SITH MASTER DIFFICULTY
Pause the game and select Input Code. Enter SITHSPAWN.

COSTUMES
Pause the game and select Input Code. Here you can enter the following codes.

COSTUME	CODE
All Costumes	SOHNDANN
Bail Organa	VICEROY
Ceremonial Jedi Robes	DANTOOINE
Drunken Kota	HARDBOILED
Emperor	MASTERMIND
Incinerator Trooper	PHOENIX
Jedi Adventure Robe	HOLOCRON
Kashyyyk Trooper	TK421GREEN

COSTUME	CODE
Kota	MANDALORE
Master Kento	WOOKIEE
Proxy	PROTOTYPE
Scout Trooper	FERRAL
Shadow Trooper	BLACKHOLE
Sith Stalker Armor	KORRIBAN
Snowtrooper	SNOWMAN
Stormtrooper	TK421WHITE
Stormtrooper Commander	TK421BLUE

SUPER HANG-ON

START ARCADE MODE WITH $10,000
Highlight Arcade Mode and press Up, Left, A, B, Start.

SUPER PUZZLE FIGHTER II TURBO HD REMIX

PLAY AS AKUMA
At the character select, highlight Hsien-Ko and press Down.

PLAY AS DAN
At the character select, highlight Donovan and press Down.

PLAY AS DEVILOT
At the character select, highlight Morrigan and press Down.

PLAY AS ANITA
At the character select, hold L1 + R1 and choose Donovan.

PLAY AS HSIEN-KO'S TALISMAN
At the character select, hold L1 + R1 and choose Hsien-Ko.

PLAY AS MORRIGAN AS A BAT
At the character select, hold L1 + R1 and choose Morrigan.

SUPER STREET FIGHTER II TURBO HD REMIX

The following codes give you the classic fighters in Classic Arcade Mode. Select the character, quickly enter the given code, and select him/her again.

CLASSIC BALROG
Right, Left, Left, Right

CLASSIC BLANKA
Left, Right (x3)

CLASSIC CAMMY
Up, Up, Down, Down

CLASSIC CHUN-LI
Down (x3), Up

CLASSIC DEE JAY
Down, Down, Up, Up

CLASSIC DHALSIM
Down, Up (x3)

CLASSIC E. HONDA
Up (x3), Down

CLASSIC FEI LONG
Left, Left, Right, Right

CLASSIC GUILE
Up, Down (x3)

CLASSIC KEN
Left (x3), Right

CLASSIC M. BISON
Down, Up, Up, Down

CLASSIC RYU
Right (x3), Left

CLASSIC SAGAT
Up, Down (x3), Up

CLASSIC T. HAWK
Right, Right, Left, Left

CLASSIC VEGA
Left, Right, Right, Left

CLASSIC ZANGIEF
Left, Right (x3)

SUPER STREET FIGHTER IV

BARREL BUSTER & CAR CRUSHER BONUS STAGES

Complete Arcade Mode in any difficulty.

COLORS & TAUNTS

Colors 1 and 2 plus the first taunt for each fighter are available from the start. For colors 11 and 12, start a game with a Street Fighter IV save game on your system. To earn the rest of the colors and taunts, you must fight a certain number of matches with that character.

COLOR	# OF MATCHES
3	2
4	4
5	6

COLOR	# OF MATCHES
6	8
7	10
8	12

COLOR	# OF MATCHES
9	14
10	16

TAUNT	# OF MATCHES
2	1
3	3
4	5

TAUNT	# OF MATCHES
5	7
6	9
7	11

TAUNT	# OF MATCHES
8	13
9	15
10	16

TIGER WOODS PGA TOUR 12: THE MASTERS

50,000 XP

If you have a save game from Tiger Woods PGA Tour 2011, you receive 50,000 XP.

TIMESHIFT

KRONE IN MULTIPLAYER

Select Multiplayer from the Options menu. Highlight Model and press △ to get to Krone. Press Y and enter RXYMCPENCJ.

TOM CLANCY'S SPLINTER CELL CHAOS THEORY HD

TEAM PICTURE

At the main menu, press R2, ○, ○, ○, ○, ○, □.

ALL LEVELS

Select your profile to play offline. Then, at the main menu, hold L1 + L2 + R1 + R2 and press □ (x5), ○ (x5).

TOM CLANCY'S SPLINTER CELL PANDORA TOMORROW HD

LEVEL SELECT

After defeating the game on hard, hold L1 + L2 at the game select and press ○, ○, □, □, Left, Right, Down, Down.

THE TOMB RAIDER TRILOGY

TOMB RAIDER: LEGEND

The following codes must be unlocked in the game before using them.

BULLETPROOF

During a game, hold L1 and press ✕, R1, △, R1, □, L2.

DRAIN ENEMY HEALTH

During a game, hold L1 and press □, ○, ✕, L2, R1, △.

INFINITE ASSAULT RIFLE AMMO

During a game, hold L2 and press ✕, ○, ✕, L1, □, △.

INFINITE GRENADE LAUNCHER AMMO

During a game, hold L2 and press L1, △, R1, ○, L1, □.

INFINITE SHOTGUN AMMO
During a game, hold L2 and press R1, Circle, Square, L1, Square, X.

INFINITE SMG AMMO
During a game, hold L2 and press Circle, Triangle, L1, R1, X, Circle.

EXCALIBUR
During a game, hold L2 and press Triangle, X, Circle, R1, Triangle, L1.

SOUL REAVER
During a game, hold L2. Then press: X, R1, Circle, R1, L1, Square.

ONE SHOT KILL
During a game, hold L1 and press Triangle, X, Triangle, Square, L2, Circle.

TEXTURELESS MODE
During a game, hold L1 and press L2, X, Circle, X, Triangle, R1.

TOMB RAIDER: UNDERWORLD

INVINCIBLE
During a game, hold L2 and press X, R2, Triangle, R2, Square, L1.

ONE SHOT KILLS
During a game, hold L2 and press hold R2 and press Triangle, X, Triangle, Square, L1, Circle.

SHOW ENEMY HEALTH
During a game, hold L2 and press Square; Circle, X, L1, R2, Triangle.

TONY HAWK'S PRO SKATER HD

ALL CHEATS
At the skater select, hold L2 and press X, Circle, Triangle.

ALL GAME MODES
At the skater select, hold L2 and press X, Triangle, Circle.

ALL LEVELS
At the skater select, hold L2 and press Triangle, Square, Circle.

ALL SKATERS
At the skater select, hold L2 and press Triangle, Circle, Square.

ALL TRICKS
At the skater select, hold L2 and press X, Square, Triangle.

MAX ALL STATS
At the skater select, hold L2 and press Triangle, Square, X.

MAX MONEY
At the skater select, hold L2 and press Triangle, Circle, X. This gives you $999,999,999.

TONY HAWK'S PROVING GROUND

Select Cheat Codes from the Options and enter the following cheats. Some codes need to be enabled by selecting Cheats from the Options during a game.

UNLOCK	CHEAT
Unlocks Boneman	CRAZYBONEMAN
Unlocks Bosco	MOREMILK
Unlocks Cam	NOTACAMERA
Unlocks Cooper	THECOOP
Unlocks Eddie X	SKETCHY
Unlocks El Patinador	PILEDRIVER
Unlocks Eric	FLYAWAY
Unlocks Mad Dog	RABBIES
Unlocks MCA	INTERGALACTIC
Unlocks Mel	NOTADUDE
Unlocks Rube	LOOKSSMELLY
Unlocks Spence	DAPPER
Unlocks Shayne	MOVERS
Unlocks TV Producer	SHAKER
Unlock FDR	THEPREZPARK
Unlock Lansdowne	THELOCALPARK
Unlock Air & Space Museum	THEINDOORPARK
Unlocks all Fun Items	OVERTHETOP
Unlocks all CAS items	GIVEMESTUFF
Unlocks all Decks	LETSGOSKATE

UNLOCK	CHEAT
Unlock all Game Movies	WATCHTHIS
Unlock all Lounge Bling Items	SWEETSTUFF
Unlock all Lounge Themes	LAIDBACKLOUNGE
Unlock all Rigger Pieces	IMGONNABUILD
Unlock all Video Editor Effects	TRIPPY
Unlock all Video Editor Overlays	PUTEMONTOP
All specials unlocked and in player's special list	LOTSOFTRICKS
Full Stats	BEEFEDUP
Give player +50 skill points	NEEDSHELP

The following cheats lock you out of the Leaderboards:

UNLOCK	CHEAT
Unlocks Perfect Manual	STILLAINTFALLIN
Unlocks Perfect Rail	AINTFALLIN
Unlock Super Check	BOOYAH
Unlocks Unlimited Focus	MYOPIC
Unlock Unlimited Slash Grind	SUPERSLASHIN
Unlocks 100% branch completion in NTT	FOREVERNAILED
No Bails	ANDAINTFALLIN

You can not use the Video Editor with the following cheats:

UNLOCK	CHEAT
Invisible Man	THEMISSING
Mini Skater	TINYTATER
No Board	MAGICMAN

TOY STORY 2: BUZZ LIGHTYEAR TO THE RESCUE!

LEVEL SELECT

At the Options menu, press Right, Left, ○, △, △.

ALL LEVELS

At the title screen, press Up (x4), Down, Down, Up, Up, Down (x3).

DEBUG MODE

At the title screen, press ✕, ○, □.

TRANSFORMERS: DARK OF THE MOON

RATCHET IN MULTIPLAYER

Select Unlockables from the Extras and enter Up, Right, Down, Left, Up, Start.

TRANSFORMERS: REVENGE OF THE FALLEN

LOW GRAVITY MODE

Select Cheat Code and enter ✕, □, △, L3, △, L3.

NO WEAPON OVERHEAT

Select Cheat Code and enter L3, □, ✕, L3, △, L1.

ALWAYS IN OVERDRIVE MODE

Select Cheat Code and enter L1, ○, L1, ✕, □, R3.

UNLIMITED TURBO

Select Cheat Code and enter ○, L3, □, R3, ✕, △

NO SPECIAL COOLDOWN TIME

Select Cheat Code and enter R3, □, R3, R3, □, ✕.

INVINCIBILITY

Select Cheat Code and enter R3, ✕, □, L3, □, □.

4X ENERGON FROM DEFEATED ENEMIES

Select Cheat Code and enter △, □, ○, R3, ✕, △.

INCREASED WEAPON DAMAGE (ROBOT FORM)

Select the Cheat Code option and enter △, △, R3, ✕, L1, △.

INCREASED WEAPON DAMAGE (VEHICLE FORM)
Select Cheat Code and enter Triangle, Circle, R1, X, R3, L3.

MELEE INSTANT KILLS
Select the Cheat Code option and enter R3, X. L1, Circle, R3, L1.

LOWER ENEMY ACCURACY
Select Cheat Code and enter X, L3, R3, L3, R3, R1.

INCREASED ENEMY HEALTH
Select Cheat Code and enter Circle, X, L1, Circle, R3, Triangle.

INCREASED ENEMY DAMAGE
Select Cheat Code and enter L1, Triangle, X, Triangle, R3, R3.

INCREASED ENEMY ACCURACY
Select Cheat Code and enter Triangle, Triangle, Circle, X, A, L1.

SPECIAL KILLS ONLY MODE
Select Cheat Code and enter Circle, Circle, R1, Circle, X, L3.

UNLOCK ALL SHANGHAI MISSIONS & ZONES
Select Cheat Code and enter Triangle, L3, R3, L1, Triangle, X.

UNLOCK ALL WEST COAST MISSIONS & ZONES
Select Cheat Code and enter L1, R1, R3, Triangle, R3, Circle.

UNLOCK ALL DEEP SIX MISSIONS & ZONES
Select Cheat Code and enter X, R1, Triangle, Circle, X, L1.

UNLOCK ALL EAST COAST MISSIONS & ZONES
Select Cheat Code and enter R3, L3, R1, X, Circle, X.

UNLOCK ALL CAIRO MISSIONS & ZONES
Select Cheat Code and enter R3, Triangle, X, Triangle, L3, L1.

UNLOCK & ACTIVATE ALL UPGRADES
Select Cheat Code and enter L1, Triangle, L1, Circle, X, X.

TWO WORLDS II

UNLOCKABLE ITEMS
Pause the game, select Bonus Code and enter the following:

ITEM	PASSWORD
Anathros Sword	6770-8976-1634-9490
Axe	1775-3623-3298-1928
Elexorien Two-handed Sword	3542-3274-8350-6064
Hammer	6231-1890-4345-5988
Lucienda Sword	9122-5287-3591-0927
Luciendar Sword	6624-0989-0879-6383
Two-handed Hammer	3654-0091-3399-0994
Dragon Scale Armor	4149-3083-9823-6545
Labyrinth Level	1797-3432-7753-9254
Scroll Bonus Map	6972-5760-7685-8477

ULTIMATE MARVEL VS. CAPCOM 3

PLAY AS GALACTUS
With a save game from Marvel vs. Capcom 3: Fate of Two Worlds on your system, Galactus becomes available. Otherwise, you need to accumulate 30,000 points on a player card. Now highlight Arcade Mode and press L1 + Select + X.

UNCHARTED 2: AMONG THIEVES

In Uncharted 2: Among Thieves, upon opening the store you'll have the option to hit the Square button to check for Uncharted: Drake's Fortune save data. You'll obtain cash for having save data! This cash can be used in the single and multiplayer stores. Could be useful if you want a head start online!

$20,000
Have a saved game of Uncharted: Drake's Fortune.

$80,000
Have a saved game of Uncharted: Drake's Fortune with the story completed at least once.

UNCHARTED 3: DRAKE'S DECEPTION

PIGGYBACK EMBLEM

Select Emblem from your Multiplayer Profile and then Image. Press Up, Right, Down, Left, Up, Left, Down, Right and Piggyback Frame appears at the end of the list. Each part of the logo is now unlocked, so next pick the Piggyback Base, followed by Piggyback Logo.

VIRTUA TENNIS 4

THERON TENNIEL

At the player select, select Load to access Custom Players. Next, press L1.

VICKY BARNEY

At the player select, select Load to access Custom Players. Next, press R1.

WALL-E

The following cheats will disable saving. The five possible characters starting with Wall-E and going down are: Wall-E, Auto, EVE, M-O, GEL-A Steward.

ALL BONUS FEATURES UNLOCKED

Select Cheats from the Bonus Features menu and enter Wall-E, Auto, EVE, GEL-A Steward.

ALL GAME CONTENT UNLOCKED

Select Cheats from the Bonus Features menu and enter M-O, Auto, GEL-A Steward, EVE.

ALL SINGLE PLAYER LEVELS UNLOCKED

Select Cheats from the Bonus Features menu and enter Auto, GEL-A Steward, M-O, Wall-E.

ALL MULTIPLAYER MAPS UNLOCKED

Select Cheats from the Bonus Features menu and enter EVE, M-O, Wall-E, Auto.

ALL HOLIDAY COSTUMES UNLOCKED

Select Cheats from the Bonus Features menu and enter Auto, Auto, GEL-A Steward, GEL-A Steward.

ALL MULTIPLAYER COSTUMES UNLOCKED

Select Cheats from the Bonus Features menu and enter GEL-A Steward, Wall-E, M-O, Auto.

UNLIMITED HEALTH UNLOCKED

Select Cheats from the Bonus Features menu and enter Wall-E, M-O, Auto, M-O.

WALL-E: MAKE ANY CUBE AT ANY TIME

Select Cheats from the Bonus Features menu and enter Auto, M-O, Auto, M-O.

WALL-EVE: MAKE ANY CUBE AT ANY TIME

Select Cheats from the Bonus Features menu and enter M-O, GEL-A Steward, EVE, EVE.

WALL-E WITH A LASER GUN AT ANY TIME

Select Cheats from the Bonus Features menu and enter Wall-E, EVE, EVE, Wall-E.

WALL-EVE WITH A LASER GUN AT ANY TIME

Select Cheats from the Bonus Features menu and enter GEL-A Steward, EVE, M-O, Wall-E.

WALL-E: PERMANENT SUPER LASER UPGRADE

Select Cheats from the Bonus Features menu and enter Wall-E, Auto, EVE, M-O.

EVE: PERMANENT SUPER LASER UPGRADE

Select Cheats from the Bonus Features menu and enter EVE, Wall-E, Wall-E, Auto.

CREDITS

Select Cheats from the Bonus Features menu and enter Auto, Wall-E, GEL-A Steward, M-O.

WORLD OF OUTLAWS: SPRINT CARS

$5,000,000

Enter your name as CHICMCHIM.

ALL DRIVERS

Enter your name as MITYMASTA.

ALL TRACKS

Enter your name as JOEYJOEJOE.

WWE '12

WWE ATTITUDE ERA HEAVYWEIGHT CHAMPIONSHIP

Select Options from My WWE. Next, choose Cheat Codes and enter OhHellYeah!

WWE ALL STARS

UNLOCK ARENAS, WRESTLERS, AND ATTIRE

At the main menu, press Left, Triangle, Down, Left, Triangle, Square, Left, Square, Triangle, Down, Right, Square, Left, Up, Square, Right.

AUSTIN AND PUNK ATTIRES

At the main menu, press Left, Left, Right, Right, Up, Down, Up, Down.

ROBERTS AND ORTON ATTIRES

At the main menu, press Up, Down, Left, Right, Up, Up, Down, Down.

SAVAGE AND MORRISON ATTIRES

At the main menu, press Down, Left, Up, Right, Right, Up, Left, Down.

WWE SMACKDOWN VS. RAW 2010

THE ROCK

Select Cheat Codes from the Options and enter The Great One.

VINCE'S OFFICE AND DIRT SHEET FOR BACKSTAGE BRAWL

Select Cheat Codes from the Options menu and enter BonusBrawl.

SHAWN MICHAEL'S ALTERNATE COSTUME

Select Cheat Codes from the Options menu and enter Bow Down.

JOHN CENA'S ALTERNATE COSTUME

Select Cheat Codes from the Options menu and enter CENATION.

RANDY ORTON'S ALTERNATE COSTUME

Select Cheat Codes from the Options menu and enter ViperRKO.

SANTINO MARELLA'S ALTERNATE COSTUME

Select Cheat Codes from the Options menu and enter Milan Miracle.

TRIPLE H'S ALTERNATE COSTUME

Select Cheat Codes from the Options menu and enter Suck IT!.

WWE SMACKDOWN VS. RAW 2011

JOHN CENA (ENTRANCE/CIVILIAN)

In My WWE, select Cheat Codes from the Options and enter SLURPEE.

ALL OF RANDY ORTON'S COSTUMES

In My WWE, select Cheat Codes from the Options and enter apexpredator.

TRIBUTE TO THE TROOPS ARENA

In My WWE, select Cheat Codes from the Options and enter 8thannualtribute.

CRUISERWEIGHT TITLE, HARDCORE TITLE, AND MILLION DOLLAR TITLE

In My WWE, select Cheat Codes from the Options and enter Historicalbelts.

XCOM: ENEMY UNKNOWN

Using the following XCOM heroes disables trophies for the rest of the game. They come loaded with abilities and a sweet weapon.

JOE KELLY

Customize your soldier with the name Joe Kelly.

KEN LEVINE

Customize your soldier with the name Ken Levine.

OTTO ZANDER

Customize your soldier with the name Otto Zander.

SID MEIER

Customize your soldier with the name Sid Meier.

X-MEN DESTINY

JUGGERNAUT SUIT

At the title screen, hold L1 + R1 and press Down, Right, Up, Left, △, ○.

EMMA FROST SUIT

At the title screen, hold L1 + R1 and press Up, Down, Right, Left, ○, △.

X-MEN ORIGINS: WOLVERINE

CLASSIC WOLVERINE UNIFORM

During a game, press ✕, □, ○, □, ✕, □, ✕, □, ✕, □, ○, ○, □, R3. Note that this code disables trophies.

INVINCIBLE

During a game, press □, ✕, ✕, □, □, □, □, ○, ○, □, R3. Note that this code disables trophies.

INFINITE RAGE

During a game, press □, □, □, □, ○, ○, □, ✕, ✕, □, R3. Note that this code disables trophies.

DOUBLES ENEMY REFLEX POINTS

During a game, press ✕, ✕, □, □, □, □, ○, ○, □, □, □, □, ✕, ✕, R3. Note that this code disables trophies.

CLASSIC WOLVERINE CHALLENGE/OUTFIT

Find any two Classic Wolverine action figures to unlock this challenge. Defeat Classic Wolverine in combat to unlock the Classic Wolverine outfit. Note that this code disables trophies.

ORIGINAL WOLVERINE CHALLENGE/OUTFIT

Find any two Original Wolverine action figures to unlock this challenge. Defeat Original Wolverine in combat to unlock the Original Wolverine outfit. Note that this code disables trophies.

X-FORCE WOLVERINE CHALLENGE/OUTFIT

Find any two X-Force Wolverine action figures to unlock this challenge. Defeat X-Force Wolverine in combat to unlock the X-Force Wolverine outfit. Note that this code disables trophies.

YOU DON'T KNOW JACK

ALL EPISODES

At the Episode Select, press Left, Left, Right, Left, □.

ZOMBIE APOCALYPSE

7 DAYS OF HELL MODE

Complete Day 55.

CHAINSAW ONLY MODE

Complete a day only using the chainsaw.

HARDCORE MODE

Survive for seven straight days.

TURBO MODE

Get a 100 multiplier.

SONY PLAYSTATION® VITA

GAMES

ARMY CORPS OF HELL

The following passwords unlock mantles that allow you to change the background music and give an effect of Help/Recover Radius +7.

GOULS ATTACK!
Enter G75i8K8a as a password.

GXSXD
Enter GUK218Jh as a password.

KING'S-EVIL
Enter KB2p3tAs as a password.

KNIGHTS OF ROUND
Enter K77w3P5a as a password.

RACHEL MOTHER GOOSE
Enter RJ53z42i as a password.

REBEL-SURVIVE
Enter S4R29dlu as a password.

UNITED
Enter U541337k as a password.

BEN 10 GALACTIC RACING

KINECELARATOR KART
Select Enter Code from Extras and enter Ben 10, Spidermonkey, Kevin, Ultimate Echo Echo.

DISGAEA 3: ABSENCE OF DETENTION

GET ACCESS TO NEW VITA CONTENT
Highlight Continue and press Triangle, Square, Circle, Triangle, Square, Circle, X. Talk to the Parallel Worlder under the stairs in the lower levels of the base.

EARTH DEFENSE 2017 PORTABLE

PALE WING
Complete the game with Storm 1.

LEGO BATMAN 2: DC SUPER HEROES

STUDS X2
Pause the game, select Extras, and then choose Enter Code. Enter 74EZUT.

SUPER BUILD
Pause the game, select Extras, and then choose Enter Code. Enter JN2J6V.

CHARACTERS
In the batcave, access the characters screen and select Cheats. These cheats still need to be purchased.

CHEAT	CODE
Clown Goon	9ZZZBP
LexBot	W49CSJ
Mime Goon	ZQA8MK
Poison Ivy Goon	M9CP6L
Riddler Goon	Q285LK
Two-Face Goon	95KPYJ

LITTLEBIGPLANET PS VITA

GOD COMPLEX SECRET PIN
Spin any of the planets 720 degrees with a single flick.

HOUSE PROUD SECRET PIN
Place 10 stickers or decorations in your pod.

PLATINUM CLUB SECRET PIN
Earn all LittleBigPlanet Vita Trophies.

WHO'S WHO SECRET PIN
Watch the credits all the way through.

The following pins are handpicked.

AWESOMESAUCE SECRET PIN
Congratulations! You are more awesome than awesome!

MASTER OF THE INTERNETS SECRET PIN
Run an awesome LBP Vita fansite!

TARSIER PIN SECRET PIN
Work at Tarsier Studios.

TEAM PICKED SECRET PIN
Have one of your levels featured in Team Picks.

MICHAEL JACKSON: THE EXPERIENCE HD

BLACK ARMGUARD
Draw 50 Perfect Shapes in a Row on Hollywood Tonight on Expert Difficulty.

EMERALD GLOVE
During Smooth Criminal, draw 45 perfect shapes in a row.

GOLDEN GLOVE
For Leave Me Alone, reach the top spot on the leaderboard.

RED RUBY GLOVE
On Ghosts, wear the alternate outfit.

STAR SAPPHIRE GLOVE
On Beat It, score 145,000.

MORTAL KOMBAT

AUGMENTED REALITY – CHANGE BACKGROUND TO REAR CAMERA VIEW
Select Practice Mode from Training. At the character select, press ▲ to access the arena select. Press L + R to enable Augmented Reality. You will hear Shao Kahn if done correctly.

MOTORSTORM RC

THUNDER LIZARD VEHICLE
Spend 1 hour in the Playground.

BEELZEBUGGY BOOM VEHICLE
Spend 2 hours in the Playground.

DUNK VEHICLE
Jump through the basketball hoop in the Playground 10 times.

HEADCASE VEHICLE
Jump through the basketball hoop in the Playground 20 times.

PATRIOT TOUCHDOWN VEHICLE
Score 10 soccer goals in the Playground.

NORD GNITRO VEHICLE
Score 20 soccer goals in the Playground.

NINJA GAIDEN SIGMA PLUS

NINJA DOG DIFFICULTY
Die 3 times on Normal difficulty.

VERY HARD DIFFICULTY
Complete game on Hard.

MASTER NINJA DIFFICULTY
Complete game on Very Hard.

FORMAL ATTIRE (RACHEL)
Clear the game on Normal

BIKER (RACHEL)
Clear the game on Hard

LEGENDARY NINJA (RYU)
Clear the game on Normal

DOPPELGANGER (RYU)
Clear the game on Hard

THE GRIP OF MURDER (RYU)
Clear the game on Very Hard.

PLANTS VS. ZOMBIES

If a code does not work, your Tree of Wisdom may not be tall enough. Try again later.

ALTERNATE LAWN MOWER
During a game, press R1 + R2 + L1 + L2 and enter trickedout.

ZOMBIE SHADES
During a game, press R1 + R2 + L1 + L2 and enter future.

ZOMBIES HAVE A MUSTACHE
During a game, press R1 + R2 + L1 + L2 and enter mustache.

ZOMBIES DANCE
During a game, press R1 + R2 + L1 + L2 and enter dance.

DEAD ZOMBIES LEAVE DAISIES BEHIND
During a game, press R1 + R2 + L1 + L2 and enter daisies.

CANDY SHOWER WHEN ZOMBIE DIES
During a game, press R1 + R2 + L1 + L2 and enter piñata.

CHANGES ZOMBIES SOUND
During a game, press R1 + R2 + L1 + L2 and enter sukhbir.

RAYMAN ORIGINS

LAND OF THE LIVING DEAD LEVEL
Collect all ten Skull Teeth and turn them in.

REALITY FIGHTERS

STORY MODE: FULL STEAM
Complete the regular Story Mode.

MR. MIYAGI
Defeat Mr. Miyagi in Story mode and Story Mode: Full Steam.

SURVIVAL EXTREME
In Survival Classic mode, win 15 fights.

RESISTANCE: BURNING SKIES

NEW GAME +
Completing the single player campaign adds New Game + to the menu.

SUPERHUMAN DIFFICULTY
Complete the single player campaign.

RETRO CITY RAMPAGE

Be careful using these codes as saving, trophies, and leaderboards are disabled until you restart the game.

$100,000
During a game, press Left, Right, Left, Right, Up, Up, Down, Down, R, ○.

ALL STAGES
During a game, press △, △, ✕, △, △, ✕, △, △, ✕, ○, ○.

ALL CHARACTERS
During a game, press Up, Up, Up, Left, Right, R, ○, R, ○, R.

ALL STYLES
During a game, press Left, Left, Right, Right, Up, Down, Up, Down, ✕, ○.

ALL WEAPONS
During a game, press Up, Up, Down, Down, Left, Right, Left, Right, ✕, ○.

LOSE THE COPS

During a game, press Up, Up, Down, Down, R, ○, R, ○, ✕.

GAWD MODE

During a game, press Up, Up, Left, Right, Left, Right, Down, Down, R, ✕.

GAWD MODE OFF

During a game, press Down, Down, Left, Right, Left, Right, Up, Up, R, ✕.

RED SWEAT MODE

During a game, press ✕, ○, ✕, △, ✕, ○, ○.

SPEED SHOES

During a game, press Right, Right, Up, Down, Left, Left, Up, Down, R, ✕.

SUPER STOMP

During a game, press Left, Left, Up, Down, Right, Right, Up, Down, R, ✕.

DESTRUCTOID STAFF PLAYABLE CHARACTERS

Go to MJ's Face-R-Us and enter DTOID as a coupon code.

MOJANG STAFF PLAYABLE CHARACTERS

Go to MJ's Face-R-Us and enter MOJANG as a coupon code.

SHINOBIDO 2: REVENGE OF ZEN

ITEM EATER

Pause the game, hold L + R and press Up, Down, Up, Down, Left, Right, □.

RAGDOLL

Pause the game, hold L + R and press Down, Up, Right, Left, Down, Up, □.

SILENT HILL: BOOK OF MEMORIES

ROBBIE DOLL WEAPON

At the main menu, press Up, Up, Down, Down, Left, Right, Left, Right, □, △, Start. This gives you the weapon and unlocks the sale of Robbie Dolls.

ULTIMATE MARVEL VS. CAPCOM 3

PLAY AS GALACTUS

Accumulate 30,000 points on a player card. Now highlight Arcade Mode and press L + Select + ✕.

UNCHARTED: GOLDEN ABYSS

CRUSHING DIFFICULTY

Complete the game on Hard.

WIPEOUT 2048

BOOST AT START

Use turbo just as the timer reaches Go.

NINTENDO DS™ / 3DS™

GAMES

3D CLASSICS: TWINBEE

10 LIVES
When starting a game, hold Up + Right and press A.

ALICE IN WONDERLAND

DORMOUSE COAT
Enter 3676 as a cheat code.

RED GUARD SHIELD
Enter 7453 as a cheat code.

RED QUEEN MASK
Enter 7675 as a cheat code.

TAN ALICE BOOK
Enter 2625 as a cheat code.

TWEEDLE OUTFIT
Enter 8946 as a cheat code.

THE AMAZING SPIDER-MAN

BLACK SPIDER-MAN SUIT
Complete Vigilante Mode

CLASSIC SPIDER-MAN SUIT
Complete all petty crimes.

BAKUGAN BATTLE BRAWLERS

1000 BP
Start a new game and enter the name as 180978772269.

5000 BP
Start a new game and enter the name as 332044292925.

10,000 BP
Start a new game and enter the name as 423482942968.

BRONZE WARIUS
Start a new game and enter the name as 449824934071.

BAKUGAN: DEFENDERS OF THE CORE

UNLOCK CODES
Select Unlock Codes from the Collection menu. Enter the verification code, HXV6Y7BF. Now you can enter the following:

EFFECT	PASSWORD
10 Vexos Passes	YQLHBBSMDC
10,000 Core Energy	QY8CLD5NJE
Earthen Armor Ability Card	JJUZDEACXX
Fire Spirit Ability Card	YJ7RGG7WGZ
Tornado Vortex Ability Card	2FKRRMNCDQ
Water Pillar Ability Card	HUUH8ST7AR
Zorch Thunder Ability Card	82D77YK6P8

BATMAN: THE BRAVE AND THE BOLD—THE VIDEOGAME

BATMAN COSTUMES

Access the terminal on the left side of the Batcave and enter the following:

COSTUME	CODE
Dark Batsuit	3756448
Medieval Batsuit	5644863
Rainbow Suit	7629863

CHALLENGE MAPS

CHALLENGE MAP	CODE
Gotham 1 & 2	4846348
Proto Sparring	6677686
Science Island 1 & 2	7262348

WEAPONS

WEAPON	CODE
Barrier	2525655
Belt Sword	2587973
Flashbangs	3527463
Smoke Pellets	7665336

BATTLE OF GIANTS: DRAGONS

Select Unlock Gold Gems from the Extras Menu and enter the following passwords:

BREATH ATTACK GOLD GEMS

LEVEL	ATTACK	PASSWORD
1	NAMGILIMA	ISAM SKNF DKTD
2	NIGHHALAMA	ZNBN QOKS THGO
3	KUGDIM	AWBF CRSL HGAT
4	KUZEN	ACLC SCRS VOSK
5	SUGZAG	XSPC LLSL KJLP

CLAW ATTACK GOLD GEMS

LEVEL	ATTACK	PASSWORD
1	USUD	NAKF HLAP SDSP
2	ULUH	SAPO RLNM VUSD
3	NIGHZU	POZX MJDR GJSA
4	GHIDRU	GPGE SMEC TDTB
5	MUDRU	ABLP CGPG SGAM

HEAD ATTACK GOLD GEMS

LEVEL	ATTACK	PASSWORD
1	MEN	PQTM AONV UTNA
2	SAGHMEN	TNAP CTJS LDUF
3	KINGAL	FHSK EUFV KALP
4	DALLA	EPWB MPOR TRTA
5	AGA	GPKT BBWT SGNR

TAIL ATTACK GOLD GEMS

LEVEL	ATTACK	PASSWORD
1	A'ASH	LSSN GOAJ READ
2	ASH	FUTY HVNS LNVS
3	ASH SAR	LPAQ KOYH TGDS
4	AHS BALA	VLQL QELB IYDS
5	NAMTAGTAG	VLDB DDSL NCJA

BATTLE OF GIANTS: MUTANT INSECTS

ELECTICITY UPGRADE
Select Unlock Rewards from Options and enter WLUA DZCN ZNKE.

ICE UPGRADE
Select Unlock Rewards from Options and enter PLAL TALG JPZV.

UNLOCK REWARDS
Select Unlock Rewards from the Options and enter the following passwords:

REWARD	PASSWORD
500 Golden Gems	SRKC RDZR KZAE
500 Golden Gems	HDTQ JCLO SSUU
750 Golden Gems	OAZN CEYQ XRDT
750 Golden Gems	FBRY CMTR KXUQ
Claw Upgrade	PLQO ILQJ YKEQ
Cyan Color	LYYD UAXR IPRT
Green Color	LCYH FVQZ XEVB
Head Upgrade	TDFS ZITF BKYE
Ice upgrade	PLAL TALG JPZV
Mutant Wasp	CHYV UEMJ QVGM
Red Color	QODI LHGH HNBN
Shock Upgrade	WLUA DZCN ZNKE
Yellow Color	TZCK AXZJ VSTW

BEN 10 GALACTIC RACING

KINECELARATOR
Select Enter Code from Extras and enter Ben, Spidermonkey, Kevin Levin, Ultimate Echo Echo.

BRAIN AGE EXPRESS: ARTS & LETTERS

ELIMINATE ENEMIES IN WORD ATTACK
In Word Attack, during the Space mode, press A, Y, X, B. You can use this once each training session.

BRAIN QUEST GRADES 5 & 6

MAD COW STICKER
Select Cheats from the Options and enter MADCOW.

BRAIN VOYAGE

ALL GOLD MEDALS
At the World Map, press A, B, Up, L, L, Y.

INFINITE COINS
At the World Tour Mode, press L, Up, X, Up, R, Y.

CALL OF DUTY: MODERN WARFARE: MOBILIZED

SURVIVAL MODE
Select Options from the War Room and press SELECT, L, R, SELECT, Y, Y, X, R, L, X, R, Y

CALL OF DUTY: WORLD AT WAR

ALL CAMPAIGN AND CHALLENGE MISSIONS
At the War Room Options screen, press Y, X, Y, Y, X, Y, X, X, Y.

CARTOON NETWORK: PUNCH TIME EXPLOSION

BATTLE MODE CHARACTERS

In Battle Mode, win the following number of matches to unlock the corresponding characters.

CHARACTER	# OF MATCHES
Captain Knuckles	3
Bubbles	7
Blossom	12
Monkey	18
Grim	25
Samurai Jack	33
Father	42
Vilgax	52
Mojo Jojo	63
Captain Planet	75

CAVE STORY

TITLE SCREEN MUSIC AND CURSOR

Complete the Sanctuary Time Attack under the following times to get new music and cursor on the title screen.

MUSIC/CURSOR	FINISH UNDER (MINUTES)
Safety / Sue	3
White / King	4
Toroko's Theme / Toroko	5
Running Hell / Curly	6

CENTIPEDE: INFESTATION

PLAY AS RIVET WITH RIVETER GUN

Select Code Entry from Extras and enter 121213.

CITY LIFE DS

1,000,000

Pause the game and press A, B, Y, L, R.

ALL BUILDINGS

Pause the game and hold B + Y + X + R for 2 seconds.

CLUB PENGUIN: ELITE PENGUIN FORCE

FLOWER HUNT MISSION

Change your system's date to April 1st.

APRIL ITEMS IN CATALOG

Change your system's date to April 1st.

SUMMER PARTY MISSION

Change your system's date to June 21st.

FIESTA HAT ON FROZEN POND

Change your system's date to June 21st.

JUNE ITEMS IN CATALOG

Change your system's date to June 21st.

HALLOWEEN PARTY MISSION

Change your system's date to October 31st.

FISH COSTUME IN LODGE ATTIC

Change your system's date to October 31st.

DELIVER THE PRESENTS MISSION

Change your system's date to December 25th.

ICE SKATES ON THE ICEBERG

Change your system's date to December 25th.

CODE OF PRINCESS

TRUE UNICORN
Win a Versus Match.

GOLD HOOP
Win 100 Versus Matches.

PEGASUS WEAPON
Complete 100 Quests.

ALL CHARACTERS FOR ONLINE CO-OP
Complete 100 quests.

SILVER HOOP MIND ACCESSORY
Complete 500 Quests.

TRUE MARS WEAPON
Clear 1000 Quests.

TRUE SERAPH
Complete 100 Co-op Quests.

BONUS CHARACTERS IN FREE MISSIONS AND BONUS QUESTS
Defeat the Campaign.

BONUS CHARACTERS

CHARACTER	COMPLETE FOLLOWING QUEST OR CAMPAIGN
Alchemia	Little Witch
Distille	Fallen Angel
General Jupponogi	Return of the Ninja
Joe the Liongate	Eclipse Calibur
Marco Neko	Epic Mandrake
Boss Jupponogi	All Free Missions and Bonus Quests
King Golgius	Complete Campaign and Watch Thousand Years with Allegro
Schwartz	Complete Campaign and Watch Thousand Years with Solange
The Guardian	Complete Campaign and Watch Thousand Years with Zozo

DINOSAUR KING

STONE CIRCLE PASSWORDS

Defeat the game to unlock the Stone Circle in South Euro. Now you can enter the following passwords to unlock dinosaurs. Find the level 1 dinosaur in a chest at the shrine.

009 DASPLETEOSARUS
Enter Grass, Water, Lightning, Lightning, Earth, Earth, Water, Wind.

012 SIAMOTYRRANUS
Enter Fire, Wind, Fire, Water, Wind, Grass, Fire, Water.

025 JOBARIA
Enter Water, Lightning, Lightning, Earth, Fire, Earth, Fire, Wind.

029 TRICERATOPS
Enter Lightning, Fire, Lightning, Fire, Water, Lightning, Grass, Earth.

038 MONOCLONIUS
Enter Lightning, Earth, Water, Water, Grass, Fire, Earth, Wind.

046 EUOPLOCEPHALUS
Enter Earth, Earth, Grass, Water, Wind, Earth, Wind, Fire.

058 ALTIRHINUS
Enter Wind, Fire, Fire, Fire, Lightning, Earth, Water, Grass.

061 CARNOTAURUS
Enter Earth, Wind, Water, Lightning, Fire, Wind, Wind, Water.

EX ACE/EX CHOMP
Enter Lightning, Grass, Fire, Earth, Water, Water, Lightning, Fire. This gives you Ace if you are playing as Rex and Chomp as Max.

EX MINI-KING
Enter Lightning, Wind, Earth, Lightning, Grass, Wind, Fire, Water.

EX PARIS
Enter Grass, Water, Water, Earth, Wind, Grass, Lightning, Lightning.

EX SAUROPHAGANAX
Enter Fire, Water, Earth, Grass, Wind, Lightning, Fire, Water.

EX SPINY
Enter Water, Earth, Fire, Water, Fire, Grass, Wind, Earth.

EX TANK
Enter Earth, Grass, Earth, Water, Wind, Water, Grass, Fire.

EX TERRY
Enter Fire, Lightning, Wind, Wind, Water, Fire, Fire, Earth.

DISGAEA DS

ETNA MODE

At the Main menu, highlight New Game and press X, Y, B, X, Y, B, A.

DISNEY FAIRIES: TINKER BELL

TINKERBELL MAGIC BOOK CODES

Talk to Queen Clarion about the Magic Book to enter the following codes.

UNLOCK	CODE
Augustus	5318 3479 7972
Baden	1199 2780 8802
Blair	6899 6003 4480
Cera	1297 0195 5747
Chipper	7980 9298 9818
Dewberry	0241 4491 0630
Elwood	3527 5660 3684
Fawn	9556 0047 1043
Idalia	2998 8832 2673
Iridessa	0724 0213 6136
Luminaria	8046 5868 5678
Magnolia	1697 4780 6430
Mariana	5138 8216 9240
Minister Autumn	2294 0281 6332
Minister Spring	2492 1155 4907
Minister Summer	2582 7972 6926
Minister Winter	2618 8587 2083
Nollie	5905 2346 9329
Olwen	7629 0545 7105
One Black Shell	1234 5678 9012
One Blue Dewdrop	0987 6543 2109

UNLOCK	CODE
One Fairy Medal	1111 1111 1111
One Green Leaf	4444 4444 4444
One Pink Petal	2222 2222 2222
One Red Leaf	5555 5555 5555
One Snow Grain	7777 7777 7777
One Weak Thread	9999 9999 9999
One White Feather	8888 8888 8888
One Yellow Leaf	6666 6666 6666
One Yellow Petal	3333 3333 3333
Party Shoes	1390 5107 4096
Party Skirt	6572 4809 6680
Party Tiara	8469 7886 7938
Party Top	0977 4584 3869
Queen Clarion	1486 4214 8147
Rosetta	8610 2523 6122
Rune	3020 5768 5351
Silvermist	0513 4563 6800
Terence	8606 6039 6383
Tinkerbell	2495 7761 9313
Vidia	3294 3220 0349

DRAGON QUEST IX: SENTINELS OF THE STARRY SKIES

MINI MEDAL REWARDS

Trade your mini medals with Cap'N Max Meddlin in Dourbridge. The effects are cumulative, so giving him 80 medals unlocks all of the rewards.

# MINI MEDALS	REWARD
4	Thief's Key
8	Mercury Bandanna
13	Bunny Suit
18	Jolly Roger Jumper
25	Transparent Tights

# MINI MEDALS	REWARD
32	Miracle Sword
40	Sacred Armor
50	Meteorite Bracer
62	Rusty Helmet
80	Dragon Robe

After giving him 80 mini medals, he will sell the following items for mini medals.

# MINI MEDALS	ITEM
3	Prayer Ring
5	Elfin Elixir
8	Saint's Ashes

# MINI MEDALS	ITEM
10	Reset Stone
15	Orichalcum
20	Pixie Boots

DOURBRIDGE SECRET SHOP

In Dourbridge, there is a secret shop behind the Dourbridge Item Shop. You need the Ultimate Key to access the shop.

DRAGON QUEST MONSTERS: JOKER 2

UNLOCK MONSTERS

MONSTER	OWN THIS MANY DIFFERENT MONSTERS
Great Argon Lizard	50
Drakularge	100
Metal King Slime	150
Grandpa Slime	200

MONSTERS FROM DRAGON QUEST VI: REALMS OF REVELATION

Activate Dreamsharing on Dragon Quest VI and then turn on Tag Mode on Dragon Quest Monsters: Joker 2. This unlocks Malevolamp, Mottle Slime, Noble Gasbagon, and Overkilling Machine.

MONSTERS FROM DRAGON QUEST IX: SENTINELS OF THE STARRY SKIES

Activate Tag Mode on Dragon Quest IX and then turn on Tag Mode on Dragon Quest Monsters: Joker 2. This unlocks Shogum, Slime Stack, and Teeny Sanguini.

DRAWN TO LIFE: THE NEXT CHAPTER

TEMPLATES

At the Creation Hall, hold L and press X, Y, B, A, A to unlock the following Templates.

- Astronaut Template
- Knight Template
- Ninja Girl Template
- Spartan Template
- Super Girl Template

DRAWN TO LIFE: SPONGEBOB SQUAREPANTS EDITION

EXTRA REWARD COINS

Select Cheat Entry and enter Down, Down, B, B, Down, Left, Up, Right, A.

ELEBITS: THE ADVENTURES OF KAI & ZERO

BIG RED BONUS OMEGA

Select Download Additional Omegas from the Extra menu. Choose Download Data and press B, Y, Up, L, Right, R, Down, Left, X, A.

GRAND THEFT AUTO: CHINATOWN WARS

FULL HEALTH AND ARMOR

During a game, press L, L, R, A, A, B, B, R.

FULL ARMOR

During a game, press L, L, R, B, B, A, A, R.

INCREASE WANTED LEVEL

During a game, press L, L, R, Y, Y, X, X, R.

DECREASE WANTED LEVEL

During a game, press R, X, X, Y, Y, R, L, L.

EXPLOSIVE PISTOL ROUND

During a game, press L, R, X, Y, A, B, Up, Down.

WEAPONS SET 1

During a game, press R, Up, B, Down, Left, R, B, Right. This gives you the Pistol, Nightstick, Minigun, Assault Rifle, Micro SMG, Stubby Shotgun, and Grenades with max ammo.

WEAPONS SET 2

During a game, press R, Up, A, Down, Left, R, A, Right. This gives you the Twin Pistol, Teaser, Flame Thrower, Carbine Rifle, SMG, Double Barreled Shotgun, and Molotovs with max ammo.

WEAPONS SET 3

During a game, press R, Up, Y, Down, Left, R, Y, Right. This gives you the Revolver, Chainsaw, Flame Thrower, Carbine Rifle, SMG, Double Barreled Shotgun, and Proximity Mines with max ammo.

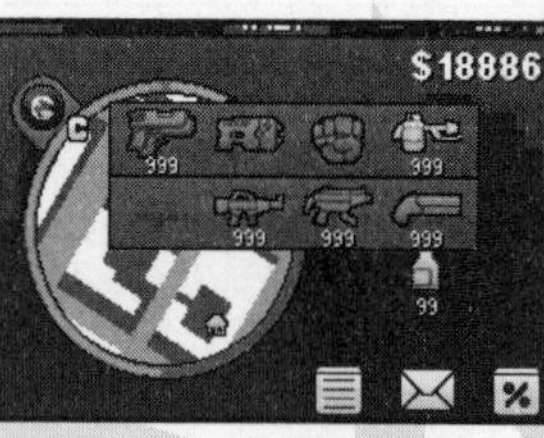

WEAPONS SET 4

During a game, press R, Up, X, Down, Left, R, X, Right. This gives you the Pistol, Baseball Bat, Carbine Rifle, RPG, Micro SMG, Shotgun, and Flashbangs with max ammo.

WEATHER: SUNNY

During a game, press Up, Down, Left, Right, A, B, L, R.

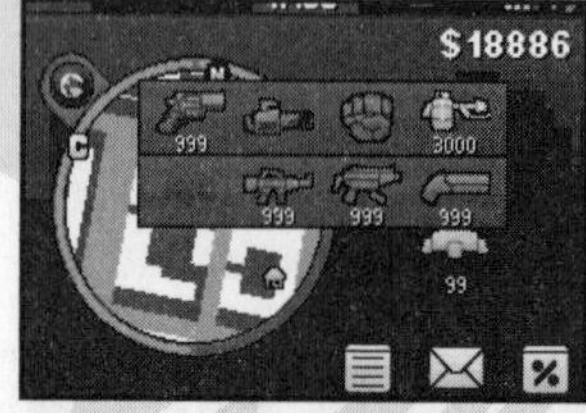

WEATHER: CLOUDY

During a game, press Up, Down, Left, Right, X, Y, L, R.

WEATHER: RAIN

During a game, press Up, Down, Left, Right, Y, A, L, R.

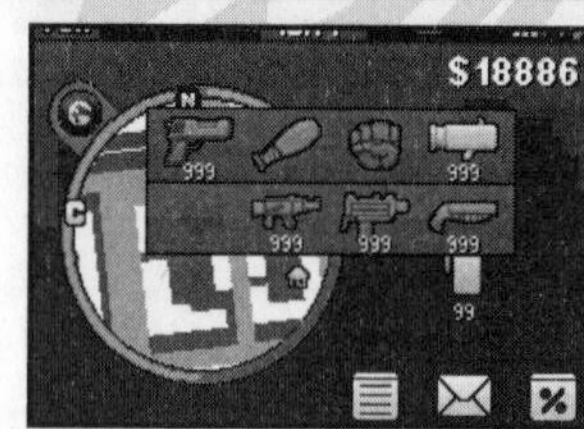

WEATHER: HEAVY RAIN

During a game, press Up, Down, Left, Right, A, X, R, L.

WEATHER: THUNDERSTORMS

During a game, press Up, Down, Left, Right, B, Y, R, L.

GRID

UNLOCK ALL

Select Cheat Codes from the Options and enter 233558.

INVULNERABILITY

Select Cheat Codes from the Options and enter 161650.

DRIFT MASTER

Select Cheat Codes from the Options and enter 789520.

PERFECT GRIP

Select Cheat Codes from the Options and enter 831782.

HIGH ROLLER

Select Cheat Codes from the Options and enter 401134.

GHOST CAR

Select Cheat Codes from the Options and enter 657346.

TOY CARS

Select Cheat Codes from the Options and enter 592014.

MM MODE

Select Cheat Codes from the Options and enter 800813.

INFINITE SPACE

NEW GAME+ & EXTRA MODE

Complete the game. New Game+ unlocks additional blue prints, while Extra Mode is another game mode with limited resources.

JAKE HUNTER: DETECTIVE CHRONICLES

PASSWORDS
Select Password from the Main menu and enter the following:

UNLOCKABLE	PASSWORD
1 Password Info	AAAA
2 Visuals	LEET
3 Visuals	GONG
4 Visuals	CARS

UNLOCKABLE	PASSWORD
5 Movies	ROSE
6 Jukebox	BIKE
7 Hints	HINT

JAKE HUNTER DETECTIVE STORY: MEMORIES OF THE PAST

JAKE HUNTER QUIZ
Select Password and enter NEET.

JAKE HUNTER SERIES
Select Password and enter MISS.

JAKE HUNTER UNLEASHED 01 BONUS
Select Password and enter NONE.

JAKE HUNTER UNLEASHED 02 BONUS
Select Password and enter ANGL.

JAKE HUNTER UNLEASHED 03 BONUS
Select Password and enter SNAP.

JAKE HUNTER UNLEASHED 04 BONUS
Select Password and enter DOOR.

JAKE HUNTER UNLEASHED 05 BONUS
Select Password and enter STOP.

JAKE HUNTER UNLEASHED DS1 BONUS
Select Password and enter KING.

JAKE HUNTER VISUALS 1
Select Password and enter LEET.

JAKE HUNTER VISUALS 2
Select Password and enter GONG.

JAKE HUNTER VISUALS 3
Select Password and enter CARS.

JAKE HUNTER VISUALS 4
Select Password and enter TREE.

JAKE HUNTER VISUALS 5
Select Password and enter PAPA.

JUKEBOX
Select Password and enter BIKE.

MOVIE GALLERY
Select Password and enter ROSE.

PASSWORD HINTS
Select Password and enter HINT.

SIDE CHARACTER'S BONUS STORY
Select Password and enter MINU.

STAFF COMMENTS 1
Select Password and enter AQUA.

STAFF COMMENTS 2
Select Password and enter MOTO.

WHAT IS A PASSWORD?
Select Password and enter AAAA.

JUICED 2: HOT IMPORT NIGHTS

$5000
At the Cheat menu, enter HSAC.

ALL CARS
At the Cheat menu, enter SRAC.

ALL RACES
At the Cheat menu, enter EDOM.

ALL TRACKS
At the Cheat menu, enter KART.

JUMBLE MADNESS

FEBRUARY 31 PUZZLE
For Daily Jumble and Jumble Crosswords, select the square under February 28, 2009.

KID ICARUS: UPRISING

BOSS RUSH MODE
Defeat the Final Boss. Boss Rush Mode can be accessed next to Chapter 25.

DIALOGUE
Complete Solo Mode. Select Other from Options and then Hidden Options to toggle Dialogue on and off.

PALUTENA OR VIRIDI LOOKS OVER MENU
Complete Chapter 21. Select Other from Options and then Hidden Options to access Palutena and Viridi.

KINGDOM HEARTS 3D: DREAM DROP DISTANCE

CRITICAL MODE
Complete the game.

NEW GAME+
Complete the game and create a new game when asked.

LEGO BATMAN

ALFRED PENNYWORTH
Use the computer in the Batcave, select Enter Code and enter ZAQ637.

BATGIRL
Use the computer in the Batcave, select Enter Code and enter JKR331.

BRUCE WAYNE
Use the computer in the Batcave, select Enter Code and enter BDJ327.

CLASSIC CATWOMAN
Use the computer in the Batcave, select Enter Code and enter M1AAWW.

CLOWN GOON
Use the computer in the Batcave, select Enter Code and enter HJK327.

COMMISSIONER GORDON
Use the computer in the Batcave, select Enter Code and enter DDP967.

FISHMONGER
Use the computer in the Batcave, select Enter Code and enter HGY748.

FREEZE GIRL
Use the computer in the Batcave, select Enter Code and enter XVK541.

FREEZE HENCHMAN
Use the computer in the Batcave, select Enter Code and enter NJL412.

JOKER GOON
Use the computer in the Batcave, select Enter Code and enter UTF782.

JOKER HENCHMAN
Use the computer in the Batcave, select Enter Code and enter YUN924.

NIGHTWING
Use the computer in the Batcave, select Enter Code and enter MVY759.

TROPICAL JOKER
Use the computer in the Batcave, select Enter Code and enter CCB199.

1 MILLION STUDS
At the Main menu, press X, Y, B, B, Y, X, L, L, R, R, Up, Down, Left, Right, Start, Select.

3 MILLION STUDS
At the Main menu, press Up, Up, B, Down, Down, X, Left, Left, Y, L, R, L, R, B, Y, X, Start, Select.

ALL CHARACTERS
At the Main menu, press X, Up, B, Down, Y, Left, Start, Right, R, R, L, R, R, Down, Down, Up, Y, Y, Y, Start, Select.

ALL EPISODES AND FREE PLAY MODE
At the Main menu, press Right, Up, R, L, X, Y, Right, Left, B, L, R, L, Down, Down, Up, Y, Y, X, X, B, B, Up, Up, L, R, Start, Select.

ALL EXTRAS
At the Main menu, press Up, Down, L, R, L, R, L, Left, Right, X, X, Y, Y, B, B, L, Up, Down, L, R, L, R, Up, Up, Down, Start, Select.

LEGO BATMAN 2: DC SUPER HEROES

STUDS X2
Pause the game, select Extras, and then choose Enter Code. Enter 74EZUT.

SUPER BUILD
Pause the game, select Extras, and then choose Enter Code. Enter JN2J6V.

CHARACTERS
In the batcave, access the characters screen and select Cheats. These cheats still need to be purchased.

CHEAT	CODE
Clown Goon	9ZZZBP
LexBot	W49CSJ
Mime Goon	ZQA8MK
Poison Ivy Goon	M9CP6L
Riddler Goon	Q285LK
Two-Face Goon	95KPYJ

LEGO BATTLES

To activate the following cheats, pause the game and tap the red brick.

INVINCIBLE HERO
At the LEGO Store, tap the Red Brick and enter HJCRAWK.

REGENERATING HEALTH
At the LEGO Store, tap the Red Brick and enter ABABLRX.

ONE-HIT KILL (HEROES)
At the LEGO Store, tap the Red Brick and enter AVMPWHK.

LONG-RANGE MAGIC
At the LEGO Store, tap the Red Brick and enter ZPWJFUQ.

SUPER MAGIC
At the LEGO Store, tap the Red Brick and enter DWFTBNS.

DOUBLE LEGO BRICKS
At the LEGO Store, tap the Red Brick and enter BGQOYRT.

FAST BUILDING
At the LEGO Store, tap the Red Brick and enter QMSLPOE.

FAST HARVESTING
At the LEGO Store, tap the Red Brick and enter PQZLJOB.

FAST MAGIC
At the LEGO Store, tap the Red Brick and enter JRTPASX.

FAST MINING
At the LEGO Store, tap the Red Brick and enter KVBPQRJ.

FULL UNIT CAP
At the LEGO Store, tap the Red Brick and enter UMSXIRQ.

SUPER EXPLOSIONS
At the LEGO Store, tap the Red Brick and enter THNBGRE.

UPGRADED TOWERS
At the LEGO Store, tap the Red Brick and enter EDRFTGY.

SHOW ENEMIES
At the LEGO Store, tap the Red Brick and enter IBGOFWX.

SHOW LEGO STUDS
At the LEGO Store, tap the Red Brick and enter CPLYREK.

SHOW MINIKIT
At the LEGO Store, tap the Red Brick and enter LJYQRAC.

SHOW RED BRICKS
At the LEGO Store, tap the Red Brick and enter RTGYPKC.

REVEAL MAP
At the LEGO Store, tap the Red Brick and enter SKQMXPL.

UNLOCK ISLANDER
At the LEGO Store, tap the Red Brick and enter UGDRSQP.

UNLOCK NINJA MASTER
At the LEGO Store, tap the Red Brick and enter SHWSDGU.

UNLOCK SPACE CRIMINAL LEADER
At the LEGO Store, tap the Red Brick and enter ZVDNJSU.

UNLOCK TROLL KING
At the LEGO Store, tap the Red Brick and enter XRCTVYB.

LEGO BATTLES: NINJAGO

SANTA CLAUS
Change your system date to December 25.

PASSWORDS
Select Cheat Codes from the LEGO shop and enter the following:

EFFECT	PASSWORD
Kruncha	HJEKTPU
Spaceman	TSDYHBZ
Show Enemies on Minimap	KMRWLSS

PASSWORDS FOR STUDS

Select Cheat Codes from the LEGO shop and enter the following:

# OF STUDS	PASSWORD
5000	GQBAUJP
10000	GALNAFE
15000	LQMZPBX
20000	PPMSUGS
25000	SLBQFSW
30000	MXQNVQP
35000	SJVPMAA
40000	WZURMZM
45000	UABBMZQ
55000	BGCHKHA
60000	JXULZZW
65000	FBMRSWG
70000	ZZXWUZJ
75000	HXMVRZP
80000	NYUXUZF

LEGO INDIANA JONES: THE ORIGINAL ADVENTURES

You should hear a confirmation sound after the following codes are entered.

ALL CHARACTERS

At the Title screen, press X, Up, B, Down, Y, Left, Start, Right, R, R, L, R, R, Down, Down, Up, Y, Y, Y, Start, Select.

ALL EPISODES AND FREE PLAY MODE

Right, Up, R, L, X, Y, Right, Left, B, L, R, L, Down, Down, Up, Y, Y, X, X, B, B, Up, Up, L, R, Start, Select.

ALL EXTRAS

Up, Down, L, R, L, R, L, Left, Right, X, X, Y, Y, B, B, L, Up, Down, L, R, L, R, Up, Up, Down, Start, Select.

1,000,000 STUDS

At the Title screen, press X, Y, B, B, Y, X, L, L, R, R, Up, Down, Left, Right, Start, Select.

3,000,000 STUDS

At the Title screen, press Up, Up, B, Down, Down, X, Left, Left, Y, L, R, L, R, B, Y, X, Start, Select.

LEGO PIRATES OF THE CARIBBEAN: THE VIDEO GAME

CODES

Pause the game and select Extras. Choose Enter Code and enter the following codes:

EFFECT	PASSWORD
Ammand the Corsair	EW8T6T
Blackbeard	D3DW0D
Clubba	644THF
Davy Jones	4DJLKR
Governor Weatherby Swann	LD9454
Gunner	Y611WB
Hungry Cannibal	64BNHG
Jack Sparrow	VDJSPW
Jacoby	BWO656
Jimmy Legs	13GLW5
Koehler	RT093G
Mistress Ching	GDETDE
Philip	WEV040
Quartermaster	RX58HU
The Spaniard	P861JO
Twigg	KDLFKD

LEGO STAR WARS III: THE CLONE WARS

RED BRICK CHEATS

Each level has a Red Brick that when found unlocks a cheat for purchase at the shop.

CHEAT	COST (STUDS)
Auto Pickup	500,000
Fast Build	500,000
Flight Weapon Power Up	2,000,000
Funny Jump	250,000
Infinite Missiles	150,000
Invincibility	4,000,000
Minigames	50,000
Regenerate Hearts	400,000
Score x2	100,000
Score x4	250,000
Score x6	500,000
Score x8	1,000,000
Score x10	2,500,000

LITTLEST PET SHOP: GARDEN

GIRAFFE PET

Select Passwords from the Options and enter LPSTRU. It is available in the Meow Market.

LITTLEST PET SHOP: JUNGLE

GIRAFFE PET

Select Passwords from the Options and enter LPSTRU. It is available in the Meow Market.

LOCK'S QUEST

REPLACE CLOCKWORKS WITH KINGDOM FORCE

After completing the game, hold R and select your profile.

ENDING STORY

After completing the game, hold L and select your profile.

MARIO KART 7

CHARACTERS

CHARACTER	FINISH 1ST IN[EL]
Daisy	Mushroom Cup 150cc
Honey Queen	Banana Cup 150cc
Lakitu	Lightning Cup 150cc
Metal Mario	Special Cup 150cc
Rosalina	Star Cup 150cc
Shy Guy	Shell Cup 150cc
Wario	Flower Cup 150cc
Wiggler	Leaf Cup 150cc

MII

Place in all cups in one of the CC levels.

MARIO TENNIS OPEN

BABY MARIO
In the Super Mario Tennis Special Game, complete 1-3.

BABY PEACH
In the Ring Shot Special Game,complete the Pro Rings.

DRY BOWSER
In the Ink Showdown Special Game, complete Inksplosion.

LUMA
In the Galaxy Rally Special Game, complete Superstar.

STAR CHARACTER
Winning the Champions Cup of the World Open gives the character you used a star. This improves the character.

FIRE MARIO
Give two characters a star.

PRO DIFFICULTY IN EXHIBITION
Complete the Champions Cup.

ACE DIFFICULTY IN EXHIBITION
Complete the Final Cup.

HIDDEN GOODIES
At the Select a File screen, hold Up and press Start. This turns on the camera. If you have found one of the QR Codes online that unlocks something for Mario Tennis Open, scan it with the camera.

MARVEL SUPER HERO SQUAD

APOCALYPSE MODE
Select Cheats from the Settings and enter Wolverine, Wolverine, Dr Doom, Abomination, Wolverine. This gives everyone one hit kills.

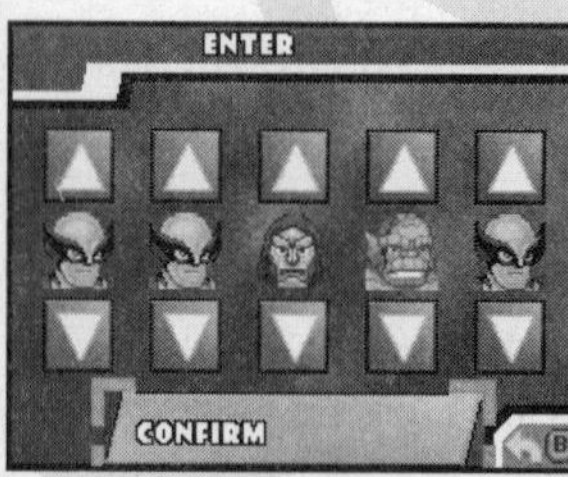

MEGA MAN STAR FORCE 3: BLACK ACE

STARS ON NEW GAME/CONTINUE SCREEN
Do the following to earn each star on the New Game/Continue screen.

NAME	HOW TO EARN
Black Ace	Defeat the game
G Comp	Collect all Giga cards
M Comp	Collect all Mega cards
S Comp	Collect all Standard cards
SS	Defeat Sirius

RANDOM SIGMA BOSSES
At the New Game/Continue screen, hold L and tap S Comp Star, G Comp Star, S Comp Star, M Comp Star, SS Star, SS Star, Black Ace Star.

FIGHT ROGUEZZ
At the New Game/Continue screen, hold L and tap G Comp Star, M Comp Star, M Comp Star, SS Star, G Comp Star, S Comp Star, Black Ace Star. RogueZZ appears in Meteor G Control CC.

MEGA MAN STAR FORCE 3: RED JOKER

STARS ON NEW GAME/CONTINUE SCREEN

Do the following to earn each star on the New Game/Continue screen.

NAME	HOW TO EARN
Red Joker	Defeat the game
G Comp	Collect all Giga cards
M Comp	Collect all Mega cards
S Comp	Collect all Standard cards
SS	Defeat Sirius

RANDOM SIGMA BOSSES

At the New Game/Continue screen, hold L and tap S Comp Star, G Comp Star, S Comp Star, M Comp Star, SS Star, SS Star, Red Joker Star.

FIGHT ROGUEZZ

At the New Game/Continue screen, hold L and tap G Comp Star, M Comp Star, M Comp Star, SS Star, G Comp Star, S Comp Star, Red Joker Star. RogueZZ appears in Meteor G Control CC.

METAL GEAR SOLID: SNAKE EATER 3D

BOSS SURVIVAL MODE

Defeat the game on any difficulty.

AUSCAM CAMO

Start a new game and select "I like MGS1!"

BANANA CAMO

Start a new game and select "I like MGS PEACE WALKER!"

DESERT TIGER CAMO AND RAIDEN MASK IN THE INTRO CUTSCENE.

Start a new game and select "I like MGS2!"

DPM CAMO

Start a new game and select "I like MGS4!"

FLECKTARN CAMO, GREEN AND BROWN FACEPAINTS.

Start a new game and select "I like MGS3!"

GRENADE CAMO

Start a new game and select "I like all the MGS games!"

MUMMY CAMO

Start a new game and select "I'm playing MGS for the first time!"

MUTANT MUDDS

PLAY AS GRANNIE

After collecting all 200 Diamonds and 40 Water Sprites, press L at the title screen to switch to Grannie.

MYSIMS KINGDOM

COW COSTUME

Pause the game and press R, X, L, Y, Up, Right, Left, Down.

COW HEADGEAR

Pause the game and press L, R, Y, X, Left, Down, Left, Right.

PATCHWORK CLOTHES

Pause the game and press Right, Down, Left, Up, L, R, L, R.

PATCHWORK PANTS

Pause the game and press Down, L, Left, R, Up, Y, Right, X.

PUNK BOTTOM

Pause the game and press Left, R, L, Right, Y, Y, X, X.

PUNK TOP

Pause the game and press Up, X, Down, Y, Left, L, Right, R.

SAMURAI ARMOR

Pause the game and press Y, X, Right, Left, L, R, Down, Up.

SAMURAI HELMET

Pause the game and press X, Y, R, L, X, Y, R, L.

N+

ATARI BONUS LEVELS

Select Unlockables from the Main menu, hold L + R and press A, B, A, B, A, A, B.

NARUTO: PATH OF THE NINJA 2

CHARACTER PASSWORDS

Talk to Konohamaru at the school to enter the following passwords. You must first complete the game for the passwords to work.

CHARACTER	PASSWORD
Gaara	DKFIABJL
Gai	IKAGDEFL
Iruka	JGDLKAIB
Itachi Uchiha	GBEIDALF
Jiraiya	EBJDAGFL
Kankuro	ALJKBEDG
Kyuubi Naruto	GJHLBFDE
Orochimaru	AHFBLEJG

NEW SUPER MARIO BROS. 2

PLAY AS LUIGI IN SINGLE PLAYER

Defeat Bowser in World 6. Then, at the file select, hold L + R as you select a file with A.

ALTERNATE TITLE SCREEN

Collect 1,000,000 coins to get a Gold Mario title screen.

ANOTHER ALTERNATE TITLE SCREEN

Collect 9,999,999 coins to get a Tanooki Mario title screen.

NINTENDOGS + CATS: FRENCH BULLDOG & NEW FRIENDS

DOG BREEDS

Unlock the following breeds with the given amount of trainer points.

DOG BREED	TRAINER POINTS REQUIRED
Beagle	3400
Boxer	3400
Bull Terrier	600
Cocker Spaniel	2100
Golden Retriever	9800
Great Dane	5800
Jack Russell Terrier	7400
Labrador Retriever	5800
Maltese	3400
Miniature Dachshund	600
Miniature Pinscher	2100
Miniature Poodle	9800
Miniature Schnauzer	5800
Pembroke Welsh Corgi	2100
Pomeranian	5800
Pug	5800
Shiba Inu	9800
Shih Tzu	600

NINTENDOGS + CATS: GOLDEN RETRIEVER & NEW FRIENDS

DOG BREEDS

Unlock the following breeds with the given amount of trainer points.

DOG BREED	TRAINER POINTS REQUIRED
Bassett Hound	9800
Boxer	5800
Bull Terrier	3400
Cavalier King Charles Spaniel	5800
Chihuahua	600
Dalmatian	3400
French Bulldog	9800
German Shepherd	2100
Jack Russell Terrier	600
Labrador Retriever	3400
Miniature Poodle	9800
Miniature Schnauzer	2100
Pembroke Welsh Corgi	7400
Pomeranian	2100
Shetland Sheepdog	600
Shih Tzu	7400
Siberian Husky	5800
Yorkshire Terrier	7400

NINTENDOGS + CATS: TOY POODLE & NEW FRIENDS

DOG BREEDS

Unlock the following breeds with the given amount of trainer points.

DOG BREED	TRAINER POINTS REQUIRED
Basset Hound	3600
Beagle	3600
Cavalier King Charles	2000
Chihuahua	5800
Cocker Spaniel	3600
Dalmatian	7400
Daschund	5800
German Shepherd	7400
Great Dane	600
Husky	2000
Maltese	2000
Mini Pinscher	7400
Pug	600
Shetland	5800
Yorkshire	600

THE OREGON TRAIL

HEIRLOOMS

HEIRLOOMS	HOW TO OBTAIN
Banjo	Finish the Gold Rush storyline.
Birch Pole	Catch 60 pounds of fish in one day.
Bugle	Bring the piano as your heirloom and complete the journey to Oregon.
Doctor's Bag	Get to the end of the trail without losing any family members.
Evil Eye	Score more than 150,000 points in a chapter.

HEIRLOOMS	HOW TO OBTAIN
Fine Suit	Score more than 120,000 points in a chapter.
Fine Whip Heirloom	Complete a trail segment without hitting an obstacle.
Fur Hat	Finish the Three Brave Brothers storyline.
Henry Rifle	Finish the Stuck in the Middle storyline.
Horseshoe	Get robbed 10 total times in one trip down the trail.
Piano	Finish the Family Affair storyline.

PEGGLE: DUAL SHOT

Q LEVEL 10

Send the trial game to another DS.

PHANTASY STAR ZERO

PASSWORD MACHINE

Check out the vending machine on the far right side of the sewers. Type in special passwords here to find free items.

ITEM	PASSWORD
Selvaria's Spear	5703-8252
Selvaria's Shield	4294-2273
Blade Cannon	7839-3594
Caduceus's Rod	5139-6877
Game Master (Ge-maga)	7162-5792
CONSOLES+ (Famitsu)	9185-6189

ITEM	PASSWORD
INGame: Greg&Kiri (Nintendo Dream)	5531-0215
Nintendo Power (Dengeki DS)	3171-0109
Puyo Soul	3470-1424
Taupy Soul	9475-6843
Lassie Soul	4775-7197

PHINEAS AND FERB

STOP CANDACE

At the Title screen, press X, Y, L, R, Select.

DOUBLE SPEED

At the Title screen, press A, B, L, R, Select.

PHOTO DOJO

FAST FIGHTERS

At the Title screen, hold Select and choose Head into Battle. Continue to hold Select and choose Vs. Mode.

POKÉMON BLACK/WHITE VERSION 2

PERMIT

See all Pokémon in Unova Pokedex. Receive from Professor Juniper.

ROUND CHARM

Catch all Pokémon in Unova Pokedex. Receive from Professor Juniper.

SHINY CHARM

Catch all Pokémon in National Pokedex. Receive from Professor Juniper.

LEGENDARY POKÉMON

POKÉMON	LOCATION	HOW TO FIND
Cobalion	Route 13	Defeat when found on Route 13. Return after defeating the Elite Four to find it at a higher level.
Terrakion	Route 22	Defeat when found on Route 22 on a small platform. Return after defeating the Elite Four to find it at a higher level.

POKÉMON	LOCATION	HOW TO FIND
Virizion	Route 11	Defeat when found on Route 11. Return after defeating the Elite Four to find it at a higher level.
Reshiram (White version)/Zekrom (Black version)	Dragonspiral Tower	After defeating the game, defeat N to get a stone. Take that to the top of Dragonspiral Tower.
Kyurem	Giant Chasm	After catching Resiram/Zekrom, return to Giant Chasm
Cresselia	Marvelous Bridge near Nimbasa City	Visit Marvelous Bridge with the Lunar Wing.
Regirock	Clay Tunnel	After defeating the game, go to the back of Clay Tunnel and find a hidden switch in an empty room. Activate the switch to find Regirock. This rewards you with an Iceberg Key (White version) or an Iron Key (Black version).
Registeel	Clay Tunnel	Use the Iron Key in the same room as before.
Regice	Clay Tunnel	Use the Iceberg Key in the same room as before.
Regigigas	Twist Mountain	With Regirock, Registeel, and Regice caught, go to the lower level of Twist Mountain.
Latias (White version)/Latios (Black version)	Dreamyard	Chase down Latias/Latios for the chance to battle.
Heatran	Reversal Mountain	Return to Reversal Mountain with Magma Stone.
Azelf	Route 23	Return to Route 23 from Victory Road, head west, cut down a shrub, and up some steps.
Mespirit	Celestial Tower	Climb to top of tower and wander around until Mespirit appears.
Uxie	Nacrene City	Walk around just outside the museum.

POKÉMON CONQUEST

PASSWORDS FOR RARE POKÉMON

Select Password from the main menu and enter the following. They appear the next month.

EFFECT	PASSWORD
Axew	BqWxXEK3xg
Beldum	CMqkZRRSRX
Chimchar	DNB3x2gCgk
Cincinno	vVALFrGTXX
Croagunk	LKpk8FRQR8
Darmanitan	pK5RgzqLG8
Deino	PKSRGpCPZJ
Dratini	Sr5Z5GqAgR
Drifloon	eqCgRvXwXX
Eevee	2rz3XFCKmR
Emolga	Jnm3kqgN8X
Gible	LTb3n3RYJ8

EFFECT	PASSWORD
Gyarados	mq2xRVNgRL
Lapras	GfV33RVN3F
Larvitar	Lpu3ggCYk8
Musharna	iMYXwqtHgL
Oshawott	frCLRpXG88
Panpour	CNZF3wpq3x
Pansage	6xSG8UCAZR
Pansear	niE33w9rwM
Pikachu	FZP8GqRZRR
Riolu	Shw8mxRAJR
Scyther	8GV3LMGrnM
Sneasel	Rc338MpqLx

KEIJI SPECIAL MISSION

Select Password and enter EDw8w2HaRn.

MOTONARI & MOTOCHIKA

Select Password and enter J2TRZXPUm3.

OKUNI SPECIAL MISSION

Select Password and enter gauRnak2nR.

RANMARU SPECIAL MISSION

Select Password and enter 2aL38Ek2Rx.

RESHIRAM EVENT

Select Password and enter 2rz3XFEKxR.

POKÉMON DREAM RADAR

#249 LUGIA

After you have earned the 3,000 points necessary to get Landorous, insert Pokémon SoulSilver into the 3DS. A new level will become available. Diving Extension becomes available and gives you Giratina.

#250 HO-OH

After you have earned the 3,000 points necessary to get Landorous, insert Pokémon HeartGold. A new level will become available. Rainbow Extension becomes available and gives you Giratina.

#483 DIALGA

After you have earned the 3,000 points necessary to get Landorous, insert Pokémon Diamond. A new level will become available. Time Extension becomes available and gives you Giratina.

#484 PALKIA

After you have earned the 3,000 points necessary to get Landorous, insert Pokémon Pearl. A new level will become available. Space Extension becomes available and gives you Giratina.

#487 GIRATINA

After you have earned the 3,000 points necessary to get Landorous, insert Pokémon Platinum. Renegade Extension becomes available and gives you Giratina.

POKEMON MYSTERY DUNGEON: EXPLORERS OF DARKNESS/TIME

Select Wonder Mail before starting your game, and then enter the following passwords to add a mission to your Job List. These are listed by the reward you receive for completing the mission.

Each password can only be used once. There are many possible passwords, here we list some examples. These passwords work on Explorers of Darkness and Explorers of Time.

ACCESSORY

ACCESSORY	PASSWORD
Gold Ribbon	5+KPKXT9RYP754&M2-58&&1-
Golden Mask	@QYPSJ@-N-J%TH6=4-SK32CR
Joy Ribbon	597C6#873795@Q6=F+TSQ68J
Mobile Scarf	R2MQ0X0&&-RN+64#4S0R+&-1
Miracle Chest	FX199P@CW@-XK54Q%4628XT#
No-Stick Cap	1@484PJ7NJW@XCHC2&-+H=@P
Pecha Scarf	8%2R-T&T1F-KR5#08P#&T=@=
Persim Band	TCX#TJQ0%#46Q6MJYMH2S#C9
Power Band	FHSM5950-2QNFTH9S-JM3Q9F
Racket Band	-F773&1XM0FRJT7Y@PJ%9C40
Special Band	752PY8M-Q1NHY#QX92836MHT
Stamina Band	F9RM4Y6W1&2T7@%SWF=R0NK&
X-Ray Specs	C#7H-#P2J9QPHCFPM5F674H=
Wonder Chest	0@R#3-+&7SC2K3@4NQ0-JQX9
Zinc Band	@WWHK8X18@C+C8KTN51H#213

ITEM

ITEM	PASSWORD
Beauty Scarf	@+CWF98#5CPYR13RJ#3YWKS5
Calcium	Y=59NRNS-#M2%C25725NJMQQ
Coronet Rock	S%9@47NTYP#Y105SR#%QH9MX
Dawn Stone	N54=MK=FSH1FCR8=R@HN14#Y
Deepseascale	WT192-H2=K@-WTJ3=JJ64C16
Deepseatooth	WQCM0-H=QH&-W+JP7FKT4CP+
Dusk Stone	X0=-JQ&X1X4KRY=8Y=23M=FH
Electrilizer	4SJYCFNX0-N@JN%NQ#+7-Q7#
Frozen Rock	YT&8WY&+278+2QJT@53TM3M8
Heal Seed	TWTN%RFRK+39-P#M2X+CXQS#
Joy Seed	PQS39&-7WC+R&QJQM2Y@@1KN
Leaf Stone	NP96N4K0HW3CJX8#FNK%=F&+
Link Box	&%8FXT9C76F4Q4SP5F8X3RW%
Lost Loot	J%0+F18XW5%P-9@&17+F8P9M
Lunar Ribbon	%-94RKFY%505XXMMC=FYK45N
Magmarizer	=TK+0KH72MNJNRW5P@RS&Y6=
Max Elixir	4Q9F-K6X66YW5TJY6MXK+RX7
Metal Coat	NP3SMTH-T&TMQFY@N1Q&SFNK
Mossy Rock	@JH#ST1&S14W3T2XJ8=7KR+7
Mystery Part	PXJ634F44Q3FQW&KYRX538+=
Oval Stone	@&FYQ977C#0YN-77TM&=X&+Q
Razor Claw	6JK2T26&MPC7&%-HWRXK2&-W
Reviver Seed	W+P0MYKJFNN3&Q%&-J12J2QH
Secret Slab	K=&4Q=@908N7=X&XHQ+Q1-CS
Shiny Stone	69-HHQX%K@#%7+5SMSPSQP#2
Sun Ribbon	7C8W308RYJ2XM@&QTYSJ%3=9
Thunderstone	+4QQK3PY84Y39P&=KN3=@XYR
Vile Seed	8#8%4496C#=JKRX9M&RKQW4%
Zinc	X=S#N&RNYSP9R2S01HT4MP8&

TM

TM	PASSWORD
Attract	Y@=JC48#K4SQ0NS9#S7@32%3
Blizzard	Y#ST42FMC4H+NM@M=T999#PR
Brick Break	@MF=%8400Y8X#T8FCTQC5XTS
Brine	9C04WP5XXN@=4NPFR08SS&03
Calm Mind	SH&YH&96C%&JK9Y0H99%3WM9
Dig	SQ96Y08RXJJXMJJ7=SSQK3K3
Embargo	1PQ7K%JX#4=HFHXPPK%7K04H
Energy Ball	5016-@1X8@&5H46#51M&+-XC
Fire Blast	W0T+NF98J13+F&NN=XNR&J-7
Flamethrower	JQ78%-CK%1PTP-77M740=F98
Flash	FS272Y61F1@MNN8FCSSTJ6TP
Gyro Ball	C#S@Y4%9YFQ+SQ6WRK36@1N0
Iron Tail	8+R006Y-&X57XX#&N-PT@R&6
Overheat	F=X5&K=FYJ3FC-N-@QXK34QJ
Payback	K3%0=W61FQCMN-FPHP=J5&W3
Poison Jab	S==YMX%92R54TSK6=F8%-%MN
Protect	Q#6762JK@967H#CMX#RQ3&M3
Psych Up	6=49WKH72&-JN%14SKNF&40N
Recycle	M@56C+=@H%K13WF4Q%RJ2JP9
Reflect	F=YTCK297HC02MT+MF13SQ4W
Rest	KR=WT#JC#@+HFS5K0JJM-0-2
Roar	C&0FWPTCRMKT&7NQ@N0&RQS+
Rock Slide	CN%+TMSHM0&3#&5YC4M1#C@2
Skill Swap	-H4TNNKY&1-P%4HSJY&XHW%Q
Sleep Talk	1M5972RY8X6NCC3CPPRS0K8J

TM	PASSWORD
Swords Dance	=633=JSY147RT=&0R9PJJ1FM
Thunder	WKY&7==@HR2%32YX6755JQ85
Vacuum-Cut	7PS2#26WN7HNX83M23J6F@C5
X-Scissor	S6P&198+-5QYR&22FJMKW1XF

POKEMON RUMBLE BLAST

The following passwords give you Pokémon that have special abilities. After the code has been entered, go to the indicated location to fight them.

EMBOAR IN ECHO VALLEY

Speak to Munna in Easterly Town and enter 8902-7356.

GALLADE IN EVERSPRING VALLEY

Speak to Munna in Easterly Town and enter 3535-6928.

GLISCOR IN SUNNY SEASHORE

Speak to Munna in Easterly Town and enter 9625-7845.

OSHAWOTT IN SHIMMERING LAKE

Speak to Munna in Easterly Town and enter 7403-2240.

PIKACHU IN VOLCANIC SLOPE

Speak to Munna in Easterly Town and enter 7746-3878.

TORNADUS IN VOLCANIC SLOPE

Speak to Munna in Easterly Town and enter 0250-7321.

LEGACY MODE

Complete the game and then at the title screen, hold L + R + Left and press A. Continue holding the buttons until you hear a sound.

POP CUTIE! STREET FASHION SIMULATION

LAYERED DRESS

At a phone, enter 7247.

POODLE OUTFIT

At a phone, enter 3107.

HOTEL PATAGONIA/EDDIE RETURNS

At a phone, enter 9901.

CALL GIBSONS

At a phone, enter 9801.

FASHION HOTLINE

At a phone enter 0000, 1111, 2222, 3333, 4444, 5555, 6666.

PRINCESS NATASHA

ALL GADGETS

Select Codes from the Extras menu and enter OLEGSGIZMO.

EXTRA LEVELS

Select Codes from the Extras menu and enter SMASHROBOT.

INFINITE LIVES

Select Codes from the Extras menu and enter CRUSHLUBEK.

RACE DRIVER: CREATE & RACE

ALL CHALLENGES

Select Cheat Codes from Extras and enter 942785.

ALL CHAMPIONSHIPS

Select Cheat Codes from Extras and enter 761492.

ALL REWARDS

Select Cheat Codes from Extras and enter 112337.

FREE DRIVE

Select Cheat Codes from Extras and enter 171923.

NO DAMAGE

Select Cheat Codes from Extras and enter 505303.

EASY STEERING

Select Cheat Codes from Extras and enter 611334.

MINIATURE CARS

Select Cheat Codes from Extras and enter 374288.

MM VIEW

Select Cheat Codes from Extras and enter 467348.

RAYMAN (DSIWARE)

Re-enter the code to toggle it off.

LEVEL SELECT (PAUSED ON THE WORLD MAP)
On the world map, enter R, Up, Left, Right, Down, Right, L.

INVINCIBILITY
Pause the game and enter L, Right, Up, Right, Left, Right, R.

99 LIVES
Pause the game and enter L Left, Right, Down, Right, Left, R.

ALL OF RAYMAN'S POWERS
Pause the game and enter R, Down, Left, Right, Left, Up, L.

10 HITPOINTS
Pause the game and enter L, Down, Up, Down, R.

25 BLUE TINGS
Pause the game and enter L, Up, Left, Right, Left, L.

RESIDENT EVIL: THE MERCENARIES 3D

CHARACTERS
Complete the following missions with a B Rank to unlock the corresponding character.

CHARACTERS	CLEAR THIS MISSION
Claire	1-3
Rebecca	2-3
Krauser	3-5
Barry	4-5
Wesker	5-5

RESIDENT EVIL: REVELATIONS

NEW GAME+
Complete the campaign.

HELL DIFFICULTY AND HYDRA SHOTGUN
Complete the campaign on Normal difficulty.

INFINITE ROCKET LAUNCHER
Complete the campaign on Hell difficulty

RAYMOND
Complete all Raid Mode stages on Chasm difficulty.

TRENCH DIFFICULTY IN RAID MODE
Complete all Raid Mode stages on Chasm Difficulty.

ABYSS DIFFICULTY IN RAID MODE
Complete all Raid Mode stages on Trench Difficulty.

FREE HERB IN RAID MODE
After completing a stage in Raid Mode, destroy the BSAA logo that appears.

RAID MODE COSTUMES
Do the following to unlock costumes for Raid Mode.

CHARACTER	HOW TO OBTAIN
Chris (Ship)	Reach Level 30.
Chris (Snow)	Complete Episodes 1-3 of the campaign.
Jessica (Ship)	Complete all Raid Mode stages on Trench difficulty.
Jessica (Snow)	Reach Level 10.
Jessica (Terragrigia)	Reach Level 40.
Jill (Beach)	Complete the first Raid stage.
Jill (Ship)	Complete Episodes 1-3 of the campaign.
Keith (HQ)	Complete 50 missions.
Keith (Snow)	Complete Episodes 4-6 of the campaign.
Parker (Beach)	Reach Level 20.
Parker (Ship)	Complete Episodes 1-3 of the campaign.

CHARACTER	HOW TO OBTAIN
Parker (Terragrigia)	Get a rare weapon.
Quint (HQ)	Reach Level 50.
Quint (Snow)	Complete 100 missions.

RAID MODE STAGES 1-7
Complete Episodes 1-3 of the campaign.

RAID MODE STAGES 8-12
Complete Episodes 4-6 of the campaign.

RAID MODE STAGES 13-17
Complete Episodes 7-9 of the campaign.

RAID MODE STAGES 18-20
Complete episodes 10-12 of the campaign.

RAID MODE STAGE 21
Complete the campaign.

RETRO GAME CHALLENGE

COSMIC GATE

HARD MODE
At the Title screen, press Down, Down, B, B, A, A, Start.

POWERED-UP INFINITY
Pause the game and press Up, Up, A, B. This cheat can only be used once per game.

SHIP POWER-UP
Pause the game and press Up, Up, A, A, B, B.

CONTINUE GAME
At the Game Over screen, press Left + Start. You will continue the game with a score of 000.

HAGGLE MAN

FULL HEALTH
Pause the game and press Down, Right, Up, Left, B, B, B, B, A, A, A, A.

SCROLLS APPEAR
Pause the game and press Up, Right, Down, Left, A, A, A, A, B, B, B, B.

INFINITE TIME
Before a level, hold Up/Left and press A + B.

HAGGLE MAN 2

STAGE SELECT
At the Title screen, hold A and press Up, Up, Right, Right, Right, Down, Down, Left, Left, Left.

FULL POWER
Pause the game and press Up, Down, Up, Down, B, B, A, A.

SCROLLS APPEAR
Pause the game and press Down, Up, Down, Up, A, A, B, B.

CONTINUE
At the Game Over screen, hold Left and press Start.

HAGGLE MAN 3

99 LIVES
Pause the game and press A, B, A, B, Left, Right, Left, Right.

9999 GEARS
Pause the game and press B, A, B, A, Right, Left, Right, Left.

WARP TO BOSS
Pause the game and press B, B, A, A, Left, Left, Right, Right.

RALLY KING

INVINCIBILITY
At the Title screen, press Select + Left.

CARS DISAPPEAR
At the Title screen, hold Select and press Down/Right.

START AT COURSE 2
At the Title screen, press A, B, A, B, Up + Select.

START AT COURSE 3
At the Title screen, press A, B, A, B, Left + Select.

START AT COURSE 4
At the Title screen, press A, B, A, B, Down + Select.

STAR PRINCE

INVINCIBILITY
At the Title screen, hold Up and press A, A, A. Then hold Down and press B, B, B.

CONTINUE
At the Game Over screen, hold Left and press Start.

RHYTHM HEAVEN

RHYTHM TOYS – TELEPHONE NUMBERS
Enter the following numbers into the telephone in Rhythm Toys to unlock sounds from Rhythm Tengoku:

5553282338
5557325937
5557268724
5557625688

RIDGE RACER 3D

CATEGORY 3 MACHINES
Complete Beginner Grand Prix Event No. 08

CATEGORY 2 MACHINES & ADVANCED GRAND PRIX
Complete Beginner Grand Prix Event No. 18

CATEGORY 1 MACHINES
Complete Advanced Grand Prix Event No. 26

EXPERT GRAND PRIX
Complete Advanced Grand Prix Event No. 36

KAMATA ANGL CONCEPT (SPECIAL CAT. 1 MACHINE)
Complete Expert Grand Prix Event No. 42

SOLDAT CRINALE (SPECIAL CAT. 1 MACHINE)
Complete Expert Grand Prix Event No. 43

AGE SOLO PETIT500 (SPECIAL CAT. 1 MACHINE)
Complete Expert Grand Prix Event No. 44

LUCKY & WILD MADBULL (SPECIAL CAT. 1 MACHINE)
Complete Expert Grand Prix Event No. 45

NAMCO PACMAN (SPECIAL CAT. 1 MACHINE) & PACMAN MUSIC CD
Complete Expert Grand Prix Event No. 46

NAMCO NEW RALLY-X (SPECIAL CAT. 1 MACHINE)
Complete Expert Grand Prix Event No. 47

MIRRORED & MIRRORED REVERSE COURSES
Complete Expert Grand Prix Event No. 48

RUBIK'S PUZZLE WORLD

ALL LEVELS AND CUBIES
At the Main menu, press X, Y, Y, X, X.

SCOOBY-DOO! FIRST FRIGHTS

DAPHNE'S SECRET COSTUME
Select Codes from the Extras menu and enter 2839.

FRED'S SECRET COSTUME
Select Codes from the Extras menu and enter 4826.

SCOOBY DOO'S SECRET COSTUME
Select Codes from the Extras menu and enter 1585.

SHAGGY'S SECRET COSTUME
Select Codes from the Extras menu and enter 3726.

VELMA'S SECRET COSTUME
Select Codes from the Extras menu and enter 6588.

SHIN MEGAMI TENSEI: STRANGE JOURNEY

SECRET DEMON PASSWORDS
Enter the following passwords when registering a demon in the Demon Compendium.

DEMON	PASSWORD
Alciel, the Black Sun	ALCARMOR
Beast Nekomata	Mai Namba
Brute Oni	Thick red skin
Cabracan	TRUSTIN SCALY — —
Deity Prometheus	Yu Namba
Demonee-Ho	You can't laugh OR cry now!
Demonica-C	Special Password+Chaos
Demonica-L	Special Password+Law
Demonica-N	Special Password+Neutral
Fairy Pixie	Madoka Ueno
Fairy Silky	Soothing ice
Genma Cu Chulainn	Trust
Hare of Inaba	X-X!Hol
Promethius	Yu Namba
Megami Ishtar	ISHTAR FIGHTS TAMMUZ ANGELS
Queen of the Faeries, Titania	summon smt.queen
Tyrant Mara	Nich Maragos
Vermin Mothman	Prophecy of wind
Vile Mishaguji	2000
Wilder Nue	James Kuroki
Yatagarasu	HELP ME
Yoma Koppa Tengu	Left hand freeze Right hand shock

SIMCITY CREATOR

99999999 MONEY
Enter MONEYBAGS as a password.

AMERICAN PROSPERITY AGE MAP
Enter NEWWORLD as a password.

ASIA AGE MAP
Enter SAMURAI as a password.

ASIA AGE BONUS MAP
Enter FEUDAL as a password.

DAWN OF CIVILIZATION MAP
Enter ANCIENT as a password.

GLOBAL WARMING MAP
Enter MODERN as a password.

GLOBAL WARMING BONUS MAP
Enter BEYOND as a password.

RENAISSANCE BONUS MAP
Enter HEREANDNOW as a password.

SONIC CLASSIC COLLECTION

SONIC THE HEDGEHOG

DEBUG MODE

At the title screen, press A, A, Up, Down, Left, Right, hold Y and press START.

LEVEL SELECT

At the title screen press Up, Down, Left, Right, hold Y and press START.

SONIC THE HEDGEHOG 2

LEVEL SELECT

At the title screen, press Up, Up, Up, Down, Down, Down, Left, Right, Left, Right, hold Y and press START.

SONIC THE HEDGEHOG 3

LEVEL SELECT

As the SEGA logo fades, quickly press Up, Up, Down, Down, Up, Up, Up, Up. Highlight Sound Test and press START.

SONIC KNUCKLES

LEVEL SELECT WITH SONIC THE HEDGEHOG 2

At the title screen, press Up, Up, Up, Down, Down, Down, Left, Right, Left, Right, hold A and press START.

SOUL BUBBLES

REVEAL ALL CALABASH LOCATIONS

Pause the game and press A, L, L, R, A, Down, A, R.

ALL LEVELS

At the World Select, press L, Up, X, Up, R, Y.

ALL GALLERY ITEMS

At the Gallery, press B, Up, B, B, L, Y.

SPIRIT CAMERA: THE CURSED MEMOIR

GOTHIC LOLITA COSTUME FOR MAYA

Complete the story mode.

PRINCESS PEACH COSTUME FOR MAYA

Complete all Battle Mode missions on Nightmare difficulty.

GOTHIC LOLITA COSTUME FOR PHOTO-OP

Complete the story mode on Nightmare difficulty.

BOY IN THE BOOK CURSED PAGES MINI-GAME

Complete all Four Strange Masks levels.

SPIRIT HOUSE CURSED PAGES MINI-GAME

Complete the first level of Boy in the Book.

SPONGEBOB SQUAREPANTS FEATURING NICKTOONS: GLOBS OF DOOM

INFINITE HEALTH

Select Unlock Codes from the Options and enter Tak, Tlaloc, Jimmy Neutron, Beautiful Gorgeous.

INSTANT KO

Select Unlock Codes from the Options and enter Dib, Tak, Beautiful Gorgeous, Plankton.

EXTRA ATTACK

Select Unlock Codes from the Options and enter Dib, Plankton, Technus, Jimmy Neutron.

EXTRA DEFENSE

Select Unlock Codes from the Options and enter Zim, Danny Phantom, Plankton, Beautiful Gorgeous.

MAX DEFENSE

Select Unlock Codes from the Options and enter Plankton, Dib, Beautiful Gorgeous, Plankton.

ITEMS +

Select Unlock Codes from the Options and enter Danny Phantom, Beautiful Gorgeous, Jimmy Neutron, Technus.

ITEMS ++
Select Unlock Codes from the Options and enter SpongeBob, Tlaloc, SpongeBob, Danny Phantom.

NO HEALTH ITEMS
Select Unlock Codes from the Options and enter Tak, SpongeBob, Technus, Danny Phantom.

LOWER PRICES
Select Unlock Codes from the Options and enter Tlaloc, Zim, Beautiful Gorgeous, SpongeBob.

SUPER BEAUTIFUL GORGEOUS
Select Unlock Codes from the Options and enter Beautiful Gorgeous, Technus, Jimmy Neutron, Beautiful Gorgeous.

SUPER DANNY PHANTOM
Select Unlock Codes from the Options and enter Danny Phantom, Zim, Danny Phantom, Beautiful Gorgeous.

SUPER DIB
Select Unlock Codes from the Options and enter Zim, Plankton, Dib, Plankton.

SUPER JIMMY
Select Unlock Codes from the Options and enter Technus, Danny Phantom, Jimmy Neutron, Technus.

SUPER PLANKTON
Select Unlock Codes from the Options and enter Tak, Plankton, Dib, Technus.

SUPER SPONGEBOB
Select Unlock Codes from the Options and enter Technus, SpongeBob, Technus, Tlaloc.

SUPER TAK
Select Unlock Codes from the Options and enter Danny Phantom, Jimmy Neutron, Tak, Tlaloc.

SUPER TECHNUS
Select Unlock Codes from the Options and enter Danny Phantom, Technus, Tak, Technus.

SUPER TLALOC
Select Unlock Codes from the Options and enter Tlaloc, Beautiful Gorgeous, Dib, SpongeBob.

SUPER ZIM
Select Unlock Codes from the Options and enter Plankton, Zim, Technus, SpongeBob.

SUPER JETPACK
Select Unlock Codes from the Options and enter Beautiful Gorgeous, Tlaloc, Jimmy Neutron, Jimmy Neutron.

COLORLESS ENEMIES
Select Unlock Codes from the Options and enter Technus, Jimmy Neutron, Tlaloc, Plankton.

BLUE ENEMIES
Select Unlock Codes from the Options and enter Beautiful Gorgeous, Zim, Plankton, Technus.

RED ENEMIES
Select Unlock Codes from the Options and enter SpongeBob, Tak, Jimmy Neutron, Danny Phantom.

DIFFICULT ENEMIES
Select Unlock Codes from the Options and enter SpongeBob, Dib, Dib, Technus.

DIFFICULT BOSSES
Select Unlock Codes from the Options and enter Plankton, Beautiful Gorgeous, Technus, Tlaloc.

INVINCIBLE PARTNER
Select Unlock Codes from the Options and enter Plankton, Tak, Beautiful Gorgeous, SpongeBob.

STAR WARS: THE FORCE UNLEASHED

INCREASED HEALTH
Select Unleashed Codes from the Extras menu and enter QSSPVENXO.

MAX OUT FORCE POWERS
Select Unleashed Codes from the Extras menu and enter CPLOOLKBF.

UNLIMITED FORCE ENERGY
Select Unleashed Codes from the Extras menu and enter TVENCVMJZ.

MORE POWERFUL LIGHTSABER
Select Unleashed Codes from the Extras menu and enter lightsaber.

UBER LIGHTSABER
Select Unleashed Codes from the Extras menu and enter MOMIROXIW.

ROM KOTA
Select Unleashed Codes from the Extras menu and enter mandalore.

CEREMONIAL JEDI ROBES
Select Unleashed Codes from the Extras menu and enter CURSEZRUX.

DAD'S ROBES
Select Unleashed Codes from the Extras menu and enter wookiee.

DARTH VADER'S COSTUME
Select Unleashed Codes from the Extras menu and enter HRMXRKVEN.

KENTO'S ROBE
Select Unleashed Codes from the Extras menu and enter KBVMSEVNM.

KOTA'S OUTFIT
Select Unleashed Codes from the Extras menu and enter EEDOPVENG.

SITH ROBE
Select Unleashed Codes from the Extras menu and enter ZWSFVENXA.

SITH ROBES
Select Unleashed Codes from the Extras menu and enter holocron.

SITH STALKER ARMOR
Select Unleashed Codes from the Extras menu and enter CPLZKMZTD.

SUPER MARIO 3D LAND

SPECIAL WORLD
Complete World 8.

PLAY AS LUIGI
Complete the castle in Special World 1. Touch the L icon to switch to Luigi.

SUPER MONKEY BALL 3D

MONKEY FIGHT CHARACTERS
Complete the following series to unlock the characters in Monkey Fight

CHARACTER	COMPLETE THIS SERIES
W-MeeMee	Basic
P-YanYan	Super Fight

MONKEY RACE CHARACTERS
Complete the following cups in Grand Prix mode to unlock the characters in Monkey Race

CHARACTER	FINISH GRAND PRIX IN GIVEN POSITION
N-Jam	1st in Sky-Way
A-Baby	2nd in Sky-Way
R-Doctor	3rd in Sky-Way
B-Jet	1st in Mt. Tyrano
P-YanYan	2nd in Mt. Tyrano
F-GonGon	3rd in Mt. Tyrano

MONKEY RACE CARS

To unlock more cars in Monkey Race, enter time trial mode and beat the given record for that track. If you beat it faster than that record, you unlock one car per level.

CAR	BEAT RECORD ON THIS TRACK
Robotron	Track 1 of Sky-Way
Mini Shooter	Track 2 of Sky-Way
Kitana	Track 3 of Sky-Way
G Caterpillar	Track 1 of Mt. Tyrano
Flying Carpet	Track 2 of Mt. Tyrano
Super Tops	Track 3 of Mt. Tyrano

SUPER ROBOT TAISEN OG SAGA: ENDLESS FRONTIER

NEW GAME +

After you have finished the game and saved, load your save to start again with your items and money.

OG1 CHOKER

Start a new game or load a saved file with the GBA game Super Robot Taisen: Original Generation in the GBA slot. This item boosts your SP by 100.

OG2 PENDANT

Start a new game or load a saved file with the GBA game Super Robot Taisen 2: Original Generation in the GBA slot. This item boosts your HP by 250.

SUPER SPEED MACHINES

UNLOCK VEHICLES

WIN GP	VEHICLE UNLOCKED
1	Haima (Rally)
2	Sandstrom (4x4)
3	Striker (Sports)

WIN GP	VEHICLE UNLOCKED
4	Copperhead (Muscle)
6	Gold Digger (Custom)
7	Blue Flame (Classic)

SUPER STREET FIGHTER IV: 3D EDITION

FIGURINES

Select Password from the Figurine Collection and enter the following:

FIGURINE	PASSWORD
Silver Akuma	RYSsPxSbTh
Silver Balrog	PqUswOobWG
Silver Chun-Li	tLWkWvrblz
Silver Cody	naMkEQgbQG
Silver Dan	rDRkkSlbqS
Silver Dhalsim	JKbsOVHbVC
Silver E. Honda	uUDsTlmbUN
Silver Hakan	rLPbyLgbUy
Silver Ibuki	ilMsRBabpB
Silver Juri	OfQkARpbJR
Silver Ken	NyosHgybuW
Silver Makoto	GHakWCTbsl
Silver Rose	GKkkXXtbSe
Silver Sakura	uzTsXzlbKn
Golden Blanka	DmdkeRvbxc
Golden Chun-Li	zAAkcHVbHk
Golden Guile	qeJkznDbKE

FIGURINE	PASSWORD
Golden M.Bison	CglsQNWbHu
Golden Ryu	KjckTnSbwK
Golden Vega	CglsQNWbHu
Golden Zangief	hinsVnebTu
Platinum Ryu	DPrkMnybCd
Special Akuma	uQHkWgYbJC

THEATRHYTHM FINAL FANTASY

COLLECTACARDS

Select Collection from the Museum menu and then choose Password. Enter the following to unlock the CollectaCard. Each password can be entered once and if you already own the Collectacard, it adds one level.

COLLECTACARD	PASSWORD
01 Warrior of Light	Class Change
01 Warrior of Light	Sarah's Lute
01 Warrior of Light	Warrior of Light
02 Firion	Cyclone
02 Firion	Wild Rose
02 Firion	Wyvern
03 Onion Knight	Pintsized Powerhouse
03 Onion Knight	Unreleased
04 Cecil	Brothers
04 Cecil	Dark Knight
04 Cecil	Holy Paladin
05 Bartz	Boko loves Koko
05 Bartz	I am Bartz
05 Bartz	Rides Boko
06 Terra	Flowered tights
06 Terra	Magitek Armor
06 Terra	Slave Crown
07 Cloud	Former SOLDIER
07 Cloud	Hardy-Daytona
07 Cloud	Lifestream
08 Squall	I'm going to pass
08 Squall	Lionheart
08 Squall	Tall, dark, and silent
09 Zidane	Beloved Dagger
09 Zidane	Tantalus
09 Zidane	Zidane Tribal
10 Tidus	Final Summoning
10 Tidus	Jecht Shot
10 Tidus	Zanarkand Abes
11 Shantotto	Ohoho!
11 Shantotto	Pain 101
11 Shantotto	Unmarried
12 Vaan	Alone in the world
12 Vaan	Denser than lead
12 Vaan	Sky Pirate wannabe
13 Lightning	Guardian Corps
13 Lightning	Serah's sister
13 Lightning	The White Knight
14 Princess Sarah	Beloved princess

COLLECTACARD	PASSWORD
14 Princess Sarah	Cornelia
14 Princess Sarah	Hostage
15 Minwu	An urban turban
15 Minwu	Likes canoeing
15 Minwu	White Mage
16 Cid	Always around?
16 Cid	The Enterprise
17 Rydia	Early bloomer
17 Rydia	Pyrophobia
17 Rydia	We're all the same
18 Faris	Beautiful pirate
18 Faris	Friend to Syldra
18 Faris	Princess of Tycoon
19 Locke	Bandana man
19 Locke	Hates mushrooms
20 Aerith	A the-TE!
20 Aerith	Cetra
20 Aerith	Mother's Materia
21 Seifer	Another gunblade
21 Seifer	Disciplinary Committee
21 Seifer	Twin Scars
22 Vivi	Black Mage
22 Vivi	Doesn't like heights
22 Vivi	Master Vivi
23 Yuna	.R.P.
23 Yuna	Eternal Calm
23 Yuna	The Gullwings
24 Prishe	Detestable Child
24 Prishe	Feed me
24 Prishe	I looo...ve lobster
25 Ashe	Amalia?
25 Ashe	Dawn Shard
25 Ashe	Then steal me.
26 Snow	Do-rag
26 Snow	Serah!
26 Snow	Sis!
27 Kain	Cecil's best friend
27 Kain	Son of Richard
28 Sephiroth	Black Materia
28 Sephiroth	Masamune
28 Sephiroth	One-winged angel
29 Cosmos	Asteraceae

COLLECTACARD	PASSWORD
29 Cosmos	Goddess of Harmony
29 Cosmos	The Great Will
30 Chocobo	Fat Chocobo
30 Chocobo	Gysahl Greens
30 Chocobo	Kweh! KWEH!
31 Moogle	Bat wings
31 Moogle	Kupo KUPO! Kupo?
31 Moogle	Red pompom
32 Shiva	Diamond Dust
32 Shiva	Heavenly Strike
32 Shiva	Ice Queen
33 Ramuh	Judgment Bolt
33 Ramuh	Love the beard
34 Ifrit	Hellfire
34 Ifrit	Infernal Blaze
35 Odin	Sleipnir's rider
35 Odin	Zantetsuken
36 Bahamut	Mega Flare
36 Bahamut	Rat tail
37 Goblin	Goblin Punch
38 Bomb	BOOM!
38 Bomb	Three strikes
39 Green Dragon	Another tail?
39 Green Dragon	Dangerous breath
39 Green Dragon	Not just green
40 Malboro	Bad breath
40 Malboro	Darkness, Silence, Poison
40 Malboro	Drooling Daisy
41 Behemoth	Surprisingly regular
41 Behemoth	What a meathead
42 Black Knight	Sun Blade
42 Black Knight	Unbeatable?
42 Black Knight	Yoichi Bow
43 Iron Giant	Reaper
43 Iron Giant	Strongest small fry
43 Iron Giant	What's under the armor?
44 Hein	Barrier Shift
44 Hein	Elemental weakness
45 Ahriman	Good at magic
46 Xande	Libra!
46 Xande	Mortality
47 Flan	Weak against Mages
48 Scarmiglione	Blighted Despot
48 Scarmiglione	Sssrrr...
48 Scarmiglione	Undead minions
49 Cagnazzo	Drowned King
49 Cagnazzo	Second life
50 Barbariccia	Lord of Wind
50 Barbariccia	Maelstrom
50 Barbariccia	The lone female
51 Rubicante	Autarch of Flame
51 Rubicante	Awesome cloak
52 Magic Pot	Miss!
52 Magic Pot	What's in the pot?

COLLECTACARD	PASSWORD
53 Tonberry	Everyone's Grudge
53 Tonberry	Knife and lantern
53 Tonberry	Voodoo
54 Gilgamesh	Bartz's rival
54 Gilgamesh	Big Bridge
55 Enkidu	Vampire
55 Enkidu	White Wind
56 Omega	Superboss
56 Omega	Wave Cannon
57 Shinryu	Ragnarok
57 Shinryu	Tidal Wave
58 Cactaur	1000 Needles
58 Cactuar	10000 Needles
58 Cactuar	Gigantuar
59 Hill Gigas	Magnitude 8
59 Hill Gigas	Once a Giant
60 Ultros	I AM an octopus!
60 Ultros	Mr. Typhon
61 Deathgaze	Level 5 Death
62 Kefka	Heartless Angel
62 Kefka	I just can't believe it!
62 Kefka	Life... Dreams... Hope...
63 Ultima Weapon	Bribes welcome
63 Ultima Weapon	Shadow Flare
64 Jenova Synthesis	Calamity from the Skies
64 Jenova Synthesis	Countdown to Ultima
64 Jenova Synthesis	Mother
65 Safer Sephiroth	I am the chosen one!
65 Safer Sephiroth	Pale Horse
65 Safer Sephiroth	Super Nova
66 Esthar Soldier	Bodysuit
66 Esthar Soldier	Shotgun
66 Esthar Soldier	Terminator
67 Gesper	Black Hole
67 Gesper	Defective weapon
67 Gesper	Degenerator
68 Pupu	Elixir please!
68 Pupu	UFO?
69 Black Waltz No. 3	Best of the Black Mages
69 Black Waltz No. 3	Triple time
70 Ozma	Curse, Meteor, Doomsday
70 Ozma	The round guy
71 Anima	Pain
71 Anima	Seymour's mother
72 Seymour Natus	One of the Guado
73 Gigas	Loves rocks
73 Gigas	Qufim Island
74 Shadow Lord	Implosion
74 Shadow Lord	The Crystal War
74 Shadow Lord	Xarcabard

COLLECTACARD	PASSWORD
75 Bangaa Thief	Hates water
75 Bangaa Thief	One of the Bangaa
76 Mandragoras	Rogue Tomato
76 Mandragoras	Sochen Cave Palace
76 Mandragoras	Too cute to hate
77 Judge	Basch's younger twin
77 Judge	Gabranth
77 Judge	Judge Magister
78 Psicom Enforcer	The Hanging Edge

COLLECTACARD	PASSWORD
78 Psicom Enforcer	The Purge
79 Manasvin Warmech	Annihilator
79 Manasvin Warmech	Crystal Rain
79 Manasvin Warmech	Targeting
80 Adamantoise	Earth Shaker
80 Adamantoise	Platinum Ingot
80 Adamantoise	Trapezohedron
81 Chaos	Demonsdance
81 Chaos	God of Discord
81 Chaos	Know despair!

UNLOCK CHARACTERS

The following characters are unlocked by collecting 8 Crystal Fragments in the given color.

CHARACTER	CRYSTAL FRAGMENT COLOR
Aerith (Final Fantasy VII)	Pink
Ashe (Final Fantasy XII)	Crimson
Cid (Final Fantasy III)	Yellow
Cosmos (Dissidia)	Rainbow
Faris (Final Fantasy V)	Red
Kain (Final Fantasy IV)	Navy Blue
Locke (Final Fantasy VI)	Blue
Minwu (Final Fantasy II)	Silver
Princess Sarah (Final Fantasy I)	Gold
Prish (Final Fantasy XI)	Purple
Rydia (Final Fantasy IV)	Emerald
Seifer (Final Fantasy VIII)	Grey
Sephiroth (Final Fantasy VII)	Black
Snow (Final Fantasy XIII)	White
Vivi (Final Fantasy IX)	Orange
Yuuna (Final Fantasy X)	Sapphire

TRANSFORMERS: WAR FOR CYBERTRON—AUTOBOTS

AUTOBOT SILVERBOLT (STORY & ARENA)

Select Cheats from the Main menu and enter 10141.

DECEPTICON RAMJET (IN ARENA)

Select Cheats from the Main menu and enter 99871.

TRANSFORMERS: WAR FOR CYBERTRON—DECEPTICONS

DECEPTICON RAMJET (STORY & ARENA)

Select Cheats from the Main menu and enter 99871.

AUTOBOT SILVERBOLT (ARENA)

Select Cheats from the Main menu and enter 10141.

TRON: EVOLUTION

THE ISLAND, TANK AND DISC BATTLE MAP

At the cheat menu, enter 25E0DE6B.

QUORRA COSTUME

At the cheat menu, enter c74f395f.

ULTIMATE MORTAL KOMBAT

VS CODES

At the VS screen, each player must use LP, BLK, and LK to enter the following codes:

EFFECT	PLAYER 1	PLAYER 2
You are now entering the realm	642	468
Blocking Disabled	020	020
Dark Kombat	448	844
Infinite Run	466	466
Play in Kahn's Kave	004	700
Play in the Kombat Temple	600	N/A
Play in the Soul Chamber	123	901
Play on Jade's Deset	330	033
Play on Kahn's Tower	880	220
Play on Noob Saibot Dorfen	050	050
Play on Rooftops	343	343
Play on Scislac Busorez	933	933
Play on Subway	880	088
Play on the Belltower	091	190
Play on the Bridge	077	022
Play on the Graveyard	666	333
Play on the Pit 3	820	028
Play on the Street	079	035
Play on the Waterfront	002	003
Play Scorpions Lair	666	444
Player 1 Half Power	033	N/A
Player 1 Quarter Power	707	N/A
Player 2 Half Power	N/A	033
Player 2 Quarter Power	N/A	707
Power Bars Disabled	987	123
Random Kombat	444	444
Revision 1.2	999	999
Sans Power	044	440
Silent Kombat	300	300
Throwing Disabled	100	100
Throwing Encouraged	010	010
Winner of round fights Motaro	969	141
Winner of round fights Noob Saibot	769	342
Winner of round fights Shao Kahn	033	564
Winner of round fights Smoke	205	205

UNLOCK ERMAC, MILEENA, CLASSIC SUB-ZERO

At the Ultimate Kombat Kode screen input the following codes:
(Note: To easily access the Ultimate Kombat Kode screen just get defeated and don't continue.)

CLASSIC SUB-ZERO

At the Ultimate Kombat Kode screen, enter 81835. You can reach this screen by losing and not continuing.

ERMAC

At the Ultimate Kombat Kode screen, enter 12344. You can reach this screen by losing and not continuing.

MILEENA

At the Ultimate Kombat Kode screen, enter 22264. You can reach this screen by losing and not continuing.

HUMAN SMOKE

Select ROBO Smoke. Hold Block + Run + High Punch + High Kick + Back before the fight begins.

UP

INVINCIBILITY

After completing the game, enter B, Y, B, Y, X, Y, X, Y, B, A at the title screen. This cheat disables saving.

WORLD CHAMPIONSHIP POKER

UNLOCK CASINOS

At the Title screen, press Y, X, Y, B, L, R. Then press the following direction:

DIRECTION	CASINO
Left	Amazon
Right	Nebula
Down	Renaissance

WWE ALL STARS

ALL CHARACTERS AND RING GEAR

At the main menu, press Left, Right, Left, Down, Up, Left, Right, Up.

SONY PLAYSTATION® PORTABLE

GAMES

THE 3RD BIRTHDAY

After you complete the game and save, you can load up that save and start a new game with your weapons and Over Energy still intact. You also get the ability to unlock cheat codes from the start menu. Press Start and select Cheat Codes to access them. Obtain more cheat codes by fulfilling certain conditions. Rank and Feat results are not recorded while cheat codes are turned on.

ASSIST CODES

CHEAT	HOW TO OBTAIN IT	DESCRIPTION
High Regen	10,000 BP	Greatly accelerates Aya's LIFE recovery rate.
Free Crossfire	10,000 BP	NPCs can join a crossfire even if not taking cover.
Infinite Ammo	Clear the game 10 times at any level.	All guns can shoot unlimited bullets.

CHALLENGE CODES

CHEAT	HOW TO OBTAIN IT	DESCRIPTION
No Armor	Accomplish 4 or more Episode 1 feats at the Hard difficulty level.	Protective gear is always at max damage.

CHEAT	HOW TO OBTAIN IT	DESCRIPTION
No Evasion Assist	Accomplish 4 or more Episode 2 feats at the Hard difficulty level.	No invulnerability while evading.
No Regen	Accomplish 3 or more Episode 3 feats at the Hard difficulty level.	LIFE does not recover automatically.
No Info	Accomplish 3 or more Episode 4 feats at the Hard difficulty level.	No on-screen battle info.
Critical Disease	Accomplish 5 or more Episode 5 feats at the Hard difficulty level.	The Liberation gauge refills at half speed.
No Over Energy	Accomplish at least 75 percent of all feats at the Hard difficulty level.	Unable to unleash Over Energy.
Static LIFE	Accomplish 4 or more Episode 1 feats at the Deadly difficulty level.	Aya gains the max LIFE amount of the NPC she dives into, regardless of her level.
Limited Weapons	Accomplish 4 or more Episode 2 feats at the Deadly difficulty level.	Unable to carry any weapon apart from the starting handgun (76SA).
Level Hold	Accomplish 3 or more Episode 3 feats at the Deadly difficulty level.	Aya is permanently at level 1 and gains no experience.
Critical Illness	Accomplish 3 or more Episode 4 feats at the Deadly difficulty level.	Constantly receive damage.
Half Ammo	Accomplish 5 or more Episode 5 feats at the Deadly difficulty level.	Ammo capacity of all guns is halved.
NPC One-Hit Death	Accomplish at least 75 percent of all feats at the Deadly difficulty level.	NPCs die with one hit.
No Haste	Complete the game at the Insane difficulty level.	Time does not slow during an Overdive.
Maintain LIFE	Complete the game at the Insane difficulty level.	LIFE doesn't increase or decrease, even during an Overdive.
Friendly Fire	Complete the game at the Insane difficulty level.	Can be damaged by allies.
No Cover	Accomplish at least 75 percent of all feats at the Hard and higher difficulties.	No barricades or plateaus.
One-Hit Death	Obtain all cheat codes.	Aya dies with one hit.

ASTRO BOY: THE VIDEO GAME

INVULNERABLE
Pause the game and press Up, Down, Down, Up, L1, R.

MAX STATS
Pause the game and press Left, Left, R, Down, Down, L1.

INFINITE SUPERS
Pause the game and press Left, L1, Right, L1, Up, Down.

INFINITE DASHES
Pause the game and press R, R, L1, R, Left, Up.

DISABLE SUPERS
Pause the game and press L1, L1, R, R, L1, Left.

COSTUME SWAP (ARENA AND CLASSIC COSTUMES)
Pause the game and press R, Up, L1, Up, Down, R.

UNLOCK LEVELS
Pause the game and press Up, L1, Right, L1, Down, L1. This allows you to travel to any level from the Story menu.

BEN 10: ALIEN FORCE: THE GAME

LEVEL LORD
Enter Gwen, Kevin, Big Chill, Gwen as a code.

INVINCIBILITY
Enter Kevin, Big Chill, Swampfire, Kevin as a code.

ALL COMBOS
Enter Swampfire, Gwen, Kevin, Ben as a code.

INFINITE ALIENS
Enter Ben, Swampfire, Gwen, Big Chill as a code.

BEN 10: ALIEN FORCE VILGAX ATTACKS

LEVEL SKIP
Pause the game and enter Portal in the Cheats menu.

UNLOCK ALL SPECIAL ATTACKS (ALL FORMS)
Pause the game and enter Everythingproof in the Cheats menu.

UNLOCK ALL ALIEN FORMS
Pause the game and enter Primus in the Cheats menu.

TOGGLE INVULNERABILITY ON AND OFF
Pause the game and enter Xlmrsmoothy in the Cheats menu.

FULL HEALTH
Pause the game and enter Herotime in the Cheats menu.

QUICK ENERGY REGENERATION
Pause the game and enter Generator in the Cheats menu.

BEN 10 ULTIMATE ALIEN: COSMIC DESTRUCTION

To remove these cheats, you must start a new game.

1,000,000 DNA
Pause the game, select Cheats, and enter Cash.

REGENERATE HEALTH
Pause the game, select Cheats, and enter Health.

REGENERATE ENERGY
Pause the game, select Cheats, and enter Energy.

UPGRADE EVERYTHING
Pause the game, select Cheats, and enter Upgrade.

ALL LEVELS
Pause the game, select Cheats, and enter Levels.

DAMAGE
Pause the game, select Cheats, and enter Hard. Enemies cause double the damage, while you inflict half damage.

CRASH: MIND OVER MUTANT

A cheat can be deactivated by re-entering the code.

FREEZE ENEMIES WITH TOUCH
Pause the game, hold R and press Down, Down, Down, Up.

ENEMIES DROP X4 DAMAGE
Pause the game, hold R and press Up, Up, Up, Left.

ENEMIES DROP PURPLE FRUIT
Pause the game, hold R and press Up, Down, Down, Up.

ENEMIES DROP SUPER KICK
Pause the game, hold R and press Up, Right, Down, Left.

ENIMIES DROP WUMPA FRUIT
Pause the game, hold R and press Right, Right, Right, Up.

SHADOW CRASH
Pause the game, hold R and press Left, Right, Left, Right.

DEFORMED CRASH
Pause the game, hold R and press Left, Left, Left, Down.

CRISIS CORE—FINAL FANTASY VII

NEW GAME+

After completing the game, you'll be prompted to make a new save. Loading a game from this new save will begin a New Game+, starting the game over while allowing Zack to retain almost everything he's earned.

The following items transfer to a New Game+: Level, Experience, SP, Gil, Playtime, Non-Key Items, Materia, and DMW Completion Rate

The following items do not transfer: Key Items, Materia/Accessory Slot Expansion, Ability to SP Convert, DMW Images, Mission Progress, Mail, and Unlocked Shops

DANTE'S INFERNO

UNLOCK EARTHLY REWARDS FOR YOUR COMPUTER

Go to www.hellisnigh.com and enter the following passwords:

Password #1: excommunicate
Password #2: scythe
Password #3: grafter
Password #4: styx
Password #5: unbaptized
Password #6: alighieri

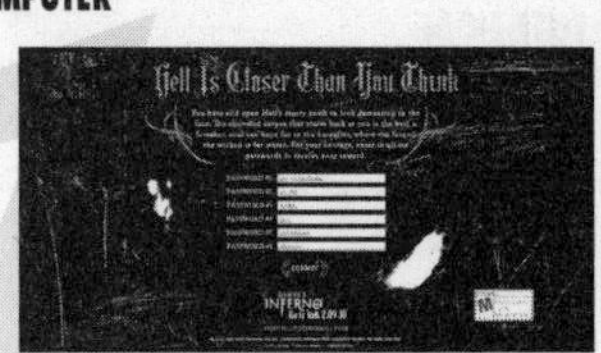

DESPICABLE ME: THE GAME

MINIONETTES COSTUME SET

In Gru's Lab, select Cheats from the Bonus menu and enter ○, ○, □, △, ✕.

VILLAGE FOLK COSTUME SET

In Gru's Lab, select Cheats from the Bonus menu and enter △, ✕, ✕, ○, ✕.

TAFFY WEB GUN

In Gru's Lab, select Cheats from the Bonus menu and enter ✕, ○, □, ✕, △.

DISGAEA 2: DARK HERO DAYS

AXEL MODE

Highlight New Game and press △, □, ○, △, □, ○, ✕.

DISSIDIA: FINAL FANTASY

SECRET PASSWORDS

The following passwords can be entered into the personal message section of your Friend Card to make the following items appear in the shop. Use the NA Version passwords for the North American version of the game and use the EU Ver. Passwords for the European version of the game.

REWARDS	NA VER.		EU VER.	
Player Icon: Chocobo (FF5)	58205	2436	62942	36172
Player Icon: Moogle (FF5)	13410	3103	84626	93120
Capricorn Recipe	87032	2642	6199	27495
Aquarius Recipe	39275	40667	3894	27509
Pisces Recipe	5310	62973	15812	2748
Friend Card: Matoya	39392	58263	1849	16360
Friend Card: Ninja	27481	73856	46490	11483
Friend Card: Fusoya	2943	2971	2971	2943
Friend Card: Siegfried	2015	1231	25496	12772
Friend Card: Vivi	37842	27940	70271	8560
Friend Card: Auron	12982	28499	33705	59603

DUNGEON SIEGE: THRONE OF AGONY

ITEM CODES

Talk to Feydwer and Klaars in Seahaven and enter the following codes. Enter the Master Code and one of the item codes.

ITEM	CODE
Master Code	MPJNKBHAKANLPGHD
Bloodstained Warboots	MHFMCJIFNDHOKLPM
Bolt Flingers	OBMIDNBJNPFKADCL
Enkindled Cleaver	MJPOBGFNLKELLLLP
Malignant Force	JDGJHKPOLNMCGHNC
Polychromatic Shiv	PJJEPCFHEIHAJEEE
Teasha's Ire	GDIMBNLEIGNNLOEG
Traveler's Handbook	PIJNPEGFJJPFALNO

ELITE MODE

Defeat the game to unlock this mode.

G.I. JOE: THE RISE OF COBRA

CLASSIC DUKE

At the Main menu, press Left, Up, □, Up, Right, △.

CLASSIC SCARLET

At the Main menu, press Right, Up, Down, Down, △.

GODS EATER BURST

CONTINUE + MODE

After defeating Arda Nova and completing the game, save the game. Load this saved game to continue with new missions.

CONTINUE ++ MODE

After defeating Corrosive Hannibal and completing Continue + Mode, save the game. Load this saved game to continue with new missions.

GRAND THEFT AUTO: CHINATOWN WARS

The following cheats will disable saving:

FULL HEALTH

During a game, press L, L, R, ○, ○, ×, ×, R.

FULL ARMOR

During a game, press L, L, R, ×, ×, ○, ○, R.

INCREASE WANTED LEVEL

During a game, press L, L, R, □, □, △, △, R.

DECREASE WANTED LEVEL

During a game, press R, △, △, □, □, R, L, L.

EXPLOSIVE PISTOL ROUND

During a game, press L, R, △, □, ○, ×, Up, Down.

WEAPONS SET 1

During a game, press R, Up, ×, Down, Left, R, ×, Right. This gives you the Pistol, Nightstick, Minigun, Assault Rifle, Micro SMG, Stubby Shotgun, and Grenades with max ammo.

WEAPONS SET 2

During a game, press R, Up, ○, Down, Left, R, ○, Right. This gives you the Twin Pistol, Teaser, Flame Thrower, Carbine Rifle, SMG, Double Barreled Shotgun, and Molotovs with max ammo.

WEAPONS SET 3

During a game, press R, Up, □, Down, Left, R, □, Right. This gives you the Revolver, Chainsaw, Flame Thrower, Carbine Rifle, SMG, Double Barreled Shotgun, and Proximity Mines with max ammo.

WEAPONS SET 4

During a game, press R, Up, △, Down, Left, R, △, Right. This gives you the Pistol, Baseball Bat, Carbine Rifle, RPG, Micro SMG, Shotgun, and Flashbangs with max ammo.

WEATHER: SUNNY

During a game, press Up, Down, Left, Right, ○, ×, L, R.

WEATHER: EXTRA SUNNY

During a game, press Up, Down, Left, Right, ✕, △, L, R.

WEATHER: CLOUDY

During a game, press Up, Down, Left, Right, △, □, L, R.

WEATHER: RAIN

During a game, press Up, Down, Left, Right, □, ○, L, R.

WEATHER: HEAVY RAIN

During a game, press Up, Down, Left, Right, ○, △, R, L.

WEATHER: THUNDERSTORMS

During a game, press Up, Down, Left, Right, ✕, □, R, L.

WEATHER: FOG

During a game, press Down, Left, Right, □, ✕, R, L.

GUILTY GEAR JUDGMENT

EXTRA SOUL IN MAIN STORY

Pause the game, press Select, and press Up, Up, Down, Left, Start.

LIFE + TENSION MAX IN MAIN STORY AND SURVIVAL

Pause the game, press Select, and press Down, Right, Right, Up, Start.

HIDDEN GALLERY TEST

First you must complete the game with each character. Then, highlight Quit on the Main Menu and press L + R + ○.

SOFT RESET

Press Start + Select + L + R.

GOLD CHARACTERS

While selecting your character, press L + R.

GUILTY GEAR XX ACCENT CORE PLUS

FIGHT EX CHARACTERS

Highlight Arcade or M.O.M. and hold R while starting the game.

FIGHT GOLD CHARACTERS

Highlight Arcade or M.O.M. and hold L while starting the game.

FIGHT GOLD/EX CHARACTERS

Highlight Arcade or M.O.M. and hold L + R while starting the game.

HELLBOY: THE SCIENCE OF EVIL

REFILL HEALTH

During a game, press Right, Down, Left, □.

REFILL RAGE

During a game, press Left, Down, Right, □.

REFILL AMMO

During a game, press Left, Down, Right, ○.

HOT BRAIN

119.99 TEMPERATURE IN ALL 5 CATEGORIES

Select New Game and enter Cheat.

INVIZIMALS

SPECIAL INVIZIMAL

At the World Map, press and hold Select and then press Up, Right, Down, Left. At the Big Secret, choose Capture Invizimals.

KINGDOM HEARTS: BIRTH BY SLEEP

FINAL EPISODE

Find all of the Xehanort Reports and complete all three stories.

TRINITY ARCHIVES

Complete the story using any character.

TROPHY	UNLOCKED BY...
Power Walker	Taking 99,999 steps.
Keyslinger	Defeating 9999 Unversed.
Clockworks	Accumulating 80 hours or more of gameplay.
Arena Sweeper	Completing all arena matches.
Dairy Devotee	Activating Frozen Fortune 30 times.
In the Munny	Earning 33,333 munny.
One Down	Completing the story using any character.
Trinity	Completing all stories in at least Proud Mode.

LEGO BATMAN

BATCAVE CODES

Using the computer in the Batcave, select Enter Code and enter the following:

CHARACTERS

CHARACTER	CODE
Alfred	ZAQ637
Batgirl	JKR331
Bruce Wayne	BDJ327
Catwoman (Classic)	M1AAWW
Clown Goon	HJK327
Commissioner Gordon	DDP967
Fishmonger	HGY748
Freeze Girl	XVK541
Joker Goon	UTF782
Joker Henchman	YUN924
Mad Hatter	JCA283
Man-Bat	NYU942
Military Policeman	MKL382
Nightwing	MVY759
Penguin Goon	NKA238

CHARACTER	CODE
Penguin Henchman	BJH782
Penguin Minion	KJP748
Poison Ivy Goon	GTB899
Police Marksman	HKG984
Police Officer	JRY983
Riddler Goon	CRY928
Riddler Henchman	XEU824
S.W.A.T.	HTF114
Sailor	NAV592
Scientist	JFL786
Security Guard	PLB946
The Joker (Tropical)	CCB199
Yeti	NJL412
Zoo Sweeper	DWR243

VEHICLES

VEHICLE	CODE
Bat-Tank	KNTT4B
Bruce Wayne's Private Jet	LEA664
Catwoman's Motorcycle	HPL826
Garbage Truck	DUS483
Goon Helicopter	GCH328
Harbor Helicopter	CHP735
Harley Quinn's Hammer Truck	RDT637
Mad Hatter's Glider	HS000W
Mad Hatter's Steamboat	M4DM4N
Mr. Freeze's Iceberg	ICYICE
The Joker's Van	JUK657

VEHICLE	CODE
Mr. Freeze's Kart	BCT229
Penguin Goon Submarine	BTN248
Police Bike	LJP234
Police Boat	PLC999
Police Car	KJL832
Police Helicopter	CWR732
Police Van	MAC788
Police Watercraft	VJD328
Riddler's Jet	HAHAHA
Robin's Submarine	TTF453
Two-Face's Armored Truck	EFE933

CHEATS

CHEAT	CODE
Always Score Multiply	9LRGNB
Fast Batarangs	JRBDCB
Fast Walk	ZOLM6N
Flame Batarang	D8NYWH
Freeze Batarang	XPN4NG
Extra Hearts	ML3KHP
Fast Build	EVG26J
Immune to Freeze	JXUDY6
Invincibility	WYD5CP
Minikit Detector	ZXGH9J

CHEAT	CODE
More Batarang Targets	XWP645
Piece Detector	KHJ554
Power Brick Detector	MMN786
Regenerate Hearts	HJH7HJ
Score x2	N4NR3E
Score x4	CX9MAT
Score x6	MLVNF2
Score x8	WCCDB9
Score x10	18HW07

MARVEL SUPER HERO SQUAD

IRON MAN BONUS COSTUME
Select Enter Code from the Options menu and enter 111111. This unlocks the bonus costume "War Machine."

HULK BONUS COSTUMES
Select Enter Code from the Options menu and enter 222222. This unlocks the bonus costumes "Grey Hulk" and "Red Hulk."

WOLVERINE BONUS COSTUMES
Select Enter Code from the Options menu and enter 333333. This unlocks the bonus costumes "Wolverine (Brown Costume)" and "Feral Wolverine."

THOR BONUS COSTUMES
Select Enter Code from the Options menu and enter 444444. This unlocks the bonus costumes "Thor (Chain Armor)" and "Loki-Thor."

SILVER SURFER BONUS COSTUMES
Select Enter Code from the Options menu and enter 555555. This unlocks the bonus costumes "Anti-Surfer" and "Gold Surfer."

FALCON BONUS COSTUME
Select Enter Code from the Options menu and enter 666666. This unlocks the bonus costume "Ultimates Falcon."

DOCTOR DOOM BONUS COSTUMES
Select Enter Code from the Options menu and enter 999999. This unlocks the bonus costumes "Ultimates Doctor Doom" and "Professor Doom."

CAPTAIN AMERICA BONUS COSTUME
Select Enter Code from the Options menu and enter 177674. This unlocks the bonus costume "Ultimate Captain America Costume."

A.I.M. AGENT BONUS COSTUME
Select Enter Code from the Options menu and enter 246246. This unlocks the bonus costume "Blue Suit A.I.M."

SUPER KNOCKBACK
Select Enter Code from the Options menu and enter 777777.

NO BLOCK MODE
Select Enter Code from the Options menu and enter 888888.

GROUNDED
Select Enter Code from the Options menu and enter 476863.

ONE-HIT TAKEDOWN
Select Enter Code from the Options menu and enter 663448.

INFINITE SHARD DURATION
Select Enter Code from the Options menu and enter 742737.

THROWN OBJECT TAKEDOWN
Select Enter Code from the Options menu and enter 847936.

MARVEL TRADING CARD GAME

COMPLETE CARD LIBRARY
At the Deck menu, select new deck and name it BLVRTRSK.

ALL PUZZLES
At the Deck menu, select new deck and name it WHOWANTSPIE.

MARVEL: ULTIMATE ALLIANCE 2

GOD MODE

At any point during a game, press Up, Up, Down, Down, Left, Right, Down.

GIVE MONEY

At the Team Select or Hero Details screen press Up, Up, Down, Down, Up, Up, Up, Down.

UNLOCK ALL POWERS

At the Team Select or Hero Details screen press Up, Up, Down, Down, Left, Right, Right, Left.

ADVANCE ALL CHARACTERS TO L99

At the Hero Details screen press Down, Up, Left, Up, Right, Up, Left, Down.

UNLOCK ALL BONUS MISSIONS

While using the Bonus Mission Simulator, press Up, Right, Down, Left, Left, Right, Up, Up.

ADD 1 CHARACTER LEVEL

During a game, press Down, Up, Right, Up, Right, Up, Right, Down.

ADD 10 CHARACTER LEVELS

During a game, press Down, Up, Left, Up, Left, Up, Left, Down.

METAL GEAR SOLID: PEACE WALKER

T-SHIRTS

From the Extras menu, select Network and then Enter Passcode. Now you can enter the following. Note that you need a PSN account and each passcode can only be used once per PSN account.

T-SHIRT	PASSCODE
Black with "Big Boss"	2000016032758
Black with "Peace Walker"	2000016032390
Black with Peace Walker Logo	2000016038415
Gray with Coffee Cup	2000016036022
Gray with MSF	2000016032567
Gray with MSF	2000016032574
Gray with Snake	2000016032338

T-SHIRT	PASSCODE
Navy Blue with MSF	2000016032635
Olive with Snake	2000016035902
Red with Big Boss	2000016537833
Tan	2000016038576
White with Big Boss	2000016756791
White with "Big Boss"	2000016032680
White with Coffee Cup	2000016032964

METAL GEAR SOLID: PORTABLE OPS PLUS

SOLDIER PASSWORDS

Enter the following as a password.

SOLDIER	PASSWORD
Alabama	BB6K768KM9
Alaska	XL5SW5NH9S
Arizona	ZHEFPVV947
Arkansas	VNRE7JNQ8WE
Black Genome	WYNGG3JBP3YS
Blue Genome	9GNPHGFFLH
California	6MSJQYWNCJ8
Colorado	W6TAH498DJ
Connecticut	2N2AB3JV2WA
Delaware	AJRL6E7TT9
Female Scientist 1	3W8WVRGB2LNN
Female Scientist 2	FUC72C463KZ
Female Scientist 3	UCAWYTMXB5V
Female Soldier 1	UZZQYRPXM86
Female Soldier 2	QRQQ7GWKHJ
Female Soldier 3	MVNDAZAP8DWE

SOLDIER	PASSWORD
Florida	A44STZ3BHY5
Fox Soldier 1	FMXT79TPV4U8
Fox Soldier 2	HGMK3WCYURM
Fox Soldier 3	6ZY5NYW4TGK
Georgia	VD5H53JJCRH
Green Genome	TGQ6F5TUHD
GRU Soldier	9V8S7DVYFTR
Gurlukovich's Soldier	6VWM6A22FSS8
Hawaii	TW7ZMZHCBL
Hideochan Soldier	RU8XRCLPUUT
High Official	ADPS2SE5UC8
High Rank Officer 1	DVB2UDTQ5Z
High Rank Officer 2	84ZEC4X5PJ6
High Ranking Officer 3	DTAZ3QRQQDU

SOLDIER	PASSWORD
High-Tech Soldier	M4MSJ6R87XPP
Idaho	XAFGETZGXHGA
Illinois	QYUVCNDFUPZJ
Indiana	L68JVXVBL8RN
Iowa	B8MW36ZU56S
Kansas	TYPEVDEE24YT
Kentucky	LCD7WGS5X5
KGB Soldier	MNBVYRZP4QH
Louisiana	EHR5VVMHUSG
Maine	T5GYHQABGAC3
KGB Soldier	MNBVYRZP4QH
Louisiana	EHR5VVMHUSG
Maine	T5GYHQABGAC3
Maintenance Crew Member 1	T8EBSRK6F38
Maintenance Crew Member 2	YHQU74J6LLQ
Maintenance Crew Member 3	MFAJMUXZHHKJ
Male Scientist 1	ZFKHJKDEA2
Male Scientist 2	QQ4N3TPCL8PF
Male Scientist 3	CXFCXF4FP9R6
Maryland	L2W9G5N76MH7
Massachusetts	ZLU2S3ULDEVF
Michigan	HGDRBUB5P3SA
Minnesota	EEBBM888ZRA
Mississippi	TBF7H9G6TJH7
Missouri	WJND6M9N738
Montana	9FYUFV29B2Y
Nebraska	MCNB5S5K47H
Nevada	Z9D4UGG8T4U6
New Hampshire	7NQYDQ9Y4KMP
New Jersey	LGHTBU9ZTGR
New Mexico	RGJCMHNLSX
New York	6PV39FKG6X
Normal Soldier Long Sleeve	QK3CMV373Y
Normal Soldier Long Sleeve Magazine Vest	D8RV32E9774
Normal Soldier Short Sleeve	N524ZHU9N4Z
Normal Soldier Short Sleeve Magazine Vest	6WXZA7PTT9Z

SOLDIER	PASSWORD
North Carolina	JGVT2XV47UZ
North Dakota	T5LSAVMPWZCY
Ocelot Female A	9FS7QYSHZ56N
Ocelot Female B	F94XDZSQSGJ8
Ocelot Female C	CRF8PZGXR28
Ocelot Unit	GE6MU3DXL3X
Ohio	AUWGAXWCA3D
Oklahoma	ZQT75NUJH8A3
Oregon	HKSD3PJ5E5
Pennsylvania	PL8GVVUM4HD
Pink Genome	7WRG3N2MRY2
Red Genome	9CM4SY23C7X8
Rhode Island	MMYC99T3QG
Seal	X56YCKZP2V
South Carolina	ZR4465MD8LK
South Dakota	RY3NUDDPMU3
Tengu Soldier	PHHB4TY4J2D
Tennessee	TD2732GCX43U
Texas	QM84UPP6F3
Tsuhan soldier	A9KK7WYWVCV
USSR Female Soldier A	2VXUZQVH9R
USSR Female Soldier B	HPMRFSBXDJ3Y
USSR Female Soldier C	QXQVW9R3PZ
USSR Female Soldier D	GMC3M3LTPVW7
USSR Female Soldier E	5MXVX6UFPMZ5
USSR Female Soldier F	76AWS7WDAV
Utah	V7VRAYZ78GW
Vermont	L7T66LFZ63C8
Virginia	DRTCS77F5N
Washington	G3S4N42WWKTV
Washington DC	Y5YCFYHVZZW
West Virginia	72M8XR99B6
White Genome	QJ4ZTQSLUT8
Wisconsin	K9BUN2BGLMT3
Wyoming	C3THQ749RA
Yellow Genome	CE5HHYGTSSB

N+

25 EXTRA LEVELS

At the Main menu, hold L + R and press ⊗, ●, ⊗, ●, ⊗, ⊗, ●.

NARUTO SHIPPUDEN: ULTIMATE NINJA HEROES

FIGURES

At the Tree of Mettle, select Enter Password and input the following passwords:

FIGURE	PASSWORD
Gods and Angels	Fire, Sheep, Ox, Tiger
Inheritor of the Will	Water, Dog, Snake, Ox
One Who Lurks in Darkness	Thunder, Dog, Tiger, Boar
Rivals	Earth, Sheep, Boar, Dog
Team Asuma	Fire, Dog, Rabbit, Tiger
Team Guy	Water, Dog, Rat, Rooster
Team Kurenai	Thunder, Snake, Dragon, Monkey
The Hokage's Office	Wind, Rabbit, Dragon, Ox
The Innocent Maiden	Water, Snake, Dragon, Ox
The Three Sand Siblings	Earth, Rooster, Ox, Snake

JUTSUS

At the Tree of Mettle, select Enter Password and input the following passwords:

NINJUTSU	PASSWORD
100m Punch	Thunder, Rat, Snake, Horse
Assault Blade	Wind, Rat, Rabbit, Ox
Bring Down the House Jutsu	Thunder, Sheep, Ox, Rooster
Cherry Blossom Clash	Fire, Monkey, Boar, Rabbit
Dead Soul Jutsu	Thunder, Monkey, Dog, Ox
Detonation Dispersion	Wind, Dragon, Horse, Rat
Dynamic Entry	Fire, Rooster, Rabbit, Boar
Feather Illusion Jutsu	Water, Dragon, Boar, Dog
Fire Style: Burning Ash	Fire, Rat, Rabbit, Monkey
Fire Style: Dragon Flame Bomb	Fire, Snake, Dragon, Rabbit
Fire Style: Fire Ball Jutsu	Fire, Dragon, Rat, Monkey
Fire Style: Yoruho'o	Fire, Horse, Rabbit, Sheep
Genjutsu: Haze	Wind, Dragon, Sheep, Rooster
Genjutsu: Madder Mist	Thunder, Rooster, Boar, Dog
Heaven Defending Kick	Earth, Rat, Boar, Monkey
Intensive Healing	Water, Rat, Tiger, Rat
Leaf Repeating Wind	Wind, Rooster, Ox, Tiger
Lightning Blade	Thunder, Monkey, Rooster, Snake
Lightning Style: Thunderbolt Flash	Thunder, Sheep, Ox, Dog
Slithering Snakes	Thunder, Tiger, Rooster, Dog
Summoning: Rashomon	Earth, Monkey, Boar, Rooster
Tunneling Fang	Wind, Dog, Boar, Horse
Water Style: Ripping Torrent	Water, Ox, Dog, Sheep
Water Style: Water Fang Bomb	Water, Horse, Rat, Ox
Weapon: Flash Kunai Ball	Fire, Sheep, Boar, Ox
Wind Style: Air Bullets	Wind, Ox, Boar, Rabbit

HOKAGE NARUTO WALLPAPER

At the Tree of Mettle, select Enter Password and enter Fire, Ox, Rabbit, Horse.

NBA 2K11

2K CHINA TEAM

In Features, select Codes from the Extras menu. Choose Enter Code and key in 2kchina.

2K SPORTS TEAM

In Features, select Codes from the Extras menu. Choose Enter Code and key in 2Ksports.

NBA 2K TEAM

In Features, select Codes from the Extras menu. Choose Enter Code and key in nba2k.

VC TEAM

In Features, select Codes from the Extras menu. Choose Enter Code and key in vcteam.

ABA BALL

In Features, select Codes from the Extras menu. Choose Enter Code and key in payrespect.

NBA 2K12

ABA BALL

Select Cheats from the Features menu and enter payrespect.

BOBCATS NASCAR RACING UNIFORM

Select Cheats from the Features menu and enter agsntrccai.

CAVS CAVFANATIC UNIFORM

Select Cheats from the Features menu and enter aifnaatccv.

HARDWOOD CLASSICS UNIFORMS

Select Cheats from the Features menu and enter Wasshcicsl. This unlocks uniforms for the Cavaliers, Jazz, Magic, Raptors, Timberwolves, Trail Blazers, and Warriors.

MARDI GRAS UNIFORMS

Select Cheats from the Features menu and enter asrdirmga. This unlocks uniforms for the Bulls, Celtics, Knicks, and Raptors.

SECONDARY ROAD UNIFORMS

Select Cheats from the Features menu and enter eydonscar. This unlocks uniforms for the Grizzlies, Hawks, Mavs, and Rockets.

ST PATRICK'S DAY UNIFORMS

Select Cheats from the Features menu and enter riiasgerh. This unlocks uniforms for the Bulls, Celtics, Knicks, and Raptors.

TRAIL BLAZERS RIP CITY UNIFORM

Select Cheats from the Features menu and enter ycprtii.

NBA LIVE 10

CHARLOTTE BOBCATS' 2009/2010 RACE DAY ALTERNATE JERSEYS

Select Options from My NBA Live and go to Select Codes. Enter ceobdabacarstcy.

NEW ORLEANS HORNETS' 2009/2010 MARDI GRAS ALTERNATE JERSEYS

Select Options from My NBA Live and go to Select Codes. Enter nishrag1rosmad0.

ALTERNATE JERSEYS

Select Options from My NBA Live and go to Select Codes. Enter ndnba1rooaesdc0. This unlocks alternate jerseys for Atlanta Hawks, Dallas Mavericks, Houston Rockets, and Memphis Grizzlies.

MORE HARDWOOD CLASSICS NIGHTS JERSEYS

Select Options from My NBA Live and go to Select Codes. Enter hdogdrawhoticns. This unlocks Hardwood Classics Nights jerseys for Cleveland Cavaliers, Golden State Warriors, Minnesota Timberwolves, Orlando Magic, Philadelphia 76ers.

ADIDAS EQUATIONS

Select Options from My NBA Live and go to Select Codes. Enter adaodqauieints1.

ADIDAS TS CREATORS WITH ANKLE BRACES

Select Options from My NBA Live and go to Select Codes. Enter atciadsstsdhecf.

ADIDAS TS SUPERNATURAL COMMANDERS

Select Options from My NBA Live and go to Select Codes. Enter andsicdsmatdnsr.

ADIDAS TS SUPERNATURAL CREATORS

Select Options from My NBA Live and go to Select Codes. Enter ard8siscdnatstr.

AIR MAX LEBRON VII

Select Options from My NBA Live and go to Select Codes. Enter ere1nbvlaoeknii, 2ovnaebnkrielei, 3rioabeneikenvl, ri4boenanekilve, ivl5brieekaeonn, or n6ieirvalkeeobn.

KOBE V

Select Options from My NBA Live and go to Select Codes. Enter ovze1bimenkoko0, m0kveokoiebozn2, eev0nbimokk3ozo, or bmo4inozeeo0kvk.

JORDAN CP3 IIIS
Select Options from My NBA Live and go to Select Codes. Enter iaporcdian3ejis.

JORDAN MELO M6S
Select Options from My NBA Live and go to Select Codes. Enter emlarmeoo6ajdsn.

JORDAN SIXTY PLUSES
Select Options from My NBA Live and go to Select Codes. Enter aondsuilyjrspxt.

NIKE HUARACHE LEGIONS
Select Options from My NBA Live and go to Select Codes. Enter aoieuchrahelgn.

NIKE KD 2S
Select Options from My NBA Live and go to Select Codes. Enter kk2tesaosepinrd.

NIKE ZOOM FLIP'NS
Select Options from My NBA Live and go to Select Codes. Enter epfnozaeminolki.

NEED FOR SPEED CARBON: OWN THE CITY

UNLOCK EVERYTHING
At the Start menu, press X, X, Right, Left, ■, Up, Down.

JET CAR
At the Start menu, press Up, Down, Left, R1, L1, ●, ▲.

LAMBORGINI MERCIALAGO
At the Start menu, press X, X, Up, Down, Left, Right, ●, ●.

TRANSFORMERS CAR
At the Start menu, press X, X, X, ■, ▲, ▲, Up, Down.

PHANTASY STAR PORTABLE 2

VISION PHONE
Use the Vision Phone to enter the following passwords:

NAME	PASSWORD
Akahara Reisou	24932278
Akahara Reisou	24932279
Akahara Reisou	24932280
Alis Landale Poster	41325468
Angry Marshmellow	32549410
Art Javelin	72401990
Blank Epoch	48168861
Blank Epoch	48168862
Bullet Lancer	32091120
Clarita Visas	29888026
Crutches	98443460
Edelweiss Figurine	54333358
Hanhei Tsunagin	41761771
Hanhei Tsunagin	41761772
Hatsune Miku's Leek Wand	12344321
Kansho Bayuka	46815464
Longinus Lance	32143166
Lovely Feathers	72401991
Lovely Feathers	72401992
Magical Princess	55687361
Magical Princess	55687362
Maverick Rifle	53962481
Miku Hatsune Dress	39395341
Miku Hatsune Dress	39395342
Miku's Leek Rifle	39395345
Miku's Leek Saber	39395343

NAME	PASSWORD
Miku's T. Leek Sabers	39395344
Mr. Ekoeko Stick	55687362
Ogi's Head	74612418
Pizza Shack D Box	89747981
Platinum Tiger	32549412
Platinum Tiger	32549414
Platinum Tiger	32549411
Platinum Tiger	32549413
Plug Suit Asuka	34336181
Plug Suit Asuka	34336182
Plug Suit Rei	46211351
Plug Suit Rei	46211352
Plug Suit Shinji	15644322
Puyo Pop Fever Gun	54186516
Puyo Pop Fists	11293398
Scouring Bubble	33286491
Sonic Knuckles	34819852
Special Pizza Cutter	34162313
Telltale Hearts	48168860
The Rappy of Hope	54684698
Toop Nasur	30495153
Trauma Bandages	98443462
Trauma Bandages	98443464
Trauma Bandages	98443461
Trauma Bandages	98443463
True Hash	41761770

POCKET POOL

ALL PICTURES AND VIDEOS

At the Title screen, press L, R, L, L, R, R, L (x3), R (x3), L (x4), R (x4).

PRINNY: CAN I REALLY BE THE HERO?

START A NEW GAME WITH THE ALTERNATE STORYLINE

At the Main menu, highlight New Game and press ▲, ■, ●, ▲, ■, ●, ✖.

PRINNY 2: DAWN OF OPERATION PANTIES, DOOD!

ASAGI WARS

Highlight New Game and press ▲, ■, ●, ▲, ■, ●, ✖.

ROCKET RACING

TRIGGER MODE

At the main menu or during a game, hold L and press Up, Down, Left, Right, ▲, release L.

TRIGGER MODE (REVERSED)

At the main menu or during a game, hold L and press Up, Down, Left, Right, ■, release L.

STICK MODE (DEFAULT)

At the main menu or during a game, hold L and press Up, Down, Left, Right, R, release L

SECRET AGENT CLANK

ACTIVATE CHALICE OF POWER

Press Up, Up, Down, Down, Left, Right, Left, Right to regain health once per level.

THE SECRET SATURDAYS: BEASTS OF THE 5TH SUN

ALL LEVELS

Select Enter Secret Code from the Secrets menu and input Zon, Zon, Zon, Zon.

UNLOCK AMAROK TO BE SCANNED IN LEVEL 2

Select Enter Secret Code from the Secrets menu and input Fiskerton, Zak, Zon, Komodo.

UNLOCK BISHOPVILLE LIZARDMAN TO BE SCANNED IN LEVEL 3

Select Enter Secret Code from the Secrets menu and input Komodo, Zon, Zak, Komodo.

UNLOCK NAGA TO BE SCANNED IN LEVEL 7

Select Enter Secret Code from the Secrets menu and input Zak, Zak, Zon, Fiskerton.

UNLOCK RAKSHASA TO BE SCANNED IN LEVEL 8

Select Enter Secret Code from the Secrets menu and input Zak, Komodo, Fiskerton, Fiskerton.

UNLOCK BILOKO TO BE SCANNED IN LEVEL 9

Select Enter Secret Code from the Secrets menu and input Zon, Zak, Zon, Fiskerton.

A SPACE SHOOTER FOR TWO BUCKS!

INVINCIBILITY

At the credits screen, press Up, Up, Down, Down, Left, Right, Left, Right, ■, Start.

MAXIMUM CASH

At the credits screen, press Left, Right, Left, Right, +, Right, ▲, ▲, ■, Start.

DISABLE SHIP INERTIA

At the credits screen, press ▲, ▲, ▲, ▲, +,+,+,+,■, Start.

FULL OVERDRIVE

At the credits screen, press Down, Left, Up, Right, ▲, ▲, +, +, ■, Start.

HIGH SPEED

At the credits screen, press ▲, +, ■, Left, Right, Left, Left, Up, ■, Start.

SLOW MOTION

At the credits screen, press +, ▲, ■, Right, Left, Right, Right, ■, ■, Start.

STAR WARS: THE FORCE UNLEASHED

CHEATS

Once you have accessed the Rogue Shadow, select Enter Code from the Extras menu. Now you can enter the following:

CHEAT	CODE
Invincibility	CORTOSIS
Unlimited Force	VERGENCE
1,000,000 Force Points	SPEEDER
All Force Powers	TYRANUS
Max Force Power Level	KATARN
Max Combo Level	COUNTDOOKU
Amplified Lightsaber Damage	LIGHTSABER

COSTUMES

Once you have accessed the Rogue Shadow, select Enter Code from the Extras menu. Now you can enter the following:

COSTUME	CODE
All Costumes	GRANDMOFF
501st Legion	LEGION
Aayla Secura	AAYLA
Admiral Ackbar	ITSATWAP
Anakin Skywalker	CHOSENONE
Asajj Ventress	ACOLYTE
Ceremonial Jedi Robes	DANTOOINE
Chop'aa Notimo	NOTIMO
Classic stormtrooper	TK421
Count Dooku	SERENNO
Darth Desolous	PAUAN
Darth Maul	ZABRAK
Darth Phobos	HIDDENFEAR
Darth Vader	SITHLORD
Drexl Roosh	DREXLROOSH
Emperor Palpatine	PALPATINE
General Rahm Kota	MANDALORE
Han Solo	NERFHERDER
Heavy trooper	SHOCKTROOP
Juno Eclipse	ECLIPSE
Kento's Robe	WOOKIEE
Kleef	KLEEF
Lando Calrissian	SCOUNDREL
Luke Skywalker	T16WOMPRAT
Luke Skywalker (Yavin)	YELLOWJCKT
Mace Windu	JEDIMASTER
Mara Jade	MARAJADE
Maris Brook	MARISBROOD
Navy commando	STORMTROOP
Obi Wan Kenobi	BENKENOBI
Proxy	HOLOGRAM
Qui Gon Jinn	MAVERICK
Shaak Ti	TOGRUTA
Shadow trooper	INTHEDARK
Sith Robes	HOLOCRON
Sith Stalker Armor	KORRIBAN
Twi'lek	SECURA

STRIKERS 1945 PLUS PORTABLE

XP-55 ASCENDER

At the Random Select screen, press Down, Up, Down, Up, Down, Down, Down, Down, Up.

TOY STORY 2: BUZZ LIGHTYEAR TO THE RESCUE

LEVEL SELECT

At the Options menu, press Right, Left, ○, △, △.

ALL LEVELS

At the title screen, press Up (x4), Down, Down, Up, Up, Down (x3).

DEBUG MODE

At the title screen, press ×, ○, □.

TOY STORY 3

For the following Toy Story 3 codes, you must activate the cheat from the Pause menu after entering it.

BUZZ USES LASER (ALL STORY LEVELS)

Select Cheat Codes from the Bonus menu and enter BLASER.

WOODY'S BANDIT OUTFIT

Select Cheat Codes from the Bonus menu and enter BANDIT.

TOY ALIENS WITH 3D GLASSES

Select Cheat Codes from the Bonus menu and enter 3DGLAS.

OLD MOVIE EFFECT

Select Cheat Codes from the Bonus menu and enter OLDMOV.

VALKYRIA CHRONICLES II

TANK STICKERS

Enter the following codes in Extra Mode for the desired effect.

STICKER	ENTER
Alicia Gunther	K1C7XKLJMXUHRD8S
Blitz Logo	VWUYNJQ8HGSVXR7J
Edy Nelson	R5PT1MXEY3BW8VBE
Edy's Squad	CR6BG1A9LYQKB6WJ
SEGA Logo	6RK45S59F7U2JLTD
Skies of Arcadia	WVZLPTYXURS1Q8TV
Crazy Taxi	38WV17PK45TYAF8V
Faldio	GWNU95RSETW1VGNQ
Gallian Military	TXU14EUV74PCR3TE
Isara Gunther and Isara's Dream	37LRK5D214VQVFYH
Prince Maximilian and Imperial Flag	H73G4L9GLJR1CHJP
Selvaria	53K8FKGP1GHQ4SBN
Sonic the Hedgehog	CUP34ASEZ9WDKBYV
Super Monkey Ball	7JMNHZ83TGH7XFKT
Yakuza	QAKVXZTALF4TU7SK
Vanquish Tank	BUNLT4EXDS74QRCR

CHARACTERS

Enter the following codes in Extra Mode for the desired effect.

CHARACTER	ENTER
Alicia Gunther	KBAFLFHICAJTKMIY
Edy's Detachment	TKBHCNBERHRKJNFG
Julius Kroze	AMNKZKYTKNBNKYMT
Lamar/Ramal	LITSGAAMEORFRCRQ

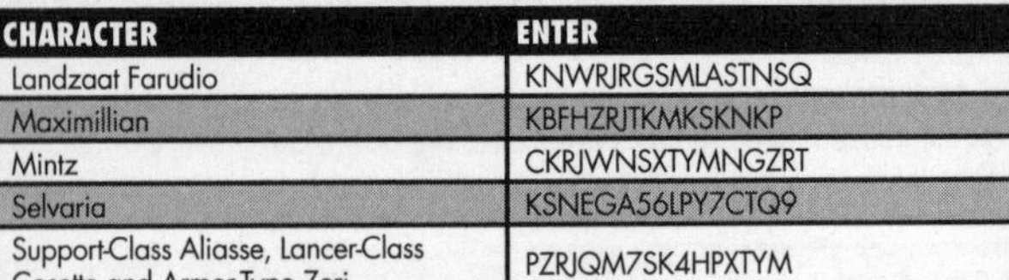

CHARACTER	ENTER
Landzaat Farudio	KNWRJRGSMLASTNSQ
Maximillian	KBFHZRJTKMKSKNKP
Mintz	CKRJWNSXTYMNGZRT
Selvaria	KSNEGA56LPY7CTQ9
Support-Class Aliasse, Lancer-Class Cosette and Armor-Type Zeri	PZRJQM7SK4HPXTYM

VELOCITY

VECTOR MODE

At the trophy screen, select the Elite trophy. Hold L and press △ (x10).

CODER ART MODE

At the Trophy screen, highlight the top-left trophy and press △. Highlight the bottom-left trophy and press △, △. Highlight the bottom-right trophy and press △ (x3). Highlight the top-right trophy and press △ (x4). Continue around the four corners again, pressing △ (x5) on the top-left trophy, △ (x6) on the bottom-left trophy, △ (x7) on the bottom-right trophy, and △ (x8) on the top-right trophy.

COLLISION BOXES

At the Minesweeper game, hold R and select the bottom-left corner, bottom-right corner, top-right corner, and then the top-left corner using X without hitting a bomb.

QUARP DRIVE POLYGONS

At the Minesweeper game, hold L and select the top-left corner, top-right corner, bottom-right corner, and then the bottom-left corner using X without hitting a bomb.

VIRTUA TENNIS 3

ALL COURTS

At the Game Mode screen, press Up, Up, Down, Down, Left, Right, Left, Right.

ALL GEAR

At the Game Mode screen, press Left, Right, ○, Left, Right, ○, Up, Down.

KING & DUKE

At the Game Mode screen, press Up, Up, Down, Down, Left, Right, L, R.

WALL-E

KILL ALL

Select Cheats and then Secret Codes. Enter BOTOFWAR.

UNDETECTED BY ENEMIES

Select Cheats and then Secret Codes. Enter STEALTHARMOR.

LASERS CHANGE COLORS

Select Cheats and then Secret Codes. Enter RAINBOWLAZER.

CUBES ARE EXPLOSIVE

Select Cheats and then Secret Codes. Enter EXPLOSIVEWORLD.

LIGHTEN DARK AREAS

Select Cheats and then Secret Codes. Enter GLOWINTHEDARK.

GOGGLES

Select Cheats and then Secret Codes. Enter BOTOFMYSTERY.

GOLD TRACKS

Select Cheats and then Secret Codes. Enter GOLDENTRACKS.

WHAT DID I DO TO DESERVE THIS, MY LORD!? 2

WHAT DID I DO TO DESERVE THIS, MY LORD!?

At the Title screen, press L, R, L, R, L, R, L, R, L, R to play the first What Did I Do to Deserve This, My Lord!?

WHAT DID I NOT DO TO DESERVE THIS, MY LORD!?

After entering the previous code and the game loads, enter the same code again at the Title screen. This unlocks the Hard Mode of What Did I Do to Deserve This, My Lord!?.

WWE ALL STARS

UNLOCK EVERYTHING

At the main menu, press Left, Right, Left, Down, Up, Left, Right, Up.

STEVE AUSTIN AND CM PUNK ATTIRES

At the main menu, press Left, Left, Right, Right, Up, Down, Up, Down.

RANDY ORTON AND JAKE ROBERTS ATTIRES

At the main menu, press Up, Down, Left, Right, Up, Up, Down, Down.

JOHN MORRISON AND RANDY SAVAGE ATTIRES

At the main menu, press Down, Left, Up, Right, Right, Up, Left, Down.

WWE SMACKDOWN VS. RAW 2011

JOHN CENA (ENTRANCE/CIVILIAN)

In My WWE, select Cheat Codes from the Options and enter SLURPEE.

ALL OF RANDY ORTON'S COSTUMES

In My WWE, select Cheat Codes from the Options and enter apexpredator.

TRIBUTE TO THE TROOPS ARENA

In My WWE, select Cheat Codes from the Options and enter 8thannualtribute.

CRUISERWEIGHT TITLE, HARDCORE TITLE, AND MILLION DOLLAR TITLE

In My WWE, select Cheat Codes from the Options and enter Historicalbelts.

YU-GI-OH! GX TAG FORCE 2

MIDDDAY CONSTELLATION BOOSTER PACK

When buying booster packs, press Up, Up, Down, Down, Left, Right, Left, Right, ⊗, ◉.

CARD PASSWORDS

CARD	PASSWORD
4-Starred Ladybug of Doom	83994646
7 Colored Fish	23771716
A Cat of Ill Omen	24140059
A Deal With Dark Ruler	06850209
A Feather of the Phoenix	49140998
A Feint Plan	68170903
A Hero Emerges	21597117
A Legendary Ocean	00295517
A Man With Wdjat	51351302
A Rival Appears!	05728014
A Wingbeat of Giant Dragon	28596933
A-Team: Trap Disposal Unit	13026402
Abare Ushioni	89718302
Absolute End	27744077
Absorbing Kid From the Sky	49771608
Abyss Soldier	18318842
Abyssal Designator	89801755
Acid Trap Hole	41356845
Acrobat Monkey	47372349
Adhesion Trap Hole	62325062
Adhesive Explosive	53828396
After the Struggle	25345186
Agido	16135253
Airknight Parshath	18036057
Aitsu	48202661
Alkana Knight Joker	06150044
Alpha the Magnet Warrior	99785935
Altar for Tribute	21070956
Amazon Archer	91869203
Amazoness Archers	67987611
Amazoness Blowpiper	73574678
Amazoness Chain Master	29654737
Amazoness Paladin	47480070
Amazoness Swords Woman	94004268
Amazoness Tiger	10979723
Ambulance Rescueroid	98927491
Ambulanceroid	36378213
Ameba	95174353
Amphibian Beast	67371383
Amphibious Bugroth MK-3	64342551
Amplifier	00303660
An Owl of Luck	23927567
Ancient Elf	93221206
Ancient Gear	31557782
Ancient Gear Beast	10509340
Ancient Gear Cannon	80045583
Ancient Gear Castle	92001300
Ancient Gear Drill	67829249
Ancient Gear Golem	83104731
Ancient Gear Soldier	56094445
Ancient Lamp	54912977
Ancient Lizard Warrior	43230671
Andro Sphinx	15013468
Anteatereatingant	13250922
Anti-Aircraft Flower	65064143
Anti-Spell	53112492

CARD	PASSWORD
Apprentice Magician	09156135
Appropriate	48539234
Aqua Madoor	85639257
Aqua Spirit	40916023
Arcane Archer of the Forest	55001420
Archfiend of Gilfer	50287060
Archfiend Soldier	49881766
Archlord Zerato	18378582
Armaill	53153481
Armed Changer	90374791
Armed Dragon LV 3	00980973
Armed Dragon LV 5	46384672
Armed Dragon LV 7	73879377
Armed Dragon LV10	59464593
Armed Ninja	09076207
Armed Samurai - Ben Kei	84430950
Armor Axe	07180418
Armor Break	79649195
Armored Lizard	15480588
Armored Starfish	17535588
Armored Zombie	20277860
Array of Revealing Light	69296555
Arsenal Bug	42364374
Arsenal Robber	55348096
Arsenal Summoner	85489096
Assault on GHQ	62633180
Astral Barrier	37053871
Asura Priest	02134346
Aswan Apparition	88236094
Atomic Firefly	87340664
Attack and Receive	63689843
Attack Reflector Unit	91989718
Aussa the Earth Charmer	37970940
Autonomous Action Unit	71453557
Avatar of the Pot	99284890
Axe Dragonute	84914462
Axe of Despair	40619825
B. Skull Dragon	11901678
B.E.S. Covered Core	15317640
B.E.S. Crystal Core	22790789
B.E.S. Tetran	44954628
Baby Dragon	88819587
Back to Square One	47453433
Backfire	82705573
Backup Soldier	36280194
Bad Reaction to Simochi	40633297
Bait Doll	07165085
Ballista of Rampart Smashing	00242146
Banisher of the Light	61528025
Bark of Dark Ruler	41925941
Barrel Dragon	81480460
Basic Insect	89091579
Battery Charger	61181383
Batteryman AA	63142001
Batteryman C	19733961
Batteryman D	55401221
Battle Footballer	48094997

CARD	PASSWORD
Battle Ox	05053103
Battle-Scarred	94463200
Bazoo The Soul-Eater	40133511
Beast Soul Swap	35149085
Beaver Warrior	32452818
Beckoning Light	16255442
Beelze Frog	49522489
Begone, Knave	20374520
Behemoth the King of All Animals	22996376
Beiige, Vanguard of Dark World	33731070
Berserk Dragon	85605684
Berserk Gorilla	39168895
Beta the Magnet Warrior	39256679
Bickuribox	25655502
Big Bang Shot	61127349
Big Burn	95472621
Big Core	14148099
Big Koala	42129512
Big Shield Gardna	65240384
Big Wave Small Wave	51562916
Big-Tusked Mammoth	59380081
Bio-Mage	58696829
Birdface	45547649
Black Illusion Ritual	41426869
Black Luster Soldier - Envoy of the Beginning	72989439
Black Pendant	65169794
Black Tyranno	38670435
Blackland Fire Dragon	87564352
Blade Knight	39507162
Blade Rabbit	58268433
Blade Skater	97023549
Bladefly	28470714
Blast Held By a Tribute	89041555
Blast Magician	21051146
Blast with Chain	98239899
Blasting the Ruins	21466326
Blazing Inpachi	05464695
Blind Destruction	32015116
Blindly Loyal Goblin	35215622
Block Attack	25880422
Blockman	48115277
Blowback Dragon	25551951
Blue-Eyes Shining Dragon	53347303
Blue-Eyes Toon Dragon	53183600
Blue-Eyes Ultimate Dragon	23995346
Blue-Eyes White Dragon	89631139
Blue-Winged Crown	41396436
Bokoichi the Freightening Car	08715625
Bombardment Beetle	57409948
Bonding - H2O	45898858
Boneheimer	98456117
Book of Life	02204140
Book of Moon	14087893
Book of Taiyou	38699854

CARD	PASSWORD
Boss Rush	66947414
Bottom Dweller	81386177
Bottomless Shifting Sand	76532077
Bottomless Trap Hole	29401950
Bountiful Artemis	32296881
Bowganian	52090844
Bracchio-Raidus	16507828
Brain Control	87910978
Brain Jacker	40267580
Branch!	30548775
Breaker the Magical Warrior	71413901
Broww, Huntsman of Dark World	79126789
Brron, Mad King of Dark World	06214884
Bubble Blaster	53586134
Bubble Illusion	80075749
Bubble Shuffle	61968753
Bubonic Vermin	06104968
Burning Algae	41859700
Burning Beast	59364406
Burning Land	24294108
Burst Breath	80163754
Burst Return	27191436
Burst Stream of Destruction	17655904
Buster Blader	78193831
Buster Rancher	84740193
Butterfly Dagger - Elma	69243953
Byser Shock	17597059
Call of The Haunted	97077563
Call of the Mummy	04861205
Cannon Soldier	11384280
Cannonball Spear Shellfish	95614612
Card of Safe Return	57953380
Card Shuffle	12183332
Castle of Dark Illusions	00062121
Cat's Ear Tribe	95841282
Catapult Turtle	95727991
Cathedral of Nobles	29762407
Catnipped Kitty	96501677
Cave Dragon	93220472
Ceasefire	36468556
Celtic Guardian	91152256
Cemetery Bomb	51394546
Centrifugal	01801154
Ceremonial Bell	20228463
Cetus of Dagala	28106077
Chain Burst	48276469
Chain Destruction	01248895
Chain Disappearance	57139487
Chain Energy	79323590
Chain Thrasher	88190453
Chainsaw Insect	77252217
Change of Heart	04031928
Chaos Command Magician	72630549
Chaos Emperor Dragon - Envoy of the End	82301904
Chaos End	61044390
Chaos Greed	97439308
Chaos Necromancer	01434352
Chaos Sorcerer	09596126
Chaosrider Gutaph	47829960
Charcoal Inpachi	13179332
Charm of Shabti	50412166
Charubin the Fire Knight	37421579
Chiron the Mage	16956455
Chopman the Desperate Outlaw	40884383
Chorus of Sanctuary	81380218
Chthonian Alliance	46910446
Chthonian Blast	18271561
Chthonian Polymer	72287557
Chu-Ske the Mouse Fighter	08508055
Clay Charge	22479888
Cliff the Trap Remover	06967870
Cobra Jar	86801871
Cobraman Sakuzy	75109441
Cold Wave	60682203
Collected Power	07565547
Combination Attack	08964854
Command Knight	10375182
Commander Covington	22666164
Commencement Dance	43417563
Compulsory Evaculation Device	94192409
Confiscation	17375316
Conscription	31000575
Continuous Destruction Punch	68057622
Contract With Exodia	33244944
Contract With the Abyss	69035382
Contract with the Dark Master	96420087
Convulsion of Nature	62966332
Cost Down	23265313
Covering Fire	74458486
Crab Turtle	91782219
Crass Clown	93889755
Creature Swap	31036355
Creeping Doom Manta	52571838
Crimson Ninja	14618326
Criosphinx	18654201
Cross Counter	37083210
Crush D. Gandra	64681432
Cure Mermaid	85802526
Curse of Aging	41398771
Curse of Anubis	66742250
Curse of Darkness	84970821
Curse of Dragon	28279543
Curse of the Masked Beast	94377247
Curse of Vampire	34294855
Cyber Dragon	70095154
Cyber End Dragon	01546123
Cyber Twin Dragon	74157028
Cyber-Dark Edge	77625948

CARD	PASSWORD
Cyber-Stein	69015963
Cyberdark Dragon	40418351
Cyberdark Horn	41230939
Cyberdark Keel	03019642
D - Shield	62868900
D - Time	99075257
D. D. Assailant	70074904
D. D. Borderline	60912752
D. D. Crazy Beast	48148828
D. D. Dynamite	08628798
D. D. M. - Different Dimension Master	82112775
D. D. Trainer	86498013
D. D. Trap Hole	05606466
D. D. Warrior Lady	07572887
Dancing Fairy	90925163
Dangerous Machine TYPE-6	76895648
Dark Artist	72520073
Dark Bat	67049542
Dark Blade	11321183
Dark Blade the Dragon Knight	86805855
Dark Driceratops	65287621
Dark Dust Spirit	89111398
Dark Elf	21417692
Dark Energy	04614116
Dark Factory of Mass Production	90928333
Dark Flare Knight	13722870
Dark Hole	53129443
Dark Magic Attack	02314238
Dark Magic Ritual	76792184
Dark Magician	46986414
Dark Magician Girl	38033121
Dark Magician of Chaos	40737112
Dark Magician's Tome of Black Magic	67227834
Dark Master - Zorc	97642679
Dark Mirror Force	20522190
Dark Paladin	98502113
Dark Room of Nightmare	85562745
Dark Sage	92377303
Dark Snake Syndrome	47233801
Dark-Piercing Light	45895206
Darkfire Dragon	17881964
Darkfire Soldier #1	05388481
Darkfire Soldier #2	78861134
Darkworld Thorns	43500484
De-Spell	19159413
Deal of Phantom	69122763
Decayed Commander	10209545
Dedication Through Light And Darkness	69542930
Deepsea Shark	28593363
Dekoichi the Battlechanted Locomotive	87621407
Delinquent Duo	44763025
Demotion	72575145
Des Counterblow	39131963

CARD	PASSWORD
Des Croaking	44883830
Des Dendle	12965761
Des Feral Imp	81985784
Des Frog	84451804
Des Kangaroo	78613627
Des Koala	69579761
Des Lacooda	02326738
Des Wombat	09637706
Desert Sunlight	93747864
Destertapir	13409151
Destiny Board	94212438
Destiny Hero - Captain Tenacious	77608643
Destiny Hero - Diamond Dude	13093792
Destiny Hero - Doom Lord	41613948
Destiny Hero - Dreadmaster	40591390
Destiny Signal	35464895
Destroyer Golem	73481154
Destruction Ring	21219755
Dian Keto the Cure Master	84257639
Dice Jar	03549275
Dimension Distortion	95194279
Dimensional Warrior	37043180
Disappear	24623598
Disarmament	20727787
Disc Fighter	19612721
Dissolverock	40826495
Divine Dragon Ragnarok	62113340
Divine Wrath	49010598
DNA Surgery	74701381
DNA Transplant	56769674
Doitsu	57062206
Dokurorider	99721536
Dokuroyaiba	30325729
Don Turtle	03493978
Don Zaloog	76922029
Doriado	84916669
Doriado's Blessing	23965037
Dragon Seeker	28563545
Dragon Treasure	01435851
Dragon Zombie	66672569
Dragon's Mirror	71490127
Dragon's Rage	54178050
Dragoness the Wicked Knight	70681994
Draining Shield	43250041
Dream Clown	13215230
Drillago	99050989
Drillroid	71218746
Dunames Dark Witch	12493482
Dust Tornado	60082867
Earth Chant	59820352
Earthbound Spirit	67105242
Earthquake	82828051
Eatgaboon	42578427
Ebon Magician Curran	46128076
Electro-Whip	37820550

CARD	PASSWORD
Elegant Egotist	90219263
Element Dragon	30314994
Elemental Burst	61411502
Elemental Hero Avian	21844576
Elemental Hero Bladedge	59793705
Elemental Hero Bubbleman	79979666
Elemental Hero Burstinatrix	58932615
Elemental Hero Clayman	84327329
Elemental Hero Electrum/ Erekshieler	29343734
Elemental Hero Flame Wingman	35809262
Elemental Hero Mariner	14225239
Elemental Hero Necroid Shaman	81003500
Elemental Hero Neos	89943723
Elemental Hero Phoenix Enforcer	41436536
Elemental Hero Shining Flare Wingman	25366484
Elemental Hero Shining Phoenix Enforcer	88820235
Elemental Hero Sparkman	20721928
Elemental Hero Thunder Giant	61204971
Elemental Mistress Doriado	99414158
Elemental Recharge	36586443
Elf's Light	39897277
Emblem of Dragon Destroyer	06390406
Embodiment of Apophis	28649820
Emergency Provisions	53046408
Emes the Infinity	43580269
Empress Judge	15237615
Empress Mantis	58818411
Enchanted Javelin	96355986
Enchanting Mermaid	75376965
Enemy Controller	98045062
Enraged Battle Ox	76909279
Enraged Muka Muka	91862578
Eradicating Aerosol	94716515
Eternal Draught	56606928
Eternal Rest	95051344
Exhausting Spell	95451366
Exile of the Wicked	26725158
Exiled Force	74131780
Exodia Necross	12600382
Exodia the Forbidden One	33396948
Fairy Box	21598948
Fairy Dragon	20315854
Fairy King Truesdale	45425051
Fairy Meteor Crush	97687912
Faith Bird	75582395
Fatal Abacus	77910045
Fenrir	00218704
Feral Imp	41392891
Fiber Jar	78706415
Fiend Comedian	81172176
Fiend Scorpion	26566878

CARD	PASSWORD
Fiend's Hand	52800428
Fiend's Mirror	31890399
Final Countdown	95308449
Final Destiny	18591904
Final Flame	73134081
Final Ritual of the Ancients	60369732
Fire Darts	43061293
Fire Eye	88435542
Fire Kraken	46534755
Fire Princess	64752646
Fire Reaper	53581214
Fire Sorcerer	27132350
Firegrass	53293545
Firewing Pegasus	27054370
Fireyarou	71407486
Fissure	66788016
Five God Dragon (Five Headed Dragon)	99267150
Flame Cerebrus	60862676
Flame Champion	42599677
Flame Dancer	12883044
Flame Ghost	58528964
Flame Manipulator	34460851
Flame Swordsman	45231177
Flame Viper	02830619
Flash Assailant	96890582
Flower Wolf	95952802
Flying Fish	31987274
Flying Kamakiri #1	84834865
Flying Kamakiri #2	03134241
Follow Wind	98252586
Foolish Burial	81439173
Forest	87430998
Fortress Whale	62337487
Fortress Whale's Oath	77454922
Frenzied Panda	98818516
Frozen Soul	57069605
Fruits of Kozaky's Studies	49998907
Fuh-Rin-Ka-Zan	01781310
Fuhma Shuriken	09373534
Fulfillment of the Contract	48206762
Fushi No Tori	38538445
Fusion Gate	33550694
Fusion Recovery	18511384
Fusion Sage	26902560
Fusion Weapon	27967615
Fusionist	01641883
Gadget Soldier	86281779
Gagagigo	49003308
Gaia Power	56594520
Gaia the Dragon Champion	66889139
Gaia the Fierce Knight	06368038
Gale Dogra	16229315
Gale Lizard	77491079
Gamble	37313786
Gamma the Magnet Warrior	11549357

CARD	PASSWORD
Garma Sword	90844184
Garma Sword Oath	78577570
Garoozis	14977074
Garuda the Wind Spirit	12800777
Gatling Dragon	87751584
Gazelle the King of Mythical Beasts	05818798
Gear Golem the Moving Fortress	30190809
Gearfried the Iron Knight	00423705
Gearfried the Swordmaster	57046845
Gemini Elf	69140098
Getsu Fuhma	21887179
Giant Axe Mummy	78266168
Giant Germ	95178994
Giant Kozaky	58185394
Giant Orc	73698349
Giant Rat	97017120
Giant Red Seasnake	58831685
Giant Soldier of Stone	13039848
Giant Trunade	42703248
Gift of the Mystical Elf	98299011
Giga Gagagigo	43793530
Giga-Tech Wolf	08471389
Gigantes	47606319
Gigobyte	53776525
Gil Garth	38445524
Gilasaurus	45894482
Giltia the D. Knight	51828629
Girochin Kuwagata	84620194
Goblin Attack Force	78658564
Goblin Calligrapher	12057781
Goblin Elite Attack Force	85306040
Goblin Thief	45311864
Goblin's Secret Remedy	11868825
Gogiga Gagagigo	39674352
Golem Sentry	82323207
Good Goblin Housekeeping	09744376
Gora Turtle	80233946
Graceful Charity	79571449
Graceful Dice	74137509
Gradius	10992251
Gradius' Option	14291024
Granadora	13944422
Grand Tiki Elder	13676474
Granmarg the Rock Monarch	60229110
Gravedigger Ghoul	82542267
Gravekeeper's Cannonholder	99877698
Gravekeeper's Curse	50712728
Gravekeeper's Guard	37101832
Gravekeeper's Servant	16762927
Gravekeeper's Spear Soldier	63695531
Gravekeeper's Spy	24317029
Gravekeeper's Vassal	99690140
Graverobber's Retribution	33737664

CARD	PASSWORD
Gravity Bind	85742772
Gray Wing	29618570
Great Angus	11813953
Great Long Nose	02356994
Great Mammoth of Goldfine	54622031
Green Gadget	41172955
Gren Maju Da Eiza	36584821
Ground Attacker Bugroth	58314394
Ground Collapse	90502999
Gruesome Goo	65623423
Gryphon Wing	55608151
Gryphon's Feather Duster	34370473
Guardian Angel Joan	68007326
Guardian of the Labyrinth	89272878
Guardian of the Sea	85448931
Guardian Sphinx	40659562
Guardian Statue	75209824
Gust Fan	55321970
Gyaku-Gire Panda	09817927
Gyroid	18325492
Hade-Hane	28357177
Hamburger Recipe	80811661
Hammer Shot	26412047
Hamon	32491822
Hand of Nephthys	98446407
Hane-Hane	07089711
Hannibal Necromancer	05640330
Hard Armor	20060230
Harpie Girl	34100324
Harpie Lady 1	91932350
Harpie Lady 2	27927359
Harpie Lady 3	54415063
Harpie Lady Sisters	12206212
Harpie's Brother	30532390
Harpies' Hunting Ground	75782277
Hayabusa Knight	21015833
Headless Knight	05434080
Heart of Clear Water	64801562
Heart of the Underdog	35762283
Heavy Mech Support Platform	23265594
Heavy Storm	19613556
Helios - The Primordial Sun	54493213
Helios Duo Megistus	80887952
Helios Tris Megiste	17286057
Helping Robo for Combat	47025270
Hero Barrier	44676200
HERO Flash!!	00191749
Hero Heart	67951831
Hero Kid	32679370
Hero Ring	26647858
Hero Signal	22020907
Hidden Book of Spell	21840375
Hidden Soldier	02047519
Hieracosphinx	82260502
Hieroglyph Lithograph	10248192
High Tide Gyojin	54579801

CARD	PASSWORD
Hiita the Fire Charmer	00759393
Hino-Kagu-Tsuchi	75745607
Hinotama Soul	96851799
Hiro's Shadow Scout	81863068
Hitotsu-Me Giant	76184692
Holy Knight Ishzark	57902462
Homunculus the Alchemic Being	40410110
Horn of Heaven	98069388
Horn of Light	38552107
Horn of the Unicorn	64047146
Horus The Black Flame Dragon LV4	75830094
Horus The Black Flame Dragon LV6	11224103
Horus The Black Flame Dragon LV8	48229808
Hoshiningen	67629977
House of Adhesive Tape	15083728
Howling Insect	93107608
Huge Revolution	65396880
Human-Wave Tactics	30353551
Humanoid Slime	46821314
Humanoid Worm Drake	05600127
Hungry Burger	30243636
Hydrogeddon	22587018
Hyena	22873798
Hyozanryu	62397231
Hyper Hammerhead	02671330
Hysteric Fairy	21297224
Icarus Attack	53567095
Illusionist Faceless Mage	28546905
Impenetrable Formation	96631852
Imperial Order	61740673
Inaba White Rabbit	77084837
Incandescent Ordeal	33031674
Indomitable Fighter Lei Lei	84173492
Infernal Flame Emperor	19847532
Infernal Queen Archfiend	08581705
Inferno	74823665
Inferno Fire Blast	52684508
Inferno Hammer	17185260
Inferno Reckless Summon	12247206
Inferno Tempest	14391920
Infinite Cards	94163677
Infinite Dismissal	54109233
Injection Fairy Lily	79575620
Inpachi	97923414
Insect Armor with Laser Cannon	03492538
Insect Barrier	23615409
Insect Imitation	96965364
Insect Knight	35052053
Insect Princess	37957847
Insect Queen	91512835
Insect Soldiers of the Sky	07019529
Inspection	16227556
Interdimensional Matter Transporter	36261276

CARD	PASSWORD
Invader From Another Dimension	28450915
Invader of Darkness	56647086
Invader of the Throne	03056267
Invasion of Flames	26082229
Invigoration	98374133
Iron Blacksmith Kotetsu	73431236
Island Turtle	04042268
Jack's Knight	90876561
Jade Insect Whistle	95214051
Jam Breeding Machine	21770260
Jam Defender	21558682
Jar of Greed	83968380
Jar Robber	33784505
Javelin Beetle	26932788
Javelin Beetle Pact	41182875
Jellyfish	14851496
Jerry Beans Man	23635815
Jetroid	43697559
Jinzo	77585513
Jinzo #7	32809211
Jirai Gumo	94773007
Jowgen the Spiritualist	41855169
Jowls of Dark Demise	05257687
Judge Man	30113682
Judgment of Anubis	55256016
Just Desserts	24068492
KA-2 Des Scissors	52768103
Kabazauls	51934376
Kagemusha of the Blue Flame	15401633
Kaibaman	34627841
Kaiser Dragon	94566432
Kaiser Glider	52824910
Kaiser Sea Horse	17444133
Kaminari Attack	09653271
Kaminote Blow	97570038
Kamionwizard	41544074
Kangaroo Champ	95789089
Karate Man	23289281
Karbonala Warrior	54541900
Karma Cut	71587526
Kelbek	54878498
Keldo	80441106
Killer Needle	88979991
Kinetic Soldier	79853073
King Dragun	13756293
King Fog	84686841
King of the Skull Servants	36021814
King of the Swamp	79109599
King of Yamimakai	69455834
King Tiger Wanghu	83986578
King's Knight	64788463
Kiryu	84814897
Kiseitai	04266839
Kishido Spirit	60519422
Knight's Title	87210505
Koitsu	69456283
Kojikocy	01184620

CARD	PASSWORD
Kotodama	19406822
Kozaky	99171160
Kozaky's Self-Destruct Button	21908319
Kryuel	82642348
Kumootoko	56283725
Kurama	85705804
Kuriboh	40640057
Kuwagata Alpha	60802233
Kwagar Hercules	95144193
Kycoo The Ghost Destroyer	88240808
La Jinn The Mystical Genie of The Lamp	97590747
Labyrinth of Nightmare	66526672
Labyrinth Tank	99551425
Lady Assailant of Flames	90147755
Lady Ninja Yae	82005435
Lady of Faith	17358176
Larvas	94675535
Laser Cannon Armor	77007920
Last Day of Witch	90330453
Last Turn	28566710
Launcher Spider	87322377
Lava Battleguard	20394040
Lava Golem	00102380
Layard the Liberator	67468948
Left Arm of the Forbidden One	07902349
Left Leg of the Forbidden One	44519536
Legendary Black Belt	96438440
Legendary Flame Lord	60258960
Legendary Jujitsu Master	25773409
Legendary Sword	61854111
Leghul	12472242
Lekunga	62543393
Lesser Dragon	55444629
Lesser Fiend	16475472
Level Conversion Lab	84397023
Level Limit - Area A	54976796
Level Limit - Area B	03136426
Level Modulation	61850482
Level Up!	25290459
Levia-Dragon	37721209
Light of Intervention	62867251
Light of Judgment	44595286
Lighten the Load	37231841
Lightforce Sword	49587034
Lightning Blade	55226821
Lightning Conger	27671321
Lightning Vortex	69162969
Limiter Removal	23171610
Liquid Beast	93108297
Little Chimera	68658728
Little-Winguard	90790253
Lizard Soldier	20831168
Lord of D.	17985575
Lord of the Lamp	99510761
Lost Guardian	45871897

CARD	PASSWORD
Luminous Soldier	57282479
Luminous Spark	81777047
Luster Dragon	11091375
Luster Dragon #2	17658803
M-Warrior #1	56342351
M-Warrior #2	92731455
Machine Conversion Factory	25769732
Machine Duplication	63995093
Machine King	46700124
Machine King Prototype	89222931
Machiners Defender	96384007
Machiners Force	58054262
Machiners Sniper	23782705
Machiners Soldier	60999392
Mad Dog of Darkness	79182538
Mad Lobster	97240270
Mad Sword Beast	79870141
Mage Power	83746708
Magic Drain	59344077
Magic Jammer	77414722
Magical Cylinder	62279055
Magical Dimension	28553439
Magical Explosion	32723153
Magical Hats	81210420
Magical Labyrinth	64389297
Magical Marionette	08034697
Magical Merchant	32362575
Magical Plant Mandragola	07802006
Magical Scientist	34206604
Magical Thorn	53119267
Magician of Black Chaos	30208479
Magician of Faith	31560081
Magician's Circle	00050755
Magician's Unite	36045450
Magician's Valkyrie	80304126
Magnet Circle	94940436
Maha Vailo	93013676
Maharaghi	40695128
Maiden of the Aqua	17214465
Maji-Gire Panda	60102563
Maju Garzett	08794435
Makiu	27827272
Makyura the Destructor	21593977
Malevolent Nuzzler	99597615
Malfunction	06137095
Malice Ascendant	14255590
Malice Dispersion	13626450
Mammoth Graveyard	40374923
Man Eater	93553943
Man-Eater Bug	54652250
Man-Eating Black Shark	80727036
Man-Eating Treasure Chest	13723605
Man-Thro' Tro'	43714890
Manga Ryu-Ran	38369349
Manju of the Ten Thousand Hands	95492061
Manticore of Darkness	77121851
Marauding Captain	02460565

CARD	PASSWORD
Marie the Fallen One	57579381
Marine Beast	29929832
Marshmallon	31305911
Marshmallon Glasses	66865880
Maryokutai	71466592
Masaki the Legendary Swordsman	44287299
Mask of Brutality	82432018
Mask of Darkness	28933734
Mask of Restrict	29549364
Mask of Weakness	57882509
Masked Dragon	39191307
Masked of the Accursed	56948373
Masked Sorcerer	10189126
Mass Driver	34906152
Master Kyonshee	24530661
Master Monk	49814180
Master of Dragon Knight	62873545
Master of Oz	27134689
Mataza the Zapper	22609617
Mavelus	59036972
Maximum Six	30707994
Mazera DeVille	06133894
Mech Mole Zombie	63545455
Mecha-Dog Marron	94667532
Mechanical Hound	22512237
Mechanical Snail	34442949
Mechanical Spider	45688586
Mechanicalchaser	07359741
Meda Bat	76211194
Medusa Worm	02694423
Mefist the Infernal General	46820049
Mega Thunderball	21817254
Mega Ton Magical Cannon	32062913
Megamorph	22046459
Megarock Dragon	71544954
Melchid the Four-Face Beast	86569121
Memory Crusher	48700891
Mermaid Knight	24435369
Messenger of Peace	44656491
Metal Armored Bug	65957473
Metal Dragon	09293977
Metallizing Parasite	07369217
Metalmorph	68540058
Metalzoa	50705071
Metamorphosis	46411259
Meteor B. Dragon	90660762
Meteor Dragon	64271667
Meteor of Destruction	33767325
Meteorain	64274292
Michizure	37580756
Micro-Ray	18190572
Mid Shield Gardna	75487237
Mighty Guard	62327910
Mikazukinoyaiba	38277918
Millennium Golem	47986555
Millennium Scorpion	82482194
Millennium Shield	32012841

CARD	PASSWORD
Milus Radiant	07489323
Minar	32539892
Mind Control	37520316
Mind Haxorz	75392615
Mind on Air	66690411
Mind Wipe	52718046
Mine Golem	76321376
Minefield Eruption	85519211
Minor Goblin Official	01918087
Miracle Dig	06343408
Miracle Fusion	45906428
Miracle Kid	55985014
Miracle Restoring	68334074
Mirage Dragon	15960641
Mirage Knight	49217579
Mirage of Nightmare	41482598
Mirror Force	44095762
Mirror Wall	22359980
Misfortune	01036974
Mispolymerization	58392024
Mistobody	47529357
Moai Interceptor Cannons	45159319
Mobius the Frost Monarch	04929256
Moisture Creature	75285069
Mokey Mokey	27288416
Mokey Mokey King	13803864
Mokey Mokey Smackdown	01965724
Molten Behemoth	17192817
Molten Destruction	19384334
Molten Zombie	04732017
Monk Fighter	03810071
Monster Egg	36121917
Monster Eye	84133008
Monster Gate	43040603
Monster Reborn	83764718
Monster Recovery	93108433
Monster Reincarnation	74848038
Mooyan Curry	58074572
Morale Boost	93671934
Morphing Jar	33508719
Morphing Jar #2	79106360
Mother Grizzly	57839750
Mountain	50913601
Mr. Volcano	31477025
Mudora	82108372
Muka Muka	46657337
Multiplication of Ants	22493811
Multiply	40703222
Musician King	56907389
Mustering of the Dark Scorpions	68191243
Mysterious Puppeteer	54098121
Mystic Horseman	68516705
Mystic Lamp	98049915
Mystic Plasma Zone	18161786
Mystic Swordsman LV 2	47507260
Mystic Swordsman LV 4	74591968
Mystic Swordsman LV 6	60482781

CARD	PASSWORD
Mystic Tomato	83011277
Mystic Wok	80161395
Mystical Beast Serket	89194033
Mystical Elf	15025844
Mystical Knight of Jackal	98745000
Mystical Moon	36607978
Mystical Sand	32751480
Mystical Sheep #2	30451366
Mystical Shine Ball	39552864
Mystical Space Typhoon	05318639
Mystik Wok	80161395
Mythical Beast Cerberus	55424270
Nanobreaker	70948327
Necklace of Command	48576971
Necrovalley	47355498
Needle Ball	94230224
Needle Burrower	98162242
Needle Ceiling	38411870
Needle Wall	38299233
Needle Worm	81843628
Negate Attack	14315573
Nemuriko	90963488
Neo Aqua Madoor	49563947
Neo Bug	16587243
Neo the Magic Swordsman	50930991
Neo-Space	40215635
Neo-Spacian Aqua Dolphin	17955766
Newdoria	04335645
Next to be Lost	07076131
Night Assailant	16226786
Nightmare Horse	59290628
Nightmare Penguin	81306586
Nightmare Wheel	54704216
Nightmare's Steelcage	58775978
Nimble Momonga	22567609
Nin-Ken Dog	11987744
Ninja Grandmaster Sasuke	04041838
Ninjitsu Art of Decoy	89628781
Ninjitsu Art of Transformation	70861343
Nitro Unit	23842445
Niwatori	07805359
Nobleman of Crossout	71044499
Nobleman of Extermination	17449108
Nobleman-Eater Bug	65878864
Non Aggression Area	76848240
Non-Fusion Area	27581098
Non-Spellcasting Area	20065549
Novox's Prayer	43694075
Nubian Guard	51616747
Numinous Healer	02130625
Nutrient Z	29389368
Nuvia the Wicked	12953226
O - Oversoul	63703130
Obnoxious Celtic Guardian	52077741
Ocubeam	86088138
Offerings to the Doomed	19230407
Ojama Black	79335209

CARD	PASSWORD
Ojama Delta Hurricane	08251996
Ojama Green	12482652
Ojama King	90140980
Ojama Trio	29843091
Ojama Yellow	42941100
Ojamagic	24643836
Ojamuscle	98259197
Old Vindictive Magician	45141844
Ominous Fortunetelling	56995655
Oni Tank T-34	66927994
Opti-Camaflauge Armor	44762290
Opticlops	14531242
Option Hunter	33248692
Orca Mega-Fortress of Darkness	63120904
Ordeal of a Traveler	39537362
Order to Charge	78986941
Order to Smash	39019325
Otohime	39751093
Outstanding Dog Marron	11548522
Overdrive	02311603
Oxygeddon	58071123
Painful Choice	74191942
Paladin of White Dragon	73398797
Pale Beast	21263083
Pandemonium	94585852
Pandemonium Watchbear	75375465
Parasite Paracide	27911549
Parasitic Ticky	87978805
Patrician of Darkness	19153634
Patroid	71930383
Penguin Knight	36039163
Penumbral Soldier Lady	64751286
People Running About	12143771
Perfect Machine King	18891691
Performance of Sword	04849037
Petit Angel	38142739
Petit Dragon	75356564
Petit Moth	58192742
Phantasmal Martyrs	93224848
Phantom Beast Cross-Wing	71181155
Phantom Beast Thunder-Pegasus	34961968
Phantom Beast Wild-Horn	07576264
Pharaoh's Servant	52550973
Pharonic Protector	89959682
Phoenix Wing Wind Blast	63356631
Photon Generator Unit	66607691
Pikeru's Circle of Enchantment	74270067
Pikeru's Second Sight	58015506
Pinch Hopper	26185991
Pineapple Blast	90669991
Piranha Army	50823978
Pitch-Black Power Stone	34029630
Pitch-Black Warwolf	88975532
Pitch-Dark Dragon	47415292
Poison Draw Frog	56840658
Poison Fangs	76539047

CARD	PASSWORD
Poison Mummy	43716289
Poison of the Old Man	08842266
Polymerization	24094653
Possessed Dark Soul	52860176
Pot of Avarice	67169062
Pot of Generosity	70278545
Pot of Greed	55144522
Power Bond	37630732
Power Capsule	54289683
Precious Card from Beyond	68304813
Premature Burial	70828912
Prepare to Strike Back	04483989
Prevent Rat	00549481
Prickle Fairy	91559748
Primal Seed	23701465
Princess Curran	02316186
Princess of Tsurugi	51371017
Princess Pikeru	75917088
Protective Soul Ailin	11678191
Protector of the Sanctuary	24221739
Protector of the Throne	10071456
Proto-Cyber Dragon	26439287
Pumpking the King of Ghosts	29155212
Punished Eagle	74703140
Pyramid of Light	53569894
Pyramid Turtle	77044671
Queen's Knight	25652259
Rabid Horseman	94905343
Rafflesia Seduction	31440542
Raging Flame Sprite	90810762
Raigeki	12580477
Raigeki Break	04178474
Rain Of Mercy	66719324
Rainbow Flower	21347810
Rallis the Star Bird	41382147
Rancer Dragonute	11125718
Rapid-Fire Magician	06337436
Rare Metalmorph	12503902
Raregold Armor	07625614
Raviel, Lord of Phantasms	69890967
Ray & Temperature	85309439
Ray of Hope	82529174
Re-Fusion	74694807
Ready For Intercepting	31785398
Really Eternal Rest	28121403
Reaper of the Cards	33066139
Reaper of the Nightmare	85684223
Reasoning	58577036
Reborn Zombie	23421244
Reckless Greed	37576645
Recycle	96316857
Red Archery Girl	65570596
Red Gadget	86445415
Red Medicine	38199696
Red Moon Baby	56387350
Red-Eyes B. Chick	36262024
Red-Eyes B. Dragon	74677422
Red-Eyes Black Metal Dragon	64335804
Red-Eyes Darkness Dragon	96561011
Reflect Bounder	02851070
Regenerating Mummy	70821187
Reinforcement of the Army	32807846
Release Restraint	75417459
Relinquished	64631466
Reload	22589918
Remove Trap	51482758
Rescue Cat	14878871
Rescueroid	24311595
Reshef the Dark Being	62420419
Respect Play	08951260
Return from the Different Dimension	27174286
Return of the Doomed	19827717
Reversal of Graves	17484499
Reversal Quiz	05990062
Revival Jam	31709826
Right Arm of the Forbidden One	70903634
Right Leg of the Forbidden One	08124921
Ring of Defense	58641905
Ring of Destruction	83555666
Ring of Magnetism	20436034
Riryoku Field	70344351
Rising Air Current	45778932
Rising Energy	78211862
Rite of Spirit	30450531
Ritual Weapon	54351224
Robbin' Goblin	88279736
Robbin' Zombie	83258273
Robolady	92421852
Robotic Knight	44203504
Roboyarou	38916461
Rock Bombardment	20781762
Rock Ogre Grotto	68846917
Rocket Jumper	53890795
Rocket Warrior	30860696
Rod of the Mind's Eye	94793422
Roll Out!	91597389
Root Water	39004808
Rope of Life	93382620
Rope of Spirit	37383714
Roulette Barrel	46303688
Royal Command	33950246
Royal Decree	51452091
Royal Keeper	16509093
Royal Knight	68280530
Royal Magical Library	70791313
Royal Surrender	56058888
Royal Tribute	72405967
Ruin, Queen of Oblivion	46427957
Rush Recklessly	70046172
Ryu Kokki	57281778
Ryu Senshi	49868263
Ryu-Kishin Clown	42647539

CARD	PASSWORD
Ryu-Kishin Powered	24611934
Saber Beetle	49645921
Sacred Crane	30914564
Sacred Phoenix of Nephthys	61441708
Saggi the Dark Clown	66602787
Sakuretsu Armor	56120475
Salamandra	32268901
Salvage	96947648
Samsara	44182827
Sand Gambler	50593156
Sand Moth	73648243
Sangan	26202165
Sanwitch	53539634
Sasuke Samurai	16222645
Sasuke Samurai #2	11760174
Sasuke Samurai #3	77379481
Sasuke Samurai #4	64538655
Satellite Cannon	50400231
Scapegoat	73915051
Scarr, Scout of Dark World	05498296
Science Soldier	67532912
Scroll of Bewitchment	10352095
Scyscraper	63035430
Sea Serpent Warrior of Darkness	42071342
Sealmaster Meisei	02468169
Second Coin Toss	36562627
Second Goblin	19086954
Secret Barrel	27053506
Self-Destruct Button	57585212
Senri Eye	60391791
Serial Spell	49398568
Serpent Night Dragon	66516792
Serpentine Princess	71829750
Servant of Catabolism	02792265
Seven Tools of the Bandit	03819470
Shadow Ghoul	30778711
Shadow Of Eyes	58621589
Shadow Tamer	37620434
Shadowknight Archfiend	09603356
Shadowslayer	20939559
Share the Pain	56830749
Shield & Sword	52097679
Shield Crash	30683373
Shien's Spy	07672244
Shift	59560625
Shifting Shadows	59237154
Shinato's Ark	60365591
Shinato, King of a Higher Plane	86327225
Shining Abyss	87303357
Shining Angel	95956346
Shooting Star Bow - Ceal	95638658
Silent Insect	40867519
Silent Magician Lv4	73665146
Silent Magician Lv8	72443568
Silent Swordsman LV3	01995985
Silent Swordsman LV5	74388798

CARD	PASSWORD
Silent Swordsman LV7	37267041
Sillva, Warlord of Dark World	32619583
Silpheed	73001017
Silver Fang	90357090
Simorgh, Bird of Divinity	14989021
Simultaneous Loss	92219931
Sinister Serpent	08131171
Sixth Sense	03280747
Skill Drain	82732705
Skilled Dark Magician	73752131
Skilled White Magician	46363422
Skull Archfiend of Lightning	61370518
Skull Descovery Knight	78700060
Skull Dog Marron	86652646
Skull Invitation	98139712
Skull Lair	06733059
Skull Mariner	05265750
Skull Red Bird	10202894
Skull Servant	32274490
Skull Zoma	79852326
Skull-Mark Ladybug	64306248
Skyscraper	63035430
Slate Warrior	78636495
Smashing Ground	97169186
Smoke Grenade of the Thief	63789924
Snatch Steal	45986603
Sogen	86318356
Soitsu	60246171
Solar Flare Dragon	45985838
Solar Ray	44472639
Solemn Judgment	41420027
Solemn Wishes	35346968
Solomon's Lawbook	23471572
Sonic Duck	84696266
Sonic Jammer	84550200
Sorcerer of Dark Magic	88619463
Soul Absorption	68073522
Soul Exchange	68005187
Soul of Purity and Light	77527210
Soul Release	05758500
Soul Resurrection	92924317
Soul Reversal	78864369
Soul Tiger	15734813
Soul-Absorbing Bone Tower	63012333
Souleater	31242786
Souls Of The Forgotten	04920010
Space Mambo	36119641
Spark Blaster	97362768
Sparks	76103675
Spatial Collapse	20644748
Spear Cretin	58551308
Spear Dragon	31553716
Spell Canceller	84636823
Spell Economics	04259068
Spell Purification	01669772
Spell Reproduction	29228529
Spell Shield Type-8	38275183

CARD	PASSWORD
Spell Vanishing	29735721
Spell-Stopping Statute	10069180
Spellbinding Circle	18807108
Spherous Lady	52121290
Sphinx Teleia	51402177
Spiral Spear Strike	49328340
Spirit Barrier	53239672
Spirit Caller	48659020
Spirit Message A	94772232
Spirit Message I	31893528
Spirit Message L	30170981
Spirit Message N	67287533
Spirit of Flames	13522325
Spirit of the Breeze	53530069
Spirit of the Harp	80770678
Spirit of the Pharaoh	25343280
Spirit Reaper	23205979
Spirit Ryu	67957315
Spiritual Earth Art - Kurogane	70156997
Spiritual Energy Settle Machine	99173029
Spiritual Fire Art - Kurenai	42945701
Spiritual Water Art - Aoi	06540606
Spiritual Wind Art - Miyabi	79333300
Spiritualism	15866454
St. Joan	21175632
Stamping Destruction	81385346
Star Boy	08201910
Statue of the Wicked	65810489
Staunch Defender	92854392
Stealth Bird	03510565
Steam Gyroid	05368615
Steamroid	44729197
Steel Ogre Grotto #1	29172562
Steel Ogre Grotto #2	90908427
Stim-Pack	83225447
Stop Defense	63102017
Storming Wynn	29013526
Stray Lambs	60764581
Strike Ninja	41006930
Stronghold	13955608
Stumbling	34646691
Success Probability 0%	06859683
Summon Priest	00423585
Summoned Skull	70781052
Summoner of Illusions	14644902
Super Conductor Tyranno	85520851
Super Rejuvenation	27770341
Super Robolady	75923050
Super Roboyarou	01412158
Supply	44072894
Susa Soldier	40473581
Swarm of Locusts	41872150
Swarm of Scarabs	15383415
Swift Gaia the Fierce Knight	16589042
Sword Hunter	51345461
Sword of Deep-Seated	98495314
Sword of Dragon's Soul	61405855

CARD	PASSWORD
Sword of the Soul Eater	05371656
Swords of Concealing Light	12923641
Swords of Revealing Light	72302403
Swordsman of Landstar	03573512
Symbol of Heritage	45305419
System Down	18895832
T.A.D.P.O.L.E.	10456559
Tactical Espionage Expert	89698120
Tailor of the Fickle	43641473
Taunt	90740329
Tenkabito Shien	41589166
Terra the Terrible	63308047
Terraforming	73628505
Terrorking Archfiend	35975813
Terrorking Salmon	78060096
Teva	16469012
The Agent of Creation - Venus	64734921
The Agent of Force - Mars	91123920
The Agent of Judgment - Saturn	91345518
The Agent of Wisdom - Mercury	38730226
The All-Seeing White Tiger	32269855
The Big March of Animals	01689516
The Bistro Butcher	71107816
The Cheerful Coffin	41142615
The Creator	61505339
The Creator Incarnate	97093037
The Dark - Hex Sealed Fusion	52101615
The Dark Door	30606547
The Dragon Dwelling in the Cave	93346024
The Dragon's Bead	92408984
The Earl of Demise	66989694
The Earth - Hex Sealed Fusion	88696724
The Emperor's Holiday	68400115
The End of Anubis	65403020
The Eye Of Truth	34694160
The Fiend Megacyber	66362965
The Flute of Summoning Dragon	43973174
The Flute of Summoning Kuriboh	20065322
The Forceful Sentry	42829885
The Forces of Darkness	29826127
The Forgiving Maiden	84080938
The Furious Sea King	18710707
The Graveyard in the Fourth Dimension	88089103
The Gross Ghost of Fled Dreams	68049471
The Hunter With 7 Weapons	01525329
The Illusionary Gentleman	83764996
The Immortal of Thunder	84926738
The Kick Man	90407382
The Last Warrior From Another Planet	86099788

CARD	PASSWORD
The Law of the Normal	66926224
The League of Uniform Nomenclature	55008284
The Legendary Fisherman	03643300
The Light - Hex Sealed Fusion	15717011
The Little Swordsman of Aile	25109950
The Masked Beast	49064413
The Portrait's Secret	32541773
The Regulation of Tribe	00296499
The Reliable Guardian	16430187
The Rock Spirit	76305638
The Sanctuary in the Sky	56433456
The Second Sarcophagus	04081094
The Secret of the Bandit	99351431
The Shallow Grave	43434803
The Spell Absorbing Life	99517131
The Thing in the Crater	78243409
The Third Sarcophagus	78697395
The Trojan Horse	38479725
The Unhappy Girl	27618634
The Unhappy Maiden	51275027
The Warrior Returning Alive	95281259
Theban Nightmare	51838385
Theinen the Great Sphinx	87997872
Thestalos the Firestorm Monarch	26205777
Thousand Dragon	41462083
Thousand Energy	05703682
Thousand Needles	33977496
Thousand-Eyes Idol	27125110
Thousand-Eyes Restrict	63519819
Threatening Roar	36361633
Three-Headed Geedo	78423643
Throwstone Unit	76075810
Thunder Crash	69196160
Thunder Dragon	31786629
Thunder Nyan Nyan	70797118
Thunder of Ruler	91781589
Time Seal	35316708
Time Wizard	71625222
Timeater	44913552
Timidity	40350910
Token Festevil	83675475
Token Thanksgiving	57182235
Tongyo	69572024
Toon Cannon Soldier	79875176
Toon Dark Magician Girl	90960358
Toon Defense	43509019
Toon Gemini Elf	42386471
Toon Goblin Attack Force	15270885
Toon Masked Sorcerer	16392422
Toon Mermaid	65458948
Toon Summoned Skull	91842653
Toon Table of Contents	89997728
Toon World	15259703
Tornado Bird	71283180
Tornado Wall	18605135

CARD	PASSWORD
Torpedo Fish	90337190
Torrential Tribute	53582587
Total Defense Shogun	75372290
Tower of Babel	94256039
Tradgedy	35686187
Transcendent Wings	25573054
Trap Dustshoot	64697231
Trap Hole	04206964
Trap Jammer	19252988
Treeborn Frog	12538374
Tremendous Fire	46918794
Tri-Horned Dragon	39111158
Triage	30888983
Trial of Nightmare	77827521
Trial of the Princesses	72709014
Triangle Ecstasy Spark	12181376
Triangle Power	32298781
Tribe-Infecting Virus	33184167
Tribute Doll	02903036
Tribute to The Doomed	79759861
Tripwire Beast	45042329
Troop Dragon	55013285
Tsukuyomi	34853266
Turtle Oath	76806714
Turtle Tiger	37313348
Twin Swords of Flashing Light	21900719
Twin-Headed Beast	82035781
Twin-Headed Behemoth	43586926
Twin-Headed Fire Dragon	78984772
Twin-Headed Thunder Dragon	54752875
Twin-Headed Wolf	88132637
Two Thousand Needles	83228073
Two-Man Cell Battle	25578802
Two-Mouth Darkruler	57305373
Two-Pronged Attack	83887306
Tyhone	72842870
Type Zero Magic Crusher	21237481
Tyranno Infinity	83235263
Tyrant Dragon	94568601
UFOroid	07602840
UFOroid Fighter	32752319
Ultimate Insect LV1	49441499
Ultimate Insect LV3	34088136
Ultimate Insect LV5	34830502
Ultimate Insect LV7	19877898
Ultimate Obedient Fiend	32240937
Ultimate Tyranno	15894048
Ultra Evolution Pill	22431243
Umi	22702055
Umiiruka	82999629
Union Attack	60399954
United Resistance	85936485
United We Stand	56747793
Unity	14731897
Unshaven Angler	92084010
Upstart Goblin	70368879

CARD	PASSWORD
Uraby	01784619
Uria, Lord of Sealing Flames	06007213
V-Tiger Jet	51638941
Valkyrion the Magna Warrior	75347539
Vampire Genesis	22056710
Vampire Lord	53839837
Vampire Orchis	46571052
Vengeful Bog Spirit	95220856
Victory D	44910027
Vilepawn Archfiend	73219648
VW-Tiger Catapult	58859575
VWXYZ-Dragon Catapult Cannon	84243274
W-Wing Catapult	96300057
Waboku	12607053
Wall of Revealing Light	17078030
Wandering Mummy	42994702
Warrior Dai Grepher	75953262
Warrior of Zera	66073051
Wasteland	23424603
Water Dragon	85066822
Water Omotics	02483611
Wave Motion Cannon	38992735
Weed Out	28604635
Whiptail Crow	91996584
Whirlwind Prodigy	15090429
White Dragon Ritual	09786492
White Horn Dragon	73891874
White Magical Hat	15150365
White Magician Pikeru	81383947
White Ninja	01571945
Wicked-Breaking Flameberge-Baou	68427465
Wild Nature's Release	61166988
Winged Dragon, Guardian of the Fortress #1	87796900
Winged Kuriboh	57116033

CARD	PASSWORD
Winged Kuriboh LV10	98585345
Winged Minion	89258225
Winged Sage Falcos	87523462
Wingweaver	31447217
Witch Doctor of Chaos	75946257
Witch of the Black Forest	78010363
Witch's Apprentice	80741828
Witty Phantom	36304921
Wolf Axwielder	56369281
Woodborg Inpachi	35322812
Woodland Sprite	06979239
Worm Drake	73216412
Wroughtweiler	06480253
Wynn the Wind Charmer	37744402
X-Head Cannon	62651957
Xing Zhen Hu	76515293
XY-Dragon Cannon	02111707
XYZ-Dragon Cannon	91998119
XZ-Tank Cannon	99724761
Y-Dragon Head	65622692
Yamata Dragon	76862289
Yami	59197169
Yata-Garasu	03078576
Yellow Gadget	13839120
Yellow Luster Shield	04542651
Yomi Ship	51534754
YZ-Tank Dragon	25119460
Z-Metal Tank	64500000
Zaborg the Thunder Monarch	51945556
Zero Gravity	83133491
Zoa	24311372
Zolga	16268841
Zombie Tiger	47693640
Zombyra the Dark	88472456
Zure, Knight of Dark World	07459013

2013 CHEAT CODE OVERLOAD

©2012 DK/BradyGAMES, a division of Penguin Group (USA) Inc. BradyGAMES® is a registered trademark of Penguin Group (USA) Inc. All rights reserved, including the right of reproduction in whole or in part in any form.

DK/BradyGames, a division of Penguin Group (USA) Inc.
800 East 96th Street, 3rd Floor
Indianapolis, IN 46240

PlayStation® 3, PSVita® and PSP® are registered trademarks or trademarks of Sony Computer Entertainment, Inc. Xbox 360® is a registered trademark or trademark of Microsoft Corporation. Nintendo DS™, Nintendo 3DS™ and Nintendo Wii™ are registered trademarks or trademarks of Nintendo of America, Inc. All rights reserved. All other trademarks and trade names are properties of their respective owners.

ISBN: 978-0-7440-1435-8

Printing Code: The rightmost double-digit number is the year of the book's printing; the rightmost single-digit number is the number of the book's printing. For example, 12-1 shows that the first printing of the book occurred in 2012.

15 14 13 12 4 3 2 1

Printed in the USA.

BRADYGAMES STAFF

Publisher
Mike Degler

Editor-In-Chief
H. Leigh Davis

Licensing Manager
Christian Sumner

Digital Manager
Tim Cox

Marketing Manager
Katie Hemlock

CREDITS

Code Editor
Michael Owen

Senior Development Editor
Ken Schmidt

Book Designer
Colin King

Production Designer
Julie Clark